# Short Story Writers

## Revised Edition

MAGILL'S CHOICE

# SHORT STORY WRITERS

## REVISED EDITION

Volume 3
Joyce Carol Oates — Richard Wright
759 – 1144
Index

*edited by*
### CHARLES E. MAY
#### CALIFORNIA STATE UNIVERSITY, LONG BEACH

SALEM PRESS, INC.

Pasadena, California          Hackensack, New Jersey

Some essays in these volumes originally appeared in *Critical Survey of Short Fiction, Second Revised Edition,* 2001. New material has been added.

∞ The paper used in these volumes conforms to the American National Standard for Permanence of Paper for Printed Library Materials, Z39.48-1992 (R1997).

**Library of Congress Cataloging-in-Publication Data**

Short story writers / edited by Charles E. May. — Rev. ed.
    v. cm. — (Magill's choice)
  Includes bibliographical references and index.
  ISBN 978-1-58765-389-6 (set : alk. paper) — ISBN 978-1-58765-390-2 (vol. 1 : alk. paper) — ISBN 978-1-58765-391-9 (vol. 2 : alk. paper) — ISBN 978-1-58765-392-6 (vol. 3 : alk. paper) 1. Short story. 2. Short stories—Bio-bibliography—Dictionaries. 3. Novelists—Biography—Dictionaries. I. May, Charles E. (Charles Edward), 1941-

PN3373.S398 2008
809.3'1—dc22

2007032789

First printing

PRINTED IN CANADA

# Contents – Volume 3

# Complete List of Contents

## Volume 1

## Volume 2

# Volume 3

# SHORT STORY WRITERS

## WRITERS

### REVISED EDITION

# Joyce Carol Oates

**Born:** Lockport, New York; June 16, 1938

**Principal short fiction** • *By the North Gate,* 1963; *Upon the Sweeping Flood,* 1966; *The Wheel of Love,* 1970; *Marriages and Infidelities,* 1972; *The Goddess and Other Women,* 1974; *The Hungry Ghosts,* 1974; *Where Are You Going, Where Have You Been?,* 1974; *The Seduction,* 1975; *The Poisoned Kiss,* 1975; *Crossing the Border,* 1976; *Night-Side,* 1977; *All the Good People I've Left Behind,* 1978; *The Lamb of Abyssalia,* 1979; *A Sentimental Education,* 1980; *Last Days,* 1984; *Raven's Wing,* 1986; *The Assignation,* 1988; *Heat, and Other Stories,* 1991; *Where Is Here?,* 1992; *Haunted: Tales of the Grotesque,* 1994; *Will You Always Love Me?,* 1994; *The Collector of Hearts,* 1998; *Faithless: Tales of Transgression,* 2001; *I Am No One You Know,* 2004; *The Female of the Species: Tales of Mystery and Suspense,* 2005; *High Lonesome: Stories, 1966-2006,* 2006.

**Other literary forms** • Joyce Carol Oates is remarkable for both the volume and breadth of her literary output. In addition to hundreds of short stories published in more than two dozen collections and various literary journals and popular magazines, she has produced ten volumes of poetry, plays, more than four dozen novels, averaging at least one novel a year after reaching the age of sixty in 1998. Through her interviews, essays, editorship of anthologies and journals, and positions at the University of Windsor and then Princeton University, she has continuously engaged in an ongoing dialogue with the North American literary community.

Oates has collected some of her literary criticism in *New Heaven, New Earth: The Visionary Experience in Literature* (1974), *(Woman) Writer: Occasions and Opportunities* (1988), *Where I've Been, and Where I'm Going: Essays, Reviews, and Prose* (1999), and *Uncensored: Views and (Re)views* (2005), and summed up some of her views in *The Faith of a Writer: Life, Craft, Art* (2003). She has also edited several anthologies, including *Night Walks* (1982), *First Person Singular* (1983), *The Best American Essays* (1991), *The Oxford Book of American Short Stories* (1992) *American Gothic Tales* (1996), and *The Best American Mystery Stories* (2005). Her other nonfiction writings cover subjects as diverse as art and boxing.

**Achievements** • Joyce Carol Oates received National Book Award nominations in 1968 and 1969; she won the award in 1970, for her novel *them* (1969). Other honors include O. Henry Awards in 1967, 1973, and 1983 for her short stories, John Simon Guggenheim Memorial Foundation and Rosenthal Fellowships, and election to the American Academy and Institute of Arts and Letters. She received the Alan Swallow award for her 1988 short-story collection *The Assignation* and the Heidemann Award for one-act plays and the Rea Award, both in 1990. She was nominated for a National Book Critics Circle Award and a Pulitzer Prize for *Black Water* (1992) and was nominated for the Nobel Prize in Literature in 1993. She was a Pulitzer finalist again in 1995. In 1996 she won the Bram Stoker Award for Horror and the Fisk Fiction Prize for *Zombie* (1995). She continued her prolific output into the twenty-first century, with novels such as *Blonde,* for which she won her National Book Award in 2001; *I'll Take You There,* and *The Falls,* as well as the short-story collections *Faithless:*

© Norman Seeff

*Tales of Transgression* (2001) and *I Am No One You Know* (2004). In 2003, she was honored with the Common Wealth Award for Distinguished Service in Literature. During that same year, the American Library Association named her *Big Mouth and Ugly Girl* (2002) as one of its Best Books for Young Adults

**Biography** • Joyce Carol Oates was born on June 16, 1938, in Lockport, New York, a small city outside Buffalo. Her father was a tool and die designer, and her childhood was spent in a rural town where she attended a one-room schoolhouse. From earliest memory, she wanted to be an author. As a small child, she drew pictures to tell stories; later, she wrote them, sometimes producing handwritten books of up to two hundred pages, with carefully designed covers. Her youth was simple and happy, and she developed a closeness to her parents that flourished in her adult years.

In 1956, Oates graduated from Williamsville Central High School, where she had written for the school newspaper, and she entered Syracuse University under a New York State Regents Scholarship. During her freshman year, a tachycardiac seizure during a basketball game profoundly affected her view of life by bringing her face to face with her mortality. She continued writing and in 1959 was selected cowinner of the *Mademoiselle* college fiction award for "In the Old World." An excellent student, she was elected Phi Beta Kappa and graduated in 1960 at the top of her class.

Oates received a Knapp Fellowship to pursue graduate work at the University of Wisconsin, where she met doctoral candidate Raymond Joseph Smith. She and Smith were married on January 23, 1961. After receiving her master's degree, Oates and Smith moved to Texas, where he taught in Beaumont and she began doctoral work at William Marsh Rice University in Houston. With one of her stories appearing on the Honor Roll of Martha Foley's *Best American Short Stories*, however, Oates decided to devote herself to writing.

Oates's first collection of stories, *By the North Gate*, appeared in 1963, followed a year later by her first novel, *With Shuddering Fall* (1964). In 1967, *A Garden of Earthly Delights* appeared as the first novel in a thematic trilogy exploring the American obsession with money. The last of the trilogy, *them* (1969), earned Oates the 1970 National Book Award.

Oates taught at the University of Detroit from 1961 to 1967; then she and Smith moved to the University of Windsor in Ontario, Canada. A prolific author, Oates continued publishing stories in such periodicals as *The Literary Review* and *Cosmopolitan* and produced a steady flow of novels, stories, and poetry. Various other writings—essays, plays, reviews—add to the unusual breadth of her works.

In 1978, Oates became the Roger S. Berlind Distinguished Professor of Creative Writing at Princeton University in New Jersey. From their home, she and Smith edited *The Ontario Review* and ran a small publishing company. As her body of work grew, so did its formal and thematic diversity. *Bellefleur* (1980), *A Bloodsmoor Romance* (1982), and *Mysteries of Winterthurn* (1984) are experimental ventures into the genres, respectively, of the family chronicle, the romance, and the gothic mystery. During the later 1980's, her work turned toward a modern naturalism.

Oates traveled and lectured widely, and in December, 1987, she was among a group of artists, writers, and intellectuals invited to greet Mikhail Gorbachev, then president of the Soviet Union, at the Soviet Embassy in Washington, D.C. During the 1990's, Oates produced a succession of works that were varied in format. From the novel *Foxfire: Confessions of a Girl Gang* (1993), about the members of an adolescent girl gang, to the gothic short stories in *Haunted: Tales of the Grotesque* and *The Collector of Hearts*, Oates continued to display her versatility and maintain her position as one of the world's most eminent authors. In 1998, she moved into the children's market with *Come Meet Muffin*, an imaginative tale of a brave, adventuresome cat. Her extensive expression as a writer, thinker, and teacher ensured Oates's role as a respected and vigorous participant in the United States' intellectual and literary life since the 1960's.

**Analysis** • Joyce Carol Oates is a very American writer. Early in her career, she drew comparisons with such predecessors as Flannery O'Connor and William Faulkner. The chiefly rural and small-town milieu of her earlier work expanded over the years, as did her vision of passion and violence in the United States in the twentieth century.

It is difficult to separate Oates's short fiction from her novels, for she consistently produced volumes in both genres throughout her career. Unlike many writers who produce both long and short fiction, Oates never subordinated her stories to her novels: They represent in sum a no less considerable achievement, and Oates is by no means a novelist who sometimes writes stories, nor for that matter a storyteller who sometimes writes novels. Both forms figure centrally in her overall work. In many cases, her stories are crystallized versions of the types of characters and dramatic moments found in larger works; over the years, the themes and stylistic approaches in the two genres maintained a parallel progression.

Oates concerns herself with the formulation of the American Dream and how it has changed and even soured through the decades of American prosperity and preeminence. Her characters are often prototypes of the nation, and their growth from naïveté to wisdom and pain reflect aspects of the national destiny that she sees in the evolving society around her. In her short stories, the naïveté is often the innocence of youth; many stories focus on adolescent girls becoming aware of the potential of their own sexuality and the dangers of the adult world. Like the United States, however, such characters retain an unbounded youthful enthusiasm, an arrogant challenge to the future and the outside world.

Relationships of individuals to the world around them are keys to many of Oates's stories. Her fascination with images of the American Dream and the power of belief and self-creation implied therein translates to an awareness of her characters' self-perceptions, and, equally, their self-deceptions. Many of her characters have a built-in isolation: That is not to say that they are not involved with other people, but that their perceptions are necessarily limited, and that they are aware, though not always specifically, of those limits. Oates often establishes their subjectivity with remarkable clarity, allowing the reader to bring wider knowledge and perspective to the story to fill it out and complete the emotional impact. Isolation, detachment, and even alienation create the obstacles that her characters struggle to overcome, and while Oates has been criticized for the darkness of her writing, as often as not her characters find redemption, hope, and even happiness. Neither the joy, however, nor the tragedy is ever complete, for human experience as Oates sees it is always a complex and mixed phenomenon.

Such complexity naturally emerges from human relationships, especially from those between the sexes. As a female writer, Oates had to deal with the "sexual question" merely in the act of sitting down at the typewriter, and her writing reveals a keen sensitivity to the interactions of men and women. Although some of her works toward the end of the 1980's manifest a more explicitly feminist outlook, Oates has never been a feminist writer. Rather, her feminism—or humanism—is subsumed in her refusal to write the kind of stories and novels that women have traditionally written or to limit her male and female characters to typically male and female behaviors, attitudes, emotions, and actions. Oates does not make the sexes equivalent but celebrates the differences and examines feminine and masculine sexual and emotional life without preconceived assumptions. Thus, reading an Oates story is peering into a vision of the world where almost anything is possible between men and women. Although they are eminently recognizable as the men and women of the contemporary United States, at the same time they are wholly independent and capable of full response to their inner lives.

Those inner lives often contain ugly possibilities. One of the major complaints that Oates faced, especially early in her career, regards the violence—often random, graphic, even obsessive—that characterizes much of her work. In 1981, in an essay in *The New York Times Book Review* entitled "Why Is Your Writing So Violent?" Oates branded such criticism as blatantly sexist and asserted the female novelist's right to depict nature as she knows it. She clearly sees the United States as a nation where violence is a fact of life. In her novels, such violence takes the form of assassinations, mass murders, rapes, suicides, arsons, autopsies, and automobile accidents. In her short stories, the same events are treated with greater economy and precision but with no less commitment to the vivid portrayal of truth. She shies away from neither the physical details of pain and atrocity nor the psychological realities that accompany them. Even when the violence of her stories is a psychological violence performed by one character upon another, with no effusion of blood and guts, the effects are no less visceral. Oates's stories are deeply felt.

Violence, however, is never the ultimate point of an Oates story. Rather, the violence acts as either catalyst or climax to a dramatic progression: Through violent events, characters undergo almost inevitable transformations, and the suddenness of violence or the sharpness of pain, either experienced or observed, jolts characters into a greater appreciation of life. Frequently, the violent event or action is very peripheral to the protagonist or prime action of the story. Rather, it is often anonymous, perpetrated by unseen hands for unknown reasons, presenting mysteries that will never be solved. Violence becomes an emphatic metaphor for the arbitrary hand of fate, destiny, chance, God—or whatever one wishes to call it. Oates generally portrays it without naming or quantifying it: For her, it is simply the way things are.

Beneath the passion, deep feeling, and violence of her stories, there is a meticulously intellectual mind that is evident, looking at the larger picture, in the wide array of approaches and devices that Oates employs over the range of hundreds of stories. She uses first-, second-, and third-person viewpoints, both male and female. Sometimes dialogue predominates; at other times, the prose is richly descriptive. Some of her stories turn on the use of imagery, tone, or rhythm, and plot is all but nonexistent; others are journalistically rich in event and sparse in stylistic embellishment. Some stories approach the length of novels, others are mere brush strokes, several pages or even a single paragraph to express the crux of a character or dramatic situation. Some stories adhere to the traditional unity and structure of the short story, recounting a single event from beginning to end; others meander, circle in upon themselves, travel backward in time, or derive unity not from the narrative but from character or mood. In brief, Oates uses stories to explore the various tools available to her as a writer. As novelist John Barth noted, "Joyce Carol Oates writes all over the aesthetical map."

In addition, while each story has integrity as a complete work of fiction, Oates devoted great attention to the composition of her collections, and each is unified structurally or thematically and forms an artistic whole as well as an anthology of smaller parts. For example, the stories in Oates's first collection, *By the North Gate*, are largely set in rural, small-town America and show individuals seeking to find order in their lives. *The Wheel of Love* consists of stories exploring varieties of love, and those in *The Goddess and Other Women* are all about women. The volume entitled *Marriages and Infidelities* contains reworkings of popular stories by such masters as Anton Chekhov, Henry James, Franz Kafka, and James Joyce; not only do the stories deal with married people and marital issues, but also the literary approach itself suggests a "marriage" between Oates's tales and the originals on which they are modeled.

The collection *The Hungry Ghosts* is unified by the stories' academic settings (places not unlike Oates's own University of Windsor and Princeton) and the vein of satire that runs throughout. The stories in *The Poisoned Kiss* were, according to a prefatory note by Oates, written by a certain Ferdinand de Briao and deal with the exotic, rustic, and more authentically European material that such a gentleman—Oates's own imaginary creation—would naturally devise. *Night-Side* and *The Seduction* contain stories that involve darker, psychologically ambiguous, sometimes surrealistic situations, and the stories in *Last Days* focus on individuals in upheaval and crisis, on the verge of emotional or physical breakdown. Many of the pieces in *Crossing the Border* are linked together by characters—Renee, Evan, Karl, Jake, Cynthia—who appear throughout, and many of those in *Raven's Wing* are set in small towns on the New Jersey coast.

**"The Census Taker"** • A small rural town in mythical Eden County, based loosely on the region of western New York where Oates grew up, is the setting of "The Census Taker," one of the notable stories from *By the North Gate*. It is a simple story involving four relatively anonymous characters—a census taker, a boy, a girl, and a mother— and it is told in simple prose against a hazy, fairy-tale-like landscape. A census taker comes to a remote home to ask questions, but instead of finding the father who can give him the facts that he needs and send him on his way, he is faced with a pair of relentlessly inquisitive children who peel away the layers of his protective delusion in an effort to bring order to their young existence. Eventually, they wear away his confidence in the meaning of any answers, factual or existential, and he leaves without having taken the simplest measure of their household. At heart is the profound mystery of life which, if not confronted with courage, will drive one to seek refuge in madness, blindness, or obsession.

**"In the Region of Ice"** • One of Oates's early triumphs in the short story, also dealing with obsession and madness, is a piece entitled "In the Region of Ice." First published in *The Atlantic Monthly* in 1965, and later in *The Wheel of Love*, it was an O. Henry Award-winner for 1967. The protagonist of "In the Region of Ice" is Sister Irene, a Shakespeare lecturer at a small Roman Catholic university. For all practical purposes, she lives "in the region of ice"—a region void of feeling and passion. Perfectly comfortable in front of a class, she is otherwise timid and essentially incapable of developing meaningful human contact.

Into her insulated existence comes Allen Weinstein, a brilliant but emotionally disturbed Jewish student. Obsessed with the reality of ideas, he comes to dominate one of Irene's classes, inspiring the hatred of his classmates but awakening intellectual and emotional life in the professor herself. The story, narrated through Irene's viewpoint, charts the emotional journey that she travels in response to Allen's erratic behavior. Their relationship, through her perception, becomes a dance of intellectual passion and spiritual magnetism.

Allen, however, stops coming to class and, after a prolonged absence, contacts Irene from a sanatorium with a plea that she intervene with his father. The Christian awakening and power that Irene feels as she approaches the Weinstein home disappear when she is faced with Allen's hateful, exasperated, unsympathetic father. Later, released from the sanatorium, Allen comes to Irene for emotional and financial support, but she painfully and inarticulately denies him, incapable of establishing a meaningful connection. Although Allen is clearly on the edge of sanity, Irene's situation is more pathetic, for she is knowingly trapped within the trivial limits of her own selfhood. At the story's end, even the almost inevitable news of Allen's suicide provokes only a longing for feeling but no true emotional response.

**"Where Are You Going, Where Have You Been?"** • Another story that details the effects of a male intruder into the life of a female protagonist and the difficulty of connection between two very different people is "Where Are You Going, Where Have You Been?," one of Oates's most anthologized early stories. This tale of confused adolescence, based on a true story of a serial killer in Tucson, Arizona, is about Connie, a fifteen-year-old who abhors her parents, haunts suburban malls, and passes the hot summer nights with her equally precocious girlfriends. Through it all, however, she privately harbors innocent dreams of ideal love. One day, while home alone, she is approached by a strange man ominously named Arnold Friend, who is determined to seduce her and take her away. Rather than use force, Friend insinuates his way into Connie's mind and subdues her vulnerable and emerging sexuality. In the end, it is clear that he is leading her to some sort of death, spiritual or physical, and that his love is empty, but she is powerless against him.

Oates tells the story naturalistically but includes dreamy and surrealistic passages that suggest allegorical interpretation. The title implies both the uncertainty of adolescence and the changelessness of feminine behavior, or, possibly, the slow pace of social progress in improving women's lives. Subtly crafted and typically Oatesian, "Where Are You Going, Where Have You Been?" is in some ways a precursor to many later Oates stories. "How I Contemplated the World from the Detroit House of Correction and Began My Life Over Again" is a first-person account of a wayward adolescent girl in search of love and self-definition; the much later "Testimony" portrays a teenage girl who is so devoted to her older boyfriend that she serves as his accomplice in the abduction, rape, and murder of her perceived "rival"; and "April" is a simple sketch of two young adolescents rebelling against maternal authority. These four, and many others, portray moments in time when youth teeters on the brink of adulthood, when innocence is subtly transformed into sophistication, and when desire and love become stronger than life itself.

**"The Scream"** • The struggles with desire, rebellion, and identity are subtler but no less intense in a story entitled "The Scream." It is a mood piece, in which little happens; the emotional impact is found in the images and the tension of stillness. The protagonist is a woman named Renée who, like many of the characters in the volume *Crossing the Border,* is an American living across the border in Canada. Floundering in a loving but lifeless marriage, she has been having an affair with a man for whom she feels passion but little trust.

The narrative of the story follows Renée as she wanders through an art museum, intentionally absent from an appointed rendezvous with her lover. An old man approaches her; she eavesdrops on talkative tourists; she peruses the art; she ruminates on her marriage, her affair, and her various uninteresting options. One photograph especially catches her attention: that of an Indian woman holding out a dead child, her face frozen in an anguished shriek. After gazing a long while at the photograph, losing herself in it, Renée swiftly leaves the museum and goes to meet her lover. The story ends as she stands outside their meeting place, no more determined to enter than when she started.

The power of the story lies in the photograph as an image. On one hand, the Indian woman's scream touches Renée's own internal anguish, which is magnified by the relative paltriness of her particular discontent. On the other hand, the static quality of the photographic image—the scream does not vanish when Renée looks away and back again—figures her own emotional paralysis. She can see and feel the inherent contradiction of her quandary—frozen in anguish—and through the experience at the museum can only barely begin to take action for self-liberation.

**"In the Autumn of the Year"** • An even more mature woman is at the center of "In the Autumn of the Year," which received an O. Henry Award in 1979, a year after its first publication in *The Bennington Review,* and which is included in the collection *A Sentimental Education.* Eleanor Gerhardt is a Pulitzer Prize-winning poet, an articulate spinster who has come to a small New England college to accept an award. Her host for the visit is Benjamin Holler, a man she knew when he was a boy in Boston when she was his father's mistress. She was never married, and her passion for Edwin Holler and the dramatic dissolution of their relationship form a memory that she sustains, though she had not seen him in the decades before his death. Upon meeting Benjamin, her consciousness shifts back and forth from the uneventful present to the tumultuous and deeply felt past. Oates here uses balance to create powerful emotional dynamics. The juxtaposition of immediate experience and memory communicates the dislocation with which Eleanor perceives her existence in the "autumn" of her life.

The second half of the story comes suddenly and unexpectedly. In a seemingly casual conversation, Benjamin expresses accumulated anger and hatred at Eleanor and his father. Confronted with the sordidness of their affair and their responsibility for the emotional misery of his childhood, Eleanor's sentimental vision of the past is shattered. Benjamin offers her the love letters and suicide threats that she sent to Edwin upon their separation, but she cannot face them and denies their authenticity. In the end, alone, she tosses the unopened letters in the fire, as if so doing will alleviate her guilt and folly. Benjamin's brutal honesty, however, has provided a missing piece to the puzzle of her life. Without the delusions by which her past drained her present of meaning, she is forced to face the past honestly and, recognizing its mixed qualities, to let go of it. Through this encounter, she can begin to take responsibility for her continued existence and her continued potential to think, feel, do, and live. As so often in Oates's stories, small encounters bring great transformations, and in pain there is redemption.

**"Raven's Wing"** • "Raven's Wing," a story in the volume of the same title, first appeared in *Esquire* and was included in *The Best American Short Stories, 1985*. It is a subtle story that portrays a rather ordinary marriage and lacks the violence and passion of much of Oates's other work. Billy and Linda have been married for barely a year. Though Linda is five months pregnant, Billy treats her with indifference; Linda, in turn, baits, teases, and spites him. A horse-racing enthusiast, Billy becomes fascinated with a prize horse named Raven's Wing after it is crippled during a race. He finds a way to visit Raven's Wing in Pennsylvania, where it is recovering from major surgery, and, eye to eye with the animal, feels a connection, an implicit mixture of awe, sympathy, and trust. The story ends soon thereafter in two brief scenes: Billy gives Linda a pair of delicate earrings and finds excitement in watching her put them on, and, weeks later, as he talks on the phone, Linda comes to him warmly, holding out a few strands of coarse black hair—a souvenir from Raven's Wing—and presses close against him.

In "Raven's Wing," rather than stating the characters' true feelings, of which they themselves are only hazily aware, Oates suggests them through the details of external reality. This is a story about perception—about how things appear differently through the blurring lens of familiarity and routine. Billy's fascination with the crippled horse betrays an unconscious awareness of his own crippled psyche, and the enormous, beautiful, and priceless creature's almost inevitable consignment to a stud farm is an ironic reminder of Linda's pregnancy and the very human power that a man and woman share to love, to support, and to create.

***The Assignation*** • The collection *The Assignation* is stylistically noteworthy, as Oates departs from standard forms and offers a variety of stories, character sketches, mood pieces, and other experiments in short fiction. Many of the pieces are deceptively short; lacking in plot information and often anonymous regarding character, they portray an emotional situation, interaction, or moment through the economic uses of detail and action. The first piece, "One Flesh," is no more than a paragraph suggesting the richly sensual relationship shared by an old couple. In "Pinch," a woman's fleeting emotions during a breast examination create a tense picture. In "Maximum Security," a woman's tour of a prison invokes a disturbing sense of isolation while invigorating her appreciation of nature and freedom. "Quarrel" and "Ace" are about how events of random violence affect, respectively, a homosexual couple's communication and a young street tough's sense of identity. In all these pieces, Oates provides the essentials of a fuller story and invites the reader's imagination to go beyond and within the story. The characters are no less unique, the prose no less picturesque, and the situations no less compelling; the economy with which Oates evokes these tales is testament to the depth of her craft.

***Will You Always Love Me?*** • *Will You Always Love Me?* is a collection of twenty-two narratives based upon childhood memories, suffering, and reason for hope. Oates cuts to the core of everyday life, revealing the truth about what people know but are not willing to admit. She portrays a profound commentary on the human condition by acting as a witness in describing the needs, cruelty, and violence displayed by humankind. Three of the stories, "You Petted Me, and I Followed You Home," "The Goose-Girl," and "Mark of Satan," won O. Henry Awards.

A lost dog is a central figure in "You Petted Me, and I Followed You Home," a story that first appeared in *TriQuarterly*. Dawn, who fears the erratic behavior and sudden violent acts of her husband, Vic, pets a little lost dog, which subsequently follows her and Vic home. Oates skillfully unveils how Dawn's feelings of fear for what lies ahead—of betrayal by loved ones and a terrible sense of lost feeling—parallel the feelings of the dog. By treating the dog with care and kindness, Dawn relays to Vic the need for similar consideration.

Oates examines some of the consequences that result from unbridled thoughts of passion in "The Goose-Girl," which first appeared in *Fiction*. Lydia, a respected suburban mother, helps her son Barry humiliate their new neighbor, Phoebe Stone. Phoebe, who reminds Lydia of the goose-girl in the fairy tales of the Brothers Grimm, propositions Barry at a neighborhood party. Struggling with deep feelings of guilt, Barry eventually reveals the incident to his mother and pleads with her to call Phoebe. After allowing Barry time to worry, Lydia finally makes the call and wittingly embarrasses Phoebe over the proposed sexual encounter with her son.

In "Mark of Satan," which first appeared in *Antaeus*, Oates brings protagonist Flash to a renewed definition of self, even a renewal of spirit. During a visit from Thelma, a female missionary, Flash attempts to seduce her by drugging her lemonade. Thelma instinctively avoids the ploy and tells Flash that Satan is present in his home. Ironically, after Thelma leaves, she returns and prays for Flash. Finally, he realizes that someone cares about him, even though he does not deserve it.

Included in *The Best American Stories, 1996*, "Ghost Girls" emerged from Oates's childhood image of a small country airport isolated between cornfields. Ingrid Boone, the child narrator, is intrigued by the mysterious lives led by her parents. Because Ingrid cannot fully comprehend or do anything about the strange adult world that surrounds her, her life, influenced by the example of her attractive mother and her frequently absent father, eventually spirals down into a tale of grotesque horrors. "Ghost Girls" is the seed of Oates's *Man Crazy* (1997), a novel of many stark images.

Perhaps the most concise articulation of the Oatesian aesthetic can be found in a story entitled "Love. Friendship" from *The Assignation*. In recollecting a friendship with a sensitive man who became obsessed with her marriage, the narrator Judith reflects:

> Our lives are narratives; they are experienced in the flesh, sometimes in flesh that comes alive only with pain, but they are recollected as poems, lyrics, condensed, illuminated by a few precise images.

Such descriptive narratives—long, short, lyrical, violent, experienced, recollected, full of precise images portraying real-life situations filled with deep heartfelt emotions—form the bulk of Oates's short fiction.

*Barry Mann*
*With updates by Alvin K. Benson and the Editors*

**Other major works**

CHILDREN'S LITERATURE: *Come Meet Muffin,* 1998; *Big Mouth and Ugly Girl,* 2002; *Freaky Green Eyes,* 2003; *Sexy,* 2005.

PLAYS: *Miracle Play,* pr. 1974; *Three Plays,* pb. 1980; *I Stand Before You Naked,* pb. 1991; *In Darkest America: Two Plays,* pb. 1991; *Twelve Plays,* pb. 1991; *The Perfectionist, and Other Plays,* pb. 1995; *New Plays,* pb. 1998.

ANTHOLOGIES: *Scenes from American Life: Contemporary Short Fiction,* 1972; *The Best American Short Stories 1979,* 1979 (with Shannon Ravenel); *Night Walks: A Bedside Companion,* 1982; *First Person Singular: Writers on Their Craft,* 1983; *The Best American Essays,* 1991; *The Oxford Book of American Short Stories,* 1992; *American Gothic Tales,* 1996; *Snapshots: Twentieth Century Mother-Daughter Fiction,* 2000 (with Janet Berliner); *The Best American Mystery Stories,* 2005 (with Otto Penzler).

NOVELS: *With Shuddering Fall,* 1964; *A Garden of Earthly Delights,* 1967, revised 2003; *Expensive People,* 1968; *them,* 1969; *Wonderland,* 1971; *Do with Me What You Will,* 1973; *The Assassins: A Book of Hours,* 1975; *Childwold,* 1976; *The Triumph of the Spider Monkey,* 1976; *Son of the Morning,* 1978; *Cybele,* 1979; *Unholy Loves,* 1979; *Bellefleur,* 1980; *Angel of Light,* 1981; *A Bloodsmoor Romance,* 1982; *Mysteries of Winterthurn,* 1984; *Solstice,* 1985; *Marya: A Life,* 1986; *Lives of the Twins,* 1987 (as Rosamond Smith); *You Must Remember This,* 1987; *American Appetites,* 1989; *Soul/Mate,* 1989 (as Smith); *Because It Is Bitter, and Because It Is My Heart,* 1990; *I Lock My Door upon Myself,* 1990; *Nemesis,* 1990 (as Smith); *The Rise of Life on Earth,* 1991; *Black Water,* 1992; *Snake Eyes,* 1992 (as Smith); *Foxfire: Confessions of a Girl Gang,* 1993; *What I Lived For,* 1994; *You Can't Catch Me,* 1995 (as Smith); *Zombie,* 1995; *First Love,* 1996; *We Were the Mulvaneys,* 1996; *Man Crazy,* 1997; *My Heart Laid Bare,* 1998; *Broke Heart Blues,* 1999; *Starr Bright Will Be With You Soon,* 1999 (as Smith); *Blonde,* 2000; *Middle Age: A Romance,* 2001; *The Barrens,* 2001 (as Smith); *Beasts,* 2002; *Rape: A Love Story,* 2003; *The Tattooed Girl,* 2003; *The Falls,* 2004; *Missing Mom,* 2005; *Black Girl/White Girl,* 2006.

NONFICTION: *The Edge of Impossibility: Tragic Forms in Literature,* 1972; *The Hostile Sun: The Poetry of D. H. Lawrence,* 1973; *New Heaven, New Earth: The Visionary Experience in Literature,* 1974; *Contraries: Essays,* 1981; *The Profane Art: Essays and Reviews,* 1983; *On Boxing,* 1987; *(Woman) Writer: Occasions and Opportunities,* 1988; *George Bellows: American Artist,* 1995; *Where I've Been, and Where I'm Going: Essays, Reviews, and Prose,* 1999; *The Faith of a Writer: Life, Craft, Art,* 2003; *Uncensored: Views and (Re)views,* 2005.

POETRY: *Women in Love,* 1968; *Anonymous Sins, and Other Poems,* 1969; *Love and Its Derangements,* 1970; *Angel Fire,* 1973; *The Fabulous Beasts,* 1975; *Women Whose Lives Are Food, Men Whose Lives Are Money,* 1978; *Invisible Woman: New and Selected Poems, 1970-1982,* 1982; *The Luxury of Sin,* 1984; *The Time Traveler,* 1989; *Tenderness,* 1996.

**Bibliography**

Bastian, Katherine. *Joyce Carol Oates's Short Stories: Between Tradition and Innovation.* Frankfurt: Verlag Peter Lang, 1983. Bastian surveys the Oatesian short story, providing occasional insights into theme and character. The focus is to place Oates in the tradition of the genre and find her links with its other masters.

Creighton, Joanne V. *Joyce Carol Oates: A Study of the Short Fiction.* New York: Twayne, 1994. After a general introduction to Oates's contribution to the short story, devotes separate chapters to feminism, the gothic, and postmodernism in several of Oates's short-story collections. Includes a number of comments by Oates on the short story, as well as brief excerpts from seven other critics.

_____. *Understanding Joyce Carol Oates*. Columbia: University of South Carolina Press, 1987. Geared to the general reader, this volume examines both Oates's major novels and some of her best-known stories. The focus is more on specific works than on Oates's overarching concerns. Easy to read, with a biography and bibliography.

Johnson, Greg. "A Barbarous Eden: Joyce Carol Oates's First Collection." *Studies in Short Fiction* 30 (Winter, 1993): 1-14. Discusses Oates's *By the North Gate* as a microcosm of her entire career in fiction. Focuses on her Faulknerian mythmaking, her view of love as a violent force through which characters strive for power, and the similarity of her stories to those of Flannery O'Connor.

_____. *Invisible Writer: A Biography of Joyce Carol Oates*. New York: Penguin Putnam, 1998. Johnson provides a thorough analysis of Oates's work and life in this full-length authorized biography. Draws on a variety of sources, including Oates's private letters and journals.

May, Charles E., ed. *Masterplots II: Short Story Series, Revised Edition*. 8 vols. Pasadena, Calif.: Salem Press, 2004. Designed for student use, this reference set contains articles providing detailed plot summaries and analyses of thirteen short stories by Oates: "Heat" (vol. 3); "How I Contemplated the World from the Detroit House of Correction and Began My Life over Again," "In the Region of Ice," and "The Lady with the Pet Dog" (vol. 4); "My Warszawa" and "Nairobi" (vol. 5); "Stalking" and "The Swimmers" (vol. 7); and "Unmailed, Unwritten Letters," "Upon the Sweeping Flood," "Waiting," "What Is the Connection Between Men and Women?," and "Where Are You Going, Where Have You Been?" (vol. 8).

Oates, Joyce Carol. *Inter/View: Talks with America's Writing Women*. Interview by Mickey Pearlman and Katherine Usher Henderson. Lexington: University Press of Kentucky, 1990. Numerous interviews with Oates have been published, but this one reveals topics germane to the poetry: class relations, gender relations, and the vital role of memory in her creativity. Oates talks about the biographers (whom Oates labels "pathographers") who ascribe sickness and deviance to women writers, conflating personal and professional lives in a very damaging way.

Wagner, Linda, ed. *Critical Essays on Joyce Carol Oates*. Boston: G. K. Hall, 1979. Good collection of twenty-eight reviews and essays, some on particular works, others on general themes or stylistic considerations. The short stories receive less attention than the novels and even, surprisingly, the poetry. Extensive and evenhanded, with a chronology and bibliography, and a short but refreshing preface by Oates herself.

Wesley, Marilyn. *Refusal and Transgression in Joyce Carol Oates's Fiction*. Westport, Conn.: Greenwood Press, 1993. Feminist analysis, this work focuses on the family as portrayed in Oates's fiction. Wesley contends that the young protagonists of many of Oates's stories and novels commit acts of transgression that serve as critiques of the American family. Wesley maintains that the acts indict the society that produces and supports these unstable, dysfunctional, and often violent, families.

Wyatt, Jennifer L., Traci S. Smrcka, and Bill Delaney. "Joyce Carol Oates." In *Critical Survey of Long Fiction, Revised Edition*, edited by Carl Rollyson. Vol. 5. Pasadena, Calif.: Salem Press, 2000. Analysis of Oates's longer fictional works that may offer insights into her short fiction.

# Edna O'Brien

**Born:** Tuamgraney, County Clare, Ireland; December 15, 1930

**Principal short fiction** • *The Love Object*, 1968; *A Scandalous Woman, and Other Stories*, 1974; *Mrs. Reinhardt*, 1978 (published in U.S. as *A Rose in the Heart*, 1979); *Returning*, 1982; *A Fanatic Heart*, 1984; *Lantern Slides*, 1990.

**Other literary forms** • Besides short stories, Edna O'Brien has written dramas (including screenplays and teleplays), poetry (*On the Bone*, 1989), children's literature (*The Dazzle*, 1981), and novels such as *A Pagan Place* (1970), *Night* (1972), *The Country Girls Trilogy and Epilogue* (1986), *House of Splendid Isolation* (1994), *Down by the River* (1996), *Wild Decembers* (1999), *In the Forest* (2001), and *The Light of Evening* (2006). She has also published nonfiction, including autobiographical travel books such as *Mother Ireland* (1976), newspaper articles, and biographical and literary criticism such as *James and Nora* (1981), and *James Joyce* (1999). She has also edited the anthology *Some Irish Loving* (1979).

**Achievements** • After a strong start in the early 1960's with three splendid short novels in the *Bildungsroman* tradition of maturation and escape (*The Country Girls*, 1960, winner of the Kingsley Amis Award; *The Lonely Girl*, 1962, reprinted as *Girl with Green Eyes*, 1964; and *Girls in Their Married Bliss*, 1964), Edna O'Brien established herself publicly in a variety of television appearances. She became a most articulate spokeswoman for a not overly romantic view of Ireland, for women trapped in an eternal mother-daughter conflict, and for some feminists. The last-mentioned achievement is reached paradoxically in O'Brien's fictions by her frequent exploration and exploitation of an unsympathetic woman in the leading role—the Caithleen (Kate) of the early novels. O'Brien has very few male leads or narrators. Her Kate-women often are whiners and losers who make poor choices in their liaisons with men (often already married), which almost inevitably bring grief. Her depiction of character, setting (particularly in Ireland—Philip Roth has praised her sense of place), and conflict is, however, so strong, so graphic, and often in such memorable language, appealing to all the senses, that the negative point is made: This is not how a woman, or indeed any person, seeking happiness should go about the search "for love or connection."

At her best, O'Brien has another counterbalancing woman present as a foil, such as the ebullient Baba, the other heroine with Kate in her early novels; this confident voice is particularly strong in *Girls in Their Married Bliss* and *Night*, an extended "Baba" monologue in the fashion of James Joyce's Molly Bloom in *Ulysses* (1922). O'Brien's achievement is to take her readers some distance along the road to realizing what it is to be an integrated, and therefore a happy, person. She is at her best when the setting of her fictions is rural Ireland, not the jet-setters' London or Mediterranean. O'Brien is most popular in the United States, where she gives frequent readings of her work. She is a gifted re-creator of the sights, smells, tastes, and feel of Ireland—with a vivid way of capturing what people might say, at their colorful best.

**Biography** • As the youngest child in a Roman Catholic family that included a brother and two sisters, Josephine Edna O'Brien was born on December 15, 1930, and grew up on a farm in the west of Ireland. She was educated at the local parochial school in Scarriff and was a boarder in the Convent of Mercy, Loughrea, County Galway. She went to Dublin to study pharmacy in the apprentice system then in vogue and began contributing to the *Irish Press*. In 1954, O'Brien married writer Ernest Gebler, author of *Plymouth Adventure* (1950); they had two sons, Carlo and Sasha.

The family moved to London, where O'Brien established her permanent residence and wrote *The Country Girls* in her first month there. She followed it quickly with the other parts of the trilogy, *The Lonely Girl* and *Girls in Their Married Bliss*. Though O'Brien and Gebler have argued in print over

© Terry O'Neill

just how much help he gave her with the trilogy (the marriage was dissolved in 1964), O'Brien was launched on a successful, high-profile career. *The Lonely Girl* was made into a film, *Girl with Green Eyes*, starring Rita Tushingham.

Based in London, very successfully bringing up her sons on her own, O'Brien had two most prolific decades of work, in a variety of genres. The novels accumulated: *August Is a Wicked Month* (1965); *Casualties of Peace* (1966); *A Pagan Place*, her favorite work; *Zee and Co.* (1971); *Johnny I Hardly Knew You* (1977); and, after what was for O'Brien a long hiatus, *The Country Girls Trilogy and Epilogue* (1986), *The High Road* (1988), and other contemporary-setting novels including *Wild Decembers* (1999). Between novels, she published short stories in a variety of magazines (*The New Yorker* in particular), the best of which have been collected. Along with prose fiction, journalism, and travel books, O'Brien also continued her interest in drama: *A Cheap Bunch of Nice Flowers* (1962), *Time Lost and Time Remembered* (1966), *X, Y, and Zee* (1971), and *Virginia* (1980).

O'Brien's biography provides the raw material for her fictions. "All fiction is fantasized autobiography," she affirms in the introduction to *An Edna O'Brien Reader* (1994). In 1984 and 1986, she published in New York a pair of matched volumes: *A Fanatic Heart*, largely from the best of her previously collected stories, and, what many would consider her best work, *The Country Girls Trilogy and Epilogue*, of which a twenty-one-page last section is entirely new. For a while, it seemed that the well of inspiration was exhausted. In 1988, however, she was back again in New York with *The High Road*, published after a ten-year novel-writing hiatus. She also presented a reading in New York in 1990 of "Brother," from her short-story collection *Lantern Slides* and autographed her poem *On the Bone* (1989).

**Analysis** • Edna O'Brien has written short stories throughout her long career. "Come into the Drawing Room, Doris" (retitled "Irish Revel" in *The Love Object* collection) first appeared in *The New Yorker* on October 6, 1962. "Cords," published as "Which of Those Two Ladies Is He Married To?" in *The New Yorker*, on April 25, 1964, deals with many of the aspects of loss and missed connections, which are O'Brien's constant themes. The missed connections are most frequently between mothers and daughters, and between women and men. O'Brien is at her most persuasively graphic when her protagonists are clearly Irish women, at home, in a vanished Ireland whose society as a whole she re-creates and often increasingly indicts most convincingly.

**"Cords"** • The question "Which of Those Two Ladies Is He Married To?," which forms the original title of "Cords," is posed in the story by Claire's scandalized, rural, Irish mother on a London visit to her sexually active, editor, lapsed Catholic, poet-daughter. The dinner guests are a husband, his pregnant wife Marigold, and his mistress Pauline—which grouping elicits the mother's question. The newer title, "Cords," more aptly focuses attention on the constrictive mother-daughter bond, which is at the center of this story. The conflict is effectively rendered; no final judgment is made on who is to blame. The Catholic, self-sacrificing mother, who masochistically sews without a thimble, is a spunky traveler. The rather precious daughter, with her "social appendages" but no friends, "no one she could produce for her mother [or herself] and feel happy about," for her part means well. The two women are deftly shown to be on a collision course, not just with their umbrellas or their differences over food. The detailed parts of the story all function smoothly. The mother looks at herself in a glass door; Claire sees herself reflected in a restaurant's mirrors. Each woman is herself and an image projected elsewhere. The constraint between them is vividly rendered from their moment of meeting until they are at the airport again, where both "secretly feared the flight number would never be called."

In the background here, in Claire's thoughts, is the father, "emaciated, crazed and bankrupted by drink," with whom the mother's unhealthy, symbiotic relationship continues: "She was nettled because Claire had not asked how he was." In "Cords," then, are many of the perennial, rush-of-memory themes: the family feuding, the malevolent Church influence, the searing, almost flawlessly detailed exposé of the tie that binds many mothers and daughters. All is rendered here with the saving grace of good humor, and even old jokes are recalled, such as those about good grazing on the Buckingham Palace lawns, about Irish planes being blessed and therefore never crashing, and about an overly heavy suitcase—"Have you stones in it?" Claire asks.

**"A Scandalous Woman"** • "A Scandalous Woman" sets the tone for O'Brien's second collection, named after it, and reveals an increasingly gloomy view of the female predicament, whether in Ireland or elsewhere. The story, published in 1974, concludes, "I thought that ours indeed was a land of shame, a land of murder, and a land of strange, [to which is added in the stronger *A Fanatic Heart* version, 'throttled'] women." Here is an indictment of a family, its church, and society, very like that in *A Pagan Place*, and to be seen again in "Savages." The anonymous narrator leads the reader through Eily's life from early courtship days until the moment when the narrator, now no longer a young girl but a mother herself, seeks out her childhood friend, to find her much changed: "My first thought was that they must have drugged the feelings out of her . . . taken her spark away." "They" and their "strange brews" are part of the "scandalous" environment of this pagan place.

The anonymous narrator graphically describes how, as a young girl, she admired and sought the company of Eily, who was a few years older and had the "face of a madonna." The narrator tells how she loved Eily and visited her home each Tuesday, even though this meant that she had to play, in the hospital game, the patient to Eily's sister's surgeon. Lying on the kitchen table, she saw "the dresser upside down" in a world whose values are far from upright either. It is Eily, however, who is hollowed out at the story's end: Her playing Juliet to her Protestant Romeo, a bank clerk named Jack, ends in Eily's sniveling at a shotgun wedding. The young narrator had acted as lookout and cover so Eily could meet her lover, "Sunday after Sunday, with one holy day, Ascension Thursday, thrown in." When Jack attempts to throw Eily over, the narrator reveals in herself the same confusion of pagan and Christian values of the others:

> I said . . . that instead of consulting a witch we ought first to resort to other things, such as novenas, putting wedding cake under our pillows, or gathering bottles of dew in the early morning and putting them in a certain fort to make a wish.

The combined forces of the family, church, and community, in a profusion of animal imagery, move events along to the marriage solution. This is a dense, beautifully put together story, packed with details of the repressive effects of society on a lively girl, who is cowed into submission. From the symbolism of the upside-down world observed by the child on the kitchen table to the loaded "Matilda" term for the female genitalia (between "ma" and "da," there "I" am), everything in this story contributes to the indictment and ironic redefinition of what is "scandalous."

***Mrs. Reinhardt, and Other Stories*** • O'Brien's pessimism about much of the female condition shows little alleviation in the *Mrs. Reinhardt, and Other Stories* collection, heavily though erratically edited and renamed *A Rose in the Heart* in the American edition. The stories overall continue to chronicle the depressing, unsuccessful search of O'Brien's heroines for happiness in, but more often out of, marriage. Other perennial themes such as loss, isolation, motherhood, and bigotry are not neglected, especially when the setting is Ireland. The gothic story "Clara" has a rare male narrator.

The stories "Number Ten" and "Mrs. Reinhardt" fit together and were in fact dramatized as a unit in a 1981 drama prepared for the British Broadcasting Corporation. Tilly, in a failing marriage with her art-dealer husband, Harold, sleepwalks her way into misery. For the normally self-centered O'Brien woman who lives, especially when in England, in an economic and social vacuum (very unlike O'Brien's own successful career), Tilly's two afternoons a week teaching autistic children is unusual and helps her credibility. In her dreams, she sees the perfect "nest"—an apartment, with one entire bedroom wall a mirror, where she and her husband can come together at night. The apartment, surreally, does exist, she discovers, and her husband uses it in the daytime with another woman. It is a rending, no-communication standoff; the unhappy O'Brien woman remains "an outsider looking in."

In the second tale, Mrs. Reinhardt heads off to color-splashed Brittany for a trial separation, determined to somnambulate no more. She resolves to forget the past and to "get even with life" by taking advantage of a brash Iowan in his mid-twenties whom she meets by the sea. It is an ugly picture that O'Brien paints of Tilly's sexual conduct, which is as predatory as that of the lobsters she observes in their tank. In this bleak tale, neither the love of the old patron at the hotel nor the arrival of Tilly's husband does much to alleviate the joyless atmosphere: "What then does a Mrs. Reinhardt do? . . . One reaches out to the face that is opposite . . . for the duration of a windy night. And by morning who knows? Who knows anything anyhow?" Such is the pessimistic conclusion to this fiction; O'Brien's aging heroine's search continues.

*Returning* • O'Brien's sharp study of a certain kind of female psychology continues in the collection *Returning*, where the external topography in all nine stories is the west of Ireland and the craggy community there. A young girl is present in all the collection's stories, either as the ostensible narrator or as the subject of mature reflection on the part of the now-experienced woman. This then-and-now tension between the innocence of childhood and the experience of fifty years, Philip Roth, in his introduction to *A Fanatic Heart*, isolates as the spring for these stories' "wounded vigor." There is no title story of the same name, but in a very real sense each of the tales here represents a return for O'Brien, a going home.

"Savages," in this collection, represents O'Brien, often accused of careless, awkward, and too-rapid writing, at her careful, three-times-reworked best. The theme bears distinct similarities to "A Scandalous Woman" in its indictment of the community. The story deals with Mabel McCann's search for love in her village community, her false pregnancy, and ostracism. The three published versions of the story that exist (the version published in *The New Yorker*, January 18, 1982; the English edition; and the version in *A Fanatic Heart*) help reveal O'Brien's artistic development, which, though it is by no means a straight-line progression, nevertheless represents work and progress. A noticeable distancing and maturing in the narrator can be seen from the first version to the second one, where she is no longer a precocious twelve-year-old. The second version introduces the five-hundred-word addition of a lugubrious scene between a deaf-and-dumb brother and sister to underscore the gothic qualities of the environment. Although all is not unequivocal, there is artistic progress in this second version, where Mabel is called a "simpleton" in the conclusion. In the third and final version, this term, removing her from the world of choices, is wisely dropped; readers are left to work out for themselves what happened. This emendation is a final improvement in the best overall version of an excellent story. The collection also includes the sensory-rich "Sister Imelda," which received the accolade of inclusion in the 1986 *Norton Anthology of English Literature*.

*A Fanatic Heart* • *A Fanatic Heart* includes twenty-five O'Brien stories previously anthologized and a quartet of *The New Yorker*, heretofore uncollected works, in a splendidly produced volume introduced by Roth. The quartet is typical of O'Brien's writing when she is on the brittle high road outside Ireland and is generally much less satisfactory. The shallow, codependent Irish woman of these stories moves in three of them through bitter, first-person musings on a current, seemingly doomed affair of the heart with a married family man. Only in the second story, "The Call," is she looked at in the third person as she does not answer the ringing telephone. It is time to cease to be strangers, she muses in "The Plan." In a later version of this tale, though, O'Brien cut the pessimistic note that follows immediately, "Though of course we would always be strangers." The "blue" narrator takes a geographical cure to forget, but that does not work, and readers are left with her wondering in "The Return" how much longer she will be able to endure.

**"Another Time"** • In "Another Time," in the collection *Lantern Slides*, the narrator, a single parent and glamorous former television announcer, gets away to her home in the west of Ireland. After a series of sharply observed encounters with and flashbacks to places and people, Nelly Nugent comes to terms with the present: "She felt as if doors or windows were swinging open all around her and that she was letting go of some awful affliction." At her best, O'Brien has the capacity in her fictions to give this release to her readers. The mirrors that appear so often in her work serve then to alert not only her recurring characters but also her readers to the roller-coaster realities of love, loss, and endurance. This work was selected for *The Best New Yorker Stories of 1989*, in which magazine four others of the dozen stories in this collection also appeared.

**"Love's Lesson"** • Whatever the question is, O'Brien's answer is love; this story, then, which appeared in *Zoetrope* (Summer, 1998), closes out a decade in which no collection appeared after *Lantern Slides*. The varieties-of-love theme continued in the 1990's to dominate O'Brien's short fictions, beginning with "No Place" (*The New Yorker*, June 17, 1991) where her well-off, ageless, lonely, Irish protagonist, her two boys still in boarding school, waits "on love" in North Africa; her man fails to show up from London's rougher-trade side. Still, in *The New Yorker* (July 11, 1994), a now aging, lonely widow, the love of her children growing "fainter and fainter," her husband's "unloving love" now a memory, shows herself in "Sin" to be far from well as she pictures her paying guests' incestuous relations with their daughter: "What reached her ears could not be called silence."

In "Love's Lesson" a jagged, uneven, disconnected, at times overwritten letter from an Irish woman in New York City reviews the course of her affair with a celebrated architect. Her relationship with him has magnified her feeling of being an outsider. Cosmopolitan and international in her experiences and sympathies, she is yet setting out for home, the mysteries of love still mysterious: "Now we will never know for sure." The lessons taught here by "love" in its various manifestations send the protagonist home to freedom, "to give up the habit of slavery." Freedom has its costs, too. Nor is there any free love, as the narrator discovers, reviewing her violent relationship with the architect, which she wishes was just physical. She shares her lesbian relationship with her friend Clarissa, who is greatly troubled by thoughts of her dead mother, as is the nameless narrator. People she meets and observes, all with their "connection" problems, cause her to book her flight home.

Given the personal-journal format here, reinforced by O'Brien's ongoing admiration for and work on master wordsmith James Joyce, the stream-of-consciousness technique is to be expected. O'Brien's best prior example of this technique is her *Night*. Here, in "Love's Lesson," she continues her alliterative reaching for metaphorical, verbal epiphanies through all the senses to establish the mood. Sometimes she is successful, sometimes not: "Skeins of sound sweetening the air." Here then O'Brien's Irish heroine, alone, courageously as ever, confronts life and the varieties and manifestations of love. The constraints of the Roman Catholic Church and rural society have no place here, but family pressures are not absent, nor is the gallant hope with which her secular heroines view life as they must live it.

*Archibald E. Irwin*

**Other major works**

CHILDREN'S LITERATURE: *The Dazzle*, 1981; *A Christmas Treat*, 1982; *The Expedition*, 1982; *The Rescue*, 1983; *Tales for the Telling: Irish Folk and Fairy Stories*, 1986.

PLAYS: *A Cheap Bunch of Nice Flowers*, pr. 1962; *A Pagan Place*, pr. 1972 (adaptation of her novel); *The Gathering*, pr. 1974; *Virginia*, pr. 1980; *Flesh and Blood*, pr. 1985; *Iphigenia*, pr., pb. 2003 (adaptation of Euripides' play).

ANTHOLOGY: *Some Irish Loving*, 1979.

NOVELS: *The Country Girls*, 1960; *The Lonely Girl*, 1962 (also known as *Girl with Green Eyes*, 1964); *Girls in Their Married Bliss*, 1964; *August Is a Wicked Month*, 1965; *Casualties of Peace*, 1966; *A Pagan Place*, 1970; *Zee and Co.*, 1971; *Night*, 1972; *Johnny I Hardly Knew You*, 1977 (published in U.S. as *I Hardly Knew You*, 1978); *The Country Girls Trilogy and Epilogue*, 1986 (includes *The Country Girls*, *The Lonely Girl*, and *Girls in Their Married Bliss*); *The High Road*, 1988; *Time and Tide*, 1992; *An Edna O'Brien Reader*, 1994; *House of Splendid Isolation*, 1994; *Down by the River*, 1996; *Wild Decembers*, 1999; *In the Forest*, 2001; *The Light of Evening*, 2006.

NONFICTION: *Mother Ireland*, 1976; *Arabian Days*, 1977; *James and Nora: A Portrait of Joyce's Marriage*, 1981; *Vanishing Ireland*, 1986; *James Joyce*, 1999.

POETRY: *On the Bone*, 1989.

SCREENPLAYS: *Girl with Green Eyes*, 1964 (adaptation of her novel); *Time Lost and Time Remembered*, 1966 (with Desmond Davis; also known as *I Was Happy Here*); *Three into Two Won't Go*, 1969; *X, Y, and Zee*, 1971 (also known as *Zee and Company*; adaptation of her novel).

TELEPLAYS: *The Wedding Dress*, 1963; *Nothing's Ever Over*, 1968; *Mrs. Reinhardt*, 1981 (adaptation of her short story); *The Country Girls*, 1983 (adaptation of her novel).

**Bibliography**

Guppy, Shusha. "The Art of Fiction: Edna O'Brien." *The Paris Review* 26 (Summer, 1984): 22-50. The topics discussed include how O'Brien got started on her writing career; the writers, such as James Joyce, Marcel Proust, and Anton Chekhov, whom she admires; feminism, into which O'Brien fits uneasily; religion; Ireland; and other areas, such as theater and film, in which O'Brien has worked. At the age of fifty-four, O'Brien affirms that she is putting the themes of love, loss, and loneliness behind her. She recommends *A Pagan Place* as her best book.

Irwin, Archibald E., and Joanne McCarthy. "Edna O'Brien." In *Critical Survey of Long Fiction, Revised Edition*, edited by Carl Rollyson. Vol. 5. Pasadena, Calif.: Salem Press, 2000. Analysis of O'Brien's longer fictional works that may offer insights into her short fiction.

May, Charles E., ed. *Masterplots II: Short Story Series, Revised Edition*. 8 vols. Pasadena, Calif.: Salem Press, 2004. Designed for student use, this reference set contains articles providing detailed plot summaries and analyses of six short stories by O'Brien: "Another Time" (vol. 1); "The Creature" (vol. 2); "Forgiveness" (vol. 3); and "Paradise," "A Rose in the Heart of New York," and "A Scandalous Woman" (vol. 6).

O'Brien, Edna. "Interview." *Paris Review* 26 (Summer, 1984): 22-50. O'Brien discusses the influence of Chekhov on her stories, the animosity of feminists to much of her writing, the theme of Ireland in her stories, and her focus on sexuality in many of her stories.

_____. "The Pleasure and the Pain." Interview by Miriam Gross. *The Observer* (April 14, 1985): 17-18. A provocative interview, interesting also in that it draws from Ernest Gebler, O'Brien's former husband, a detailed rebuttal of her statements about him (*The Observer*, April 28, 1985) and an incendiary interview with him (*Sunday Independent*, April 28, 1985, 7).

_____. *Publishers Weekly* 239 (May 18, 1992): 48-49. O'Brien discusses her relationship with her mother, her calling to become a writer, her interest in the Gospels and the writings of Catholic mystics, and her relationship with her editors.

O'Brien, Peggy. "The Silly and the Serious: An Assessment of Edna O'Brien." *The Massachusetts Review* 28 (Autumn, 1987): 474-488. An overview of O'Brien's work, discussing her central themes and critiquing critical reception of her stories. Argues that her obsession with a father figure makes her portray sexually insatiable women in disastrous relationships with hurtful men.

O'Hara, Kiera. "Love Objects: Love and Obsession in the Stories of Edna O'Brien." *Studies in Short Fiction* 30 (Summer, 1993): 317-326. Discusses O'Brien's characters' obsession with love, which stands in the way of love's attainment. Discusses "Irish Revel" from her 1969 collection *The Love Object* as the birth of the obsession and the title story of her 1990 collection *Lantern Slides* as the epitome of it.

Shumaker, Jeanette Roberts. "Sacrificial Women in Short Stories by Mary Lavin and Edna O'Brien." *Studies in Short Fiction* 32 (Spring, 1995): 185-197. Examines sacrificial women in two stories by Lavin and two by O'Brien; claims that in the stories, female martyrdom engendered by the Madonna myth takes different forms, from becoming a nun to becoming a wife, mother, or "fallen woman."

Woodward, Richard B. "Edna O'Brien: Reveling in the Heartbreak." *The New York Times Magazine* (March 12, 1989): 42, 50, 52. An up-close and unsympathetic portrait, with a color photo, of O'Brien, whom Woodward, after several meetings and much research, calls "a poet of heartbreak." This careful essay shows an off-putting, publicity-hunting, and difficult side of the deliberately apolitical O'Brien. Woodward does not find that *The High Road* breaks any new ground, in contrast to the affirmation of Shusha Guppy; he finds her short fiction more accomplished.

# Flannery O'Connor

**Born:** Savannah, Georgia; March 25, 1925
**Died:** Milledgeville, Georgia; August 3, 1964

**Principal short fiction** • *A Good Man Is Hard to Find*, 1955; "Good Country People," 1955; "Revelation," 1964; *Everything That Rises Must Converge*, 1965; *The Complete Stories*, 1971.

**Other literary forms** • In addition to writing thirty-one short stories, Flannery O'Connor wrote two short novels, *Wise Blood* (1952) and *The Violent Bear It Away* (1960). A collection of her essays and occasional prose entitled *Mystery and Manners* (1969) was edited by Robert and Sally Fitzgerald, and a collection of letters entitled *The Habit of Being* (1979) was edited by Sally Fitzgerald. More correspondence is collected in *The Correspondence of Flannery O'Connor and Brainard Cheneys* (1986), edited by C. Ralph Stephens. O'Connor also wrote book reviews, largely for the Roman Catholic press; these are collected in *The Presence of Grace* (1983), which was compiled by Leo J. Zuber and edited by Carter W. Martin.

**Achievements** • The fiction of Flannery O'Connor has been highly praised for its unrelenting irony, its symbolism, and its unique comedy. O'Connor is considered one of the most important American writers of the short story, and she is frequently compared with William Faulkner as a writer of short fiction.

For an author with a relatively small literary output, O'Connor has received an enormous amount of attention. More than twenty-five books devoted to her have appeared beginning in the early 1960's, when significant critics worldwide began to recognize O'Connor's gifts as a fiction writer. Almost all critical works have emphasized the bizarre effects of reading O'Connor's fiction, which, at its best, powerfully blends the elements of traditional southwestern humor, the southern grotesque, Catholic and Christian theology and philosophy, atheistic and Christian existentialism, realism, and romance. Most critics have praised and interpreted O'Connor from a theological perspective and noted how unusual her fiction is, as it unites the banal, the inane, and the trivial with Christian, though fundamentally humorous, tales of proud Georgians fighting battles with imaginary or real agents of God sent out to shake some sense into the heads of the protagonists.

As an ironist with a satirical bent, O'Connor may be compared with some of the best in the English language, such as Jonathan Swift and George Gordon, Lord Byron. It is the comic irony of her stories that probably attracts most readers—from the orthodox and religious to the atheistic humanists whom she loves to ridicule in some of her best fiction. Thus, as a comedian, O'Connor's achievements are phenomenal, since through her largely Christian stories, she is able to attract readers who consider her beliefs outdated and quaint.

In her lifetime, O'Connor won recognition, but she would be surprised at the overwhelming response from literary critics that her fiction has received since her death. O'Connor won O. Henry Awards for her stories "The Life You Save May Be Your Own," "A Circle in the Fire," "Greenleaf," "Everything That Rises Must Converge," and "Revelation." *The Complete Stories,* published posthumously in 1971, won the National Book Award for Fiction. O'Connor received many other honors, including several grants and two honorary degrees.

**Biography** • Flannery O'Connor's relatively short life was, superficially, rather uneventful. O'Connor was born on March 25, 1925, in Savannah, Georgia, to Regina Cline and Edward Francis O'Connor, Jr. She was their only child. O'Connor's father worked in real estate and construction, and the family lived in Savannah until 1938, when they moved to Atlanta. In that year, Edward O'Connor became a zone real estate appraiser for the Federal Housing Administration (FHA). Shortly thereafter, O'Connor and her mother moved to Milledgeville, Georgia, and her father became so ill that he had to resign from his job in Atlanta and move to Milledgeville. On February 1, 1941, Edward O'Connor died.

From the fall of 1938 until her death, O'Connor spent most of her life in Milledgeville, except for brief hiatuses. After graduating from the experimental Peabody High School in 1942, O'Connor entered Georgia State College for Women (subsequently renamed Georgia College) in Milledgeville, where she majored in sociology and English and graduated with a bachelor's degree in June, 1945. While in college, she was gifted both in drawing comic cartoons and in writing. In September, 1945, O'Connor enrolled at the State University of Iowa with a journalism scholarship, and in 1946, her first story, "The Geranium" (later revised several times until it became "Judgement Day," her last story), was published in *Accent.* In 1947, she received the master of fine arts degree and enrolled for postgraduate work in the prestigious Writers' Workshop. She was honored in 1948 by receiving a place at Yaddo, an artists' colony in Saratoga Springs, New York.

Planning never to return to the South, O'Connor lived briefly in New York City in 1949 but later moved to Ridgefield, Connecticut, to live with Robert and Sally Fitzgerald. Robert Fitzgerald is best known as a classics scholar and a translator of such works as Homer's *Odyssey* (c.725 B.C.E) and Sophocles' *The Theban Plays.* City life was too much for O'Connor, but she became quickly acclimated to life in slower-paced Ridgefield. In January, 1950, she underwent an operation while visiting her mother during Christmas. She remained in Milledgeville until she returned to Ridgefield in March.

In December, 1950, O'Connor became extremely ill en route to Milledgeville for Christmas. At first, it was believed that she was suffering from acute rheumatoid arthritis, but in February, after being taken to Emory University Hospital in Atlanta, O'Connor was diagnosed with disseminated lupus erythematosus. As a result of her illness, O'Connor would remain under the care of her mother for the rest of her life, and in March, 1951, she and her mother moved from the former governor's mansion in Milledgeville to Andalusia, the Cline family's farm, which was on the outskirts of town. O'Connor's mother, a Cline, was part of a family who had played a significant part in the history of the town of Milledgeville and the state of Georgia. Like many O'Connor protagonists, her mother, using hired help probably very often similar to the "white trash" and black field hands of O'Connor fiction, ran Andalusia as a dairy farm.

Meanwhile, O'Connor continued to write when she was not too weak. During the rest of her lifetime, she wrote fiction and befriended many people, some, such as the woman referred to in the collected letters as "A," through correspondence, others through frequent trips to college campuses for lectures, and still others through their visits to see her at Andalusia. Though her illness restricted her life considerably, she was able to achieve greatness as a writer, with a literary output that had already become a permanent part of the canon of American literature since World War II.

Physicians were able to control the effects of lupus for years through the use of cortisone and other drugs, but in early 1964, O'Connor, suffering from anemia, was diagnosed with a fibroid tumor. The operation to rid her of the tumor reactivated the lupus, and O'Connor died of kidney failure in August, 1964. In her last months, most of which were spent in hospitals, O'Connor worked slowly but conscientiously on the fiction that was to appear in her second (and posthumous) collection of short stories, *Everything That Rises Must Converge.*

Throughout her life, O'Connor remained faithful to her Catholic and Christian beliefs. Although her letters and fiction indicate frequent humor and self-mockery over her illness, it seems clear that O'Connor did not wish to be treated like an invalid. She did not fear death, because she held to the Christian belief in immortality. Although some critics recognize elements of anger, bitterness, and frustration in the fiction, perhaps it was through her craft that she was able to vent her feelings in a more fruitful way. Friends and acquaintances admired her for her wit, her intelligence, and her sharpness of tongue, but they also admired her for her courage.

**Analysis** • Flannery O'Connor is uncharacteristic of her age. In writing about the pervasive disbelief in the Christian mysteries during modern times, O'Connor seems better suited to the Middle Ages in her rather old-fashioned and conventional Catholic and Christian conviction that the central issue in human existence is salvation through Christ. Perhaps the recognition that such conviction in the postmodern world is rapidly fading and may soon be lost makes O'Connor's concerns for the spiritual realm, what she called the "added dimension" in her essay entitled "The Church and the Fiction Writer," more attractive for a dubious audience.

Although O'Connor completed thirty-one short stories and two novels, she is best remembered for nearly a dozen works of short fiction. These major stories may be classified as typical O'Connor short stories for a number of reasons. Each story concerns a proud protagonist, usually a woman, who considers herself beyond reproach and is boastful about her own abilities, her Christian goodness, and her property and possessions. Each central character has hidden fears that are brought to surface through an outsider figure, who serves as a catalyst to initiate a change in the protagonist's perception. O'Connor's primary theme, from her earliest to her last stories, is hubris—that is, overweening pride and arrogance—and the characters' arrogance very often takes on a spiritual dimension.

Closely connected with the theme of hubris is the enactment of God's grace (or Christian salvation). In an essay entitled "A Reasonable Use of the Unreasonable," O'Connor states that her stories are about "the action of grace in territory held largely by the devil" and points out that the most significant part of her stories is the "moment" or "action of grace," when the protagonist is confronted with her own humanity and offered, through an ironic agent of God (an outsider) and, usually through violence, one last chance at salvation. O'Connor's protagonists think so highly of themselves that they are unable to recognize their own fallenness because of Original Sin, so the characters typically are brought to an awareness of their humanity (and their sinfulness) through violent confrontations with outsider figures.

**"The Geranium"** • O'Connor's six earliest stories first appeared in her thesis at the University of Iowa. The most memorable in terms of O'Connor's later themes are "The Geranium," her first published story, and "The Turkey." "The Geranium," an early version of O'Connor's last story, "Judgement Day," deals with the experience of a southerner living in the North. In the story, an old man is treated as an equal by a black man in his apartment building but longs to return home to the South. More modernist in its pessimistic outlook than the later, more characteristic (and religious) O'Connor works, "The Geranium" shows the effects of fading southern idealism and resembles O'Connor's later stories concerned with home and displacement—other central themes of her fiction.

**"The Turkey"** • "The Turkey" describes an encounter between a young boy named Ruller and a turkey. Receiving little recognition from home, Ruller manages to capture the turkey, only to be outwitted by a leathery confidence woman, a forerunner of O'Connor's later outsider figures. Thematically, the story concerns the initiation of Ruller into adult consciousness and paves the way for O'Connor's later concern with theological issues. Ruller, who resembles the prophetlike figures of the novels and several stories, blames God for allowing him to catch the turkey and then taking it away from him.

*A Good Man Is Hard to Find* • The first collection of O'Connor's fiction, *A Good Man Is Hard to Find*, consists mostly of previously published short stories and a short novella, *The Displaced Person*. The title story, which may be O'Connor's most famous, deals with a Georgia family on its way to Florida for vacation. As the story opens, the main character, the grandmother, tries to persuade her son, Bailey, to go to east Tennessee because she has just read about an escaped convict, The Misfit, who is heading to Florida. The next day, the family, including the nondescript mother, a baby, the other children, John Wesley and June Star, and Pitty Sing, the grandmother's cat, journeys to Florida. They stop at Red Sammy's Famous Barbeque, where the proprietor discusses his views of the changing times, saying "A good man is hard to find" to the grandmother, who has similar views.

The seemingly comic events of the day turn to disaster as the grandmother, upsetting the cat, causes a car wreck, and The Misfit and two men arrive on the scene. The grandmother recognizes The Misfit, and as a result, brings about the death of the entire family. Before she dies, however, the grandmother, who has been portrayed as a self-centered, judgmental, self-righteous, and hypocritical Protestant, sees the humanity of The Misfit and calls him "one of my babies." This section of the story represents what O'Connor calls "the action or moment of grace" in her fiction. Thematically, the story concerns religious hypocrisy, faith and doubt, and social and spiritual arrogance. The Misfit, who strikes comparison with Hazel Motes of *Wise Blood* (1952), is a "prophet gone wrong" (from "A Reasonable Use of the Unreasonable"), tormented by doubt over whether Christ was who he said he was.

**"The Life You Save May Be Your Own"** • Another important story, "The Life You Save May Be Your Own," portrays a drifter named Tom T. Shiftlet, a one-armed man who covets the automobile of a widow named Lucynell Crater and marries her daughter, a deaf-mute, in order to obtain it. He tells the mother that he is a man with "a moral intelligence." Shiftlet, who is searching for some explanation for the mystery of human existence, which he cannot quite comprehend, reveals himself to be just the opposite: one with amoral intelligence. An outsider figure who becomes the story's protagonist, Shiftlet leaves his wife, also named Lucynell, at a roadside restaurant, picks up a hitchhiker, and flies away to Mobile as a thunderstorm approaches. The story's epiphany concerns the irony that Shiftlet considers the hitchhiker a "slime from this earth," when in reality it is Shiftlet who fits this description. In rejecting his wife, he rejects God's grace and, the story suggests, his mother's valuation of Christianity.

**"The Artificial Nigger"** • The next major tale, "The Artificial Nigger," is one of O'Connor's most important and complex. It has been subjected to many interpretations, including the suggestion by some critics that it contains no moment of grace on the part of Mr. Head and Nelson, the two main characters. The most Dantesque of all O'Connor stories, "The Artificial Nigger" concerns a journey to the city (hell), where Nelson is to be introduced to his first black person. As O'Connor ridicules the bigotry of the countrified Mr. Head and his grandson, she also moves toward the theological and philosophical. When Nelson gets lost in the black section of Atlanta, he identifies with a big black woman and, comparable to Saint Peter's denial of Christ, Mr. Head denies that he knows him. Nevertheless, they are reunited when they see a statue of an African American, which represents the redemptive quality of suffering and as a result serves to bring about a moment of grace in the racist Mr. Head. The difficulty of this story, other than the possibility that some may see it as racist itself, is that O'Connor's narrative is so ironic that critics are unsure whether to read the story's epiphany as a serious religious conversion or to assume that Mr. Head is still as arrogant and bigoted as ever.

Of all O'Connor's stories—with the possible exceptions of "The Life You Save May Be Your Own" and "Good Country People"—"The Artificial Nigger" most exemplifies the influence of the humor of the Old Southwest, a tradition that included authors such as Augustus Baldwin Longstreet, Johnson Jones Hooper, and George Washington Harris. In "The Artificial Nigger," the familiar motif of the country bumpkin going to the city, which is prevalent in southwestern humor in particular and folk tradition in general, is used.

**"Good Country People"** • "Good Country People," which is frequently anthologized, concerns another major target of O'Connor's satirical fictions: the contemporary intellectual. O'Connor criticizes modern individuals who are educated and who believe that they are capable of achieving their own salvation through the pursuit of human knowledge. Hulga Hopewell, a doctor in philosophy and an atheistic existentialist, resides with her mother, a banal woman who cannot comprehend the complexity of her daughter, because Hulga has a weak heart and has had an accident that caused her to lose one leg.

Believing herself to be of superior intellect, Hulga agrees to go on a picnic with a young Bible salesman and country bumpkin named Manley Pointer, hoping that she can seduce him, her intellectual inferior. Ironically, he is a confidence man with a peculiar affection for the grotesque comparable to characters in the humor of the Old Southwest. As he is about to seduce Hulga, he speeds away with her wooden leg and informs her, "I been believing in nothing since I was born," shattering Hulga's illusion that she is sophisticated and intelligent and that her atheism makes her special. As the story ends, Hulga is prepared for a spiritual recognition that her belief system is as weak and hollow as the wooden leg on which she has based her entire existence. Pointer, whose capacity for evil has been underestimated by the logical positivist Mrs. Hopewell but not by her neighbor Mrs. Freeman, crosses "the speckled lake" in an ironic allusion to Christ's walking on water.

***The Displaced Person*** • The final piece in the collection, a novella entitled *The Displaced Person*, portrays the most positive of O'Connor's outsider figures, Mr. Guizac, a Pole. The story is divided into two sections. In the first part, to escape incarceration in the refugee camps after World War II, Mr. Guizac agrees to work for Mrs. McIntyre, a widow who runs a dairy farm. Unknown to him, Mr. Guizac arouses jealousy and fear in the regular tenant farmers, the Shortleys, and the black field hands. Because Mr. Shortley is lazy and lackadaisical, he particularly resents the productivity of Mr. Guizac. The story moves toward the spiritual dimension when Mrs. Shortley, who considers herself a model Christian, begins to see Mr. Guizac and his family as agents of the devil. After Mrs. Shortley learns that her husband is to be fired the next morning, the Shortleys drive away, and Mrs. Shortley dies of a stroke and sees her "true country," which is defined in one of O'Connor's essays as "what is eternal and absolute" ("The Fiction Writer and His Country"). At the time of her death, Mrs. Shortley, displaced like the poor victims of the Holocaust, which she has witnessed in newsreels, is redeemed through displacement and enters her spiritual home.

The story's second part concerns Mrs. McIntyre's growing fear of outsiders. Mr. Shortley reappears after his wife's death and learns that Mr. Guizac is arranging a marriage for, and taking money from, Sulk, a Negro field hand, so that Mr. Guizac's niece can earn passage to the United States. The southern racial taboos are portrayed as fundamentally inhumane when confronted with the reality of human suffering, as seen in the niece, who is in a refugee camp. Father Flynn, the priest who has arranged for Mr. Guizac and his family to come to the United States to work for Mrs. McIntyre, tries to teach Mrs. McIntyre the importance of Christian charity and the fine points of Catholic theology. Unconcerned with these matters, which she considers unimportant, Mrs. McIntyre becomes neurotic about Mr. Guizac's inappropriateness and overlooks the spiritual for the material. Throughout the novella, O'Connor links the peacock, a symbol of Christ's Transfiguration, with Mr. Guizac, and in the end, Mr. Shortley "accidentally" allows a tractor to run over Mr. Guizac while Mrs. McIntyre and the other field hands watch. As the human race is complicit in the persecution and crucifixion of Christ, so are Mrs. McIntyre and the others in the death of Mr. Guizac, a Christ figure. At the story's end, Mrs. McIntyre, losing her dairy farm and all the material possessions in which she has put so much faith all of her life, becomes displaced, as do the others who have participated in the "crucifixion" of Mr. Guizac.

*Everything That Rises Must Converge* • The second collection of O'Connor's short fiction, *Everything That Rises Must Converge*, shows the author's depth of vision as she moved away from stories rooted primarily in the tradition of southwestern humor to heavily philosophical, though still quite humorous, tales of individuals in need of a spiritual experience. Most apparent is the influence of Pierre Teilhard de Chardin, the French paleontologist and Catholic theologian, on the title story as well as the vision of the entire collection. Teilhard de Chardin argued that through the course of time, it was almost inevitable, even in the evolution of the species, that there was a process moving toward convergence with God.

**"Everything That Rises Must Converge"** • This idea, though perhaps used ironically, appears as the basis for "Everything That Rises Must Converge," which is considered one of O'Connor's greatest works. O'Connor once said that this story was her only one dealing with the racial issue; even so, the tale still transcends social and political commentary. The main character, Julian, is another typical O'Connor protagonist. Arrogant and unjust to his more conventional southern and racist mother, the adult college graduate Julian angrily hopes that his mother will be given a lesson in race relations by having to sit next to a black woman wearing the same hat that she is wearing. Outwardly friendly to the black woman's child, Julian's mother, with characteristic O'Connor violence, converges with the oppressed black race after she offers a penny to Carver, the child. After the black woman hits Julian's mother with her purse, Julian is as helpless, lost, and innocent as Carver is. He recognizes that his mother is dying and enters the world of "guilt and sorrow." Through this story, O'Connor reflects on the rising social status of blacks and connects this rise with a spiritual convergence between the two races.

**"Greenleaf"** • "Greenleaf," also a major work, portrays still another woman, Mrs. May, attempting to run a dairy farm. Her two ungrateful bachelor sons refuse to take her self-imposed martyrdom seriously when she complains of the Greenleafs and their bull, which, at the beginning of the story, is hanging around outside her window. The Greenleafs are lower-class tenant farmers whose grown children are far more productive and successful than the bourgeois Mrs. May's. O'Connor moves to pagan mythology as she characterizes the bull as a god (compared to Zeus) and unites the Greenleaf bull symbolically with peculiarly Christian elements. The coming of grace in this story is characteristically violent. Mrs. May is gored by a bull, which, like the ancient Greek gods, is both pagan lover and deity (although a Christian deity).

**"The Lame Shall Enter First"** • The next significant story in the collection, "The Lame Shall Enter First," strikes comparison with the novel *The Violent Bear It Away*, for the main character, Rufus Johnson, a sociopathic teenage criminal, reminds readers of Francis Marion Tarwater, the hero of the novel. There is also Sheppard, the intellectual social worker who, like Tarwater's Uncle Rayber, is a secular humanist and believes that if he takes away the biblical nonsense that the adolescent protagonist has been taught, he will be saved.

Ironically, Sheppard spends all of his time trying to analyze and improve Rufus while at the same time neglecting his own son, Norton. Although Rufus is clearly a demonic figure, he nevertheless believes in God and the Devil and convinces the child that he can be with his dead mother through Christian conversion. The child, misunderstanding, kills himself, and Sheppard is left to recognize the emptiness of his materialist philosophy. O'Connor's attitude toward the secular humanist is again satirical; without a divine source, there can be no salvation.

**"Revelation"** • O'Connor's last three stories, according to most critics, ended her career at the height of her powers. "Revelation," one of the greatest pieces of short fiction in American literature, is O'Connor's most complete statement concerning the plight of the oppressed. Although her fiction often uses outsiders, she seldom directly comments on her sympathies with them, but through Ruby Turpin's confrontation with the fat girl "blue with acne," who is named Mary Grace, O'Connor is able to demonstrate that in God's Kingdom the last shall be first. Mary Grace calls Mrs. Turpin, who prides herself on being an outstanding Christian lady, a "wart hog from hell," a phrase that Mrs. Turpin cannot get out of her mind. Later, Mrs. Turpin goes to "hose down" her hogs, symbols of unclean spirits, and has a vision of the oppressed souls entering heaven ahead of herself and her husband (Claud). Critical disagreement has centered largely on whether Mrs. Turpin is redeemed after her vision or whether she remains the same arrogant, self-righteous, bigoted woman she has been all of her life.

**"Parker's Back"** • "Parker's Back" is one of the most mysterious of O'Connor's stories. Obadiah Elihue Parker, a nonbeliever, marries Sarah Ruth, a fundamentalist bent on saving her husband's soul. After a mysterious accident in which he hits a tree, Parker gradually experiences religious conversion and, though tattooed all over the front of his body, is drawn to having a Byzantine tattoo of Christ placed on his back, thinking that his wife will be pleased. She is not, however, accusing him instead of idolatry. In reality, she is the heretic, for she is incapable of recognizing that Christ was both human and divine. Beating welts into her husband's back, Sarah Ruth fails to recognize the mystical connection between the suffering of her husband and that of the crucified Christ. By this point in her career, O'Connor was using unusual symbols to convey her sense of the mystery of God's redemptive power.

**"Judgement Day"** • O'Connor's last completed story, "Judgement Day," is a revised version of her first published story, "The Geranium." The central character, a displaced southerner living with his daughter in New York City, wishes to return home to die. Tanner, while an old and somewhat bigoted man, remembers fondly his relationship with a black man and hopes to befriend a black tenant in his daughter's apartment building. This story concerns Tanner's inability to recognize differences in southern and northern attitudes toward race, and, as with earlier O'Connor stories, "home" has more than a literal meaning (a spiritual destiny or heaven). Unlike almost all other O'Connor works, this story portrays racial relations as based on mutual respect. Also, Tanner, while attacked violently by the black tenant, is portrayed as a genuine believer and is sent to his eternal resting place (heaven), the destiny of a Christian. By the end of her life, O'Connor considered a return to a heavenly home much more significant than any other subject.

*D. Dean Shackelford*

**Other major works**

NOVELS: *Wise Blood*, 1952; *The Violent Bear It Away*, 1960.

MISCELLANEOUS: *Collected Works*, 1988.

NONFICTION: *Mystery and Manners*, 1969; *The Habit of Being: Letters*, 1979; *The Presence of Grace*, 1983; *The Correspondence of Flannery O'Connor and Brainard Cheneys*, 1986.

**Bibliography**

Asals, Frederick. *Flannery O'Connor: The Imagination of Extremity*. Athens: University of Georgia Press, 1982. In one of the best books on O'Connor's fiction, Asals focuses on the use of the doppelgänger (double) motif in the novels and short fiction, the most thorough and intelligent treatment of this subject. Asals also concentrates on O'Connor's religious extremity, which is evident in her fiction through her concern with polarities and extremes. Contains extensive endnotes and a good bibliography.

_____. *"A Good Man Is Hard to Find": Flannery O'Connor*. New Brunswick, N.J.: Rutgers University Press, 1993. Critical essays on O'Connor's story from a variety of perspectives. Critics discuss the pros and cons of O'Connor's shift in point of view from the grandmother to The Misfit, the nature of grace in a materialistic world, and the theological significance of the story's concluding confrontation.

Bacon, Jon Lance. *Flannery O'Connor and Cold War Culture*. New York: Cambridge University Press, 1993. Reads O'Connor's stories in relation to social issues of their milieu. Discusses the context of Cold War politics, popular culture, media, and consumerism that form the backdrop to O'Connor's stories.

Cash, Jean W. *Flannery O'Connor: A Life*. Knoxville: University of Tennessee, 2002. Painstakingly researched portrait of O'Connor. Includes a bibliography and index.

Desmond, John F. *Risen Sons: Flannery O'Connor's Vision of History*. Athens: University of Georgia Press, 1987. Desmond's argument is that O'Connor's fictions reenact Christian history and Catholic theology through an art O'Connor herself saw as an "incarnational act." Discussing several major stories and the two novels, the book focuses on the metaphysical and the Christian historical vision as observed through reading O'Connor's fiction and emphasizes that *The Violent Bear It Away* represents the fullest development of her vision. Includes an extensive bibliography and useful endnotes.

Enjolras, Laurence. *Flannery O'Connor's Characters*. Lanham, Md.: University Press of America, 1998. Chapters on O'Connor's descriptions of the body, of wicked children, of "conceited, self-righteous Christians," of "intellectuals and would-be artists." Includes notes and bibliography.

May, Charles E., ed. *Masterplots II: Short Story Series, Revised Edition*. 8 vols. Pasadena, Calif.: Salem Press, 2004. Designed for student use, this reference set contains articles providing detailed plot summaries and analyses of eleven short stories by O'Connor: "The Artificial Nigger" (vol. 1); "The Displaced Person" and "The Enduring Chill" (vol. 2); "Everything That Rises Must Converge," "Good Country People," "A Good Man Is Hard to Find," and "Greenleaf" (vol. 3); "The Life You Save May Be Your Own" (vol. 4); and "Parker's Back," "Revelation," and and "The River" (vol. 6).

Paulson, Suzanne Morrow. *Flannery O'Connor: A Study of the Short Fiction.* Boston: Twayne, 1988. Useful resource for the beginner. Paulson's book includes primary and secondary material on O'Connor's fiction and concentrates on the predominant issues, themes, and approaches to O'Connor's fiction. Paulson divides O'Connor's stories into four categories: death-haunted questers, male/female conflicts, "The Mystery of Personality" and society, and good/evil conflicts. Supplemented by a chronology of O'Connor's life and a bibliography of primary and secondary works.

Rath, Sura P., and Mary Neff Shaw, eds. *Flannery O'Connor: New Perspectives.* Athens: University of Georgia Press, 1996. The new perspectives illustrated in this collection of essays are primarily feminist and Bakhtinian, with one essay using discourse theory and one focusing on race and culture. Stories discussed include "A View from the Woods," "The Artificial Nigger," and "The Crop."

Spivey, Ted R. *Flannery O'Connor: The Woman, the Thinker, the Visionary.* Macon, Ga.: Mercer University Press, 1995. Attempts to understand O'Connor first as a southerner, then as a modernist intellect, and finally as a visionary thinker. Argues that O'Connor reflects the personal and social issues of the twentieth century.

# Frank O'Connor

**Born:** Cork City, Ireland; September 17, 1903
**Died:** Dublin, Ireland; March 10, 1966

**Principal short fiction** • *Guests of the Nation*, 1931; *Bones of Contention, and Other Stories*, 1936; *Crab Apple Jelly*, 1944; *Selected Stories*, 1946; *The Common Chord*, 1947; *Traveller's Samples*, 1951; *The Stories of Frank O'Connor*, 1952; *More Stories*, 1954; *Stories by Frank O'Connor*, 1956; *Domestic Relations*, 1957; *My Oedipus Complex, and Other Stories*, 1963; *Collection Two*, 1964; *A Set of Variations*, 1969; *Collection Three*, 1969; *Collected Stories*, 1981.

**Other literary forms** • Frank O'Connor was a prolific writer who wrote in nearly every literary genre. His published books include poems, translations of Irish poetry, plays, literary criticism, autobiographies, travel books, and essays. His two novels—*The Saint and Mary Kate* (1932) and *Dutch Interior* (1940)—are interesting complements to the many short-story collections, for which he is best known.

**Achievements** • Frank O'Connor was a masterful short-story writer. He was a realist who closely observed his characters and their world. He was not a pitiless realist, however, but he always seemed to have great sympathy for his characters, even those who insisted on putting themselves in absurd situations. It follows that one of his major techniques was humor. There is a place for humor in nearly all of his works, including those that border on tragedy. His stories tend to deal with a domestic rather than a public world, and the characters make up what he has called a "submerged population."

Structurally, the stories are simple. O'Connor likes to use a sudden reversal to bring about the necessary change in the plot. The plots tend to be simple, and the reconciliation of the conflict is always very clear. One of the special devices he employed to give the stories some distinction is his use of a narrator. Whether the narrator is a child or an old priest, there is always a distinctive voice telling the reader the story. This voice has some of O'Connor's special qualities: warmth, humor, sympathy, and a realistic appraisal of the circumstances.

**Biography** • Educated at the Christian Brothers College, Cork, Frank O'Connor (Michael Francis O'Donovan) joined the Irish Volunteers and participated on the Republican side in the Irish Civil War (1922-1923), for which activity he was imprisoned. He supported himself as a librarian, first in Cork, and later in Dublin, where he met George (Æ) Russell and William Butler Yeats, and began his literary career on Æ's *Irish Statesman*. He was until 1939 a member of the board of directors of the Abbey Theatre. From 1940 he coedited *The Bell*, a literary journal, with Seán O'Faoláin. In addition to his editorial work, O'Connor was writing the stories that ensured his fame. From *Guests of the Nation* on, O'Connor wrote a number of superb collections of short stories. In recognition of this feat, O'Connor was invited to teach at a number of prestigious American universities. In 1939 he married Evelyn Bowen, with whom he had two sons and a daughter. During part of World War II he lived in London, working for the Ministry of Information. In 1951 he took up a creative writing position at Harvard, was divorced in 1952, and remarried in 1953 (to Harriet Randolph Rich, with whom he had one daughter). He returned to Ireland permanently in 1961. He received a Litt.D. from Dublin University in 1962, where for a time he held a Special Lectureship. He died in Dublin on March 10, 1966.

**Analysis** • Although widely read in Western literature, Frank O'Connor's literary character is most profoundly influenced by tensions within the literature and life of Ireland, ancient and modern. He was a dedicated student of the literature of Ireland's native language, a keen observer of the life of the folk, intimately fa-

miliar with Ireland's topography, and an active participant in its revolutionary and literary politics. These interests shaped his art. His literary vocation, however, like so many others of his generation, begins with Yeats's literary nationalism and continues through a dialectic between his perceptions of that poet's idealism and James Joyce's early naturalism. O'Connor's predominantly realistic fiction attempts a fusion of these two influences, while also recalling the popular origin—in the oral art of the *shanachie*—of the short story. He found that Yeats and Joyce were too "elitist" for the "common reader"; and with O'Faoláin, he is associated with the development of the realistic Irish short story, the most representative art of the Irish Literary Revival.

**"Guests of the Nation"** • "Guests of the Nation," the title story of O'Connor's first collection, is probably his single finest work. All the stories in this volume reflect his involvement in the War of Independence; and this one distinguishes itself by its austere transcendence of the immediate circumstances, which in the rest of the stories here trammel the subjects with excessive patriotic enthusiasm. During the War of Independence, the protagonist's (Bonaparte's) cadre of Volunteers has been charged with the task of holding hostage two British soldiers, Belcher and Hawkins; during their captivity, the forced intimacy of captors and hostages leads to a reluctantly admitted mutual respect which develops through their card-playing, arguments, and sharing of day-to-day chores. As the reader observes the exchanges of sympathy, idiom, and gesture between Irish and English soldiers, the two Englishmen become distinct from their roles, and from each other. The narrative develops the issues of religion, accent, and political allegiances as only superficially divisive, so that when the order arrives from headquarters to execute the hostages in military reprisal, the moral conflict is joined.

The story nicely dramatizes the contrasting reactions to this order among the various figures, captors and hostages: Donovan's giving grim precedence to national duty over "personal considerations"; Noble's pious reflections, which short-circuit his comprehension of the enormity of his actions; and Bonaparte's reflective agony. The change in the attitudes of the Englishmen, once they know the truth of the directive, poignantly reveals new dimensions in these men's characters. The argument to the last of Hawkins, the intellectual, dramatizes the limitations of rational discussion; but the stoicism of the more effective Belcher, his unflappability in the face of his own annihilation, drives the story to its height of feeling, a height to which only Bonaparte is equal. Noble's moral earnestness and Donovan's objectivity provide contrasts and contexts for Bonaparte's tragic anagnorisis.

O'Connor achieves the inimitable effects of the fine conclusion by a combination of devices: the shreds of partisan argument about religion and politics, the range of attitudes embodied by the various characters, the carefully modulated speaking voice of the narrator—steady, intelligent, slightly uncouth, bitter—the spare use of images (ashes, spades, light and dark), and the figure of the old woman who observes the whole affair. This woman, at once a representative of the "hidden powers" of the universe, the irrationality behind the appearances of coherence, and also a representative of the affinity between such forces in the human psyche and the justifiable cause of Mother Ireland, gives the story both historical and universal resonances. Thus as one considers the story as a tragic examination of the theme of duty (to self, friends, institutions, nation, God), and of the tension between the claims of individual conscience and communal obligation, between commitments to the personal and the abstract, developed with psychological accuracy in a modern setting, one notes its roots in the soil of Irish literature and tradition. The political situation, the various elements of local color, the allusively named characters, the figure of the old woman, the precedence of the ancient Celtic ritual of bog-burial, and the echoes of the tension in Celtic society between the obligations to provide hospitality to strangers and at the same time to protect the clan's rights through the insurance of hostage-taking: All these elements blend the modern with the archaic. Taken in combination, they achieve the result of casting these English soldiers as "guests" of the nation as an imaginative entity.

The restrained lyricism of the last paragraph, coming as it does on the heels of a rather colloquial narrative, shows how moved is the storyteller by his recollections. The bathetic solecism of the summary comment, however—"And anything that happened to me afterwards, I never felt the same about again"—certifies that the narrator's education is unfinished. This sentence mirrors the dislocation of his feelings, while it also nicely preserves the integrity of O'Connor's characteristic fictional device, the speaking voice.

**"In the Train"** • The story "In the Train" (*Bones of Contention, and Other Stories*) dramatizes the reactions of a group of South-of-Ireland villagers toward an accused murderer in their midst, as they all return homeward by train from the Dublin criminal court. They have all conspired to prevent the woman's conviction, planning to punish her in their own manner when they return home. By a series of interconnected scenes, observed in a sequence of compartments of the train as it traverses the dark countryside, the story develops the theme of the villagers' common opposition to the law of the state and, by implication, their allegiance to the devices of their ancient community. From the bourgeois pretensions of the sergeant's wife to the dialogue that reveals the tensions and boredom among the policemen, to the stoicism of the peasants, to the huddled figure of the accused herself, the focus narrows from the humor of the opening scenes to the brooding interior monologue of the isolated woman in the final scene. The various parts of the story are interconnected by the characters' common motion west, their agreed attitude toward the legal apparatus of the Free State, by the Chaplinesque rambling drunk, and by the fated, defiant pariah. The story proceeds by indirection: Its main action (the murder and trial) is over and revealed only in retrospect; and its focus (the accused) is not fully identified until the final section. O'Connor develops these suspensions, however, in a resourceful manner, by focusing on the secondary tension in the community occasioned by the presence of the sergeant's carping wife, and by having the shambling drunk lead the reader to the transfixed woman.

The apparent naïveté of the narrator's voice—colloquial, amused, relishing the folksy scenes—is belied by the complex structure of the piece. Moreover, the narrative is rich with echoes of Anton Chekhov, touches of melodrama and vaudeville, devices from folktales and folkways, as it portrays the residue of the ancient legal unit of Celtic society, the *derb-fine*, persisting under the "foreign" order of the Irish Free State. In these contexts, the ambiguities of the sergeant's position and that of the local poteen manufacturer are richly developed, while one discerns that the woman's guilt is never firmly established. The story ends with a choric circle around the tragic complaint of the woman, whose community has preserved her only to impose their own severe penalty: ostracism from the only community she knows. O'Connor shares and enlarges her despair. The initial amusement of his story yields to chagrin at the loss both of the ideals of the Irish revolution in the Free State and of humaneness in the dying rural communities of Ireland.

**"The Long Road to Ummera"** • "The Long Road to Ummera" concerns an old woman's conflict with her son over her desire for burial in her ancestral ground in the remote West Cork village of Ummera. Abby, Batty Heig's daughter, has followed her son Pat to the city of Cork, but feeling the approach of death, desires to be returned to Ummera, not by the modern highway but by the ancient "long road." A tragicomic test of wills between mother and son ensues, pitting against each other the desires for established ritual against modern efficiency, uncouth rural mannerisms and polite town manners, homage to ancestors and modern progressivism. Because of her son's insensitivity, the old woman is forced to engage in comic subterfuge to achieve her last wish, and by grotesque turns of events involving a cobbler, a jarvey, and a priest, she has her way in all its details: Her body is transported along the prescribed road and announced ritually to the desolate countryside.

This is a moving portrait of an old woman, dignified by a lively sense of the presence of the dead and by lyrical evocations of the scenery of West Cork. In contrast to these qualities is the philistinism of her businessman son. The story itself has ritual quality, woven as it is with repeated phrases, scenes, arguments, events, recurrent images of death, various addictions, and the rehearsals of rituals themselves. The story represents O'Connor's criticism of bourgeois Ireland and the triumph of profit and respectability, major themes of his sweet-and-sour stories from the 1930's and 1940's contained in this, perhaps his best collection, *Crab Apple Jelly*. Although the speaking voice remains the norm, the tone here is more knowing than in the earlier stories. O'Connor, like Abby, is keeping promises to ancient values, including the language, family loyalty, community, and rootedness. If the old woman's loyalty to her circuitous way is bypassed by Ireland's new one, however, the narrator's sad lyricism suggests that he can tread neither.

**"First Confession"** • Of O'Connor's childhood stories, "First Confession," "My Oedipus Complex," and "The Drunkard," developed over the 1940's, are his most famous, although not his most distinguished, works. The much-anthologized "First Confession" humorously exploits the mildly exotic Roman Catholic rite, as the little boy finds that the image of religion fostered by his female educators is not borne out in the encounter with the priest-confessor. Hearing that the boy's chief sin is his desire to murder his ill-mannered grandmother, the priest humors the impenitent child by having him articulate the fantasy and sends him back to the sunny street. The idiom of an Irish child carries the narration here, although with the injection of some adult irony directed at the boy's naïve literalism. The story might be faulted for its slapstick and cuteness, as if O'Connor indulges too liberally in the mood of his creation. Many of O'Connor's stories portray insensitive and repressive priests, but not this one. Rather, it is the women who are the agents of terrifying, dogmatic religiosity, in contrast with the priest's personification of a paternal, forgiving, and humorous God.

**"My Oedipus Complex" and "The Drunkard"** • "My Oedipus Complex" and "The Drunkard" are charming examples of O'Connor's mastery of the narrator-as-child. In them, the themes of marital tension, domestic evasiveness, and the dependence of Irish men on their mothers are treated with light irony. By means of an unexpected turn of events, the severe social controls on incest and alcoholism are toyed with as the jealous conspiracies of women; thus moral awareness commences with male bonding. In each of these three childhood stories, the antagonist at first appears as male—priest, bed-rival, drunken father—until the possessiveness of women emerges as the substantial moral antagonist. In these much-revised stories, O'Connor has refined the instrument of the speaking voice to a point that is perhaps too ingratiating, too calculatedly smooth, so that the spontaneity of the "rough narrative voice" is lost, and with it, some of his cold and passionate isolation. The attraction of these stories, however, is readily apparent in their author's recorded versions, which he narrates with considerable relish.

**"A Story by Maupassant"** • O'Connor's tendency to reread his own work with disapproval led to constant revisions, so that there are two, three, or more variants of many of his most popular works. A case in point is "A Story by Maupassant," which first appeared in *The Penguin New Writing* (No. 24, 1945) and in a significantly revised version in *A Set of Variations*. This story of the corruption of an Irish intellectual, observed by his more concrete-minded friend, climaxes when Terry Coughlan admits to the narrator that his appreciation of Maupassant's grasp of "what life can do to you" came during a sleepless night in the bed of a Parisian prostitute. A comparison of the two versions shows several changes: He expands the proportion of more precise and graphic details and reduces dialectal, self-conscious, and repetitive elements; he achieves a more complex ironic effect by a stronger investment in double perspective; he condemns more forthrightly the hypocrisy of the Catholic school, as he renders more deft the function of religious metaphor; he enlarges the sympathy for Terry Coughlan by an enlargement of oblique cultural references and a softening of the narrator's moralizing. O'Connor's own view of Maupassant—that the mainspring of his art lay in the mixture of creative and destructive tendencies interacting as perversity—is brought to bear on the bitter conclusion of the story: Maupassant, at least, has not abandoned these self-destructive characters. In his revisions, O'Connor strengthens Maupassant's perspective, focusing in the end on the prostitute's baby, a symbol of the naïveté of new life. O'Connor bitterly notes that nature, like Maupassant's fiction, without an ideal that is informing, seeks the lowest level. Here is a story that, by the intervention of O'Connor's matured hand, gains considerably in power and perspective, subtlety and professionalism.

**"Introverted" Ireland** • The general subject of O'Connor's fiction is a critique of the "introverted religion" and "introverted politics" of bourgeois Ireland—sectarian obscurantism, the abuses of clerical power, class snobbery, family rivalries, disingenuous piety, Anglophobia, and thwarted idealism—although these criticisms are usually modified by warm portraits of energetic children, humane clerics, and unpretentious peasants. His central object in these stories is "to stimulate the moral imagination" by separating his characters from their assumed social roles and having them stand, for a moment, alone. In many of his most distinguished works, and indeed throughout his whole career as a writer of short fiction, one may discern such a movement from the depiction of the comfortably communal to that of the isolated, enlightened individual. He proposes a nexus between such a contrast of perspectives and the short-story form.

***The Lonely Voice*** • In his study entitled *The Lonely Voice* (1963), O'Connor holds as central that "in the short story at its most characteristic [there is] something we do not often find in the novel—an intense awareness of human loneliness." This collection of essays on selected practitioners of the modern short story (Ivan Turgenev, Anton Chekhov, Rudyard Kipling, James Joyce, Katherine Mansfield, D. H. Lawrence, Ernest Hemingway, A. E. Coppard, Isaac Babel, and Mary Lavin) draws on seminar notes from O'Connor's classes at various universities in the 1950's. The discussions are genial, opinionated, and not academic, and afford brilliant comments on individual artists and works, although they suffer from diffuseness and overextension at certain points in the argument. The study rests on the theory that the distinction of the short story from the novel is less a formal than an ideological one: It is the expression of "an attitude of mind that is attracted by submerged population groups . . . tramps, artists, lonely idealists, dreamers, and spoiled priests . . . remote from the community—romantic, individualistic, and intransigent."

From this position, O'Connor argues that "the conception of the short story as a miniature art is inherently false," holding that, on the contrary, "the storyteller differs from the novelist in this: he must be much more of a writer, much more of an artist . . . more of a dramatist." From the same vantage point he evaluates his selected authors as they severally identify with some "submerged population group," finding that as each author compromised or found less compelling the vision of his subjects as outsiders or social or political minorities, he either failed as a short-story writer or found another form more expressive of his vision.

Although O'Connor's claims for these theories are maintained in the face of easily adduced contrary evidence, they have limited, and in some ways startling, application to certain authors and works. As a critic, O'Connor possessed brilliant intuitions, although he did not have the power to systematize. In *The Lonely Voice* his remarks on Joyce's and Hemingway's rhetorical styles, his contrasting Chekhov and

Mansfield, his accounting for Kipling's artistic failure, and, in *The Mirror in the Roadway* (1956), his discussion of Joyce's "dissociated metaphor" have useful application to the contribution of each of these authors to the literature of the short story.

From various accounts by former students and colleagues, as well as from these critical works, it is quite clear that O'Connor was a brilliantly successful teacher of fiction-writing. His seminars were guided with authority and seriousness, and he placed great emphasis on the perfection of technique. He trained his students to begin with a "prosaic kernel" which the "treatment" takes to its crisis. The finished work takes its power from the cumulation of the drama, poetry, and emotion developed throughout the narrative, finally resolving itself in universalizing mystery. The short story is not concerned with the passage of time or with particularities of character; ideally it is based on an incident and a briefly stated theme, which technique elaborates to the final formula; it should not proceed on technique alone (Hemingway's fault) or follow a preconceived symbolic pattern (Joyce's fault), but ideally it is a fusion of the opposites of naturalism and symbolism.

*Cóilín Owens*
*With updates by James Sullivan*

**Other major works**

PLAYS: *In the Train*, pr. 1937 (with Hugh Hunt); *The Invincibles: A Play in Seven Scenes*, pr. 1937 (with Hunt); *Moses' Rock*, pr. 1938 (with Hunt); *The Statue's Daughter: A Fantasy in a Prologue and Three Acts*, pr. 1941.

NOVELS: *The Saint and Mary Kate*, 1932; *Dutch Interior*, 1940.

MISCELLANEOUS: *A Frank O'Connor Reader*, 1994.

NONFICTION: *Death in Dublin: Michael Collins and the Irish Revolution*, 1937; *The Big Fellow*, 1937; *A Picture Book*, 1943; *Towards an Appreciation of Literature*, 1945; *Irish Miles*, 1947; *The Art of the Theatre*, 1947; *The Road to Stratford*, 1948; *Leinster, Munster, and Connaught*, 1950; *The Mirror in the Roadway*, 1956; *An Only Child*, 1961; *The Lonely Voice*, 1963; *The Backward Look: A Survey of Irish Literature*, 1967; *My Father's Son*, 1968; *The Happiness of Getting It Down Right: Letters of Frank O'Connor and William Maxwell, 1945-1966.*, 1996.

POETRY: *Three Old Brothers, and Other Poems*, 1936.

TRANSLATIONS: *The Wild Bird's Nest*, 1932 (of selected Irish poetry); *Lords and Commons*, 1938 (of selected Irish poetry); *The Fountain of Magic*, 1939 (of selected Irish poetry); *Lament for Art O'Leary*, 1940 (of Eileen O'Connell); *The Midnight Court: A Rhythmical Bacchanalia from the Irish of Bryan Merryman*, 1945 (of Brian Merriman's *Cuirt an mheadhoin oidhche*); *Kings, Lords, and Commons*, 1959 (of selected Irish poetry); *The Little Monasteries*, 1963 (of selected Irish poetry); *A Golden Treasury of Irish Poetry*, 1967 (with David Greene).

**Bibliography**

Alexander, James D. "Frank O'Connor in *The New Yorker*, 1945-1967." *Eire-Ireland* 30 (1995): 130-144. Examines how O'Connor changed his narrative style during the twenty years he was writing for *The New Yorker*—contracting the presence of a narrator to a voice and developing a double-leveled view of "experienced innocence" in his young boy stories. Argues that O'Connor created a genial persona in his stories that diverted attention from his more serious subject matter of Irish social problems.

Bordewyk, Gordon. "Quest for Meaning: The Stories of Frank O'Connor." *Illinois Quarterly* 41 (Winter, 1978): 37-47. Discusses O'Connor's concern with fundamental qualities of everyday life and his sense of wonder in the mundane in four major groups of stories of war, religion, youth, and marriage. Examines how the search for meaning changes the lives of characters in these four groups.

Evans, Robert C., and Richard Harp, eds. *Frank O'Connor: New Perspectives.* West Cornwall, Conn.: Locust Hill Press, 1998. Fresh, thoughtful interpretations of O'Connor's works.

McKeon, Jim. *Frank O'Connor: A Life.* Edinburgh: Mainstream, 1998. Brief, readable life of O'Connor; comments on the biographical sources of some of the short stories; discusses O'Connor's literary career.

Matthews, James H. *Frank O'Connor.* Lewisburg, Pa.: Bucknell University Press, 1976. This book is an excellent introduction to O'Connor's fiction since it deals with the social context of the stories and the critical theory underlying them. Part of the Irish Writers series.

May, Charles E., ed. *Masterplots II: Short Story Series, Revised Edition.* 8 vols. Pasadena, Calif.: Salem Press, 2004. Designed for student use, this reference set contains articles providing detailed plot summaries and analyses of these nine short stories by O'Connor: "Christmas Morning" and "The Drunkard" (vol. 2), "First Confession" and "Guests of the Nation" (vol. 3), "Judas" and "Legal Aid" (vol. 4), "The Man of the World" and "My Oedipus Complex" (vol. 5), and "A Story by Maupassant" (vol. 7).

Neary, Michael. "The Inside-Out World in Frank O'Connor's Stories." *Studies in Short Fiction* 30 (Summer, 1993): 327-336. Discusses O'Connor's use of smallness to accent the collision between the world of the self and the vast world outside. Discusses "The Story Teller" as the most emphatic embodiment of this tension in O'Connor's stories, for the protagonist confronts characters who refuse to take her quest for magic and meaning seriously.

Renner, Stanley. "The Theme of Hidden Powers: Fate vs. Human Responsibility in 'Guests of the Nation.'" *Studies in Short Fiction* 27 (Summer, 1990): 371-378. Argues that the story's moral design emphasizes the existence of mysterious "hidden powers" or forces of chance and fate that control human lives. Suggests that the moral judgment of the story is against the protagonist-teller Bonaparte, who contributes to the world's brutality by mistakenly believing people have no choice.

Steinman, Michael. *Frank O'Connor at Work.* Syracuse, N.Y.: Syracuse University Press, 1990. Study of O'Connor's life and works.

Tomory, William M. *Frank O'Connor.* Boston: Twayne, 1980. Introductory book on O'Connor that briefly sketches his life and then gives an overview of his work. Tomory touches on a few stories, but most of the analysis is on themes and character types.

Wohlgelernter, Maurice. *Frank O'Connor: An Introduction.* New York: Columbia University Press, 1977. Full critical study on O'Connor's fiction. The author is especially good at articulating O'Connor's theory of the story and in applying those concepts to individual short stories.

# Seán O'Faoláin

**Born:** Cork City, Ireland; February 22, 1900
**Died:** Dublin, Ireland; April 20, 1991

**Principal short fiction** • *Midsummer Night's Madness, and Other Stories,* 1932; *A Purse of Coppers,* 1937; *Teresa, and Other Stories,* 1947; *The Man Who Invented Sin, and Other Stories,* 1948; *The Finest Stories of Seán O'Faoláin,* 1957; *I Remember! I Remember!,* 1961; *The Heat of the Sun: Stories and Tales,* 1966; *The Talking Trees, and Other Stories,* 1970; *Foreign Affairs, and Other Stories,* 1976; *The Collected Stories of Seán O'Faoláin,* 1980-1982 (3 volumes).

**Other literary forms** • Seán O'Faoláin's literary production includes novels, biographies, travel books, social analysis, and literary criticism. He wrote a number of well-received novels and several biographies of prominent Irish political figures. O'Faoláin's most notable work of literary criticism is his study of the short story, *The Short Story,* published in 1948. O'Faoláin also wrote a memorable autobiography, *Vive Moi!* (1964).

**Achievements** • Seán O'Faoláin is one of the acknowledged Irish masters of the short story. His stories are realistic and closely dissect the social world of the ordinary Irishman of the twentieth century. His protagonists are usually forced to accept the limitations and defeats that life in modern Ireland enforces. O'Faoláin, however, is not a social critic or satirist. Such an accommodation with society is often seen as welcome and necessary. The central theme in many of O'Faoláin's stories is the defeat of rigid principle and idealism by social and individual compromise. O'Faoláin seems to resist any appeal to pure principle and to celebrate a healthy realism and recognition of the limits that life imposes.

O'Faoláin's most important structural device is the reversal, in which a character's situation is suddenly altered. These reversals may be embarrassing or even humiliating, but O'Faoláin often softens the ending to show something human and positive even in the defeat that the reversal effects. O'Faoláin progressed as a writer of short fiction from his early autobiographical stories, focusing on the Irish troubles and civil war, to stories dealing with a variety of Irish people in different sections and social situations. The autobiography became a more flexible and distanced art as O'Faoláin approached the ideal of his master, Anton Chekhov.

**Biography** • Seán O'Faoláin was born John Francis Whelan in the city of Cork, Ireland, in 1900. His parents led an untroubled conventional life; his father was a constable for the Royal Irish Constabulary and his mother a pious Roman Catholic. By the time that John grew up, however, the problems of Ireland and England were becoming acute. The 1916 uprising in Dublin declared an Irish Republic, and a war broke out between Irish revolutionaries and British soldiers. John Whelan knew on which side he had to be and joined the Irish Volunteers in 1918 and later the Irish Republican Army. He changed his name to its Gaelic form of Seán O'Faoláin in 1918 to signal his new identity.

During the Irish troubles, O'Faoláin was educating himself; he received his bachelor's and master's degrees from University College, Cork, and a fellowship to Harvard University in 1928. In 1932, he published his first collection of short stories, *Midsummer Night's Madness, and Other Stories*. After that O'Faoláin became a prolific writer, as he produced novels, travel books, biographies, and studies of the national character of Ireland. Above all, however, he was a masterly writer of short stories.

O'Faoláin's *Midsummer Night's Madness, and Other Stories* contains a number of stories dealing with the Irish Civil War. Most of these treat broken promises and the destruction of idealism and romantic dreams. The later collections contain a considerable amount of irony, as the ordinary Irishman, with little hope of engaging in a historic event, tries to find some distinction in a bleak society. O'Faoláin, however, often modulates his irony and finds some compensatory victory even in defeat.

After having found his style and subject matter, O'Faoláin published a number of excellent collections of stories, culminating in *The Collected Stories of Seán O'Faoláin*. O'Faoláin became one of the finest Irish writers of the twentieth century and a master in his chosen genre, the short story.

**Analysis** • Seán O'Faoláin's stories are varied. The earliest ones deal with the immediate political concerns of the Irish Civil War. Others use irony, although the irony tends to be gentle rather than harsh. O'Faoláin never merely mocked or made fun of his characters; there is always affection and sympathy for those he created. Another group of stories expose idealism or abstract principles. O'Faoláin had little use for such general principles; he was consistently on the side of the specific case and the demands of realism and life. The later stories deal with sexuality and relationships between man and woman, especially the problems of husbands and wives.

A few constants do exist, however, in the stories. O'Faoláin's strength is in the portrayal and development of character and world. Each of his major characters fully exists in a well-defined environment. Ireland, as portrayed by O'Faoláin, is nearly a character in the story, and the limitations created by that world are significant. Whether it be religion or a narrow-minded social system, Ireland often restricts in various ways the opportunities for expression and a fuller and freer life.

**"The Old Master"** • "The Old Master," from *A Purse of Coppers*, is an early story that punctures the claims of a character to a privileged position; it uses a sudden and surprising reversal to bring about its resolution. The use of irony in this story is direct and amusing, if not very sophisticated. The protagonist, John Aloysius Gonzaga O'Sullivan, spends his time mocking the provincialism and lack of culture in his small Irish town. He has a sinecure as a law librarian and refuses to practice law; he spends his time, instead, berating the locals for their lack of sophistication. He is "the only man left in Ireland with a sense of beauty . . . the old master deserted in the abandoned house."

One day, the Russian Ballet comes to town, and he is ecstatic. A conflict arises, however, from the presence of the Russian Ballet. When O'Sullivan attempts to see a performance, he is stopped by men from the Catholic Church who oppose "Immoral Plays." O'Sullivan holds his sinecure from the county council, and he can lose his job if he offends the Catholic Church. Therefore, he compromises and walks away from the door; he has apparently failed to live up to his ideals. He tries, however, to make amends by sneaking in the back way and reassuring the Russian performers that he is with them.

O'Sullivan returns to the front of the theater and is immediately involved in a march against the ballet company. If he is seen by the people at the courthouse, he will be ruined, but if he is seen abandoning the march, he may lose his job. He tries to resolve his conflict by escaping to an outhouse and cursing the local leaders, as he has done so often in the past. He remains in the outhouse all night and catches pneumonia from this exposure and soon dies. The people in the town had seen him earlier as a "public show" and only at his death did they see him as a "human being." "The Old Master" is a typical O'Faoláin story. The unnatural idealism and pomposity of the main character have to be exposed. He is not mocked, however, for his fall; he has instead joined a fallible human community and rid himself of false pretensions.

**"Childybawn"** • "Childybawn" was published in *The Finest Stories of Seán O'Faoláin*, and it is a delightful study of the Irish character in which O'Faoláin reverses the usual view of the Irishman's dominance by his mother. The story is simple in its structure, and its effect depends on a reversal of expectations. O'Faoláin is not really a comic writer in the traditional sense; in later stories, the humor is much more subtle and becomes a part of the story, not the only element as it is here. The plot begins when Benjy Spillane's mother receives an anonymous note telling her that her son, fat and forty, is carrying on with a bank teller. Her strategy to retain the dedication and presence of her son is to remind him incessantly of Saint Augustine's love for his mother, Monica. This has little effect until Benjy becomes seriously ill and begins to read religious texts and change his life.

Suddenly the relationship is reversed; the religious Benjy begins complaining about the drinking and excessive betting of his mother. His mother now wishes that he would get married and leave her alone. The climax of the story is another reversal, as Benjy returns to his riotous ways and finally gains the promise of the bank clerk to wed him. There is a five-year engagement until his mother dies. After all, Benjy notes, "a fellow has to have *some* regard for his mother!"

"Childybawn" is a comic story and plays on many Irish stereotypes. There is the dominating mother and the middle-aged son who worships his mother. O'Faoláin gives the story and the types an original twist when he shows what would happen if a middle-aged son actually behaved the way a mother wished him to behave. Mrs. Spillane realizes that she has not had a peaceful moment since her son took up religion; she longs for the old, irreverent, and natural relationship that works on conflict and confrontation.

**"The Fur Coat"** • "The Fur Coat" is a poignant story taken from *The Man Who Invented Sin, and Other Stories*. It is concerned with social class, a somewhat unusual area for an O'Faoláin story. Most of his characters seem to live in a static environment, and such social change in Ireland is very different from that in the earlier stories. The plot is very simple, since it emphasizes character rather than action. Paddy Maguire receives an important promotion, so his wife, Molly, immediately determines that she must have a fur coat to go with her new status. She immediately becomes defensive over such a purchase, however, asking her husband if he thinks that she is "extravagant." The conflict grows between husband and wife as they discuss the fur coat, but it is really within Molly. Her own doubts about such a purchase are projected onto her husband, and they end up fighting, with her accusing him of being "mean." The climax of the story comes when Paddy gives Molly a check for £150 and she rips it up. She wants the coat desperately, but she cannot afford it. "I couldn't,

Paddy. I just couldn't." The story ends with Paddy asking her why she cannot purchase what she most desires and receiving the despairing answer, "I don't know."

"The Fur Coat" is a social story as well as a character study. The sudden rise in class and position leaves Molly between the old ways that have sustained her and the new ones that she cannot embrace. O'Faoláin has found a new subject for Irish fiction. The focus is no longer the enduring and unchanging peasant but an urban middle-class character who must deal with changes in his or her social position and personal life.

**"The Sugawn Chair"** • "The Sugawn Chair," from *I Remember! I Remember!*, is a perfect example of O'Faoláin's gentle irony; the story pokes fun at the illusions of an ideal rural life with economy and humor. O'Faoláin seems dedicated to exposing the various illusions that are endemic in Ireland. The chair, as the story opens, is abandoned and without a seat in the attic of the narrator. He associates the chair with memories of a yearly sack of apples that would be delivered, smelling of "dust, and hay, and apples." The sack and the chair both signify another world, the country.

The chair also has a history. It was an object of comfort in which "my da could tilt and squeak and rock to his behind's content." One night while rocking, his father went through the seat of the chair, where he remained stuck and cursing, much to the amusement of his wife and son. The father decides to repair his chair with some straw that he bought in a market. He enlists the aid of two of his country comrades. They soon, however, begin to argue about the different regions that they came from in rural Ireland. These arguments subside, but a new argument erupts about the type of straw needed to repair the chair. One claims that this straw is too moist, while another says that it is too short. Finally, they abandon the project and return to their earlier pursuits.

The story ends with the father symbolically admitting defeat by throwing a potato back into the sack and sitting on one of the city-made "plush" chairs. The Sugawn chair remains as it had been, shattered without a seat. The narrator comes upon the chair one day when he is cleaning out the attic after his mother has died. It recalls to his mind not only the country smells but also his mother and father embracing and "laughing foolishly, and madly in love again." "The Sugawn Chair" modulates its irony at the very end, so that the mocking at the illusions of an ideal rural life are tempered by the real feelings and memories that they share. O'Faoláin is by no means a James Joyce who fiercely indicts the false dreams of his Dubliners. O'Faoláin has a place even in his irony for true affections and relationships.

**"Dividends"** • "Dividends," from *The Heat of the Sun: Stories and Tales*, is a more ambitious story than many of the earlier ones, and it shows both a greater tolerance for the foibles of the characters and a subtlety in structure. Its primary subject is the clash between principle and reality, a favorite O'Faoláin theme. The story begins with the narrator's Aunt Anna coming into a legacy of £750. The narrator advises her to invest her legacy in secure stocks, so that she will receive a steady income. An old friend of the narrator, Mel Meldrum, arranges the transaction. The conflict arises when Aunt Anna sells her shares and continues to demand her dividends from Mel. Mel finally gives in and pays her the money, even though it is against his principles.

In order to resolve the dispute, the narrator is forced to return to Cork from Dublin. He finds that Mel is very well situated, with a country cottage and a beautiful young girl as a servant. Mel reveals that Aunt Anna has sold the shares not for a chair and some Masses for her soul but for a fancy fur coat. Mel now refuses to compromise and pay Anna her dividends. This intensifies the conflict as the narrator urges Mel to be his old self and take a chance on life, abandon his principles, pay Aunt Anna the dividends, and marry the young girl. Mel, however, is unable to change; if he marries the girl, he may be unhappy; if he pays the dividends, he is compromised and is no longer his ideal self.

Mel resolves the problem by abandoning his relationship with the young girl and hiring Aunt Anna as a servant. He will remain logical and consistent. The ending of the story, however, is not an indictment of Mel's principled consistency but a confession by the narrator that he has done something terrible by demanding that Mel remain the Mel that he had known as a boy at school. He had "uncovered his most secret dream and destroyed it by forcing him to bring it to the test of reality." He also has been narrow-minded in demanding a consistency of character and exposed a life-giving illusion no less than Mel had. "Dividends" is a complex narrative and a psychological study of how characters live upon illusions rather than principles. There is no neat exposure of illusions as in "The Old Master" but instead an unmasking of those who are all too eager to uncover dreams.

**"Hymeneal"** • "Hymeneal" is a story from O'Faoláin's latest period, and it is one of the fullest explorations of marriage, as O'Faoláin scrutinizes the relationship between husband and wife. "Hymeneal" covers the many years of a couple's marriage, but it focuses on the period of retirement. It is one of O'Faoláin's best-plotted stories, with a sudden and surprising reversal. It begins peacefully, detailing the enduring relationship of a married couple, Phil and Abby Doyle, who have been rooted in one spot in the North Circular section of Dublin. They have lived in this section for some thirty-five years. Phil, however, is to retire in a year, and he knows that Abby needs some help with the house, but he cannot afford it on his pension. He then decides—without consulting his wife—to sell their house and move to West Clare, where he can hire a servant and have the peace and time to write the book that he has been planning to write for years, which will expose the Education Department and Ministry.

The conflict between Phil and Abby develops quickly. She hates the isolation of West Clare, especially since it means moving away from her Dublin-based sister, Molly. Phil is also unhappy, although he refuses to admit it. He does none of the things that he has talked about for years; he does not fish or hunt, and he makes no progress on his book, although he continues to talk about it. Phil talks incessantly about exposing the department, where he has worked for such a long time, and the current minister, Phelim Quigley, the husband of Molly, Abby's sister. He sees Phelim as the perfect example of a man who has sacrificed principle to sentiment and convenience. When Phelim refuses to fire a teacher who drinks and quarrels with his wife, Phil Doyle is outraged at this lack of action. The book will reveal all.

The plot turns when Phelim Quigley suddenly dies in a car crash and Phil and Abby return to Dublin to console Molly and set her affairs in order. Phil assigns himself to work alone to sort out Phelim's papers. In those papers, Phil finds a number of surprising documents that alter his life. First of all, he finds that Phelim has acquired a decent sum of money and has recently purchased Phil's old house in Dublin. He then finds a sequence of poems that Phelim has written about his love for Abby rather than his wife, Molly. Phil is enraged at this soiling of his own love for Abby. Phil changes once more, however, when he comes upon some letters of Abby to Phelim that tell of Phelim's advice to Abby to stick to Phil and not divorce or leave him. Phelim also praises Phil's great ability as a civil servant; it is just those rigid qualities, however, that have made it so difficult to live with him. The whole tone and attitude of the last part of the story changes. The weather changes from stormy to sunny and clear. Molly announces that she would like to rent the Dublin house that she and Phelim had bought recently to Phil and Abby. Phil has become more accommodating. He will abandon his book and his inhuman principle for a fuller and less rigid life.

**"The Patriot"** • O'Faoláin's fiction shows clear lines of development. The early stories that focus on the Irish Civil War are filled with bitterness at the failure of leaders to live up to the republican ideal. They also tend to lack the smooth narrative surface, and some, such as "The Patriot," are quite simple and undemanding in their structure. The collections that followed showed an increasing mastery of the short-story form. They also avoid the simple structure and tiresome bitterness at the failures of ideals. "The Old Master," for example, shows an exposure of ideals that can deepen a character's humanity.

By the time of *I Remember! I Remember!*, O'Faoláin had mastered the short story; the stories from this period demonstrate a subtlety of characterization, plot, and theme that was not found in the earlier works. In addition, O'Faoláin changes his attitude toward the world of his fiction. He now was able to distance himself and find amusement in the dreams of his characters, as "The Sugawn Chair" makes clear. The last phase of O'Faoláin's development can be seen in the stories of *The Heat of the Sun: Stories and Tales* and *The Talking Trees, and Other Stories*. He began more fully to investigate the place and role of sexuality in Ireland. Stories such as "One Man, One Boat, One Girl" and "Falling Rocks, Narrowing Road, Cul-de-Sac Stop" are humorous explorations of human relationships. The Irishman's fear of women is handled with grace and sympathy, while at the same time acknowledging its absurdity. One other aspect of human relationships in O'Faoláin's fiction needs to be mentioned. "Hymeneal" is a haunting portrayal of marriage in which the main character's illusions are punctured so that he might re-create and strengthen his relationship with his wife.

*James Sullivan*

**Other major works**

PLAY: *She Had to Do Something,* pr. 1937.

ANTHOLOGY: *The Silver Branch: A Collection of the Best Old Irish Lyrics Variously Translated,* 1938.

NOVELS: *A Nest of Simple Folk,* 1933; *Bird Alone,* 1936; *Come Back to Erin,* 1940; *And Again?,* 1979.

NONFICTION: *The Life Story of Eamon De Valera,* 1933; *Constance Markievicz: Or, The Average Revolutionary,* 1934; *King of the Beggars: A Life of Daniel O'Connell,* 1938; *An Irish Journey,* 1940; *The Great O'Neill: A Biography of Hugh O'Neill, Earl of Tyrone, 1550-1616,* 1942; *The Story of Ireland,* 1943; *The Irish: A Character Study,* 1947; *The Short Story,* 1948; *A Summer in Italy,* 1949; *Newman's Way,* 1952; *South to Sicily,* 1953 (pb. in U.S. as *An Autumn in Italy,* 1953); *The Vanishing Hero,* 1956; *Vive Moi!,* 1964.

**Bibliography**

Bonaccorso, Richard. *Seán O'Faoláin's Irish Vision*. Albany: State University of New York Press, 1987. Excellent study that places O'Faoláin and his work in a social and literary context. Bonaccorso's readings of the stories are thorough and ingenious, if not always convincing.

Butler, Pierce. *Seán O'Faoláin: A Study of the Short Fiction*. New York: Twayne, 1993. Introduction to O'Faoláin's short fiction in which Butler claims that O'Faoláin shifts from an early focus on individuals in conflict with repressive Irish forces to more universal human conflicts. Examines O'Faoláin's realistic style and narrative voice as it changes throughout his career. Includes O'Faoláin's comments on the short story, some contemporary reviews, and three previously published critical studies.

Davenport, Guy. "Fiction Chronicle." *The Hudson Review* 32 (1979): 139-150. In a review article, Davenport has high praise for O'Faoláin's ability as a writer of short fiction. He finds the central themes of the stories to be the Irish character and Irish Catholicism.

Doyle, Paul A. *Sean O'Faoláin*. New York: Twayne, 1968. Life-and-works study of O'Faoláin in the Twayne series. It is good on the novels and the literary context in which O'Faoláin wrote but only adequate on the short fiction.

Hanley, Katherine. "The Short Stories of Seán O'Faoláin: Theory and Practice." *Eire-Ireland* 6 (1971): 3-11. An excellent introduction to O'Faoláin's stories. Hanley briefly sketches the theoretical base of the stories and then traces the development of O'Faoláin from the early romantic stories to the more sophisticated ones.

Harmon, Maurice. *Seán O'Faoláin*. London: Constable, 1994. Harmon first analyzes O'Faoláin's biographies on Irish figures to provide a social context and then examines briefly each book of short stories. Useful for an understanding of the Irish political and social scene.

May, Charles E., ed. *Masterplots II: Short Story Series, Revised Edition*. 8 vols. Pasadena, Calif.: Salem Press, 2004. Designed for student use, this reference set contains articles providing detailed plot summaries and analyses of seven short stories by O'Faoláin: "Childybawn" (vol. 2), "The Fur Coat" (vol. 3), "Innocence" (vol. 4), "The Man Who Invented Sin" and "Midsummer Night Madness" (vol. 5), "The Trout" (vol. 7), and "Up the Bare Stairs" (vol. 8).

Neary, Michael. "Whispered Presences in Seán O'Faoláin's Stories." *Studies in Short Fiction* 32 (Winter, 1995): 11-20. Argues that O'Faoláin confronts his Irishness in his stories in a way that refuses closure or the comfort of the telling detail. Asserts that many of his stories create a feeling of characters being haunted by some event from the past of which no sense can be made.

# Liam O'Flaherty

**Born:** Gort na gCapell, Aran Islands, Ireland; August 28, 1896
**Died:** Dublin, Ireland; September 7, 1984

**Principal short fiction** • *Spring Sowing*, 1924; *Civil War*, 1925; *Darkness*, 1926; *The Tent, and Other Stories*, 1926; *The Terrorist*, 1926; *The Mountain Tavern, and Other Stories*, 1929; *The Ecstasy of Angus*, 1931; *The Short Stories of Liam O'Flaherty*, 1937; *Two Lovely Beasts, and Other Stories*, 1948; *Dúil*, 1953; *The Stories of Liam O'Flaherty*, 1956; *The Pedlar's Revenge, and Other Stories*, 1976; *The Wave, and Other Stories*, 1980; *Liam O'Flaherty: The Collected Stories*, 1999 (A. A. Kelly, editor).

**Other literary forms** • Liam O'Flaherty wrote four regional novels, of which *Thy Neighbour's Wife* (1923), *The Black Soul* (1924), and *Skerrett* (1932) are set on Inishmore, the largest of the Aran Islands; the fourth, *The House of Gold* (1929), is set in Galway City. Four novels of Dublin city life are *The Informer* (1925), *Mr. Gilhooley* (1926), *The Assassin* (1928), and *The Puritan* (1931). *The Return of the Brute* (1929) concerns O'Flaherty's World War I experiences in trench warfare; *The Martyr* (1933), *Famine* (1937), *Land* (1946), and *Insurrection* (1950) are Irish historical novels for the years 1845-1922. O'Flaherty wrote three books of autobiography, *The Life of Tim Healy* (1927), several essays on social conditions and on literature, poems, and stories in Gaelic.

**Achievements** • The source of many of Liam O'Flaherty's achievements is his birthplace off the coast of the west of Ireland. The Aran Islands' remoteness and stark natural beauty, the dependence of their scattered population on the vagaries of wind and sea, the inhabitants' preservation of the Irish language as their primary means of communication, and the virtually mythological status accorded such phenomena by leading figures in the Irish Literary Revival such as William Butler Yeats and John Millington Synge all exerted a crucial influence on the development of O'Flaherty's work.

Both his short fiction and novels are noteworthy for their unsentimental treatment of island life, the vivid directness of their style, and their attention to natural detail. Although by no means all, or even all the best, of O'Flaherty's work draws on his Aran background, the marked degree to which all of his work emphasizes the spontaneity and volatility of all living things is the product of his formative exposure to the life forces of Aran. One of the consequences of this background's influence is plots that deal with the problematical socialization of natural energy. These plots tend to take on a melodramatic or expressionistic coloration that can mar the overall balance and objectivity of the work. Such coloration also, however, unwittingly reveals O'Flaherty's essential opposition to the aesthetic and cultural codes of the Irish Literary Revival and lends his work an often overlooked but crucial, critical dimension.

O'Flaherty won the James Tait Black Memorial Prize in 1926 for his novel *The Informer.* That same novel won him several other awards and honors in France and England, including two Academy Awards in 1935. O'Flaherty was honored with a doctorate in literature from the National University of Ireland in 1974, and with the Irish Academy of Letters Award for literature in 1979.

**Biography** • Liam O'Flaherty was educated in seminaries and at University College, Dublin, from which in 1915 he joined the British army. He served in France and Belgium and, shell-shocked, became an invalid in 1918. He traveled to the United States and Canada and returned to Ireland in 1920 and became a Communist and Socialist activist. Forced to escape to England in 1922, he began writing steadily. He married Margaret Barrington in 1926, but they separated in 1932, the same year he helped to found the Irish Academy of Letters. During World War II he lived in Connecticut, the Caribbean region, and South America. Despite his controversial participation in the Irish struggle for independence and the general political militancy of his twenties, and despite his active contribution to the establishment of the Irish Academy of Letters, O'Flaherty absented himself from public involvement for virtually the last forty years of his life. Unlike most Irish writers of his generation, O'Flaherty did not continue to develop. The widespread public congratulations that greeted his eightieth birthday in 1976 and the republication of many of his best-known novels during the last decade of his life did nothing of significance to break the immense silence of his later years.

**Analysis** • To experience the full range of Liam O'Flaherty's stories, one must deal with the exceptions in the collection *The Stories of Liam O'Flaherty*, notably "The Mountain Tavern," which, like his historical novels, treats the revolutionaries in the 1920's, and "The Post Office," a humorous account of visitors' attempts to send a telegram from a small Irish town. The bulk of his stories, however, deal with nature and with people close to nature. In his publication entitled *Joseph Conrad* (1930), O'Flaherty distinguishes himself from Joseph Conrad and other novelists, saying, "I have seen the leaping salmon fly before the salmon whale, and I have seen the sated buck horn his mate and the wanderer leave his wife in search of fresh bosoms with the fire of joy in his eye." Such firsthand observance characterizes twelve of the forty-two stories in the collection, for all twelve are animal stories with little or no intrusion of a human being.

The raw guts of nature, its tenderness and its viciousness, appear in these stories, with both wild and domesticated animals. A cow follows the trail of its stillborn calf to where it has been thrown over a cliff, the maternal instinct so strong that, when a wave washes the calf's body away, the cow plunges to her death in pursuit. A rockfish fights for its life against a fisherman's hook, winning the battle by leaving behind a torn piece of its jaw. A proud black mare overruns a race and falls to her death; a huge conger eel tears up a fisherman's net in making its escape; a wild goat, protecting its kid, attacks and kills a marauding dog. In "Birth," the people watch through the night for a newborn calf. Among several bird stories, a blackbird, proud of its song, barely escapes the claws of a cat; a baby seagull conquers fear and learns to fly; a wild swan's mate dies and, forlorn and desperate, he woos, fights for, and flies away with another mate. A wounded cormorant, outcast from its flock, tries to gain acceptance, but the others tear at it and destroy it. A hawk captures a lark to feed his mate and by his very presence drives peaceful birds out of the territory; but then the hawk loses his life in attacking a man climbing up to his nest, and the man captures the mate and takes the eggs.

Yet the objective study of nature, impassioned alike with tenderness and viciousness, yields a delicate study of erotica. The laws of nature are so closely observed in primitive living conditions and so necessary to the barren efforts of survival that any slight aberration seems marked by a higher intelligence. In O'Flaherty's stories, this phenomenon seems to take two directions. Ordinary living conditions become bound by rigid customs so that anything not traditional, the peasants say, has "the law of God" against it. Some creatures, however, respond to a different divinity. In these cases the law of nature may permit more individuality than does social custom or the Church. Caught between these baffling natural and socioreligious forces, the people may switch their allegiances with remarkable speed and use the same kind of logic to support two different kinds of action. Some of O'Flaherty's best stories—"The Fairy Goose," "The Child of God," "Red Barbara," "Two Lovely Beasts"—deal with the reaction of the people not so much to adversity as to difference. "The Red Petticoat" and "The Beggars" deal with people who are different.

**"The Fairy Goose"** • The title creature of "The Fairy Goose" from before its birth evokes undue emotion; sitting on the egg with two others, an old woman's pet hen dies. Of the three eggs, only one hatches, into a scrawny, sickly thing obviously better off dead. The woman's husband intervenes with his admonition of "the law of God" not to kill anything born in a house. So unlike a goose is its subsequent behavior that the people begin to treat it as a fairy, adorn it with ribbons, and bestow other favors. Regarding it as sacred, O'Flaherty writes, "All the human beings in the village paid more respect to it than they did to one another." On the basis of its supernatural powers, its owner becomes a wise woman sought far and near, but jealousy intervenes: A woman who herself casts spells informs the local priest. He destroys the goose's nest and calls its admirers idolaters. Confronted with the powers of the Church, the former adherents of the goose now denounce it and threaten to burn the old woman's house. Only those villagers hitherto unconcerned manage to restrain the threatened violence, but eventually young men during the night approach and kill the goose. The old woman's only defense, a traditional curse, seems to linger in the air, for thereafter the villagers become quarrelsome drunkards.

**"The Child of God"** • No doubt based on his own disaffection with the Church, O'Flaherty's stories do not present priests as dispensers of benevolence or wisdom. For the people themselves, religion, custom, and superstition equally make up the law of God. Tradition, moreover, curbs the active intelligence and promotes baleful ironies; a thing may be blessed and cursed in rapid succession. Such is the career of Peter O'Toole in "The Child of God." The farmer O'Toole and his wife, in their forties, have an embarrassing "late from the womb" child. The baby's uncommon ill health provokes the first accusation that he is a fairy child, but the mother maintains that he is a child of God. The wife's unusual attention to the child seems in itself to be a miracle and alters the conduct of the father, who gives up his drinking bouts. The mother believes the child will bring prosperity to the house, and she makes the older children take jobs and save. At the age of ten, as if to confirm the mother's faith, Peter announces his ambition to become a priest—an honor higher than his parents could have dreamed for him. After six years, however, with the family driven into debt to support his education, Peter is expelled because, as he explains later, he does not believe in God. Further, they learn upon his return home at the age of nineteen that he has become an artist. To their horror, his books of pictures show "naked women . . . like French postcards." Peter's difference becomes a threat, and the artist, like the satirists of old, becomes feared for his sketching the people in unflattering poses.

After some six months, an "orgy" occurs at a wake. It would be bad enough for Peter as a participant, but it is much worse for him when the people discover that he is stone sober. As if spellbound, they watch while he sketches the entire shameful scene;

afterward outraged, they call his art sacrilege and threaten to stone him. His mother now believes he has brought a curse with his birth, and his father believes God will strike all of the villagers dead for what Peter has done. The priest intervenes and dispels a stone-throwing mob; but, exhibiting no more compassion, benevolence, or enlightenment than do the people, he denounces Peter for having brought a curse on the parish and banishes him. The mother, left alone, weeps for her lost child, not aware of the irony that her son's creativity indeed makes him a child close to God.

**"Red Barbara"** • Between the alternatives of a blessing or a curse, one who thrives—provided he is not too different—surely must be blessed. So Barbara's second husband in "Red Barbara," although a weaver and a flower grower, gains acceptance until his marriage proves unfruitful; then he proves himself limited to the prevailing viewpoint. Barbara, accustomed to beatings and violent lovemaking by a frequently drunken husband, shrinks from Joseph's gentle touch and soon despises him as a "priestly lecher." Sharing the people's belief in the importance of a family, he grows fearful of his own failure to father a child, becomes strange, solitary, and emaciated, and eventually dies deranged. Barbara returns to her wild ways with her third husband, and Joseph is remembered only as "a fable in the village."

**"Two Lovely Beasts"** • So closely knit is a small Aran community that the owner of a cow shares its milk, free, with his neighbors. Thus a crisis occurs in "Two Lovely Beasts" when Colm Derrane consents to buy a motherless calf from a poor widow and feed it alongside his own calf. The widow, Kate Higgins, assures Colm that he is different from everybody else. The difference in his decision to raise a calf on the people's milk definitely breaks the law of God and of the community, and the family becomes outcast. Kate herself cannot find another cow to buy, uses the sale money to feed her children, and turns against Colm with the accusation that his money was cursed. Forcing his family to live frugally in order to feed both calves, Colm beats his wife into submission; this evidence of male sanity restores her confidence in him. Hereafter all the children work hard to save, the tide of public opinion turns as the family prospers, and now the people say that God has blessed the family's efforts to rise in the world.

Two of the Higgins children die without proper nourishment; the distraught mother, removed to an asylum, leaves behind a plot of grassland which Colm rents through a difficult winter. He demands of his starving and threadbare family another year of sacrifice while the two beasts grow into bullocks and he can save money to open a shop. At last, with the community's belief that God blesses those who prosper, the shop brings financial success, and the calves become champions on fair day. Envy intrudes, also, but as Colm and his family drive away to open a shop in the town, he appears unaware of the people's hostility and derision. "Two Lovely Beasts" in this way shows the possible rise of a merchant class, who as money lenders became known as the hated gombeen men—those who live off the peasants by buying their produce at low prices and selling it elsewhere for a profit, a topic O'Flaherty treated in *The House of Gold*.

**"The Red Petticoat"** • Most of the stories, however, relate the peasants' situation at home—their contention with the forces of nature, their primitive living conditions, and their sensitivity to social order and ideals. Often conditions seem to be fixed at the close of a story, but occasionally good wit or good fortune alters the circumstances, at least temporarily, as in "The Red Petticoat" and "The Beggars." The ankle-length skirt of red or blue wool called a petticoat is a colorful part of the native costume of women of the Aran Islands. Often paired with a heavy, long shawl, it stands out against a somber background of rocks and grey houses. "The Red Petticoat" begins with Mrs. Mary Deignan and her four children, with no food in the house, trying to think of a way to obtain provisions. This unusual family does not work consistently, although all work valiantly when they have work; they enjoy laughing together and composing poems, some of them satires against their enemies. Unlike most residents of Aran, they can laugh in the midst of near-starvation. Out of such a background and the family's rehearsals come the expediency that Mrs. Deignan contrives to relieve their want—a melodrama spawned in her own brain, using the stock character of a witch or "wise woman," and acted out against the village storekeeper.

Mrs. Deignan, known as "Mary of the bad verses" because her poems are "scurrilous and abusive, and at times even indecent and in a sense immoral," is not powerless when she sets forth wearing her shawl and her new check apron to visit Mrs. Murtagh, the local storekeeper who has somewhat the character of a gombeen. In her "wise woman" role Mrs. Deignan terrifies Mrs. Murtagh with a hissing account of Mrs. Murtagh's sins in the traditional style of name-calling, out of which eventually Mrs. Deignan shoots a question: "Where is the red petticoat you were wearing last Sunday night, when you went to visit the tailor?" Tricking Mrs. Murtagh into denying it was red and admitting it was a black skirt, Mrs. Deignan now has what she wanted—the means of blackmail. Mrs. Murtagh launches into a vicious battle with Mrs. Deignan and knocks her into a corner but attracts passersby. Mrs. Deignan only pretends to be unconscious and, at the propitious moment, she changes character and becomes a pitiful beggar, blessing Mrs. Murtagh for having agreed to provide whatever she wants on six-months' credit. The neighbors understand that something is wrong, but they are totally mystified. Mrs. Deignan returns home with her shawl turned into a grocery sack slung over her shoulder; Mrs. Murtagh knows she will be subject to further blackmail but comforts herself with thoughts of spending more time with the tailor.

**"The Beggars"** • "The Beggars" features as protagonist a blind man who with "priestly arrogance" exhorts people to beware the hour of their deaths, although he knows from experience that a church is not a place to beg alms; cemeteries and missions are better. His repeated cry, totally incongruous with his surroundings, earns him nothing near the gateway to a racetrack. Changing to angry curses when he thinks a man jeers at him, the beggar gains the sympathy and the aid of other beggars—a tipster, a singing woman, and an accordionist. The honor and generosity he finds among beggars seem sufficient to confirm his dream that he would find good fortune in a strange place on this day; but then the formerly cursed man returns to count into his hand five one-pound banknotes, part of two hundred pounds earned from an intuitive flash at the sight of the blind man and the memory of a horse named "Blind Barney."

**"The Mountain Tavern"** • In "The Mountain Tavern" O'Flaherty records some of the political upheaval caused by the Act of Partition in 1921. Three Republican revolutionaries trudge through a night snowstorm to reach a tavern and obtain aid for their wounded. When they arrive, the tavern is a smoking ruin, destroyed in a shootout between the Republicans and the Free Staters. Their incredulity on finding that the destitute survivors can do nothing for them parallels the anger of the tavern owner's wife, who tongue-lashes them for the three years she has suffered in their war. The wounded man dies, and the other two are taken prisoner.

**"The Post Office"** • In an opposite and humorous vein, O'Flaherty in "The Post Office" assembles on old-age pension day the most traditional elements of a small Gaelic town; to them, the telephone, a newfangled gadget, complicates former lives of simplicity which relied on donkeys, carts, and rowboats. Three tourists speaking French and arriving in a New York Cadillac have a tourist's reason for sending a telegram to California—a friend's ancestor is from this town—and create great humor and confusion because the postmaster considers telegrams the bane of his existence. Even a priest forgets to be scandalized by the two women's clothing when he learns the visitors' purpose. The local old people take the male visitor to be a government spy because of his fluent Gaelic, consider that the women's painted toenails are a disease on their feet, believe the Spanish girl to be a duke's daughter, and appraise the American girl for her obvious reproductive capacities. The postmaster refuses to send a telegram in Spanish because it may be obscene, relents upon a recitation of Lorca's poetry, and tries to place the call to Galway; but he finds himself on the telephone at first cursed as a fishmonger, then receives news of a neighbor's operation and death, and finally hears a wrong-number grievance from a schoolteacher. "We are all in it," says one native upon pronunciation of the town's name, Praiseach Gaelic for confusion, disorder, and shapelessness.

The best character, the mocking young man who has graduated from his native background, lends himself to the confusion for the humor of it, reads a letter to oblige an old soldier, and with quick wit constructs tales appropriate for the native credulity. O'Flaherty's depiction of the clash of two cultures, his ear for the local diction, and his intelligence for the local logic and laughter here show him at his very best.

*Grace Eckley*
*With updates by George O'Brien*

## Other major works

CHILDREN'S LITERATURE: *All Things Come of Age and the Test of Courage*, 1984.

NOVELS: *Thy Neighbour's Wife*, 1923; *The Black Soul*, 1924; *The Informer*, 1925; *Mr. Gilhooley*, 1926; *The Assassin*, 1928; *The House of Gold*, 1929; *The Return of the Brute*, 1929; *The Puritan*, 1931; *Skerrett*, 1932; *The Martyr*, 1933; *Hollywood Cemetery*, 1935; *Famine*, 1937; *Land*, 1946; *Insurrection*, 1950.

NONFICTION: *The Life of Tim Healy*, 1927; *Joseph Conrad*, 1930; *Two Years*, 1930; *I Went to Russia*, 1931; *Shame the Devil*, 1934; *The Letters of Liam O'Flaherty*, 1996 (A. A. Kelly, editor).

## Bibliography

Cahalan, James M. *Liam O'Flaherty: A Study of the Short Fiction*. Boston: Twayne, 1991. Introduction to O'Flaherty's stories by an expert in Irish literature. Discusses the peasant consciousness in the stories, as well as the stories' relationship to the Irish language. Comments on issues of gender and politics raised by the stories. Also includes many comments by O'Flaherty from letters and articles, as well as secondary sources.

Costello, Peter. *Liam O'Flaherty's Ireland.* Dublin: Wolfhound Press, 1996. Explores O'Flaherty's life and times, how his environment influenced his writings.

Daniels, William. "Introduction to the Present State of Criticism of Liam O'Flaherty's Collection of Short Stories: *D il.*" *Eire-Ireland* 23 (Summer, 1988): 122-134. A summary of criticism of O'Flaherty's stories in *D il.* Takes issue with a number of criticisms of the stories, such as their lack of focus on setting, plot, and point of view. Argues that the stories deserve much better criticism than they have received from critics in both Irish and English.

Doyle, Paul A. *Liam O'Flaherty.* Boston: Twayne, 1972. The first comprehensive overview of O'Flaherty's life and work. The author's reading of O'Flaherty's short fiction tends to be more illuminating than that of the novels. Although superseded by later studies, this volume is still helpful as a means of orientating the newcomer to O'Flaherty's work. Contains an extensive bibliography.

Jefferson, George. *Liam O'Flaherty: A Descriptive Bibliography of His Works.* Dublin: Wolfhound Press, 1993. Useful tool for the student of O'Flaherty. Includes bibliographical references and an index.

Kelly, A. A. *Liam O'Flaherty: The Storyteller.* London: Macmillan, 1976. Exhaustive treatment of the themes and techniques of O'Flaherty's short fiction. Although somewhat disjointed in organization, this study ultimately makes a convincing case for the distinctiveness of O'Flaherty's achievements in the form. Particular emphasis is placed on the range and variety of his stories. Supplemented by an excellent bibliography.

Kilroy, James R. "Setting the Standards: Writers of the 1920's and 1930's." In *The Irish Short Story: A Critical History,* edited by James F. Kilroy. Boston: Twayne, 1984. Introduction to O'Flaherty's stories, emphasizing their ethical implications and naturalism. Discusses his simple narrative technique and style and how the short story suits his single-minded vision.

May, Charles E., ed. *Masterplots II: Short Story Series, Revised Edition.* 8 vols. Pasadena, Calif.: Salem Press, 2004. Designed for student use, this reference set contains articles providing detailed plot summaries and analyses of four short stories by O'Flaherty: "The Mountain Tavern" (vol. 5), "The Post Office" (vol. 6), "The Sniper" (vol. 7), and "Two Lovely Beasts" (vol. 8).

O'Brien, James H. *Liam O'Flaherty.* Lewisburg, Pa.: Bucknell University Press, 1973. Brief introduction to O'Flaherty's life and work. Its longest chapter is devoted to O'Flaherty's short stories, but the study also contains biographical information and analyses of the novels. O'Flaherty's achievements as a short-story writer are considered in the context of those of his Irish contemporaries. The stories' themes and motifs are also discussed.

Thompson, Richard R. "The Sage Who Deep in Central Nature Delves: Liam O'Flaherty's Short Stories." *Eire-Ireland* 18 (Spring, 1983): 80-97. A discussion of the central themes in O'Flaherty's stories, focusing primarily on the moral lessons inherent in his nature stories, which urge a turning away from intellectualism.

Zneimer, John. *The Literary Vision of Liam O'Flaherty.* Syracuse, N.Y.: Syracuse University Press, 1970. Ambitious approach to O'Flaherty's work. The author sees a strong religious component in O'Flaherty's novels and stories and a tension between the two forms. The novels are said to be despairing, while the stories are claimed to offer a redemptive alternative. Some important insights do not ultimately make the author's argument persuasive.

# Tillie Olsen

**Born:** Omaha, Nebraska; January 14, 1912
**Died:** Oakland, California; January 1, 2007

**Principal short fiction** • *Tell Me a Riddle*, 1961.

**Other literary forms** • Besides her short stories and the novel *Yonnondio: From the Thirties* (1974), Tillie Olsen was the author of "A Biographical Interpretation," the afterword published in Rebecca Davis's *Life in the Iron Mills* (1972), which she edited, and *Silences* (1978), a collection of essays about women and writing. She edited two books: *Mother to Daughter, Daughter to Mother: Mothers on Mothering—A Daybook and Reader* (1984), a collection of excerpts, and *Mothers and Daughters: That Special Quality—An Exploration in Photographs* (1987). In addition, she wrote uncollected magazine articles on women and writing and many uncollected poems, several of which appeared in *Partisan Review, Prairie Schooner, New World Writing, Ms., Harper's,* and *College English.*

**Achievements** • Even though Olsen secured her literary reputation on the strength of one collection of short fiction, her voice as a humanist and feminist extended her influence beyond this small output. Olsen wrote about working-class people who, because of class, race, or sex, have been denied the opportunity to develop their talents. Frequently she focused on the obstacles women have experienced. She understood them well. She herself was exactly such a victim of poverty during the 1930's, and then she worked and raised a family for more than twenty years until she could begin writing. Both her fiction and her nonfiction deal with the problem women face: developing individual talents while combating socially imposed views.

Olsen was also known as a leading feminist educator. Her courses introduced students to forgotten writings, such as journals, to teach them about women's lives. The reading lists she developed have provided models for other women's studies courses throughout the United States. Besides the O. Henry Award for the best American short story of 1961 for "Tell Me a Riddle," Olsen also won the Award for Distinguished Contribution to American Literature from the American Academy and the National Institute of Arts and Letters. Her other awards included a John Simon Guggenheim Memorial Foundation Fellowship in 1975-1976, an honorary doctorate from the University of Nebraska in 1979, a Ministry to Women Award from the Unitarian Women's Federation in 1980, a Bunting Institute Fellowship from Radcliffe College in 1985, and a Rea Award for the short story in 1994. Her short fiction appears in more than one hundred anthologies, including *The Best American Short Stories* for 1957, 1961, and 1971, and *Fifty Best American Stories, 1915-1965.*

**Biography** • The daughter of Russian-Jewish immigrant parents, Tillie L. Olsen spent her youth in Nebraska and Wyoming. Her parents were active union members, so political commitment as well as economic pressures accompanied her early years. Her father served as state secretary in the Socialist Party. In 1933, she moved to California, where, in 1936, she married printer Jack Olsen. Because she raised four daughters and worked at full-time clerical jobs, she did not publish her first book until she was in her late forties. She worked as a pork trimmer in meat-packing houses, a hotel maid, a jar-capper, and a waitress. Then, with the help of a Stanford University Creative Writing Fellowship and a Ford grant in literature she put together *Tell Me a Riddle,* the title story of which received the O. Henry Award for the best American short story of 1961. There followed a fellowship at the Radcliffe Institute for Independent Study, grants from the National Endowment for the Arts, and a Guggenheim Fellowship. A grant from the MacDowell Colony allowed her to complete *Yonnondio: From the Thirties,* a novel she began in the 1930's which was originally published in 1934 in the *Partisan Review.* After its revision and publication in 1974, Olsen continued writing essays and articles as well as editing collections of women's writings. In addition, she taught at Amherst College, Stanford University, the Massachusetts Institute of Technology, and the University of Minnesota, among others. In the introduction of her

Leonda Fiske

nonfiction book *Silences* (1978), Olsen wrote, "For our silenced people, century after century, their beings consumed in the hard everyday essential work of maintaining human life. Their art, which still they made—anonymous; refused respect, recognition; lost." She was twice arrested for her activism.

After experiencing years of deteriorating health, Olsen died on January 1, 2007, in Oakland, California. She was was two weeks shy of her ninety-fifth birthday.

**Analysis** • Tillie Olsen's *Tell Me a Riddle* contains four stories arranged chronologically in the order in which they were written: "I Stand Here Ironing," "Hey Sailor, What Ship?," "O Yes," and "Tell Me a Riddle." All but the first story contain, as major or minor characters, members of the same family, whose parents emigrated from Russia. The characters in the first story could also belong to the same family, although there is no evidence to prove it and the names of the children are different; nevertheless in "I Stand Here Ironing" characters, situation, and tone are similar to those found in the other three stories. A difference between "I Stand Here Ironing" and the remaining stories in the volume is that the former story is told in the first person, being a kind of interior monologue (actually an imagined dialogue), whereas "Hey Sailor, What Ship?," "O Yes," and "Tell Me a Riddle" are told in varieties of the third person.

**"I Stand Here Ironing"** • Exterior action in "I Stand Here Ironing" is practically nonexistent, consisting of a woman moving an iron across an ironing board. Interior action is much more complicated, being a montage of times, places, and movements involving a mother in interaction (or lack of interaction) with her firstborn, a daughter, Emily. Questions arise as to whether the montage can define or even begin to define the daughter; whether the mother or anyone else can help the daughter or whether such help is needed; whether the daughter will continue to be tormented like the mother, who identifies herself with the iron moving inexorably back and forth across the board; or whether, as the mother hopes, the daughter will be more than the dress on the ironing board, "helpless before the iron." "She will leave her seal," the mother says, the only words spoken aloud in the story; but the words could express only the mother's fervent hope for the well-being of a daughter born to a mother of nineteen, impoverished, alone, distracted, in an age of depression, war, and fear.

**"Hey Sailor, What Ship?"** • "Hey Sailor, What Ship?" introduces Lennie and Helen and their children, Jeannie, Carol, and Allie; but the story is not so much about them as it is about Whitey (Michael Jackson, a sailor and friend of the family who seems more lost at sea than at home in any port or ship). Filtering through Whitey's consciousness, the story explores his frustrations and anger, pain and despair. At the same time, however, the living conditions of Lennie and Helen and their children and the relationships among the family and between various members of the family and Whitey are carefully delineated.

Whitey is a mariner, a perpetual wanderer whose only contact with family life is with Lennie, a boyhood friend. As the story opens, Whitey is drunk, a condition he finds himself in more and more, and with almost nothing left of his pay. His anguish, born of his desire to be with Lennie and the family and his reluctance to bear the pain of such a visit, is evident from the beginning, as is also the shame and degradation he feels associated with his lifestyle. What had started out as a dream, a life of adventure on the sea, with comrades who shared the good and the bad, has become a parade of gin mills and cathouses, clip joints, hock shops, skid rows, and lately hospitals. Lennie's dreams, however, have also been frustrated. Lennie is a worn likeness of his former self; Helen is graying and tired from holding a job as well as caring for house and home. They live in poverty in cramped quarters. Still, as Helen explains to her oldest daughter, Jeannie, this house is the only place in which Whitey does not have to buy his way. The tragedy is that he feels he does. He comes bearing presents, distributing dollars and at the same time too drunk to share in meaningful interaction with the family he loves, where he is brother, lover, and father to a family not his own.

**"O Yes"** • "O Yes" picks up the family several years later when Carol, the second daughter, is twelve and about to experience the pain of parting with a close friend, Parry, a black girl. Carol and her mother, Helen, have accompanied Parry and her mother, Alva, to a black church to witness Parry's baptism. Carol is uncomfortable, however, both with the surroundings and with Parry, who is growing away from her. As the services rise to a crescendo of passion, Carol asks her mother to take her home and then faints. Later Alva tries to explain to Carol that the religion is like a hope in the blood and bones and that the music offers a release to despair, but Carol will not listen.

Later Jeannie tries to explain to her mother that Carol and Parry are undergoing an almost inevitable "sorting out" process, a sorting out demanded by the culture—their environment, their peers, their teachers—a sorting out that "they" demand. The separation is hard on both girls. Nevertheless, Parry seems better equipped to handle the crisis, while Carol continues to suffer and question. Helen knows that Carol, too, has been baptized, immersed in the seas of humankind, and she suffers with her daughter. The irony is that white people have no means of catharsis through their religion; they are unable to cry "O Yes."

**"Tell Me a Riddle"**   •   The most haunting story in the collection *Tell Me a Riddle* is the title story. Longer than the other stories, this one focuses on Lennie's mother and father while at the same time it brings to a culmination themes Olsen explores in the other stories: the frustration of dreams unrealized; the despair of never having enough money; the anger and hostility of women who have had to cope with too much with too little and who have lost themselves in the process; the search for meaning and explanation; the continuing hope of the young in spite of the tensions around them; the pain of mortality. If the story has a fault, it may be that it is too painful as it grasps readers and pulls them too close to raw feeling. "Tell me a riddle, granny," a grandchild demands. "I know no riddles, child," the grandmother answers; but she knows, and the reader knows, that the riddle is of existence itself. Why claw and scratch; why hold on? Aged and consumed by cancer, the grandmother's body will not let go.

Russian emigrants of Jewish extraction who have fled persecution to come to the American land of promise, the grandfather and grandmother have been married forty-seven years and have reared seven children, all of whom are married and have families of their own. Now the grandfather wants to sell the house and move to The Haven, a retirement community, where he will have freedom from responsibility, from fretting over money, and will be able to share in communal living, to fish or play cards or make jokes with convivial companions. The grandmother refuses, however, countering every argument her husband puts forth. She was the one who worked eighteen hours a day without sufficient money to keep the house together. Not once did he scrape a carrot or lift a dish towel or stay with the children. He is the one who needs companions; she lived a life of isolation. "You trained me well," she tells him. "I do not need others to enjoy." She is adamant: "Never again to be forced to move to the rhythms of others." The argument between them erupts continually, fanned by his desires and her anger and resentment.

The children do not understand. How can people married forty-seven years and now at a time of life when they should be happy get themselves into a power struggle that threatens to pull them apart? Unknowingly the children take their father's side, considering their mother to be unreasonable or sick. They advise him to get her to a doctor. The doctor finds nothing seriously wrong and advises a diet and a change in lifestyle—"start living like a human being." The grandmother continues to deteriorate; more and more she keeps to herself, stays in bed, and turns her face to the wall. One night she realizes that although the doctor said she was not sick, she feels sick, and she asks her husband to stay home with her. He refuses, once again bringing up the old argument, and as he leaves she sobs curses at him. When he returns he finds that she has left their bed and retired to a cot. They do not speak to each other for a week until one night he finds her outside in the rain singing a love song of fifty years ago. The husband and the children bring her to a son-in-law who is a physician, and during surgery he finds cancer. The children advise their father to travel with her and visit all the children; and now begins an exodus of pain. She does not yet realize she is terminally ill, and the constant movement causes her utter despair when all she wants is to be at home. From house to house they carry her and she refuses to participate, will not touch a baby grandchild, and retreats finally to sit in a closet when they believe she is napping. Once a granddaughter, herself upset, hauls her little body into the closet and finds her grandmother there—"Is this where you hide, too, Grammy?"

Finally the grandfather brings her to a new apartment close to a seaside resort, dismal in the off-season and filled with the impoverished aged. The grandmother, ill in bed for several days, is tended by her granddaughter, Jeannie, daughter of Lennie and Helen, and now a visiting nurse. When she is better, the grandmother wants to go by the sea to sit in the sand. More and more now she loses control of her conscious self, sings snatches of songs, remembers pieces of quotations, tries in herself to find meaning while noticing that death, decay, and deterioration are all around her. Then she realizes that she, too, is dying and knows that she cannot tell her husband of her realization because a fiction is necessary to him; and she wants to go home.

One day Jeannie brings her a cookie in the shape of a real little girl who has died and tells her of a Spanish custom of partying at funerals, singing songs, and picnicking by the graves. From this interaction Jeannie draws solace, from what she takes to be a promise from her grandmother that at death she will go back to when she first heard music, to a wedding dance, where the flutes "joyous and vibrant tremble in the air." For the others there is no comfort. "Too late to ask: and what did you learn with your living, Mother, and what do we need to know?"

*Mary Rohrberger*
*With updates by Louise M. Stone and Nika Hoffman*

**Other major works**

ANTHOLOGIES: *Life in the Iron Mills,* 1972, revised 1984; *Mother to Daughter, Daughter to Mother: Mothers on Mothering—A Daybook and Reader,* 1984; *Mothers and Daughters: That Special Quality—An Exploration in Photographs,* 1987 (with others).

NOVELS: *Yonnondio: From the Thirties,* 1974.

NONFICTION: "A Biographical Interpretation," 1972; *Silences,* 1978.

**Bibliography**

Barstow, Jane M. "Tell Me a Riddle." In *Masterplots II: Short Story Series,* edited by Charles E. May. Rev. ed. Vol. 7. Pasadena, Calif.: Salem Press, 2004. Analysis of "Tell Me a Riddle" with sections on themes and meaning and style and technique. Also includes a detailed synopsis of the story.

Bauer, Helen Pike. "'A Child of Anxious, Not Proud, Love': Mother and Daughter in Tillie Olsen's 'I Stand Here Ironing.'" In *Mother Puzzles: Daughters and Mothers in Contemporary American Literature,* edited by Mickey Pearlman. Westport, Conn.: Greenwood Press, 1989. Analyzes the story as a dialogue between a number of opposites in which the basic issues are how much of the past determines the daughter's future, how much of the mother is in the daughter, and how much responsibility the mother has for her daughter's passivity and repression.

Cardoni, Agnes Toloczko. *Women's Ethical Coming-of-Age: Adolescent Female Characters in the Prose Fiction of Tillie Olsen.* Lanham, Md.: University Press of America, 1998. Survey of Olsen's adolescent female characters, comparing and contrasting their milieux. Includes a bibliography and an index.

Coiner, Constance. *Better Red: The Writing and Resistance of Tillie Olsen and Meridel Le Sueur.* New York: Oxford University Press, 1995. Compares these two authors' activism and writing styles. Includes a bibliography and an index.

Faulkner, Mara. *Protest and Possibility in the Writing of Tillie Olsen.* Charlottesville: University Press of Virginia, 1993. Examines the themes of motherhood, relationships between men and women, community, and language in Olsen's fiction.

Frye, Joanne S. *Tillie Olsen: A Study of the Short Fiction.* New York: Twayne, 1995. One of the most extensive discussions of the four stories in *Tell Me a Riddle* and "Requa." Frye contends that Olsen's readings are embedded in history—both cultural and personal. The book also contains a long conversation Frye had with Olsen about her five short stories.

Gawthrop, Betty G. "I Stand Here Ironing." In *Masterplots II: Short Story Series,* edited by Charles E. May. Rev. ed. Vol. 4. Pasadena, Calif.: Salem Press, 2004. Student-friendly analysis of "I Stand Here Ironing" that covers the story's themes and style and includes a detailed synopsis.

Jacobs, Naomi. "Earth, Air, Fire, and Water in *Tell Me a Riddle.*" *Studies in Short Fiction* 23 (Fall, 1986): 401-406. Jacobs analyzes the plot of Olsen's story by showing the development of a series of images derived from the four basic elements. Jacobs then relates this interpretation to Olsen's theme of spiritual rebirth.

Nelson, Kay Hoyle, and Nancy Huse, eds. *The Critical Response to Tillie Olsen.* Westport, Conn.: Greenwood Press, 1994. Collection of the most important articles, reviews, and parts of books about Olsen, arranged in chronological order; includes essays from a variety of approaches on the stories "I Stand Here Ironing," "Tell Me a Riddle," and "O Yes."

Niehus, Edward L., and Teresa Jackson. "Polar Stars, Pyramids, and *Tell Me a Riddle.*" *American Notes and Queries* 24 (January/February, 1986): 77-83. Niehus and Jackson analyze one incident recalled by Eva, the dying woman, by relating it to a pole or center of life, an idea that derives from basic astronomy and late nineteenth century pyramidology. The authors explore how Olsen handles this theme when circumstances change so that the pole does not remain stable.

Pearlman, Mickey, and Abby H. P. Werlock. *Tillie Olsen.* Boston: Twayne, 1991. General introduction to Olsen's life and work that tries to redress previous critical neglect and to suggest new directions for further study of her work. Includes an interview and extensive discussions of the four stories in Olsen's *Tell Me a Riddle,* especially "I Stand Here Ironing" and the title story.

# Cynthia Ozick

**Born:** New York, New York; April 17, 1928

**Principal short fiction** • *The Pagan Rabbi, and Other Stories*, 1971; *Bloodshed and Three Novellas*, 1976; *Levitation: Five Fictions*, 1982; *The Shawl*, 1989; *The Puttermesser Papers*, 1997.

**Other literary forms** • Cynthia Ozick is the author of poems, articles, reviews, and essays, as well as short stories. She has also published several novels, including *Trust* (1966), *The Cannibal Galaxy* (1983), *The Messiah of Stockholm* (1987), and *Heir to the Glimmering World* (2004; also known as *The Bear Boy*). Her poems have appeared in journals such as *Epoch*, *Commentary*, *The Literary Review*, and *Judaism*. Her other short works have been published frequently in journals such as those mentioned above and also in a wide variety of others. She also adapted her short story "The Shawl" to the stage as *Blue Light*, a play that was produced in 1994. In 1998, she edited the anthology *The Best American Essays*. Ozick's criticism and nonfiction writings have been collected in more than a half-dozen volumes, including *Art and Ardor* (1983), *Metaphor and Memory: Essays* (1989), *What Henry James Knew, and Other Essays on Writers* (1993), *Portrait of the Artist as a Bad Character, and Other Essays on Writing* (1996), *Quarrel and Quandry: Essays* (2000), and *The Din in the Head* (2006).

**Achievements** • Often characterized as difficult and involved in syntax and idea, Cynthia Ozick's works have, nevertheless, received many awards. The short fiction especially has been judged prizeworthy, winning for her such prestigious awards and honors as the Best American Short Stories award (several times), the National Book Award, the American Academy of Arts and Letters Award for Fiction, the O. Henry Award, the PEN/Faulkner Award, and the Jewish Book Council Award. Immediately consequent to the publication of "Rosa," one of her prizewinning stories, Ozick was invited to deliver the Phi Beta Kappa oration at Harvard University, and she became the first person to receive the Michael Rea Award for career contribution to the short story. She has received a number of honorary degrees from schools like Adelphi University, Williams College, Brandeis University, and Skidmore College as well as Yeshiva University, Hebrew Union College, and the Jewish Theological Seminary.

**Biography** • Born of Russian immigrants who took up residence in the Bronx borough of New York, Cynthia Ozick and her parents and siblings worked in the family drugstore, which kept them in comfort and relative prosperity even through the years of the Great Depression. As a female child, Ozick was not marked for extensive education by her family and community. Nevertheless, she was enrolled at the age of five and a half in a Yiddish-Hebrew school, so she could take religious instruction, and her family insisted that she be allowed to stay. The rabbi giving the instruction soon found that she had what he called a "golden head." Successful as she was in religious instruction, however, her public school experiences were difficult and humiliating. It was not until her entrance into Hunter College High School in Manhattan that she was once again made to feel part of an intellectual elite. Her years at New York University, where she earned a bachelor's degree in 1949, were followed by attendance at Ohio State University, where she received her master's degree in 1951.

In 1952, she married Bernard Hallote. One daughter, Rachel, was born in 1965. Early in her career, Ozick became interested in the Jewish textual tradition, and over the years she became an expert in it. In fiction and nonfiction, she has argued with passion concerning the vital role Judaism has played in Western culture, and she has become for many a spokesperson for the importance of art and artists in the Jewish tradition and for the role of women in Jewish culture.

Julius Ozick

**Analysis** • Cynthia Ozick's thesis for her master's degree was titled "Parable in the Later Novels of Henry James," an exercise that she later thought of as a first step in an act of devotion that resulted in her belief in the exclusivity of art. In effect, as a result of studying Henry James, she became, she believed, a worshiper at the altar of art, a devotee of the doctrine of art for art's sake. This idea—one that many believe places art before life, form before content, beauty before truth, aesthetic enjoyment before moral behavior—became the belief system that led Ozick to conclude that to worship art is to worship idols—in effect, to break the Mosaic law. This kind of understanding led Ozick to study the Jewish textual tradition and the role of Judaism in Western culture.

During the 1980's, Ozick began to realize that creative writers needed to use the highest powers of imagination to posit an incorporeal god, as exists in the Jewish faith, and to put forth a vision of moral truth rooted in the history, traditions, and literature of the Jewish people. Ozick's success in this endeavor is manifested not only in her identification as a Jewish American author but also in the number of awards she has received from representatives of the Jewish people. Perhaps most important, however, is her own satisfaction that in her writing she is serving and has continued to serve the cause of moral truth according to Mosaic law.

A highly serious approach to art as embodying moral imperatives, however, is not necessarily one that eschews metafictional techniques, repetitions, reworkings, and story sequences. Happily, in her use of self-referential devices and other dazzling postmodern presentations of the fantastic, the irreverent, and the grotesque, Ozick's techniques are relevant to the traditions and teachings of Judaism, where magic, dreams, and fantastic occurrences are ways to embody and convey truth.

**"The Pagan Rabbi"** • "The Pagan Rabbi" is a case in point. It is the story of Isaac Kornfeld, a pious and intelligent man who one day hangs himself from the limb of a tree. Isaac's story is told by a friend who has known Isaac since they were classmates in the rabbinical seminary and who is a parallel character to Isaac. In the same way that the narrator and Isaac are counterparts, the fathers of both men are set up as opposites who agree on one thing only—that philosophy is an abomination that must lead to idolatry (the worship of false gods). Though the fathers are rivals, the sons accept the apparent differences in their own personalities and remain friends. In time, their different ambitions and talents separate them. The narrator leaves the seminary, marries a Gentile, and becomes a furrier; Isaac continues his brilliant career in the seminary and achieves the peak of his renown at the time of his death, when he has almost reached the age of thirty-six. The narrator, now a bookseller separated from his wife, learns that Isaac has hanged himself with his prayer shawl from a tree in a distant park. Immediately, the narrator takes a subway to the site of the suicide; Isaac's behavior seems totally alien to his character and personality.

In the remainder of the story, Ozick attempts to explain the odd circumstances of Isaac's death, and, by means of the parallelisms, inversions, and doublings, point to the ramifications of leaving the intellectual path for the mysteries and seductions of the unknown world of fantasy, magic, and dream. Apparently Isaac, shortly after his marriage, began to seek different kinds of pleasure than those associated with the marriage bed and the beautiful Scheindel. In line with marriage customs, Scheindel covers her lustrous black hair after the wedding ceremony and subsequently bears Isaac seven daughters, one after another. As he fathers each daughter, Isaac invents bedtime stories for each, relating to such aberrations as speaking clouds, stones that cry, and pigs with souls. At the same time, Isaac shows an inordinate interest in picnics in strange and remote places.

As Isaac behaves in odder and odder ways for a rabbi, exhibiting unhealthy (because excessive) interest in the natural world, Scheindel becomes more and more puzzled and estranged, since she has no interest in old tales of sprites, nymphs, gods, or magic events. Scheindel's refusal to countenance anything magical is in counterpoint to her escape from the electrified fences of the concentration camp, which seemed a miracle of chance. Isaac's notebook offers little explanation for his behavior, though it is filled with romantic jottings, quotations from lyric poets, and a strange reference to his age, using the means of counting rings as for a tree. Below this unusual computation, Isaac has written a startling message: "Great Pan lives."

The narrator begins to understand more as Scheindel reads a letter written by Isaac and left tucked in his notebook. The letter makes clear that Isaac has eschewed deeply held Jewish beliefs to accept a kind of animism or pantheism, where all matter has life and, moreover, soul, although all matter except for human beings can live separate from their souls and thus are able to know everything around them. Humans cannot live separate from their souls and thus are cursed with the inability to escape from their bodies except through death. Isaac concludes that there may be another route to freedom—exaltation and ecstasy by means of coupling with a freed soul. The idea, once conceived, needs a trial, and Isaac's efforts are subsequently rewarded by the appearance of a dryad, the soul of a tree. The dryad's lovemaking brings Isaac to marvels and blisses that no man, it is said, has experienced since Adam. Isaac errs, however, in trying to trap the dryad into his own mortal condition. In so doing, he loses his own soul. His soul free, Isaac's body is doomed to death. More important, however, the soul retains the visage of the rabbi, who has been and will be the one who walks indifferently through the beauties of the fields, declaring that the sound, smells, and tastes of the law are more beautiful than anything to be found in the natural world.

Scheindel's repugnance toward, and lack of charity for, her husband's folly surprises the narrator and turns him away from her. The narrator is able to appreciate the subtlety of the rabbi's thinking and the bravery of the pursuit, but Scheindel is one who guarded the Mosaic law with her own wasted body during the Holocaust, and Scheindel is the issue here—not intellectual subtlety—she who seemed doomed to death when she was seventeen years old, she who traded her youth and vitality for marriage to a Jewish rabbi. After his conversation with Scheindel, and as an ironic afterthought, the narrator goes home to clear his house of his three paltry houseplants. His gesture next to Isaac's forthright penetration into the forest, however, indicates something of the struggle of every Jew seduced by the pleasures of the beautiful but charged to interpret and guard the laws instead.

**"The Shawl"** • By the time of the publication of "The Shawl" in *The New Yorker* and "Rosa," also in *The New Yorker,* Ozick had come to articulate fairly clearly her recognition that imagination need not be a negative, leading to idolatry, but a positive, allowing Jews to imagine a god without image. These stories are of exceptional importance and significance in the Ozick canon. In them, Ozick deals directly with the horror of the Holocaust. Rosa is the focal character of both stories, each of which exists as a separate entity coherent in itself, but also, when juxtaposed as in a diptych or modified story sequence, each takes on added significance as the two parts interact with each other.

In "The Shawl," Rosa is a young woman with a baby in her arms wrapped in a shawl that serves not only to shelter the child, called Magda, but also to hide it, to muffle its cries, and to succor it. With Rosa is her young niece, Stella, who is jealous of Magda and takes the shawl for her own comfort. Deprived of her shawl, the baby begins to cry and crawl around on the ground. Rosa's dilemma must be excruciatingly painful. She understands that her adolescent niece took the shawl, trying to cling to her own life, and she understands that if she chances picking up the baby without the shawl to cover it up, she is likely to lose both her life and Magda's. She chooses to go after the shawl first, and the fatal moment arrives too soon. A German officer finds the child wandering around and hurls her against the electrified fence.

Complicating the issue is the question of who is Magda's father. Early in the story, it is suggested that the father is no Jew, since Magda has blue eyes and blond hair and seems a pure Aryan, a situation that causes Stella to react even more bitterly. As in any nightmare, the dreaded occurs. Stella steals the shawl; the baby cries, wanders about, and is killed. Rosa survives the horrible ordeal as she has survived others, including repeated rapes by German soldiers. She knows that any action will result in her death, so she stuffs the shawl in her own mouth and drinks Magda's saliva to sustain herself.

**"Rosa"** • For "Rosa," Ozick won four awards. On the basis of the story's publication, she was named one of three best short-story writers in the United States. Because the story does not proceed chronologically, a brief plot summary is helpful. After Rosa and Stella are rescued from the camps, Rosa brings Stella to the United States, where Stella gets a job and Rosa opens an antique shop. The action takes place some thirty-five years after the occurrences described in "The Shawl." Rosa is still very angry with Stella for her role in Magda's death, and she is able to get little personal satisfaction from her activities in the antique shop. Apparently, her customers do not want to listen to the stories she has to tell, and one day, extremely angry and apparently insane,

Rosa destroys her shop. To escape institutionalization, she agrees to move to what appears to be a poverty-stricken retirement hotel in Miami Beach. Life is difficult for her. The intense heat makes it hard for her to get out into the sunlight in order to shop. When she does eat, she scavenges or makes do with tiny portions, such as a cracker with grape jelly or a single sardine. The condition of her clothes seems to indicate that she has nothing to wear. One morning, however, Rosa makes her way to a supermarket, and there, she meets Simon Persky. Persky is not a person in the ordinary mold. He notices Rosa on a personal level and insists that she respond to him. While Rosa's relationship with Simon Persky is developing, Ozick establishes two parallel plot lines having to do with Rosa's request of Stella that she send Magda's shawl and a request from a Dr. Tree asking Stella to help him conduct research on Rosa's reaction to her imprisonment and ill treatment.

These three plot lines weave about one another, providing the matrices for the action. Rosa is responsible for saving Stella's life in the concentration camp and bringing her to the United States, and Stella is indirectly responsible for Magda's death, perhaps the single most horrible thing that happened to Rosa in a life full of horrors—the internment, the death of family and friends, assaults and rape by brutal Nazis, near starvation, and finally Magda's execution by electric shock. Since Magda's death, Rosa has teetered on the brink of insanity, managing to hold herself together by working and by the creative act of writing letters to an imaginary Magda who, in Rosa's fantasy, has survived and become a professor of Greek philosophy at Columbia University. Stella too has survived in Rosa's imagination in another guise. She is a thief, a bloodsucker, evil personified, and the Angel of Death. To Magda, Rosa writes letters in perfect Polish, literary and learned. To Stella, Rosa writes in crude English, a language she never bothered to learn. To Stella, Rosa admits that Magda is dead; to Magda, Rosa explains that Stella is unable to accept and cannot be told the truth.

The shawl, which Stella agrees to send to Rosa and which finally arrives, acted in Poland during the worst years as an umbrella covering the three people—Rosa, prepubescent Stella, and baby Magda—and providing sustenance and security, even though illusionary. After Magda's death, the shawl becomes for Rosa an icon; "idol," "false god," Stella says, since Rosa worships it and prays to it.

Dr. Tree is another threat to Rosa; he is a kind of parasite, living to feed off the horrors attached to other people's lives. He wants to interview Rosa for a book that he is writing on Holocaust survivors. His letter to Rosa calling her a survivor is replete with jargon, with clinical terms naming the horrible conditions with neutral language and hiding the grotesque reality under the name of his own Institute for Humanitarian Context. Rosa objects to being called a "survivor" because the word dehumanizes her and every other person on the planet. Persky, on the other hand, offers Rosa an actual friendship, a human relationship in concrete, not abstract, terms. Thus he emerges as winner of Rosa's attention, with Dr. Tree dismissed and memories of Magda put on hold for a while.

***The Puttermesser Papers*** • *The Puttermesser Papers* consists of a series of five previously published short stories about Ruth Puttermesser. In the stories, it is often difficult to distinguish between what actually happens to her and what she fantasizes. In the first story, "Puttermesser: Her Work History, Her Ancestry, Her Afterlife," for example, she visits her Uncle Zindel for Hebrew lessons, but the narrator says that Uncle Zindel died before Puttermesser was born. In the second story, "Puttermesser and Xanthippe," Puttermesser creates a female golem, a person made of clay, from the dirt in the flowerpots in her apartment. The golem, named Xanthippe, helps Putter-messer get elected mayor of New York City and helps Puttermesser transform New York into a kind of paradise. The golem discovers sex, however, and as a result destroys all of the wonderful things she has helped Puttermesser achieve.

In each story, Puttermesser is a loser. She tries to achieve some kind of ideal and ends up with an unpleasant reality. In the long run, things never go right for her. In the third story, "Puttermesser Paired," she finds someone she considers to be a true soul mate, Rupert Rubeeno, a copyist. Rubeeno and Puttermesser share a love of literature, especially an interest in the British authors and lovers George Eliot, the novelist, and George Lewes, the essayist. Eventually they marry, but Rubeeno leaves her on their wedding night, apparently without consummating the marriage.

In the fourth story, "Puttermesser and the Muscovite Cousin," one of her relatives in the Soviet Union calls her and asks her to save the relative's child. The child, Lidia Klavdia Girshengornova, turns out to be a grown woman interested in making a fortune in America. Eventually, she returns to the Soviet Union to rejoin her boyfriend. The final section, "Puttermesser in Paradise," is probably the saddest of all. In it, Puttermesser is killed by a man who rapes her after she is dead. She enters a Paradise in which all things seem to go well for her, but in Paradise, she ultimately finds no happiness, for even there, "nothing is permanent." She discovers the secret meaning of Paradise: "It too is hell." Each thing she enjoys there disappears in turn, leaving her longing to be back on earth in spite of earth's having also been in many ways unpleasant for her.

Discussions of Cynthia Ozick's fiction often include the descriptors "uncompromising," "demanding," "difficult"—characteristics that can diminish a writer's popularity and, consequently, status. For Ozick, however, no such diminution has taken place. Indeed, her reputation has grown steadily and strongly, her writings gaining more attention and Ozick herself more recognition. The phenomenon is not, after all, that surprising. If her protestations are stronger than those of other Jewish American writers, her demands are based more clearly in moral imperatives of the Jewish tradition; yet there is another tradition as truly her own—one commentators sometimes forget—an American literary heritage, with Nathaniel Hawthorne, Herman Melville, Edgar Allan Poe, William Faulkner, those writers who clearly work like Ozick in a realm where the "power of blackness" wrestles with us all.

*Mary Rohrberger*
*With updates by Richard Tuerk and the Editors*

**Other major works**

PLAY: *Blue Light*, pr. 1994 (adaptation of her short story "The Shawl").

ANTHOLOGY: *The Best American Essays, 1998*, 1998.

NOVELS: *Trust*, 1966; *The Cannibal Galaxy*, 1983; *The Messiah of Stockholm*, 1987; *Heir to the Glimmering World*, 2004 (also known as *The Bear Boy*).

MISCELLANEOUS: *A Cynthia Ozick Reader*, 1996.

NONFICTION: *Art and Ardor*, 1983; *Metaphor and Memory: Essays*, 1989; *What Henry James Knew, and Other Essays on Writers*, 1993; *Fame and Folly: Essays*, 1996; *Portrait of the Artist as a Bad Character, and Other Essays on Writing*, 1996; *Quarrel and Quandry: Essays*, 2000; *The Din in the Head*, 2006.

POETRY: *Epodes: First Poems*, 1992.

**Bibliography**

Alkana, Joseph. "'Do We Not Know the Meaning of Aesthetic Gratification?' Cynthia Ozick's *The Shawl*, the Akedah, and the Ethics of Holocaust Literary Aesthetics." *Modern Fiction Studies* 43 (Winter, 1997): 963-990. Argues that Ozick takes a stance against universalism in the two stories, the tendency to level human suffering under an all-inclusive existential or theological quandary.

Bloom, Harold, ed. *Cynthia Ozick: Modern Critical Views*. New York: Chelsea House, 1986. Excellent collection of essays, including brief book reviews as well as lengthy articles. Much of value for both the beginning student and a scholarly audience involved in an examination of complications of idea and form.

Cohen, Sarah Blacher. *Cynthia Ozick's Comic Art: From Levity to Liturgy*. Bloomington: Indiana University Press, 1994. Places Ozick in the context of the Jewish comic tradition but argues that levity in her fiction must serve a higher purpose than laughter for laughter's sake, usually the satiric purpose of attacking vices, follies, and stupidities.

Friedman, Lawrence S. *Understanding Cynthia Ozick*. Columbia: University of South Carolina Press, 1991. Critical study of Ozick, which includes a bibliography and an index.

Kauvar, Elaine M. *Cynthia Ozick's Fiction: Tradition and Invention*. Bloomington: Indiana University Press, 1993. Examines the sources and contexts of Ozick's fiction, focusing on tensions between Hebraism and Hellenism, Western culture and Judaism, artistic imagination and moral responsibility; discusses Ozick's relationship to psychoanalysis, feminism, and postmodernism.

Lowin, Joseph. *Cynthia Ozick*. New York: Twayne, 1988. This excellent overview of Ozick's canon includes an annotated bibliography and full notes. Most valuable for beginning students whose knowledge of Holocaust literature and Ozick is limited. Offers perceptive and lucid analyses of all the major works.

_____. "Cynthia Ozick, Rewriting Herself: The Road from 'The Shawl' to 'Rosa.'" In *Since Flannery O'Connor: Essays on the Contemporary American Short Story*, edited by Loren Logsdon and Charles W. Mayer. Macomb: Western Illinois University Press, 1987. Contends Ozick paints not the thing itself but, like the French Symbolists, the effect produced by the thing; each of the three characters in the story uses the shawl as a life preserver.

May, Charles E., ed. *Masterplots II: Short Story Series, Revised Edition*. 8 vols. Pasadena, Calif.: Salem Press, 2004. Designed for student use, this reference set contains articles providing detailed plot summaries and analyses of five short stories by Ozick: "Envy; Or, Yiddish in America" (vol. 2); and "The Pagan Rabbi," "Puttermesser Paired," "Rosa," and "The Shawl" (vol. 6).

Ozick, Cynthia. "An Interview with Cynthia Ozick." Interview by Elaine M. Kauvar. *Contemporary Literature* 26 (Winter, 1985): 375-401. Contains references to Ozick's religion, history, intelligence, feminism, postmodern techniques, and philosophy of art. A good introduction to her views, personality, and level of intelligence.

_____. "An Interview with Cynthia Ozick." *Contemporary Literature* 34 (Fall, 1993): 359-394. Ozick discusses Jewish culture, other Jewish writers, her own fiction, and the Holocaust with her friend Elaine M. Kauvar.

Pinsker, Sanford. *The Uncompromising Fiction of Cynthia Ozick*. Columbia: University of Missouri Press, 1987. Brief analysis of major works, including several of the more important short stories. Excellent for a reader new to Ozick's fiction. Emphasizes postmodern aspects of Ozick's work.

# Grace Paley

**Born:** New York, New York; December 11, 1922
**Died:** Thetford, Vermont; August 22, 2007

**Principal short fiction** • *The Little Disturbances of Man: Stories of Men and Women in Love*, 1959; *Enormous Changes at the Last Minute*, 1974; *Later the Same Day*, 1985; *The Collected Stories*, 1994; *Here and Elsewhere*, 2007 (with Robert Nichols).

**Other literary forms** • In addition to her short fiction, Grace Paley published the poetry collections *Leaning Forward* (1985), *New and Collected Poems* (1992), and *Begin Again: Collected Poems* (2000), the nonfiction works *Conversations with Grace Paley* (1997) and *Just as I Thought* (1998). She also published essays on teaching.

**Achievements** • Grace Paley received a John Simon Guggenheim Memorial Foundation Fellowship, a National Council on the Arts grant, and a National Institute of Arts and Letters Award for short-story writing. She was elected to the American Academy of Arts and Letters in 1980, and in 1988 and 1989 she received the Edith Wharton Award. In 1993, she was awarded the Michael Rea Award for the short story and the Vermont Governor's Award for excellence in the arts. In 1994, she was a nominee for the National Book Award and a finalist for the Pulitzer Prize. In 1997, she was awarded the Lannan Foundation Literary Award.

**Biography** • The daughter of Russian immigrants, Grace Paley was born and raised in New York City. Both her parents, Mary (Ridnyik) Goodside and Isaac Goodside, M.D., were political exiles in their early years and passed on their political concerns to their daughter. At home they spoke Russian and Yiddish as well as English, exposing their daughter to both old and new cultures. She studied in city schools and attended Hunter College in 1938 and later New York University. Paley, however, was not interested in formal academic study and dropped out of college. She had begun to write poetry and in the early 1940's studied with W. H. Auden at the New School for Social Research. In 1942 she married Jess Paley, a motion-picture cameraman. The couple had two children and then separated, although they were not legally divorced for twenty years. During the 1940's and 1950's, Paley worked as a typist, while raising her children and continuing to write. At this time she began her lifelong political involvement by participating in New York City neighborhood action groups.

After many rejections, her first collection of eleven stories, *The Little Disturbances of Man*, was published in 1959. Even though the book was not widely reviewed, critics admired her work, and Paley's teaching career flourished. During the early 1960's, she taught at Columbia University and Syracuse University and also presented summer workshops. She also began writing a novel, a project that she did not complete. She increased her political activism, participating in nonviolent protests against prison conditions in New York City and the government's position on the war in Vietnam. A prominent member in the peace movement, she was a member of a 1969 mission that went to Hanoi to negotiate for the release of prisoners of war. In 1973, she was a delegate to the World Peace Conference in Moscow. In 1974, her second collection of stories appeared. It received condemnation from reviewers, partially because of her political views but also because the writing was deemed uneven in quality.

During the 1970's and 1980's, Paley continued her political activism as well as her writing and teaching. She joined with other activists in condemning Soviet repression of human rights, was a leader in the 1978 demonstrations in Washington, D.C., against nuclear weapons, and in 1985, along with campaigning against American government policy in Central America, visited Nicaragua and El Salvador. Her stories have appeared in *The Atlantic, Esquire, Accent,* and other magazines. Paley settled in Greenwich Village in New York City, with her second husband, poet, playwright, and landscape architect Robert Nichols. During the 1990's Paley continued to teach in the New York City area, particularly at Sarah Lawrence College, but she retired by the end of the decade. She divided her time between Vermont and the Greenwich Village apartment that was so often a backdrop for her fiction. She died from breast cancer at her Vermont home on August 22, 2007.

**Analysis** • Despite her small literary output, Grace Paley's innovative style and the political and social concerns she advocates in her work have enabled her to generate significant critical attention. Her stories treat traditional themes, focusing on the lives of women and the experiences of love, motherhood, and companionship that bind them together. She presents these themes, however, in inventive rather than traditional structures. Her stories are frequently fragmented and open-ended, without conventional plot or character development, structural innovations that make her work more true to life. The stories gain their vitality by Paley's use of distinctive language—the voice, idiom, tone, and rhythms of the New York City locale. She writes best when rendering the razor-tongued Jewish American urban female, with an ironic wit, who does not hesitate to voice her opinions.

To speak out is a basic theme in Paley's stories, and it reflects her own life and political principles. The women in her stories are like her; they are political activists who speak on nuclear energy, on the environment, and on all conditions that affect the world into which their children are born. This intermingling of politics and art brought Paley mixed reviews, but she has continued to stretch the limits of the short story, in both form and content.

***The Little Disturbances of Man*** • "Goodbye and Good Luck," the first story in Grace Paley's first collection, *The Little Disturbances of Man*, shows her characteristic style and theme. The story begins, "I was popular in certain circles, says Aunt Rose. I wasn't no thinner then, only more stationary in the flesh." Aunt Rose knows what her sister—Lillie's "mama"—does not, that time rushes by relentlessly, that the old generation is quickly forgotten as the new generation supplants it, and that mama's life of stodgy domesticity (the "spotless kitchen") has meant little to her or anyone else as her life slips away. Mama, however, feels sorry for "poor Rosie" because Aunt Rose has not married or led a virtuous life.

As a young girl, Rose cannot stand her safe but boring job in a garment factory and takes instead a job selling tickets at the Russian Art Theatre, which puts on Yiddish plays. The man who hires her says "Rosie Lieber, you surely got a build on you!" These attributes quickly gain the attention of the Yiddish matinee idol Volodya Vlashkin, "the Valentino of Second Avenue."

Although he is much older than she and has a wife and family elsewhere, he sets her up in an apartment. Their affair continues on—and off—over the years while he has many other lovers, but Rose is not lonely herself when he is gone. She never complains but worships him when she has him and is philosophical about his infidelities: An actor needs much practice if he is to be convincing on the stage. Although she never asks anything from him, "the actresses . . . were only interested in tomorrow," sleeping lovelessly with wealthy producers for advancement. They get their advancement: Now they are old and forgotten. Vlashkin himself is old and retired, Aunt Rose fat and fifty, when his wife divorces him for all his past adulteries. He comes back to Rosie, the only woman who never asked anything of him, and they decide to get married. She has had her warm and love-filled life, and now she will have a bit of respectability, a husband—and, "as everybody knows, a woman should have at least one before the end of the story."

The theme is seen most clearly when Rose contrasts her life with her own mother's. Her mother had upbraided her when she moved in with Vlashkin, but her mother had "married who she didn't like. . . . He never washed. He had an unhappy smell . . . he got smaller, shriveled up little by little, till goodbye and good luck." Rosie, therefore, "decided to live for love." No amount of respectability, no husband, advancement, or wealth will save one from imminent change, decay, and death; so live for love, Aunt Rose would say, and you will have the last laugh.

**"The Pale Pink Roast"** • The characters and tone may change in other stories, but the theme remains the same. In "The Pale Pink Roast" Anna sees her former husband and asks him to help her move into her new apartment. He is in "about the third flush of youth," a handsome, charming, but "transient" man. In the midst of hanging her curtains, he stops and makes love to her. Then, admiring her fancy apartment and stylish clothes, he asks archly who is paying for it. "My husband is," she responds. Her former husband is furious with her. The new husband, she tells him, is a "lovely" man, in the process of moving his business here. Why did you do it, then, her former husband wants to know: "Revenge? Meanness? Why?" "I did it for love," she says.

**"An Interest in Life"** • Over and over the female characters must choose between the safe but boring man and the charming but worthless lover. In "An Interest in Life," the girl has her secure but dull boyfriend yet dreams of the husband who deserted her. In "Distance," Paley tells the same story over again, but this time from the point of view of another character in the story, a bitter old woman full of destructive meanness. She was wild in youth, but then opted for the safe, loveless marriage, and it has so soured her life that she has tried to force everyone else into the same wrong pattern. Her own very ordinary son is the analogue of the boring boyfriend from "An Interest in Life." At heart, the bitter old woman understands the young girl, and this is her redeeming humanity.

**"Wants" and "Come On, Ye Sons of Art"** • In a slight variation of theme, "Wants" demonstrates why the love relationship between man and woman must be transitory. The desirable man wants everything out of life; the loving woman wants only her man. "You'll always want nothing," the narrator's former husband tells her bitterly, suggesting a sort of ultimate biological incompatibility between the sexes. The result assuredly is sadness and loneliness, but with islands of warmth to make it endurable. In "Come On, Ye Sons of Art," Kitty is spending Sunday morning with her boyfriend ("Sunday was worth two weeks of waiting"). She is pregnant by him and already has a houseful of children by other fathers. She takes great pleasure in the fine morning she can give her boyfriend. The boyfriend, a traveling salesman, delights in his skill as a salesman. He only regrets he is not more dishonest, like his sister who, ignoring human relationships, has devoted herself to amassing an immense fortune by any means. Kitty's boyfriend wistfully wishes he too were corrupt, high, and mighty. They are listening to a beautiful piece of music by English composer Henry Purcell on the radio, which the announcer says was written for the queen's birthday; in reality, the music was not written for the queen but rather for Purcell's own delight in his art, in the thing he did best, and no amount of wealth and power equals that pleasure.

**"In the Garden"** • In her later stories, Paley struck out in new directions, away from the inner-city unwed mothers and the strongly vernacular idiom, to sparse, classical, universal stories. The theme, however, that there is no safe harbor against change and death, and that the only salvation is to live fully, realistically, and for the right things, has not changed. "In the Garden" has, essentially, four characters who appear to be in some country in the West Indies. Lush gardens of bright flowers and birds surround them, suggesting a particularly bountiful nature. One character is a beautiful young woman whose children were kidnapped eight months earlier and now are certainly dead, but she cannot face this fact, and her talk is constantly about "when they come home." Her husband is a rich landlord, who did not give the kidnappers their ransom money; he shouts constantly in a loud voice that everything is well. There is a vacationing communist renting one of the landlord's houses, who, out of curiosity, asks the neighbors about the case. He learns that the landlord had once been poor but now is rich and has a beautiful wife; he could not believe that anything had the power to hurt his luck, and he was too greedy to pay the ransom. It is known that it was "his friends who did it." There is an elderly neighbor woman who is dying of a muscle-wasting disease. She had spent much time with the beautiful woman listening to her talk about when the children would return, but now she is fed up with her and cannot stand the husband's shouting. For a while, since she is too wasted to do much more, she follows with her eyes the movements of the communist, but "sadly she had to admit that the eyes' movement, even if minutely savored, was not such an adventurous journey." Then "she had become interested in her own courage."

At first it may appear that nothing happens in the story, but it is all there. The garden is the world. The young woman with her beauty has won a rich husband; the landlord, through aggressiveness, has clawed his way to the top. Both these states of being—beauty and aggressiveness—have succeeded only for a while, but almost inevitably whatever is gained in the world is lost because human beings are all mortal. The communist—by being a communist, "a tenderhearted but relentless person"—suggests someone who will try to find a political way to stave off chance and mortality, but in fact he merely leaves, having done nothing. The old woman, who realizes the fecklessness of trying to help, and who has found mere observation of process insufficient, becomes more interested in the course of her own courage in facing up to almost inevitable change. She and her husband are the only ones who admit to change, and this seems the right position, the tragic sense of life which makes life supportable.

**The Collected Stories** • *The Collected Stories* gathers over thirty years of stories from Paley's previous collections, allowing the reader to track the development of Paley's feminism and pacifism, as well as her depiction of urban family life. *The Collected Stories* also brings with it an opportunity to examine one of Paley's most enduring fictional characters, a major figure in thirteen stories, and a minor figure in several more. This character, Faith Darwin, first appeared in the "The Used Boy-Raisers," where it was clear that she served as her author's alter ego, so that Faith, like Paley, is of Jewish descent, lives in Greenwich Village, has married, divorced and remarried, has two children, and is also a writer.

In addition to paralleling Paley's own life to some degree, the Faith Darwin stories track the various political movements in which Paley has been involved. For instance, in "Faith in a Tree," Faith's personal life is restrained in the light of her political principles, indicated by a demonstration against the war in Vietnam. In "Dreamer in a Dead Language," Faith's father, whom she had loved and admired uncritically, is critically reassessed in the light of her growing feminism. In later stories, however, Faith herself is subjected to criticism and revaluation. In "Listening," Faith is confronted by her lesbian friend Cassie, who accuses her of ignoring her in her fiction. Faith is also criticized by other characters in "Friends," "Zagrowsky Tells," and "Love," the latter story detailing the breaking up of friendships over disagreements concerning the Soviet Union.

In these later stories, Faith must deal with changing times. In "The Long-Distance Runner" Faith faces her own aging process by returning to the old Jewish neighborhood in which she and her parents had once lived, and which is now populated by African Americans. When Faith decides to live in her old apartment for three weeks with four African American children and their mother, Mrs. Luddy, she discovers that, despite their differences, they share a sense of sisterhood because they are both women and mothers. The centrality of motherhood in the life of women is a continuing theme in the Faith Darwin stories, beginning with "The Used Boy Raisers" and emerging again in such stories as "The Long Distance Runner" and "The Exquisite Moment."

Stories such as "The Long-Distance Runner," with its African American family, and "The Exquisite Moment," involving a Chinese houseguest, also remind the reader of the multicultural element in Paley's fiction. Faith's own neighborhood—a Greenwich village community of artists, left-wing political activists, and people from minority ethnic and racial groups—is different from what is considered mainstream

America, but at the same time it reminds the reader that this world, too, is part of the American scene. This urban community, which blends and mixes ethnicities, religions, and radical politics, along with her role as a fictional version of Paley herself, makes Faith Darwin's stories a particularly representative aspect of Grace Paley's collected work.

*Norman Lavers*
*With updates by Louise M. Stone and Margaret Boe Birns*

**Other major works**
MISCELLANEOUS: *Long Walks and Intimate Talks: Stories and Poems*, 1991 (with paintings by Vera Williams).
NONFICTION: *Conversations with Grace Paley*, 1997 (Gerhard Bach and Blaine H. Hall, editors); *Just as I Thought*, 1998.
POETRY: *Leaning Forward*, 1985; *New and Collected Poems*, 1992; *Begin Again: Collected Poems*, 2000.

**Bibliography**
Aarons, Victoria. "Talking Lives: Storytelling and Renewal in Grace Paley's Short Fiction." *Studies in American Jewish Literature* 9 (1990): 20-35. Asserts that Paley empowers her characters through their penchant for telling stories. In telling their stories, her characters try to gain some control over their lives, as if by telling they can reconstruct experience.
Arcana, Judith. *Grace Paley's Life Stories: A Literary Biography*. Urbana: University of Illinois Press, 1993. Biography of Paley that includes a bibliography and an index.
Bach, Gerhard, and Blaine Hall, eds. *Conversations with Grace Paley*. Jackson: University Press of Mississippi, 1997. Collection of interviews with Paley from throughout her career as a writer, in which she comments on the sources of her stories, her political views, her feminism, and the influences on her writing.
Iannone, Carol. "A Dissent on Grace Paley." *Commentary* 80 (August, 1985): 54-58. Iannone states that Paley's first collection of stories reveals talent. Her second, however, written when she was deeply involved in political activity, shows how a writer's imagination can become trapped by ideologies, not able to rise above them to make sense of the world. Iannone's comments on the intermingling of politics and art result in interesting interpretations of Paley's stories.
Isaacs, Neil D. *Grace Paley: A Study of the Short Fiction*. Boston: Twayne, 1990. Introduction to Paley's short fiction, strong on a summary and critique of previous criticism. Also contains a section of Paley quotations, in which she talks about the nature of her fiction, her social commitment, and the development of her narrative language. Emphasizes Paley's focus on storytelling and narrative voice.
Marchant, Peter, and Earl Ingersoll, eds. "A Conversation with Grace Paley." *The Massachusetts Review* 26 (Winter, 1985): 606-614. A conversation with novelist Mary Elsie Robertson and writer Peter Marchant provides insights into Paley's transition from poetry to short stories, her interest in the lives of women, and the connection between her subject matter and her politics.
May, Charles E., ed. *Masterplots II: Short Story Series, Revised Edition*. 8 vols. Pasadena, Calif.: Salem Press, 2004. Designed for student use, this reference set contains articles providing detailed plot summaries and analyses of seven short stories by Paley:

"A Conversation with My Father" and "Dreamers in a Dead Language" (vol. 2), "Faith in a Tree" (vol. 3), "An Interest in Life" and "The Long-Distance Runner" (vol. 4), "The Loudest Voice" (vol. 5), and "The Used-Boy Raisers" (vol. 8).

Meyer, Adam. "Faith and the 'Black Thing': Political Action and Self-Questioning in Grace Paley's Short Fiction." *Studies in Short Fiction* 31 (Winter, 1994): 79-89. Discusses how Paley, through the character of Faith, examines someone very much like herself while distancing herself from that person's activities.

Taylor, Jacqueline. *Grace Paley: Illuminating the Dark Lives.* Austin: University of Texas Press, 1990. Taylor focuses on what she calls Paley's "woman centered" point of view. Asserts that "Conversation with My Father" allows discussion of many of the narrative conventions her fiction tries to subvert. The story reveals the connection between Paley's recognition of the fluidity of life and her resistance to narrative resolution.

# Dorothy Parker

**Born:** West End, New Jersey; August 22, 1893
**Died:** New York, New York; June 7, 1967

**Principal short fiction** • "Big Blonde," 1929; *Laments for the Living*, 1930; *After Such Pleasures*, 1933; *Here Lies: The Collected Stories*, 1939; *The Portable Dorothy Parker*, 1944; *The Penguin Dorothy Parker*, 1977; *Complete Stories*, 1995.

**Other literary forms** • Dorothy Parker's principal writings, identified by Alexander Woolcott as "a potent distillation of nectar and wormwood," are short stories and verse—not serious "poetry," she claimed. Her poetic volumes include *Enough Rope* (1926), *Sunset Gun* (1928), and *Death and Taxes* (1931)—mostly lamentations for loves lost, never found, or gone awry. An edition of her complete poems was published in 1999. She also wrote witty drama reviews for *Vanity Fair* (1918-1920), *Ainslee's* (1920-1933), and *The New Yorker* (1931); and terse, tart book reviews for *The New Yorker* (1927-1933) and *Esquire* (1959-1962). "Tonstant Weader Fwowed Up," her provoked, personal reaction to A. A. Milne's *The House at Pooh Corner* (1928), typifies her "delicate claws of . . . superb viciousness" (Woolcott). Parker's major plays are *The Coast of Illyria* (about Charles and Mary Lamb's tortured lives) and *The Ladies of the Corridor* (1953; three case studies of death-in-life among elderly women).

**Achievements** • Dorothy Parker's career flashed brilliantly out in the 1920's and early 1930's and then faded equally quickly as the world she portrayed in her stories and poems disappeared into the hardships of the Depression. Her stories are sharp, witty portraits of an age when social and sexual conventions were changing rapidly. Her dramatic monologues, usually spoken by unselfconfident women, her sharp social satires, and her careful delineations of scenes and situations reveal the changing mores of the 1920's. They also, however, portray the attendants of rapid social change: anxiety, lack of communication, and differing expectations of men and women on what social and sexual roles should be. These problems continue into contemporary times, and Parker's incisive writing captures them well. Her writings are like herself—witty and sad.

Parker's stories, verse, and reviews appeared in, and helped to set the tone of, the newly founded *The New Yorker*, which began publication in 1925, and she remained an occasional contributor until 1955.

**Biography** • Educated at Miss Dana's School in Morristown, New Jersey, Dorothy Rothschild Parker wrote fashion blurbs and drama criticism for *Vanity Fair*, short stories for *The New Yorker* irregularly, Hollywood screenplays at intervals (1934-1954), and *Esquire* book reviews (1959-1962). Her marriage to Edwin Pond Parker (1917-1928) was succeeded by two marriages to bisexual actor-writer Alan Campbell (1934-1947; 1950-1963, when Campbell died). Campbell, Lillian Hellman, and others nurtured Parker, but they could not control her drinking and her worsening writer's block that kept her from finishing many of her literary attempts during her last fifteen years.

**Analysis** • Dorothy Parker's best-known stories are "The Waltz," "A Telephone Call," and her masterpiece, "Big Blonde," winner of the O. Henry Memorial Prize for the best short story of 1929.

**"The Waltz"** • "The Waltz" and "A Telephone Call," both dramatic monologues, present typical Parker characters, insecure young women who derive their social and personal acceptance from the approval of men and who go to extremes, whether sincere or hypocritical, to maintain this approbation. The characters, anonymous and therefore legion, elicit from the readers a mixture of sympathy and ridicule. They evoke sympathy because each is agonizing in an uncomfortable situation which she believes herself powerless to control. The waltzer is stuck with a bad, boorish dancer—"two stumbles, slip, and a twenty-yard dash."

Library of Congress

The other woman is longing for a telephone call from a man she loves who does not reciprocate her concern: "Please, God, let him telephone me now, Dear God, let him call me now. I won't ask anything else of You. . . ."

These predicaments are largely self-imposed as well as trivial, and so they are ludicrous, unwittingly burlesqued through the narrators' hyperbolic perspectives. Both women are trapped in situations they have permitted to occur but from which they lack the resourcefulness or assertiveness to extricate themselves. The waltzer not only accepts the invitation to dance but also hypocritically flatters her partner: "Oh, they're going to play another encore. Oh, goody. Oh, that's lovely. Tired? I should say I'm not tired. I'd like to go on like this forever." These cloying words mask the truth, which she utters only to herself and to the eavesdropping audience: "I should say I'm not tired. I'm dead, that's all I am. Dead . . . and the music is never going to stop playing. . . ." Enslaved by an exaggerated code of politeness, therefore, she catches herself in the network of her own lies: "Oh, they've stopped, the mean things. They're not going to play any more. Oh, darn." Then she sets herself up for yet another round of hypocritical self-torture: "Do you really think so, if you gave them twenty dollars? . . . Do tell them to play this same thing. I'd simply adore to go on waltzing."

**"A Telephone Call"** • Like the waltzer, the narrator in "A Telephone Call" is her own worst enemy. Suffering from too much time on her hands—she is evidently not occupied with a job or responsibility for anyone but herself—she can afford the self-indulgence to spend hours focused exclusively on the dubious prospect of a phone call. She plays games with God; her catechism is a parody: "You see, God, if You would just let him telephone me, I wouldn't have to ask You . . . for anything more." She plays games with herself: "Maybe if I counted five hundred by fives, it might ring by that time. I'll count slowly. I won't cheat." She is totally preoccupied with herself and her futile efforts to fan the embers of a dying love; having violated the social code by phoning her former admirer at his office, by the monologue's end she is desperately preparing to violate it again by calling him at home. Nevertheless, she is ludicrous rather than pathetic because her concern is so superficial (although her concentration on the anticipated phone call is also a barrier against the more serious reality of the estrangement); her calculations so trivial ("I'll count five hundred by fives, and if he hasn't called me then, I will know God isn't going to help me, ever again"); and the stakes for which she prays so low (attempting to manipulate God's will in such a minor matter). She, like the waltzer, envisions a simplistic fairy-tale solution dependent on the agency of another.

Thus the plots of these slight stories are as slender as the resources of the monologist narrators, for whom formulaic prayers or serial wisecracks ("I'd like to [dance] awfully, but I'm having labor pains. . . . It's so nice to meet a man who isn't a scaredy-cat about catching my beri-beri") are inadequate to alter their situations. Such narratives, with their fixed perspectives, exploitation of a single, petty issue, and simple characters, have to be short. To be any longer would be to add redundance without complexity, to bore rather than to amuse with verbal pyrotechnics.

**"Big Blonde"** • Although "Big Blonde" shares some of the features of the monologues, it is far more complex in narrative mode and in characterization. Rather than anatomizing a moment in time, as do the monologues, "Big Blonde" covers an indefinite span of years, perhaps a dozen. The story moves from comedy into pathos as its protagonist, Hazel Morse, moves from genuine gaiety to forced conviviality, undergirded by the hazy remorse that her name connotes.

Hazel, "a large, fair," unreflective, voluptuous blonde, has been, in her twenties, by day a "model in a wholesale dress establishment," and for "a couple of thousand evenings . . . a good sport among her [numerous] male acquaintances." Having "come to be more conscientious than spontaneous" about her enjoyment of men's jokes and drunken antics, she escapes into what she unthinkingly assumes will be a stereotype of marriage, isolation from the outer world *à deux*, but what instead becomes a travesty. She revels in honesty—the freedom to stop being incessantly cheerful and to indulge in the other side of the conventional feminine role that is her life's allotment, the freedom to weep sentimental tears over various manifestations, large and small, of "all the sadness there is in the world."

Hazel's husband, Herbie, is "not amused" at her tears and impersonal sorrows: "crab, crab, crab, that was all she ever did." To transform her from "a lousy sport" into her former jocular self he encourages her to drink, "Atta girl! . . . Let's see you get boiled, baby." Having neither the intellectual, imaginative, nor domestic resources to hold her marriage together any other way, Hazel acquiesces, even though she hates "the taste of liquor," and soon begins to drink steadily. Herbie, however, is as barren of human resources as is his wife, and alcohol only ignites their smoldering anger, despite Hazel's "thin and wordless idea that, maybe, this night, things would begin to be all right." They are not; Herbie fades out of Hazel's alcohol-blurred existence as Ed merges into it. He, too, insists "upon gaiety" and will not "listen to admissions of aches or weariness." Nor will Ed's successors, Charley, Sydney, Fred, Billy, and others, to whom Hazel responds with forced cordiality through her alcoholic haze in which the days and year lose "their individuality."

By now perpetually "tired and blue," she becomes frightened when her "old friend" whiskey fails her, and she decides, having no ties, no talents, and no purpose in living, to commit suicide by taking twenty sleeping pills—"Well, here's mud in your eye." In her customary vagueness she fails again, however, causing the impersonal attendants, a reluctant doctor and housemaid, more annoyance than concern. She concludes that she might as well live, but with a paradoxical prayer of diabolic self-destructiveness: "Oh, please, please, let her be able to get drunk, please keep her always drunk."

Although in both "Big Blonde" and the monologues Parker satirizes vapid, unassertive women with empty lives, her work carries with it satire's inevitable message of dissatisfaction with the status quo and an implicit plea for reform. For in subtle ways Parker makes a feminist plea even through her most passive, vacuous characters. Women ought to be open, assertive, independent; they should think for themselves and act on their own behalf, because men cannot be counted on to do it for them. They should be their own persons, like Geoffrey Chaucer's Wife of Bath, "wel at ease," instead of allowing their happiness to depend on the waxing and waning affections and attentions of inconstant men.

To the extent that Dorothy Parker was a satirist she was also a moralist. In satirizing aimless, frivolous, or social-climbing lives, she implied a purposeful ideal. In ridiculing self-deception, hypocrisy, obsequiousness, and flattery, she advocated honesty in behavior and communication. In her epigrams, the moralist's rapiers, she could hone a razor-edge with the best. In her portraits, cameos etched in acid, the touchstone of truth shines clear.

*Lynn Z. Bloom*
*With updates by Karen M. Cleveland Marwick*

### Other major works

PLAYS: *Nero*, pr. 1922 (with Robert Benchley); *Close Harmony: Or, The Lady Next Door*, pr. 1924 (with Elmer Rice); *The Coast of Illyria*, pr. 1949 (with Ross Evans); *The Ladies of the Corridor*, pr., pb. 1953 (with Arnaud d'Usseau).

POETRY: *Enough Rope*, 1926; *Sunset Gun*, 1928; *Death and Taxes*, 1931; *Not So Deep as a Well*, 1936; *Not Much Fun*, 1996; *Complete Poems*, 1999.

SCREENPLAYS: *Business Is Business*, 1925 (with George S. Kaufman); *Here Is My Heart*, 1934 (with Alan Campbell); *Big Broadcast of 1936*, 1935 (with Campbell); *Hands Across the Table*, 1935; *Mary Burns, Fugitive*, 1935; *One Hour Late*, 1935 (with Campbell); *Paris in Spring*, 1935; *Lady Be Careful*, 1936 (with Campbell and Harry Ruskin); *Suzy*, 1936 (with Campbell, Horace Jackson, and Lenore Coffee); *The Moon's Our Home*, 1936; *Three Married Men*, 1936 (with Campbell); *A Star Is Born*, 1937 (with Campbell and Robert Carson); *Woman Chases Man*, 1937 (with Joe Bigelow); *Crime Takes a Holiday*, 1938; *Flight into Nowhere*, 1938; *Sweethearts*, 1938 (with Campbell); *Trade Winds*, 1938 (with Campbell and Frank R. Adams); *Five Little Peppers and How They Grew*, 1939; *The Little Foxes*, 1941; *Weekend for Three*, 1941 (with Campbell); *Saboteur*, 1942 (with Campbell, Peter Viertel, and Joan Harrison); *A Gentle Gangster*, 1943; *Mr. Skeffington*, 1944; *Smash-Up: The Story of a Woman*, 1947 (with Frank Cavett); *The Fan*, 1949 (with Walter Reisch and Ross Evans); *Queen for a Day*, 1951; *A Star Is Born*, 1954.

**Bibliography**

Calhoun, Randall. *Dorothy Parker: A Bio-bibliography.* Westport, Conn.: Greenwood Press, 1993. Helpful guide for the student of Parker. Includes bibliographical references and an index.

Edward, Ann. "Big Blonde." In *Masterplots II: Short Story Series,* edited by Charles E. May. Rev. ed. Vol. 1. Pasadena, Calif.: Salem Press, 2004. Analysis of "Big Blonde" with sections on themes and meaning and style and technique. Also includes a detailed synopsis of the story.

Freibert, Lucy M. "Dorothy Parker." In *Dictionary of Literary Biography: American Short Story Writers, 1910-1945,* edited by Bobby Ellen Kimbel. Vol. 86. Detroit: Gale Research, 1989. Freibert's excellent entry on Dorothy Parker provides some general biographical information and close readings of some of her most important stories. Includes a bibliography of Parker's work and a critical bibliography.

Keats, John. *You Might as Well Live: The Life and Times of Dorothy Parker.* New York: Simon & Schuster, 1970. Keats's book was the first popular biography published on Parker, and it is quite thorough and readable. Supplemented by a bibliography and an index.

Kinney, Arthur F. *Dorothy Parker.* Rev. ed. Boston: Twayne, 1998. In this excellent study of Parker's life and work, Kinney incorporates facts recorded for the first time and provides the first full critical assessment of her writing. Kinney calls Parker the best epigrammatic American poet of her century. Contains a bibliography and extensive notes and references.

Meade, Marion. *Dorothy Parker: What Fresh Hell Is This?* London: Heinemann, 1987. Meade has produced a good, thorough biography that relates events in Parker's fiction to situations in her life. Nevertheless, Meade's focus is biographical, and the discussion of Parker's work is mostly in passing. Includes notes and an index.

Melzer, Sondra. *The Rhetoric of Rage: Women in Dorothy Parker.* New York: Peter Lang, 1997. Explores Parker's representation of female characters in her works.

Pettit, Rhonda S. *A Gendered Collision: Sentimentalism and Modernism in Dorothy Parker's Poetry and Fiction.* Madison, N.J.: Fairleigh Dickinson University Press, 2000. Study that attempts to shift the focus of Parker criticism from the poet's life to the wider literary environment.

Simpson, Amelia. "Black on Blonde: The Africanist Presence in Dorothy Parker's 'Big Blonde.'" *College Literature* 23 (October, 1996): 105-116. Claims that "Big Blonde" exposes the way race and gender are mutually constitutive and how blackness contests and constructs the privilege of whiteness; argues that three seemingly unimportant African figures are the key to this narrative about the subjugation of white women in America.

Walker, Nancy A. "The Remarkably Constant Reader: Dorothy Parker as Book Reviewer." *Studies in American Humor,* n.s. 3, no. 4 (1997): 1-14. A discussion of Parker's book reviews for *The New Yorker* from 1927 to 1933 and for *Esquire* from 1957 to 1962 as a reflection of her literary sensibility.

# S. J. Perelman

**Born:** Brooklyn, New York; February 1, 1904
**Died:** New York, New York; October 17, 1979

**Principal short fiction** • *Dawn Ginsbergh's Revenge*, 1929; *Parlor, Bedlam, and Bath*, 1930 (with Quentin J. Reynolds); *Strictly from Hunger*, 1937; *Look Who's Talking*, 1940; *The Dream Department*, 1943; *Crazy Like a Fox*, 1944; *Keep It Crisp*, 1946; *Acres and Pains*, 1947; *Westward Ha! Or, Around the World in Eighty Clichés*, 1948; *Listen to the Mocking Bird*, 1949; *The Swiss Family Perelman*, 1950; *A Child's Garden of Curses*, 1951; *The Ill-Tempered Clavichord*, 1952; *Hold That Christmas Tiger!*, 1954; *Perelman's Home Companion*, 1955; *The Road to Miltown: Or, Under the Spreading Atrophy*, 1957; *The Most of S. J. Perelman*, 1958; *The Rising Gorge*, 1961; *Chicken Inspector No. 23*, 1966; *Baby, It's Cold Inside*, 1970; *Vinegar Puss*, 1975; *Eastward Ha!*, 1977.

**Other literary forms** • S. J. Perelman's more than twenty-five books include essays, stories, plays, and an autobiography. He has also written screenplays for film and television, and he is best known for his work with the Marx Brothers on *Monkey Business* (1931) and *Horse Feathers* (1932).

**Achievements** • S. J. Perelman was a highly successful and well-loved humorist whose best writing appeared in *The New Yorker* and then was collected in popular books for five decades, from the 1930's to the 1970's. He wrote the book upon which the Broadway hit *One Touch of Venus* (1943) was based, and he wrote one other acclaimed Broadway comedy, *The Beauty Part* (1961). For his contribution to *Around the World in Eighty Days*, he shared an Academy Award in 1956 and also received a New York Film Critics Award. In 1978, he received the special National Book Award for his lifetime contribution to American literature.

Perelman's influence on other writers is difficult to measure because, although he was the leader of the "dementia praecox" school of humor closely associated with *The New Yorker*, he was not the inventor of the techniques of verbal humor he used so well, and his type of writing has been on the decline. There seem to be clear mutual influences between Perelman and several of his contemporaries: James Thurber, Dorothy Parker, Groucho Marx, and Nathanael West, his brother-in-law. French Surrealists admired his style, and contemporary black humorists often use the techniques he mastered; but one hesitates to assert direct influence on writers such as Joseph Heller and Kurt Vonnegut. Perelman's type of writing seems to have been taken over by television, film, and perhaps the New Journalism. Woody Allen admired Perelman and is often mentioned as one of his disciples. In his critiques of American style, Perelman may be a predecessor of writers such as Tom Wolfe, Hunter Thompson, and Terry Southern.

**Biography** • Sidney Joseph Perelman was born in Brooklyn, New York, on February 1, 1904, the son of Sophia Charren and Joseph Perelman, a Jewish poultry farmer. He briefly attended Brown University, where he edited the *College Humor* magazine. After leaving the university in 1925, he began his career as a writer and cartoonist for *Judge* magazine. Following a brief time at *College Humor* and his marriage to Laura Weinstein on July 4, 1929, he began writing full-time and in 1931 became a regular contributor to *The New Yorker* and other major magazines. He and Laura had a son and a daughter. He worked occasionally in Hollywood, writing motion-picture screenplays, but he spent most of his life in New York City and on his Pennsylvania farm. He collaborated to write several successful plays; his usual collaborator on films as well as plays was his wife, although on *One Touch of Venus*, he worked with Ogden Nash, and for a television musical, *Aladdin*, with Cole Porter.

After his wife's death in 1970, Perelman lived for two years in England but then returned to Manhattan, where he remained until his death on October 17, 1979.

**Analysis** • Parody, satire, and verbal wit characterize S. J. Perelman's works. Most of them are very short and tend to begin as conversational essays that develop into narrative or mock dramatic episodes and sometimes return to essay. Perelman called them feuilletons (little leaves), "comic essays of a particular type." They seem formally related to the earliest American forms of short story, Benjamin Franklin's bagatelles and early American humor. Norris Yates best summarizes the worldview reflected in Perelman's work: Perelman values normal life, "integrity, sincerity, skepticism, taste, a respect for competence, a striving after the golden mean, and a longing for better communication and understanding among men." Yates sees Perelman's typical persona (the "I" of the pieces) as a Little Man resisting the forces of American cultural life that would "invade and corrupt his personality and impel him toward neuroses," the forces which seem determined to destroy the values Perelman holds. According to Yates, these forces manifest themselves for Perelman most decisively in "the mass media, which are, on the whole, the offspring of technology's unconsecrated marriage with Big Business."

Perelman's "autobiographical" work reveals his version of the Little Man. A favorite type of *The New Yorker* humorists, the Little Man is a caricature of a typical middle-class, early twentieth century American male, usually represented as helpless before the complexities of technological society, cowed by its crass commercialism, dominated by desperate, unfulfilled women, sustaining himself on heroic fantasies of a bygone or imaginary era. James Thurber's Walter Mitty has become the classic presentation of this character type. Perelman's personae seem related to the type, but vary in several significant ways.

*Acres and Pains* • In *Acres and Pains*, the major collection of his adventures on his farm, he makes his persona into a city dweller who has naïvely tried to realize a romantic agrarian dream on his country estate but who has come to see the error of his ways. Perelman uses this reversal of the rube in the city to debunk a sentimental picture of country life by exaggerating his trials. Many episodes show good country people betraying the ideal with which they are associated. Contractors, antique dealers, and barn painters rob him of purse and peace. "Perelman" differs from the Little Man type in that, although he may at any time fall victim to another illusion, he knows and admits that country life is no romance. In these sketches, he also differs from the Little Man type in his relationship to wife and family. He is not dominated by a frustrated woman. He and his wife are usually mutual victims of pastoral illusion, although often she suffers more than he.

This "Perelman" is most like the typical Little Man when he deals with machines. For example, when his water pump goes berserk during a dinner party, he handles the problem with successful incompetence: "By exerting a slight leverage, I succeeded in prying off the gasket or outer jacket of the pump, exactly as you would a baked potato. . . . This gave me room to poke around the innards with a sharp stick. I cleaned the pump thoroughly . . . and, as a final precaution, opened the windows to allow the water to drain down the slope." The major difference between this persona and Walter Mitty is that the former is competent; he escapes neurosis and resists with some success his crazy world. By splitting the narrator into a present sophisticate (a mask that often slips) and a former fool, he tends to shift the butt of humor away from the present narrator and toward the man who believes in romantic

Library of Congress

ideals and toward the people who so completely fail to live up to any admirable ideals. The latter are typified by the contractor who digs "Perelman's" pool in a bad place although he knows the best place for it. Asked why he offered his advice when the pool was dynamited rather than before it was begun, he virtuously replies. "It don't pay to poke your nose in other people's business." Implied in these tall tales of mock pastoral life are criticisms of the values which oppose those Yates lists: dishonesty, hypocrisy, greed, naïveté, incompetence, overenthusiasm, deliberately created confusion, and lying.

Looking over the full range of Perelman's first-person sketches, one sees significant variation in the presentation of the persona. In *Acres and Pains*, the narrator is much more concrete than in many other sketches in which the "I" is virtually an empty mind waiting to take shape under the power of some absurd mass-media language. Perelman is acutely sensitive to this language as a kind of oppression. Many of his sketches explore "sub-dialects" of American English in order to expose and ridicule the values that underlie them. "Tomorrow—Fairly Cloudy" is a typical example of the author's probing of a sample of American language.

**"Tomorrow—Fairly Cloudy"** • In "Tomorrow—Fairly Cloudy," Perelman notices a new advertisement for a toothpaste which promises its users rescue from humdrum ordinary life and elevation into romance and success. In his introduction, Perelman emphasizes the absurdity of taking such ads seriously, describes the ad in detail, then introduces a dramatic scenario by observing that this ad heralds the coming demise of a desperate industry: "So all the old tactics have finally broken down—wheedling, abuse, snobbery and terror. I look forward to the last great era in advertising, a period packed with gloom, defeatism, and frustration." In the following spectacle, the children bubble excited "adese" while father despairs over his drab life:

**Bobby**—Oh, Moms, I'm so glad you and Dads decided to install a Genfeedco automatic oil burner and air conditioner with the new self-ventilating screen flaps plus finger control! It is noiseless, cuts down heating bills, and makes the air we breathe richer in vita-ray particles. . . .

**Mr. Bradley** (tonelessly)—Well, I suppose anything is better than a heap of slag at this end of the cellar.

Soon the Fletchers arrive to sneer at their towels and to make the Bradleys aware of all the products they do not have. The sketch ends in apocalypse as their inferior plumbing gives way, and they all drown in their combination cellar and playroom. It remains unclear throughout whether this episode forecasts the forms of future advertising or its effects on the public.

Perelman exposes the absurdity of this language of conspicuous consumption by imagining its literal acceptance. In the world this language implies, happiness is possessing the right gadgets. If sales are to continue, it must be impossible for most people ever to have all the right things, and so impossible ever to be happy. The Bradleys have the right oil burner, but their towels disintegrate in two days, and they failed to use Sumwenco Super-Annealed Brass Pipe. This last omission costs them their lives. Not only their happiness but also their very survival depend on their ability to possess the right new product.

**"Entered as Second-Class Matter"** • Perelman's many sketches of this type culminate perhaps in "Entered as Second-Class Matter," which is apparently a montage of fragments lifted (and, one hopes, sometimes fabricated) from magazine fiction and advertising. The resulting silliness may be intended as a portrait of the mass feminine mind as perceived by American magazines, 1930-1944. It ends:

> We have scoured the fiction market to set before you *Three Million Tiny Sweat Glands Functioning* in that vibrant panorama of tomorrow so that *Your Sensitive Bowel Muscles Can* react to the almost inevitable realization that only by enrichment and guidance *plus a soothing depilatory* can America face its problems confidently, unafraid, *well-groomed mouth-happy, breaking hair off at the roots without undue stench. Okay, Miss America!*

In such pieces, Perelman's values are clearly those Yates names. Especially important in these works is the humorous attempt to clear away the garbage of American language culture through ridicule. This aim is central to the series "Cloudland Revisited," in which he reexamines the popular literature of his youth. Perelman varies this formula with attacks on absurd fashion and the language of fashion, one of the best of which is "Farewell, My Lovely Appetizer."

**Verbal Wit** • Perelman is deservedly most admired for his faculty of verbal wit. In several of his more conventional stories which seem less restrained by satiric ends, his playfulness dazzles. Among the best of these are "The Idol's Eye," "Seedlings of Desire," and "The Love Decoy." Based on the sensational plots of teen-romance, "The Love Decoy" is narrated by a coed who seeks revenge on an instructor who once failed to make a pass and who later humiliated her before her classmates by accusing her of "galvanizing around nights." Her plan is to lure him to her room after hours, then expose him as a corrupter of undergraduates. This plan backfires in a non sequitur when a lecherous dean arrives to assault her. The reader expects the plot to complicate, but instead it is transformed when the dean is unmasked as Jim the Penman who framed the girl's father and sent him to the pen. Other identities are revealed, and the reader arrives at the end of a detective thriller. Although there is parody here of sentimental language and plot, the story seems more intent on fun than ridicule. It contains a number of Perelman's most celebrated witticisms. For example:

> He caught my arm in a vice-like grip and drew me to him, but with a blow I sent him groveling. In ten minutes he was back with a basket of appetizing fresh picked grovels. We squeezed them and drank the piquant juice thirstily.

At the center of this wit is the double entendre. Multiple meanings of words suggest the multiple contexts in which they may apply. Perelman juxtaposes these contexts, makes rapid shifts between them, and sometimes uses a suggestion to imagine a new context. The effects are sometimes surreal. The double meaning of "sent" suggests a transformation from a blow to the groin to an activity such as berrying. "Groveling" gathers an imaginary context which generates a new noun, "grovels." Although this reading seems most plausible, in another reading there are no transformations, and gathering grovels becomes a euphemistic way to describe the amorous instructor's reaction to her literal attack or to her unusually expressed affection.

Perelman creates this slipperiness of meaning and encourages it to reverberate in this passage and in the language and structure of the whole work. One result is a heightened alertness in the reader to the ambiguity of language and the elusiveness of meaning, a first but important step on the way to the sort of respect for language Perelman implies in his many critiques of its abuses. This concern connects Perelman most closely with James Joyce, whom he considered the greatest modern comic writer, with a number of his contemporaries, including William Faulkner and James Thurber. Although Perelman has not the stature of these great writers, he shares with them a consciousness of the peculiar problems of modern life and a belief that how one uses language is important to recognizing and dealing with those problems. Among *The New Yorker* humorists with whom S. J. Perelman is associated, he is probably one of the lesser lights, showing neither the versatility, the variety, nor the universality of Dorothy Parker or of Thurber. Although critical estimates of his achievement vary, there is general agreement that his best work, done mostly before 1950, shows a marvelous gift for verbal wit.

*Terry Heller*

## Other major works

PLAYS: *The Night Before Christmas*, pr. 1941 (with Laura Perelman); *One Touch of Venus*, pr. 1943 (with Ogden Nash); *The Beauty Part*, pr. 1961.

MISCELLANEOUS: *That Old Gang o' Mine: The Early and Essential S. J. Perelman*, 1984 (Richard Marschall, editor).

NONFICTION: *The Last Laugh*, 1981; *Don't Tread on Me: Selected Letters of S. J. Perelman*, 1987; *Conversations with S. J. Perelman*, 1995 (Tom Teicholz, editor).

SCREENPLAYS: *Monkey Business*, 1931; *Horse Feathers*, 1932; *Around the World in Eighty Days*, 1956.

**Bibliography**

Adams, Michael. "A Critical Introduction to *The Best of S. J. Perelman by Sidney Namlerep.*" In *Masterplots II: Short Story Series*, edited by Charles E. May. Rev. ed. Vol. 2. Pasadena, Calif.: Salem Press, 2004. Analysis of "A Critical Introduction to The Best of S. J. Perelman by Sidney Namlerep" with sections on themes and meaning and style and technique. Also includes a detailed synopsis of the story.

Epstein, Joseph. "Sid, You Made the Prose Too Thin." *Commentary* 84 (September, 1987): 53-60. A biographical sketch of Perelman, suggesting that his best writing occurred when he was angry, as in *Acres and Pains*, a collection of stories about an idealistic city man being taken advantage of by rural hustlers; claims that elsewhere his natural penchant for gloom, suspicion, and pessimism led him merely to make wisecracks about banal subjects or unpleasantly callous pokes at barely disguised real people.

Fowler, Douglas. *S. J. Perelman.* Boston: Twayne, 1983. This critical study examines influences on Perelman, the development of his career, his relationships with his contemporaries, his technique, and his importance. Includes a chronology, a biographical sketch, and an annotated bibliography.

Gale, Steven. *S. J. Perelman: A Critical Study.* New York: Greenwood Press, 1987. Gale examines Perelman's prose, screenplays, and plays, then studies his themes and techniques. Gale gives special attention to Perelman's background in Jewish humor and his use of clichés and allusions. The volume is supplemented by a chronology and a bibliographical essay.

_____. *S. J. Perelman: An Annotated Bibliography.* New York: Garland, 1985. This useful, annotated bibliography lists 650 Perelman publications and 380 items written about Perelman.

Gale, Steven H., ed. *S. J. Perelman: Critical Essays.* New York: Garland, 1992. Includes two dozen essays, articles, and critiques of Perelman from academic studies, newspapers, and popular journals over a seventy-year period of his career. Gale's introduction places Perelman in the tradition of such great humorists as Geoffrey Chaucer and Mark Twain.

Herrmann, Dorothy. *S. J. Perelman: A Life.* New York: Putnam, 1986. This complete biography makes use of recollections of his acquaintances to shed light on the life of a very private man. It includes select bibliographies of writing by and about Perelman.

Katona, Cynthia Lee. "The Love Decoy." In *Masterplots II: Short Story Series*, edited by Charles E. May. Rev. ed. Vol. 5. Pasadena, Calif.: Salem Press, 2004. Student-friendly analysis of "The Love Decoy" that covers the story's themes and style and includes a detailed synopsis.

Perelman, S. J. *Conversations with S. J. Perelman.* Edited by Tom Teicholz. Jackson: University Press of Mississippi, 1995. Collection of interviews with the author.

Plimpton, George, ed. *Writers at Work: The Paris Review Interviews, Second Series.* New York: Viking Press, 1963. In an interview appearing on pages 241-256, Perelman offers glimpses into his creative process and his artistic purposes.

Yates, Norris Wilson. "The Sane Psychoses of S. J. Perelman." In *The American Humorist: Conscience of the Twentieth Century.* Ames: Iowa State University Press, 1964. Though this study has to some extent been superseded by more extensive and later works, it still provides a good, brief introduction to Perelman.

# Ann Petry

**Born:** Old Saybrook, Connecticut; October 12, 1908
**Died:** Old Saybrook, Connecticut; April 28, 1997

**Principal short fiction** • *Miss Muriel, and Other Stories*, 1971.

**Other literary forms** • Ann Petry has received her greatest critical recognition for her adult novels: *The Street* (1946), *Country Place* (1947), and *The Narrows* (1953). In 1949 she began a distinguished career as a writer of children's literature with the publication of *The Drugstore Cat*, to be followed by the now-classic biographical novels *Harriet Tubman: Conductor of the Underground Railroad* (1955) and *Tituba of Salem Village* (1964). She also published a devotional work, *Legends of the Saints* (1970), in addition to various articles for small periodicals.

**Achievements** • Ann Petry's receipt of a Houghton Mifflin Literary Fellowship in 1945 (and an award of twenty-five hundred dollars) enabled her to complete *The Street*, which went on to become the first novel by an African American woman to sell more than one million copies. In 1977 she was awarded a National Endowment for the Arts grant and in 1983 received a D. Litt. from Boston's Suffolk University. In 1992 the reissuing of *The Street* renewed Petry's reputation as an important American writer and introduced a new generation to her work. Her death in April, 1997, was eulogized publicly by Connecticut senator Christopher Dodd, and the following year MacArthur Fellow Max Roach premiered "Theater Pieces" (December, 1998), an adaptation of Petry's tale of a jazz love triangle, "Solo on the Drums," featuring Ruby Dee and Ossie Davis along with Roach.

**Biography** • Ann Lane Petry was born to Peter Clarke Lane and Bertha James Lane on October 12, 1908, joining a family that had lived for several generations as the only African American citizens of the resort community of Old Saybrook, Connecticut. The descendant of a runaway Virginian slave, Petry admitted to never having believed herself to be a true New Englander; her cultural legacy was not that of the typical Yankee, and as a small child she came to know the isolating effects of racism after being stoned by white children on her first day of school. Nevertheless, her family distinguished itself within the community and boasted numerous professionals: Her grandfather was a licensed chemist; her father, aunt, and uncle became pharmacists; and her mother worked as a chiropodist. In 1902 Peter Lane opened a pharmacy in Old Saybrook, for which Ann herself trained. Inspired by the example of her many independent female relatives—women who had, she explained, "abandoned the role of housewife in the early twentieth century"—in 1931 Ann secured a degree in pharmacology from the University of Connecticut, the only black graduate in her class. She worked in family-owned pharmacies until 1938, when she met and married Louisiana-born George D. Petry and moved with him to his home in Harlem.

Petry had begun writing fiction seriously in high school after an antagonistic teacher grudgingly praised her work as having real potential, and she wrote steadily thereafter (although to no immediate success). With the move to New York City, her writing career began in earnest. She quickly secured jobs with various Harlem newspapers as a reporter, editor, and copywriter, working for the *Amsterdam News* and *The People's Voice* (the latter a weekly begun by African American clergyman and politician Adam Clayton Powell, Jr.). She also briefly acted in the American Negro Theatre and worked on a study conducted by the New York Foundation investigating the effects of segregation on black children.

Participation in a creative writing seminar at Columbia University greatly influenced Petry during this time. Her first published short story, "On Saturday the Siren Sounds at Noon," appeared in a 1943 issue of *The Crisis* (a magazine published by the National Association for the Advancement of Colored People) and not only earned her twenty dollars but also led to her discovery by an editor at Houghton Mifflin. He encouraged her to submit preliminary work on what would become *The Street*, for which Petry received the 1945 Houghton Mifflin Literary Fellowship and a stipend of twenty-five hundred dollars. Thus she was able to complete her novel, translating nearly a decade spent observing the difficulties of aspiring African Americans in the urban North into the powerful story of single mother Lutie Johnson and her star-crossed eight-year-old, Bub. Although her trenchant insights into the play of race and class as conjoined factors stifling Lutie's dreams recall Richard Wright's landmark *Native Son* (1940), Petry's recognition of the role of gender in the discriminatory equation made *The Street* a groundbreaking work on its own and another expression of the woman-centered ethic she had learned from her family. Published in 1946, *The Street* received both critical and popular acclaim and sold 1.5 million copies—at the time the largest audience ever reached by an African American woman. The fame accompanying that success overwhelmed Petry, however, and in 1948 she and George returned to the obscurity of Old Saybrook, where they bought the two-hundred-year-old house of an old sea captain and reared their daughter, Elizabeth Ann.

Petry's subsequent fiction did not receive the same kind of praise accorded her first novel, despite her continued willingness to tackle difficult racial themes (*The Narrows*, 1953) and explore the terrain of small-town white America from its own assumed vantage point, a project seldom undertaken by black writers even today (*Country Place*, 1947). In 1971 she issued a collection of her short fiction, *Miss Muriel, and Other Stories*. She also contributed stories and essays to numerous magazines and journals. Perhaps in response to the indifference accorded her adult fiction, she began writing for children during the time she was raising Elizabeth and produced such classics as *The Drugstore Cat*, *Harriet Tubman*, and *Tituba of Salem Village*. The latter two novels, about actual historical personages, reflect her determination to place art in the service of an honest picture of American racial history; they have become young adult classics and are perhaps more widely read than the adult fiction on which her initial reputation was built.

Petry spent the second half of her life away from the hurly-burly of publishing centers and for the most part outside the rarefied walls of the university; David Streitfeld of *The Washington Post* said that she "had little tolerance for fools or academics, two categories she regarded as essentially synonymous." She did hold a visiting professorship at the University of Hawaii in 1974-1975 and in 1977 received a grant from the National Endowment for the Arts. Boston's Suffolk University awarded her a D.Litt. degree in 1983. She had the satisfaction of seeing her daughter continue the legacy of strong female achievement by becoming an attorney.

Petry died at the age of eighty-eight in a convalescent home in the same community where she was born, still married to the man who had briefly taken her out of New England and made possible the launching of her lifelong career.

**Analysis** • Although Ann Petry's fiction typically involves African Americans struggling against the crippling impact of racism, her overarching theme involves a more broadly defined notion of prejudice that targets class and gender as well as race. Thus her aims are consistently broader than racial critique, since she regularly exposes the consequences of America's hierarchical social systems and its capitalistic materialism. That vision explains what might otherwise seem to be inconsistencies of direction in Petry's career: her decision, for example, following the potent racial protest of *The Street* to focus her next novel, *Country Place*, on a white community's postwar crises of adjustment or her movement into the realm of children's literature. Like her contemporaries, black and white alike, who came of age in the 1930's, she adopted a social realist aesthetic committed to documenting the obstacles to human fulfillment imposed on those at the margins of American prosperity. As she explained,

> I find it difficult to subscribe to the idea that art exists for art's sake. It seems to me that all truly great art is propaganda . . . [and fiction], like all other forms of art, will always reflect the political, economic, and social structure of the period in which it was created.

Her work also reveals an increasingly overt Christian existentialist vision celebrating the individual's potential for spiritual liberation, through which an entire culture might come to relinquish its crippling prejudices.

Rather than celebrating the American ideal of self-making with which her native New England is so closely associated, Petry exposes the illusions it has fostered and depicts their graphic costs to those relegated to the periphery of American possibility. Racism invites Petry's most scathing attacks, not only for the material hardship it forces upon people of color but also for the psychological and cultural distortions it produces. At her most biting, Petry lampoons the absurdist systems of human classification into which racist societies ultimately fall. Generally, her perspective is a tragic one, however, grounded in the recognition that confronting racism necessitates confronting history itself.

One of Petry's most insistent indictments of America's hypocrisy targets the class distinctions that parallel and overlap racism as forces negating individual hope for a better life, a more just world. Repeatedly she shows how Americans in quest of the material security, comfort, and status that propel middle-class striving acquiesce to soul-numbing labor and retreat into a moral inflexibility that blindly sanctions aggressive self-interest. In Petry's fiction the culture's high-flown rhetoric is belied by rigid social hierarchies that produce venal, grasping have-nots at the bottom, whose ambitions mimic the ruthless acquisitiveness of those at the top.

Petry's most important characters are those who reject the fallacy of the self-made individual existing independently of the world or the continuing legacy of the past. Though that perspective assumes certain mechanistic dimensions in her work, she does not concede full authority to deterministic necessity; the dice may be loaded against her protagonists, but the game is not inexorably mandated to play itself out to any single predetermined end. Her characters sometimes prove capable of personal growth that moves them toward a common humanity with the potential to fuel real and far-reaching change in the social order itself. Petry's narratives of personal transformation often grow from characters' chance movements across rigid cultural boundaries; the resulting crises test the spiritual flexibility of many others besides her protagonists.

Overlooked by academic critics, Petry's children's books offer tantalizing clues to her larger agenda. Their emphasis upon personal fearlessness in rethinking entrenched assumptions and disengaging from unjust systems invites comparison with numerous figures from her adult fiction. Moreover, in applying their new insights, these characters undertake subtly revolutionary actions that defy the cultural boundaries that had previously defined their lives. It takes a saint, perhaps, to challenge a predatory universe with an alternative vision of love, but having told children in *Legends of the Saints* that true sanctity is a function of bravery, Petry seems to evaluate her other fictional characters on their receptivity to grace as an antidote to hate.

***Miss Muriel, and Other Stories*** • Although Petry's reputation rests primarily on her novels, she saw herself quite differently at the start of her career:

> I set out to be a writer of short stories and somehow ended up as a novelist—possibly because there simply wasn't room enough within the framework of the short story to do the sort of thing I wanted to do.

Yet the pieces in *Miss Muriel, and Other Stories*, written over the course of several decades, provide a compact and provocative introduction to her imaginative concerns, chief among them her sensitivity to racism's psychological as well as material consequences.

**"Like a Winding Sheet"** • In the prizewinning story "Like a Winding Sheet," she depicts the physical and mental toll exacted by the nature of work in an industrial society where laborers are treated as interchangeable machines. The story dramatizes how the corrosive humiliations of prejudice, when added to work stresses, can trigger blind and catastrophic violence. A husband's inability to challenge the string of racist assaults on his dignity delivered both during and after his exhausting night shift at a World War II defense plant not only makes him incapable of imagining benign white behavior (even in the face of apologies) but also causes him to respond to his wife's affectionate teasing with the beating he is forbidden to direct at his real oppressors. Although racism provides the context for his rage, however (her unwitting use of the word "nigger" echoing the hostile epithet regularly used against him by the outside world), his reaction exposes the starkness of the struggle between male and female in Petry's world and the sobering betrayals it can provoke. The title image begins as the bedsheet in which he has tossed and turned all day in a futile effort to sleep, but his wife jokingly casts it as a burial linen—a reference ironically appropriate to his sense of himself as the walking dead. By story's end that reference has assumed sinister dimensions as he feels trapped by the violence he is committing but cannot control, "and he thought it was like being enmeshed in a winding sheet."

**"In Darkness and Confusion"** • "In Darkness and Confusion" fictionalizes the Harlem Riot of 1943, an event sparked by the wounding of a black soldier whose uniform provided scant protection on his own home front. The story's protagonist, William Jones, a drugstore porter who, despite endless humiliations, has worked hard all his life to secure a better world for his son Sam, suddenly loses that son to the wartime draft and the dangers of a Jim Crow world at the southern training camp to which he is sent. When Sam, who once aspired to college and his share of the American Dream, protests an order to move to the back of the bus and then shoots the aggressive military police officer who gave it, he is court-martialed and sentenced to twenty years of hard labor.

As Jones broods over this news in a Harlem bar, he watches as another uniformed black G.I., this one standing in the supposedly more egalitarian North, tries to help a black woman being beaten by a white policeman, punches the lawman, runs, and is summarily gunned down. Jones erupts into a violence ignited by grief and rage and becomes the leader of a mob. When his churchgoing wife learns of their son's fate, she too turns to retributive action with an explosive passion that kills her: Her religion proves unable to provide her with the strength to resume her burden and go on with her life. Nor is the mob's looting of local merchants legitimized, for it is produced by the intoxicating siren song of white capitalist materialism, with which the culture regularly deflects attention from matters of real social justice. The riot leaves Jones more completely bereft than he had been before, for it literally costs him his heart and soul, even as it finally allows him to understand the anomie of his disaffected teenage niece, who has baldly scorned his lifetime of exhausting effort for the whites, who in the end allow them "only the nigger end of things."

**"The New Mirror"** • Petry as skillfully evokes the impact of racism on the black bourgeoisie as she does on the proletariat, and in several tales she demonstrates how a lifetime of belittlement and intimidation can erode one's ability to act ethically in the world. In "Miss Muriel" and "The New Mirror," Petry creates a black family much like her own—the Layens are professionals who own the pharmacy in a small New England town. The adolescent girl who narrates these tales speaks of "the training in issues of race" she has received over the years, not only through the casual bigotries she has witnessed but also through the painful self-consciousness of respectable people like her parents, whose behavior is a continual exercise in refuting cultural stereotypes while carefully preserving proudly held racial loyalties. In "The New Mirror" the ironies are more overt, cleaner. Mr. Layen's decision to take a day off to outfit himself with a new pair of false teeth leads his unknowing wife to an excruciating encounter with police, from whom she withholds her fear that the absent Layen may have become another black man who deserts his family as a delayed response to a lifetime of indignities within the white patriarchal social order. Layen's surprising secrecy leads his daughter to realize that even securing a new set of teeth subjects a black male to humiliation, in this case taking the form of the grinning Sambos and toothless Uncle Toms he fears his dental problems will call to mind. The child learns to use the codes by which the black middle class shields itself from white contempt— just as she shoulders her own share of the burden of always acting with an eye on the reputation of "the Race": She thus learns why "all of us people with this dark skin must help hold the black island inviolate."

**"Miss Muriel"** • The title story of the volume, "Miss Muriel," operates more subtly in its exploration of the racist preoccupations inculcated within and often unwillingly relinquished by its victims. The title itself refers to a white racist joke the young narrator innocently relates to one of Aunt Sophronia's black suitors—a joke in which an African American trying to buy a Muriel cigar is upbraided for not showing the proper respect for white womanhood by asking instead for a "Miss" Muriel. The child is bluntly chastised for voicing such "nigger" put-downs in one of the many moments of confusion she suffers over the inconsistent and seemingly arbitrary management of prejudices operating among the adults around her: her aunt's unpopular courtship by Bemish, a white member of their upstate New York community; the equal dismay with which Mr. Layen regards Sophronia's other suitor, the "tramp piano player" Chink, who evokes the "low" culture of the black masses, from which the bourgeois Layen has distanced himself as part of his accommodation to a scornful white world; the contempt quietly directed against the homosexual partner of her cherished Uncle Johno; the colorist hierarchies of all the African Americans she knows (even when the lightest skinned among them eschew the opportunity to "pass"). At the end of the story, when the black men in her circle have effectively driven Bemish out of town for his persistent wooing of Sophronia, the narrator brokenheartedly confronts their hypocrisy, yelling, "You both stink. You stink like dead bats. You and your goddamn Miss Muriel." Internalizing such divisiveness as they have just enforced directly clashes with the other set of values she has been taught, and the two are starkly juxtaposed early in the story when the child muses:

> If my objections to Mr. Bemish are because he's white . . . then I have been 'trained' on the subject of race just as I have been trained to be a Christian. . . .

It is one of the paradoxes of bigotry that its victims may become its emissaries, at the price of their most cherished beliefs.

**"The Witness"** • Petry revisits this theme in a number of ways throughout the collection. Against the most aggressive forms of white hatred directed at her characters, there is no defense except a temporary abandonment of one's human dignity. "The Witness" presents the case of a retired black college professor who takes a high school teaching position in a northern white community. Called upon to assist the local pastor in counseling delinquent adolescents, he finds himself their prey as they kidnap him and force him to watch their sexual abuse of a young white woman. Having at one point coerced him to place his hand on the girl, they effectively blackmail him into complicit silence about their crime, for he is paralyzed by the specter of being publicly accused of the ultimate racial taboo. His exemplary life and professional stature cannot protect him from such sordid insinuations, and he bitterly describes himself in his moral impotence as "another poor scared black bastard who was a witness."

**"The Necessary Knocking on the Door"** • In "The Necessary Knocking on the Door" a similar loss of agency is made bitingly ironic by the context in which Alice Knight's dilemma unfolds: A participant at a conference about the role of Christianity in the modern world, she finds herself unable to master her dislike for a white woman dying in the hotel room across the hall from hers—a woman who had earlier in the day refused to be seated next to a "nigger" and had thus awakened in Alice the bitterness that a lifetime of such indignities has nurtured. Her hardened heart is jolted the next day by news of the woman's death during the night—and her own guilty knowledge that she alone had heard the woman's distress but had let the hated epithet reduce her to that "animal," "outcast," "obscene" state it implies—not because it had been leveled at her but because she had let it rob her of her Christian commitment to do good to those who harm her. Even her own dreams indict Alice: "The octopus moonlight" pitilessly asserts, "Yours is the greater crime. A crime. A very great crime. It was a crime. And we were the witnesses." Like other African American writers before and since, Petry warns that prejudice delivers its most sinister harm when it saps its victims' capacity for decency and compassion and enlists them in the service of a gospel of irreparable division. In these stories Petry vividly captures the spiritual anguish of discovering that one's own grievances can weaken rather than deepen one's moral courage.

**"The Bones of Louella Brown"** • Petry's handling of white perspectives on racism is more unyielding. The absurdities into which segregationist practices lead multiracial societies (including the pseudosciences hunting frantically for physical evidence of racial "difference") are lampooned in "The Bones of Louella Brown." The most prestigious family in Massachusetts, the Bedfords, find their plans to build a chapel for its deceased members compromised when an undertaker's assistant confuses the bones of an African American maid with the sole noblewoman in their clan and, because of the "shocking" similarities of hair, teeth, height, and bone mass between the two skeletons, cannot differentiate the two. That alone is newsworthy enough to attract a Boston reporter sniffing for scandal, but the story gets juicier when it becomes clear there is every likelihood that the segregation that has been a hallmark of the cemetery in question will be permanently breached once it can no longer guarantee that "black" bones will not commingle in the same park with "white" bones. After Mrs. Brown makes a series of ghostly visitations to principals in the story, they decide to acknowledge the truth with an epitaph explaining that either woman (or both) may lie in the crypt, along with the admission of their common humanity: "They both wore the breastplate of faith and love, and for a helmet, the hope of salvation." Here too Petry moves her reader beyond social contexts and into metaphysical ones by reminding readers that this story of dry bones (an unmistakable homage to a favorite trope of black oral tradition) is also a meditation on mortality itself, which exposes such preoccupation with earthly pecking orders for the consummate folly it is.

**"The Migraine Workers"** • "The Migraine Workers" offers another example of white protagonists brought up short in the knowledge of their moral blindness in following the unquestioned attitudes of a lifetime. Pedro Gonzalez, proud owner of a successful truck stop, suddenly finds himself staring into a trailer full of migrant laborers exuding a human misery more palpable than anything he has ever encountered. Outraged by the black driver, who blithely explains how he usually hides such scenes from public scrutiny, Pedro feeds the people with the surplus food left on his premises by other haulers. When he later discovers that an elderly man from the crew has hidden himself in the area and is living off what he can scavenge from the truckstop, his first impulse is to have the man removed by the police. It is only when his longtime assistant challenges his callousness and points to the resources they could easily spare for the man's upkeep that Pedro realizes how his own fleshy body indicts him of complicity in a system of polarized haves and have-nots: migraine-producing epiphanies indeed in the land of equal opportunity.

**"Mother Africa"** • Other stories in the collection evoke the mysterious private centers of grief hidden in the human heart: "Olaf and His Girl Friend" and "Solo on the Drums" show Petry's interest in African American music as an exquisite, untranslatable evocation of that pain. "Mother Africa" introduces Emanuel Turner, another of Petry's junk men, whose business indicts the acquisitive mandate of American consumer culture. Years earlier, the loss of his wife and baby in childbirth had robbed him of any further desire for self-improvement; as a junk dealer he is free from anxious adherence to other people's standards of worth or accomplishment, and because he is his own man, he is a welcome figure to those around him. All that changes when a friend blesses him with the huge sculpture of a female nude being discarded by a wealthy white woman. The statue seduces Turner back into a realm of self-conscious striving as he tries to live up to its grandeur; in the process he loses his liberty and the easy rapport he has had with his neighbors. Convinced that she is a mythic evocation of Africa itself, he resents the prudish efforts of others to clothe her as missionaries had once done to his ancestors. Thus he is stunned to learn that this dark madonna is not a black woman at all but a white woman—the oxidized metal had misled him.

By parodying the assumed black male obsession with white women in this way, Petry implies that the real hunger at work is for authentic enunciation of the African American experience, a hunger left unsatisfied when Turner hurriedly rushes to sell the piece for scrap. In succumbing to the desire to make a world fit for his queenly companion, Turner submits himself for the first time in twenty-five years to the pressures of conformity and material acquisition. Is it love which so compromises him?—or are the statue's racial associations Petry's warnings against the lure of cultural standards derived from the spiritually bankrupt spheres of white consumer capitalism? Taken together, the stories in this collection offer tantalizing variations upon Petry's most insistent themes.

*Barbara Kitt Seidman*

## Other major works

CHILDREN'S LITERATURE: *The Drugstore Cat*, 1949; *Harriet Tubman: Conductor on the Underground Railroad*, 1955; *Tituba of Salem Village*, 1964; *Legends of the Saints*, 1970.
NOVELS: *The Street*, 1946; *Country Place*, 1947; *The Narrows*, 1953.

## Bibliography

Bell, Bernard. "Ann Petry's Demythologizing of American Culture and Afro-American Character." In *Conjuring: Black Women, Fiction, and Literary Tradition*, edited by Marjorie Pryse and Hortense J. Spillers. Bloomington: Indiana University Press, 1985. Argues that Petry should be moved out of the shadow of male contemporaries such as Richard Wright to permit her fiction the proper reevaluation it deserves.
Clark, Keith. "A Distaff Dream Deferred? Ann Petry and the Art of Subversion." *African-American Review* 26 (Fall, 1992): 495-505. A study of Petry's interest in the ways black women respond to the American Dream while subverting it to their own ends.
Ervin, Hazel Arnett, and Hilary Holladay, eds. *Ann Petry's Short Fiction: Critical Essays.* Westport, Conn.: Praeger, 2004. Collection of essays addressing Petry's less studied short stories, including issues of gender, race, and folklore.
Gross, Theodore. "Ann Petry: The Novelist as Social Critic." In *Black Fiction: New Studies in the Afro-American Novel Since 1945*, edited by A. Robert Lee. New York: Barnes & Noble Books, 1980. Discussion of Petry's strong commitment to an aesthetic of social realism that puts art in the service of political, economic, and societal transformation and justice.

Hernton, Calvin. "The Significance of Ann Petry." In *The Sexual Mountain and Black Women Writers*. New York: Doubleday, 1987. Analysis of the relationship between Petry's fiction and that of contemporary black women writers, particularly in its wedding of social protest and violence.

May, Charles E., ed. *Masterplots II: Short Story Series, Revised Edition*. 8 vols. Pasadena, Calif.: Salem Press, 2004. Designed for student use, this reference set contains articles providing detailed plot summaries and analyses of four short stories by Petry: "In Darkness and Confusion" and "Like a Winding Sheet" (vol. 4), "Solo on the Drums" (vol. 7), and "The Witness" (vol. 8).

Washington, Gladys. "A World Made Cunningly: A Closer Look at Ann Petry's Short Fiction." *College Language Association Journal* 30 (September, 1986): 14-29. A critical argument for tracing Petry's important themes and their evolving nuances through her understudied short stories.

Wilson, Mark. "A *MELUS* Interview: Ann Petry—The New England Connection." *MELUS* 15 (Summer, 1988): 71-84. A discussion with Petry about her early life and the first decades of her writing career.

# Luigi Pirandello

**Born:** Girgenti (now Agrigento), Sicily, Italy; June 28, 1867
**Died:** Rome, Italy; December 10, 1936

**Principal short fiction** • *Amori senza amore*, 1894; *Beffe della morte e della vita*, 1902-1903 (2 volumes); *Quando'ero matto . . .* , 1902; *Bianche e nere*, 1904; *Erma bifronte*, 1906; *La vita nuda*, 1910; *Terzetti*, 1912; *Le due maschere*, 1914; *Erba del nostro orto*, 1915; *La trappola*, 1915; *E domani, lunedì*, 1917; *Un cavallo nella luna*, 1918; *Berecche e la guerra*, 1919; *Il carnevale dei morti*, 1919; *A Horse in the Moon and Twelve Short Stories*, 1932; *Better Think Twice About It! and Twelve Other Stories*, 1933; *The Naked Truth and Eleven Other Stories*, 1934; *Four Tales*, 1939; *The Medals, and Other Stories*, 1939; *Short Stories*, 1959; *Selected Stories*, 1964; *Short Stories*, 1964; *The Merry-Go-Round of Love and Selected Stories*, 1964.

**Other literary forms** • In addition to publishing 233 short stories, Luigi Pirandello produced several volumes of poetry, seven novels, and forty-four plays. Through his many essays, Pirandello established himself as an influential literary philosopher, commentator, and critic.

**Achievements** • In 1934, Luigi Pirandello was awarded the Nobel Prize in Literature in recognition of his lifetime achievement in all the major literary genres. Pirandello was the preeminent figure in the European revolt against the pretentiousness and sentimentality of nineteenth century Romantic literature. With compassion for the reality of human misery, he labored through more than fifty years of creative activity to present one central thesis: the bittersweet comedy of life in which sorrow and joy are inextricably commingled, the absurd contradictoriness of the human condition. He appealed to generations disillusioned by the failure of numerous revolutions designed to bring harmony within countries terrorized by the chaos of a truly world war and confounded by their own inability to establish harmony even in their personal relationships with those they loved. His tragicomic view that the paradox of human reality could be resolved only in black laughter was masterfully presented in his seminal essay *L'umorismo* (1908, revised 1920; partial translation *On Humour*, 1966, complete translation, 1974), a view that caught the attention of the literary world and gave rise to the literary movements that coalesced by midtwentieth century as absurdism and existentialism. Pirandello is recognized as a key figure in the modern exploration of the crisis of the interior life.

**Biography** • Born June 28, 1867, to wealthy parents in a small village on the island of Sicily, Luigi Pirandello was brought up with the expectation that he would work in the family sulfur-mining business. From an early age, however, he showed little interest or talent in business matters. Instead, he began writing poetry and short stories and, in 1886, persuaded his father to allow him to pursue a classical education at the University of Palermo. In 1887, he went on to the University of Rome, transferring from there to the University of Bonn, Germany, where he completed his doctorate in 1891 with a dissertation in philology: a rhetorical study of the dialect of his native Sicilian area.

At the age of twenty-seven, he entered an arranged marriage with the daughter of his father's business partner and settled in a career as a novelist and short-story writer, while teaching at a girls' academy in order to support his growing family of three children. In 1903, the emotional trauma of the failure of the family's sulfur business so affected Pirandello's wife that she became mentally unstable. For more than a dozen years, she plagued him with paranoiac jealousy, spying on his movements and raging about his every relationship both within and without the home. Pirandello devoted himself at great sacrifice to caring for her personally until, in 1919, he finally conceded to placing her in a nursing institution, where she remained until 1959.

During these same troubled years, Europe was enmeshed in the internecine destructiveness of World War I. Pirandello was torn between his dual allegiance to Germany as the land where he had so enjoyed the intellectual stimulation of his graduate studies, and his love for his homeland of Italy, which entered the war in support of France and England. His writings during the years 1903 to 1920 reflect the turmoil of his circumstances and establish his basal premise of the inability of persons to find truth and peace in an existence driven by appearances. Repeatedly, he delineated the hopelessness of his characters' willing assumption of roles to be played—of masks to be worn and so cherished that they cease to be masks at all and become the very reality of the person within.

Pirandello achieved international recognition primarily for his plays, a genre to which he turned most seriously after 1915, when a few of his earliest plays were first performed. He founded a theater company in Rome in 1925 and managed there a sort of national theater until its financial collapse in 1928. After this, he traveled and worked extensively in Europe and the United States, writing and producing drama and even spending some time in Hollywood studying cinematic form. In December, 1936, he died in Rome and was cremated, following the austere and simple service that he had requested. The world community mourned the loss of a truly great poet, painter, novelist, critical essayist, short-story writer, and dramatist.

**Analysis** • Luigi Pirandello's earliest short stories are tales of the insular environment of his native Sicily. Originally written in Sicilian dialect and later translated into Italian, they deal in naturalistic style with the traditions and customs of the peasant peoples. He admired the writings of the Italian Verists (realists) but moved beyond them in his view that reality is individual and psychologically determined. External realism was for Pirandello insufficient for the expression of internal states. He strove to transform naturalistic determinism into a broad philosophical commentary on the inner meaning of the human person, proclaiming that a single reality does not exist. All is illusion, experience is ambiguous, and each person lives behind a self-constructed mask, concealing one's essential nature and adapting to the environment for the protection of the fragile ego within. As his world experience grew, his stories, too, grew to be blends of philosophy and human emotion, brave attempts to express the inexpressible dilemma of humankind's inability to communicate honestly in a world of false appearances and deceitful words.

Pirandello's characters are victims of insecurity and self-doubt, combined with a great capacity for love. They live their lives as in a mirror, reaching always from behind a mask of reality for elusive and illusionary happiness. His characters move out from a core of circumstantial suffering, attempting to discover meaning and truth in the very suffering itself and discovering instead the perverse comedy of decep-

© The Nobel Foundation

tion upon deception—of mask upon mask. Only through ironic laughter could humankind endure such contradiction. Humor, for Pirandello, is an amalgam of laughter and tears, a coming together of the power to mock with the power to sympathize. He treats his characters with pity rather than derision for their follies and with compassion for their inescapable miseries.

Pirandello's stories appeal to the intellect searching for answers to the puzzling contradictions of life. They contain frequent asides, some long disquisitions, and occasional intellectual debates with the self. Characters seem at times to be delivering speeches for the author rather than revealing themselves through action. The narrative line seems fragmented and convoluted, with the reader's interest not drawn steadily along with the unfolding plot but instead concentrated on particular discrete moments of paradox and inversion of fortune.

All of this comes to the non-Italian reader in translations that may seem tedious because of the double problem of language and cultural differences. Since he was chiefly known as a dramatist, Pirandello's stories have been overlooked, many never translated, and often even these few translations are questionable renderings of his thought rather than of his rhetoric. Nevertheless, those few tales that are available will give the thoughtful reader a sampling of the philosophy and view of life of a writer whose works provide a bridge from nineteenth century Romanticism, on through realism, to twentieth century relativism.

**"Sunlight and Shadow"** • Among Pirandello's earliest short stories is "Sole e ombra" ("Sunlight and Shadow"), a tale of the suicide of an elderly gentleman, Ciunna, who has stolen money from the company for which he works in order to help his poverty-stricken son and his young family. On the day after the theft, Ciunna plans to journey to the nearby coastal town where he will throw himself into the sea, thereby escaping judgment and guaranteeing that his son may keep the stolen money.

Here, Pirandello uses the unusual technique of extended "dialogue soliloquies." Ciunna walks about the street of his village on the night of the theft, carrying on vocalized conversations with the inspector who will discover his crime the following day. He speaks also with his son, telling of his great happiness in being able to sacrifice his life for the boy. He chats also with the chemist from whom he has received a few crystals of arsenic in preparation for his suicide.

For two weeks, Ciunna has been going about the streets muttering to himself as he formed his plan, but no one has bothered to ask what is disturbing him. He feels himself an outsider among his friends, a man alienated from others and even from himself. This sense of total alienation from life is a repeated theme in Pirandello's stories and plays, and the response of suicide—or at least the contemplation of it as a possibility for escaping life's harsh realities—is the basis of some two dozen of his better-known tales.

On the morning after the theft, Ciunna sets out by horse and carriage on his journey to the sea. As he goes through the countryside, he continues his "dialogue," greeting in a whisper the peasants he sees laboring long hours for a few coins, inviting them to join him on his journey. He calls out within himself "Let's be merry! Let's all go and throw ourselves into the sea! . . . Life's a beautiful thing and we shouldn't trouble it with the sight of us." The motif of life as a ridiculous journey of futility lived among strangers with whom one cannot communicate is a further common element of Pirandellian stories.

Ciunna's plan for death in the sea is foiled when he meets a young friend at the coast who spends the whole day with him. That evening, as he is returning to his village in the same carriage, he swallows the arsenic crystals and dies, alone and in agony, unnoticed even by the driver who is singing overhead.

**"Adrianna Takes a Trip"** • A suicide tale of a different sort is "La viaggio" ("Adrianna Takes a Trip"). Adrianna, a widow of thirteen years, lives simply with her two teenage sons in the home of her brother-in-law Cesare. It is the custom in this Sicilian mountain village that mourning for a husband is perpetual, that all widows live in seclusion and in submisiveness to some male of her own or her deceased husband's family. It was Adrianna's accepted role to live this life of repression, this pinched and narrow existence in a barren, parched land, and it was a role that she carried well.

Adrianna's marriage to her husband had been an arranged, loveless affair. He had married her to spite his older brother, who truly loved her as she had come to love him in return through the years of her widowhood. Though neither, by custom, could express their true feelings in any way, each came to understand and accommodate the masks imposed upon them by circumstances and by village expectations.

In time, Adrianna begins to experience some pain in her shoulder and chest. Local doctors advise Cesare to take her to Palermo for diagnosis. She resists the idea of such a journey, fearful of venturing beyond the village after thirty-five years of confinement there. The trip is arranged, however, and she must go despite her terror both at the newness of the experience and at the prospect of being alone with Cesare beyond the village for the first time.

After the diagnosis of a fatal tumor and the procurement of a potentially lethal medicine for her pain, Cesare prevails on Adrianna to continue their trip to the mainland for a short holiday, as is his annual custom. They journey on to Naples, Rome, and finally Venice, each city another revelation to her of the fullness of life, which can never be hers. In the course of their journey, they are at last able to express and consummate their deep love for each other. Adrianna knows, however, that they can never return to Sicily as man and wife—an action considered sacrilegious there. After a day of surrender to perfect joy together in Venice, she sends Cesare on an errand and drinks the whole of her medicine in one draft, choosing an immediate death of the body over a return to Sicily and a lingering death of the heart.

This tale shows clearly Pirandello's insight concerning women such as Adrianna, the falseness of the life that they were forced to lead, the masks that they were required to wear to hide their true selves, the masks that in turn they forced upon those around them. Adrianna and Cesare were victims of what Pirandello frequently referred to as the "reciprocity of illusion," the mutual life-lie that each human being must assume in order to survive within the black comedy of a world filled with deception and false expectations.

**"Signora Frola and Her Son-in-Law, Signor Ponza"** • Adrianna's refusal to continue the mutual deception required by her life circumstances stands in sharp contrast to the positions of the protagonists of "La signora Frola e il signor Ponza, suo genero" ("Signora Frola and Her Son-in-Law, Signor Ponza"). One of Pirandello's most popular and typical tales, it is a highly compressed comic presentation of multiple planes of illusion and reality, a trenchant satire on pious busybodies and their rationalization of gross curiosity. More than that, however, it is his clearest statement of the ironic comedy of humankind's search for the one truth among the many truths that make up the reality of interrelationships and of the compassionate necessity of supporting one another's mutual deceits.

The plot is both simple and complex: A husband, wife, and mother-in-law have come to a small town where their background is unknown. Local gossips are eager to solve the mystery of their past and to discover why the two women are maintained in separate households by the husband, Signor Ponza, and why he visits his mother-in-law daily but apparently does not allow her to visit with her daughter except through shouted conversations from courtyard to a third-floor window and through occasional letters. First the husband and then the mother-in-law explain their unusual arrangement, each stating that the other is mad and under a delusion concerning the true identity of the wife: Signor Ponza declares her to be his second wife, taken after the death of Signora Frola's daughter, who had been his first wife, a death that her mother has never accepted and has convinced herself never happened; Signora Frola maintains that the woman is her own daughter and Ponza's only wife, though married to him in a second ceremony after a serious illness of a year's duration during which time he convinced himself that she was dead.

Strangely, each of these two is aware of the other's version of the truth, and not only aware of it but also at pains to help maintain the other's belief in order to preserve their carefully constructed arrangement for living with their mutual tragedy. To believe either of the stories would provide an adequate explanation of the mysterious relationship among the three. To have two apparently "real" explanations, however, is not acceptable to the townspeople, who are bent on discovering "the truth"—even though both the husband and the mother-in-law beseech them to drop their investigation, as further probing can only cause deeper suffering for the little family.

Here, Pirandello illustrates the immutable failure of the desire for truth in a world where individuals know so little of themselves that they can never hope to know the full reality of others. He would have his reader accept the *construziones*, the masks that members of the family have created as a protection from the encroachment of a third reality too terrible to realize. This tale is a Pirandellian conundrum in which nothing is as it seems. Perceptions are not reality; apparent reality may be no more than perceptions. Here, as in all of his works, Pirandello holds that life itself strives to give the perfect illusion of reality. People are all make-believe. Their pretense is their reality, and that is the horror. Through such depiction of ordinary characters enmeshed in the chance circumstances of life and sharing compassionate, redeeming love, Pirandello accomplishes in his short fiction universal statements of lasting human value.

*Gabrielle Rowe*

## Other major works

PLAYS: *La morsa,* pb. 1898 (as *L'epilogo,* pr. 1910; *The Vise,* 1928); *Scamandro,* pb. 1909, pr. 1928; *Lumìe di Sicilia,* pr. 1910, pb. 1911 (*Sicilian Limes,* 1921); *Il dovere del medico,* pb. 1912, pr. 1913 (*The Doctor's Duty,* 1928); *Se non così . . .,* pr. 1915, pb. 1916; *All'uscita,* pr. 1916, pb. 1922 (*At the Gate,* 1928); *Liolà,* pr. 1916, pb. 1917 (English translation, 1952); *Pensaci, Giacomino!,* pr. 1916, pb. 1917; *Così è (se vi pare),* pr. 1917, pb. 1918 (*Right You Are [If You Think So],* 1922); *Il berretto a sonagli,* pr. 1917, pb. 1920 (*Cap and Bells,* 1957); *Il piacere dell'onestà,* pr. 1917, pb. 1918 (*The Pleasure of Honesty,* 1923); *La giara,* pr. 1917, pb. 1925 (*The Jar,* 1928); *Il giuoco delle parti,* pr. 1918, pb. 1919 (*The Rules of the Game,* 1959); *La patente,* pb. 1918, pr. 1919 (*The License,* 1964); *Ma non è una cosa seria,* pr. 1918, pb. 1919; *L'innesto,* pr. 1919, pb. 1921; *L'uomo, la bestia, e la virtù grave;,* pr., pb. 1919 (*Man, Beast, and Virtue,* 1989); *Come prima, meglio di prima,* pr. 1920, pb. 1921; *La Signora Morli, una e due,* pr. 1920, pb. 1922; *Tutto per bene,* pr., pb. 1920 (*All for the Best,* 1960); *Sei personaggi in cerca d'autore,* pr., pb. 1921 (*Six Characters in Search of an Author,* 1922); *Enrico IV,* pr., pb. 1922 (*Henry IV,* 1923); *L'imbecille,* pr. 1922, pb. 1926 (*The Imbecile,* 1928); *Vestire gli ignudi,* pr. 1922, pb. 1923 (*Naked,* 1924); *L'altro figlio,* pr. 1923, pb. 1925 (*The House with the Column,* 1928); *L'uomo dal fiore in bocca,* pr. 1923. pb. 1926 (*The Man with the Flower in His Mouth,* 1928); *La vita che ti diedi,* pr. 1923, pb. 1924 (*The Life I Gave You,* 1959); *Ciascuno a suo modo,* pr., pb. 1924 (*Each in His Own Way,* 1923); *Sagra del Signore della nave,* pb. 1924, pr. 1925 (*Our Lord of the Ship,* 1928); *Diana e la Tuda,* pr. 1926 (in Switzerland), pr., pb. 1927 (*Diana and Tudo,* 1950); *Bellavita,* pr. 1927, pb. 1928 (English translation, 1964); *L'amica della mogli,* pr., pb. 1927 (*The Wives' Friend,* 1949); *La nuova colonia,* pr., pb. 1928 (*The New Colony,* 1958); *The One-Act Plays of Luigi Pirandello,* pb. 1928; *Lazzaro,* pr., pb. 1929 (*Lazarus,* 1952); *O di uno o di nessuno,* pr., pb. 1929; *Sogno (ma forse no),* pb. 1929, pr. 1936 (*I'm Dreaming, but Am I?,* 1964); *Come tu mi vuoi,* pr., pb. 1930 (*As You Desire Me,* 1931); *Questa sera si recita a soggetto,* pr., pb. 1930 (*Tonight We Improvise,* 1932); *I giganti della montagna,* act 1 pb. 1931, act 2 pb. 1934, act 3 pr. 1937 (*The Mountain Giants,* 1958); *Trovarsi,* pr., pb. 1932 (*To Find Oneself,* 1943); *Quando si è qualcuno,* pr. 1933 (*When Someone Is Somebody,* 1958); *La favola del figlio cambiato,* pr., pb. 1934; *Non si sa come,* pr. 1934, pb. 1935 (*No One Knows How,* 1960); *Naked Masks: Five Plays,* pb. 1952.

NOVELS: *L'esclusa,* 1901 (*The Outcast,* 1925); *Il turno,* 1902 (*The Merry-Go-Round of Love,* 1964); *Il fu Mattia Pascal,* 1904 (*The Late Mattia Pascal,* 1923); *Suo marito,* 1911, revised 1941 (*Her Husband,* 2000); *I vecchi e i giovani,* 1913 (*The Old and the Young,* 1928); *Si gira . . .,* 1916 (*Shoot! The Notebooks of Serafino Gubbio, Cinematograph Operator,* 1926); *Uno, nessuno, centomila,* 1925 (*One, None and a Hundred Thousand,* 1933); *Tutti i romanzi,* 1941 (collected novels).

MISCELLANEOUS: *Opere,* 1966.

NONFICTION: *Arte e scienze,* 1908; *L'umorismo,* 1908, revised 1920 (partial translation *On Humour,* 1966; complete translation, 1974); *Saggi,* 1939.

POETRY: *Mal giocondo,* 1889; *Pasqua di Gea,* 1891; *Pier Gudrò,* 1894; *Elegie renane,* 1895; *Elegie romane,* 1896 (translation of Johann von Goethe's *Römische Elegien*); *Scamandro,* 1909 (dramatic poem); *Fuori de chiave,* 1912; *Saggi,* 1939.

## Bibliography

Alessio, A., D. Pietropaolo, and G. Sanguinetti-Katz, eds. *Pirandello and the Modern Theatre.* Ottawa, Ont.: Canadian Society for Italian Studies, 1992. Selection from the proceedings of the International Conference on Pirandello and the Modern Theatre, held in Toronto in November, 1990. Includes bibliography.

Bassanese, Fiora A. "Luigi Pirandello." In *Critical Survey of Long Fiction, Revised Edition,* edited by Carl Rollyson. Vol. 5. Pasadena, Calif.: Salem Press, 2000. Analysis of Pirandello's longer fictional works that may offer insights into his short fiction.

_____. *Understanding Luigi Pirandello.* Columbia: University of South Carolina Press, 1997. Introduction to Pirandello's work, focusing largely on his thought and the relationship of his life to his work.

Biasin, Gian-Paolo, and Manuela Gieri, eds. *Luigi Pirandello: Contemporary Perspectives.* Toronto: University of Toronto Press, 1999. This collection of essays provides modern perspectives on the work of Pirandello, including his quest for truth, his use of theater-within-the-theater, and use of characters and actors on the stage.

Caesar, Ann. *Characters and Authors in Luigi Pirandello.* Oxford, England: Clarendon Press, 1998. Good study focusing on Pirandello's characters. Includes bibliographical references and an index.

Dashwood, Julie, ed. *Luigi Pirandello: The Theater of Paradox.* Lewiston, N.Y.: Edwin Mellen Press, 1996. This volume examines the works of Pirandello, particularly his creation of paradoxical scenes in his drama. Includes bibliography and index.

DiGaetani, John Louis, ed. *A Companion to Pirandello Studies.* New York: Greenwood Press, 1991. Comprehensive volume, twenty-seven essays on Pirandello's biography and work, with an excellent introduction and several appendices, including production histories and an extensive bibliography.

Kleine-Ahlbrandt, Wm. Laird. "War." In *Masterplots II: Short Story Series,* edited by Charles E. May. Rev. ed. Vol. 8. Pasadena, Calif.: Salem Press, 2004. Analysis of "War" with sections on themes and meaning and style and technique. Also includes a detailed synopsis of the story.

O'Grady, Deidre. *Piave, Boito, Pirandello: From Romantic Realism to Modernism.* Lewiston, N.Y.: Edwin Mellen Press, 2000. O'Grady traces the development of Italian literature, from romantic realism to modernism, examining the works of Pirandello, Arrigo Boito, and Francesco Maria Piave, among others. Includes bibliography and index.

Radcliff-Umstead, Douglas. *The Mirror of Our Anguish: A Study of Luigi Pirandello's Narrative Writing.* Madison, N.J.: Fairleigh Dickinson University Press, 1978. The introductory segment on Pirandello's philosophy of literature and its role in literary history is excellent. Of particular interest is the study of his short fiction complemented by a full treatment of his rhetorical style and themes. Extensive bibliography, index.

Stella, M. John. *Self and Self-Compromise in the Narratives of Pirandello and Moravia.* New York: P. Lang, 2000. Stella examines the concept of self in literature, comparing and contrasting the works of Pirandello and Alberto Moravia.

# Edgar Allan Poe

**Born:** Boston, Massachusetts; January 19, 1809
**Died:** Baltimore, Maryland; October 7, 1849

**Principal short fiction** • *Tales of the Grotesque and Arabesque,* 1840; *The Prose Romances of Edgar Allan Poe,* 1843; *Tales,* 1845; *The Short Fiction of Edgar Allan Poe,* 1976 (Stuart Levine and Susan Levine, editors).

**Other literary forms** • During his short literary career, Edgar Allan Poe produced a large quantity of writing, most of which was not collected in book form during his lifetime. He published one novel, *The Narrative of Arthur Gordon Pym* (1838), and several volumes of poetry, the most famous of which is *The Raven, and Other Poems* (1845). Poe earned his living mainly as a writer and as an editor of magazines. For magazines, he wrote reviews, occasional essays, meditations, literary criticism, and a variety of different kinds of journalism, as well as poetry and short fiction.

**Achievements** • During his life, Edgar Allan Poe was a figure of controversy and so became reasonably well known in literary circles. Two of his works were recognized with prizes: "Manuscript Found in a Bottle" and "The Gold-Bug." "The Raven," his most famous poem, created a sensation when it was published and became something of a best-seller. After his death, Poe's reputation grew steadily—though in the United States opinion remained divided—until by the middle of the twentieth century he had clear status as an author of worldwide importance. Poe's achievements may be measured in terms of what he has contributed to literature and of how his work influenced later culture.

Poe was accomplished in fiction, poetry, and criticism, setting standards in all three that distinguish him from most of his American contemporaries. In fiction, he is credited with inventing the conventions of the classical detective story, beginning the modern genre of science fiction, and turning the conventions of gothic fiction to the uses of high art in stories such as "The Fall of the House of Usher." He was also an accomplished humorist and satirist. In poetry, he produced a body of work that is respected throughout the world and a few poems that have endured as classics, notably "The Raven," as well as several poems that, in part because of their sheer verbal beauty, have persistently appealed to the popular imagination, such as "The Bells" and "Annabel Lee." In criticism, Poe is among the first to advocate and demonstrate methods of textual criticism that came into their own in the twentieth century, notably in his essay "The Philosophy of Composition," in which he analyzed with remarkable objectivity the process by which "The Raven" was built in order to produce a specified effect in its readers.

Poe's influence on later culture was pervasive. Nearly every important American writer after Poe shows signs of his influence, especially when working in the gothic mode or with grotesque humor. The French, Italians, and writers in Spanish and Portuguese in the Americas acknowledge and demonstrate their debts to Poe in technique and vision. Only to begin to explore Poe's influence on twentieth century music and film would be a major undertaking. In terms of his world reputation, Poe stands

Library of Congress

with William Faulkner and perhaps T. S. Eliot as one of the most influential authors of the United States.

**Biography** • Edgar Allan Poe was born in Boston on January 19, 1809. His parents, David and Elizabeth Arnold Poe, were actors at a time when the profession was not widely respected in the United States. David was making a success in acting when alcohol addiction brought an end to his career. He deserted his family a year after Edgar's birth; Elizabeth died a year later in 1811, leaving Edgar an orphan in Richmond, Virginia. There, he was taken in by John Allan, who educated him well in England and the United States. Poe was a sensitive and precocious child; during his teens, his relations with his foster father declined. Stormy relations continued until Allan's first wife died and his second wife had children. Once it became unlikely that he would inherit anything significant from the wealthy Allan, Poe, at the age of twenty-one, having already published a volume of poetry, began a literary career.

From 1831 to 1835, more or less dependent on his Poe relatives, he worked in Baltimore, writing stories and poems, a few of which were published. In 1835, he secretly married his cousin, Virginia Clemm, when she was thirteen. From 1835 to 1837, he was assistant editor of *The Southern Literary Messenger,* living on a meager salary, tending to drink enough to disappoint the editor, publishing his fiction, and making a national reputation as a reviewer of books. When he was fired, he moved with his wife (by then the marriage was publicly acknowledged) and her mother to New York City, where he lived in poverty, selling his writing for the next two years. Though he published *The Narrative of Arthur Gordon Pym* in 1838, it brought him no income. He moved to Philadelphia that same year and for several months continued to live on only a small income from stories and other magazine pieces. In 1839, he became coeditor of *Burton's Gentleman's Magazine.* Before drinking led to his losing this job, he wrote and published some of his best fiction, such as "The Fall of the House of Usher." He took another editing position with *Graham's Magazine* that lasted about a year. He then lived by writing and working at occasional jobs. In 1844, he went with his family back to New York City. His wife, Virginia, had been seriously ill, and her health was declining. In New York, he wrote for newspapers. In 1845, he published "The Raven" and *Tales,* both of which were well received ("The Raven" was a popular success), though again his income from them was small. During the early nineteenth century, an author could not easily earn a satisfactory income from writing alone, in part because of the lack of international copyright laws. He was able to purchase a new weekly, *The Broadway Journal,* but it failed in 1846.

After 1845, Poe was famous, and his income, though unstable, was a little more dependable. His life, however, did not go smoothly. He was to some extent lionized in literary circles, but his combination of desperation for financial support with alcoholism and a combative temper kept him from dealing well with being a "star." Virginia died in 1847, and Poe was seriously ill for much of the next year. In 1849, he found himself in Richmond, and for a few months he seemed quite well. His Richmond relatives received and cared for him kindly, and he stopped drinking. In October, however, while on a trip, he paused in Baltimore, became drunk, was found unconscious, and was carried to a local hospital, where he died on October 7, 1849.

**Analysis** • The variety of Edgar Allan Poe's short fiction cannot be conveyed fully in a short introduction. Though he is best known for his classics of gothic horror such as "The Fall of the House of Usher" and his portraits of madmen and grotesques such as "The Tell-Tale Heart" and "The Cask of Amontillado," he is also the author of detective stories, "The Purloined Letter"; science fiction, *The Narrative of Arthur Gordon Pym*; parodies, "The Premature Burial"; satires, "The Man That Was Used Up"; social and political fiction, "The System of Dr. Tarr and Prof. Fether"; and a variety of kinds of humor, "Diddling Considered as One of the Exact Sciences" and "Hop-Frog."

Three stories that illustrate some of this variety while offering insight into Poe's characteristic themes are "A Descent into the Maelström," "The Purloined Letter," and "The Fall of the House of Usher." Among Poe's central themes is an emphasis on the mysteries of the self, of others, of nature, and of the universe. His stories usually function in part to undercut the kinds of easy optimism and certainty that were characteristic of popular thought in his time.

**"A Descent into the Maelström"** • "A Descent into the Maelström," which first appeared in *Graham's Magazine* in May, 1841, and was collected in *Tales*, opens with a declaration of mystery: "The ways of God in Nature, as in Providence, are not as our ways; nor are the models that we frame any way commensurate to the vastness, profundity, and unsearchableness of His works, which have a depth in them greater than the well of Democritus." In using this epigraph, slightly altered from the seventeenth century English essayist Joseph Glanvill, Poe announces several motifs for the story that follows. One of these is the mystery of how God acts and, therefore, may be revealed in nature. Another is inadequacy of humanly devised models for explaining nature or God's presence in nature. Yet another is the idea of the multiple senses of depth, not merely the physical depth of a well or a maelstrom, but also the metaphorical depths of a mystery, of God, of nature, of God's manifestation in nature.

The story is relatively simple in its outline, though interestingly complicated by its frame. In the frame, the narrator visits a remote region of Norway to look upon the famous maelstrom, an actual phenomenon described in contemporary reference books that were Poe's sources. There, he encounters an apparently retired fisherman, who guides him to a view of the whirlpool and who then tells the story of how he survived being caught in it. In the main body of the story, the guide explains how a sudden hurricane and a stopped watch caused him and his two brothers to be caught by the maelstrom as they attempted to return from a routine, if risky, fishing trip. He explains what the experience was like and how he managed to survive even though his boat and his brothers were lost. Poe carefully arranges the frame and the fisherman's narration to emphasize his themes.

The frame narrator is a somewhat comic character. The guide leads him to what he calls a little cliff and calmly leans over its edge to point out the sights, but the narrator is terrified by the cliff itself: "In truth so deeply was I excited by the perilous position of my companion, that I fell at full length upon the ground, clung to the shrubs around me, and dared not even glance upward at the sky—while I struggled in vain to divest myself of the idea that the very foundations of the mountain were in danger from the fury of the winds." On one level this is high comedy. The narrator professes to be worried about his companion's safety but cannot help revealing that he is personally terrified, and his resulting posture contrasts humorously with the equanimity of his guide. On another level, however, Poe is also suggesting at least two serious ideas. The narrator's description of the cliff, with its sheer drop of sixteen hundred feet, should remind most readers that in a strong wind, they would feel and behave much the same as the narrator. This realization makes the next idea even more significant: The pose the narrator has adopted is pointedly a pose of worship drawn from the Old Testament of the Bible. The narrator abases himself full-length, not daring to look up while clinging to the earth. He behaves as if he is in the presence of God, and this is before the tide turns and the maelstrom forms. The tame scene evokes in the narrator the awe of a mortal in a god's presence; when he sees the maelstrom, he feels he is looking into the heart of awesome, divine mystery.

When the maelstrom forms, when the earth really trembles and the sea boils and the heavens shout and the guide asks him what he sees and hears, he replies, "this *can* be nothing else than the great whirlpool of the Maelström." The narrator continues to see it as a more than natural phenomenon. Unable to accept the naturalistic account of it offered by the *Encyclopædia Britannica*, he is drawn instead by the power that it exerts over his imagination to see it as a manifestation of occult powers, an eruption of supernatural power into the natural world. This view forms the context within which the guide tells his tale.

An important feature of the guide's story is the contrast between his sense of chaotic threat and his repeated perceptions that suggest an ordered purpose within this chaos. It almost seems at times as if the episode were designed to teach the fisherman a lesson that he would then pass on through the narrator to the reader, though conveying a simple moral seems not to be the fisherman's purpose. For the fisherman, it was good fortune, assisted perhaps by a kind Providence, that allowed him to find a means of escape once his fishing boat had been sucked into the gigantic whirlpool and had begun its gradual descent toward the rushing foam at the bottom of the funnel of water. The main sign of design in these events is that just as the boat is blown into the whirlpool by the sudden and violent hurricane, a circle opens in the black clouds, revealing a bright moon that illuminates the scene of terror. This event makes the weather into a symmetrical picture: An inverted funnel of clouds ascending to an opening where the moon appears, over a funnel of whirling seawater descending into an obscured opening where a rainbow appears, "like that narrow and tottering bridge which Musselmen say is the only pathway between Time and Eternity." This view of a tremendous overarching cosmic order composing a scene of mortal chaos produces other kinds of order that help to save the fisherman.

Bewitched by the beauty that he sees in this scene, the fisherman, like the narrator on the cliff-top, gains control of himself, loses his fear, and begins to look around, merely for the sake of enjoying it: "I began to reflect how magnificent a thing it was to die in such a manner . . . in view of so wonderful a manifestation of God's power." Studying the beauty, he regains his self-possession, and in possession of his faculties, no longer terrified, he begins to understand how the whirlpool works, and he learns that different shapes and sizes of objects descend its sides at different rates. Attaching himself to a cylindrical barrel, he slows his descent enough that instead of going to the bottom and so across the mystical bridge he envisions there, he is borne up until the maelstrom stops and he finds himself again in comparatively calm water.

For the fisherman, his narrow escape is a tale of wonder, luck, and divine mercy. For the reader, however, carefully prepared by the narrator and supported by elements in the fisherman's story upon which he does not comment, the story also illustrates the inscrutability of the God that may be visible in nature. This is not a God who operates nature solely for human benefit, though he has given humanity reason, aesthetic sense, and the power of faith that can allow people to survive in, and even enjoy, the terrors of nature. The fisherman's brother, who survives the onslaught of the storm to experience the maelstrom with him, is never able to move by means of faith or the appreciation of beauty beyond his terror; this makes his despair at impending death insuperable, so he cannot discover a way of escape or even attempt the one offered by the fisherman.

Though not necessarily unique in this respect, the United States has throughout its history been a nation where large groups of people tended to assume that they had discovered the one truth that explained the universe and history and where it seemed easy to believe that a benevolent God had designed a manifest destiny for the nation and, perhaps, for humankind as a whole if led by American thought. Poe was among those who distrusted such thinking deeply. "A Descent into the Maelström" is one of many Poe stories in which part of the effect is to undercut such assumptions in his readers by emphasizing the mysteries of nature and the inadequacy of human ideas to encompass them, much less encompass the divinity of which nature might be a manifestation.

**"The Purloined Letter"** • Although "A Descent into the Maelström" emphasizes the inadequacy of human intelligence to comprehend God's purposes in the universe, it also emphasizes the crucial importance of people using what intelligence they have to find truth and beauty in nature and experience. "The Purloined Letter," one of Poe's best detective stories, places a greater emphasis on the nature and importance of intelligence, while still pointing at mysteries of human character. This story first appeared in two magazine versions in 1844: a shorter version in *Chamber's Edinburgh Journal* and what has become the final version in *The Gift*. It was then collected in *Tales*.

The narrator and his friend C. Auguste Dupin are smoking and meditating in Dupin's darkened library, when they are interrupted by the comical Monsieur G—, the prefect of the Paris police. The prefect tries to pretend that he is merely paying a friendly call, but he cannot help making it clear that he has come to Dupin with a troubling problem. He eventually explains that the Minister D— has managed, in the presence of an important lady, presumably the queen, to steal from her a compromising letter with which he might damage her severely by showing it to her husband. He has since been using the threat of revealing the letter to coerce the queen's cooperation in influencing policy. As the prefect repeats, to Dupin's delight, getting the letter back without publicity ought to be simple for an expert policeman. One merely finds where it is hidden and takes it back. The letter must be within easy reach of the minister to be useful, and so by minute searching of his home and by having a pretended thief waylay him, the letter should surely be found. All these things have been done with great care, and the letter has not been found. The prefect is stumped. Dupin's advice is to search again. A few weeks later, the prefect returns, still without success. Dupin then manipulates the prefect into declaring what he would pay to regain the letter, instructs him to write Dupin a check for that amount, and gives him the letter. The prefect is so astonished and gratified that he runs from the house, not even bothering to ask how Dupin has managed this feat.

The second half of the story consists of Dupin's explanation to the narrator, with a joke or two at the prefect's expense, of how he found and obtained the letter. As in Dupin's other cases, notably the famous "The Murders in the Rue Morgue," the solution involves a rigorous and seemingly miraculous application of rationality to the problem. Although in these stories Poe was establishing conventions for detection and stories about it that would flower richly in Arthur Conan Doyle's tales of Sherlock Holmes, the principles upon which Dupin works are slightly but significantly different from Holmes's principles.

One key difference is the importance of poetic imagination to the process. Most of Dupin's explanation of his procedure has to do with how one goes about estimating the character and ability of one's opponent, for understanding what the criminal may do is ultimately more important to a solution than successful deduction. It requires a kind of poet to penetrate the criminal's mind; a "mere" mathematician can make competent deductions from given ideas, as the prefect has done. It takes a combination of poet and mathematician—in short, Dupin—to solve such a crime dependably. The prefect has greatly underestimated the minister because he is known to be a poet and the prefect believes poets are fools. Dupin says that the police often fail because they assume that the criminal's intelligence mirrors their own, and therefore over- or underestimate the criminal's ability. Having established that the minister is a very cunning opponent who will successfully imagine the police response to his theft, Dupin is able to deduce quite precisely how the minister will hide the letter, by placing it very conspicuously, so as not to appear hidden at all, and by disguising it. Dupin's deduction proves exactly right, and by some careful plotting, he is able to locate and regain it.

The two main portions of the story, presenting the problem and the solution, illustrate the nature and powers of human reason. The end of the story emphasizes mystery by raising questions about morality. Although reason is a powerful instrument for solving problems and bringing about actions in the world, and solving problems is a satisfying kind of activity that makes Dupin feel proud and virtuous, his detecting occurs in a morally ambiguous world. The end of the story calls attention repeatedly to the relationship between Dupin and the Minister D—, a final quotation from a play even hinting that they could be brothers, though there is no other evidence that this is the case. Dupin claims intimate acquaintance and frequent association with the minister; indeed, these are the foundation of his inferences about the man's character and ability. They disagree, however, politically. The nature of this disagreement is not explained, but the story takes place in nineteenth century Paris, and Dupin's actions seem to support the royal family against a rebellious politician. Dupin, in leaving a disguised substitute for the regained letter, has arranged for the minister's fall from power and may even have endangered his life.

By providing this kind of information at the end, Poe raises moral and political questions, encouraging the reader to wonder whether Dupin's brilliant detection serves values of which the reader might approve. To those questions, the story offers no answers. In this way, Dupin's demonstration of a magnificent human intellect is placed in the context of moral mystery, quite unlike the tales of Sherlock Holmes and related classical detectives. On a moral level, who are Dupin and the minister, and what are the meanings of their actions with regard to the well-being of French citizens? Although Poe invented what became major conventions in detective fiction—the rational detective, his less able associate, the somewhat ridiculous police force, the solution scene—his detective stories show greater moral complexity than those of his best-known followers.

**"The Fall of the House of Usher"** • "The Fall of the House of Usher" has everything a Poe story is supposed to have according to the popular view of him: a gothic house, a terrified narrator, live burial, madness, and horrific catastrophe. One of his most popular and most discussed stories, this one has been variously interpreted by critics, provoking controversy about how to read it that remains unsettled. This story was first published in 1839, and it appeared in both of Poe's fiction collections.

The narrator journeys to the home of his boyhood chum, Roderick Usher, a man of artistic talent and generous reputation. Usher has been seriously ill and wishes the cheerful companionship of his old friend. The narrator arrives at the grimly oppressive house in its equally grim and oppressive setting, determined to be cheerful and helpful, but finds himself overmatched. The house and its environs radiate gloom, and though Usher alternates between a kind of creative mania and the blackest depression, he tends also on the whole to radiate gloom. Usher confides that he is upset in part because his twin sister, Madeline, is mortally ill. It develops, however, that the main reason Usher is depressed is that he has become in some way hypersensitive, and this sensitivity has revealed to him that his house is a living organism that is driving him toward madness. The narrator does not want to believe this, but the longer he stays in the house with Usher, the more powerfully Usher's point of view dominates him. Madeline dies and, to discourage grave robbers, Usher and the narrator temporarily place her in a coffin in a vault beneath the house. Once Madeline is dead, Usher's alternation of mood ceases, and he remains always deeply gloomy.

On his last evening at Usher, the narrator witnesses several events that seem to confirm Usher's view that the house is driving him mad. Furthermore, these confirmations seem to suggest that the house is just one in a nest of Chinese boxes, in a series of closed, walled-in enclosures that make up the physical and spiritual universe. This oft-repeated image is represented most vividly in one of Usher's paintings, what appears to be a burial vault unnaturally lit from within. This image conveys the idea of the flame of human consciousness imprisoned, as if buried alive in an imprisoning universe. The terrifying conviction of this view is one of the causes of Usher's growing madness. On the last evening, a storm seems to enclose the house as if it were inside a box of wind and cloud, on which the house itself casts an unnatural light. The narrator tries to comfort both himself and Usher by reading a story, but the sound effects described in the story are echoed in reality in the house. Usher, as his reason crumbles, interprets these sounds as Madeline, not really dead, breaking through various walls behind which she has been placed—her coffin and the vault—until finally, Usher claims, she is standing outside the door of the room where they are reading. The door opens, perhaps supernaturally, and there she stands. The narrator watches the twins fall against each other and collapse; he rushes outside only to see the house itself collapse into its reflection in the pool that stands before it, this last event taking place under the unnatural light of a blood-red moon.

Such a summary helps to reveal one of the main sources of conflicting interpretation. How could such events really occur? Is not this a case of an unreliable narrator, driven toward a horrific vision by some internal conflicts that might be inferred from the content of the vision? This viewpoint has tended to dominate critical discussion of the story, provoking continuous opposition from more traditionally minded readers who argue that "The Fall of the House of Usher" is a supernatural tale involving occult forces of some kind. Both modes of interpretation have their problems, and so neither has been able to establish itself as superior to the other.

One of the main difficulties encountered by both sides is accounting for the way that the narrator tells his story. He seems involved in the same sort of problem that the community of literary critics experiences. He is represented as telling the story of this experience some time after the events took place. He insists that there are no supernatural elements in his story, that everything that happened at the House of Usher can be accounted for in a naturalistic way. In this respect, he is like the narrator of "A Descent into the Maelström." He "knows" that the natural world operates according to regular "natural" laws, but when he actually sees the whirlpool, his imagination responds involuntarily with the conviction that this is something supernatural. Likewise, the narrator of "The Fall of the House of Usher" is convinced that the world can be understood in terms of natural law and, therefore, that what has happened to him at Usher either could not have happened or must have a natural explanation. Like the narrator of "The Black Cat," another of Poe's most famous stories, this narrator hopes that by telling the story, perhaps again, he will arrive at an acceptable explanation or that his listener will confirm his view of the events.

Perhaps "The Fall of the House of Usher" is a kind of trap, set to enmesh readers in the same sort of difficulty in which the narrator finds himself. If this is the case, then the story functions in a way consistent with Poe's theme of the inadequacy of models constructed by human intelligence to map the great mysteries of life and the universe. The narrator says he has had an experience that he cannot explain and that points toward an inscrutable universe, one that might be conceived as designed to drive humans mad if they find themselves compelled to comprehend it. Likewise, in reading the story, the reader has an experience that finally cannot be explained, that seems designed to drive readers mad if they insist upon achieving a final view of its wholeness. The story itself may provide an experience that demonstrates the ultimate inadequacy of human reason to understand the mysteries of creation.

Although Poe wrote a variety of stories, he is best remembered for his tales of terror and madness. His popular literary reputation is probably a distorted view of Poe, both as person and as artist. Although he was tragically addicted to alcohol and while he did experience considerable difficulty in a milieu that was not particularly supportive, he was nevertheless an accomplished artist whose work, especially when viewed as a whole, is by no means the mere outpouring of a half-mad, anguished soul. To look closely at any of his best work is to see ample evidence of a writer in full artistic control of his materials, calculating his effects with a keen eye. Furthermore, to examine the range and quantity of his writing, to attend to the quantity of his humor—of which there are interesting examples even in "The Fall of the House of Usher"—to notice the beauty of his poetry, to study the learned intelligence of his best criticism—in short, to see Poe whole—must lead to the recognition that his accomplishments far exceed the narrow view implied by his popular reputation.

*Terry Heller*

## Other major works

PLAY: *Politian*, pb. 1835-1836.

NOVELS: *The Narrative of Arthur Gordon Pym*, 1838.

MISCELLANEOUS: *The Complete Works of Edgar Allan Poe*, 1902 (17 volumes); *Collected Works of Edgar Allan Poe*, 1969, 1978 (3 volumes).

NONFICTION: *The Letters of Edgar Allan Poe*, 1948; *Literary Criticism of Edgar Allan Poe*, 1965; *Essays and Reviews*, 1984.

POETRY: *Tamerlane, and Other Poems*, 1827; *Al Aaraaf, Tamerlane, and Minor Poems*, 1829; *Poems*, 1831; *The Raven, and Other Poems*, 1845; *Eureka: A Prose Poem*, 1848; *Poe: Complete Poems*, 1959; *Poems*, 1969 (volume 1 of *Collected Works*).

## Bibliography

Brown, Arthur A. "Literature and the Impossibility of Death: Poe's 'Berenice.'" *Nineteenth-Century Literature* 50 (March, 1996): 448-463. Argues that Poe's stories of the dead coming back to life and of premature burial dramatize the horror of the impossibility of dying.

Burluck, Michael L. *Grim Phantasms: Fear in Poe's Short Fiction*. New York: Garland, 1993. Considers the question of why Poe focused primarily on portraying weird events in his stories. Discusses the gothic conventions Poe used to achieve his effects. Argues that neither drugs nor insanity are responsible for Poe's gothic tales, but rather they were a carefully thought out literary tactic meant to appeal to current public taste and the general human reaction to fear.

Carlson, Eric, ed. *Critical Essays on Edgar Allan Poe*. Boston: G. K. Hall, 1987. Offers a cross section of writing about Poe from the 1830's to the 1980's. Many of the essays deal with short stories, illustrating a variety of interpretive strategies.

Crisman, William. "Poe's Dupin as Professional, the Dupin Stories as Serial Text." *Studies in American Fiction* 23 (Autumn, 1995): 215-229. Part of a special section on Poe. Argues that the Dupin stories bear out his mesmeric revelation that mind forms one continuum with inert substance.

Frank, Lawrence. "'The Murders in the Rue Morgue': Edgar Allan Poe's Evolutionary Reverie." *Nineteenth-Century Literature* 50 (September, 1995): 168-188. Claims that Poe's story explores the implications of the nebular hypothesis and did not reinforce the prevailing orthodoxy; rather it may have been in the service of an emerging Darwinian perspective.

Kennedy, J. Gerald. *A Historical Guide to Edgar Allan Poe*. New York: Oxford University Press, 2001. Considers the tensions between Poe's otherworldly settings and his representations of violence, delivers a capsule biography situating Poe in his historical context, and addresses topics such as Poe and the American publishing industry, Poe's sensationalism, his relationships to gender constructions, and Poe and American privacy. Includes bibliographical essay, chronology of Poe's life, bibliography, illustrations, and index.

May, Charles E. *Edgar Allan Poe: A Study of the Short Fiction*. Boston: Twayne, 1991. Introduction to Poe's short stories that attempts to place them with the nineteenth century short narrative tradition and within the context of Poe's aesthetic theory. Suggests Poe's contributions to the short story in terms of his development of detective fiction, fantasy, satire, and self-reflexivity. Includes passages from Poe's narrative theory and three essays by other critics illustrating a variety of critical approaches.

_____, ed. *Masterplots II: Short Story Series, Revised Edition.* 8 vols. Pasadena, Calif.: Salem Press, 2004. Designed for student use, this reference set contains articles providing detailed plot summaries and analyses of thirteen short stories by Poe: "The Black Cat" and "The Cask of Amontillado" (vol. 1), "A Descent into the Maelström" (vol. 2), "The Fall of the House of Usher" and "The Gold-Bug" (vol. 3), "Ligeia" (vol. 4), "The Masque of the Red Death," "Ms. Found in a Bottle," "The Murders in the Rue Morgue" (vol. 5), "The Pit and the Pendulum" and "The Purloined Letter" (vol. 6), "The Tell-Tale Heart" (vol. 7), and "William Wilson" (vol. 8).

Peeples, Scott. *Edgar Allan Poe Revisited.* New York: Twayne, 1998. Introductory critical study of selected works and a short biography of Poe. Includes bibliographical references and index.

Sova, Dawn B. *Edgar Allen Poe, A to Z: The Essential Reference to His Life and Work.* New York: Facts On File, 2001. Thorough guide to the life and works of Poe.

Thoms, Peter. *Detection and Its Designs: Narrative and Power in Nineteenth-Century Detective Fiction.* Athens: Ohio University Press, 1998. Study of early detective fiction from readings of Poe's Dupin stories to Arthur Conan Doyle's *The Hound of the Baskervilles.*

Whalen, Terence. *Edgar Allan Poe and the Masses: The Political Economy of Literature in Antebellum America.* Princeton, N.J.: Princeton University Press, 1999. Brilliant study of Poe that provides an inventive understanding of his works and his standing in American literature.

# Katherine Anne Porter

**Born:** Indian Creek, Texas; May 15, 1890
**Died:** Silver Spring, Maryland; September 18, 1980

**Principal short fiction** • *Flowering Judas, and Other Stories*, 1930; *Hacienda*, 1934; *Noon Wine*, 1937; *Pale Horse, Pale Rider: Three Short Novels*, 1939; *The Leaning Tower, and Other Stories*, 1944; *The Old Order*, 1944; *The Collected Stories of Katherine Anne Porter*, 1965.

**Other literary forms** • Katherine Anne Porter wrote, in addition to short stories, one novel, *Ship of Fools* (1962), parts of which were published separately from 1947 to 1959, in such magazines and journals as *The Sewanee Review, Harper's*, and *Mademoiselle*. She wrote essays of various kinds, some of which she published under the title of one of them, *The Days Before* (1952); these included critical analyses of Thomas Hardy's fiction and biographical studies of Ford Madox Ford and Gertrude Stein. Porter was a reporter with unsigned journalism for the Fort Worth weekly newspaper *The Critic* in 1917 and the Denver *Rocky Mountain News* in 1918-1919. Early in her career, she worked on a critical biography of Cotton Mather, which she never finished; she did, however, publish parts in 1934, 1940, 1942, and 1946. Her few poems and most of her nonfictional prose have been collected in *The Collected Essays and Occasional Writings* (1970) under the following headings: "Critical," "Personal and Particular," "Biographical," "Cotton Mather," "Mexican," "On Writing," and "Poems." In 1967, she composed *A Christmas Story*, a personal reminiscence of her niece, who had died in 1919. Her memoir of the Sacco and Vanzetti trial, *The Never-Ending Wrong*, was published in 1977 on the fiftieth anniversary of their deaths. She was a prodigious writer of personal letters; many have been published, first, by her friend Glenway Wescott, as *The Selected Letters of Katherine Anne Porter* (1970), and later by another friend, Isabel Bayley, as *Letters of Katherine Anne Porter* (1990).

**Achievements** • Katherine Anne Porter is distinguished by her small literary production of exquisitely composed and highly praised short fiction. Although she lived to be ninety years old, she produced and published only some twenty-five short stories and one long novel. Nevertheless, her work was praised early and often from the start of her career; some of her stories, such as "Flowering Judas," "Pale Horse, Pale Rider," and "Old Mortality," have been hailed as masterpieces. Sponsored by Edmund Wilson, Allen Tate, Kenneth Burke, and Elizabeth Madox Roberts, Porter won a Guggenheim Fellowship in 1931 and went to Berlin and Paris to live while she wrote such stories as "The Cracked Looking-Glass" and "Noon Wine," for which she won a Book-of-the-Month Club award in 1937. After publication of the collection *Pale Horse, Pale Rider: Three Short Novels* in 1939, she received a gold medal for literature from the Society of Libraries of New York University, in 1940. Elected a member of the National Institute of Arts and Letters in 1943, Porter was also appointed as writer-in-residence at Stanford University in 1949, and, in the same year, she received an honorary degree, doctor of letters, from the University of North Carolina. Such awards and honors continued, with writer-in-residence appointments at the University of Michigan in 1954 and the University of Virginia in 1958, honorary degrees at the University of Michigan, Smith College, and La Salle College. In 1959, she received a Ford Foundation grant, in 1962 the Emerson-Thoreau gold medal from the American Academy of Arts and Sciences, and in 1966-1967, the National Book Award for Fiction, the Pulitzer Prize in fiction, and the Gold Medal for fiction, National Institute of Arts and Letters.

**Biography** • There are conflicting reports of dates from Katherine Anne Porter's life, partly because Porter herself was not consistent about her biography. Nevertheless, the main events are fairly clear. Her mother, Mary Alice, died fewer than two years after Katherine Anne's birth. Subsequently, her grandmother, Catherine Anne Porter, was the most important adult woman in her life, and after the death of her grandmother in 1901, Katherine Anne was sent away by her father to an Ursuline convent in New Orleans, then in 1904 to the Thomas School for Girls in San Antonio. She ran away from her school in 1906 to marry John Henry Kroontz, the twenty-year-old son of a Texas rancher. She remained with him seven years (some reports say her marriage lasted only three years), and in 1911 she went to Chicago to earn her own way as a reporter for a weekly newspaper and as a bit player for a film company. From 1914 to 1916, she traveled through Texas, earning her way as a ballad singer. Then she returned to journalism, joining the staff of the Denver *Rocky Mountain News* in 1918. At about this time, Porter was gravely ill, and she thought she was going to die. Her illness was a turning point in the development of her character, and it was the basis for her story "Pale Horse, Pale Rider," which she finished twenty years later.

After she recovered her health, Porter lived briefly in New York and then Mexico, where she studied art while observing the Obregón revolution in 1920. Her experiences in Mexico provided material for her earliest published stories, "María Concepción" and "The Martyr" in 1922 and 1923. She married and promptly divorced Ernest Stock, a young English art student in New York, in 1925. Soon after, she participated in protests against the trial of Nicola Sacco and Bartolomeo Vanzetti, and then, in 1928, she began work on her biography of Mather, which was never completed. Porter traveled often during these years, but she wrote some of her greatest stories at the same time, including "He," "The Jilting of Granny Weatherall," "Theft," and "Flowering Judas."

After publication of her collection *Flowering Judas, and Other Stories* in 1930, Porter was awarded a Guggenheim Fellowship to support her while living in Berlin and

Paris, from 1931 to 1937. While in Europe, she composed "The Leaning Tower" and "The Cracked Looking-Glass," and she wrote an early draft of "Noon Wine." In 1933, she married Eugene Pressly, whom she divorced to marry Albert Erskine in 1938, when she returned to the United States to live with her new husband in Baton Rouge, Louisiana. At that time, she became a friend of Tate and his family.

In 1941, Porter appeared on television with Mark Van Doren and Bertrand Russell; in 1944, she worked on films in Hollywood; and in 1947, she undertook a lecture tour of several southern universities. The novel that she began as a story, "Promised Land," in 1936, was finally published in 1962 as *Ship of Fools* to mixed reviews. Apart from her work on this long fiction, Porter wrote little except for occasional essays and reviews, some of which she published as *The Days Before* in 1952. Porter spent most of her life after 1950 lecturing, traveling, buying and selling property, and slowly composing her novel along with her biography of Mather. In October, 1976, she read her essay "St. Augustine and the Bullfight" at the Poetry Center in New York City, and in 1977, she published a memoir of Sacco and Vanzetti, whose trials of injustice had haunted her for fifty years. When she died, in 1980, in Silver Spring, Maryland, she left behind a small canon of fiction and a great achievement of literary art.

**Analysis** • Katherine Anne Porter's short fiction is noted for its sophisticated use of symbolism, complex exploitation of point of view, challenging variations of ambiguously ironic tones, and profound analyses of psychological and social themes. Her career can be divided into three main (overlapping) periods of work, marked by publications of her three collections: The first period, from 1922 to 1935, saw the publication of *Flowering Judas, and Other Stories*; the second, from 1930 to 1939, ended with the publication of *Pale Horse, Pale Rider: Three Short Novels*; and the third, from 1935 to 1942, shaped many of her characters that later appear in the collection *The Leaning Tower, and Other Stories*. Her one novel and two stories "The Fig Tree" and "Holiday" were published long after the last collection of short stories, in 1962 and 1960, respectively. These constitute a coda to the body of her work in fiction.

From 1922 to 1935, Porter's fiction is concerned with the attempts of women to accommodate themselves to, or to break the bounds of, socially approved sexual roles. They usually fail to achieve the identities that they seek; instead, they ironically become victims of their own or others' ideas of what they ought to be. Violeta of "Virgin Violeta" fantasizes about her relationship with her cousin Carlos, trying to understand it according to the idealistic notions that she has learned from church and family; when Carlos responds to her sensual reality, she is shocked and disillusioned. The ironies of Violeta's situation are exploited more fully, and more artfully, in "María Concepción," "Magic," and "He."

In the first, María manages, through violence, to assert her identity through the social roles that she is expected to play in her primitive society; she kills her sensual rival, María Rosa, seizes the baby of her victim, and retrieves her wandering husband. Social norms are also triumphant over poor Ninette, the brutalized prostitute of "Magic," in which the narrator is implicated by her own ironic practice of distance from her story and her employer, Madame Blanchard. The mother of "He," however, cannot maintain her distance from the image that she has projected of her mentally disabled son; she is willing to sacrifice him, as she had the suckling pig, to preserve the social image she values of herself toward others. In the end, however, Mrs. Whipple embraces, helplessly and hopelessly, the victim of her self-delusion: She holds her son in tragic recognition of her failures toward him, or she holds him out of ironic disregard for his essential need of her understanding. "He" does not resolve easily into reconciliation of tone and theme.

Images of symbolic importance organize the ironies of such stories as "Rope," "Flowering Judas," "Theft," and "The Cracked Looking-Glass." In the first story, a husband and wife are brought to the edge of emotional chaos by a piece of rope that the husband brought home instead of coffee wanted by his wife. As a symbol, the rope ties them together, keeps them apart, and threatens to hang them both. "Flowering Judas," one of Porter's most famous stories, develops the alienated character of Laura from her resistance to the revolutionary hero Braggioni, to her refusal of the boy who sang to her from her garden, to her complicity in the death of Eugenio in prison. At the center of the story, in her garden and in her dream, Laura is linked with a Judas tree in powerfully mysterious ways: as a betrayer, as a rebellious and independent spirit. Readers will be divided on the meaning of the tree, as they will be on the virtue of Laura's character.

**"The Cracked Looking-Glass"** • The same ambivalence results from examining the symbolic function of a cracked mirror in the life of Rosaleen, the point-of-view character in "The Cracked Looking-Glass." This middle-aged Irish beauty sees herself as a monster in her mirror, but she cannot replace the mirror with a new one any more than she can reconcile her sexual frustration with her maternal affection for her aged husband, Dennis. This story twists the May-December stereotype into a reverse fairy tale of beauty betrayed, self deceived, and love dissipated. Rosaleen treats young men as the sons she never had to rear, and she represses her youthful instincts to nurse her impotent husband in his old age. She does not like what she sees when she looks honestly at herself in the mirror, but she will not replace the mirror of reality, cracked as she sees it must be.

**"Theft"** • More honest and more independent is the heroine of "Theft," an artist who chooses her independence at the cost of sexual fulfillment and social gratification; she allows her possessions, material and emotional, to be taken from her, but she retains an integrity of honesty and spiritual independence that are unavailable to most of the other characters in these early stories. A similar strength of character underlies the dying monologue of Granny Weatherall, but her strength has purchased her very little certainty about meaning. When she confronts death as a second jilting, Granny condemns death's cheat as a final insult to life; she seems ironically to make meaningful in her death the emptiness that she has struggled to deny in her life.

**"Old Mortality"** • In the middle period of her short fiction, Porter's characters confront powerful threats of illusion to shatter their tenuous holds on reality. Romantic ideals and family myths combine to shape the formative circumstances for Miranda in "Old Mortality." Divided into three parts, this story follows the growth of the young heroine from 1885, when she is eight, to 1912, when she is recently married against her father's wishes. Miranda and her older sister, Maria, are fascinated by tales of their legendary Aunt Amy, their father's sister whose honor he had risked his life to defend in a duel, and who died soon after she married their Uncle Gabriel. The first part of the story narrates the family's anecdotes about Aunt Amy and contrasts her with her cousin Eva, a plain woman who participated in movements for women's rights. Part 2 of the story focuses on Miranda's disillusionment with Uncle Gabriel, whom she meets at a racetrack while she is immured in a church school in New Orleans; he is impoverished, fat, and alcoholic, remarried to a bitter woman who hates his family, and he is insensitive to the suffering of his winning racehorse.

Part 3 describes Miranda's encounter with cousin Eva on a train carrying them to the funeral of Uncle Gabriel. Here, Miranda's romantic image of Aunt Amy is challenged by Eva's skeptical memory, but Miranda refuses to yield her vision entirely to Eva's scornful one. Miranda hopes that her father will embrace her when she returns home, but he remains detached and disapproving of her elopement. She realizes that from now on she must live alone, separate, and alienated from her family. She vows to herself that she will know the truth about herself, even if she can never know the truth about her family's history. The story ends, however, on a note of critical skepticism about her vow, suggesting its hopefulness is based upon her ignorance.

**"Noon Wine"** • Self-delusion and selfish pride assault Mr. Thompson in "Noon Wine" until he can no longer accept their terms of compromise with his life. A lazy man who lets his south Texas farm go to ruin, he is suddenly lifted to prosperity by the energetic, methodical work of a strangely quiet Swede, Mr. Helton. This man appears one day in 1896 to ask Mr. Thompson for work, and he remains there, keeping to himself and occasionally playing the tune of "Noon Wine" on his harmonica. The turn into failure and tragedy is more sudden than the turn to prosperity had been. Mr. Hatch, an obnoxious person, comes to Mr. Thompson looking for Helton, wanted for the killing of Helton's brother in North Dakota. Thompson angrily attacks and kills Hatch, and Helton flees. Helton, however, is captured, beaten, and thrown in jail, where he dies. Thompson is acquitted of murder at his trial.

Thompson, however, cannot accept his acquittal. He believes that his neighbors think that he is really guilty. His wife is uncertain about his guilt, and his two sons not only are troubled by his part in the deaths but also accuse him of mistreating their mother. Burdened by pains of conscience, Thompson spends his days after the trial visiting neighbors and retelling the story of Hatch's visit. Thompson believes he saw Hatch knife Helton, but no one else saw it, and Helton had no knife wound. The problem for Thompson is that he cannot reconcile what he saw and what was real. All of his life has been spent in a state of delusion, and this crisis of conscience threatens to destroy his capacity to accept life on his own visionary terms. The irony of the story is that Thompson must kill himself to vindicate his innocence, but when he does so, he paradoxically accepts the consequences of his delusions even as he asserts his right to shape reality to fit his view of it.

**"Pale Horse, Pale Rider"** • Love and death mix forces to press Miranda through a crisis of vision in "Pale Horse, Pale Rider." This highly experimental story mixes dreams with waking consciousness, present with past, and illness with health. Set during World War I, it analyzes social consequences of a military milieu, and it uses that setting to suggest a symbolic projection of the pressures that build on the imagination and identity of the central character. Miranda is a writer of drama reviews for a newspaper; her small salary is barely enough to support her, and so when she balks at buying Liberty Bonds, she has her patriotism questioned. This worry preoccupies her thoughts and slips into her dreaming experience. In fact, the opening of the story seems to be an experience of a sleeper who is slowly coming awake from a dream of childhood in which the adult's anxieties about money are mixed. Uncertainty about the mental state of Miranda grows as she mixes her memories of past with present, allowing past feelings to affect present judgments.

Miranda meets a young soldier, Adam, who will soon be sent to battle. They both know that his fate is sealed, since they are both aware of the survival statistics for soldiers who make assaults from trenches. Miranda becomes gravely ill just before Adam leaves for the war front, and he nurses her through the earliest days of her sickness. Her delirium merges her doctor with Adam, with the German enemy, and with figures of her dreams. By this process, Miranda works through her attractions to Adam, to all men, and she survives to assert her independence as a professional artist. The climax of her dream, echoing certain features of Granny Weatherall's, is her refusal to follow the pale rider, who is Death. This feature of her dream is present at the beginning of the story, to anticipate that Miranda will have to contend with this, resolve her inner battle, even before the illness that constitutes her physical struggle with death. The men of her waking life enter her dreams as Death, and so when Adam actually dies in battle, Miranda is symbolically assisted in winning her battle for life. The story makes it seem that her dreaming is the reality of the men, that their lives are figments of her imagination. Her recovery of health is a triumph, therefore, of her creative energies as well as an assertion of her independent feminine identity.

In the final, sustained period of her work in short fiction, from 1935 to 1942, Porter subjects memories to the shaping power of creative imagination, as she searches out the episodes that connect to make the character of Miranda, from "The Source" to "The Grave," and she traces the distorting effects of social pressures on children, wives, and artists in the remaining stories of the third collection. The crucial, shaping episodes of Miranda's childhood constitute the core elements of several stories in the collection called *The Leaning Tower, and Other Stories.* Beginning with a sequence under the title "The Old Order," Miranda's growth is shaped by her changing perceptions of life around her. Helping her to interpret events are her grandmother, Sophia Jane, and her grandmother's former black slave and lifetime companion, Aunt Nannie; in addition, Great-Aunt Eliza plays an important role in Miranda's life in the story that was later added to the sequence, "The Fig Tree." Two of the stories of this collection, "The Circus" and "The Grave," are examples of remarkable compression and, particularly in "The Grave," complex artistry.

**"The Circus"** • Miranda cries when she sees a clown perform high-wire acrobatics in "The Circus." Her fear is a child's protest against the clown's courtship with death. There is nothing pleasurable about it for Miranda. In fact, she seems to see through the act to recognize the threat of death itself, in the white, skull-like makeup of the clown's face. The adults enjoy the spectacle, perhaps insensitive to its essential message or, on the other hand, capable of appreciating the artist's defiance of death. In any event, young Miranda is such a problem that her father sends her home with one of the servants, Dicey. The point of poignancy is in Miranda's discovery of Dicey's warm regard for her despite the fact that Dicey had keenly wanted to stay at the circus. When Miranda screams in her sleep, Dicey lies beside her to comfort her, to protect her even from the dark forces of her nightmares. This sacrifice is not understood by the child Miranda, although it should be apparent to the adult who recalls it.

**"The Grave"** • "The Grave" is more clear about the function of time in the process of understanding. Miranda and her brother Paul explore open graves of their family while hunting. They find and exchange a coffin screw and a ring, then skin a rabbit that Paul killed, only to find that the rabbit is pregnant with several young that are "born" dead. The experience of mixing birth with death, sexual awareness with marriage and death, is suddenly illuminated for Miranda years later when she recalls her brother on that day while she stands over a candy stand in faraway Mexico.

**"The Downward Path to Wisdom"** • Other stories of *The Leaning Tower, and Other Stories* collection have disappointed readers, but they have virtues of art nevertheless. The strangely powerful story of little Stephen in "The Downward Path to Wisdom" has painful insights that may remind one of some of the stories by Flannery O'Connor, a friend of Porter. The little boy who is the object of concern to the family in this story grows to hate his father, mother, grandmother, and uncle; in fact, he sings of his hate for everyone at the end of the tale. His hatred is understandable, since no one genuinely reaches out to love him and help him with his very real problems of adjustment. His mother hears his song, but she shows no alarm; she may think that he does not "mean" what he sings, or she may not really "hear" what he is trying to say through his "art." A similar theme of hatred and emotional violence is treated in the heartless marital problems of Mr. and Mrs. Halloran of "A Day's Work." Here, however, the violence is borne by physical as well as emotional events, as the story ends with a deadly battle between the aging husband and wife. First one, and then the other, believes the other one is dead. The reader is not sure if either is right.

**"The Leaning Tower"** • Charles Upton, the artist hero of "The Leaning Tower," encounters emotional and physical violence during his sojourn in Berlin in 1931. When he accidentally knocks down and breaks a replica of the Leaning Tower, Charles expresses in a symbolic way his objection to values that he finds in this alien city. He must endure challenges by various other people, with their lifestyles and their foreign values, to discover an underlying humanity that he shares with them. Although he is irritated when he finds that his landlady, Rosa, has repaired the Leaning Tower, he cannot say exactly why he should be so. German nationalism and decadent art have combined to shake Charles's integrity, but he searches for inner resources to survive. The story concludes with a typically ambiguous gesture of Porter's art: Charles falls into his bed, telling himself he needs to weep, but he cannot. The world is invulnerable to sorrow and pity.

**"The Fig Tree"** • The coda of her work in short fiction, "The Fig Tree" and "Holiday," are revisits to earlier stories, as Porter reexamines old themes and old subjects with new emphases: "The Fig Tree" relocates Miranda in the matriarchal setting of her childhood, and "Holiday" reviews ironies of misunderstanding alien visions. In "The Fig Tree," young Miranda buries a dead baby chicken beneath a fig tree, and then thinks she hears it chirping from beneath the earth. Frantic with anxiety, she is unable to rescue it because her grandmother forces her to leave with the family for the country. Later, Miranda's Great-Aunt Eliza, who constantly studies nature through telescopes and microscopes, explains to Miranda that she hears tree frogs when Miranda thinks she is hearing the weeping of the dead chicken. Her guilt is relieved by this, and since Miranda has emotionally mixed her burial of the chicken with burials of family members, resolution of guilt for one functions as resolution of guilt for the other.

**"Holiday"** • The story of "Holiday" is much different in subject and setting, but its emotional profile is similar to "The Fig Tree." The narrator spends a long holiday with German immigrants in the backlands of Texas. The hardworking Müllers challenge, by their lifestyle, the values of the narrator, who only gradually comes to understand them and their ways. The most difficult experience to understand, however, is the family's attitude toward one of the daughters, Ottilie; at first, this girl seems to be only a crippled servant of the family. Gradually, however, the narrator understands that Ottilie is in fact a member of the family. She is mentally disabled and unable to communicate except in very primitive ways. Just when the narrator believes she can appreciate the seemingly heartless ways Ottilie is treated by her family, a great storm occurs and the mother dies. Most of the family follow their mother's corpse to be buried, but Ottilie is left behind. The narrator thinks Ottilie is desperate to join the funeral train with her family, and so she helps Ottilie on board a wagon and desperately drives to catch up with the family. Suddenly, however, the narrator realizes that Ottilie simply wants to be in the sunshine and has no awareness of the death of her mother. The narrator accepts the radical difference that separates her from Ottilie, from all other human beings, and resigns herself, in freedom, to the universal condition of alienation.

The critical mystery of Katherine Anne Porter's work in short fiction is in the brevity of her canon. Readers who enjoy her writing must deplore the failure of the artist to produce more than she did, but they will nevertheless celebrate the achievements of her remarkable talent in the small number of stories that she published. Whatever line of analysis one pursues in reading her stories, Porter's finest ones will repay repeated investments of reading them. They please with their subtleties of technique, from point of view to patterned images of symbolism; they inform with their syntheses of present feeling and past sensation; and they raise imaginative energy with their ambiguous presentations of alien vision. Porter's stories educate the patiently naïve reader into paths of radical maturity.

*Richard D. McGhee*

### Other major works

NOVELS: *Ship of Fools*, 1962.

NONFICTION: *My Chinese Marriage*, 1921; *Outline of Mexican Popular Arts and Crafts*, 1922; *What Price Marriage*, 1927; *The Days Before*, 1952; *A Defence of Circe*, 1954; *A Christmas Story*, 1967; *The Collected Essays and Occasional Writings*, 1970; *The Selected Letters of Katherine Anne Porter*, 1970; *The Never-Ending Wrong*, 1977; *Letters of Katherine Anne Porter*, 1990.

POETRY: *Katherine Anne Porter's Poetry*, 1996 (Darlene Harbour Unrue, editor).

### Bibliography

Bloom, Harold, ed. *Katherine Anne Porter: Modern Critical Views*. New York: Chelsea House, 1986. Bloom introduces twelve classic essays, by Robert Penn Warren, Robert B. Heilman, Eudora Welty, and others. The symbolism of "Flowering Judas," the ambiguities of "He," and the dreams in "Pale Horse, Pale Rider" are focuses of attention. Porter is compared with Flannery O'Connor. Includes a chronology, a bibliography, and an index.

Brinkmeyer, Robert H., Jr. *Katherine Anne Porter's Artistic Development: Primitivism, Traditionalism, and Totalitarianism*. Baton Rouge: Louisiana State University Press,

1993. Applying Mikhail Bakhtin's theory of the dialogic and monologic to Porter's fiction, Brinkmeyer argues that when she created a memory-based dialogue with her southern past, she achieved her height as an artist, producing such important stories as "The Jilting of Granny Weatherall" and "Noon Wine."

Fornataro-Neil, M. K. "Constructed Narratives and Writing Identity in the Fiction of Katherine Anne Porter." *Twentieth Century Literature* 44 (Fall, 1998): 349-361. Discusses "Old Mortality," "He," "Noon Wine," and "Holiday" in terms of Porter's fascination with characters who cannot or do not speak; claims that her silent characters are alienated because they communicate by a sign system that others cannot understand.

Graham, Don. "Katherine Anne Porter's Journey from Texas to the World." *Southwest Review* 84 (1998): 140-153. Argues that because the dominant figure in Texas literary mythology was the heroic cowboy, Porter, who had nothing to say about cowboys in her writing, chose instead to identify herself as southerner.

May, Charles E., ed. *Masterplots II: Short Story Series, Revised Edition.* 8 vols. Pasadena, Calif.: Salem Press, 2004. Designed for student use, this reference set contains articles providing detailed plot summaries and analyses of eleven short stories by Porter: "The Downward Path to Wisdom" (vol. 2); "Flowering Judas" and "The Grave" (vol. 3); "The Jilting of Granny Weatherall" and "The Leaning Tower" (vol. 4); "María Concepción," "Noon Wine," and "Old Mortality" (vol. 5); "Pale Horse, Pale Rider" and "Rope" (vol. 6); and "Theft" (vol. 7).

Spencer, Virginia, ed. *"Flowering Judas": Katherine Anne Porter.* New Brunswick, N.J.: Rutgers University Press, 1993. A volume in the Women Writers: Texts and Contexts series, this collection of critical discussions of Porter's most famous story features background material and important essays, from Ray B. West's influential 1947 discussion of the story to debates about the character of Eugenio as Christ figure.

Stout, Janis. *Katherine Anne Porter: A Sense of the Times.* Charlottesville: University Press of Virginia, 1995. Chapters on Porter's background in Texas, her view of politics and art in the 1920's, her writing and life between the two world wars, and her relationship with the southern agrarians. Also addresses the issue of gender, the problem of genre in *Ship of Fools*, and the quality of Porter's "free, intransigent, dissenting mind." Includes notes and bibliography.

Titus, Mary. *The Ambivalent Art of Katherine Anne Porter.* Athens: University of Georgia Press, 2005. Look at the ways in which Porter confronted issues of gender in her work and her life, including a study of some of her unpublished papers.

Unrue, Darlene Harbour. *Katherine Anne Porter: The Life of an Artist.* Jackson: University Press of Mississippi, 2005. Comprehensive biography of Porter that offers insight into her turbulent personal life and her writing.

Walsh, Thomas F. *Katherine Anne Porter and Mexico.* Austin: University of Texas Press, 1992. Chapters on Porter and Mexican politics, her different periods of residence in Mexico, and *Ship of Fools*. Includes notes and bibliography.

# J. F. Powers

**Born:** Jacksonville, Illinois; July 8, 1917
**Died:** Collegeville, Minnesota; June 12, 1999

**Principal short fiction** • *Prince of Darkness, and Other Stories,* 1947; *The Presence of Grace,* 1956; *Lions, Harts, Leaping Does, and Other Stories,* 1963; *Look How the Fish Live,* 1975; *The Old Bird: A Love Story,* 1991 (a short story, originally pb. in *Prince of Darkness, and Other Stories*); *The Stories of J. F. Powers,* 2000.

**Other literary forms** • J. F. Powers is the author of two novels: *Morte d'Urban,* which received the National Book Award for fiction in 1962, and *Wheat That Springeth Green* (1988), a National Book Award nominee. In addition, he published essays and reviews.

**Achievements** • Like Flannery O'Connor, a Roman Catholic writer with whom he is often compared, J. F. Powers is widely recognized as a distinctive figure in the modern American short story despite having produced only a small body of work. A master of comedy whose range encompasses cutting satire, broad farce, and gentle humor, Powers explores fundamental moral and theological issues as they are worked out in the most mundane situations. Although he is best known for stories centering on priests and parish life, Powers, in several early stories of the 1940's, was among the first to portray the circumstances of black people who had migrated from the South to Chicago and other urban centers.

**Biography** • John Farl Powers was born into a Catholic family in a town in which the "best" people were Protestant, a fact which he said "to some extent made a philosopher out of me." He attended Quincy Academy, taught by Franciscan Fathers, and many of his closest friends there later went into the priesthood. Powers himself was not attracted to clerical life, principally because of the social responsibilities, although he has said the praying would have attracted him. After graduation he worked at Marshall Field and Co., sold insurance, became a chauffeur, and clerked in Brentano's bookshop. During World War II, Powers was a conscientious objector; as a result, he spent more than a year in a federal prison. His first story was published in 1943. In 1946, he married Elizabeth Wahl, also a writer. They were to have five children; at the time of her death, in 1988, they had been married for forty-two years.

After the war, Powers and his family lived in Ireland as well as in the United States. He supplemented income from writing by teaching at various colleges and universities; in addition, he received a Guggenheim Fellowship and two fellowships from the Rockefeller Foundation. In 1976, Powers settled in Collegeville, Minnesota, where he became Regents Professor of English at St. John's University.

**Analysis** • The most frequently reprinted of J. F. Powers's short stories and therefore the best known are not the title stories of his two collections—"Prince of Darkness" and "The Presence of Grace"—but rather "Lions, Harts, Leaping Does," "The Valiant Woman," and "The Forks"—stories that are firmly rooted in social observation and realistic detail but have at their center specifically moral and theological issues. Powers is a Catholic writer, not a writer who happens to be a Catholic or one who proselytizes for the Church, but rather (as Evelyn Waugh has said) one whose "art is everywhere infused and directed by his Faith."

For Powers the central issue is how in the midst of a fallen world to live up to the high ideals of the Church. Since that issue is most sharply seen in the lives of those who have chosen the religious life as their vocation, parish priests, curates, friars, nuns, and archbishops dominate Powers's stories. As might be expected of a religious writer who admires, as Powers does, the art of James Joyce and who learned the satiric mode from Sinclair Lewis and Evelyn Waugh, Powers's stories are frequently ironic and often satiric portraits of clerics who fail to measure up to the ideals of their priestly vocation. Many are straightforward satires.

**"Prince of Darkness"** • "Prince of Darkness," for example, is the fictional portrait of a priest, Father Burner, who in his gluttony, his ambition for material rewards and professional success, and his lack of charity toward sinners in the confessional, reveals himself to be a modern incarnation of the devil himself. In opposition to Father Burner is the Archbishop, an elderly cleric in worn-out slippers who in the proper spirit of moral firmness and Christian compassion reassigns Father Burner not to the pastorate he covets but to another parish assistant's role where, presumably, his power of darkness will be held in check.

**"The Devil Was the Joker"** • "The Devil Was the Joker" from Powers's second collection resembles "Prince of Darkness" in theme and conception, except here the satanic figure is a layman who has been hired by a religious order to sell its publication in Catholic parishes. Mac, the salesman—"Fat and fifty or so, with a candy-pink face, sparse orange hair, and popeyes"—hires a young former seminarian to travel about with him as his companion-driver.

Myles Flynn, the former seminarian, also becomes the drinking companion and confidant of Mac, who gradually reveals himself to be totally cynical about the religious wares he is peddling, and who is, moreover, neither religious nor Catholic. Mac exploits the priests he encounters on his travels and attempts to use Myles to further his financial interests. As a way of making a sale, for example, he will frequently "take the pledge," that is, promise to refrain from alcohol. In return, he usually manages to extract from the priest to whom he made the pledge a large order for his wares. One day, after drunkenly confessing to Myles that he is not Catholic, he tries to repair the damage he imagines has been done to his position by trying to get Myles to baptize him, alleging that

Hugh Powers

Myles has been responsible for his sudden conversion. It is through Myles's response that Powers provides the perspective for understanding and judging Mac. Myles perceives that Mac "was the serpent, the nice old serpent with Glen-plaid markings, who wasn't very poisonous." In conclusion, Myles not only refuses to baptize Mac but also leaves him and attempts once more to get back into the seminary.

"Prince of Darkness" and "The Devil Was the Joker" are both loosely constructed revelations of character rather than stories of conflict and action. Powers's two best-known pieces are also among the best things he has done, including those in *Look How the Fish Live*. Both are told from the point of view of a priest caught in a moral dilemma.

**"The Forks"** • In "The Forks," a young curate, Father Eudex, assistant to a Monsignor in a middle-class parish, is presented with a check from a manufacturing company that has been having labor trouble. Father Eudex, born on a farm, a reader of the *Catholic Worker*, and a sympathizer with the strikers, regards the check as hush money and therefore finds it unacceptable. His superior, the Monsignor, who drives a long black car like a politician's and is friendly with bankers and businessmen, suggests that Father Eudex use the check as down payment on a good car. The Monsignor is a man of impeccable manners, concerned with the appearance of things, with laying out a walled garden, with the perfection of his salad, and disturbed by the fact that Father Eudex strips off his shirt and helps the laborer spade up the garden, and that he uses the wrong fork at dinner. Quite clearly the Monsignor represents to Powers a modern version of the secularized church, Father Eudex, the traditional and, in this story, powerless Christian virtues. At the end of the story, Father Eudex, who has considered sending the check back to the company or giving it to the strikers' fund, merely tears it up and flushes it down the toilet, aware that every other priest in town will find some "good" use for it. True goodness in Powers's stories tends to be helpless in the face of such worldliness.

**"The Valiant Woman"** • In "The Valiant Woman" the same issue is raised in the conflict between a priest and his housekeeper. The occasion in this story is the priest's fifty-ninth birthday celebration, a dinner from which his one remaining friend and fellow priest is driven by the insistent and boorish presence of the housekeeper. The theological and moral issue is dramatized by the priest's dilemma: According to church law he can rid himself of the housekeeper, but he can only do so by violating the spirit of Christian charity. The housekeeper, being totally unconscious of the moral implications of her acts, naturally has the advantage. Like the wily mosquito who bites the priest, her acts are of the flesh only, while his, being conscious and intellectual, are of the will. The priest cannot bring himself to fire her, and so in a helpless rage at being bitten by a mosquito (after having been, in effect, stung by the housekeeper), he wildly swings a rolled up newspaper at the mosquito and knocks over and breaks a bust of Saint Joseph.

When summarized, Powers's stories sound forbidding, when, in fact, they are— despite the underlying seriousness—delightfully humorous. About the housekeeper in "The Valiant Woman," for instance, Powers has the priest think:

> [She] was clean. And though she cooked poorly, could not play the organ, would not take up the collection in an emergency and went to card parties, and told all— even so, she was clean. She washed everything. Sometimes her underwear hung down beneath her dress like a paratrooper's pants, but it and everything she touched was clean. She washed constantly. She was clean.

Not all of Powers's stories have been about priests. Four of those in his first collection deal with racial and religious prejudice; three are about blacks ("The Trouble," about a race riot, "He Don't Plant Cotton," in which black entertainers in a northern nightclub are badgered by a visitor from Mississippi and quit their jobs, and "The Eye," about a lynching of an innocent black), and one about anti-Semitism ("Renner"). Two stories from *The Presence of Grace* are also not explicitly religious: "The Poor Thing" and "Blue Island." Even these apparently secular stories arise out of the same moral concern that may be seen more clearly in the overtly religious ones.

**"The Poor Thing"** • In "The Poor Thing" a disabled woman, Dolly, who goes through the motions of being religious, is revealed as a pious hypocrite when she slyly exploits an elderly spinster, forcing her to serve for little pay as her constant companion. The elderly woman had been talked into accepting the position in the first place and then, when she tried to leave, was falsely accused by Dolly of having stolen from her. The woman then has the choice of either returning to Dolly or having her reputation at the employment office ruined.

**"Blue Island"** • In "Blue Island" the oppressor is a woman who sells pots and pans by arranging "coffees" in other women's houses and then arriving to "demonstrate" her wares. Under the guise of neighborly concern for a young woman who has recently moved into the neighborhood and is unsure of herself (and ashamed of her origins), she persuades the young woman to have a coffee to which all of the important neighbor women are invited; then the saleswoman arrives with her wares, and the young woman, the victim, stricken by the deception practiced on her and on the neighbors she has tried to cultivate, rushes to her bedroom and weeps, while downstairs the neighbor women file out, leaving her alone with her oppressor. In both "The Poor Thing" and "Blue Island," Powers also shows that the victims participate in their victimization, the spinster through her pride and the young woman in "Blue Island" by denying her past and attempting to be something she is not.

**"Lions, Harts, Leaping Does"** • Powers's best stories are undoubtedly those that bring the moral and religious issue directly into the main action. The story still most widely admired is the one written when Powers was twenty-five that established his early reputation as a master of the short story: "Lions, Harts, Leaping Does." The popularity of this story may result not only from the high level of its art but also from the way it deals so gently with the issues and creates in Father Didymus and in the simple Friar Titus two appealing characters. Indeed, one of Powers's major achievements is his ability in many of his stories to create characters with the vividness and complexity one expects only from the longer novel. For this reason, if for no other, the stories of J. F. Powers will continue to engage the attention of discriminating readers.

*W. J. Stuckey*

**Other major works**

NOVELS: *Morte d'Urban*, 1962; *Wheat That Springeth Green*, 1988.

## Bibliography

Evans, Fallon, ed. *J. F. Powers*. St. Louis: Herder, 1968. Collection of essays and appreciations emphasizing the Catholic context of Powers's fiction. Among the contributors are Hayden Carruth, W. H. Gass (whose essay "Bingo Game at the Foot of the Cross" is a classic), Thomas Merton, and John Sisk. Also includes an interview with Powers and a bibliography.

Gussow, Mel. "J. F. Powers, 81, Dies." *The New York Times*, June 17, 1999, p. C23. In this tribute to Powers, Gussow traces his literary career, commenting on his first important story, "Lions, Harts, Leaping Does," and his best-known collection, *Prince of Darkness, and Other Stories*, noting his frequent focus on priests.

Hagopian, John V. *J. F. Powers*. New York: Twayne, 1968. The first book-length study of Powers, this overview comprises a biographical sketch and a survey of Powers's work through *Morte d'Urban*. Gives extensive attention to Powers's stories. Includes a useful bibliography.

Long, J. V. "Clerical Character(s)." *Commonweal*, May 8, 1998, 11-14. Long offers a retrospective analysis of the leading characters in *Morte d'Urban* and *Wheat That Springeth Green* and the sacred-versus-secular issues confronting them. It is an interesting look back in the light of changes in American Catholicism since the 1950's.

McCarthy, Colman. "The Craft of J. F. Powers." *The Washington Post*, June 12, 1993, p. A21. A brief tribute to Powers, commenting on his teaching and fiction, and recounting an interview, in which Powers laments the fact that college students do not read any more.

McInerny, Dennis Q., and William Hoffman. "J. F. Powers." In *Critical Survey of Long Fiction, Revised Edition*, edited by Carl Rollyson. Vol. 5. Pasadena, Calif.: Salem Press, 2000. Analysis of Powers's longer fictional works that may offer insights into his short fiction.

May, Charles E., ed. *Masterplots II: Short Story Series, Revised Edition*. 8 vols. Pasadena, Calif.: Salem Press, 2004. Designed for student use, this reference set contains articles providing detailed plot summaries and analyses of five short stories by Powers: "The Forks" (vol. 3); "Lions, Harts, Leaping Does" (vol. 4); "The Old Bird: A Love Story" (vol. 5); "Prince of Darkness" (vol. 6); and "The Valiant Woman" (vol. 8).

Meyers, Jeffrey. "J. F. Powers: Uncollected Stories, Essays, and Interviews, 1943-1979." *Bulletin of Bibliography* 44 (March, 1987): 38-39. Because Powers has published relatively little in his long career, it is particularly useful to have a list of his uncollected stories. The essays and interviews listed here provide valuable background.

Powers, J. F. "The Alphabet God Uses." Interview by Anthony Schmitz. *Minnesota Monthly* 22 (December, 1988): 34-39. At the time of this interview, occasioned by the publication of Powers's novel *Wheat That Springeth Green*, Schmitz himself had just published his first novel, which also deals with the Catholic clergy. He makes an ideal interviewer, and his conversation with Powers provides an excellent introduction to the man and his works.

Powers, Katherine A. "Reflections of J. F. Powers: Author, Father, Clear-Eyed Observer." *The Boston Globe*, July 18, 1999, p. K4. A reminiscence of Powers by his daughter; discusses the writers who most influenced Powers, particularly his admiration for Evelyn Waugh, and comments on his writing and reading habits.

# V. S. Pritchett

**Born:** Ipswich, England; December 16, 1900
**Died:** London, England; March 20, 1997

**Principal short fiction** • *The Spanish Virgin, and Other Stories,* 1930; *You Make Your Own Life, and Other Stories,* 1938; *It May Never Happen, and Other Stories,* 1945; *Collected Stories,* 1956; *The Sailor, the Sense of Humour, and Other Stories,* 1956 (also known as *The Saint, and Other Stories,* 1966); *When My Girl Comes Home,* 1961; *The Key to My Heart,* 1963; *Blind Love, and Other Stories,* 1969; *The Camberwell Beauty, and Other Stories,* 1974; *Selected Stories,* 1978; *The Fly in the Ointment,* 1978; *On the Edge of the Cliff,* 1979; *Collected Stories,* 1982; *More Collected Stories,* 1983; *A Careless Widow, and Other Stories,* 1989; *Complete Collected Stories,* 1990.

**Other literary forms** • V. S. Pritchett's sixty-year career as a writer, apart from his many short stories, produced several novels (not well received), two autobiographies (*A Cab at the Door,* 1968, and *Midnight Oil,* 1972), several travel books (the noteworthy ones including *The Spanish Temper,* 1954, and *The Offensive Traveller,* 1964), volumes of literary criticism, literary biographies (*George Meredith and English Comedy,* 1970; *Balzac,* 1973; *The Gentle Barbarian: The Life and Work of Turgenev,* 1977), essays (among them *New York Proclaimed,* 1965, and *The Working Novelist,* 1965), and journalistic pieces from France, Spain, Ireland, and the United States that remain in the literary canon, so well are they written.

**Achievements** • In his long and distinguished career, V. S. Pritchett, who preferred the abbreviation V. S. P., produced an impressive number of books in all genres—from novels and short stories, on which rests his fame, to literary criticism, travel books, and journalistic pieces written for *The Christian Science Monitor* when he covered Ireland, Spain, and France. His most successful genre was the short story, which resulted from his razor-sharp characterizations of all classes, both in England and on the Continent, his focus on the moment of epiphany, his graceful writing, and his ironic, bittersweet wit. Pritchett has the uncanny ability to select a commonplace moment and through imagery, wit, and irony lift it to a transfiguration. He focuses on the foibles of all people without malice, anger, or sentimentality but rather with humor, gentleness, and understanding. In his preface to *Collected Stories,* Pritchett states that although some people believe that the short story has lost some of its popularity, he does not think so: "[T]his is not my experience; thousands of addicts still delight in it because it is above all memorable and is not simply read, but re-read again and again. It is the glancing form of fiction that seems to be right for the nervousness and restlessness of contemporary life."

**Biography** • Victor Sawden Pritchett was born in Ipswich, Suffolk, England, of middleclass parents. His father, Walter, a Yorkshireman, espoused a strict Congregationalism. He married Beatrice of London, whom he had met when both worked in a draper's shop. Enthralled by wild business schemes, Walter often left his family for months as he pursued dreams that shattered and left the family destitute, forcing it

© Nancy Crampton

into innumerable moves and frequent sharing of flats with relatives. Often a traveling salesman, Pritchett's father, despite his long absences, caused the family unmitigated misery when he returned. Pritchett's dictatorial father is reflected in many of his stories and novels, and Pritchett is completely frank in his autobiography about his father's brutality.

Most remarkable, Pritchett received only the barest of formal training at Alleyn's Grammar School, which he left when he was only sixteen to enter the leather trade. Clever with languages, he soon showed proficiency in French. He read omnivorously. In his stories, he reflects a cerebral ability, perceptiveness, and imagism. Despite his lack of formal training in literature, he is considered to be one of the best writers of the short story in England. In 1975, he was knighted as Sir Victor for his contributions to literature.

After working in the leather trade for several years as a tanner, he left for a two-year interlude in Paris. Those years as a tanner were fruitful, he once declared, for he encountered all classes of people in England, a factor noted in his short stories, depicting the monied aristocrats and the working classes, together with the middle classes that he fixes in amber. In Paris, he worked in a photography shop as clerk and letter writer but soon wearied of the routines and determined to become a writer. His connection with *The Christian Science Monitor* became the key transitional phase, for he wrote and published for this newspaper a series of articles. When there was no longer a need for these articles written in Paris, *The Christian Science Monitor* sent him to Ireland, where the civil war raged. Pritchett soaked up experiences from his wide travels as he journeyed from Dublin to Cork, Limerick, and Enniskillen. A year later the newspaper editors informed him that they needed him in Spain, and he left for Iberia with Evelyn Maude Vigors, whom he married at the beginning of 1924. There are virtually no details about his first wife, except that she was an actor. Their marriage turned out not to be a happy one; the couple was divorced in 1936, and during that same year, Pritchett married Dorothy Roberts. His wife continued to assist him in his literary work, and he has invariably dedicated his work to her, one inscription reading "For Dorothy—always."

The years in Spain were productive, with Pritchett writing novels, short stories, travel books, and journalistic pieces. While there, he learned Spanish easily and immersed himself in its literature, especially being influenced by Miguel de Unamuno y Jugo, whose philosophic themes often concern the intensity of living near the jaws of death, and by Pío Baroja, whose books often focus on atheism and pessimism. Pritchett especially was influenced by Baroja's empathy for character. After two years in Spain, Pritchett visited Morocco, Algeria, Tunisia, the United States, and Canada, travels that further shaped his contours of place and people. During the 1930's, his writing approached the luminous. In the second volume of his autobiography, *Midnight Oil*, Pritchett wrote to this point:

> If I began to write better it was for two reasons: in my thirties I had found my contemporaries and had fallen happily and deeply in love. There is, I am sure, a direct connection between passionate love and the firing of the creative power of the mind.

Critics agree that Pritchett reached a high level of achievement in the short story in the 1930's. He continued writing on a high level until all was interrupted, as it was for many other writers, by the onset of World War II, during which he served in the Ministry of Information.

Pritchett became literary editor of *New Statesman* in 1945, resigning this position in 1949 to become its director from 1951 to 1978. Along the way, he had been given lectureships at Princeton University (1953, Christian Gauss Lecturer) and the University of California at Berkeley (1962, Beckman Professor), and he was appointed as writer-in-residence at Smith College in 1966. Brandeis University, Columbia University, and the University of Cambridge also invited him to teach.

Honors poured on Pritchett. He was elected fellow by the Royal Society of Literature, receiving a C.B.E. in 1969. Two years later he was elected president of the British PEN and was made honorary member of the American Academy of Arts and Letters. In 1974, he was installed as international president of PEN for two years. One of his greatest honors came from Queen Elizabeth as she received him into knighthood in 1975 for his services to literature. Also, Pritchett through the years received academic honors from several universities in the Western world, including honorary D.Litt. degrees from Leeds (1972) and Columbia Universities (1978).

Pritchett continued to contribute to journals in the United States and Europe and England. Not wishing to rest on his innumerable laurels, this grand master of the short story continued to write and to select stories for his collections. By many, he is thought to be a writer's writer. He died on March 20, 1997, at the age of ninety-six, in London.

**Analysis** • V. S. Pritchett writes in *Midnight Oil*,

> I have rarely been interested in what are called "characters," i.e., eccentrics; reviewers are mistaken in saying I am. They misread me. I am interested in the revelations of nature and (rather in Ibsen's fashion) of exposing the illusions or received ideas by which they live or protect their dignity.

An approach to the short stories reveals that Pritchett is projecting comic incongruities. He captures the moment of revelation when his men and women recognize an awareness of their plight. His panoply of people ranges from sailors, divers, clerks, blind men, and shopgirls to piano accompanists, wastrels, and the penurious wealthy. Pritchett concentrates on selected details with tart wit and irony in dialogue that characterizes those who people his short stories. Two highly discrete characters often interrelate to their despair or to their joy. With such irony, the reader may conclude that in reading a Pritchett story, nothing is but what is not.

One of the earliest collections of short stories by Pritchett, *You Make Your Own Life, and Other Stories*, already reflects the mature touch of the writer. Although showing some slight inconsistency, the tales attest variety in narrative, theme, tone, and style. Some stories are stark and Kafkaesque, especially "The Two Brothers," in which a nightmarish suicide is the central concern. The longest story in this group is "Handsome Is as Handsome Does," set on the French Mediterranean.

**"Handsome Is as Handsome Does"** • The focus is on Mr. and Mrs. Coram, an English couple, both of whom are unusually ugly. Their ugliness is their only similarity. He is rude, inarticulate, and slow-witted, and he quarrels with everyone. He is especially rude to M. Pierre, the proprietor of the hotel, insulting him in English which he does not understand. Mrs. Coram is left to play the role of diplomat and apologist. Soon after the English couple's arrival, Alex, whose forebears are flung throughout Europe, also vacations at the inn. He is young and handsome and delights in swimming. Childless, Mrs. Coram views Alex as the son she might have had. Yet one day, she attempts to seduce him while he watches unfeelingly, and she, scorned, feels ridiculous. One day, the Corams, Alex, and M. Pierre go to a deserted beach that is known for its dangerous undertow. M. Pierre dives in and before long, it is apparent to all that he is drowning. Alex rescues him while Mr. Coram looks on, never even thinking of saving the innkeeper. His wife is silently furious at him. Later, as M. Pierre brags at the hotel about his narrow escape, Mrs. Coram blandly tells some recent English arrivals that her husband saved M. Pierre's life.

Clearly, the Corams are loathsome people, but through Pritchett's portrayal of them as wounded, frustrated, and vindictive, even grotesque, they emerge as human beings, capable of eliciting the reader's empathy. Alex, protected by his "oily" youth, remains the catalyst, rather neutral and asexual. The aging couple, in Pritchett's lightly satirical portraiture, in the end claim the reader's sympathy.

**"Sense of Humour"** • Another well-known and often-quoted story in this collection is "Sense of Humour." Arthur Humphrey, a traveling salesman, is the narrator. On one of his trips, he meets Muriel MacFarlane, who is dating a local boy, Colin Mitchell, who always rides a motorcycle. Colin is obsessively in love with Muriel. Arthur courts Muriel, who stops dating Colin. Nevertheless, the motorcyclist compulsively follows the couple wherever they go. Muriel says that she is Irish, and she has a sense of humor. Yet she never exhibits this so-called Irish trait. When Colin, who is also an auto mechanic, announces that he cannot repair Humphrey's car and thereby hopes to ruin the couple's plan, they take the train to Humphrey's parents' house. Shortly after their arrival, Muriel receives a call from the police: Colin has been killed in a motorcycle crash nearby. That night, Muriel is overwhelmed with grief for Colin; Arthur begins to comfort her, and they eventually, for the first time, have sex. All the while, Muriel is crying out Colin's name. To save Colin's family the expense, Colin's body is returned to his family in a hearse belonging to Arthur's father. Both Muriel and the obtuse Arthur feel like royalty when the passing drivers and pedestrians doff their hats in respect. Arthur says, "I was proud of her, I was proud of Colin, and I was proud of myself and after what happened, I mean on the last two nights, it was like a wedding." Colin is following them for the last time. When Arthur asks Muriel why she stopped seeing Colin, she answers that he never had a sense of humor.

Critics believe that Pritchett in this story exerts complete control in keeping the reader on tenterhooks between crying and guffawing. The narrator, like the reader, never concludes whether Muriel is marrying Arthur for his money or for love or whether she loves Colin or Arthur, in the final analysis. The story underscores one of Pritchett's favorite techniques: peeling away at the character with grim irony and even then not providing enough details to see the character's inner self. As Pritchett declared, however, his interest is in the "happening," not in overt characterization. Yet, in death, Colin after all does seem to win his love. Still, in the conclusion, it appears that all three people have been deluded. Some of the grim gallows humor in this story reminds the reader of Thomas Hardy, whom Pritchett acknowledged as an important influence.

**"When My Girl Comes Home"** • More than a decade after the end of World War II, *When My Girl Comes Home* was published. The mature style of Pritchett is readily discernible in this collection. The stories become somewhat more complex and difficult in morality, in situations, and in the greater number of characters. The moral ambiguities are many. The title story, "When My Girl Comes Home," is Pritchett's favorite short story.

Although World War II is over, the bankruptcy of the war ricochets on many levels. The "girl" coming home is Hilda Johnson, for whom her mother has been working and scrimping to save money. Residents of Hincham Street, where Mrs. Johnson lives, had for two years implored the bureaucracies of the world to obtain news about the whereabouts and the condition of Hilda, who was believed to be wasting away in a Japanese concentration camp. Now Hilda has come home, not pale and wan but sleek and relaxed. Only gradually does the story emerge, but never completely. In fact, because Hilda's second husband was a Japanese officer, she survived the war comfortably. She does not need the money that her mother saved from years of sewing. En route home, Hilda met two men, one of whom, Gloster, a writer, wished to write Hilda's story. The narrator observes, when he first sees her, that

her face was vacant and plain. It was as vacant as a stone that has been smoothed for centuries in the sand of some hot country. It was the face of someone to whom nothing had happened; or, perhaps, so much had happened to her that each event wiped out what had happened before. I was disturbed by something in her—the lack of history, I think. We were worm-eaten by it.

Hilda sleeps with her mother in a tiny bedroom while she waits for help from Gloster, who never appears. She seems to become involved with a real prisoner of the Japanese, Bill Williams, who survived through the war, as he terms it, with "a bit of trade." Some of the neighbors begin to understand that Hilda, too, survived by trading as well. At one point in the tale, Hilda begs her friends to save her from Bill Williams, and she stays away from her apartment that night. When she returns to her flat, she discovers that Bill Williams has robbed her flat completely and has disappeared. Soon after, Hilda leaves London and surfaces only in a photograph with her two boyfriends, Gloster and someone else. Gloster does publish a book, not about Hilda's war experiences but about the people on Hincham Street.

The story's subtext may suggest that it might have been better for Hincham Street had the "girl" not come home, for then they would have retained their illusions about her. The illusion versus reality theme is one often used by Pritchett. Mrs. Johnson, now dead, seemed to have kept the street together in a kind of moral order, now destroyed on Hincham Street. After her death, Hilda and Bill were involved in seamy happenings. In the Hincham Street pubs, the war is discussed but only fitfully and inconclusively because "sooner or later, it came to a closed door in everybody's conscience." Hilda and Bill, surviving the Japanese camps through moral bankruptcy, form a mirror image of those Englishman who became black marketers, malingerers, ration thieves, and hoodlums. Moral codes were shattered by Englishmen—whether at home or abroad. Pritchett is deliberately murky in theme and relationships, but the story suggests that just as the Japanese disturbed the civil and moral order thousands of miles away, the disruption caused a moral decay at home at the same time that the war was fought to reestablish the world order. Perhaps Pritchett is suggesting that England during the war and after was a microcosm. Despite the disillusionment that touches the entire street and the gravity of the theme, Pritchett never fails to use the restorative of humor and subtle satire, watchwords of the writer.

At the end of the 1960's, *Blind Love, and Other Stories* appeared. This collection reflects Pritchett's admiration of Anton Chekhov and Ivan Turgenev, whose bittersweet irony enfolds the characters as they experience, at the end, self-revelation. In his later years, Pritchett continued to grow as an artist in many ways. The story lines are compelling, and no matter what the theme, Pritchett's wit provides humor and pathos. The transition between time present and time past is accomplished with laser-beam precision.

**"The Skeleton"** • "The Skeleton," concerning George Clark, fleshes out a skinny man who has never loved. Cantankerous, selfish, perfectionistic, and thoroughly narcissistic, George is painted to perfection with satirical brushes. His encounter with Gloria Archer, whom George accuses of corrupting his favorite painter, transforms him. The comic becomes almost caricature and is flawless. Pritchett shows him guarding his whiskey bottle like a Holy Grail, but his valet finds it mistakenly left on the table, drinks a bit, and then dilutes the bottle with water. Dean R. Baldwin, who wrote the excellent Twayne biography of Pritchett, wrote, "George is the skeleton, until Gloria puts a bit of meat on his emotional bare bones."

**"Blind Love"** • Like many of Pritchett's best stories used as title stories, "Blind Love" is a masterful portrait of two people who are scarred by nature but who succumb to pride before their fall. Mr. Armitage, a wealthy lawyer living in the country and blind for twenty years, has been divorced because of his affliction. He interviews Mrs. Johnson by feeling her face and hands, and he hires her as a secretary/housekeeper. As Thomas Gray would say, nothing disturbed the even tenor of their ways for a few years. One day, Armitage, walking in his garden, loses his balance when a dog chases a rabbit, and he falls into his pool. Mrs. Johnson sees the fall but before she can rush out to help him, he is rescued. When Mrs. Johnson tries to help him change his clothes in his room, she breaks the cardinal rule of never changing the physical order of things because Armitage has memorized the place for every item. He screams at her to get out and leave him alone. This verbal attack stimulates a flashback that reveals that Mrs. Johnson had heard "almost exactly those words, before. Her husband had said them. A week after the wedding." She recalls that he was shocked and disgusted at

> a great spreading ragged liver-coloured island of skin which spread under the tape of her slip and crossed her breast and seemed to end in a curdle of skin below it. She was stamped with an ineradicable bloody insult.

After Armitage's rudeness, Mrs. Johnson decides to leave, for, in addition to those scorching words, she disliked the country. Armitage apologizes and begs her to stay. Soon thereafter, he gropes toward her and kisses her, and they make love. Mrs. Johnson, initially motivated by the pleasure of revenge against her husband, begins in time to enjoy Armitage's lovemaking. Religion is woven into the story when Armitage mocks Mrs. Johnson for going to church, and at one time, he insists that she use spit- tle and dirt on his eyes to mock a miracle of Christ: "Do as I tell you. It's what your Jesus Christ did when he cured the blind man."

Armitage then goes to Mr. Smith, an expensive faith healer, actually a charlatan manqué, to regain his sight. Once, Mrs. Johnson accompanies him. As she leaves, Armitage hears her telling Smith that she loves Armitage as he is. Earlier, Smith ap- peared when Mrs. Johnson had been sunbathing nude at the pool. After wondering whether he saw her, Mrs. Johnson concludes that he did not. When Armitage later asks her whether Smith had seen her at the pool, Mrs. Johnson explodes and says that Smith saw everything. Unzipping her dress, she cries, "You can't see it, you silly fool. The whole bloody Hebrides, the whole plate of liver."

Later, when Mrs. Johnson for some strange reason is found lying face down in the pool, she, like Armitage earlier, is rescued. Both have had their "fall." This parallel happening seems to be a moment of epiphany, and the story ends with the couple liv- ing in Italy, where Mrs. Johnson describes churches and gallery pictures to her "per- haps" husband. In the last paragraph, Mrs. Johnson proclaims her love for her hus- band as she eyes the lovely Italian square below. She says that she feels "gaudy," leaving the reader wrestling over her selection of the word. Long after the reading, the poignancy of the story resonates.

This title story, an intensely poignant one, forthright and absorbing, shows the handicaps bringing people together and almost tearing them apart. They are both anointed by their "fall" from pride, and in their moment of epiphany, they see their need of each other and the love accompanying the need. Through each other and by self-analysis, they transcend their limitations and experience the joy of seeing them- selves anew. Again, this revelatory process is a mainstay of Pritchett.

**"The Diver"** • Five years later, Pritchett continued his consistent stream of produc- tivity by publishing *The Camberwell Beauty, and Other Stories.* This volume particularly focuses on the eccentric foibles of the middle class. "The Diver," set in Paris, is an en- joyable tale of a diver who is a metaphor for sexual encounters. This diver is sent to retrieve bundles of leather goods that a Dutch ship accidentally spews into the Seine. A young clerk for the leather tannery is assigned to count the sodden bales. Quite by chance, he himself falls into the Seine and is fished out by the onlookers. His boss takes him across the street to a bar and expects the lad to pay for his own brandy. Mme Chamson, feeling sorry for the youth, takes him to her shop for a change of clothing. As he disrobes, she notices his inflamed member and becomes furious at his disrespect. A few minutes later, she calls him into her bedroom, where he finds her nude, and she initiates a sexual encounter. The youth, yearning to become a writer, feels inarticulate. This encounter with Mme Chamson, his first sexual experi- ence, has released his creative wellsprings. A simple tale, "The Diver" is rib-tickling in its theme of innocence lost and creativity gained. Pritchett elsewhere has written of the link between sexuality and creativity.

**"The Camberwell Beauty"** • Again, the long title story, "The Camberwell Beauty," is one of the most arresting. The ambience is that of the antique dealers of London, a cosmos of its own. Each antique dealer has his own specialty, and "within that spe- cialty there is one object he broods on from one year to the next, most of his life; the thing a man would commit murder to get his hands on if he had the nerve."

The narrator is a former antique dealer. A current art dealer, Pliny, an elderly man, has married a beautiful woman, and the narrator is determined to get hold of the Camberwell beauty, who is essentially a work of art. Once more, Pritchett writes of illusion, this time using the art world and the gulf between the greed of the dealers and the loveliness of the art and the artifacts. Isabel, the Camberwell beauty, is exploited by being held captive, like any objet d'art. The narrator fails in his attempt at seduction, which might have replicated another sexual exploitation. Isabel insists that Pliny is a good lover, but Pritchett strongly suggests that there is no intimacy between them. She, like William Blake's Thel, seems not to descend into generation (or sexuality). Remaining under the illusion that she is safe and protected in her innocence, and content to be in stasis and in asexuality, she never does reach a moment of self-awareness. She might just as well have been framed and hung on a wall.

**"The Accompanist"** • The last collection of original stories, *On the Edge of the Cliff*, was published in 1979, and it contains stories wrought with a heightened sensibility and subtlety. The humor and technical brilliance are very much in evidence. Marital infidelity is the theme of several tales, especially in "The Fig Tree" and "A Family Man." A well-carved cameo, "The Accompanist" also portrays an unfaithful mate. William, the narrator, on leave from his Singapore job, is having an affair with Joyce, a piano accompanist, married to Bertie, impotent but particularly likable by a circle of friends who gather for dinner in his flat. The furniture, Victorian monstrosity, obsesses Bertie, since it is a link to the past. For undisclosed reasons, the furniture may almost affirm his asexuality. Critics invariably remark on a Henry James-like subtlety of sensitivity and particularity of detail. This texture surfaces when Bertie, accompanied by his wife, sings a French bawdy song about a bride who was murdered on her wedding night. Despite Bertie's problems with sex, he seems not to be aware of the irony in singing this song and in being anchored in the protected illusion of bygone Victorian days. His wife, Joyce, may emerge from the decadence of her marriage if, as the narrator says at the end, she will hear her tune: "And if she heard it, the bones in her legs, arms, her fingers, would wake up and she would be out of breath at my door without knowing it." William is saying that *if* she arrives out of a sexual impulse, there will be hope for her liberation from Bertie and from the historical frost symbolized by the Victorian furnishings.

**"On the Edge of the Cliff"** • The centerpiece story, "On the Edge of the Cliff," unravels the tale of a May-December liaison. Harry, a botanist in his seventies, and Rowena, an artist and twenty-five, have a happy affair in his house on the edge of a cliff. Driving down to a nearby village fair, they engage in role playing. The omniscient narrator declares, "There are rules for old men who are in love with young girls, all the stricter when the young girls are in love with them. It has to be played as a game." The game stimulates the love affair. At the fair, Harry meets Daisy Pyke, who was a former mistress and who has a young man in tow, mistakenly thought by Harry and Rowena to be her son but actually her lover. Daisy subsequently visits Harry, not to resume any romance but to beg Harry to keep the two young people apart so that her own love life will not be jeopardized. She cries, "I mean it, Harry. I know what would happen and so do you and I don't want to *see* it happen."

Ironically, both Harry and Rowena rarely venture into society. When Harry denies that Rowena is being kept prisoner, Daisy shrewdly insists, "You mean *you* are the prisoner. That is it! So am I!" Harry replies, "Love is always like that. I live only for her." In this tale, as in many of Pritchett's stories, there are contrasting sets of people who are often foils for each other. Both Daisy and Rowena are jealous of their lovers and want their May-December relationships to continue. Pritchett is undoubtedly concerned with the aging process and the capacity to sustain love. Both Daisy and Harry find their capacity to love undiminished with age. Yet, although their love affairs are alive, Pritchett's metaphor of the house on the cliff may suggest that the lovers are aware of inherent dangers because of the differences in ages. At the same time, Pritchett may be implying that even with no age differences between lovers, there is an element of risk. Illusion in this and many other of Pritchett's tales plays an important role. As Harry and Daisy discuss their younger lovers, illusion is implicit. Yet, in their confronting the reality of age differences, they become intensely aware of their predicament, and it is at this moment that they experience a Pritchett epiphany. This realization will help them to savor the time spent on the edge of the cliff.

In his short fiction, Pritchett fashions a host of unique characters, uses witty and humorous dialogue, employs a variety of "happenings," and leaves readers with the sense that they themselves have been mocked, not with bitterness or caustic wit but with gentleness and love.

*Julia B. Boken*

**Other major works**

NOVELS: *Claire Drummer,* 1929; *Shirley Sanz,* 1932 (also known as *Elopement into Exile*); *Nothing Like Leather,* 1935; *Dead Man Leading,* 1937; *Mr. Beluncle,* 1951.

MISCELLANEOUS: *The Pritchett Century,* 1997.

NONFICTION: *Marching Spain,* 1928; *In My Good Books,* 1942; *The Living Novel and Later Appreciations,* 1946; *Why Do I Write? An Exchange of Views Between Elizabeth Bowen, Graham Greene, and V. S. Pritchett,* 1948; *Books in General,* 1953; *The Spanish Temper,* 1954; *London Perceived,* 1962; *The Offensive Traveller,* 1964 (also known as *Foreign Faces*); *New York Proclaimed,* 1965; *Shakespeare: The Comprehensive Soul,* 1965; *The Working Novelist,* 1965; *Dublin: A Portrait,* 1967; *A Cab at the Door,* 1968; *George Meredith and English Comedy,* 1970; *Midnight Oil,* 1972; *Balzac: A Biography,* 1973; *The Gentle Barbarian: The Life and Work of Turgenev,* 1977; *The Myth Makers: Literary Essays,* 1979; *The Tale Bearers: Literary Essays,* 1980; *The Other Side of the Frontier: A V. S. Pritchett Reader,* 1984; *A Man of Letters,* 1985; *Chekhov: A Spirit Set Free,* 1988; *Lasting Impressions,* 1990; *The Complete Essays,* 1991; *Balzac,* 1992.

**Bibliography**

Angell, Roger. "Marching Life." *The New Yorker* 73 (December 22-29, 1997): 126-134. In this biographical sketch, Angell contends that although Pritchett was called First Man of Letters, the title never fit properly because he was neither literary nor stylist, and he liked to say he was a hack long before he was a critic.

Baldwin, Dean. *V. S. Pritchett.* Boston: Twayne, 1987. This slim book of 133 pages contains a superb short biography of Pritchett, followed by a clear-cut analysis of his novels, short stories, and nonfiction. One caution is to be noted: Baldwin says there is no article analyzing any of Pritchett's short stories, yet the *Journal of the Short Story in English,* an excellent journal published in Angers, France, devoted an entire volume to Pritchett. It may be that Baldwin's book was already in the process of publication when the journal issue was completed.

Johnson, Anne Janette. "V(ictor) S(awdon) Pritchett." In *Contemporary Authors, New Revision Series,* edited by James G. Lesniak. Vol. 31. Detroit: Gale Research, 1990.

This article includes general material on Pritchett's life and work, with a wide range of critical comments by magazines and literary journals such as *The Times Literary Supplement, The New York Times,* and *The New Republic.* Contains a listing of Pritchett's writings divided into genres and biographical and critical sources, especially those articles that appeared in newspapers, magazines, and literary journals. Geared for the general reader, with the variety of quotes appealing to a specialist.

May, Charles E., ed. *Masterplots II: Short Story Series, Revised Edition.* 8 vols. Pasadena, Calif.: Salem Press, 2004. Designed for student use, this reference set contains articles providing detailed plot summaries and analyses of five short stories by Pritchett: "The Camberwell Beauty" (vol. 1), "It May Never Happen" (vol. 4), "Many Are Disappointed" (vol. 5), and "The Saint" and "Sense of Humour" (vol. 6).

Oumhani, Cecile. "Water in V. S. Pritchett's Art of Revealing." *Journal of the Short Story in English* 6 (1986): 75-91. Oumhani probes the immersion motif in the pattern of water imagery in Pritchett's short stories, especially in "On the Edge of a Cliff," "The Diver," "The Saint," and "Handsome Is as Handsome Does." Oumhani believes that Pritchett's views about sensuality can be intuited from the stories she analyzes.

Pritchett, V. S. "An Interview with V. S. Pritchett." Interview by Ben Forkner and Philippe Sejourne. *Journal of the Short Story in English* 6 (1986): 11-38. Pritchett in this interview reveals a number of salient details about writing in general and the influences of people like H. G. Wells and Arnold Bennett. He talks at length about the Irish predilection for storytelling and the Irish ideas about morality and the art of concealment. Pritchett reveals his penchant for the ironic and pays homage to Anton Chekhov, one of his models. He believes that the comic is really a facet of the poetic. The interview is written in a question-answer style and is a straightforward record of Pritchett's views.

Stinson, John J. *V. S. Pritchett: A Study of the Short Fiction.* New York: Twayne, 1992. Introduction to Pritchett's short fiction. Suggests that Pritchett's stories have been largely ignored by critics because they do not have the symbolic image pattern favored by formalist critics. Provides interpretations of a number of Pritchett's stories. Includes Pritchett's own comments on writers who have influenced him, as well as essays on his short fiction by Eudora Welty and William Trevor.

Theroux, Paul. "V. S. Pritchett." *The New York Times Book Review* 102 (May 25, 1997): 27. A biographical tribute, claiming that Pritchett was probably the last man who could be called a man of letters; notes that Pritchett worked slowly and with confidence.

Treglown, Jeremy. *V. S. Pritchett: A Working Life.* New York: Random House, 2004. Admiring and engaging biography of Pritchett that examines both the breadth of Pritchett's literary production and the highs and lows of his personal life.

Tunick, Linda F. "V. S. Pritchett." In *Critical Survey of Long Fiction, Revised Edition,* edited by Carl Rollyson. Vol. 6. Pasadena, Calif.: Salem Press, 2000. Analysis of Pritchett's longer fictional works that may offer insights into his short fiction.

# E. Annie Proulx

**Born:** Norwich, Connecticut; August 22, 1935

**Principal short fiction** • *Heart Songs, and Other Stories*, 1988; *Close Range: Wyoming Stories*, 1999; *Bad Dirt: Wyoming Stories 2*, 2004.

**Other literary forms** • E. Annie Proulx has published in many different genres. Early in her career, she was a freelance journalist, writing cookbooks, how-to manuals, and magazine articles on everything from making cider to building fences. During the 1980's, she published eleven nonfiction books, ranging from *Great Grapes! Grow the Best Ever* in 1980 to *The Gourmet Gardener: Growing Choice Fruits and Vegetables with Spectacular Results* in 1987. During the 1990's, she began publishing long fictional works. Her first novel, *Postcards* (1992), received good reviews. However, it was the enthusiastic reception of her second novel, *The Shipping News* (1993), that brought her international fame and popular success. The Pulitzer Prize-winner was made into a successful film in 2001. Her novel *Accordion Crimes* (1996) did not enjoy the same acclaim. Her fourth novel, *That Old Ace in the Hole* (2002) is about land swindlers in the Texas Panhandle. Proulx also shared screenwriting credit for the film adapted from her short story "Brokeback Mountain" that won multiple Academy Awards. She later contributed a chapter to *Brokeback Mountain: Story to Screenplay* (2006), which contains Larry McMurtry and Diana Ossana's complete screenplay.

**Achievements** • For her *Postcards*, E. Annie Proulx was the first woman to win the PEN/Faulkner Award for fiction. In 1993, *The Shipping News* won many awards, including the *Chicago Tribune* Heartland Prize, *The Irish Times* International Fiction Prize, the National Book Award, and the Pulitzer Prize. Four stories from her collection *Close Range: Wyoming Stories* were selected for the 1998 and 1999 editions of *The Best American Short Stories* and *Prize Stories: The O. Henry Awards*. "The Half-Skinned Deer" was selected for *The Best American Short Stories of the Century*. Proulx also shared several awards for the screenplay of *Brokeback Mountain*.

**Biography** • Edna Annie Proulx was born in Norwich, Connecticut, in 1935, the oldest of five daughters. Her father worked his way up in the textile mills to the position of vice president; her mother painted landscapes in watercolors. Because her father was frequently transferred, the family moved several times when she was young. She entered Colby College in the 1950's but dropped out to, as she says, "experience two terrible marriages, New York City, the Far East, and single-mother-with-two-children poverty." She returned to school in 1963, graduating Phi Beta Kappa. She entered the graduate program at Sir George Williams University (now Concordia University), in Montreal, specializing in Renaissance economic history, and finished all the work for the doctoral degree except the dissertation.

By this time Proulx had been married and divorced three times and was the mother of three sons. She worked as a freelance journalist from 1975 to 1988, writing books and articles on a wide range of subjects. During the mid-1990's, Proulx moved from Vermont to Centennial, Wyoming (population 100), where she lives and writes in relative isolation. She travels part of the year to Australia and Ireland and across the United States.

**Analysis** • Although E. Annie Proulx's first collection, *Heart Songs, and Other Stories*, was relatively conventional in structure and language, her interest in what one of her characters calls the "rural downtrodden" is much in evidence here. The stories, featuring such quaintly named characters as Albro, Eno, and Snipe, take place in rural Vermont and New Hampshire. Without condescension, Proulx describes trailer-dwelling men and women who drink, smoke, feud, and fornicate without much introspection or analysis.

***Close Range: Wyoming Stories*** • In *Close Range: Wyoming Stories*, Proulx shifts her milieu to the rural West, where her characters are similarly ragged and rugged, but where, either because of her increased confidence as a writer or because she was inspired by the landscape and the fiercely independent populace, her characters are more compellingly caught in a world that is grittily real and magically mythical at once. Claiming that her stories gainsay the romantic myth of the West, Proulx admires the independence and self-reliance she has found there, noting that the people "fix things and get along without them if they can't be fixed. They don't whine."

Place is as important as the people who populate it in *Close Range*, for the Wyoming landscape is harsh yet beautiful, real yet magical, deadly yet sustaining. In such a world, social props are worthless and folks are thrown back on their most basic instincts, whether they be sexual, survival, or sacred. In such a world, as one character says in "Brokeback Mountain," "It's easier than you think to yield up to the dark impulse." Proulx's Wyoming is a heart of darkness both in place and personality.

**"Brokeback Mountain"** • The most remarkable thing about "Brokeback Mountain" is that although it is about a sexual relationship between two men, it cannot be categorized as a homosexual story; it is rather a tragic love story that simply happens to involve two men. The fact that the men are Wyoming cowboys rather than San Francisco urbanites makes Proulx's success in creating such a convincing and emotionally affecting story all the more wonderful.

Jack Twist and Ennis del Mar are "high-school drop-out country boys with no prospects" who, while working alone at a sheep-herding operation on Brokeback Mountain, abruptly and silently engage in a sexual encounter, after which both immediately insist, "I'm not no queer." Although the two get married to women and do not see each other for four years, when they meet again, they grab each other and hug in a gruff masculine way, and then, "as easily as the right key turns the lock tumblers, their mouths came together."

Neither has sex with other men, and both know the danger of their relationship. Twenty years pass, and their infrequent encounters are a combination of sexual passion and personal concern. The story comes to a climax when Jack, who unsuccessfully tries to convince Ennis they can make a life together, is mysteriously killed on the roadside. Although officially it was an accident, Ennis sorrowfully suspects that Jack has been murdered after approaching another man. Although "Brokeback Mountain" ends with Jack a victim of social homophobia, this is not a story about the social plight of the homosexual. The issues Proulx explores here are more basic and primal than that. Told in a straightforward, matter-of-fact style, the story elicits a genuine sympathy for a love that is utterly convincing.

**"The Half-Skinned Steer"** • Chosen by writer John Updike for *The Best American Short Stories of the Century,* this brief piece creates a hallucinatory world of shimmering significance out of common materials. The simple event on which the story is based is a cross-country drive made by Mero, a man in his eighties, to Wyoming for the funeral of his brother. The story alternates between the old man's encounters on the road, including an accident, and his memories of his father and brother. The central metaphor of the piece is introduced in a story Mero recalls about a man who, while skinning a steer, stops for dinner, leaving the beast half skinned. When he returns, he sees the steer stumbling stiffly away, its head and shoulders raw meat, its staring eyes filled with hate. The man knows that he and his family are doomed.

The story ends with Mero getting stuck in a snowstorm a few miles away from his destination and trying to walk back to the main highway. As he struggles through the wind and the drifts, he notices that one of the herd of cattle in the field next to the road has been keeping pace with him, and he realizes that the "half-skinned steer's red eye had been watching for him all this time." In its combination of stark realism and folktale myth, "The Half-Skinned Steer" is reminiscent of stories by Eudora Welty and Flannery O'Connor, for Mero's journey is an archetypal one toward the inevitable destiny of death.

**"The Mud Below"** • Proulx has said that this is her favorite story in *Close Range,* for "on-the-edge situations" and the rodeo interest her. The title refers to the mud of the rodeo arena, and the main character is twenty-three-year-old Diamond Felts, who, at five foot three, has always been called "Shorty," "Kid," "Tiny," and "Little Guy." His father left when he was a child, telling him, "You ain't no kid of mine." His mother taunts him about his size more than anyone else, always calling him Shorty and telling him he is stupid for wanting to be a bull rider in the rodeo.

The force of the story comes from Diamond's identification with the bulls. The first time he rides one he gets such a feeling of power that he feels as though he were the bull and not the rider; even the fright seems to fulfill a "greedy physical hunger" in him. When one man tells him that the bull is not supposed to be his role model, Diamond says the bull is his partner. The story comes to a climax when Diamond is thrown and suffers a dislocated shoulder. Tormented by the pain, he calls his mother and demands to know who his father is. Getting no answer, Diamond drives away thinking that all of life is a "hard, fast ride that ended in the mud," but he also feels the euphoric heat of the bull ride, or at least the memory of it, and realizes that if that is all there is, it must be enough.

**"The Bunchgrass Edge of the World"** • Like most of the stories in *Close Range,* "The Bunchgrass Edge of the World" is about surviving. As Old Red, a ninety-six-year-old grandfather, says at the end, "The main thing in life was staying power. That was it: stand around long enough, you'd get to sit down." Picked by Amy Tan to be included in *The Best American Short Stories 1999,* it is one of the most comic fictions in the collection. A story about a young woman named Ottaline, with a "physique approaching the size of a propane tank," being wooed by a broken-down John Deere 4030 tractor could hardly be anything else.

Ottaline's only chance for a husband seems to be the semiliterate hired man, Hal Bloom, with whom she has silent sex, that is, until she is first approached by the talking tractor, who calls her "sweetheart, lady-girl." Tired of the loneliness of listening to cellular phone conversations on a scanner, Ottaline spends more and more time with the tractor, gaining confidence until, when made to take on the responsibility of cattle trading by her ill father, she meets Flyby Amendinger, whom she soon marries. The story ends with Ottaline's father getting killed in a small plane he is flying. The ninety-six-year-old grandfather, who sees how things had to go, has the powerfully uncomplicated final word—that the main thing in life is staying power.

*Charles E. May*
*With updates by the Editors*

**Other major works**

ANTHOLOGY: *The Best American Short Stories, 1997: Selected from U.S. and Canadian Magazines*, 1997 (with Katrina Kenison).

NOVELS: *Postcards*, 1992; *The Shipping News*, 1993; *Accordion Crimes*, 1996; *That Old Ace in the Hole*, 2002.

MISCELLANEOUS; *Brokeback Mountain: Story to Screenplay*, 2006 (with Larry McMurtry and Diana Ossana)

NONFICTION: *Great Grapes! Grow the Best Ever*, 1980; *Making the Best Apple Cider*, 1980; *Sweet and Hard Cider: Making It, Using It, and Enjoying It*, 1980 (also known as *Cider: Making, Using, and Enjoying Sweet and Hard Cider*, 1997; with Lew Nichols); *"What'll You Take for It?": Back to Barter*, 1981; *Make Your Own Insulated Window Shutters*, 1981; *The Complete Dairy Foods Cookbook: How to Make Everything from Cheese to Custard in Your Own Kitchen*, 1982 (with Nichols); *Plan and Make Your Own Fences and Gates, Walkways, Walls, and Drives*, 1983; *The Gardener's Journal and Record Book*, 1983; *The Fine Art of Salad Gardening*, 1985; *The Gourmet Gardener: Growing Choice Fruits and Vegetables with Spectacular Results*, 1987.

**Bibliography**

Elder, Richard. "Don't Fence Me In." *The New York Times*, May 23, 1999, p. 8. An extended review of *Close Range: Wyoming Stories*. Says the strength of the collection is Proulx's feeling for place and how it affects her characters. Claims Proulx's extraordinary knowledge of male behavior is most remarkable in "Brokeback Mountain." Argues that the best story in the collection is "The Mud Below."

Hustak, Alan. "An Uneasy Guest of Honor." *The Montreal Gazette*, June 10, 1999, p. D10. An interview-story on the occasion of Proulx's receiving an honorary degree from her alma mater, Concordia University. Provides biographical information about her education and her literary career. Proulx discusses her years as a freelance journalist, the film production based on *The Shipping News*, and the relationship of character to place in her fiction.

Liss, Barbara. "Wild, Wearying Wyoming." Review of *Close Range: Wyoming Stories*, by E. Annie Proulx. *The Houston Chronicle*, June 20, 1999, p. Z23. Praises the book's Magical Realism, but suggests that its "downbeat weirdness" will not be to everyone's taste. Says that "Brokeback Mountain" is the best story, with Proulx pouring a great deal of sympathy on the two young men and their passionate relationship.

May, Charles E., ed. *Masterplots II: Short Story Series, Revised Edition*. 8 vols. Pasadena, Calif.: Salem Press, 2004. Designed for student use, this reference set contains articles providing detailed plot summaries and analyses of three short stories by Proulx: "Brokeback Mountain" and "The Bunchgrass Edge of the World" (vol. 1), and "The Half-Skinned Steer" (vol. 3).

Rood, Karen L. *Understanding Annie Proulx.* Columbia: University of South Carolina Press, 2001. Rood provides a biography, introduces the themes and techniques used in Proulx's fiction, and discusses her early work as a nonfiction writer. Includes an annotated bibliography of writings by and about Proulx.

See, Carolyn. "Proulx's Wild West." *The Washington Post,* July 2, 1999, p. C2. See says she is in awe of *Close Range,* claiming that Proulx has the most amazing combination of things working for her: an exquisite sense of place, a dead-on accurate sense of working class, hard-luck Americans, and a prose style that is the best in English today.

Singleton, Janet. "Proulx's Keen Insights Focus on Life, not Awards." *The Denver Post,* June 6, 1999, p. F3. In this interview-based story, Proulx talks about her research, her nomadic lifestyle, and the stories in *Close Range: Wyoming Stories*; says she writes stories that question the romantic myth of the West. Singleton claims Proulx's characters may live in God's country, but they seem godforsaken.

Steinbach, Alice. "E. Annie Proulx's Novel Journey to Literary Celebrity Status." *The Baltimore Sun,* May 15, 1994, p. 1K. An interview-based story that reveals Proulx's lighter side. Provides biographical information about her education, marriages, divorces, and rise to fame. Proulx discusses her love of writing, her male characters, and feminism.

Steinberg, Sybil. "E. Annie Proulx: An American Odyssey." *Publishers Weekly* 243, no. 23 (July, 1996): 57-58. Discusses how Proulx has been inspired by harsh landscapes and her development of *Postcards, The Shipping News,* and *Accordion Crimes* through meticulous research.

Streitfeld, David. "The Stuff of a Writer." *The Washington Post,* November 16, 1993, p. B1. A long, interview-based story on Proulx on the occasion of *The Shipping News* being nominated for the National Book Award. Provides much insight into Proulx's life in rural Vermont, her preference for "the rough side of things" and her rugged independence.

# James Purdy

**Born:** Fremont, Ohio; July 17, 1923

**Principal short fiction** • *Don't Call Me by My Right Name, and Other Stories*, 1956; *Sixty-three: Dream Palace*, 1956; *Color of Darkness: Eleven Stories and a Novella*, 1957; *The Candles of Your Eyes*, 1985; *The Candles of Your Eyes, and Thirteen Other Stories*, 1987; *Sixty-three: Dream Palace: Selected Stories, 1956-1987*, 1991; *Moe's Villa, and Other Stories*, 2000.

**Other literary forms** • James Purdy, in more than four decades of literary work, beginning in the 1950's, has written—besides his short fiction—a number of novels (including *Malcolm*, published in 1959, and *In a Shallow Grave*, published in 1976) several collections of poetry, and numerous plays, some of which have been staged in the United States as well as abroad.

**Achievements** • James Purdy has received a National Institute of Arts and Letters grant in literature (1958), John Simon Guggenheim Memorial Foundation Fellowships (1958, 1962), and a Ford Foundation grant (1961). *On Glory's Course* was a finalist for the PEN/Faulkner Award (1985). He also received a Rockefeller Foundation grant, a Morton Dauwen Zabel Fiction award from the American Academy of Arts and Letters (1993), and an Oscar Williams and Gene Derwood award for poetry and art (1995).

**Biography** • James Otis Purdy was born near Fremont, Ohio, on July 14, 1923, the son of William and Vera Purdy, and he has told many interviewers that the exact location of his birthplace is now unknown, since the community no longer exists. Purdy's parents were divorced when he was quite young. He lived, as he once said, with his father for a time in various locations and at other times with his mother and an aunt who had a farm, an experience which he has recalled favorably.

Purdy has explained that his ethnic background was that of a very long line of Scotch-Irish Presbyterians, but that most of his family is now deceased, as are many of his oldest friends. Purdy's formal education began with his attendance at the University of Chicago, where he was to drop out during World War II to serve with the U.S. Air Corps. He has indicated that he was not the best of soldiers but that his military service gave him the necessary background for his later novel *Eustace Chisholm and the Works* (1967).

Purdy also attended for a time the University of Puebla, Mexico, and enrolled in graduate school at the University of Chicago. He taught from 1949 to 1953 at Lawrence College in Appleton, Wisconsin, and later worked as an interpreter in Latin America, France, and Spain. In 1953, however, he gave up other work to pursue a full-time career as a writer.

Although he has been a prolific writer throughout his career, Purdy's fiction, while enjoying considerable critical success, has not been commercially successful, a fact that Purdy often attributes to a conspiratorial elite in New York that foists more commercial, but less substantive, literature on the American public.

Purdy's early work was rejected by most major American publishing houses, and his first fiction was published privately by friends in the United States and later through the help of writers such as Carl Van Vechten and, in Great Britain, Edith Sitwell. Both Purdy's volumes *Sixty-three: Dream Palace* and *Don't Call Me by My Right Name, and Other Stories* were printed privately in 1956, and in 1957, the novella *Sixty-three: Dream Palace* appeared with additional stories under the title *Color of Darkness,* published by Gollancz in London. These early works gained for Purdy a small, devoted following, and his allegorical novel *Malcolm* followed in 1959. In that work, Malcolm, a beautiful young man, is led by older persons through a wide range of experiences, until he finally dies of alcoholism and sexual hyperesthesia. In a way, Malcolm is a forerunner of many Purdy characters, whose driven states of being take them ultimately to disaster. (*Malcolm* was

Library of Congress

later adapted to play form by Edward Albee, an admirer of Purdy's work. The 1966 New York production, however, was not successful.)

Two Purdy novels of the 1960's expanded the author's literary audience: *The Nephew* (1960) explores small-town life in the American Midwest and centers on the attempt of an aunt to learn more about her nephew (killed in the Korean War) than she had known about him in his lifetime, and *Cabot Wright Begins* (1964) is a satirical attack on the totally materialistic American culture of consumers and competitors, where all love is either suppressed or commercialized. *Cabot Wright Begins* relates the comic adventures of a Wall Street broker-rapist who manages to seduce 366 women. The novel was sold to motion-picture firms, but the film version was never made.

The inability of people to deal with their inner desires—a major theme of Purdy's fiction—and the resultant violence provoked by that inability characterize Purdy's next novel, *Eustace Chisholm and the Works.* Another recurring Purdy theme is that of the self-destructive, cannibalistic American family, in which parents refuse to let go of their children and give them an independent life of their own. That self-destructive family theme and his earlier motif—the search for meaning in an unknown past—mark his trilogy of novels *Sleepers in Moon-Crowned Valleys,* the first volume of which, *Jeremy's Version,* appeared in 1970 to considerable critical acclaim. The second and third volumes of the trio of novels, however, *The House of the Solitary Maggot* (1974) and *Mourners Below* (1981), received little critical notice. Purdy once said that parts of the trilogy had come from stories that his grandmother had related to him as a child at a time when he was living with her.

Perhaps the most bizarre of Purdy's novels, *I Am Elijah Thrush,* was published in 1972. Set in New York, the novel deals with an aged male dancer (once a student of

Isadora Duncan and known as "the most beautiful man in the world") who becomes obsessed with a mysterious blond, angelic child known as Bird of Heaven, a mute who communicates by making peculiar kissing sounds.

Purdy's later works reinforce these themes of lost identity and obsessive but often suppressed loves: *In a Shallow Grave* concerns a disfigured Vietnam War veteran who has lost that most personal form of identity, his face; *Narrow Rooms* (1978) details the complex sexual relationships of four West Virginia boys who cannot cope with their emotional feelings for one another and who direct their feelings into garish violence. That novel, Purdy said, was partially derived from fact; Purdy said that he frequently ran into hillbilly types in New York who told him such terrible stories of their lives.

Purdy's later works include *On Glory's Course* (1984), *In the Hollow of His Hand* (1986), and the 1989 novel dealing with acquired immunodeficiency syndrome (AIDS), *Garments the Living Wear.* His novel *In a Shallow Grave* was made into a motion picture in 1988.

**Analysis** • James Purdy is one of the more independent, unusual, and stylistically unique of American writers, since his fiction—novels, plays, and short stories—maintains a dark vision of American life while stating that vision in a literary voice unlike any other American writer. In more than a dozen novels, several collections of short fiction, and volumes of poetry and plays, Purdy has created an unrelentingly tragic view of human existence, in which people invariably are unable to face their true natures and thus violate—mentally and physically—those around them. In an interview in 1978, Purdy said:

> I think that is the universal human tragedy. We never become what we could be. I believe life is tragic. It's my view that nothing ever solves anything. Oh yes, life is full of many joys . . . but it's essentially tragic because man is imperfect. He can't find solutions by his very nature.

As a result of his tragic view of humankind, Purdy's fiction often contains unpleasant, violent, even repellent actions by his characters.

The short fiction of James Purdy is marked—as are many of his novels—by the recurrence of several themes, among them the conflict in the American family unit caused by the parental inability to relinquish control over children and allow them to live their own lives, a control to which Purdy has often referred as the "cannibalization" present in the family. A second theme frequently found in Purdy's short fiction is that of obsessive love that cannot be expressed, both heterosexual and homosexual. This inability of individuals to express their emotional yearning and longing often is turned into an expression of violence against those around them. The homoerotic element in Purdy's fiction only accentuates this propensity to violence, since Purdy often sees the societal repression of the homosexual emotion of love as one of the more brutal forms of self-denial imposed on an individual. Thus, many of his stories deal with such a latent—and tension-strained—homoeroticism. These two themes are conjoined occasionally in many of his novels and short stories to produce the unspeakable sense of loss: the loss of self-identity, of a loved one, or of a wasted past.

**"Color of Darkness"** • In "Color of Darkness," the title story of the collection by the same name, a husband can no longer recall the color of the eyes of his wife, who has left him. As his young son struggles with the memory of his lost mother, he begins to suck regularly on the symbol of his parents' union, their wedding ring. In a confrontation with his father—who is concerned for the boy's safety because of the metal object in his mouth—the youngster suddenly kicks his father in the groin and reduces him to a suffering, writhing object at whom the boy hurls a crude epithet.

This kind of terrible family situation, embodying as it does loss, alienation from both a mate and a parent, and violence, is typical of the kind of intense anguish that Purdy's short stories often portray. In the world of Purdy, the American family involves a selfish, possessive, and obsessive struggle, which, over time, often becomes totally self-destructive, as individuals lash out at one another for hurts that they can no longer endure but that they cannot explain.

**"Don't Call Me by My Right Name"** • Elsewhere in the collection *Color of Darkness,* "Don't Call Me by My Right Name" portrays a wife who has begun using her maiden name, Lois McBane, because after six months of marriage she finds that she has grown to hate her new name, Mrs. Klein. Her loss of name is, like many such minor events in Purdy's fiction, simply a symbol for a larger loss, that of her self-identity, a theme that Purdy frequently invokes in his novels (as in his later novel *In a Shallow Grave*). The wife's refusal to accept her husband's name as her new label leads to a violent physical fight between them following a party which they both attend.

**"Why Can't They Tell You Why?"** • This potential for violence underlying the domestic surface of the American family is seen again in one of the author's most terrifying early stories, "Why Can't They Tell You Why?" A small child, Paul, who has never known his father, finds a box of photographs. These photographs become for the boy a substitute for the absent parent, but his mother, Ethel, who appears to hate her late soldier-husband's memory, is determined to break the boy's fascination with his lost father. In a final scene of real horror, she forces the child to watch as she burns the box of photographs in the furnace, an act that drives the boy into, first, a frenzy of despair and then into a state of physical and emotional breakdown, as she tries to force the child to care for her and not for his dead father. Again, Purdy has captured the awful hatreds that lie within a simple family unit and the extreme malice to which they can lead.

**"Sleep Tight"** • A similar tale of near-gothic horror affecting children is found in Purdy's story "Sleep Tight," which appears in his 1985 collection, *The Candles of Your Eyes.* In it, a fatally wounded burglar enters the bedroom of a young child who has been taught to believe in the Sandman. The child, believing the man to be the Sandman whom his sister, Nelle, and his mother have told him about, does not report the presence of the bleeding man, who takes refuge in the child's closet. After the police have come and gone, the child enters the closet where the now-dead man has bled profusely. He believes the blood to be watercolors and begins painting with the burglar's blood, and he comes to believe that he has killed the Sandman with his gun.

**"Cutting Edge"** • Domestic violence within the family unit is but one of Purdy's terrible insights into family life in America. Subdued family tensions—beneath the surface of outright and tragic violence—appear in "Cutting Edge," in which a domineering mother, her weak-willed husband, and their son (an artist home from New York wearing a beard) form a triangle of domestic hatred. The mother is determined that her son must shave off his beard while visiting, so as to emasculate her son symboli-cally, the way she has emasculated his father. The son is aware of his father's reduced status at his mother's hands and even suggests, at one point, that his father use physi-cal violence against the woman to gain back some control over her unpleasant and demanding, dictatorial manner. Purdy directly states in the story that the three are truly prisoners of one another, seeking release but unable to find it. Purdy thus in-vokes once again the entrapment theme that he sees typical of American families. The father, in insisting on his son's acquiescence to the mother's demand for the re-moval of the beard, has lost all credibility with his son. (The father had told the son that if the offending beard was not shaved off, then the mother would mentally tor-ture her husband for six months after their son had returned to New York.)

The story's resolution—when the son shaves off the beard and mutilates his face in the process as a rebuke to his parents—is both an act of defiance and an almost lit-eral cutting of the umbilical cord with his family, since he tells his parents that he will not see them at Christmas and that they cannot see him in New York, since he will again have his beard. This story also introduces another theme upon which Purdy frequently touches: the contempt for artistic pursuit by the narrow and materialistic American middle class. The parents, for example, see art as causing their son's defi-ance of their restrictive lives.

**"Dawn"** • A similar mood is found in the story "Dawn," from the collection *The Can-dles of Your Eyes*. Here, a father, outraged because his son has posed for an underwear advertisement, comes to New York, invades the apartment where his son Timmy lives with another actor, Freddy, and announces that he is taking Timmy home to the small town where the father still lives. The father, Mr. Jaqua, resents his son's attempt to become an actor. He has urged the boy into a more respectable profession: the law. The story turns on Timmy's inability to resist his father's demands and his ultimate acquiescence to them. After Timmy has packed and left the apartment, Freddy is left alone, still loving Timmy but aware that he will never see him again.

This inability of American middle-class culture to accept or deal logically with ho-mosexual love as a valid expression in men's emotional makeup is also found in Purdy's novels and elsewhere in his short fiction. The theme occurs in *Eustace Chis-holm and the Works* as well as in *The Nephew, In a Shallow Grave, Malcolm,* and *Narrow Rooms,* and this denial of one's homosexual nature often leads Purdy's characters to violent acts.

**"Everything Under the Sun"** • A slightly suppressed homoeroticism is also found in "Everything Under the Sun," in Purdy's collection *Children Is All.* Two young men, Jesse and Cade, two of those flat-spoken country (or hillbilly) types who often appear in Purdy's fiction, are living together in an apartment on the south end of State Street (Chicago possibly). Their basic conflict is whether Cade will work or not, which Jesse desires but which Cade is unwilling to do. Cade ultimately remains in full control of the tense erotic relationship by threatening to leave permanently if Jesse does not let him have his own way. Although there is talk of liquor and women, the real sexual tension is between the two men, who, when they bare their chests, have identical tattoos of black panthers. Although neither would acknowledge their true relationship, their sexual attraction is seen through their ungrammatically accurate speech patterns and the subtle erotic undertones to their pairing.

**"Some of These Days"** • The stories in *The Candles of Your Eyes* exhibit a homoerotic yearning as part of their plot. In "Some of These Days," a young man (the first-person narrator of the story) is engaged in a pathetic search for the man to whom he refers as his "landlord." His quest for the elusive "landlord" (who comes to be known merely as "my lord") takes him through a series of sexual encounters in pornographic motion-picture theaters as he tries desperately to find the man whose name has been obliterated from his memory.

**"Summer Tidings"** • "Summer Tidings," in the same collection, portrays a Jamaican working as a gardener on an estate, where he becomes obsessed with the young blond boy whose parents own the estate. In a subtle ending, the Jamaican fancies the ecstasy of the perfume of the blond boy's shampooed hair.

**"Rapture"** • In "Rapture," an army officer visits his sister, who is fatally ill, and she introduces the man to her young son, Brice. The soldier develops a fetish for the boy's golden hair, which he regularly removes from the boy's comb. After the boy's mother dies and her funeral is held, the uncle and his nephew are united in a wild love scene, a scene that the mother had foreseen when she thought of leaving her son to someone who would appreciate him as she had been appreciated and cared for by her bridegroom.

**"Lily's Party"** • "Lily's Party," in the same collection, is even more explicit in its homosexual statement. In this story, Hobart, a man obsessed with his brother's wife, follows the woman to her rendezvous with a new lover, a young preacher. Hobart then watches as the woman, Lily, and the preacher make love. Then, the two men alternately make love with Lily and take occasional breaks to eat pies that Lily had cooked for a church social. Finally, the two men smear each other with pies and begin— much to Lily's consternation—to nibble at each other. As their encounter becomes more explicitly sexual, Lily is left alone, weeping in the kitchen, eating the remains of her pies, and being ignored by the two men.

Purdy's fiction has a manic—almost surreal—quality, both in the short works and in the novels. In his emphasis on very ordinary individuals plunging headlong into their private hells and their nightmarish lives, Purdy achieves the same kind of juxtaposition of the commonplace, seen through warped configuration of the psyche, that one finds in surrealist art.

*Sixty-three: Dream Palace* • Nowhere is that quality as clearly to be found as in Purdy's most famous piece of short fiction, his early novella *Sixty-three: Dream Palace*, a work that, by its title, conveys the grotesque vision of shattered illusion and the desperation of its characters. Not only does *Sixty-three: Dream Palace* have the surreal quality of nightmare surrounding its action, but also it contains the latent homoeroticism of many of Purdy's other works and the distinctive speech rhythms, this time in the conversation of its principal character, the West Virginia boy Fenton Riddleway.

Fenton Riddleway, together with his sick younger brother Claire, has come from his native West Virginia to live in an abandoned house, on what he calls "sixty-three street," in a large city. In a public park, Fenton encounters a wealthy, largely unproductive "writer" named Parkhearst Cratty. Parkhearst seeks to introduce the young man to a wealthy woman named Grainger (but who is referred to as "the great woman"). Ostensibly, both Parkhearst and Grainger are attracted to the youth, and it is suggested that he will be cared for if he will come and live in Grainger's mansion. Fenton also likes to spend time in a film theater (somewhat like Purdy's main character in "Some of These Days"). At one point in the story, Fenton is picked up by a handsome homosexual named Bruno Korsawski, who takes the boy to a production of William Shakespeare's *Othello,* starring an actor named Hayden Banks. A violent scene with Bruno serves to let readers realize Fenton's capability for violence, a potentiality that is revealed later when readers are told that he has killed his younger brother, who would not leave the abandoned house to go and live in the Grainger mansion. Faced with his younger brother's reluctance, his own desire to escape from both his derelict life, and the burden of the child Claire, Fenton killed the child, and the story's final scene has Fenton first trying to revive the dead child and then placing the child's body in a chest in the abandoned house.

Desperation, violence, an inability to deal with sexual longing, and the capacity to do harm even to ones who are loved are found in *Sixty-three: Dream Palace,* and it may be the most representative of Purdy's short fiction in its use of these thematic elements, strands of which mark so many of his various short stories. The tragic vision of life that Purdy sees as the human condition thus haunts all of his short fiction, as it does his most famous story.

In 1981 Purdy published *Sixty-three: Dream Palace, Selected Stories, 1956-1987,* a collection of reprints of twenty-six stories and one novella from the author's earlier works, including *Color of Darkness, Children Is All,* and *The Candles of Your Eyes.* The collection provides readers the opportunity to reappraise the unconventional literary style and trademark blend of quirky characters and bizarre settings Purdy uses to confront racial and sexual stereotypes in American culture.

**"You May Safely Gaze"** • In "You May Safely Gaze," one of his less successful efforts, two narcissistic male exhibitionists put on an open display of affection at a beach, while a male colleague, obsessed with their behavior, complains to his disinterested female companion. Not only does the female companion appear detached, but also the author, who in an attempt to infuse a superficiality to the entire scene, never appears to rise above the surface level himself in constructing a meaningful framework that would help establish the motivations behind his characters' actions.

**"Eventide"** • Emotional voids, another favorite Purdy theme, is explored with more piercing insight in "Eventide," the tale of two African American sisters grieving over lost young sons, one of whom simply disappeared, the other having died. Faced with a life without their offspring, the sisters seek their solace in the darkness that surrounds them, as if life beyond it is a threat to the memory of their sons, which represents the only security they have left.

**"Man and Wife"** • Husbands and wives fare badly in Purdy's America when faced with personal crises. In "Man and Wife," a mentally disabled husband is fired from his job for an alleged sexual deviancy, prompting his wife to accuse him of having no character because "he had never found a character to have" and the husband to bemoan a marriage invaded by "something awful and permanent that comes to everybody." Only the sense of hopelessness that pervades the marriage is left to bind them in the end. In "Sound of Talking," the reality of a marriage turned sour becomes starkly evident when a wife's patience in catering to the demands of a wheelchair-bound husband runs dry. In both stories Purdy's characters are only able to raise their voices in plaintive cries, unable to explain to their spouses or themselves the source of their discomfort and disdain for each other. Attempts at escape often appear feeble, as in the wife's recommendation in "Sound of Talking" that she and her husband purchase a pet as a remedy for their trouble.

If the promise of marriage seems a distant memory in "Man and Wife" and "Sound of Talking," it becomes a cruel reality in the author's "Ruthanna Elder" when a young man learns his prospective bride has been sexually violated by her uncle, causing the groom-to-be to suddenly take his own life. It is a tragic tale, simply told, yet one that illustrates perhaps Purdy's most enduring theme, that of the human heart's great potential for great good or great evil.

*Jere Real*
*With updates by William Hoffman*

## Other major works

PLAYS: *Mr. Cough Syrup and the Phantom Sex*, pb. 1960; *Cracks*, pb. 1962, pr. 1963; *Wedding Finger*, pb. 1974; *Clearing in the Forest*, pr. 1978, pb. 1980; *True*, pr. 1978, pb. 1979; *A Day After the Fair*, pb. 1979; *Now*, pr. 1979, pb. 1980; *Two Plays*, pb. 1979 (includes *A Day After the Fair* and *True*); *What Is It, Zach?*, pr. 1979, pb. 1980; *Proud Flesh: Four Short Plays*, pb. 1980; *Strong*, pb. 1980; *Scrap of Paper*, pb. 1981; *The Berry-Picker*, pb. 1981, pr. 1984; *In the Night of Time, and Four Other Plays*, pb. 1992 (includes *In the Night of Time, Enduring Zeal, The Paradise Circus, The Rivalry of Dolls*, and *Ruthanna Elder*); *The Rivalry of Dolls*, pr., pb. 1992.

NOVELS: *Malcolm*, 1959; *The Nephew*, 1960; *Cabot Wright Begins*, 1964; *Eustace Chisholm and the Works*, 1967; *Jeremy's Version*, 1970; *I Am Elijah Thrush*, 1972; *The House of the Solitary Maggot*, 1974; *In a Shallow Grave*, 1976; *Narrow Rooms*, 1978; *Mourners Below*, 1981; *On Glory's Course*, 1984; *In the Hollow of His Hand*, 1986; *Garments the Living Wear*, 1989; *Out with the Stars*, 1992; *Gertrude of Sony Island Avenue*, 1997.

MISCELLANEOUS: *Children Is All*, 1961 (10 stories and 2 plays); *An Oyster Is a Wealthy Beast*, 1967 (story and poems); *Mr. Evening: A Story and Nine Poems*, 1968; *On the Rebound: A Story and Nine Poems*, 1970; *A Day After the Fair: A Collection of Plays and Stories*, 1977.

POETRY: *The Running Sun*, 1971; *Sunshine Is an Only Child*, 1973; *She Came Out of the Mists of Morning*, 1975; *Lessons and Complaints*, 1978; *The Brooklyn Branding Parlors*, 1986.

## Bibliography

Adams, Stephen D. *James Purdy*. New York: Barnes & Noble Books, 1976. Adams's study covers Purdy's major work from the early stories and *Malcolm* up through *In a Shallow Grave*. Of particular interest is his discussion of the first two novels in Purdy's trilogy *Sleepers in Moon-Crowned Valleys*.

Ladd, Jay L. *James Purdy: A Bibliography*. Columbus: Ohio State University Libraries, 1999. Annotated bibliography of works by and about James Purdy.

May, Charles E., ed. *Masterplots II: Short Story Series, Revised Edition*. 8 vols. Pasadena, Calif.: Salem Press, 2004. Designed for student use, this reference set contains articles providing detailed plot summaries and analyses of four short stories by Purdy: "Color of Darkness," "Daddy Wolf" and "Don't Call Me by My Right Name" (vol. 2); and "Why Can't They Tell You Why?" (vol. 8).

Peden, William. *The American Short Story: Front Line in the National Defense of Literature.* Boston: Houghton Mifflin, 1964. Peden discusses Purdy in comparison with some of the "southern gothic" writers, such as Truman Capote and Carson McCullers, and in relation to Purdy's probing of themes about the strange and perverse in American life.

Purdy, James. "Out with James Purdy: An Interview." Interview by Christopher Lane. *Critique* 40 (Fall, 1998): 71-89. Evaluates reasons for critical hostility to Purdy's writings. Presents Purdy's views on racial and sexual stereotyping, violence in art, and the effect of political correctness. Analyzes theme and subject, presenting real-life counterparts to characters in several novels.

Renner, Stanley. "'Why Can't They Tell You Why?' A Clarifying Echo of *The Turn of the Screw.*" *Studies in American Fiction* 14 (1986): 205-213. Compares the story with Henry James's famous tale; argues that both are about a female suppressing a male's sexual identity.

Schwarzchild, Bettina. *The Not-Right House: Essays on James Purdy.* Columbia: University of Missouri Press, 1968. Although the primary focus of these essays is on Purdy's novels, there is some comparative discussion of such early works as *Sixty-three: Dream Palace* and "Don't Call Me by My Right Name."

Skaggs, Calvin. "The Sexual Nightmare of 'Why Can't They Tell You Why?'" In *The Process of Fiction*, edited by Barbara McKenzie. New York: Harcourt, Brace and World, 1969. Argues that the mother tries to destroy the boy's masculine identification because of her own ambiguous sexual identity. Claims that in the final scene a strong female emasculates a weak male.

Turnbaugh, Douglas Blair. "James Purdy: Playwright." *PAJ* 20 (May, 1998): 73-75. Discusses Purdy's international acclaim and publication history. Praises his uses of dialogue and vernacular in the novels. Critical evaluation of dramatizations of Purdy's novels, specifically focusing on the Public Broadcasting Service (PBS) distortion of *In a Shallow Grave.*

# Saki

**Born:** Akyab, Burma (now Myanmar); December 18, 1870
**Died:** Beaumont Hamel, France; November 14, 1916

**Principal short fiction** • *Reginald*, 1904; *Reginald in Russia*, 1910; *The Chronicles of Clovis*, 1911; *Beasts and Super-Beasts*, 1914; *The Toys of Peace*, 1919; *The Square Egg*, 1924; *The Short Stories of Saki (H. H. Munro) Complete*, 1930.

**Other literary forms** • Saki's fame rests on his short stories, but he also wrote novels, plays, political satires, a history of imperial Russia, and journalistic sketches.

**Achievements** • The brilliant satirist of the mind and manners of an upper-crust Great Britain that World War I would obliterate, Saki operates within a rich national tradition that stretches from the towering figure of Jonathan Swift well into the present, in which fresh wits such as Douglas Adams have obtained a certain stature. An intelligent, perceptive, and uncannily unsentimental observer, Saki focuses many of his deeply sarcastic pieces, which fill six volumes, on the criminal impulses of a privileged humanity. In his tightly wrought stories, for which surprise endings, ironic reversals, and practical jokes are de rigueur, Saki's mischievous protagonists thus arrive on the scene to wreak havoc on victims who have invited their tormentors out of folly or a streak of viciousness of their own. The frequent inclusion of intelligent, independent, and improbable animal characters further betrays Saki's fondness for the supernatural as a powerful satirical device.

**Biography** • Born in colonial Burma (now Myanmar) to a family that had for generations helped to rule the British Empire, Hector Hugh Munro grew up in a Devonshire country house where, reared along with his brother and sister by two formidable aunts, he had the secluded and strictly supervised sort of childhood typical of the Victorian rural gentry. This upbringing decisively shaped—or perhaps warped, as some sources suggest—his character. After finishing public school at Bedford, Munro spent several years studying in Devonshire and traveling on the Continent with his father and sister. In 1983, he went to Burma to accept a police post obtained through his father's influence. Much weakened by recurrent malaria, he returned to Devonshire to convalesce and write. In the first years of the twentieth century he turned to journalism, wrote political satires, and served as a foreign correspondent in Eastern Europe and Paris. At this time he adopted the pseudonym "Saki," which may refer to the cupbearer in *The Rubáiyát of Omar Khayyám* (1859) or may contract "Sakya Muni," one of the epithets of the Buddha. After 1908, Saki lived and wrote in London. Despite being over-age and far from robust, he volunteered for active duty at the outbreak of World War I. Refusing to accept a commission, to which his social position entitled him, or a safe job in military intelligence, for which his education and experience equipped him, Munro fought as an enlisted man in the trenches of France. He died in action.

**Analysis** • Saki is a writer whose great strength and great weakness lie in the limits he set for himself. Firmly rooted in the British ruling class that enjoyed "dominion over palm and pine," Saki wrote about the prosperous Edwardians among whom he moved. His stories, comedies of manners, emphasize the social side of the human animal as they survey the amusements, plots, and skirmishes that staved off boredom for the overripe leisure class whose leisure ended in August, 1914, with the onset of World War I.

Just as Saki wrote about a particular class, so he aimed his stories at a comparatively small and select readership. Although he was indifferent to wealth, Saki subsisted by his pen; he was, therefore, obliged to write stories that would sell. From the first, he succeeded in producing the "well-made" story savored by literate but not necessarily literary readers of such respected journals as the liberal *Westminster Gazette* and the conservative *Morning Post*. His debonair, carefully plotted stories full of dramatic reversals, ingenious endings, and quotable phrases do not experiment with new literary techniques but perfect existing conventions. Without seeming to strain for effect, they make of Hyde Park an enchanted forest or treat the forays of a werewolf as an ordinary country occurrence. Like the Paris gowns his fictional duchesses wear, Saki's stories are frivolous, intricate, impeccable, and, to some eyes, obsolete.

If Saki's background, subjects, and techniques were conventional, however, his values and sympathies certainly were not. As a satirist, he mocked the people he entertained. His careful portraits of a complacent ruling class are by no means flattering: They reveal all the malice, pettiness, mediocrity, and self-interest of people intent on getting to the top or staying there. His heroes—Reginald, Clovis, Bertie, and the like—are aristocratic iconoclasts who share their creator's distaste for "dreadful little everyday acts of pretended importance" and delight in tripping the fools and hypocrites who think themselves exceptional but walk the well-worn path upward. "Cousin Theresa," a variation on the theme of the Prodigal Son, chronicles the frustration of one such self-deluder.

**"Cousin Theresa"** • In Saki's version of the parable, the wandering brother—as might be expected in an age of far-flung Empire—is the virtuous one. Bassett Harrowcluff, a young and successful bearer of the "white man's burden," returns from the colonies after having cheaply and efficiently "quieted a province, kept open a trade route, enforced the tradition of respect which is worth the ransom of many kings in out of the way regions." These efforts, his proud father hopes, might earn Bassett a knighthood as well as a rest.

The elder brother Lucas, however, a ne'er-do-well London bachelor, claims to have his own scheme for certain success—a refrain that, appended to a song and embodied in a musical revue, should catch the ear of all London: "Cousin Theresa takes out Caesar,/ Fido, Jock, and the big borzoi." Fate bears out Lucas's prophecy. Theresa and her canine quartet enthrall the city. Orchestras acquire the four-legged accessories necessary for proper rendition of the much-demanded melody's special effects. The double thump commemorating the borzoi rings throughout London: Diners pound tables, drunks reeling home pound doors, messenger boys pound smaller messenger boys. Preachers and lecturers discourse on the song's "inner meaning." In Society, the perennial mystifications of politics and polo give way to discussions of "Cousin Theresa." When Colonel Harrowcluff's son is knighted, the honor goes to Lucas.

Saki's parable offers two lessons: an obvious one for the "eminent," a subtler one for the enlightened. If the reader takes the story as an indictment of a foolish society that venerates gimmicks and ignores achievements, that rewards notoriety rather than merit, he classes himself among the Bassett Harrowcluffs. For the same delicate irony colors Saki's accounts of both brothers' successes: Whether this treatment whimsically elevates the impresario or deftly undercuts the pillar of empire is problematic. As Saki sees it, administering the colonies and entertaining the populace are equally trivial occupations. To reward Lucas, the less self-righteous of two triflers, seems just after all.

Saki, then, does not profess the creed of the society he describes; both the solid virtues and the fashionable attitudes of the adult world come off badly in his stories. In contrast to other adults, Saki's dandy-heroes and debutante-heroines live in the spirit of the nursery romp; and when children and animals appear (as they often do) he invariably sides with them. "Laura," a fantasy in which a mischievous lady dies young but returns to life first as an otter and then as a Nubian boy to continue teasing a pompous fool, is one of many stories demonstrating Saki's allegiance to *Beasts and Super-Beasts* at the expense of men and supermen.

Saki's favorites are never sweetly pretty or coyly innocent. The children, as we see in "The Lumber-Room," "The Penance," and "Morlvera," are cruel, implacable, the best of haters. The beasts, almost as fierce as the children, tend to be independent or predatory: wolves and guard dogs, cats great and small, elk, bulls, and boars figure in Saki's menagerie. Embodied forces of nature, these animals right human wrongs or counterpoise by their example the mediocrity of man throughout Saki's works, but nowhere more memorably than in the chilling tale of "Sredni Vashtar."

**"Sredni Vashtar"** • In "Sredni Vashtar," Conradin, a rather sickly ten-year-old, suffers under the restrictive coddling of his cousin and guardian, Mrs. De Ropp, a pious hypocrite who "would never, in her honestest moments, have confessed to herself that she disliked Conradin, though she might have been dimly aware that thwarting him 'for his good' was a duty which she did not find completely irksome." Conradin's one escape from her dull, spirit-sapping regime is the toolshed where he secretly cherishes Sredni Vashtar, the great ferret around whom he has fashioned a private religious cult. Offering gifts of red flowers, scarlet berries, and nutmeg that "had to be stolen," Conradin prays that the god Sredni Vashtar, who embodies the rude animal vitality the boy lacks, will smite their common enemy the Woman. When Mrs. De Ropp, suspecting that the toolshed harbors something unsuitable for invalids, goes to investigate, Conradin fears that Sredni Vashtar will dwindle to a simple ferret and that he, deprived of his god, will grow ever weaker under the Woman's tyranny.

Eventually, however, Conradin sees Sredni Vashtar the Terrible, throat and jaws wet with a dark stain, stalk out of the shed to drink at the garden brook and slip away. Mrs. De Ropp does not return from the encounter, and Conradin, freed from his guardian angel, helps himself to the forbidden fruit of his paradise—a piece of toast, "usually banned on the ground that it was bad for him; also because the making of it 'gave trouble,' a deadly offense in the middle-class feminine eye."

**"The Open Window"** • The brutal vengeance of "Sredni Vashtar" demonstrates that Saki's preference is not founded on the moral superiority of children and animals. "The Open Window," probably Saki's most popular story, makes the point in a more plausible situation, where a "self-possessed young lady of fifteen" spins from the most ordinary circumstances a tale of terror that drives her visitor, the nervous and hypochondriacal Mr. Frampton Nuttel, to distraction. In the Saki world the charm and talent of the liar makes up for the cruelty of her lie; the reader, cut adrift from his ordinary values, admires the unfeeling understatement of Saki's summing up: "Romance at short notice was her specialty." The reader joins in applauding at the story's end not injustice—the whimpering Nuttel gets no worse than he deserves—but justice undiluted by mercy, a drink too strong for most adults most of the time.

What Saki admires about the people and animals he portrays is their fidelity to absolutes. They follow their natures single-mindedly and unapologetically; they neither moralize nor compromise. Discussing the preferences of a character in his novel *When William Came* (1913), Saki indirectly explains his own austere code: "Animals . . . accepted the world as it was and made the best of it, and children, at least nice children, uncontaminated by grown-up influences, lived in worlds of their own making." In this judgment the satirist becomes misanthrope. Saki endorses nature and art but rejects society.

It is this moral narrowness, this refusal to accept compromise, that makes Saki, despite the brilliance of his artistry, an unsatisfying writer to read in large doses. His dated description of a vanished world is really no flaw, for he does not endorse the dying regime but clearly shows why it ought to die. His lack of sentiment is refreshing; his lack of emotion (only in such rare stories as "The Sheep," "The Philanthropist and the Happy Cat," and "The Penance" does Saki credibly present deep or complex feelings) does not offend present-day readers long inured to black comedy. Saki's defect is sterility. He refuses to be generous or make allowances as he considers society, that creation of adults, and he sends readers back empty-handed to the world of compromise where they must live.

*Peter W. Graham*
*With updates by R. C. Lutz*

**Other major works**

PLAYS: *Karl-Ludwig's Window*, pb. 1924; *The Death-Trap*, pb. 1924; *The Square Egg, and Other Sketches, with Three Plays*, pb. 1924; *The Watched Pot*, pr., pb. 1924 (with Cyril Maude).

NOVELS: *The Unbearable Bassington*, 1912; *When William Came*, 1913.

NONFICTION: *The Rise of the Russian Empire*, 1900; *The Westminster Alice*, 1902.

## Bibliography

Birden, Lorene M. "Saki's 'A Matter of Sentiment.'" *Explicator* 5 (Summer, 1998): 201-204. Discusses the Anglo-German relations in the story "A Matter of Sentiment" and argues that the story reflects a shift in Saki's image of Germans.

Gillen, Charles H. *H. H. Munro (Saki)*. New York: Twayne, 1969. Comprehensive presentation of the life and work of Saki, with a critical discussion of his literary output in all of its forms. Balanced and readable, Gillen's work also contains an annotated bibliography, which naturally does not include studies since then.

Lambert, J. W. Introduction to *The Bodley Head Saki*. London: Bodley Head, 1963. Perceptive, concise, and persuasive review of Saki's work. Written by a biographer who enjoyed a special and productive working relationship with Saki's estate.

Langguth, A. J. *Saki*. New York: Simon & Schuster, 1981. Probably the best biography, enriching an informed, analytical presentation of its subject with a fine understanding of Saki's artistic achievement. Eight pages of photos help bring Saki and his world to life.

May, Charles E., ed. *Masterplots II: Short Story Series, Revised Edition*. 8 vols. Pasadena, Calif.: Salem Press, 2004. Designed for student use, this reference set contains articles providing detailed plot summaries and analyses of five short stories by Saki: "The Interlopers" and "Laura" (vol. 4), "The Open Window" (vol. 5), "The Schartz-Metterklume Method" (vol. 6), and "Sredni Vashtar" (vol. 7).

Munro, Ethel M. "Biography of Saki." In *The Square Egg and Other Sketches, with Three Plays*. New York: Viking Press, 1929. Warm account of the author by his beloved sister, who shows herself deeply appreciative of his work. Valuable for its glimpses of the inner workings of Saki's world and as a basis for late twentieth century evaluations.

Salemi, Joseph S. "An Asp Lurking in an Apple-Charlotte: Animal Violence in Saki's *The Chronicles of Clovis*." *Studies in Short Fiction* 26 (Fall, 1989): 423-430. Discusses the animal imagery in the collection, suggesting reasons for Saki's obsessive interest in animals and analyzing the role animals play in a number of Saki's major stories.

Spears, George J. *The Satire of Saki*. New York: Exposition Press, 1963. Interesting and revealing study of Saki's wit, which combines careful textual analysis with a clear interest in modern psychoanalysis. The appendix includes four letters by Ethel M. Munro to the author, and the bibliography lists many works that help to place Saki in the context of the satirical tradition.

# J. D. Salinger

**Born:** New York, New York; January 1, 1919

**Principal short fiction** • *Nine Stories*, 1953; *Franny and Zooey*, 1961; *Raise High the Roof Beam, Carpenters, and Seymour: An Introduction*, 1963.

**Other literary forms** • Although J. D. Salinger has lived well into the twenty-first century, his literary reputation rests almost entirely on work he did many decades earlier. Indeed, much like novelist Harper Lee, the author of *To Kill a Mockingbird* (1960), Salinger is known primarily for his single novel, *The Catcher in the Rye* (1951). That book influenced a generation of readers and is still considered a classic.

**Achievements** • The precise and powerful creation of J. D. Salinger's characters, especially *The Catcher in the Rye*'s Holden Caulfield and the Glass family of his short fiction, has led them to become part of American folklore. Salinger's ironic fiction and enigmatic personality captured the imagination of post-World War II critics and students. His authorized books were published over the course of twelve years, from 1951 to 1963, yet his works still remain steadily in print in many languages throughout the world.

Salinger received a number of awards in his career. "This Sandwich Has No Mayonnaise" was selected as one of the distinguished short stories published in American magazines for 1945 and was later included in *The Best Short Stories 1946*. "Just Before the War with the Eskimos" was reprinted in *Prize Stories of 1949*. "A Girl I Know" was selected for *The Best American Short Stories 1949*. "For Esmé—with Love and Squalor" was selected as one of the distinguished short stories published in American magazines in 1950 and is included in *Prize Stories of 1950*. The novel *The Catcher in the Rye* was a Book-of-the-Month Club selection for 1951.

Martin Green remarked that Salinger is not so much a writer who depicts life as one who celebrates it, an accurate characterization of the humor and love in his work. Ultimately, the most serious charge against him is that his output is too small. Ironically, Salinger's small output and his extreme reclusiveness have enhanced his reputation by adding an aura of mystery. Both scholars and journalists have pursued him, trying—usually without success—to learn more about his mind and his thoughts on writing.

**Biography** • Jerome David Salinger is the second child—his sister, Doris, was born eight years before him—and only son of Sol and Miriam Jillich Salinger, a Jewish father and a Christian mother. His father was a successful importer of hams and cheeses. Salinger was a serious child who kept mostly to himself. His IQ test score was above average, and his grades, at public schools in the upper West Side of Manhattan, were in the "B" range. Socially, his experiences at summer camp were more successful than in the Manhattan public schools. At Camp Wigwam, in Harrison, Maine, he was voted at the age of eleven "the most popular actor of 1930."

In 1934, Salinger entered Valley Forge Military Academy, in Pennsylvania, a school resembling Pencey Prep in *The Catcher in the Rye*. Salinger, however, was more successful at Valley Forge than Holden had been at Pencey, and in June, 1936, Valley Forge gave him his only diploma. He was literary editor of the school yearbook and wrote a poem that was set to music and sung at the school.

In 1937, he enrolled in summer school at New York University but left for Austria and Poland to try working in his father's meat importing business. In 1938, after returning to the United States, he briefly attended Ursinus College in Collegeville, Pennsylvania. There, he wrote a column, "Skipped Diploma," which featured film reviews for the college newspaper. In 1939, he signed up for a short-story course at Columbia University, given by Whit Burnett, editor of *Story* magazine. In 1940, his first short story, "The Young Folks," was published in the March/April issue of *Story*, and he was paid twenty-five dollars for it.

The story "Go See Eddie" was pub-

National Archives

lished in the December issue of the University of Kansas City *Review.* In 1941, "The Hang of It" appeared in *Collier's* and "The Heart of a Broken Story" in *Esquire.* Salinger sold his first story about Holden Caulfield to *The New Yorker,* but publication was delayed until 1946 because of the United States' entry into World War II.

In 1942, Salinger was drafted. He used his weekend passes to hide in a hotel room and write. He attended Officers, First Sergeants, and Instructors School of the Signal Corps. He engaged in a brief romantic correspondence with Oona O'Neill, daughter of the playwright Eugene O'Neill and later to be the wife of Charles Chaplin. In 1943, he was stationed in Nashville, Tennessee, with the rank of staff sergeant and transferred to the Army Counter-Intelligence Corps. "The Varioni Brothers" was his first story in *The Saturday Evening Post.* He received counterintelligence training in Devonshire, England. During the war, he landed on Utah Beach in Normandy as part of the D-Day invasion force and participated in five campaigns. It was during this period that he met war correspondent Ernest Hemingway.

In 1945, Salinger was discharged from the Army. He continued to publish stories, including two stories with material later to be used in *The Catcher in the Rye.* In 1948, he began a long, exclusive association with *The New Yorker* with "A Perfect Day for Bananafish," the first story about Seymour Glass. Early in 1950, Salinger began studying Advaita Vedanta, Eastern religious philosophy, in New York City. In 1951, *The Catcher in the Rye* was published, and in 1953, he moved to Cornish, New Hampshire.

In the following years, several of his stories were published in *The New Yorker,* including "Franny," "Raise High the Roof Beam, Carpenters," "Zooey," "Seymour: An

Introduction," and "Hapworth 16, 1924." Salinger married Claire Douglas on February 17, 1955. A daughter, Margaret Ann, was born in 1955, and a son, Matthew, in 1960. Salinger was divorced from his wife in 1967. In 1987, Matthew Salinger starred in a made-for-television film. During the mid-1980's, Salinger, known to be a reclusive person, became the center of public attention when he protested the publication of an unauthorized biography by Ian Hamilton. The suit led to the rewriting of Hamilton's biography, which was published in 1988.

Salinger has continued to refuse all requests for interviews and has ignored correspondents. However, his daughter, Margaret Salinger, went against his wishes by publishing a book about her family, _Dream Catcher: A Memoir_ in 2000. Meanwhile, Salinger has continued to comment publicly on his published work, saying, "The stuff's all there in the stories; there's no use talking about it."

**Analysis** • The main characters of J. D. Salinger, neurotic and sensitive people, search unsuccessfully for love in a metropolitan setting. They see the phoniness, egotism, and hypocrisy around them. There is a failure of communication between people: between husbands and wives, between soldiers in wartime, between roommates in schools. A sense of loss, especially the loss of a sibling, recurs frequently. Many of his stories have wartime settings and involve characters who have served in World War II. Some of these characters cannot adjust to the military, some have unhappy marital relationships, and others are unsuccessful in both areas. The love for children occurs frequently in his stories—for example, the love for Esmé, Phoebe, and Sybil. Like William Wordsworth, Salinger appreciates childhood innocence. Children have a wisdom and a spontaneity that is lost in the distractions and temptations of adult life.

Salinger's early stories contain elements foreshadowing his later work. Many of these stories are concerned with adolescents. In "The Young Folks," however, the adolescents resemble the insensitive schoolmates of Holden Caulfield more than they resemble Holden himself. Salinger demonstrates his admirable ear for teenage dialogue in these stories.

The reader sees how often members of the Glass family are present in the stories or novelettes. Looking back at Salinger's early works, one sees how these selections can be related to events in the actual life of Salinger as well as how they contain characters who are part of the Glass family saga.

**"For Esmé—with Love and Squalor"** • An early example is the character of Sergeant X in "For Esmé—with Love and Squalor," from the collection _Nine Stories_. The time and setting of this story tie it into the experiences of Salinger abroad during World War II. At the same time, Sergeant X is Seymour Glass. The reader is shown the egotism of the wife and mother-in-law of Sergeant X, who write selfish civilian letters to the American soldier about to be landed in France, requesting German knitting wool and complaining about the service at Shrafft's restaurant in Manhattan.

This behavior is the same as that of the insensitive wife of "A Perfect Day for Bananafish" and that of the wife and mother-in-law of "Raise High the Roof Beam, Carpenters." The only person who offers love to Sergeant X is the brave British orphan Esmé, who sings with a voice like a bird and offers him the wristwatch of her deceased father. Esmé is too proper a British noblewoman to kiss Sergeant X, but she drags her five-year-old brother, Charles, back into the tearoom to kiss the soldier good-bye and even invites him to her wedding, five years later. Esmé's love restores Sergeant X from the breakdown that he suffered from the war. The gestures of love from Esmé lead to Sergeant X finally being able to go to sleep, a sign of recovery in the Glass family.

The love of Esmé is contrasted to the squalor of the other people around Seymour. His wife, "a breathtakingly levelheaded girl," discourages Sergeant X from attending the wedding of Esmé because his mother-in-law will be visiting at the same time (another selfish reason). The "squalor" that is contrasted to the pure, noble love of Esmé is also exemplified in the letter of the older brother of Sergeant X, who requests "a couple of bayonets or swastikas" as souvenirs for his children. Sergeant X tears up his brother's letter and throws the pieces into a wastebasket into which he later vomits. He cannot so easily escape the squalor of the "photogenic" Corporal Z, from whom readers learn that Sergeant X had been released from a hospital after a nervous breakdown. Corporal Clay, the jeep-mate of Sergeant X, personifies even more the squalor that Sergeant X is "getting better acquainted with," in one form or another. Clay has been "brutal," "cruel," and "dirty" by unnecessarily shooting a cat and constantly dwelling upon the incident.

Clay has a name that represents earth and dirt. He is obtuse and insensitive. He is contrasted to the spirituality, sensitivity, and love expressed by Esmé. Clay brings news of the officious character Bulling, who forces underlings to travel at inconvenient hours to impress them with his authority, and of Clay's girlfriend Loretta, a psychology major who blames the breakdown of Sergeant X not on wartime experiences but on lifelong instability, yet excuses Clay's sadistic killing of the cat as "temporary insanity." The killing of the cat is similar to Hemingway's killing a chicken in the presence of Salinger when the two men met overseas. The love of Esmé redeems and rejuvenates Sergeant X from his private hell in this well-written and moving story.

**"Uncle Wiggily in Connecticut"** • References to other members of the Glass family tie other stories to the saga of the Glass children. Eloise, the Connecticut housewife in "Uncle Wiggily in Connecticut" had been in love with a soldier named "Walt." Walt was one of the twin brothers in the Glass family. He had been killed during the war not in battle but in a senseless accident. The central characters in the story are Eloise, a frustrated housewife, living trapped in a wealthy Connecticut home with a man she does not love and her memories of the soldier Walt whom she had loved dearly; and Ramona, her young daughter. Salinger himself was living in Connecticut at the time he wrote this story.

Ramona may lack the nobility and capacity to show affection that Esmé had, yet she is an imaginative child, with abilities that her mother does not understand or appreciate. Ramona compensates for her loneliness by creating imaginary friends, such as "Jimmy Jimmereeno." This imaginative spontaneity in Ramona is in danger of being stifled by Eloise. Once when drunk, Eloise frightens her daughter by waking her up during the night after seeing her sleeping on one side of the bed to leave space for her new playmate, "Mickey Mickeranno." Eloise herself was comforted by memories of her old beloved Walt but did not permit Ramona also to have an imaginary companion. The suburban mother suddenly realizes what has happened to her and begins to cry, as does her frightened daughter. All Eloise has left is the small comfort of her memories of Walt. She now realizes that she had been trying to force Ramona to give up her fantasies about imaginary boyfriends too. In this Salinger story, again there is a contrast between the "nice" world of love that Eloise remembers she once had and the rude, "squalid" Connecticut world in which she is currently living.

*The Glass Family Cycle* • The writings of Salinger can be best discussed by dividing them into three sections: his early writings, his great classic works, and the Glass family cycle. The later works of Salinger are more concerned with religion than the earlier ones. Most of these later works deal with members of the Glass family, characters who have elements in common with Salinger himself. They are sensitive and introspective, they hate phoniness, and they have great verbal skill. They are also interested in mystical religion. "Glass" is an appropriate name for the family. Glass is a clear substance through which a person can see to acquire further knowledge and enlightenment, yet glass is also extremely fragile and breakable and therefore could apply to the nervous breakdowns or near breakdowns of members of the family. The Glass family also attempts to reach enlightenment through the methods of Zen Buddhism. Professor Daisetz Suzuki of Columbia University, whose work is said to have influenced Salinger, commented that "the basic idea of Zen is to come in touch with the inner workings of our being, and to do this in the most direct way possible, without resorting to anything external or superadded. . . . Zen is the ultimate fact of all philosophy and religion."

What Seymour, Zooey, and Franny Glass want to do is to come in touch with the inner workings of their being in order to achieve nonintellectual enlightenment. With all religions at their fingertips, the Glass siblings utilize anything Zen-like, and it is their comparative success or failure in this enterprise that forms the basic conflict in their stories. In "Raise High the Roof Beam, Carpenters," the point made is that Seymour, who has achieved the satori, or Zen enlightenment, is considered abnormal by the world and loved and admired only by his siblings. He is despised by other people who cannot comprehend his behavior. The maid of honor at the wedding that Seymour failed to attend describes him as a schizoid and latent homosexual. His brother Buddy, the only Glass family member attending the wedding, is forced to defend his brother by himself. After enduring all the misinformed verbal attacks on his brother, Buddy replies: "I said that not one God-damn person, of all the patronizing, fourth-rate critics and column writers, had ever seen him for what he really was. A poet, for God's sake. And I mean a *poet.*"

The central figure around whom all the stories of the Glass family revolve is Seymour, Seymour alive, Seymour quoted by Zooey, and the memory of Seymour when he is no longer physically alive. Once the Zen experience is understood by the reader, the meaning of earlier stories about the Glass siblings becomes more intelligible as contributing to Salinger's goal in his later stories. Zen is a process of reduction and emptying of all the opinions and values that one has learned and has been conditioned to that interfere with one's perceptions.

**"A Perfect Day for Bananafish"** • The first Glass story, "A Perfect Day for Bananafish," is a kind of koan, or paradox, one whose meaning the Glass children will be mediating upon for years to come. Seymour is the Bananafish. He has taken in so much from outside himself, knowledge and sensations, and he is so stuffed that he cannot free himself and climb out of the banana hole.

Seymour, in this first story, is married to Muriel and is in a world of martinis and phony conversations in Miami Beach. He discovers that Muriel looks like Charlotte, the girl at whom he threw a stone in his earlier life because her physical loveliness was distracting him from his spiritual quest. He cannot communicate with his wife either. Muriel Fedder was aptly named because her presence serves as a "fetter" to Seymour. The only one with whom he *can* communicate is Sybil, the young child who is still so uncorrupted by the opinions and values of the world that her clear perceptions give her the status of the mythological Sybil.

Seymour has found, unfortunately, that Muriel Fedder Glass will not serve, teach, or strengthen him, as Seymour's diary entry before his marriage had indicated: "Marriage partners are to serve each other. Elevate, help, teach, strengthen each other, but above all, serve." Boo Boo Glass wrote a more admiring tribute to Seymour on the bathroom mirror than one senses from Muriel. Muriel is found reading a *Reader's Digest* article, "Sex Is Fun—or Hell." Marriage to Muriel has turned out not to be a spiritually enlightening experience. The only move that Seymour can make in his spiritual quest is to empty himself totally of all the opinions, values, and drives, of all sensations that distract and hinder him in achieving his spiritual goal. He is best able to move forward in his search by committing suicide and becoming pure spirit. Warren French wrote, "When Muriel then subsequently fails to live up to his expectations of a spouse, he realizes the futility of continuing a life that promises no further spiritual development."

The critic Ann Marple noted that "Salinger's first full-length novel, *The Catcher in the Rye*, emerged after scattered fragments concerning his characters appeared over a seven-year span. For some time now it has been evident that Salinger's second novel may be developing in the same way." Salinger wrote of *Franny and Zooey*: "Both stories are early, critical entries in a narrative series I am doing about a family of settlers in 20th Century New York, the Glasses." The remaining stories deal with Zen Buddhism and the effort to achieve a Zen-inspired awakening. They continue to deal with Seymour Glass and his influence on his siblings. In addition, the work of Salinger becomes increasingly experimental as he continues to write.

***Franny and Zooey*** • When "Franny" was first published in the January 29, 1955, issue of *The New Yorker*, no mention was made that Franny was a member of the Glass family. All the reader knows is that Franny is visiting her boyfriend Lane for a football weekend at an Ivy League college. Lane is an insensitive pseudointellectual who brags about his successful term paper on Gustave Flaubert as he consumes frogs' legs. Lane is not interested in the religious book *The Way of the Pilgrim* that Franny describes to him or in hearing about the Jesus prayer that has a tremendous mystical effect on the whole outlook of the person who is praying. The luncheon continues, with Lane finishing the snails and frogs' legs that he had ordered. The contrast has deepened between the mystical spirituality of Franny and Lane's interest in satisfying his physical appetites. The reader is shocked at the part of the story when Franny faints. She is apparently suffering from morning sickness. The implication is that Lane is the father of her unborn child.

Almost two and a half years pass before the title character is identified as Franny Glass. "Zooey" was published in the May 4, 1957, issue of *The New Yorker*. It continued the story of Franny Glass, the youngest of the siblings of Seymour Glass. It is made clear in this story that Franny was not pregnant in the earlier story but was suffering from a nervous breakdown as a result of her unsuccessful attempt to achieve spiritual enlightenment. In "Zooey," her brother identifies the book that Franny is carrying to their mother as *The Pilgrim Continues His Way*, a sequel to the other book, both of which she had gotten from the old room of Seymour. Zooey cannot console his sister at first. Franny is crying uncontrollably. Zooey finally goes into the room that had been occupied previously by Seymour and Buddy. Zooey attempts to impersonate Buddy when he calls Franny on the telephone, but Franny eventually recognizes the voice of the caller. Zooey is finally able to convince his sister that the mystical experience she should strive for is not of seeing Christ directly but that of seeing Christ through ordinary people. "There isn't anyone anywhere who isn't Seymour's Fat Lady," who is really "Christ himself, buddy." Reassured by the words of her brother, Franny can finally fall asleep.

In "Franny," as in many other Salinger short stories, character is revealed through a series of actions under stress, and the purpose of the story is reached at the moment of epiphany, an artistic technique formulated by James Joyce, in which a character achieves a sudden perception of truth. In "Franny," Salinger uses the theatrical tricks of a telephone in an empty room and of one person impersonating another. He often uses the bathroom of the Glass apartment as a place where important messages are left, important discussions are conducted, important documents are read. It is on the bathroom cabinet mirror that Boo Boo Glass leaves the epithalamium prayer for her brother on his wedding day, from which the title of the story "Raise High the Roof Beams, Carpenters" is taken. The Glass bathroom is almost a sacred temple. Bessie Glass, in the "Zooey" portion of *Franny and Zooey*, goes in there to discuss with Zooey how to deal with Franny's nervous breakdown. Buddy closes the bathroom door of the apartment he had shared with Seymour to read the diary of Seymour on his wedding day. He reads that Seymour is so happy that he cannot attend his wedding on that date (although he subsequently elopes with Muriel Fedder). The reader sees in *Franny and Zooey* the role Seymour played in the lives of his youngest brother and sister, the influence he had over them and their religious education. The reader sees in "Franny" a spiritual crisis in her efforts to retain her spiritual integrity, to live a spiritual life in an egotistical, materialistic society, a society personified by Lane Coutell.

"Franny" can be considered as a prologue to "Zooey," which carries the reader deeply into the history of the Glass family. The last five pieces that Salinger published in *The New Yorker* could constitute some form of a larger whole. The narrative possibly could constitute parts of two uncompleted chronicles. One order in which the stories could be read is with Buddy as the narrator, the order in which they were published (this is the order in which Buddy claims to have written them); the other order is the one suggested by the chronology of events in the stories. Arranged one way, the stories focus on Buddy and his struggle to understand Seymour by writing about him; arranged the other way, the stories focus on the quest of Seymour for God. J. D. Salinger has for some years been a devoted student of Advaita Vedanta Hinduism, and the teachings of Seymour Glass reflect this study.

If one focuses on Seymour Glass, his spiritual quest, and how this quest is reflected in the behavior and beliefs of his siblings, one sees as a result an unfinished history of the Glass family. Salinger announced, in one of his rare statements about his intentions, on the dust jacket of a later book, that he had "several new Glass family stories coming along," but, by the close of the century, only "Hapworth 16, 1924" had appeared, in 1965. Readers see in this story the presence of Seymour, a presence that is evident in the four stories published after that time.

These four stories became more experimental in literary technique and are also involved with the Eastern mystical religious beliefs studied by Salinger and promoted by his character Seymour Glass. One interpretation of the stories that deal with Seymour (that of Eberhard Alsen) is that together these selections constitute a modernist hagiography, the account of the life and martyrdom of a churchless saint. "Raise High the Roof Beam, Carpenters" is the first story to be published after "Franny" and the first to introduce all the members of the Glass family. "Zooey" continues the account of specific events introduced in "Franny," and the reader learns that the behavior of Franny is influenced by two books of Eastern religion that she found in the old room of Seymour. In "Zooey" the name of Seymour is evoked when Franny wants to talk to him. In "Raise High the Roof Beam, Carpenters," the reader learns what Seymour has written in his diary, although Seymour is not physically present. In "Seymour: An Introduction," the reader is offered a much wider range of what he said and wrote, conveyed by his brother Buddy. In "Hapworth 16, 1924," which appeared in *The New Yorker* on June 19, 1965, Buddy, now at the age of forty-six, tries to trace the origins of the saintliness of his older brother in a letter that Seymour wrote home from Camp Simon Hapworth in Maine when he was seven.

In giving the reader the exact letter, Buddy provides one with a full example of how things are seen from the point of view of Seymour and introduces the reader to the sensitivity and psychic powers that foreshadow his spirituality. The reader sees the incredibly precocious mind of Seymour, who reflects on the nature of pain and asks his parents to send him some books by Leo Tolstoy, Swami Vivekananda of India, Charles Dickens, George Eliot, William Makepeace Thackeray, Jane Austen, and Frederick Porter Smith.

**"Seymour: An Introduction" and "Hapworth 16, 1924"** • In these last two works, "Seymour: An Introduction" and "Hapworth 16, 1924," the reader sees Seymour Glass more closely than anywhere before. The reader sees the brilliance of Seymour, his spirituality, his poetic ability, and his capacity for love. With the character of Seymour, Salinger is trying to create a modern-day saint.

Salinger's last works received mixed critical reception. Some critics believe that Salinger has lost the artistic ability he had showed during his classic period. His characters write, and others subsequently read, long, tedious letters filled with phrases in parentheses and attempts at wit. Buddy describes "Zooey" as "a sort of prose home movie." Some critics criticize these last works, calling "Zooey" the longest and dullest short story ever to appear in *The New Yorker,* but others recognize that Salinger is no longer trying to please conventional readers but, influenced by his many years of study of Eastern religious philosophy, is ridding himself of conventional forms and methods accepted by Western society. In his later years, Salinger has continued to become increasingly innovative and experimental in his writing techniques.

*Linda S. Gordon*
*With updates by the Editors*

**Other major works**

NOVELS: *The Catcher in the Rye*, 1951.

**Bibliography**

Alexander, Paul. *Salinger: A Biography.* New York: Renaissance Books, 2000. Attempt to explain Salinger's reclusiveness, which the author relates to themes in Salinger's fiction.

Alsen, Eberhard. *A Reader's Guide to J. D. Salinger.* Greenwood, 2003. Offers an insightful analysis of *The Catcher in the Rye,* as well as useful indexes and appendices covering all of Salinger's fiction.

Bloom, Harold, ed. *J. D. Salinger.* Broomall, Pa.: Chelsea House, 1999. Nine original essays on Salinger by prominent writers.

_____. *J. D. Salinger: Modern Critical Views:* New York: Chelsea House, 1987. Collection of criticism by respected critics who deal with topics ranging from Salinger and Zen Buddhism to Salinger's heroes and love ethic. Includes an introduction, chronology, and bibliography.

Bruni, Domenic, and James Norman O'Neill. "J. D. Salinger." In *Critical Survey of Long Fiction, Revised Edition,* edited by Carl Rollyson. Vol. 6. Pasadena, Calif.: Salem Press, 2000. Analysis of Salinger's longer fictional works that may offer insights into his short fiction.

Kotzen, Kip, and Thomas Beller, eds. *With Love and Squalor: Fourteen Writers Respond to the Work of J. D. Salinger.* New York: Broadway, 2001. Collection of essays by contemporary writers on their personal first impressions of Salinger's work.

May, Charles E., ed. *Masterplots II: Short Story Series, Revised Edition.* 8 vols. Pasadena, Calif.: Salem Press, 2004. Designed for student use, this reference set contains articles providing detailed plot summaries and analyses of four short stories by Salinger: "De Daumier-Smith's Blue Period" (vol. 2), "For Esmé—with Love and Squalor" (vol. 3), "A Perfect Day for Bananafish" (vol. 6), and "Uncle Wiggily in Connecticut" (vol. 8).

Purcell, William F. "Narrative Voice in J. D. Salinger's 'Both Parties Concerned' and 'I'm Crazy.'" *Studies in Short Fiction* 33 (Spring, 1996): 278-280. Argues that "I'm Crazy" lacks the essential characteristic of *skaz* narrative that communicates the illusion of spontaneous speech.

Silverberg, Mark. "A Bouquet of Empty Brackets: Author-Function and the Search for J. D. Salinger." *Dalhousie Review* 75 (Summer/Fall, 1995): 222-246. Examines the consequences of J. D. Salinger's "disappearance" from the literary scene and looks at the obsessive desire to find him; explores how Salinger's characters and name have been freed from his person and re-created in various fictional and nonfictional contexts, concluding that while Salinger may have disappeared, his name and creations remain.

Steinle, Pamela Hunt. *In Cold Fear: "The Catcher in the Rye" Censorship Controversies and Postwar American Character.* Columbus: Ohio State University Press, 2000. Study of the impact of the novel on its release during a nervous period in American social history.

# William Saroyan

**Born:** Fresno, California; August 31, 1908
**Died:** Fresno, California; May 18, 1981

**Principal short fiction** • *The Daring Young Man on the Flying Trapeze, and Other Stories,* 1934; *Inhale and Exhale,* 1936; *Three Times Three,* 1936; *Little Children,* 1937; *The Gay and Melancholy Flux: Short Stories,* 1937; *Love, Here Is My Hat, and Other Short Romances,* 1938; *The Trouble with Tigers,* 1938; *Peace, It's Wonderful,* 1939; *Three Fragments and a Story,* 1939; *My Name Is Aram,* 1940; *Saroyan's Fables,* 1941; *The Insurance Salesman, and Other Stories,* 1941; *Forty-eight Saroyan Stories,* 1942; *Dear Baby,* 1944; *Some Day I'll Be a Millionaire: Thirty-four More Great Stories,* 1944; *The Saroyan Special: Selected Stories,* 1948; *The Fiscal Hoboes,* 1949; *The Assyrian, and Other Stories,* 1950; *The Whole Voyald, and Other Stories,* 1956; *William Saroyan Reader,* 1958; *Love,* 1959; *After Thirty Years: The Daring Young Man on the Flying Trapeze,* 1964; *Best Stories of William Saroyan,* 1964; *The Tooth and My Father,* 1974; *The Man with the Heart in the Highlands, and Other Early Stories,* 1989.

**Other literary forms** • William Saroyan published almost fifty books, including novels, plays, and several autobiographical memoirs. Among his most famous plays are *My Heart's in the Highlands* (pr., pb. 1939) and *The Time of Your Life* (pr., pb. 1939). The latter was awarded the Pulitzer Prize in 1939, but Saroyan rejected it because he "did not believe in official patronage of art." His screenplay, *The Human Comedy* (1943), was one of the most popular wartime films and was later revised into a successful novel. Saroyan's talents also extended to songwriting, his most famous song being "Come Ona My House." His last work, *My Name Is Saroyan,* a potpourri of stories, verse, play fragments, and memoirs, was published posthumously in 1983.

**Achievements** • William Saroyan's reputation rests mainly on his pre-World War II plays and fictional sketches that embraced an upbeat, optimistic, and happy view of people during a period of deep economic depression and increasing political upheaval. His immense popularity and critical acclaim in the United States declined after the war, though in Europe, notably France and Italy, his reputation has remained high. His plays and fiction have been translated into several languages.

Although highly diversified in technique, Saroyan's best works all bear an irrepressible faith in the goodness of the human spirit. His unique, multifaceted style has been emulated by other writers who lack his sanguine outlook and control of craft. Occasional flashes of brilliance partially restored Saroyan's reputation after World War II, and his memoir, *Obituaries* (1979), was nominated for the American Book Award. Saroyan's greatest and most influential works, however, belong to his early, experimental period.

**Biography** • William Saroyan was born in Fresno, California, in 1908. His father, who died when William was two, was a minister turned grape farmer; upon his death, young Saroyan spent seven years in an orphanage, after which his family was reunited. He worked at many odd jobs, including a stint as a telegraph operator, spending most of his time in Fresno and San Francisco. His first short stories began to appear in 1934 and found instant success. In his first year as a writer his work appeared in the O'Brien volume of *The Best Short Stories*, and he published what is still his best-received volume of short stories, *The Daring Young Man on the Flying Trapeze*. Thereafter he produced an amazingly prolific stream of short stories, plays, novels, and memoirs. Saroyan was twice married to Carol Marcus, with whom he had two children. In 1959, after his second divorce, he declared himself a tax exile and went to live in Europe. He returned in 1961 to teach at Purdue University and later returned to live in Fresno. He was actively writing right up to his death from cancer in 1981.

**Analysis** • Although William Saroyan cultivated his prose to evoke the effect of a "tradition of carelessness," of effortless and sometimes apparently formless ruminations and evocations, he was in reality an accomplished and conscious stylist whose influences are varied and whose total effect is far more subtle than the seemingly "breezy" surface might at first suggest. His concern for the lonely and poor—ethnic outsiders, barflies, working girls, children—and their need for love and connectedness in the face of real privation recalls Sherwood Anderson. All of Saroyan's best work was drawn from his own life (although the central character must be regarded as a persona, no matter how apparently connected to the author). In this aspect, and in his powerful and economical capacity to evoke locale and mood, Saroyan is in the tradition of Thomas Wolfe. The empathetic controlling consciousness and adventurous experiments with "formless form" also place Saroyan in the tradition that includes Walt Whitman and Gertrude Stein. It might also be noted that Saroyan's work shows the influence of Anton Chekhov in his use of seemingly "plotless" situations which

nevertheless reveal some essential moment in the characters' lives and philosophical insight into the human condition.

Certainly, while the tone of Saroyan's stories evolves from the comic to the stoical to the sadly elegiac mood of his later work, his ethos stands counter to the naturalists and the ideologically programmatic writers of the 1930's, the period during which he produced some of his best work. Often his stories portray the world from the perspective of children, whose instinctual embrace of life echoes the author's philosophy. Saroyan wrote, "If you will remember that living people are as good as dead, you will be able to perceive much that is very funny in their conduct that you might never have thought of perceiving if you did not believe that they were as good as dead." Both the tone and outlook of that

Courtesy, D.C. Public Library

statement are paradigmatic.

**"The Daring Young Man on the Flying Trapeze"** • The title story of his first and most enduring collection, "The Daring Young Man on the Flying Trapeze," is still one of the most ambitious stylistic exercises of the Saroyan canon and an embodiment of the first phase of his career. The impressionistic style uses a welter of literary allusions in a stream-of-consciousness technique to portray the inner mind of an educated but destitute writer during the Depression who is literally starving to death as his mind remains lucid and aggressively inquiring. The poignant contrast between the failing body and the illuminated mind might evoke pity and compassion on the part of the reader, but somehow Saroyan invokes respect and acceptance as well.

The story begins with the random associated thoughts of the half-dreaming writer which reveal both the chaos of the present era—"hush the queen, the king, Karl Franz, black Titanic, Mr. Chaplin weeping, Stalin, Hitler, a multitude of Jews . . ."— and the young protagonist's literary erudition: "Flaubert and Guy de Maupassant, a wordless rhyme of early meaning, Finlandia, mathematics highly polished and slick as green onions to the teeth, Jerusalem, the path to paradox."

Upon awakening, the writer plunges into "the trivial truth of reality." He is starving, and there is no work. He ironically contemplates starvation as he combines the food in a restaurant into a mental still life; yet without a shred of self-pity, and with great dignity in spite of a clerk's philistine and patronizing attitude, he attempts to obtain a job at an employment agency where the only skill which the writer can offer to a pragmatic world is the ability to type. He is relieved when there is no work because he can now devote his remaining energies to writing a literary last will and testament, an "Apology for Permission to Live."

The writer drinks copious amounts of water to fill his empty belly, steals some writing paper from the Y.M.C.A., and repairs to his empty apartment to compose his manifesto. Before beginning to write, he polishes his last remaining coin—a penny (he has sold his books for food, an act of which he feels ashamed)—and savors the "absurd act." As he contemplates the words on the coin which boast of unity, trust in God, and liberty, he becomes drowsy, and he takes final leave of the world with an inner act of grace and dignity reminiscent of the daring young man of the title. His last conscious act of thought is the notion that he ought to have given the coin to a child.

> A child could buy any number of things with a penny. Then swiftly, neatly, with the grace of the young man on the trapeze he was gone from his body. . . . The city burned. The herded crowd rioted. The earth circled away, and knowing that he did so, he turned his lost face to the empty sky and became dreamless, unalive, perfect.

The story embodies Saroyan's control of his materials and the sensitive and ironic understatement for which he is famous. Although the stories written during the Depression express bitterness about the situation, Saroyan eschews political solutions of any particular stripe and emphasizes the dignity of the individual and his tenacious connection to the forces of life and survival with grace and good humor.

***My Name Is Aram*** • A second collection which gained worldwide fame is the series of interconnected stories which form the book *My Name is Aram*. Told through the eyes of the title character, a young boy in the milieu of Armenian Fresno, the collection reveals the characteristics of the stories of the middle part of Saroyan's career and foreshadows the direction taken in his later work. The reader sees childlike adults and children imbued with the burdens of adulthood. Throughout, the collection explores the often contradictory claims of emotional, poetic, and instinctive needs and the claims of reality. The author's vision is dualistic. Some of the stories show a happy symbiosis between the poetic and the rational needs of his characters; others portray the conflicting demands unresolved. Even in the latter case, however, his characters cheerfully accept their fate, not with a stoicism so much as with a recognition that such a condition is a necessity to life and does not preclude savoring the moments of beauty which occur even in the midst of squalor or hardship.

**"The Summer of the Beautiful White Horse"** • The first aspect of the mature and late phase of Saroyan's writing is aptly illustrated by the story "The Summer of the Beautiful White Horse." Typical of Saroyan's boyhood reminiscences, this tale concerns the seven-year-old Aram Garoghlanian and his slightly older cousin Mourad, who "borrow" a horse from their neighbor's barn and keep him for months at an abandoned farm, enjoying clandestine early morning rides. The owner of the horse, John Byro, complains to the boys' uncle Khosrove, a Saroyan eccentric who responds, "It's no harm. What is the loss of a horse? Haven't we all lost the homeland? What is this crying over a horse?" When the owner complains that he must walk, the uncle reminds him that he has two legs. When Byro laments that the horse had cost him sixty dollars, the uncle retorts, "I spit on money." Byro's loss of an agent to pull his surrey brings a roar of "Pay no attention to it!"

Uncle Khosrove's attitude is typical of the charming impracticality of many of Saroyan's characters. When the boys at last secretly return the animal, the farmer is merely thankful that it has been returned and makes no attempt to find out who had stolen it. He marvels that the horse is in better condition than when it had been stolen. The story charmingly resolves the conflicting demands of the poetic and the practical (in favor of the poetic).

**"Pomegranate Trees"** • "Pomegranate Trees" illustrates the darker and more elegiac side of the later Saroyan canon. Uncle Melik purchases some arid desert land which he intends to farm. The land is obviously impossible to render productive; yet the uncle persists in tilling the soil, planting his crops, and beating back the encroaching cactus while holding little dialogues with Aram and the prairie dogs. He decides against all reason to produce pomegranate trees, since he associates the fruit with his Assyrian past, but the trees are stunted, and the fruit yield is merely enough to fill a few boxes. When the meager harvest fails to bring a high enough price to suit Melik, he has the fruit sent back to him at still more expense. For the uncle, the enterprise has nothing to do with agriculture. "It was all pure aesthetics. . . . My uncle just liked the idea of planting trees and watching them grow."

The real world of unpaid bills intrudes, however, and the man loses the land. Three years later Aram and his uncle revisit the land which had given Melik such quixotic pleasure. The trees have died and the desert has reclaimed the land. "The place was exactly the way it had been all the years of the world." Aram and his uncle walk around the dead orchard and drive back to town. "We didn't say anything because there was such an awful lot to say, and no language to say it in."

There is nominal defeat, yet the still wistfully remembered joy in attempting the impossible for its own sake is a counterweight to the sadness of the finality of the experience. Such a resonance is at the heart of Saroyan's ethos, expressed in countless stories which have made him a popular favorite, and which are beginning to elicit a high critical acclaim as well.

*David Sadkin*
*With updates by John W. Fiero*

## Other major works

CHILDREN'S LITERATURE: *Me*, 1963; *Horsey Gorsey and the Frog*, 1968; *The Circus*, 1986.

PLAYS: *My Heart's in the Highlands*, pr., pb. 1939; *The Hungerers: A Short Play*, pb. 1939, pr. 1945; *The Time of Your Life*, pr., pb. 1939; *Love's Old Sweet Song*, pr., pb. 1940; *Subway Circus*, pb. 1940; *The Beautiful People*, pr. 1940, pb. 1941; *The Great American Goof*, pr. 1940, pb. 1942; *The Ping-Pong Game*, pb. 1940 (one act); *Three Plays: My Heart's in the Highlands, The Time of Your Life, Love's Old Sweet Song*, pb. 1940; *Across the Board on Tomorrow Morning*, pr., pb. 1941; *Hello Out There*, pr. 1941, pb. 1942 (one act); *Jim Dandy*, pr., pb. 1941; *Three Plays: The Beautiful People, Sweeney in the Trees, Across the Board on Tomorrow Morning*, pb. 1941; *Razzle Dazzle*, pb. 1942 (collection); *Talking to You*, pr., pb. 1942; *Get Away Old Man*, pr. 1943, pb. 1944; *Sam Ego's House*, pr. 1947, pb. 1949; *A Decent Birth, a Happy Funeral*, pb. 1949; *Don't Go Away Mad*, pr., pb. 1949; *The Slaughter of the Innocents*, pb. 1952, pr. 1957; *The Cave Dwellers*, pr. 1957, pb. 1958; *Once Around the Block*, pb. 1959; *Sam the Highest Jumper of Them All: Or, The London Comedy*, pr. 1960, pb. 1961; *Settled Out of Court*, pr. 1960, pb. 1962; *The Dogs: Or, The Paris Comedy, and Two Other Plays*, pb. 1969; *An Armenian Trilogy*, pb. 1986 (includes *Armenians, Bitlis*, and *Haratch*); *Warsaw Visitor and Tales from the Vienna Streets: The Last Two Plays of William Saroyan*, pb. 1991.

NOVELS: *The Human Comedy*, 1943; *The Adventures of Wesley Jackson*, 1946; *Rock Wagram*, 1951; *Tracy's Tiger*, 1951; *The Laughing Matter*, 1953 (reprinted as *The Secret Story*, 1954); *Mama I Love You*, 1956; *Papa You're Crazy*, 1957; *Boys and Girls Together*, 1963; *One Day in the Afternoon of the World*, 1964.

MISCELLANEOUS: *My Name Is Saroyan*, 1983 (stories, verse, play fragments, and memoirs); *The New Saroyan Reader*, 1984 (Brian Darwent, editor).

NONFICTION: *Harlem as Seen by Hirschfield*, 1941; *Hilltop Russians in San Francisco*, 1941; *Why Abstract?*, 1945 (with Henry Miller and Hilaire Hiler); *The Twin Adventures: The Adventures of William Saroyan*, 1950; *The Bicycle Rider in Beverly Hills*, 1952; *Here Comes, There Goes, You Know Who*, 1961; *A Note on Hilaire Hiler*, 1962; *Not Dying*, 1963; *Short Drive, Sweet Chariot*, 1966; *Look at Us*, 1967; *I Used to Believe I Had Forever: Now I'm Not So Sure*, 1968; *Letters from 74 Rue Taitbout*, 1969; *Days of Life and Death and Escape to the Moon*, 1970; *Places Where I've Done Time*, 1972; *Sons Come and Go, Mothers Hang in Forever*, 1976; *Chance Meetings*, 1978; *Obituaries*, 1979; *Births*, 1983.

SCREENPLAY: *The Human Comedy*, 1943.

## Bibliography

Balakian, Nona. *The World of William Saroyan*. Lewisburg, Pa.: Bucknell University Press, 1998. Balakian, formerly a staff writer for *The New York Times Book Review*, knew Saroyan personally in his last years, and her observations of him color her assessment of his later works. She viewed it as her mission to resurrect his reputation and restore him to his place among the finest of twentieth century American writers. Traces his evolution from ethnic writer to master of the short story, to playwright, and finally to existentialist.

Dyer, Brenda. "Stories About Stories: Teaching Narrative Using William Saroyan's 'My Grandmother Lucy Tells a Story Without a Beginning, a Middle, or an End.'" In *Short Stories in the Classroom*, edited by Carole L. Hamilton and Peter Kratzke. Urbana, Ill.: National Council of Teachers of English, 1999. Offers some suggestions for teaching Saroyan's story as a story about storytelling; argues that the story provides tools that empower and enrich when taught this way.

Floan, Howard R. *William Saroyan*. New York: Twayne, 1966. Floan's study remains one of the best extensive critical monographs on Saroyan's work. It focuses on Saroyan's early literature, glossing over the post-World War II period as less productive and durable. Contains a valuable annotated bibliography through 1964.

Foster, Edward Halsey. *William Saroyan: A Study of the Short Fiction*. New York: Twayne, 1991. Introduction to Saroyan's short stories that discusses his use of the oral tradition, his Armenian heritage, and his usual themes and experimental techniques. Includes Saroyan's own comments on his fiction as well as previously published essays by other critics.

Haslam, Gerald W. "William Saroyan and San Francisco: Emergence of a Genius (Self-Proclaimed)." In *San Francisco in Fiction: Essays in a Regional Literature*, edited by David Fine and Paul Skenazy. Albuquerque: University of New Mexico Press, 1995. Discusses the influence of San Francisco in a number of Saroyan's stories. Suggests that his stylistic triumph in "The Daring Young Man on the Flying Trapeze" is to force the readers to become co-creators in the story.

Keyishian, Harry, ed. *Critical Essays on William Saroyan*. New York: G. K. Hall, 1995. Collection of essays on Saroyan, from early reviews to critical articles. Helpful essays to a study of Saroyan's short stories are Edward Halsey Foster's discussion of Saroyan's relationship to Gertrude Stein and Walter Shear's essay on Saroyan's ethnicity.

Lee, Lawrence, and Barry Gifford. *Saroyan: A Biography*. New York: Harper and Row, 1984. Lee and Gifford's study is rich with anecdotes and segments of interviews with Saroyan's family, friends, and associates. Supplemented by a chronology and a bibliography.

Leggett, John. *A Daring Young Man*. New York: Alfred A. Knopf, 2003. Leggett relies heavily on Saroyan's journals to produce a sustained glimpse of the author that is neither admiring nor forgiving.

May, Charles E., ed. *Masterplots II: Short Story Series, Revised Edition*. 8 vols. Pasadena, Calif.: Salem Press, 2004. Designed for student use, this reference set contains articles providing detailed plot summaries and analyses of three short stories by Saroyan: "The Daring Young Man on the Flying Trapeze" (vol. 2), "The Parsley Garden" (vol. 6), and "The Summer of the Beautiful White Horse" (vol. 7).

Whitmore, Jon. *William Saroyan: A Research and Production Sourcebook*. Westport, Conn.: Greenwood Press, 1994. Whitmore provides a bibliography citing resources to help determine how Saroyan's plays were staged and produced. Indexes.

# Alan Sillitoe

**Born:** Nottingham, England; March 4, 1928

**Principal short fiction** • *The Ragman's Daughter*, 1963; *A Sillitoe Selection*, 1968; *Guzman Go Home, and Other Stories*, 1968; *Men, Women, and Children*, 1973; *The Second Chance, and Other Stories*, 1981; *The Far Side of the Street*, 1988; *Collected Stories*, 1995; *Alligator Playground: A Collection of Short Stories*, 1997; *New and Collected Stories*, 2003.

**Other literary forms** • Alan Sillitoe's more than five dozen published books include nearly two dozen novels, more than a dozen collections of poetry, five books for children, and volumes of travel literature, essays, and plays. Four of his books, including *The Loneliness of the Long-Distance Runner* and *The Ragman's Daughter*, have been made into films. His first novel, *Saturday Night and Sunday Morning* (1958), was also produced in a stage adaptation, and his second, *The General* (1960), carried the film title *Counterpoint*. Athough he wrote his best-known novels during the late 1950's and 1960's, he continued writing long fiction into his seventies, producing such novels as *The Broken Chariot* (1998), *The German Numbers Woman* (1999), and *Birthday* (2001).

**Achievements** • Alan Sillitoe's early novels and stories fall within the tradition of British working-class fiction established by Charles Dickens and Mrs. Elizabeth Gaskell in the 1840's and carried on by George Gissing, Arthur Morrison, and Walter Greenwood. *Saturday Night and Sunday Morning* won the Author's Club Prize as the best English novel in 1958, and Sillitoe's best-known story, "The Loneliness of the Long-Distance Runner," won the Hawthornden Prize in 1959 and is widely accepted as a modern classic on proletarian life. *The General*, which began as a short story in 1950, won the Nottingham Writers' Club competition in 1960. Believing the concept of class is a degradation, Sillitoe is not so political in his later work, which shows a willingness to experiment in form and style. His stories have been frequently anthologized and have been translated into more than twenty languages.

**Biography** • Born into a working-class family in the English industrial city of Nottingham, Alan Sillitoe was educated to the age of fourteen at Radford Boulevard School for Boys and worked in local factories until he joined the Royal Air Force in 1946. He served in Malaya for two years, followed by sixteen months spent in an English sanatorium recuperating from tuberculosis. During this period he read voraciously and began to write. From 1952 to 1958, he lived in France and Spain, where he became friends with Robert Graves. On the publication of *Saturday Night and Sunday Morning*, he returned to England, and he settled in Kent. He has traveled frequently and widely and has made extended visits to North Africa, Israel, and the Soviet Union. He married the poet Ruth Fainlight in 1959 and has one son, David. His avocations are wireless telegraphy and collecting maps.

**Analysis** • "The Loneliness of the Long-Distance Runner," the title story of Alan Sillitoe's first collection of short fiction, quickly became one of the most widely read stories of modern times. Its basic theme, that one must be true to one's own instincts and beliefs despite intense social pressure to go against them, is echoed in many of his best-known stories, including "On Saturday Afternoon," "The Ragman's Daughter," "The Good Women," and "Pit Strike." Such an attitude strikes a responsive chord in modern readers who feel hemmed in by the dictates of "official" bureaucracies and by government interference in their personal lives. It is important for Sillitoe's characters to establish their independence in a conformist world, yet at the same time they often subscribe to a class-oriented code of values which pits the disadvantaged working class against the rest of society.

**"Uncle Ernest"** • Many of Sillitoe's stories are located in urban working-class slums and reflect the environment he knew himself. In story after story these ghetto-dwellers are seen as society's underdogs, as victims of a series of injustices, real or imagined, which undermine their sense of personal dignity and self-esteem. Ernest Brown, for example, the protagonist in "Uncle Ernest," is a lonely, aging upholsterer who befriends Alma and Joan, two young schoolgirls he meets at a local café. In a series of encounters, always at the café and in public view, he buys them food and small gifts and takes pleasure in learning something of their lives. He asks nothing of the girls in return, and they come to think of him affectionately as "Uncle Ernest." After a few weeks, however, he is accosted by two detectives who accuse him of leading the girls "the wrong way" and forbid him to see them again. Unable to cope with this "official" harassment, Ernest Brown retreats into alcohol and despair.

In one sense "Uncle Ernest" is an anomaly in Sillitoe's short fiction, for although it illustrates the victimization his characters often face, it chronicles a too-ready acceptance of the larger society's interference and power. For the most part his characters remain defiant in the face of directives from those in positions of authority.

**"On Saturday Afternoon"** • "On Saturday Afternoon," the story of an unnamed working-class man's attempt to commit suicide, offers a sardonic example of this defiance. The man first tries to hang himself from a light fixture, but before he can succeed the police arrive and arrest him. In response to his bitter comment, "It's a fine thing if a bloke can't tek his own life," the police tell him "it ain't your life." They take him to a psychiatric hospital and unwittingly put him in a sixth floor room and fail to restrain him. That night he jumps from the window and succeeds in killing himself.

"On Saturday Afternoon" is typical of Sillitoe's stories in its assumed attitude to social authority: Although "they" interfere and place controls on an individual's right to act as he pleases, they can usually be outwitted. Here and in other stories Sillitoe's workers place great stress on "cunning," the ability to preserve individual freedom of action in a restrictive or oppressive social environment.

**"The Loneliness of the Long-Distance Runner"** • This attitude of cunning is well illustrated in Sillitoe's best-known story, "The Loneliness of the Long-Distance Runner." The protagonist in this story is simply called Smith, the modern equivalent of Everyman. He is a seventeen-year-old boy who has been put in a Borstal, a reform school, for theft from a baker's shop. He is also an accomplished long-distance runner and has been chosen by the governor, or warden, to represent the Borstal in a competition for the All-England Championship. As the reader meets Smith, he is running alone over the early-morning countryside, and as he runs he considers his situation. It soon becomes apparent that he has rejected the warden's platitudes ("if you play ball with us, we'll play ball with you") and has seen through the hypocrisy of his promises as well. He recognizes the difference between his own brand of honesty, which allows him to be true to his own instincts, and the warden's, which rejects the needs of the individual in favor of social expediency. Smith's only counter to the warden's attempt to use him for his own ends is cunning. As he sees it, the warden is "dead from the toenails up," living as he does in fear of social disapproval and manipulating the inmates of his Borstal to gain social prestige. Smith, however, resolves to fight against becoming swallowed up in social convention, to be true to his own concept of honesty. Adopting such a stance means recognizing "that it's war between me and them" and leads to his decision to lose the upcoming race.

In the second part of his three-part story the reader shares Smith's reminiscences about his boyhood in a Nottingham slum. He first engages sympathy by telling how he impulsively took part in the theft for which he was sent to Borstal, and then moves quickly to describe the confrontations with police who investigated the robbery. In this section Sillitoe manages a difficult feat by maintaining support for his protagonist even though readers know the boy is guilty of theft. He does this by turning the investigation into a series of skirmishes between Smith and the authorities which allow the reader to be caught up in admiration of the boy's ability to outwit for a time a vindictive, slow-thinking policeman. Not unexpectedly, persistence pays off for the investigators, and in a highly original and amusing climax the stolen money is found and Smith is taken into custody. The facts are less important here, however, than Sillitoe's narrative skill in sustaining the reader's sympathetic involvement with his protagonist. Having manipulated the reader into becoming Smith's ally by allowing conventional notions of right and wrong to be suspended, he also paves the way for the acceptance of Smith's dramatic gesture in the final section of the story.

The third part brings the reader back to time present and the day of the race. The warden, anticipating Smith's win and the reflected glory it will bring to him, has invited numbers of influential friends to witness the competition. Ironically, none of the boys' parents is present, their invitations having been worded so that they would be likely to mistrust or misunderstand them. Details such as this add to the impression of the callousness of the Borstal authorities and help to confirm Smith's conviction that they are using the boys as pawns in a selfish social game. The purity of Smith's intentions, however, is underscored during the race by his sense of communication with the natural surroundings through which he runs and his Edenic perception of himself as "the first man ever to be dropped into this world." As he runs, his thoughts alternate between lyrical commentary on the physical satisfaction of running well and consideration of his decision to lose the race and the punitive consequences this will bring him. Nevertheless he remains firm in his decision, committed to showing the warden "what honesty means if it's the last thing I do." In the end he does lose the race and makes his point, but in much more dramatic manner than he had foreseen. Arriving at the finish line well in advance of the other runners, he is virtually forced to mark time in front of the grandstand until one of his competitors passes him and crosses the line. Smith has made his point: Like so many other of Sillitoe's protagonists, he refuses to be manipulated.

**"The Good Women"** • The fierce independence espoused by Sillitoe's working-class characters, and the rejection of what they see as unwarranted interference by society's authority figures in their personal affairs, is also evident in "The Good Women." The heroine of this story is Liza Atkin, a vital and earthy woman whom one critic called "a Nottingham Mother Courage." Liza's life, like that of Bertolt Brecht's protagonist, is plagued by economic hardship and marked by injustice and the stupidity of war. Although the story has no real plot—readers are shown a series of disconnected events which take place over a period of years—they are caught up in the problems of Liza's life and come to applaud her feisty, tough-minded manner of coping with them.

Dogged by poverty, she ekes out a precarious existence supporting her out-of-work husband and two young boys by filling a decrepit baby carriage with old rags and bits of metal from local dumps and selling them to scrap dealers, and by taking in washing from troops stationed nearby. When the means-test man attempts to deny her welfare payments because of her "business," she shouts him down so the whole street can hear. She makes her gesture of protest against war by harboring a deserter; and standing up for workers' rights in the factory where she eventually finds work, she quickly becomes known to management as "the apostle of industrial unrest." Later, when her son dies because Allied planes bombed his unit by mistake, she is devastated. She recovers, however, to become a passionate advocate of violent revolution at a time in life when most women would be settling into comfortable grandmother roles.

"The Good Women," like many of Sillitoe's stories, has strong didactic overtones. Liza Atkin, along with Smith, Ernest Brown, and the unnamed protagonist in "On Saturday Afternoon," finds herself in a world in which the dictates of society at large often contradict her personal convictions. Yet she is able to resist the pressure to conform, partly because of her strong belief in what is right (harboring the deserter to protest against war, for example), partly because she shares the habitual working-class mistrust of "them" (the authority figures who come from outside and above her own social station) and their motives. From her perspective, and from Sillitoe's, society is badly flawed, and it is up to the individual to strive for a new order in which the unjust exercise of power and the suffering it can cause are eliminated. Memorable characters such as Liza Atkin are meant to show the reader how to begin.

**"Pit Strike"** • In "Pit Strike," which was filmed for British Broadcasting Corporation Television, Sillitoe offers yet another working-class hero, a champion of fairness and integrity. Joshua, a fifty-year-old Nottingham miner, journeys to the south of England with a number of his friends to support a strike by fellow colliers. In a well-organized program of action, the men race from one coal-powered generating station to another to form picket lines and halt deliveries of coal. In a number of cases they are confronted by policemen whose job it is to see that deliveries are uninterrupted. Clashes between the workers, who feel they are being treated unjustly, and the police, representing the power of society as a whole, are almost inevitable in such circumstances. Although Joshua acts to restrain his more belligerent companions in these confrontations, he makes his own mark in a dramatic and courageous manner. When a fully loaded coal truck is seen crawling up an incline away from a picketed power station to make its delivery at another, Joshua daringly and at great personal risk runs after it and forces open the rear gate safety catches, allowing tons of coal to fall on the highway. Although he narrowly escapes death, the gesture seems worth making, and soon after this the strike is settled in the miners' favor.

Like Joshua, the characters in Sillitoe's other stories are usually agitators, passionately and defiantly reaffirming the value of the individual spirit in a world that too often encourages unthinking conformity to social norms. Sillitoe's audience may not always concur with the views his characters express, nor wish to accept the methods they use to further their aims, but their stories nevertheless touch readers and stay tenaciously with them disturbing, provoking, and making them more aware of the imperfect world and of themselves.

*Stanley S. Atherton*
*With updates by Jerry Bradley and the Editors*

## Other major works

CHILDREN'S LITERATURE: *The City Adventures of Marmalade Jim*, 1967; *Big John and the Stars*, 1977; *The Incredible Fencing Fleas*, 1978; *Marmalade Jim at the Farm*, 1980; *Marmalade Jim and the Fox*, 1984.

PLAYS: *All Citizens Are Soldiers*, pr. 1967 (adaptation of Lope de Vega; with Ruth Fainlight); *Three Plays*, pb. 1978.

NOVELS: *Saturday Night and Sunday Morning*, 1958; *The Loneliness of the Long-Distance Runner*, 1959 (novella); *The General*, 1960; *Key to the Door*, 1961; *The Death of William Posters*, 1965; *A Tree on Fire*, 1967; *A Start in Life*, 1970; *Travels in Nihilon*, 1971; *The Flame of Life*, 1974; *The Widower's Son*, 1976; *The Storyteller*, 1979; *Her Victory*, 1982; *The Lost Flying Boat*, 1983; *Down from the Hill*, 1984; *Life Goes On*, 1985; *Out of the Whirlpool*, 1987; *The Open Door*, 1989; *Last Loves*, 1990; *Leonard's War*, 1991; *Snowstop*, 1993; *The Broken Chariot*, 1998; *The German Numbers Woman*, 1999; *Birthday*, 2001.

NONFICTION: *The Road to Volgograd*, 1964; *Raw Material*, 1972; *Mountains and Caverns: Selected Essays*, 1975; *The Saxon Shore Way: From Gravesend to Rye*, 1983 (with Fay Weldon); *Nottinghamshire*, 1986 (with David Sillitoe); *Every Day of the Week*, 1987; *Leading the Blind: A Century of Guidebook Travel, 1815-1914*, 1996; *Life Without Armor*, 1996.

POETRY: *Without Beer or Bread*, 1957; *The Rats, and Other Poems*, 1960; *A Falling out of Love, and Other Poems*, 1964; *Love in the Environs of Voronezh, and Other Poems*, 1968; *Shaman, and Other Poems*, 1968; *Poems*, 1971 (with Ted Hughes and Ruth Fainlight); *Barbarians, and Other Poems*, 1974; *Storm: New Poems*, 1974; *Snow on the North Side of Lucifer*, 1979; *More Lucifer*, 1980; *Sun Before Departure*, 1984; *Tides and Stone Walls*, 1986; *Collected Poems*, 1993.

SCREENPLAYS: *Saturday Night and Sunday Morning*, 1960 (adaptation of his novel); *The Loneliness of the Long-Distance Runner*, 1961 (adaptation of his novella); *Che Guevara*, 1968; *The Ragman's Daughter*, 1974 (adaptation of his novel).

## Bibliography

Atherton, Stanley S. *Alan Sillitoe: A Critical Assessment.* London: W. H. Allen, 1979. This study primarily emphasizes the revolutionary spirit of Sillitoe's first novels, but it deals with short fiction and lesser works as well.

Hanson, Gillian Mary. *Understanding Alan Sillitoe.* Columbia: University of South Carolina Press, 1999. Useful volume of Sillitoe criticism and appreciation.

Hensher, Philip. "Radical Sentiments." *Sunday Telegraph*, July 23, 1995, p. B9. A discussion of the life and works of Sillitoe, focusing on his autobiography *Life Without Armour* and his *The Collected Stories*; discusses briefly "The Loneliness of the Long Distance Runner" and the political nature of some of Sillitoe's short stories.

Hitchcock, Peter. *Working-Class Fiction in Theory and Practice: A Reading of Alan Sillitoe.* Ann Arbor, Mich.: UMI Research Press, 1989. Good examination of the writer's themes and execution.

Kalliney, Peter. "Cities of Affluence: Masculinity, Class, and the Angry Young Man." *Modern Fiction Studies* 47 (Spring, 2001): 92-117. Studies the class element in Sillitoe's work and the way in which gender dynamics illustrate class dynamics.

May, Charles E., ed. *Masterplots II: Short Story Series, Revised Edition.* 8 vols. Pasadena, Calif.: Salem Press, 2004. Designed for student use, this reference set contains articles providing detailed plot summaries and analyses of three short stories by Sillitoe: "The Loneliness of the Long-Distance Runner" (vol. 4), "The Ragman's Daughter" (vol. 6), and "The Sniper" (vol. 7).

Penner, Allen Richard. *Alan Sillitoe.* Boston: Twayne, 1972. Useful midcareer overview of Sillitoe's work. Penner offers a short biography and a helpful bibliography. The discussion covers Sillitoe's poetry and fiction.

Sawkins, John. *The Long Apprenticeship: Alienation in the Early Work of Alan Sillitoe.* New York: P. Lang, 2001. Semiotic reading of Sillitoe's work that looks for symbols and explores Sillitoe's semantics.

Sillitoe, Alan. "The Growth of a Writer: An Interview with Alan Sillitoe." Interview by Joyce Rothschild. *Southern Humanities Review* 20 (Spring, 1986): 127-140. This interview reveals Sillitoe's career and the irrelevance of class on his artistic sensibility. Sillitoe stresses the importance of character in his fiction.

Skovmand, Michael, and Steffen Skovmand, eds. *The Angry Young Men.* Aarhus, Denmark: Akademisk Forlag, 1975. Hans Hauge's essay on Sillitoe considers *Saturday Night and Sunday Morning* as a representative novel from an angry generation of young writers that included John Osborne, John Wain, John Braine, and Kingsley Amis.

# Isaac Bashevis Singer

**Born:** Leoncin, Poland; July 14 or November 21, 1904
**Died:** Surfside, Florida; July 24, 1991

**Principal short fiction** • *Gimpel the Fool, and Other Stories*, 1957; *The Spinoza of Market Street*, 1961; *Short Friday, and Other Stories*, 1964; *The Séance, and Other Stories*, 1968; *A Friend of Kafka, and Other Stories*, 1970; *A Crown of Feathers, and Other Stories*, 1973; *Passions, and Other Stories*, 1975; *Old Love*, 1979; *The Collected Stories*, 1982; *The Image, and Other Stories*, 1985; *The Death of Methuselah, and Other Stories*, 1988.

**Other literary forms** • Among Isaac Bashevis Singer's prodigious output are several translations; numerous novels, including *Der Sotn in Gorey* (1935; *Satan in Goray*, 1955), *Der Knekht* (1961; *The Slave*, 1962), and *Sonim, de Geshichte fun a Liebe* (1966; *Enemies: A Love Story*, 1972); several volumes of memoirs and autobiographical stories; more than a dozen collections of children's stories; and a variety of adaptations of his stories or novels for other media, including opera, stage, and film.

**Achievements** • Isaac Bashevis Singer, more than any other writer in the twentieth century, kept alive the rich traditions of a vanishing language and culture. Born into Eastern European Orthodox Judaism, Singer witnessed both the gradual assimilation of his generation into Gentile culture and the tragic Nazi Holocaust that ravaged Eastern Europe's Jewish populations.

Yiddish, a language written in Hebrew characters and derived from German, with borrowings from Polish, Lithuanian, and other languages, was spoken by millions of Jews. Inextricably connected to it are centuries of traditional beliefs and customs, as well as fascinating folklore, demonology, and mysticism that evolved from religious teaching. Writing exclusively in Yiddish (though translating much of his work into English himself) and mining both the language and the culture, Singer nourished a population stricken with tragedy and dispersed by exile.

Singer's greatest achievement, however, lay in expressing the universality of that very particular milieu. Never did Singer cater to audiences unfamiliar with Yiddish culture, yet, by finding the truly human aspects of the people and conflicts in his stories, he earned impressive popularity among a wide and varied audience. It is no doubt the profound universality of his vision that earned for Singer election to the National Institute of Arts and Letters in 1964, as the only member writing in a language other than English, and the Nobel Prize in Literature in 1978.

**Biography** • Isaac Bashevis Singer was born in Leoncin, Poland, on either July 14 or November 21, 1904. His grandfathers had been rabbis, and his father was a Hasidic scholar, whom Singer's mother chose over other suitors for his scholarly excellence. The Singers moved to Warsaw in 1908, and the young Bashevis (a name adapted from his mother's name Bathsheba) grew up with his sister and two brothers in a ghetto tenement at 10 Krochmalna Street, which was his father's rabbinical court.

Rabbi Pinchos-Mendel Singer was a warm, mystical, and deeply spiritual man who was loved and revered by the entire community. Bathsheba Singer was a cool, sharp,

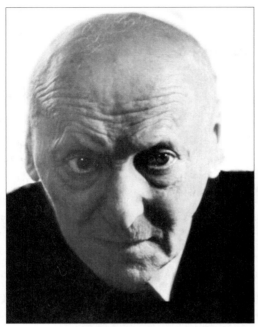

© The Nobel Foundation

practical, and rational woman who in many ways held the family together. The young Singer grew up among parental balances and contrasts that inform much of his writing. Singer read widely, including Fyodor Dostoevski's *Prestupleniye i nakazaniye* (1866; *Crime and Punishment*, 1886) in Yiddish at the age of nine, and studied languages. In addition, his older brother, Israel Joshua, eleven years his senior, was an intelligent and rebellious spirit who very early began to influence Singer's intellectual development.

In 1917, Singer accompanied his mother to her native Bilgoray, where they lived for four years. There, he taught Hebrew—considered an affront to tradition, as the language of the Scriptures was not to be used for mundane purposes. In 1921, Singer's father took a rabbinical post in a small town in Galicia; Singer, then seventeen, refused to follow, and instead stayed in Warsaw to study at the Tachkemoni Rabbinical Seminary. He later characterized his stay in Warsaw as the worst year of his life: Undernourished and ill fit to follow in his forefathers' footsteps, Singer left the seminary after a year to rejoin his family, only to return to Warsaw in 1923. He would never see his parents and younger brother, Moishe, again.

Singer's father wrote religious tracts, and Israel Joshua wrote secular pieces: It was almost inevitable that Singer too would write. During his year at the seminary, he had translated Knut Hamsun's novel *Sult* (1890; *Hunger*, 1899). In 1923 he became a proofreader for six dollars a week at the *Literarische Bletter*, a Yiddish literary magazine. He translated popular novels into Yiddish for newspaper serialization and experimented with writing in both Hebrew and Yiddish. During the late 1920's, the *Literarische Bletter* and *Warshaver Shriften* began accepting his Yiddish stories, such as "Women," "Grandchildren," and "The Village Gravedigger" for publication; meanwhile, his brother Israel Joshua's first novel, *Blood Harvest*, appeared in 1927.

Singer became involved with a young Communist woman, Runia; they lived in common-law marriage, and in 1929 they had a son, Israel. They became estranged, however, and Runia and the child left for Russia, then Turkey and Palestine. Singer would not meet his son again for decades.

During the 1930's, the Singer brothers' lives and careers became interwoven. In 1932, Isaac Bashevis became the editor of *Globus*, another literary magazine, and Israel Joshua published *Yoshe Kalb*, the popularity of which led to serial publication in the *Jewish Daily Forward* in New York. Isaac Bashevis's first novel, *Satan in Goray*, was serialized in *Globus* in 1933; in 1934, the older brother left for New York to escape the rise of European Nazism and to find success in the thriving Yiddish American community; and in 1935 the younger brother followed.

Singer moved into the Williamsburgh section of Brooklyn. The poverty and hunger that he met there were not new to him, but exile brought on an unprecedented spiritual collapse. He felt isolated from his family in Poland, his wife and child in Palestine, and his beloved culture devastated by war and genocide across Europe. He could not write, virtually forgot Yiddish, despaired for the future of Yiddish literature, and even at times became suicidal.

In 1937, Singer met Alma, a married German Jew with a son and daughter, who captured his mind and heart. She was divorced from her husband in 1939, and the following year they married. He was freelancing for the *Forward*, which continually encouraged him to resume his writing, in Yiddish. In 1943, he became an American citizen, and in 1944, with World War II raging, Singer was struck by a personal tragedy: His brother Israel Joshua, to whom he was devoted personally and artistically, died suddenly at the age of fifty-one.

The following year, the war ended and Singer began work on a novel, *Di Familye Muskat* (1950; *The Family Moskat*, 1950), which was serialized in the *Forward* over the next three years, broadcast on a Jewish radio station, chosen by publisher Alfred A. Knopf for translation into English, and awarded the Louis Lamed Prize in 1950. He began to write steadily, and in the early 1950's, nearing the age of fifty himself, Singer came to the attention of the American literary community. Editor Cecil Hemley and his wife Elaine Gottlieb helped Singer in several ways: They translated his stories, got them placed in major periodicals such as *Commentary* and *Partisan Review*, and published his novels through their Noonday Press, which in 1960 became part of Farrar, Straus and Giroux.

During the 1960's and 1970's, Singer produced a steady stream of stories and novels. His stories were published in numerous magazines as well as collections; some collections included reissues of much older pieces; translations appeared under his own hand or those of his nephew Joseph, Hemley, Gottlieb, writer Saul Bellow, or others. During the late 1960's, well past his sixtieth birthday, Singer took the suggestion of a friend and began writing stories for children as well. He also taught widely, serving as writer-in-residence at such institutions as Oberlin College and the University of Wisconsin.

Ironically, though well known in Yiddish and literary circles, Singer did not enjoy mass popularity and recognition until the 1983 release of the film *Yentl*, featuring Barbra Streisand, based on Singer's 1952 story "Yentl der Yeshive Bucher" ("Yentl the Yeshiva Boy"). A similar success was enjoyed by the 1989 film *Enemies: A Love Story*, based on Singer's 1972 novel.

For much of his later life, Singer lived with his wife Alma on West Eighty-sixth Street in New York; he later divided his time between New York and Miami Beach, where he ultimately retired. He died of a stroke on July 24, 1991, ten days after his eighty-seventh birthday.

**Analysis** • Isaac Bashevis Singer relished the short story; he believed that it offered, much more than the novel, the possibility of perfection. His stories, however, seldom reveal signs of a painstaking artisan conscious of form; rather, they flow naturally, even mindlessly, without any sense of manipulation. Indeed, Singer's art grows out of a thriving tradition of oral storytelling that had been fermenting through Eastern Europe for centuries.

Like many authors, Singer writes about the places and lives he knows. He sets most of his stories in pre-World War II Poland, in the small villages (Shtetlach) or the urban ghettoes of his childhood and youth. In his stories, these places are the Polish cities of Warsaw and Kraków, or semifictional towns such as Goray and Frampol; they appear over and over again with recurring motifs and character types, until most of Singer's tales seem to happen in the same prototypical settings.

Given the specificity of Singer's cultural milieu, the individual's relationship to his or her community becomes important, whether that relationship focuses on the collective attitude toward unusual characters and behavior or the individual's dislocation from family, community, and nation. Singer spent most of his life with such dislocation; it is not surprising that many of his characters are in some sort of exile. That exile can involve a new country, a new language, a new culture, or a new identity. Later in his career, Singer set stories among the expatriate Yiddish communities of New York or Israel and dealt explicitly with issues faced by an aging writer in exile.

As de facto chronicler of twentieth century Jewish experience, Singer chooses to leave untouched its central event: the Holocaust and the slaughter of six million European Jews under Adolf Hitler's Third Reich. Believing that a simple storyteller could never tell such an incomprehensible and horrific story, he rather evokes it through the richness with which he portrays the culture that it eradicated and the scattered pathos that it left in its wake. Like the Jewish people as a whole, Singer's characters struggle with identity in a changing world, they confront incomprehensible horrors and either surrender or survive. The individual in his community and his world is ultimately the individual in his universe, often alone with the supernatural powers that govern it.

Singer borrows from and embellishes on the wide array of Jewish mysticism and demonology to personify such powers and their involvement in the human condition. Sometimes the result is explicitly mythological; sometimes it explores the depths of possibility in very real circumstances. Whatever the form, Singer never hesitates to explore life and death, sin and redemption, good and evil, and heaven and hell in broad, literal terms. For him, imagination is paramount, and there are never any limits to what is possible. Much of the charm in his stories comes from the striking juxtaposition of the astoundingly cosmic with the laughably trivial, the apocalyptic with the quotidian, the macabre with the sentimental.

Nowhere is this approach more successful than in Singer's treatment of human sexuality. He never takes for granted the difficulties that sex engenders or the social rules and taboos that it confronts; at the same time, however, he consistently attributes to it its role as a driving force, and a truly beautiful one, in human affairs. His characters—be they rabbis, devils, simpletons, maidens, or whores—are all of flesh and blood, and they act accordingly. Singer portrays violence, rape, and hatred as unflinchingly as he portrays the deepest romantic love or most spiritual piety, never with judgment or disapproval, always striving to plumb the depths of the human heart.

**"Two Corpses Go Dancing"** • One of Singer's early stories shows the playfulness with which he treats death, demons, and infidelity. "Two Corpses Go Dancing," first published in *The Jewish Daily Forward* in 1943, is told from the point of view of the so-called Evil One, a device Singer also employs in such stories as "The Destruction of Kreshev" and "The Unseen." In "Two Corpses Go Dancing," the Evil One amuses himself by reinvigorating the corpse of a forgotten pauper named Itche-Godl, who "had been a corpse even when alive." Itche-Godl returns to his home, only to find his widow remarried to a more substantial man. His two appearances at her door inspire terror, but, believing himself to be alive, Itche-Godl cannot understand her behavior.

Itche-Godl soon encounters Finkle Rappaport, a widow who had gone to Vienna with a serious illness a year before and had long been believed dead but had recently reappeared in Warsaw. Finkle and Itche-Godl soon become betrothed; the couple's mysterious romance and macabre appearance astonish those around them. After the wedding, they retire to their wedding chamber only to find themselves transformed into corpses again and to realize that their return to life was only an illusion.

In "Two Corpses Go Dancing," Singer avoids all pretense of realism and rather depicts a surreal universe where no assumptions are valid. The physical and spiritual worlds are interwoven: Corpses are visible to the outside world but lack self-knowledge; they possess desire but are ultimately incapable of consummating it; they have superhuman powers but are essentially powerless.

**"Taibele and Her Demon"** • A story that similarly plays on the border between the real and spiritual realms but does not in the end sacrifice literal plausibility is "Taibele and Her Demon." Taibele is an abandoned wife in the shtetl of Frampol. Forbidden to remarry until her husband is proven dead, she is sentenced to a life of solitude. The village prankster Alchonon one day overhears Taibele's fascination with a story of a woman seduced by a demon, and he devises a scheme to take advantage of her credulity. One night he appears naked in her bedroom claiming to be the demon Hurmizah. He testifies that her husband is dead, charms her with tales of the demon world, and is welcomed into her bed. Though at first fearful and ashamed, Taibele gradually becomes dependent on Hurmizah's biweekly visits.

Winter comes, however, and with it the inescapable truth of Alchonon's humanity. His naked body cannot tolerate the cold during his nocturnal visits; he is taken ill and stops coming to see Taibele. She despairs at Hurmizah's absence and takes it as a pronouncement on her. Then one day, she sees a modest funeral procession on the snowy village street. When she realizes that the deceased is the idler Alchonon, whom she often mocked at the well, she feels a deep sympathy and accompanies him to the cemetery. She lives the rest of her life alone and carries her secret to the grave.

The power of this story lies in the irony of Taibele's passion for the demon Hurmizah. Here, the surreal world exists only in the minds of the characters: So long as people believe in demons, their existence is real enough. Singer is suggesting the unseen and unknown connections that can be forged between individuals when the imagination is free. At the same time, the love that results is not without its price. For Alchonon, that price is untimely death; for Taibele, it is the burden of sin, mystery, and desertion.

**"Gimpel the Fool"** • One of Singer's most celebrated stories, "Gimpel the Fool," also locates the individual's happiness in his or her power to believe. This, however, is a lighthearted tale where the willingness to let go of belief, to distrust one's senses and logic, defines the shape of the story. Gimpel the baker is known throughout Frampol for his gullibility. He recounts the nicknames that people have given him and the tricks that they have played on him but does not regret his simpleness, for he feels that he must always be open to all possibilities.

As such, he allows himself to be prodded into marrying an unprincipled woman named Elka. He accepts her bastard son as her little brother and believes her explanation of a premature birth when she bears another son seventeen weeks after their wedding night. She is repeatedly unfaithful to him; he accuses and even catches her but always eventually accepts her explanations and returns to his natural state of contentment. They live in this way for twenty years. Finally, on her deathbed, Elka confesses that she has lived sinfully and deceived him constantly. Soon after her death, Gimpel is tempted by the Evil Angel to have revenge on the scornful townsfolk by baking urine into their bread, but a vision of Elka returns and stops him. With his innocence restored, he leaves Frampol and travels the world, witnessing falsehood and truth in people. At the story's end, he is old, wise, accepting, prepared for death, free of regret, and full of love.

Throughout the story, Gimpel knows that the true factuality of events is less important than their effect on people's minds and hearts. He knows that he is incapable of skepticism but that his innocence and belief are his strength. Though Singer makes it clear that Gimpel is indeed a gullible fool, the simple joy with which he approaches life ultimately reveals itself to be a subversive wisdom. "Whatever doesn't really happen is dreamed at night," he says. "It happens to one if it doesn't happen to another, tomorrow if not today, or a century hence if not next year. What difference can it make?" Gimpel's doctrine is essentially Singer's affirmation of the power and validity of creating and telling stories.

**"The Spinoza of Market Street"** • "The Spinoza of Market Street" is another of Singer's most popular and most often reprinted tales. It is the story of Dr. Nahum Fischelson, a librarian, teacher, and revered philosopher who has devoted his life to studying the ideas of the seventeenth century Dutch Jewish philosopher Baruch Spinoza. Spinoza's *Ethics* dictates a rigid rational philosophy that Fischelson strives to embody. He contemplates the heavens and the mysteries of astronomy and contrasts them with the world below, in which the mindless rabble represents the antithesis of reason.

Then, as World War I descends on Warsaw, Fischelson's bitterness and stomach problems worsen, and he takes to a sickbed, where he has a stunning apocalyptic dream that he immediately dismisses as irrational. He seems to be on the verge of death, but a grotesque old spinster neighbor named Black Dobbe comes to take care of him. She nurses him back to health with simple attention and conversation, and soon Fischelson's study of Spinoza begins to seem less relevant. Before long, Black Dobbe announces to the rabbi that she and Fischelson will wed, and the story ends with their wedding night. When Black Dobbe comes to the so-called Spinoza of Market Street, he drops the *Ethics* to which he has devoted his life, and in his new wife's arms miraculously regains his health, his youth, and his passion for living.

**"Zeitl and Rickel"** • In "Zeitl and Rickel," Singer again focuses on an unpredictable relationship and the depth of human love and obsession, this time setting it more firmly in a context of social attitudes. The narrator says that the incredible tale she is about to relate demonstrates that anything is possible. She tells of two women, Zeitl and Rickel, one the daughter of a follower of the false Messiah, and the other an abandoned wife and the daughter of the town's ritual slaughterer. Rickel comes to attend on Zeitl's dying father, and the two women become absorbed in each other. Their relationship becomes steady and secretive, as seen from outside by the women of the community. They are overheard one day in a seeming catechism regarding hell and their shared future and eventually commit suicide in succession by throwing themselves into the well.

On one level, this is a story about an obsessive love shared by two women (with the suggestion, though never explicit, of lesbianism) and the mystical and eventually self-destructive form it assumes. On another level, it is about community perception: As told by one of Rickel's former students, the tale is an accumulation of gossip ennobled into spiritual mystery. Implicit in the story is a view of the place of women as daughters and wives in shtetl society, and the unorthodoxy of two women forging a spiritual connection and devoting their lives to each other. Although Singer has never been accused of feminism, he is sometimes keenly aware, and even in awe, of the shape and power of the female psyche.

**"Grandfather and Grandson"** • "Grandfather and Grandson" powerfully reflects the tension between the old insularity of Yiddish culture and the new worldliness that comes with greater exposure and assimilation. Reb Mordecai Meir is a widowed Hasid who devotes his life to his study of Judaism. He abhors everything worldly, including newspapers, theater, atheism, religious reform, and even the integration of the sexes. Having disowned his liberal-minded daughter, he is surprised when his long-forgotten grandson Fulie shows up on his Warsaw doorstep. Fulie, dressed like a Gentile, is a Communist sought by the authorities for political subversion. Though his presence and beliefs threaten Reb Mordecai Meir, blood flows deep, and the grandfather welcomes the fugitive into his home. Their shared life is precarious: Each wants to convert the other, each has guarded distrust, and ultimately they find a silent and respectful balance.

When Fulie announces that he must leave, possibly never to return, and asks his grandfather to keep an envelope to be passed on to a contact from the movement, Reb Mordecai Meir is put to a test of faith and conscience. He begrudgingly complies, and even when he later sees his grandson's revolver, accepts with silence the world's intrusion into his life. Finally, Fulie's dead body is returned to his bewildered grandfather, who utters prayers over the slain youth as best he can, finding reaffirmation of his faith and identity in their tragic blood connection.

"Grandfather and Grandson" reflects a larger awareness of the political events that shook European Jewry through the twentieth century. Though still set in prewar Poland, it is a story that reaches beyond to a universal experience of the painful changes that mark the passage of generations.

**"The Manuscript"** • "The Manuscript" also reflects larger historical realities and creates a sense of political urgency. Set at the outbreak of World War II, it is a story, retold much later in a café in Tel Aviv, of a woman's sacrifice for the man she loves and her response to his betrayal.

Shibtah is an actor married to a writer and womanizer named Menasha. When war comes to Warsaw, they flee to Białystok, leaving behind all Menasha's writing except a promising novel called *Rungs*. When a Białystok publisher expresses interest in the piece, they discover that they have someone else's manuscript; *Rungs* was left in Warsaw. Seeing no other option, and against Menasha's wishes, Shibtah undertakes a perilous ten-day journey back to Warsaw to retrieve it. On her return to Białystok, however, she finds Menasha in bed with another woman. She impulsively tosses the manuscript in the stove and leaves Białystok alone the following day.

Shibtah was never obsessively jealous; it is the particular infidelity, set against her journey and the backdrop of war, that constitutes a deception she cannot tolerate. Singer is not telling a simple story of broken vows; rather, he portrays the response of the human heart to a unique and complex set of circumstances, where love, sex, art, politics, and history find dramatic junction in a particular moment of time. As in much of his later work, the world of all possibility becomes a world where the individual can depend on nobody and nothing but his or her own heart and will to act.

**"Schloimele"** • Many of Singer's stories are loosely biographical, drawn from specific people and events from his own experience. "Schloimele," written during the period that the adaptation was being done for the film *Yentl*, is about a virtually unknown Yiddish writer in New York and a fast-talking aspiring stage producer whose perennial promise of a lucrative deal for the narrator dissolves into a humorous and pathetic refrain. In a series of vignettes tracing the two men's encounters over the course of several years, the pretentious Schloimele becomes a symbol first for the artifice of "showbiz" and ultimately for the narrator's own idleness, professional failure, mediocre love life, and general discontent. At the story's end, the two men escape the city on a bus to bucolic Monticello, but their departure is more like a funeral than a vacation.

"Schloimele" no doubt draws on both the despair that Singer felt at times in his career and the type of ambitious businessman that he knew well. Although free of the tortures of demons or melodrama of lost worlds, straightforward, unsensational narratives such as "Schloimele" evoke, in their understated realism, an amazingly strong and personal sense of tragedy and longing.

**"The Smuggler"** • There are certainly links from Taibele to Rickel to Shibtah, from Dr. Fischelson to Reb Mordecai Meir, or from Alchonon to Gimpel to Schloimele, and while no story can be said to sum up Singer's vision, some come strikingly close to a clear articulation of deep existential belief. An example is "The Smuggler," published three years before the author's death. It is a simple tale, most certainly based in truth (if only loosely), about a stranger's visit to the narrator (an author himself, living in a small New York apartment), seeking autographs for a cartload of his books. The man is a gentle old bum who met the narrator years before at a speech in Philadelphia; he does not want to intrude, only to get his books signed and leave.

During his short visit, however, he offers samples of the wisdom by which he has lived. Born to a family of Polish Jews, he learned to smuggle for a living, until he eventually realized that he survived by smuggling himself. He has come to recognize the intrinsic corruptibility of human beings, that power breeds wickedness, and that victims who overcome tyrants become tyrants themselves. He knows that evil and good are not mutually exclusive opposites, that there is nothing strange or inhuman about a Nazi leaving a concentration camp, where humans are systematically killed, and returning home to write heartfelt poetry. Finding security in this knowledge, the smuggler is at peace.

Although the message is harsh, it is for Singer, as for the smuggler of the story, only a starting point. Beyond it is a world of possibilities—for goodness and evil, love and violence, sex and piety—in which the human heart and mind rule. In his clever and paradoxical way, Singer affirms, "We must believe in free will. We have no choice."

*Barry Mann*

## Other major works

CHILDREN'S LITERATURE: *Zlateh the Goat, and Other Stories,* 1966; *Mazel and Shlimazel: Or, The Milk of a Lioness,* 1967; *The Fearsome Inn,* 1967; *When Shlemiel Went to Warsaw, and Other Stories,* 1968; *A Day of Pleasure: Stories of a Boy Growing Up in Warsaw,* 1969; *Elijah the Slave,* 1970; *Joseph and Koza: Or, The Sacrifice to the Vistula,* 1970; *Alone in the Wild Forest,* 1971; *The Topsy-Turvy Emperor of China,* 1971; *The Wicked City,* 1972; *The Fools of Chelm and Their History,* 1973; *Why Noah Chose the Dove,* 1974; *A Tale of Three Wishes,* 1975; *Naftali the Storyteller and His Horse, Sus, and Other Stories,* 1976; *The Power of Light: Eight Stories,* 1980; *The Golem,* 1982; *Stories for Children,* 1984.

PLAYS: *The Mirror,* pr. 1973; *Shlemiel the First,* pr. 1974; *Yentl, the Yeshiva Boy,* pr. 1974 (with Leah Napolin); *Teibele and Her Demon,* pr. 1978.

NOVELS: *Der Sotn in Gorey,* 1935 (*Satan in Goray,* 1955); *Di Familye Mushkat,* 1950 (*The Family Moskat,* 1950); *Der Hoyf,* 1953-1955 (*The Manor,* 1967, and *The Estate,* 1969); *Shotns baym Hodson,* 1957-1958 (*Shadows on the Hudson,* 1998); *Der Kuntsn-makher fun Lublin,* 1958-1959 (*The Magician of Lublin,* 1960); *Der Knekht,* 1961 (*The Slave,* 1962); *Sonim, de Geshichte fun a Liebe,* 1966 (*Enemies: A Love Story,* 1972); *Der Bal-Tshuve,* 1974 (*The Penitent,* 1983); *Neshome Ekspeditsyes,* 1974 (*Shosha,* 1978); *Reaches of Heaven: A Story of the Baal Shem Tov,* 1980; *Der Kenig vun di Felder,* 1988 (*The King of the Fields,* 1988); *Scum,* 1991; *The Certificate,* 1992; *Meshugah,* 1994.

NONFICTION: *Mayn Tatn's Bes-din Shtub,* 1956 (*In My Father's Court,* 1966); *The Hasidim,* 1973 (with Ira Moskowitz); *A Little Boy in Search of God: Mysticism in a Personal Light,* 1976; *A Young Man in Search of Love,* 1978; *Isaac Bashevis Singer on Literature and Life,* 1979 (with Paul Rosenblatt and Gene Koppel); *Lost in America,* 1980; *Love and Exile,* 1984; *Conversations with Isaac Bashevis Singer,* 1985 (with Richard Burgin); *More Stories from My Father's Court,* 2000.

TRANSLATIONS: *Romain Rolland,* 1927 (of Stefan Zweig); *Die Volger,* 1928 (of Knut Hamsun); *Victoria,* 1929 (of Hamsun); *All Quiet on the Western Front,* 1930 (of Erich Remarque); *Pan,* 1931 (of Hamsun); *The Way Back,* 1931 (of Remarque); *The Magic Mountain,* 1932 (of Thomas Mann); *From Moscow to Jerusalem,* 1938 (of Leon Glaser).

## Bibliography

Alexander, Edward. *Isaac Bashevis Singer: A Study of the Short Fiction.* Boston: Twayne, 1990. Introduction to Singer's stories in terms of their themes, types, and motifs, for example: moral tales, holocaust stories, supernatural tales, tales of apocalypse and politics, stories of faith and doubt. Focuses on Singer's universal appeal rather than his Jewish appeal. Includes a section of quotations from Singer about his work, as well as essays on Singer by Irving Howe and two other critics.

Buchen, Irving H. *Isaac Bashevis Singer and the Eternal Past.* New York: New York University Press, 1968. Buchen provides an interesting though not painstakingly detailed look at Singer's early career. Although his efforts to relate the author to other contemporary writers and the overall tradition of English and American literature are excessive, he explores and understands the balances of Singer's writing. Includes a chapter on selected early stories and a good bibliography.

Farrell, Grace, ed. *Critical Essays on Isaac Bashevis Singer.* New York: G. K. Hall, 1996. Extensive introduction on Singer's critical reception and the issues that have preoccupied him and his critics. Collects both contemporary reviews and a wide range of essays, including Leslie Fiedler's "I. B. Singer: Or, The American-ness of the American Jewish Writer."

_____. *Isaac Bashevis Singer: Conversations.* Jackson: University Press of Missis-
sippi, 1992. Collection of interviews with Singer that reveal the connections
among his philosophy of life, his perspective on literature, and his mode of living.
Guzlowski, John. "Isaac Bashevis Singer's 'Satan in Goray' and Bakhtin's Vision of the
Carnivalesque." *Critique* 39 (Winter, 1998): 167-175. Argues that Mikhail Bakhtin's
notion of the grotesque illuminates Singer's and that Wolfgang Kayser's theories
of the grotesque oversimplify his message; concludes, however, that Singer departs from Bakhtin is in his less hopeful belief about society's ability to build a new
order out of carnival.
Hadda, Janet. *Isaac Bashevis Singer: A Life.* New York: Oxford University Press, 1997.
Focusing on both the forces of family and that social environment that influenced
Singer, Hadda uncovers the public persona to reveal a more complex man than
heretofore understood.
_____. "Isaac Bashevis Singer in New York." *Judaism* 46 (Summer, 1997): 346-
363. Discusses the transformation of Singer from Bashevis, the sharp-witted, con-
flicted, occasionally harsh, literary genius, to Isaac Bashevis Singer—and even
Isaac Singer—the quaint, pigeon-feeding vegetarian, the serene and gentle embodiment of the timeless values of Eastern European Jews.
May, Charles E., ed. *Masterplots II: Short Story Series, Revised Edition.* 8 vols. Pasadena,
Calif.: Salem Press, 2004. Designed for student use, this reference set contains
articles providing detailed plot summaries and analyses of eight short stories by
Singer: "The Admirer" (vol. 1); "A Friend of Kafka," "The Gentleman from Cra-
cow," and "Gimpel the Fool" (vol. 3); "Moon and Madness" (vol. 5); "Short Friday"
(vol. 6); "The Spinoza of Market Street" (vol. 7); and "Yentl, the Yeshiva Boy"
(vol. 8).
Sinclair, Clive. *The Brothers Singer.* London: Allison and Busby, 1983. Fascinating examination of Singer and his work in the context of one of the most important personal and literary relationships of the author's life. Sinclair effectively interweaves
biography and literary analysis, conveying a deep understanding of the lives and
works of Isaac and Joshua Singer.
Wolitz, Seth L., ed. *The Hidden Isaac Bashevis Singer.* Austin: University of Texas Press,
2001. Collection of essays focusing on Singer's use of Yiddish language and cultural experience, themes that persist through his writing, his interface with other
times and cultures, his autobiographical work, and a translation of a previously
unpublished "gangster" novel.

# Muriel Spark

**Born:** Edinburgh, Scotland; February 1, 1918
**Died:** Florence, Italy; April 13, 2006

**Principal short fiction** • *The Go-Away Bird, and Other Stories*, 1958; *Voices at Play*, 1961 (with radio plays); *Collected Stories I*, 1967; *Bang-Bang You're Dead, and Other Stories*, 1981; *The Stories of Muriel Spark*, 1985; *Open to the Public: New and Collected Stories*, 1997; *All the Stories*, 2001 (also pb. as *The Complete Short Stories*).

**Other literary forms** • Muriel Spark is known primarily for her novels and short fiction, but her body of work also includes works of nonfiction, children's literature, poetry, film adaptations, and radio plays. She began her career writing news articles as a press agent. Later she expanded her range to include works of poetry and literary criticism, contributing poems, articles, and reviews to magazines and newspapers, occasionally using the pseudonym Evelyn Cavallo. Spark published her first short story in 1951. In 1954, she began writing novels, her best known being *The Prime of Miss Jean Brodie*. She eventually published two dozen novels, including two that she wrote after she reached the age of eighty: *Aiding and Abetting* (2000) and *The Finishing School* (2004).

**Achievements** • Muriel Spark's honors and awards include the Prix Italia (1962) for her radio play adaptation of *The Ballad of Peckham Rye* (1960); the *Yorkshire Post* Book of the Year Award (1965) and the James Tait Black Memorial Prize (1966), both for *The Mandelbaum Gate* (1965); Commander, Order of the British Empire (1967); the Booker McConnell Prize nomination (1981) for *Loitering with Intent* (1981); the Scottish Book of the Year Award (1987) for The Stories of Muriel Spark; Officier de l'Ordre des Arts et des Lettres (1988); the Ingersoll T. S. Elliot Award (1992); Dame, Order of the British Empire (1993); and the David Cohen British Literature Prize for Lifetime Achievement (1997).

**Biography** • Muriel Sarah Spark, née Camberg, was born and educated in Edinburgh, Scotland. In 1937, she went to Rhodesia. During her stay in Africa, she married S. O. Spark but was divorced a short time later. She had one child, her son Robin. Spark's parents, Bernard and Sarah Elizabeth Camberg, held diverse religious faiths; her father was Jewish, while her mother was Presbyterian. Spark practiced the Anglican faith until her interest in the writings of John Henry Newman, a nineteenth century Roman Catholic theologian, persuaded her to convert to Catholicism in 1954. Her personal search for spiritual belief is reflected in many of the themes of her fiction. Consequently her works often express some moral or spiritual truth.

Spark spent several years living in British colonies in Central Africa. In 1944, she returned to England. During World War II, she wrote news articles for the political intelligence department of the British government. After the war, she held various posts in the publishing field, including a position as founder of the short-lived literary magazine *The Forum*. During the early 1950's, Spark began to produce serious work in literary criticism and poetry. Hand and Flower Press published her first volume of poetry in 1952. At the same time, she was involved in editing and researching critical and biographical work on several nineteenth century literary figures, including William Wordsworth, Mary Wollstonecraft Shelley, and Emily Brontë.

Spark's initial attempt at fiction writing received considerable attention when her short story "The Seraph and the Zambesi" won top honors in a writing contest in 1951. She was encouraged to expand the scope of her fiction in 1954, when Macmillan, Spark's publisher, persuaded her to write a full-length novel. At the same time that Spark began to develop a technique for composing a novel, she was also struggling with her religious beliefs and her decision to convert to Catholicism. Consequently, her first novel, *The Comforters*, completed in 1957, examines theological issues, reflecting Spark's own private search for a belief that was consistent with her personal need for an adequate faith during the time that she was writing the novel. The link between her conception of the world, both physically and spiritually, and the subjects of her fiction is evident in her later novels as well.

Spark presented facts about her life and the beginnings of her writing career in her autobiography, *Curriculum Vitae* (1992). She lived in Italy from the late 1960's until her death in Florence on April 13, 2006.

**Analysis** • Muriel Spark was an adept storyteller with a narrative voice that was often distant or aloof. Her tales are psychologically interesting because Spark was reluctant to reveal all that her characters think and feel; in consequence, readers are forced to evaluate the stories, think about issues from a different perspective, and try to fill in the gaps. Critics regard Spark's novels as her strongest genre, but her short stories are also well constructed and intriguing. Her volumes of short stories, published over four decades, contain many of the same stories reprinted, with new stories added to each new edition.

Spark's tales are often set in England, British colonies in Africa, or European locations. Her works reflect a sense of moral truth, which some critics view as the influence of her conversion to Catholicism in 1954. Her narrative is rarely wordy. The story line relies on the impressions and dialogue of the characters or narrator to convey the plot. She made frequent use of first-person narrative, but none of her voices "tells all." One of the distinguishing elements in Spark's style was her penchant for leaving gaps that her readers must fill for themselves.

**"The Seraph and the Zambesi"** • Spark's first short story, "The Seraph and the Zambesi," won an award in a Christmas contest sponsored by *The Observer* in 1951. In characteristic Spark style, this story does not mince words but focuses on action and sparse dialogue. Set in Africa at Christmastime, the story portrays the events surrounding preparations for a Christmas pageant. Besides sweltering temperatures, curious natives, and preoccupied performers, the presentation is "hindered" by the presence of a heavenly Seraph, complete with six wings and a heat-producing glow. The writer of the nativity play is incensed when a real angel appears. He expresses rage rather than awe and destroys the stage in his attempts to banish the Seraph. Though Spark refuses to offer a moral at the close of "The Seraph and the Zambesi," the story resembles a parable, illustrating the egocentrism of human beings, especially "artists." The narrative also serves as a metaphor for the definition of genuine "art."

A related story dealing with art and creativity is entitled "The Playhouse Called Remarkable." This story, published several years after "The Seraph and the Zambesi," features a character named Moon Biglow. Moon confesses to the narrator that he is really a native of the moon who migrated to Earth on the "Downfall of [the] Uprise" some time in the distant past. His primary mission was to save earth's residents from suffocating aesthetic boredom. It seems human beings had no form of recreation other than that of gathering in groups to chant "Tum tum ya" each evening. The moon migrants organize the "playhouse called Remarkable" to offer alternative entertainment and also to give earthlings a creative outlet for their imaginations.

**"The Pawnbroker's Wife"** • Often Spark's short fiction depicts varied types of female personalities. These stories, narrated in first person and set in Africa, tell little about the narrators themselves but focus on the manipulative power of the central female characters. In "The Pawnbroker's Wife," the narrator tells the story of Mrs. Jan Cloote, who is never identified by her first name. Her pawnbroker husband has disappeared, and Mrs. Cloote carries on the business herself but denies the slightly sordid reputation of her vocation by claiming that she is only the pawnbroker's wife. Thus, in her name and her speech, she tries the separate her actions from her image. Such "distancing" allows Mrs. Cloote freedom in refusing to accept responsibility for her conduct, no matter how cruel or petty, as she performs the duties of a pawnbroker (and ironically she is far more successful in business than her husband had been). She uses a show of politeness to remain corrupt without having to admit fault or make concessions. She breaks her promises to customers and sells the pawned items of her friends at the first opportunity. Mrs. Cloote's poor taste, grasping manipulation, and innocent pretense give her character an insidious cast. Yet the narrator who reveals these facts refuses to pass judgment regarding Mrs. Cloote's morality. That matter is left to the reader.

© Jerry Bauer

**"The Curtain Blown by the Breeze"** • In a similar story, Sonia Van der Merwe, the female protagonist in "The Curtain Blown by the Breeze," gains power over her domain in the absence of her husband. Mr. Van der Merwe, who lives in the remote territory of Fort Beit, is imprisoned for fatally shooting a young native boy who was a Peeping Tom. Although her husband's conviction and imprisonment might have prompted a feeling of tragedy, the opposite occurs. Sonia finds that she has considerable financial resources at her disposal with her husband gone. Like Mrs. Cloote, Sonia takes charge, encouraged on by the British medical women serving in the colony. She soon learns to use her feminine wiles to access power and control in Fort

Beit. The male British medical workers seek her attention, captivated by her "eccentric grandeur." Much to the chagrin of the British women who helped to create the "new Sonia," Sonia gains influence even over government officials. Just as the English nurse, however, who narrates the story can never truly decide what she wants, the same applies to Sonia. At the close of the story, Mr. Van der Merwe returns from prison unexpectedly. When he discovers his wife, Sonia, in the company of another man, he shoots them both. Thus, Sonia and her image are quickly eliminated. In her stories, Spark explores the roles of greedily ambitious women, the irony of their plight, and their cloaks of politeness.

Often Spark deals with themes of childhood or adolescent memories in her short fiction. She may contrast the innocent but terrifyingly real fears of children with the more serious cruelty of adults or reverse the irony and explore the cruelty of "devilish" children, who are shielded by a guise of adult politeness. For example, "The Twins" is a story about two seemingly polite children who exercise some invisible but insidious control over their parents and other adults who enter their household.

**"The Portobello Road" and "Bang-Bang You're Dead"** • "The Portobello Road" and "Bang-Bang You're Dead" juxtapose the childhood memories of two young girls with their lives as "grown-ups." These stories explore the serious ramifications of situations in which childish conceptions or antagonisms are transferred into adulthood. Both stories are examples of Muriel Spark's ability to create unique narrative forms. "The Portobello Road" is narrated by Needle, a young girl whose childhood nickname was given to her because she found a needle in a haystack. When the story opens, Needle is dead and her ghostly voice chronicles the events that led to her murder—when she becomes the "Needle" who is murdered and buried in a haystack by a childhood friend.

"Bang-Bang You're Dead" connects the present and the past in a complex narrative using a series of flashbacks. In the present, represented in the story's opening scene, a group of Sybil's friends gather to view four reels of eighteen-year-old films from Sybil's past years spent in Africa. As the group views the "silent movies," the third-person narrative reveals Sybil's memories—not those seen by the spectators of the film but as Sybil remembers them. As each reel ends, Sybil's mental narrative is interrupted by the surface chatter of her friends, who are impressed by the appearance of the people and exotic scenes revealed in the film. When the final reel ends, the reader finds, through Sybil's mental recollections, that two murders were committed shortly after the scenes were recorded on film. As the acquaintances agree to view the last reel again because it is their "favorite," Sybil remains stoically unmoved by the memories of the tragedy. Her indifference and objectivity regarding the memories of her deceased friends reveal a chilling aspect of her personality. Coldly intellectual and detached, Sybil remains indifferent and unmoved by the recorded memories even though she was largely responsible for the murders.

**"The Go-Away Bird" and "The First Year of My Life"** • "The Go-Away Bird" is one of the longest of Spark's stories. It is also about a woman and murder. Daphne, the central female figure, is reared in a British colony in Africa. Caught between two cultures, that of the Dutch Afrikaners and the English colonists, Daphne searches for her identity—for a world in which she can not only belong but also find safety. Set in Africa and England during World War II, "The Go-Away Bird" presents characters who reflect diverse backgrounds, personalities, motivations, and societies. Daphne's struggles and her relationship with the African Go-Away Bird illustrate an individual's difficulty in trying to fulfill one's need for love and identity within diverse cultural and social structures.

At the opposite end of the spectrum, "The First Year of My Life" does not struggle with maturing in society but presents the first-person commentary of an infant, born during World War I. The adults who care for the baby treat the child as an "innocent infant," unaware of the newborn's ability to grasp the tragedy of war. Such diversity in narrative voice, subject, and style is a trademark of Muriel Spark. As a writer, she avoided classification and was unafraid of experimentation.

**Open to the Public: New and Collected Stories** • Spark's collection *Open to the Public* contains ten stories not included in the previous volume, *The Stories of Muriel Spark* (1985). The title story "Open to the Public" is a sequel to "The Fathers' Daughters." "The Fathers' Daughters" centers on a thirty-year-old intellectual, Ben, who pursues the daughters of famous writers in order to meet the authors themselves. When the young, beautiful Carmelita is unable to gain an audience for Ben with her father, a successful novelist, Ben abandons her to marry Dora, the forty-six-year-old daughter of an aged author whose popularity has faded. Spark creates an ironic situation in which the characters use one another for their own purposes. Ben wants to write essays based on another author's work; Dora's father craves an audience for his forgotten books; and Dora needs someone to provide income for their impoverished household.

The sequel "Open to the Public" presents Ben and Dora five years later. Dora's father dies, but Ben's promotion of his works restores the family's fortune. However, the dead man's memory is not enough to sustain the relationship; the couple separate. Their plans to open the writer's house and personal documents to the public are abandoned when both Ben and Dora realize that museums "have no heart." In a humorous turn, they burn the father's archives instead. The story demonstrates the hopelessness of trying to maintain perpetual fame, and the futility of attempting to build one's future on another's achievements.

In a story with similar elements, "The Executor," the protagonist Susan, who is a middle-aged spinster like Dora, must dispose of her uncle's literary estate. She sells his papers to a university foundation but retains an unfinished manuscript which she hopes to complete and publish as her own. However, her plans are thwarted when her uncle's ghost returns to write warning messages to her. Thus Susan, like the women in "The Father's Daughters," must abandon her schemes to find success vicariously and learn to build her own future.

The remaining additions in the *Open to the Public* collection are stylized and brief. Some plots turn on a single ironic twist as in "The Girl I Left Behind Me" when the narrator finds her own body "lying strangled on the floor." Other stories feature the troubling imposition of the supernatural into the natural world. For example, in "The Pearly Shadow" a shady specter haunts the staff and patients in a medical clinic. The specter finally disappears when doctors begin dispensing sedatives to his "stressed-out" victims. "Going Up and Coming Down" is a poetic vignette about a man and woman who ride to work in the same elevator every day. Once the couple actually meet, their speculations about each other disappear in the face of "plain real facts."

The stories included in *Open to the Public* demonstrate Spark's mastery of the short-story form. Her plots expose human foibles with an ironic, mysterious, or sarcastic tone. She was adept at illustrating the slightly macabre or deceitful nature of human actions. Her characters may be subtly malevolent or sinisterly civilized, but evil is punished and hypocrisy exposed in Spark's comic tales.

*Paula M. Miller*
*With updates by the Editors*

## Other major works

CHILDREN'S LITERATURE: *The Very Fine Clock*, 1968; *The Small Telephone*, 1993.

PLAY: *Doctors of Philosophy*, pr. 1962.

ANTHOLOGIES: *Tribute to Wordsworth*, 1950 (with Derek Stanford); *My Best Mary: The Selected Letters of Mary Shelley*, 1953 (with Stanford); *The Brontë Letters*, 1954 (pb. in U.S. as *The Letters of the Brontës: A Selection*, 1954); *Letters of John Henry Newman*, 1957 (with Stanford).

NOVELS: *The Comforters*, 1957; *Robinson*, 1958; *Memento Mori*, 1959; *The Bachelors*, 1960; *The Ballad of Peckham Rye*, 1960; *The Prime of Miss Jean Brodie*, 1961; *A Muriel Spark Trio*, 1962 (contains *The Comforters*, *Memento Mori*, and *The Ballad of Peckham Rye*); *The Girls of Slender Means*, 1963; *The Mandelbaum Gate*, 1965; *The Public Image*, 1968; *The Driver's Seat*, 1970; *Not to Disturb*, 1971; *The Hothouse by the East River*, 1973; *The Abbess of Crewe: A Modern Morality Tale*, 1974; *The Takeover*, 1976; *Territorial Rights*, 1979; *Loitering with Intent*, 1981; *The Only Problem*, 1984; *A Far Cry from Kensington*, 1988; *Symposium*, 1990; *The Novels of Muriel Spark*, 1995; *Reality and Dreams*, 1996; *Aiding and Abetting*, 2000; *The Finishing School*, 2004.

NONFICTION: *Child of Light: A Reassessment of Mary Wollstonecraft Shelley*, 1951 (revised as *Mary Shelley*, 1987); *Emily Brontë: Her Life and Work*, 1953 (with Derek Stanford); *John Masefield*, 1953; *Curriculum Vitae*, 1992 (autobiography); *The Essence of the Brontës: A Compilation with Essays*, 1993.

POETRY: *The Fanfarlo, and Other Verse*, 1952; *Collected Poems I*, 1967; *Going Up to Sotheby's, and Other Poems*, 1982; *All of the Poems of Muriel Spark*, 2004.

## Bibliography

Bold, Alan, ed. *Muriel Spark: An Odd Capacity for Vision*. Totowa, N.J.: Barnes & Noble Books, 1984. Bold has compiled a collection of nine essays from different contributors, regarding various aspects of Spark's fiction. The volume is organized into two sections. The first four essays explore Spark's background and the content of her work. The remaining chapters contain critical articles centered on the diverse forms of Spark's writings, including discussions of her use of satire, her poetry, and an essay by Tom Hubbard that deals exclusively with her short stories.

Edgecombe, Rodney Stenning. *Vocation and Identity in the Fiction of Muriel Spark*. Columbia: University of Missouri Press, 1990. Critical and historical study of the psychological in Scottish literature. Includes a bibliography and index.

Hague, Angela, and Isabel Bonnyman Stanley. "Muriel Spark." In *Critical Survey of Long Fiction, Revised Edition*, edited by Carl Rollyson. Vol. 6. Pasadena, Calif.: Salem Press, 2000. Analysis of Spark's longer fictional works that may offer insights into her short fiction.

Hynes, Joseph, ed. *Critical Essays on Muriel Spark*. New York: G. K. Hall, 1992. Comprehensive collection of reviews, essays, and excerpts from books on Spark's fiction, by both her detractors and her admirers. Includes autobiographical essays and a survey and critique of past criticism.

May, Charles E., ed. *Masterplots II: Short Story Series, Revised Edition*. 8 vols. Pasadena, Calif.: Salem Press, 2004. Designed for student use, this reference set contains articles providing detailed plot summaries and analyses of three short stories by Spark: "The Black Madonna" (vol. 1), "The Father's Daughters" (vol. 3), and "The Portobello Road" (vol. 6).

Randisi, Jennifer Lynn. *On Her Way Rejoicing: The Fiction of Muriel Spark*. Washington, D.C.: Catholic University of America Press, 1991. Argues that Spark's vision is metaphysical, combining piety and satire, deception and anagogical truth. Discusses the tension between mysticism and satire in Spark's novels and stories.

Richmond, Velma B. *Muriel Spark*. New York: Frederick Ungar, 1984. Richmond explores Spark's writing in terms of content and emphasis. Spark's novels, poetry, and short stories are discussed in relation to their themes rather than their chronology. The closing chapter includes a discussion of Spark's "comic vision." Richmond includes biographical material along with a detailed chronology, a bibliography, and an extensive index.

Spark, Muriel. *Curriculum Vitae: Autobiography*. Boston: Houghton Mifflin, 1993. Spark examines her life and literary career.

Walker, Dorothea. *Muriel Spark*. Boston: Twayne, 1988. Informative study on the main themes of Spark's work, with emphasis given to the wit and humor of her characters. The extensive bibliography is particularly helpful.

Whittaker, Ruth. *The Faith and Fiction of Muriel Spark*. New York: St. Martin's Press, 1982. Whittaker's work elaborates on the diversity of Spark's themes, meanings, and purpose. The chapter divisions are organized according to topics—religion, style, structure, and form. The book is limited primarily to a discussion of Spark's novels. Whittaker includes a biographical section as well as an extensive bibliography, notes, and an index.

# John Steinbeck

**Born:** Salinas, California; February 27, 1902
**Died:** New York, New York; December 20, 1968

**Principal short fiction** • *Saint Katy the Virgin*, 1936; *The Long Valley*, 1938.

**Other literary forms** • Besides two volumes of short fiction, John Steinbeck produced numerous novels, among which is his masterpiece, *The Grapes of Wrath* (1939). He also authored several screenplays and three dramas, two of which were based on his novels *Of Mice and Men* (1937) and *The Moon Is Down* (1942). Among his nonfiction are several travel books and a collection of war sketches. His last work was a translation of Sir Thomas Malory's Arthurian stories. A volume of letters was published posthumously.

**Achievements** • John Steinbeck assumes an important place in American literature chiefly for his powerful and deft portrayal of the common people—the migrant worker, the ranch hand, and the laborer—whose capacity for survival surpassed the attempts of economic and corporate forces to defeat them. His novels, especially, render the human condition with sensitivity and lyrical grace. His work often shows a versatility unrivaled among his contemporaries. The comic, the tragic, the whimsical, and the naturalistic all merge in such a way as to make Steinbeck one of the United States' most popular writers, one whose art form is particularly suited to the cinema. Many of his books have been turned into successful films. Though much of Steinbeck's best work was written in the 1930's, he is not only a propagandist of the Great Depression era but also a writer who is deeply concerned with the dignity of human beings. A human being as an individual may pass away, but the human being as a group, humankind as a species, is immortal. As Ma Joad remarked in the final pages of *The Grapes of Wrath*: "We're the people. We go on."

**Biography** • The Salinas Valley, where John Steinbeck was born, lies about a hundred miles south of San Francisco. It is a fertile, temperate trough between two mountain ranges and encompasses some of central California's most picturesque areas, notably Pacific Grove and the serenity of Monterey Bay. Such a landscape was at the heart of Steinbeck's boyhood experience and forms a crucial link with the characteristics of the writer's work. The son of a mill owner and a schoolteacher, Steinbeck grew up in the small railroad town just entering the twentieth century, a town not quite pastoral yet not quite industrial, whose people were farmers and ranchers and shopkeepers but whose location and natural resources were quickly making it an agricultural and mercantile hub. This unique duality of the Salinas Valley—the long valley of Steinbeck's fiction—became a formative agent in the quality of Steinbeck's work, stories at once gently romantic and mythic as they were also realistic and proletarian. His early reading was evidence of his growing dualism. The realistic novels of Gustave Flaubert and Thomas Hardy were supplemented by his readings in Greek and Roman mythology, the Bible, and especially Sir Thomas Malory's *Le Morte d'Arthur* (c. 1469, printed 1485), the first book given to him as a child and the last to serve as a source for his fiction.

(A retelling of the King Arthur stories was published posthumously in 1976).

By the time Steinbeck entered Salinas High School in 1915, he was a widely read young man, tall, with rugged good looks and a desire to write. At the age of seventeen, he entered Stanford University, already convinced that he was going to be a writer. Like many creative artists before and since, Steinbeck found the discipline of the college curriculum too irksome. Though he enjoyed reading contemporary European and American writers such as Theodore Dreiser and Sinclair Lewis, he was uninterested in much else and took a leave of absence after two years. For the next few years, he worked in the San Francisco area as a clerk and a field hand on a ranch, gaining the invaluable experience of ranch life and ranch hands that was to figure in such works as *Of Mice and Men* and *The Long Valley.*

© The Nobel Foundation

Steinbeck returned to Stanford University briefly as an English major but finally left in 1925 without a degree. He had written two stories for the *Stanford Spectator,* one a satire on college life and the other a bizarre tale about a strangely inarticulate woman and her marriage to a migrant worker who kept horses' heads in a rain barrel. The story is insignificant but interesting for its odd mixture of the real and the whimsical, a characteristic typical of much of Steinbeck's mature work.

Steinbeck was in New York during the late 1920's, working as a construction worker on the original Madison Square Garden by day and writing stories by night. Unsuccessful, he returned to California, married, and settled in his family's cottage in Pacific Grove. He wrote constantly, and in 1929, his first novel, *Cup of Gold,* was published. This thinly fictionalized account of the pirate Henry Morgan was both an artistic and a financial failure. *The Pastures of Heaven* (1932), Steinbeck's second book, was a collection of short stories about the people of an almost mythically beautiful valley. Influenced by Sherwood Anderson's *Winesburg, Ohio* (1919), published a decade earlier, neither it nor his next novel, *To a God Unknown* (1933), brought Steinbeck much critical or popular success.

Steinbeck's apprenticeship, however, was over. Beginning in 1935 with the publication of *Tortilla Flat,* Steinbeck was to produce half a dozen books over the next ten years, works that were to establish his reputation as a writer of power and versatility. *Tortilla Flat* was followed by *In Dubious Battle* (1936), regarded by some as one of the best strike novels ever written. *Of Mice and Men* was followed by *The Long Valley*, containing his best short stories. His masterpiece, on which he had been working for three years, was published as *The Grapes of Wrath* in 1939.

During World War II, Steinbeck wrote propaganda scripts for the U.S. Army and published *The Moon Is Down*, a short novel set in Nazi-occupied Norway. His postwar work shows a marked decline. Aside from the massive *East of Eden* (1952), the works of this period are marked by a bland whimsy. *Cannery Row* (1945) is generally recognized as the novel that signaled the beginning of Steinbeck's decline. Throughout the 1950's and 1960's, Steinbeck, then a national celebrity, continued to produce a variety of fiction, novels such as *Sweet Thursday* (1954), *The Short Reign of Pippen IV* (1957), and *The Winter of Our Discontent* (1961). They are works of minor importance and show little of the narrative strength that won for Steinbeck the Nobel Prize in Literature in 1962.

Steinbeck's last years were spent quietly in New York City and on Long Island. By then he had become an honored American writer. In 1963, he was selected as honorary consultant in American literature for the Library of Congress. He was elected to the National Arts Council in 1966. Steinbeck died peacefully in his sleep on December 20, 1968.

**Analysis** • The qualities that most characterize the work of John Steinbeck are a supple narrative style, a versatility of subject matter, and an almost mystical sympathy for the common human being. His fiction is peopled with men and women somehow shoaled from society's mainstream yet possessed of a vision that is itself a source of strength. His characteristic narrative method is to portray these people with an unerring mixture of realism and romance.

Although the Great Depression is the central social focus of Steinbeck's best work, his characters respond to those social forces not only in terms of realistic confrontation but also in the form of a romantic, intuitive escape. His characters become not so much victims of social or economic failure but celebrants of a life-force beyond society and economics. The best of Steinbeck's work maintains this tension—developed by a narrative tone—between the world of harsh reality and the world of animal-like freedom. Even in a late novel such as *East of Eden*, his best books behind him, Steinbeck symbolically construed this duality in the reference to the two mountain ranges that defined the territory of his narrator's childhood, the "sunny" flowered slopes of the Gabilans to the east and the dark, brooding peaks of the Santa Lucias to the west.

*The Pastures of Heaven* • Nowhere is this duality—the tension between realism and romance—more evident than in Steinbeck's earliest short stories, those forming his first major work, *The Pastures of Heaven*. Structurally the book shows the influence of Anderson's *Winesburg, Ohio*, a series of short stories, each independent but each connected by the locale and the theme of psychic isolation.

Using the frame narrative of Winesburg as a model, *The Pastures of Heaven* deals with the lives of a number of characters living in the peaceful, idyllic valley in the hills beyond Monterey. Secluded like some medieval bower or enchanted castle, the place evokes images of romance and peace. Yet for all the outward tranquillity, the valley cannot remain isolated from the real world of economic hardship and violence.

The Munroe farm, for example, is cursed, and the curse executes itself on all the characters who come into contact with the Munroes. The theme of this collection of short stories is the conflict inherent in the tension between the characters' desire to live in the peaceful valley and their own human weaknesses, which prevent them from fulfilling their desires. Put in another way, the stories form a latter-day Garden of Eden myth. The land is beautiful, fruitful, prosperous; but the people of the land are thwarted by the serpent of human frailty.

Though some of the characters are spiritual kin to the "grotesques of Anderson's famous collection," they are markedly different in their attempts to reconcile their romantic intuition with the reality of social convention. Tularecito, for example, is all instinct. Though an idiot, he possesses great strength and an intuitive ability to draw. The title of the story, "The Legend of Tularecito," suggests that, like a legend, Tularecito is a child of romance. In his contradictory nature, he is the archetype of all the characters in the collection. Foreshadowing the half-witted giant, Lenny, in *Of Mice and Men*, Tularecito brings destruction on himself when he attacks Bert Munroe and is sent to a state asylum outside the valley. His punishment is not physical death, as in Lenny's case, but banishment from the valley, from Eden. Tularecito has come into contact with the reality of social convention and is defeated. Intuition is thwarted in the interest of social stability.

The conflict between an idyllic life, communing with nature, and the demands of middle-class respectability is the focus of another story, "Junius Maltby." Like prelapsarian man, Junius lives innocently off the land. Reminiscent of the *paisanos*, such as Danny and Mac in later novels such as *Tortilla Flat* and *Cannery Row,* Junius is shiftless and, by society's standards, an irresponsible dreamer. Like Tularecito, Junius is intuitive, instinctual, indifferent to the economic imperatives of being a farmer, and casually indecorous in his personal appearance. To Mrs. Munroe, Junius's life of the imagination is a threat. Junius is forced to abandon his farm and to leave the valley. There is no place for the poor and the romantic in Eden.

**"The Chrysanthemums"** • The garden as instinct, as the life of the spirit, is a prominent image in two stories in a later collection. Published in 1938, *The Long Valley* contains some of Steinbeck's most brilliant work in the genre of short fiction. In "The Chrysanthemums," Steinbeck presents the figure of Eliza Allen, a woman whose romantic gentleness conflicts with the brusque matter-of-factness of her husband and the deceitful cunning of a tinker. The story reveals a skillful meshing of character and setting, of symbol and theme. The garden is at once the chief setting and abiding symbol that define Eliza's character and her predicament as a woman.

Dressed in a man's clothing, Eliza is working in her garden when the story opens. Already the contrast is clear between Eliza's sensitive nature and the man-like indifference of her dress, her husband and life on the ranch, bathed in "the cold greyflannel fog of winter." Eliza's only emotional outlet, her only contact with a deeper life-pulse, is her growing of chrysanthemums, symbolic of both her sexual need and her recognition of the dominance in her nature of the life of the instinct. Like the virgin queen Elizabeth, Eliza has no children and her mannish ways merely disguise her sensitivity, a sensitivity that her husband, Henry, does not understand.

When a tinker stops his wagon at the ranch, looking for pots to repair, Eliza at first has no work for him, but when he praises her chrysanthemums, implying an understanding of her nature, Eliza gives him the flowers in a pot. That night, on their way to town for dinner and—the husband teases—to the prizefights, Eliza sees the discarded flowers on the road and realizes that the tinker had deceived her. Like her husband, the tinker did not really understand her; he had merely used her to his own advantage. At the end of the story, Eliza cries quietly, "like an old woman."

**"The White Quail"** • Still another story in the collection presents the image of the garden as both physical and psychic landscape. The garden that Mary Tiller tends in "The White Quail," however, is symbolic not of a healthy life of the spirit but of self-love and egotism. Mary's happiness with her garden, complete when she sees a white quail in it one night, is at the expense of her love for her husband. Harry is shut out of her love, often forced to sleep alone, though he virtually idolizes her. Mary's garden is her dream of an ordered, nonthreatening, and nonsexual existence. In a sense, Mary "quails" before a life of passion or the body. When a cat one day wanders into the garden, Mary is fearful of its potential as a predator and demands that Harry shoot it. Inexplicably, he shoots the quail; in destroying Mary's dream, he has brought his wife back to the real world, to a sexuality that she had refused to admit.

**"Flight"** • A story of maturity and death is the much-praised "Flight." Opening amid the rocky crags of the Torres farm, the story centers on Pepe, the oldest son of the widow Torres. A tall, lazy youth, Pepe has inherited his father's knife and yearns for the day when he will become, like his father, a man. Sent into Monterey on an errand, Pepe is insulted by a townsman and kills the man with his knife. Returning, he bids his mother good-bye and, armed with his father's rifle and horse, leaves his home to flee into the mountains. Gradually, he loses his rifle, then his horse. Now alone, he faces the threat of natural forces and the human pursuers. In the end, he is shot by one of the unseen "dark watchers."

Significantly, Pepe relies more on his own strength and courage as he flees deeper into the wild mountain passes; as he leaves his childhood behind, however, he also approaches his own death. Pepe's journey has become not only a physical escape from society's retribution but also a symbolic pilgrimage toward manhood and a redemptive death.

*Edward Fiorelli*

**Other major works**

PLAYS: *Of Mice and Men*, pr., pb. 1937; *The Moon Is Down*, pr. 1942; *Burning Bright*, pb. 1951.

NOVELS: *Cup of Gold*, 1929; *The Pastures of Heaven*, 1932; *To a God Unknown*, 1933; *Tortilla Flat*, 1935; *In Dubious Battle*, 1936; *Of Mice and Men*, 1937; *The Red Pony*, 1937, 1945; *The Grapes of Wrath*, 1939; *The Moon Is Down*, 1942; *Cannery Row*, 1945; *The Pearl*, 1945 (serial), 1947 (book); *The Wayward Bus*, 1947; *Burning Bright*, 1950; *East of Eden*, 1952; *Sweet Thursday*, 1954; *The Short Reign of Pippen IV*, 1957; *The Winter of Our Discontent*, 1961.

NONFICTION: *Their Blood Is Strong*, 1938; *Sea of Cortez*, 1941 (with Edward F. Ricketts); *The Forgotten Village*, 1941; *Bombs Away*, 1942; *A Russian Journal*, 1948 (with Robert Capa); *Once There Was a War*, 1958; *Travels with Charley: In Search of America*, 1962; *Letters to Alicia*, 1965; *America and Americans*, 1966; *Journal of a Novel*, 1969; *Steinbeck: A Life in Letters*, 1975 (Elaine Steinbeck and Robert Wallsten, editors); *America and Americans, and Selected Nonfiction*, 2002 (Susan Shillinglaw and Jackson J. Benson, editors).

SCREENPLAYS: *The Forgotten Village*, 1941; *Lifeboat*, 1944; *A Medal for Benny*, 1945; *The Pearl*, 1945; *The Red Pony*, 1949; *Viva Zapata!*, 1952.

TRANSLATION: *The Acts of King Arthur and His Noble Knights*, 1976.

## Bibliography

DeMott, Robert J., ed. *Steinbeck's Typewriter: Essays on His Art.* Troy, N.Y.: Whitston, 1996. Good collection of criticism of Steinbeck. Includes bibliographical references and an index.

French, Warren. *John Steinbeck's Fiction Revisited.* New York: Twayne, 1994. The chapter on *The Long Valley* in this revision of French's earlier Twayne book on Steinbeck provides brief discussions of the major stories, including "Flight" and "Chrysanthemums."

George, Stephen K., ed. *John Steinbeck: A Centennial Tribute.* New York: Praeger, 2002. Collection of reminiscences from Steinbeck's family and friends as well as wide-ranging critical assessments of his works.

Hayashi, Tetsumaro, ed. *Steinbeck's Short Stories in "The Long Valley": Essays in Criticism.* Muncie, Ind.: Steinbeck Research Institution, 1991. Collection of new critical essays on the stories in *The Long Valley* (excluding *The Red Pony*), from a variety of critical perspectives.

Hughes, R. S. *John Steinbeck: A Study of the Short Fiction.* New York: Twayne, 1989. General introduction to Steinbeck's short fiction, focusing primarily on critical reception to the stories. Also includes some autobiographical statements on short-story writing, as well as four essays on Steinbeck's stories by other critics.

McElrath, Joseph R., Jr., Jesse S. Crisler, and Susan Shillinglaw, eds. *John Steinbeck: The Contemporary Reviews.* New York: Cambridge University Press, 1996. Fine selection of reviews of Steinbeck's work.

May, Charles E., ed. *Masterplots II: Short Story Series, Revised Edition.* 8 vols. Pasadena, Calif.: Salem Press, 2004. Designed for student use, this reference set contains articles providing detailed plot summaries and analyses of six short stories by Steinbeck: "The Chrysanthemums" (vol. 2), "Flight" and "The Gift" (vol. 3), "The Leader of the People" (vol. 4), "The Pearl" (vol. 6), and "The Snake" (vol. 7).

Noble, Donald R. *The Steinbeck Question: New Essays in Criticism.* Troy, N.Y.: Whitston, 1993. Collection of essays on most of Steinbeck's work; most important for a study of the short story is the essay by Robert S. Hughes, Jr., on "The Art of Story Writing," Charlotte Hadella's "Steinbeck's Cloistered Women," and Michael J. Meyer's "The Snake."

Parini, Jay. *John Steinbeck: A Biography.* New York: Henry Holt, 1995. This biography suggests psychological interpretations of the effect of Steinbeck's childhood and sociological interpretations of his fiction. Criticizes Steinbeck for his politically incorrect gender and social views; also takes Steinbeck to task to what he calls his blindness to the political reality of the Vietnam War.

Timmerman, John H. *The Dramatic Landscape of Steinbeck's Short Stories.* Norman: University of Oklahoma Press, 1990. Formalist interpretation of Steinbeck's stories, focusing on style, tone, imagery, and character. Provides close readings of such frequently anthologized stories as "The Chrysanthemums" and "Flight," as well as such stories as "Johnny Bear" and "The Short-Short Story of Mankind."

# Robert Louis Stevenson

**Born:** Edinburgh, Scotland; November 13, 1850
**Died:** Vailima, near Apia, Samoa; December 3, 1894

**Principal short fiction** • *The New Arabian Nights*, 1882; *More New Arabian Nights*, 1885; *The Merry Men, and Other Tales and Fables*, 1887; *Island Nights' Entertainments*, 1893.

**Other literary forms** • Despite poor health, Robert Louis Stevenson was a prolific writer, not only of juvenile fiction but also of poetry, plays, and essays. He is best known for adventure romances such as *Treasure Island* (1881-1882, serial; 1883, book), *Kidnapped* (1886), and the horror-suspense novel *The Strange Case of Dr. Jekyll and Mr. Hyde* (1886), works that appeal principally to youthful readers. A habitual voyager, Stevenson also wrote travelogues and sketches recounting his personal experiences. His children's poems, published in *A Child's Garden of Verses* (1885), remain perennial favorites, as do several of his beautiful family prayers.

**Achievements** • For clarity and suspense, Robert Louis Stevenson is a rarely equaled raconteur. He reveals his mastery of narrative in his economical presentation of incident and atmosphere. Yet, despite his sparse, concise style, many of his tales are notable for dealing with complex moral ambiguities and their diagnoses. Although influenced by a host of romantic writers, including Charles Lamb, William Hazlitt, William Wordsworth, and Nathaniel Hawthorne, Stevenson's theories of prose fiction were most directly provoked by Henry James's *The Art of Fiction* (1884). Stevenson placed himself in literary opposition to James and the "statics of character," favoring instead an action-fiction whose clear antecedents are allegory, fable, and romance. His tales of adventure and intrigue, outdoor life and old-time romance, avidly read by children and young adults, have had a continuous and incalculable influence since their first publication in the 1880's.

**Biography** • The only child of a prosperous civil engineer and his wife, Robert Louis Stevenson was a sickly youth, causing his formal education to be haphazard. He reacted early against his parents' orthodox Presbyterianism, donning the mask of a liberated Bohemian who abhorred the hypocrisies of bourgeois respectability. As a compromise with his father, Stevenson did study law at Edinburgh University in lieu of the traditional family vocation of lighthouse engineer. In 1873, however, he suffered a severe respiratory illness, and, although he completed his studies and was admitted to the Scottish bar in July, 1875, he never practiced. In May, 1880, Stevenson married Fanny Van de Grift Osbourne, a divorcé from San Francisco and ten years his senior. The couple spent most of the next decade in health resorts for Stevenson's tuberculosis: Davos in the Swiss Alps, Hyéres on the French Riviera, and Bournemouth in England. After his father's death, Stevenson felt able to go farther from Scotland and so went to Saranac Lake in the Adirondack Mountains of New York, where treatment arrested his disease. In June, 1888, Stevenson, his wife, mother, and stepson sailed for the South Seas. During the next eighteen months they saw the Marquesas, Tahiti, Australia, the Gilberts, Hawaii, and Samoa. In late 1889, Stevenson decided to settle and bought "Vailima," three miles from the town of Apia, Up-olu, Samoa, and his home until his death. His vigorous crusading there against the white exploita-tion of native Samoans almost led to expulsion by both German and English authorities. Stevenson's tu-berculosis remained quiescent, but he suddenly died of a cerebral hemorrhage on December 3, 1894, while working on the novel *Weir of Hermiston* (1896), a fragment which many modern readers think to be his best writing. Known to the na-tives as "Tusitala," the Storyteller, Stevenson was buried on the sum-mit of Mount Vaea.

Library of Congress

**Analysis** • Robert Louis Stevenson has long been relegated to either the nursery or the juvenile section in most libraries, and his mixture of romance, horror, and allegory seems jejune. In times narrative and well-ordered structure have be-come the facile tools of Harlequin paperbacks and irrelevant to high-quality "litera-ture," Stevenson's achievement goes quietly unnoticed. To confine this technique of "Tusitala" solely to nursery and supermarket, however, is to confuse Stevenson's tal-ents with his present audience.

Stevenson's crucial problem is the basic one of joining form to idea, made more difficult because he was not only an excellent romancer but also a persuasive essayist. In Stevenson, however, these two talents seem to be of different roots, and their com-bination was for him a lifelong work. The aim of his narratives becomes not only to tell a good story, constructing something of interest, but also to ensure that all the materials of that story (such as structure, atmosphere, and character motivation) contribute to a clear thematic concern. Often Stevenson's fictional talents alone can-not accomplish this for him, and this accounts—depending in each instance on whether he drops his theme or attempts to push it through—for both the "pulp" feel of some stories and the "directed" feel of others.

**"A Lodging for the Night"** • Appearing in the *Cornhill Magazine* for May, 1874, an es-say on Victor Hugo was Stevenson's very first publication. The short stories he began writing soon after demonstrate a strong tendency to lapse into the more familiar ex-pository techniques either as a solution to fictional problems or merely to bolster a sagging theme. A blatant example of this stylistic ambiguity is the early story "A Lodging for the Night."

The atmosphere of the first part of the story is deftly handled. It is winter, and its buffets upon the poor are reemphasized in every descriptive detail. Paris is "sheeted up" like a body ready for burial. The only light is from a tiny shack "backed up against the cemetery wall." Inside, "dark, little, and lean, with hollow cheeks and thin black locks," the medieval poet François Villon composes "The Ballade of Roast Fish" while Guy Tabard, one of his cronies, sputters admiringly over his shoulder. Straddling before the fire is a portly, purple-veined Picardy monk, Dom Nicolas. Also in the small room are two more villains, Montigny and Thevenin Pensete, playing "a game of chance." Villon cracks a few pleasantries, quite literally gallows humor, and begins to read aloud his new poem. Suddenly, between the two gamesters:

> The round was complete, and Thevenin was just opening his mouth to claim another victory, when Montigny leaped up, swift as an adder, and stabbed him to the heart. The blow took effect before he had time to utter a cry, before he had time to move. A tremor or two convulsed his frame; his hands opened and shut, his heels rattled on the floor; then his head rolled backward over one shoulder with the eyes wide open; and Thevenin Pensete's spirit had returned to Him who made it.

Tabard begins praying in Latin, Villon breaks into hysterics, Montigny recovers "his composure first" and picks the dead man's pockets. Naturally, they must all leave the scene of the murder to escape implication, and Villon departs first.

Outside, in the bitter cold, two things preoccupy the poet as he walks: the gallows and "the look of the dead man with his bald head and garland of red curls," as neat a symbol as could be for the fiery pit of hell where Villon eventually expects to find himself. Theme has been handled well, Stevenson's fiction giving one the feeling of a single man thrown by existence into infernal and unfavorable circumstances, being pursued by elements beyond his control, the gallows and Death, survival itself weaving a noose for him with his own trail in the snow, irrevocably connecting him to "the house by the cemetery of St. John." The plot is clear and the situation interesting. On this cold and windy night, after many rebuffs, Villon finally finds food and shelter with a "refined," "muscular and spare," "resonant, courteous," "honorable rather than intelligent, strong, simple, and righteous" old knight.

Here, the structure of "A Lodging for the Night" abruptly breaks down from fiction, from atmospheric detail, plot development, and character enlargement, to debate. What Stevenson implied in the first part of his story, he reasserts here in expository dialogue, apparently losing faith in his fictional abilities as he resorts back to the directness of the essay.

Villon takes the side of duty to one's own survival; he is the first modern skeptic, the prophet of expediency. In contrast, the knight stands for honor, *bonne noblesse*, with allegiance always to something greater than himself. The moral code of the criminal is pitted against the hypocrisy of the bourgeoisie. One's chances in life are determined by birth and social standing, says Villon. There is always the chance for change, implores the knight. In comparison to Stevenson's carefully built atmosphere and plot, this expository "solution" to his story is extremely crude.

**"Markheim"** • "Markheim," a ghost story that deals with a disturbing problem of conscience, also contains a dialogue in its latter half. This dialogue, however, is a just continuation of the previous action. Different from "crawlers" such as "The Body-Snatcher," "Markheim" reinforces horror with moral investigation. Initial atmospherics contribute directly to Stevenson's pursuit of his thematic concern, and the later debate with the "visitant" becomes an entirely fitting expression for Markheim's own madness.

An allegory of the awakening conscience, "Markheim" also has the limits of allegory, one of which is meaning. For readers to understand, or find meaning in, an allegory, characters (or actors) must be clearly identified. In "Markheim" this presents major difficulties. Not only is an exact identity (or role) for the visitant finally in doubt, but also the identity of the dealer is unclear. It can be said that he usually buys from Markheim, not sells to him, but exactly what the dealer buys or sells is a good question. Whatever, on this particular occasion (Christmas Day), Markheim will have to pay the dealer extra "for a kind of manner that I remark in you today very strongly."

Amid the "ticking of many clocks among the curious lumber" of the dealer's shop, a strange pantomime ensues. Markheim says he needs a present for a lady, and the dealer shows him a hand mirror. Markheim grows angry:

> "A glass," he said hoarsely, and then paused, and repeated it more clearly. "A glass? For Christmas? Surely not!"
> "And why not?" cried the dealer. "Why not a glass?"
> Markheim was looking upon him with an indefinable expression. "You ask me why not?" he said. "Why, look here—look at it—look at yourself! Do you like to see it? No! nor I—nor any man."

After damning the mirror as the "reminder of years, and sins, and follies—this hand-conscience," Markheim asks the dealer to tell something of himself, his secret life. The dealer puts Markheim off with a chuckle, but as he turns around for something more to show, Markheim lunges at him, stabbing him with a "long, skewerlike dagger." The dealer struggles "like a hen" and then dies. The murder seems completely gratuitous until Markheim remembers that he had come to rob the shop: "To have done the deed and yet not to reap the profit would be too abhorrent a failure."

Time, "which had closed for the victim," now becomes "instant and momenteous for the slayer." Like Villon, Markheim feels pursued by Death, haunted by "the dock, the prison, the gallows, and the black coffin." The blood at his feet begins "to find eloquent voices." The dead dealer extracts his extra payment, becoming the enemy who would "lift up a cry that would ring over England, and fill the world with the echoes of pursuit." Talking to himself, Markheim denies that this evil murder indicates an equally evil nature, but his guilt troubles him. Not only pursued by Death, Markheim is pursued by Life as well. He sees his own face "repeated and repeated, as it were an army of spies"; his own eyes meet and detect him. Although alone, he feels the inexplicable consciousness of another presence:

> Ay, surely; to every room and corner of the house his imagination followed it; and now it was a faceless thing, and yet had eyes to see with; and again it was a shadow of himself; and yet again beheld the image of the dead dealer, reinspired with cunning and hatred.

Eventually, Markheim must project an imaginary double, a doppelgänger or exteriorized voice with which to debate his troubles. Here, action passes from the stylized antique shop of the murdered to the frenzied mind of the murderer. The visitant, or double, is a product of this mind. Mad and guilty as Markheim appears to be, his double emerges as a calm-sounding sanity who will reason with him to commit further evil. Thus, the mysterious personification of drives buried deep within Markheim's psyche exteriorizes evil as an alter ego and allows Markheim the chance to act against it, against the evil in his own nature. Stevenson's sane, expository technique of debate erects a perfect foil for Markheim's true madness.

In the end, although Markheim thinks himself victorious over what seems the devil, it is actually this exteriorized aspect of Markheim's unknown self that conquers, tricking him into willing surrender and then revealing itself as a kind of redemptive angel:

> The features of the visitor began to undergo a wonderful and lovely change; they brightened and softened with a tender triumph; and, even as they brightened, faded and dislimned. But Markheim did not pause to watch or understand the transformation.

Material and intention are artistically intertwined in "Markheim," but the moral ambiguities of Stevenson's theme remain complex, prompting various questions: is Markheim's martyrdom a victory over evil or merely a personal cessation from action? Set on Christmas Day, with its obvious reversal of that setting's usual significance, is "Markheim" a portrayal of Christian resignation as a purely negative force, a justification for suicide, or as the only modern solution against evil? What is the true nature and identity of the visitant? Finally, can the visitant have an identity apart from Markheim's own? Even answers to these questions, like Markheim's final surrender, offer only partial consolation to the reader of this strange and complex story of psychological sickness.

**"The Beach of Falesá"** • With Stevenson's improved health and his move to the South Seas, a new type of story began to emerge, a kind of exotic realism to which the author brought his mature talents. "The Bottle Imp," for example, juxtaposes the occult of an old German fairy tale (interestingly enough, acquired by Stevenson through Sir Percy Shelley, the poet's son) with factual details about San Francisco, Honolulu, and Papeete. These settings, however, seem used more for convenience than out of necessity.

The long story "The Beach of Falesá" fulfills Stevenson's promise and gives evidence of his whole talents as a writer of short fiction. Similar to Joseph Conrad's *Heart of Darkness* (1902), Stevenson's story deals with a person's ability or inability to remain decent and law-abiding when the external restraints of civilization have been removed. Action follows simply and naturally a line laid down by atmosphere. Stevenson himself called it "the first realistic South Sea story," while Henry James wrote in a letter the year before Stevenson's death, "The art of 'The Beach of Falesá' seems to me an art brought to a perfection and I delight in the observed truth, the modesty of nature, of the narrator."

In this adventure of wills between two traders on a tiny island, Stevenson is able to unify fitting exposition with restrained description through the voice of first-person narrator John Wiltshire. Three decades later, using Stevenson as one of his models, W. Somerset Maugham would further perfect this technique using the same exotic South Sea setting.

Stevenson's "The Beach of Falesá," along with the incomplete *Weir of Hermiston* and perhaps the first part of *The Master of Ballantrae* (1888), rests as his best work, the final integration of the divergent roots of his talents. If he had lived longer than forty-four years, "Tusitala" might have become one of the great English prose writers.

As history stands, however, Stevenson's small achievement of clear narrative, his victory of joining form to idea, remains of unforgettable importance to students and practitioners of the short-story genre.

*Kenneth Funsten*
*With updates by John W. Fiero*

**Other major works**

PLAYS: *Deacon Brodie*, pb. 1880 (with William Ernest Henley); *Admiral Guinea*, pb. 1884 (with Henley); *Beau Austin*, pb. 1884 (with Henley); *Macaire*, pb. 1885 (with Henley); *The Hanging Judge*, pb. 1887 (with Fanny Van de Grift Stevenson).

NOVELS: *Treasure Island*, 1881-1882 (serial), 1883 (book); *Prince Otto*, 1885; *Kidnapped*, 1886; *The Strange Case of Dr. Jekyll and Mr. Hyde*, 1886; *The Black Arrow*, 1888; *The Master of Ballantrae*, 1889; *The Wrong Box*, 1889; *The Wrecker*, 1892 (with Lloyd Osbourne); *Catriona*, 1893; *The Ebb-Tide*, 1894 (with Osbourne); *Weir of Hermiston*, 1896 (unfinished); *St. Ives*, 1897 (completed by Arthur Quiller-Couch).

NONFICTION: *An Inland Voyage*, 1878; *Edinburgh: Picturesque Notes*, 1878; *Travels with a Donkey in the Cévennes*, 1879; *Virginibus Puerisque*, 1881; *Familiar Studies of Men and Books*, 1882; *The Silverado Squatters: Sketches from a Californian Mountain*, 1883; *Memories and Portraits*, 1887; *The South Seas: A Record of Three Cruises*, 1890; *A Footnote to History*, 1892; *Across the Plains*, 1892; *Amateur Emigrant*, 1895; *Vailima Letters*, 1895; *In the South Seas*, 1896; *The Letters of Robert Louis Stevenson to His Family and Friends*, 1899 (2 volumes), 1911 (4 volumes); *The Lantern-Bearers, and Other Essays*, 1988; *The Letters of Robert Louis Stevenson*, 1994-1995 (8 volumes); *R. L. Stevenson on Fiction: An Anthology of Literary and Critical Essays*, 1999 (Glenda Norquay, editor).

POETRY: *Moral Emblems*, 1882; *A Child's Garden of Verses*, 1885; *Underwoods*, 1887; *Ballads*, 1890; *Songs of Travel, and Other Verses*, 1896.

**Bibliography**

Bell, Ian. *Dreams of Exile: Robert Louis Stevenson: A Biography.* New York: Henry Holt, 1992. Bell, a journalist rather than an academic, writes evocatively of Stevenson the dreamer and exile. This brief study of Stevenson's brief but dramatic life does a fine job of evoking the man and the places he inhabited. It is less accomplished in its approach to the work.

Bevan, Bryan. "The Versatility of Robert Louis Stevenson." *Contemporary Review* 264 (June, 1994): 316-319. A general discussion of Stevenson's work, focusing on his versatility in a number of genres; discusses early influences on his writing, and comments on his essays and his fiction.

Calder, Jenni. *Robert Louis Stevenson: A Life Study.* New York: Oxford University Press, 1980. This excellent study, by the daughter of literary historian David Daiches, is richly documented with Stevenson's letters. Less a biography than a study of the writer's mind, it focuses on the personal values and attitudes informing Stevenson's work.

Callow, Philip. *Louis: A Life of Robert Louis Stevenson.* Chicago: Ivan R. Dee, 2001. Engaging biography that draws on the work of other biographers to present for the general reader a cohesive life of the novelist.

Chesterton, G. K. *Robert Louis Stevenson.* Poughkeepsie, N.J.: House of Stratus, 2001. First published in 1927, this distinguished critical study of Stevenson is still highly regarded for its insights as well as for its wit and lucidity.

Hammond, J. R. *A Robert Louis Stevenson Companion: A Guide to the Novels, Essays, and Short Stories.* London: Macmillan, 1984. The first three sections cover the life and literary achievements of Stevenson and contain a brief dictionary which lists and describes his short stories, essays, and smaller works. The fourth section critiques his novels and romances, and the fifth is a key to the people and places of Stevenson's novels and stories.

McLaughlin, Kevin. "The Financial Imp: Ethics and Finance in Nineteenth-Century Fiction." *Novel* 29 (Winter, 1996): 165-183. Examines the key issue of finance that can be found at the center of some works of British fiction during this time, focusing particularly on Stevenson's treatment of these issues in his short story "The Bottle Imp."

McLynn, Frank. *Robert Louis Stevenson: A Biography.* New York: Random House, 1993. The author traces Robert Louis Stevenson's career, noting the malignant influence of his wife and stepson and concluding that Stevenson "is Scotland's greatest writer of English prose."

May, Charles E., ed. *Masterplots II: Short Story Series, Revised Edition.* 8 vols. Pasadena, Calif.: Salem Press, 2004. Designed for student use, this reference set contains articles providing detailed plot summaries and analyses of five short stories by Stevenson: "The Bottle Imp" (vol. 1), "A Lodging for the Night" (vol. 4), "Markheim" (vol. 5), and "The Sire de Malétroit's Door" and "The Suicide Club" (vol. 7).

# Amy Tan

**Born:** Oakland, California; February 19, 1952

**Principal short fiction** • *The Joy Luck Club*, 1989.

**Other literary forms** • Amy Tan's most important volume of short fiction, *The Joy Luck Club*, is also often categorized as a novel. That book has been translated into twenty languages. Her second novel, *The Kitchen God's Wife*, was a *Booklist* editor's choice. Her later novels include *The Hundred Secret Senses* (1995), *The Bonesetter's Daughter* (2001), and *Saving Fish from Drowning* (2005). Tan has also written two children's books, *The Moon Lady* (1992) and *The Chinese Siamese Cat* (1994). Her essays include "The Language of Discretion" and "Mother Tongue." Her first nonfiction work, *The Opposite of Fate: A Book of Musings* (2003), collects her casual writings that supplement her fiction and her life.

**Achievements** • One of the most important works of modern fiction by an Asian American writer, Tan's *The Joy Luck Club* was a finalist for the National Book Award and the National Book Critics Circle Award. Tan also cowrote, with Ronald Bass, the screenplay for a film based on the novel that was released in 1993. Her essay "Mother Tongue" was included in *Best American Essays of 1991*, edited by Joyce Carol Oates. She received an honorary doctorate from Dominican College in 1991.

**Biography** • Amy Ruth Tan was born in Oakland, California, on February 19, 1952, the middle child and only daughter of John Yuehhan and Daisy Tu Ching Tan, who had emigrated from China. Her father was an electrical engineer in China, but he became a minister in the United States. The family moved frequently, finally settling in Santa Clara, California. After the death of her husband and older son when Amy was fifteen years old, Daisy took the family to Switzerland and enrolled her children in schools there, but she returned to California in 1969.

Tan's parents hoped she would become a physician and concert pianist. She began a premedical course of study but switched to English and linguistics, much to her mother's dismay. She received her bachelor's degree in 1973 and her master's degree in 1974 from San Jose State University. She attended the University of California, Berkeley, from 1974 to 1976, beginning studies toward a doctorate. In 1974, she married Louis M. DeMattei, a tax attorney; they settled in San Francisco.

Tan was a language consultant, a reporter, a managing editor, and a freelance technical writer before she turned to fiction writing. She joined a writing workshop in 1985 and submitted a story about a Chinese American chess prodigy. The revised version was first published in a small literary magazine and reprinted in *Seventeen* magazine as "Rules of the Game." When Tan learned that the story had appeared in Italy and had been translated without her knowledge, she obtained an agent, Sandra Dijkstra, to help handle publication. Although Tan had written only three stories at that time, Dijkstra encouraged her to write a book. At her suggestion, Tan submitted an outline for a book of stories and then went on a trip to China with her mother. On her return, she learned that her proposal had been accepted by G. P. Putnam's Sons.

**Analysis** • Amy Tan's voice is an important one among a group of "hyphenated Americans" (such as African Americans and Asian Americans) who describe the experiences of members of ethnic minority groups. Her short fiction is grounded in a Chinese tradition of "talk story" (*gong gu tsai*), a folk art form by which characters pass on values and teach important lessons through narrative. Other writers, such as Maxine Hong Kingston, employ a similar narrative strategy.

A central theme of Tan's stories is the conflict faced by Chinese Americans who find themselves alienated both from their American milieu and from their Chinese parents and heritage. Other themes include storytelling, memory, and the complex relationships between mother and daughter, husband and wife, and sisters. By using narrators from two generations, Tan explores the relationships between past and present. Her stories juxtapose the points of view of characters (husband and wife, mother and daughter, sisters) who struggle with each other, misunderstand each other, and grow distant from each other. Like Tan, other ethnic writers such as Louise Erdrich use multiple voices to retell stories describing the evolution of a cultural history.

Tan's stories derive from her own experience as a Chinese American and from stories of Chinese life her mother told her. They reflect her early conflicts with her strongly opinionated mother and her growing understanding and appreciation of her mother's past and her strength in adapting to her new country. Daisy's early life, about which Tan gradually learned, was difficult and dramatic. Daisy's mother, Jing-mei (Amy Tan's maternal grandmother), was forced to become the concubine of a wealthy man after her husband's death. Spurned by her family and treated cruelly by the man's wives, she committed suicide. Her tragic life became the basis of Tan's story "Magpies," retold by An-mei Hsu in *The Joy Luck Club*. Daisy was raised by relatives and married to a brutal man. After her father's death, Tan learned that her mother had been married in China and left behind three daughters. This story became part of *The Joy Luck Club* and *The Kitchen God's Wife*.

Tan insists that, like all writers, she writes from her own experienceand is not representative of any ethnic group. She acknowledges her rich Chinese background and combines it with typically American themes of love, marriage, and freedom of choice. Her first-person style is also an American feature.

***The Joy Luck Club*** • Although critics call it a novel, Tan wrote *The Joy Luck Club* as a collection of sixteen short stories told by the club members and their daughters. Each chapter is a complete unit, and five of them have been published separately in short-story anthologies. Other writers, such as the American authors Sherwood Anderson (*Winesburg, Ohio*) and Gloria Naylor (*The Women of Brewster Place*), and the Canadian Margaret Laurence (*A Bird in the House*), have also built linked story collections around themes or groups of characters.

The framework for *The Joy Luck Club* is formed by members of a mah-jongg club, immigrants from China, who tell stories of their lives in China and their families in the United States. The first and fourth sections are the mothers' stories; the second and third are the daughters' stories. Through this device of multiple narrators, the conflicts and struggles of the two generations are presented through the contrasting stories. The mothers wish their daughters to succeed in American terms (to have professional careers, wealth, and status), but they expect them to retain Chinese values (filial piety, cooking skills, family loyalty) as well. When the daughters become Americanized, they are embarrassed by their mothers' old-fashioned ways, and their mothers are disappointed at the daughters' dismissal of tradition. Chasms of misunderstanding deepen between them.

Jing-mei (June) Woo forms a bridge between the generations; she tells her own stories in the daughters' sections and attempts to take her mother's part in the mothers' sections. Additionally, her trip to China forms a bridge between her family's past and present, and between China and America.

**"The Joy Luck Club"** • The first story, "The Joy Luck Club," describes the founding of the club by Suyuan Woo to find comfort during the privations suffered in China during World War II. When the Japanese invaders approached, she fled, abandoning her twin daughters when she was too exhausted to travel any farther. She continued the Joy Luck Club in her new life in San Francisco, forming close friendships with three other women. After Suyuan's death, her daughter Jing-mei, "June," is invited to take her

Robert Foothorap

place. June's uncertainty of how to behave there and her sketchy knowledge of her family history exemplify the tensions experienced by an American daughter of Chinese parents. The other women surprise June by revealing that news has finally arrived from the twin daughters Suyuan left in China. They present June with two plane tickets so that she and her father can visit her half-sisters and tell them her mother's story. She is unsure of what to say, believing now that she really did not know her mother. The others are aghast, because in her they see the reflection of their daughters, who are also ignorant of their mothers' stories, their past histories, their hopes and fears. They hasten to tell June what to praise about their mother: her kindness, intelligence, mindfulness of family, "the excellent dishes she cooked." In the book's concluding chapter, June recounts her trip to China.

**"Rules of the Game"** • One of the daughters' stories, "Rules of the Game," describes the ambivalent relationship of Lindo Jong and her six-year-old daughter. Waverly Place Jong (named after the street on which the family lives) learns from her mother's "rules," or codes of behavior, to succeed as a competitive chess player. Her mother teaches her to "bite back your tongue" and to learn to bend with the wind. These techniques help her persuade her mother to let her play in chess tournaments and then help her to win games and advance in rank. However, her proud mother embarrasses Waverly by showing her off to the local shopkeepers. The tensions between mother and daughter are like another kind of chess game, a give and take, where the two struggle for power. The two are playing by different rules, Lindo by Chinese rules of behavior and filial obedience, Waverly by American rules of self-expression and independence.

**"Two Kinds"** • Another daughter's story, "Two Kinds," is June's story of her mother's great expectations for her. Suyuan was certain that June could be anything she wanted to be; it was only a matter of discovering what it was. She decided that June would be a prodigy piano player, and outdo Waverly Jong, but June rebelled against her mother and never paid attention to her lessons. After a disastrous recital, she stops playing the piano, which becomes a sore point between mother and daughter. On her thirtieth birthday, the piano becomes a symbol of her reconciliation with her mother, when Suyuan offers it to her.

**"Best Quality"** • "Best Quality" is June's story of a dinner party her mother gives. The old rivalries between June and Waverly continue, and Waverly's daughter and American fiancé behave in ways that are impolite in Chinese eyes. After the dinner Suyuan gives her daughter a jade necklace she has worn in the hope that it will guide her to find her "life's importance."

**"A Pair of Tickets"** • This is the concluding story of *The Joy Luck Club*. It recounts Jing-mei (June) Woo's trip to China to meet her half-sisters, thus fulfilling the wish of her mother and the Joy Luck mothers and bringing the story cycle to a close, completing the themes of the first story. June learns from her father how Suyuan's twin daughters were found by an old school friend. He explains that her mother's name means "long-cherished wish" and that her own name Jing-mei means "something pure, essential, the best quality." When at last they meet the sisters, she acknowledges her Chinese lineage: "I also see what part of me is Chinese. It is so obvious. It is my family. It is in our blood."

*Karen F. Stein*

**Other major works**

NOVELS: *The Kitchen God's Wife*, 1991; *The Hundred Secret Senses*, 1995; *The Bonesetter's Daughter*, 2001; *Saving Fish from Drowning*, 2005.

CHILDREN'S LITERATURE: *The Moon Lady*, 1992; *The Chinese Siamese Cat*, 1994.

NONFICTION: "The Language of Discretion," 1990 (in *The State of the Language*, Christopher Ricks and Leonard Michaels, editors); *The Opposite of Fate: A Book of Musings*, 2003.

**Bibliography**

Becerra, Cynthia S. "Two Kinds." In *Masterplots II: Short Story Series*, edited by Charles E. May. Rev. ed. Vol. 8. Pasadena, Calif.: Salem Press, 2004. Analysis of "Two Kinds" with sections on themes and meaning and style and technique. Also includes a detailed synopsis of the story.

Bloom, Harold, ed. *Amy Tan*. Philadelphia: Chelsea House, 2000. Bloom also provides an introduction to the installment in the Modern Critical Views series. Pulls together the comments of contemporary critics.

Chua, C. L., and Ka Ying Vu. "Rules of the Game." In *Masterplots II: Short Story Series*, edited by Charles E. May. Rev. ed. Vol. 6. Pasadena, Calif.: Salem Press, 2004. Student-friendly analysis of "Rules of the Game" that covers the story's themes and style and includes a detailed synopsis.

Cooperman, Jeannette Batz. *The Broom Closet: Secret Meanings of Domesticity in Post-feminist Novels by Louise Erdrich, Mary Gordon, Toni Morrison, Marge Piercy, Jane Smiley, and Amy Tan.* New York: Peter Lang, 1999. Study of the role of traditionally feminine concerns, such as marriage and family, in the works of these postfeminist writers.

Ho, Wendy. *In Her Mother's House: The Politics of Asian American Mother-Daughter Writing.* Walnut Creek, Calif.: AltaMira Press, 1999. Includes two chapters dedicated specifically to Tan, "Losing Your Innocence But Not Your Hope: Amy Tan's Joy Luck Mothers and Coca-Cola Daughters," and "The Heart Never Travels: The Incorporation of Fathers in the Mother-Daughter Stories of Maxine Hong Kingston, Amy Tan, and Fae Myenne Ng."

Huh, Joonok. *Interconnected Mothers and Daughters in Amy Tan's 'The Joy Luck Club.'* Tucson, Ariz.: Southwest Institute for Research on Women, 1992. Examines the mother and adult child relationship in Tan's novel. Includes a bibliography.

_____. *Amy Tan: A Critical Companion.* Westport, Conn.: Greenwood Press, 1998. Discusses Tan's biography and analyzes her novels in the context of Asian American literature. Analyzes major themes such as the crone figure, food, clothing, language, biculturalism, mothers and daughters. Includes useful bibliography.

Pearlman, Mickey, and Katherine Usher Henderson. "Amy Tan." *Inter/View: Talks with America's Writing Women.* Lexington: University Press of Kentucky, 1990. Provides biographical information on Tan, revealing the sources of some of the stories in *The Joy Luck Club.*

Snodgrass, Mary Ellen. *Amy Tan: A Literary Companion.* Jefferson, N.C.: McFarland, 2004. Replete with tools for further research, including study questions, an extensive bibliography, and a glossary of Chinese terms found in Tan's works, Snodgrass presents a readable, engaging introduction to both Tan's life and works.

Tan, Amy. "Amy Tan." Interview by Barbara Somogyi and David Stanton. *Poets and Writers* 19, no. 5 (September 1, 1991): 24-32. One of the best interviews with Tan. Tan speaks about her childhood and her early career as a business writer, her decision to write fiction, her success with *The Joy Luck Club,* and some of its autobiographical elements.

# Peter Taylor

**Born:** Trenton, Tennessee; January 8, 1917
**Died:** Charlottesville, Virginia; November 2, 1994

**Principal short fiction** • *A Long Fourth, and Other Stories*, 1948; *The Widows of Thornton*, 1954; *Happy Families Are All Alike*, 1959; *Miss Leonora When Last Seen, and Fifteen Other Stories*, 1963; *The Collected Stories of Peter Taylor*, 1968; *In the Miro District, and Other Stories*, 1977; *The Old Forest, and Other Stories*, 1985; *The Oracle at Stoneleigh Court*, 1993.

**Other literary forms** • In addition to his short fiction, Peter Taylor published the novels *A Woman of Means* (1950), *A Summons to Memphis* (1986), and *In the Tennessee Country* (1994), as well as plays. Several of his plays were performed at Kenyon College, and three of them have been published separately; a collection of seven dramas was also published in 1973. Taylor was one of three editors of a memorial volume, *Randall Jarrell, 1914-1965* (1967).

**Achievements** • The publication of *The Collected Stories of Peter Taylor* brought general acknowledgment that he was one of the most skillful practitioners of the modern short story in the United States. Although his reputation prior to that volume had for the most part been limited to a fairly small circle of enthusiastic readers, the list of his awards indicates the respect in which he was always held by his peers. Taylor was honored twelve different times by inclusion in the annual volume of *The Best American Short Stories* and was included six times in the *O. Henry Award Stories*.

Taylor was awarded a John Simon Guggenheim Memorial Foundation Fellowship (1950), a National Institute of Arts and Letters grant (1952), a Fulbright Fellowship (1955), first prize from the O. Henry Memorial Awards (1959), an Ohioan Book Award (1960), a Ford Foundation Fellowship (1961), a Rockefeller Foundation grant (1964), second prize from the *Partisan Review-Dial* and a National Institute of Arts and Letters gold medal (1979), a Ritz Paris Hemingway Award and the PEN/Faulkner Award (1986), and a Pulitzer Prize (1987).

Although acknowledging his admiration for the work of Anton Chekhov, Ivan Turgenev, and Henry James, Taylor has put his own unique mark on the short story. Much of his fiction is set in the South, recalling the work of William Faulkner and Flannery O'Connor, but he is less concerned with violence and moral themes than either of those writers, concentrating instead on social relationships and the inevitability of betrayal in the interactions between men and women.

**Biography** • Peter Hillsman Taylor grew up in middle-class circumstances in border states. His family moved to Nashville when he was seven, spent several years in St. Louis, and settled in Memphis when he was fifteen. Expected to follow his father and older brother into the practice of law, Taylor chose early to try to make his career as a writer. He studied with the poet Allen Tate. After a brief enrollment at Vanderbilt University, he preferred to follow the poet, editor, and teacher John Crowe Ransom to Kenyon College in Ohio. At Kenyon College, he was befriended by the poet and critic Randall Jarrell and shared a room with the poet Robert Lowell.

After service in the U.S. Army during World War II, Taylor took up teaching as a profession. Between 1945 and 1963, he held faculty appointments at Indiana State University and Ohio State University, and on three different occasions he was appointed to teaching positions at the University of North Carolina at Greensboro. In 1967, he accepted a professorship at the University of Virginia, where he remained until his retirement in 1984.

Success as a short-story writer came fairly early in his career. Prestigious magazines such as *The Southern Review* and *The New Republic* published some of his stories written while he was still in college, and his first recognition in *Best American Short Stories* came in 1941, just after his graduation from Kenyon College. By 1948, his work was appearing in *The New Yorker*, which over the next three decades would publish more than two dozen of his works. Popular success, however, waited until the publication of *A Summons to Memphis* in 1986. The novel was a best-seller and won for Taylor the Pulitzer Prize for fiction. One scholar has hypothesized that Taylor saw this as a means of gaining validation for his short stories, the genre he considered more demanding of real artistry. Taylor died on November 2, 1994, in Charlottesville, Virginia.

**Analysis** • The art of Peter Taylor is ironic and subtle. In a typical story, the narrator or point-of-view character is an observer, perhaps a member of a community who remembers someone or something in the town's past that is puzzling or strange, or a character whose understanding of his or her life falls short of reality. In tone, the stories are deceptively simple and straightforward, masking their complex ironies in seemingly ordinary actions. Taylor does not experiment with form or structure in the manner of a Jorge Luis Borges or a Robert Coover, but his stories are not always about commonplace experience; the grotesque plays a major role in such stories as "The Fancy Woman" and "Venus, Cupid, Folly, and Time."

Low-keyed and rarely involving violent action, the stories are more complex in their effect than at first appears, often revealing more about the narrator or the society than about the character being described. Their settings are often in small towns or minor cities in the upper South, Tennessee or Missouri, places such as those where Taylor lived as a boy and young man. Familial relationships, including those between husband and wife, are often central. Racial and economic matters enter into many of the stories, but such major social issues are generally depicted in the context of the social interactions of ordinary people. Nevertheless, Taylor provides considerable insight into the effects of the radical changes that affected the South in the 1960's and 1970's.

**"Dean of Men"** • Betrayal is a recurrent theme in Taylor's short fiction, and it is no accident that the story he chose to place first in *The Collected Stories of Peter Taylor* is the relatively late "Dean of Men," a recital of the history of the men in a family. The narrator, an older man and a successful academic, tries in the story to explain to his son the background of his career and his divorce from his first wife, the son's mother. The story unfolds by an examination of the past, in which the narrator's grandfather was a successful politician, governor of his state, and then U.S. senator. Younger men in his party persuaded him to give up his Senate seat and run for governor again to save the party from a man he despised, and he agreed. It turned out that the plan was intended to get him out of his Senate seat. As a result, he gave up politics in disgust and lived out his life an embittered man.

The narrator's father was similarly betrayed by a man he had known all his life, who had installed the father on the board of a bank. During the Great Depression of the 1930's, the friend promised to come from New York to explain doubtful investments he had made, but he never arrived, and the father was left holding the bag. In his turn, the narrator, as a young instructor in a small college, was used by other faculty members to block an appointment they all feared, but when the move was avenged by its target, the young man was left to suffer the consequences alone. In the aftermath, he left to take another job, but his wife did not go with him; both later remarried. The story is the narrator's attempt to explain his life to the son who grew up without him. What the narrator is unaware of is the decline in the importance and stature of his family through the generations; his achievements and his place in life, of which he is unduly proud, are notably less important than those of his father, which were in turn significantly less than those of the grandfather. The entire family's history is flawed by the men's lack of initiative, their acceptance of what others do to them. This lack of self-knowledge on the part of a narrator will characterize Taylor's first-person fictions as late as "The Captain's Son."

**"A Spinster's Tale"** • The narrator's or central figure's ignorance of her or his own attitudes is present from the beginning of Taylor's career, in his first published story, "A Spinster's Tale," a study of sexual repression. Taylor's only explicit investigation of sexual deviance would come much later, in "The Instruction of a Mistress," although "Venus, Cupid, Folly, and Time" contains strong overtones of incest. In "A Spinster's Tale," the narrator, the spinster of the title, is a woman whose youth was blighted by her fear of an old drunk who often passed the house in which she lived with her father and brother. As she tells the story, it is clear that her fear of "Mr. Speed" is a transference of her inadmissible attraction to her older brother, who also drinks, often and to excess. She is unaware that her irrational fear is really fear of any kind of departure from the most repressed kinds of behavior. In the old man, drunkenness is revolting; in her brother, she fears it only because her dead mother had told the young man that he would go to hell if he continued, but her brother's antic behavior when drunk exercises an attraction on her that she struggles to deny. In her old age, she still has revealing dreams laden with sexual implications. The betrayal in this story, of which she is only dimly aware, is the narrator's calling the police to haul away Mr. Speed when he stumbles onto their lawn during a driving rainstorm. She acknowledges late in life that she had acted "with courage, but without wisdom."

**"What You Hear from 'Em?"** • Betrayal of one kind or another seems to be almost inevitable in the relations between races, especially as those relations undergo the changes brought about by the Civil Rights movement and the push for integration. Since most of Taylor's stories are set in the South of the 1930's and 1940's, those relations are often between masters and servants, but that will change in the later tales. "What You Hear from 'Em?" is written from the point of view of an old black servant, Aunt Munsie, who lives in retirement, raising pigs and dogs and a few chickens. Her only real interest is in the lives of the two white men she reared when their mother died, and the question she addresses to people she meets in her daily rounds asks when they will return to the small town where she still lives. Their visits to her, bringing wives and children and eventually grandchildren, do not matter to Aunt Munsie; things will not be right until they again live in Thornton, a Nashville suburb. The betrayal is by the two men. Worried by her refusal to acknowledge automobiles or traffic rules as she goes through town collecting slop for her pigs, they arrange for an ordinance to be enacted that will forbid pig farming within the town limits. Aunt Munsie knows what they have done; she sells her pigs and loses her individuality, becoming a kind of parody of an old former servant.

**"A Wife of Nashville"** • A different kind of betrayal and a different kind of response occur in another early story, "A Wife of Nashville." On the surface, this is a story about a marriage between John R. and Helen Ruth Lovell, in some ways a typical southern couple. He has succeeded in the insurance business, but he has spent much of his time over the years with other businessmen, hunting and traveling. Helen Ruth, as a result, has been occupied with rearing her children, and her chief companions over the years have been the black women who have cooked and cleaned for her: Jane Blackemore, when they were first married; Carrie, during the time their two younger boys were born; Sarah, who at the age of sixty-eight left for Chicago and a new marriage; and Jess, hired during the Depression and the most durable and helpful of them all.

"A Wife of Nashville," however, is only partly about the marriage and the rearing of a family. It becomes clear as the story develops that Helen Ruth's genuine emotional life has increasingly been centered on her relationships with her servants and that they have been an integral part of the family. Jess, who does not drive a car herself, is essential to the boys' learning to drive, a symbol of their adulthood. In the end, she concocts a scene to explain her leaving the family; Helen Ruth knows that the explanation is false and that Jess and a friend are leaving Nashville for what they think is a more glamorous life in California. The husband and sons are shocked and resentful at the way they think Helen Ruth has been treated by Jess; Helen Ruth herself, however, rejects their sympathy and refuses to share their anger. It is clear that she wishes she had a means of escape, even one as improbable as that taken by Jess and her friend. On another level, it is clear also that she, unlike the men in the family, recognizes the social changes that are under way, changes that will alter the ways in which the races will survive. Other stories having to do with difficult marital relations were written throughout Taylor's career and include the early "Cookie," "Reservations," and "The Elect."

**"Miss Leonora When Last Seen"** • Perhaps the story most typical of Taylor's work, and one of the most powerful, is the one he chose to conclude *The Collected Stories of Peter Taylor,* "Miss Leonora When Last Seen." Narrated by one of the middling-successful men who populate this fiction, a small-town druggist, the story operates on several levels. It encompasses the narrator's sadness at having to carry bad news to the woman who was his teacher and who had encouraged him to aspire to greater things than he was able to achieve. At the same time, it is a story about a town's revenge on Miss Leonora's family, the wealthiest and most powerful residents of the town; over the years, they had prevented every "improvement" that might have brought business and "progress" to Thomasville, using their influence to keep out the railroad, the asylum, and other projects that would have changed the town. Most of them moved away, but they retained the home place, and they continued to exercise their influence. Now the town has decided to condemn the old manor house in which Miss Leonora lives in order to build a new high school. The irony that Miss Leonora had been a superb teacher in the old school is not lost on the narrator.

More important, "Miss Leonora When Last Seen" shows the mixed blessings and curses of the old ways and of the changes that are coming to the "New South." The old ways were autocratic and sometimes unfair, and they depended upon a servant class descended from slaves, such as the blacks who still live on Miss Leonora's place. Modernity, however, may not be much of an improvement; the new high school is being pushed as a final attempt to avoid the supposed horrors of racial integration. The narrator is caught between these times and has nothing to look to for support.

While these elements are at work, and the narrator is showing his own lack of understanding of Miss Leonora, the story is presenting a picture of an eccentric but fascinating individual who has lived in Thomasville all her life, teaching, trying to inspire the young men who were her favorites to achievement, and living close to the blacks who still reside on the family property, which she has inherited. In her retirement, she has taken to traveling by car, driving always at night in an open convertible, wearing one of two strange costumes, and stopping at "tourist homes," which were the motels of the time. Informed of the town's decision, she has taken to the road. Postcards come from surrounding states, but "She seems to be orbiting her native state of Tennessee." There is no sign that she will ever return; the old ways are indeed dead, and those who lived in the old way are anachronisms.

**"The Old Forest"** • "The Old Forest" is a good example of Taylor's interest in the tensions between the Old and New South. The story's action takes place in Memphis in 1937, although the story is told more than forty years later by Nat, the central character. Nat relates how in the 1930's a young man in Memphis, even if he was engaged, might continue to go out with the bright young women he and his friends jokingly called *demimondaines*. These were intelligent young women who had good jobs, read good books, and attended concerts and plays. Nevertheless, they were not quite in the social class of Nat and his friends. The two groups went out for their mutual amusement without expecting long-term commitments, either sexual or matrimonial. Young men like Nat intended to marry duller girls of their own class who lived by the standards of the Memphis Country Club. Nat says that the *demimondaines* were at least two generations ahead of themselves in their sexual freedom, for although they did not usually sleep with Nat and his friends, they often entered sexual relationships with men they truly loved.

Although Nat is already working for his father's cotton firm, he is also studying Latin in a lackadaisical way at the local college. His family ridicules his interest in Horace's *Odes*, but he enjoys the distinction it brings him among his friends, even though he is nearly failing the course. This particular Saturday, about a week before Nat's December wedding to Caroline Braxton, he invites Lee Ann Deehart, his "other" girl, to come out to the college with him while he studies for a test. On snow-packed roads in the primeval forest near the Mississippi, they have a car accident. Nat is slightly hurt and hardly notices that Lee Ann has climbed out of the car and disappeared in the snow and virgin forest. When she does not return to her boarding-house that evening, Nat knows he must confess the affair to Caroline, who is surprisingly understanding and agrees that he must find her.

Lee Ann's friends know where she is, but Nat soon realizes that she is deliberately hiding from him, and he fears the scandal when the story hits the newspapers. Especially he fears that Caroline will break off their engagement. In the end, Caroline is the one who finds Lee Ann and discovers her motives for hiding, motives which ironically involve her own fear of publicity and the identification of her family.

Throughout, Nat contrasts the Memphis of 1937 with the present Memphis and the two sorts of girls represented by Lee Ann and Caroline. Typically, Taylor invites the reader to take a slightly different view from Nat's. For all her supposed dullness, Caroline uses real intelligence in finding Lee Ann and real compassion in responding to her crisis. Moreover, ten years later she supports Nat's decision to leave cotton for a career teaching college. Caroline's own analysis of what happened, however, is straight from the old forest of Memphis convention. She has not set herself free, she says, like Lee Ann, so in protecting Nat she has protected for herself "the power of a woman in a man's world," the only power she can claim.

*John M. Muste*
*With updates by Ann D. Garbett*

## Other major works

PLAYS: *Tennessee Day in Saint Louis: A Comedy*, pr. 1956; *A Stand in the Mountains*, pb. 1965; *Presences: Seven Dramatic Pieces*, pb. 1973.

ANTHOLOGY: *Randall Jarrell, 1914-1965*, 1967 (with Robert Lowell and Robert Penn Warren).

NOVELS: *A Woman of Means*, 1950; *A Summons to Memphis*, 1986; *In the Tennessee Country*, 1994.

NONFICTION: *Conversations with Peter Taylor*, 1987 (Hubert H. McAlexander, editor).

## Bibliography

Graham, Catherine Clark. *Southern Accents: The Fiction of Peter Taylor.* New York: P. Lang, 1994. Insightful study. Includes bibliographical references.

Griffith, Albert J. *Peter Taylor.* Rev. ed. Boston: Twayne, 1990. Excellent introductory study.

Kramer, Victor A., Patricia A. Bailey, Carol G. Dana, and Carl H. Griffin. *Andrew Lytle, Walker Percy, Peter Taylor: A Reference Guide.* Boston: G. K. Hall, 1983. One of the later and most complete bibliographies of Taylor's work and the reviews and criticism.

McAlexander, Hubert H. *Peter Taylor: A Writer's Life.* Baton Rouge: Louisiana State University Press, 2001. Biography written with the close cooperation of its subject. In fact, McAlexander, who edited *Conversations with Peter Taylor* and a collection of essays on the writer, was hand-picked by Taylor, and his portrait is admiring.

May, Charles E., ed. *Masterplots II: Short Story Series, Revised Edition.* 8 vols. Pasadena, Calif.: Salem Press, 2004. Designed for student use, this reference set contains articles providing detailed plot summaries and analyses of six short stories by Taylor: "The Fancy Woman" (vol. 3); "Miss Leonora When Last Seen" and "The Old Forest" (vol. 5); "Reservations: A Love Story" (vol. 6); and "Venus, Cupid, Folly, and Time" and "What You Hear from 'Em?" (vol. 8).

Oates, Joyce Carol. "Realism of Distance, Realism of Immediacy." *The Southern Review* 7 (Winter, 1971): 295-313. A novelist's sensitive appreciation of other writers, including Taylor.

Robison, James C. *Peter Taylor: A Study of the Short Fiction.* Boston: Twayne, 1987. This volume not only is the sole extended study of Taylor's short stories but also contains two interviews with the author as well as essays by a number of critics. Robison's comments are occasionally wide of the mark, but he is an earnest and generally intelligent reader of Taylor's work. Essential reading.

Samarco, C. Vincent. "Taylor's 'The Old Forest.'" *The Explicator* 57 (Fall, 1998): 51-53. Argues that the car accident represents a collision between Nat Ramsey's pursuit of knowledge and the history of his upbringing within the narrow walls of privilege.

Stephens, C. Ralph, and Lynda B. Salamon, eds. *The Craft of Peter Taylor.* Tuscaloosa: University of Alabama Press, 1995. Collection of essays on Taylor's work, including discussions of his poetics, his focus on place, his relationship to the Agrarians, his treatment of absence, his role in American pastoralism, and such stories as "The Other Times," "The Old Forest," and "The Hand of Emmagene."

Taylor, Peter. "Interview with Peter Taylor." Interview by J. H. E. Paine. *Journal of the Short Story in English* 9 (Fall, 1987): 14-35. The most extended interview with Taylor, dealing with his techniques and influences.

# Dylan Thomas

**Born:** Swansea, Wales; October 27, 1914
**Died:** New York, New York; November 9, 1953

**Principal short fiction** • *Portrait of the Artist as a Young Dog*, 1940; *Selected Writings of Dylan Thomas*, 1946; *A Child's Christmas in Wales*, 1954; *A Prospect of the Sea, and Other Stories*, 1955; *Adventures in the Skin Trade, and Other Stories*, 1955; *Early Prose Writings*, 1971; *The Followers*, 1976; *The Collected Stories*, 1984.

**Other literary forms** • In addition to his short fiction, Dylan Thomas published several collections of poetry, including *Eighteen Poems* (1934), *Twenty-five Poems* (1936), *New Poems* (1943), and *Collected Poems: 1934-1952* (1952). *Under Milk Wood* (1954) is a verse drama that affectionately portrays a day in the life of the inhabitants of a tiny Welsh fishing village. Thomas also wrote many screenplays, most notably *The Doctor and the Devils* (1953) and a comic detective novel *The Death of the King's Canary* (1976).

**Achievements** • The lyricism of Dylan Thomas's poetry probably constitutes his most powerful contribution to twentieth-century verse and is also a notable characteristic of his prose. One source of that lyric quality is surely Thomas's Welsh origins and his awareness of the depth and richness of Welsh poetic traditions. He also paid homage to Wales in his short fiction, lovingly (if sometimes satirically) describing it in works such as *A Child's Christmas in Wales* and in the stories that make up *Portrait of the Artist as a Young Dog* and *Adventures in the Skin Trade*. In those works appear characters and events from his childhood in Swansea and his early work as a news reporter.

Thomas's poetry won the "Poet's Corner" Prize of the *Sunday Referee* in 1934, the Blumenthal Poetry Prize in 1938, the Levinson Poetry Prize in 1945, and Foyle's Poetry Prize (for *Collected Poems: 1934-1952*) in 1952. Thomas also received a grant from The Authors' Society Traveling Scholarship Fund in 1947.

**Biography** • Dylan Marlais Thomas's father, John David Thomas, was an embittered schoolmaster, emotionally remote from his son, but he possessed a fine library of contemporary fiction and poetry which his son was free to read. His father's distance and unhappiness may have made Thomas more susceptible to the indulgences of his mother, Florence Williams Thomas. It is her family who appears in Thomas's work as the chapel-going farmers, and it is her oldest sister whose husband owned the farm near Llangain where the young Thomas often spent summer vacations. Thomas also had a sister, Nancy, nine years older than he. The family home at 5 Cwmdonkin Drive, Swansea, was across the street from the park which sometimes appears in his poems ("The Hunchback in the Park," for example). Likewise the beautiful Gower peninsula and his aunt's farm appeared in his adult work as subjects for his poetry and memoirs (most notably in "Fern Hill"). Thomas's early life in Wales furnished him with material that surfaced in his work for the rest of his life.

Thomas was a lackadaisical student at Swansea Grammar School. Talented in English, he edited the school magazine while he was there, and he began to keep the notebooks that reveal his early attempts to form his style, but he gave little attention

Library of Congress

to subjects that did not interest him. It was at school that he began his friendship with Dan Jones, with whom he composed poems and played elaborate word games. In adulthood, Jones became Dr. Daniel Jones, musical composer and editor of Thomas's work.

Thomas left school in 1931 to work—not very successfully—as a reporter for the *South Wales Evening Post,* a job which gave him material for many of his stories. During the next three years, he also experienced a period of exciting poetic growth, learning about Welsh poets of the past and producing much work of his own. Late in 1934, he moved to London where he cultivated a conscious bohemianism and began to gain a reputation as drinker, brilliant conversationalist, and poet of merit. Through the rest of his life, the two parts of his personality—the serious poet who cared about his craft and the hard-drinking bohemian—were at odds in dominating his behavior.

In 1937, he married Caitlin Macnamara, a strong-willed, passionate dancer with whom he was intensely in love. They had three children—Llewelyn, Aeron, and Colm. During the war, Thomas, a conscientious objector, wrote mostly prose. Afterward, his life alternated between London and the Welsh fishing village of Laugharne, where he lived with his family and did his most profitable work. In London, when he was in need of money (as he usually was), he often worked for the British Broadcasting Corporation, but there, too, his drinking began to cause him more and more troubles.

In 1950, he made the first of four tours to the United States, reading his work at colleges and universities. It was an enormous success, but it documented his reputation as an "outlaw" poet—a hard drinker and womanizer who spent the proceeds of his readings on women and whiskey while his family went without necessities. The subsequent tours intensified that legend. He died of alcohol poisoning in St. Vincent's Hospital in New York City in 1953.

**Analysis** • Dylan Thomas's ten stories in *Portrait of the Artist as a Young Dog* are charming reminiscences of his relatives, school friends, and neighbors in the town where he grew up. Their wit and accessibility made them immediately popular, in contrast to the dark, subjective stories he had written prior to 1938, for which he had difficulty finding a publisher. In March, 1938, he wrote to Vernon Watkins that "A Visit to Grandpa's" was "the first of a series of short, straightforward stories about Swansea." Published on March 10, 1939, in the *New English Weekly,* it told of a boy's waking up on a mild summer night to the sounds of "gee-up and whoa" in the next room where his grandfather, wearing his red waistcoat with its brass buttons, is reining invisible horses. On their morning walks, the grandfather has expressed his wish not to be buried in the nearby churchyard. When he is missing a few days later, the entire village is summoned to go in search of him, and they find him on Carmarthen Bridge in his Sunday trousers and dusty tall hat on his way to Llangadock to be buried. They try to persuade him to come home to tea instead.

**"The Peaches"** • In "The Peaches," first published in the October, 1938, issue of *Life and Letters Today*, the naïve narrator tells of his spring holiday on a farm in Gorsehill. His uncle Jim drives him there in a green cart late one April evening, stopping for a drink at a public house. The squeal coming from the wicker basket he takes inside with him prepares the reader for the fact that cousin Gwilym will note that one of the pigs is missing the next day. The terror of being abandoned in a dark alley is assuaged by Aunt Annie's warm welcome of him later that night at the farmhouse. He enters, small, cold, and scared, as the clock strikes midnight, and is made to feel "among the shining and striking like a prince taking off his disguise." Next morning, Gwilym takes him to see the sow, who has only four pigs left. "He sold it to go on the drink," whispers Gwilym rebukingly. The boy imagines Jim transformed into a hungry fox: "I could see uncle, tall and sly and red, holding the writhing pig in his two hairy hands, sinking his teeth in its thigh, crunching its trotters up; I could see him leaning over the wall of the sty with the pig's legs sticking out of his mouth." Gwilym, who is studying to be a minister, takes him to the barn which he pretends is his chapel and preaches a thunderous sermon at him, after which he takes up a collection.

Next, the complication begins. Gwilym and Jim are told to dress up for Jack Williams, whose rich mother will bring him in an automobile from Swansea for a fortnight's visit. A tin of peaches has been saved from Christmas; "Mother's been keeping it for a day like this." Mrs. Williams, "with a jutting bosom and thick legs, her ankles swollen over her pointed shoes," sways into the parlor like a ship. Annie precedes her, anxiously tidying her hair, "clucking, fidgeting, excusing." (The string of participles is typical of Thomas's prose style; one sentence [in "Return Journey"] contains fifteen.) The rich guest declines refreshments. "I don't mind pears or chunks, but I can't bear peaches." The boys run out to frolic, climb trees, and play Indians in the bushes. After supper, in the barn, Gwilym demands confessions from them, and Jack begins to cry that he wants to go home. That night in bed, they hear Uncle Jim come in drunk and Annie quietly relating the events of the day, at which he explodes into thunderous anger: "Aren't peaches good enough for her!" At this, Jack sobs into his pillow. The next day Mrs. Williams arrives, sends the chauffeur for Jack's luggage, and drives off with him, as the departing car scatters the hens and the narrator waves good-bye.

Two aspects of the point of view are significant. The first, its tone, is what made all the stories so immediately beloved. The genial Chaucerian stance, which perceives and accepts eccentricities, which notes and blesses all the peculiarities of humanity, is endearing without being sentimental, because the acuteness of the observations stays in significant tension with the nonjudgmental way in which they are recorded. This combination of acuity and benevolence, of sharpness and radiance, is the special quality of Thomas's humor. The second aspect of the author's style is its expansion and contraction, which indicates the view of a visionary poet. The narrator is both a homesick, cold, tired little boy, and "a royal nephew in smart town clothes, embraced and welcomed." The uncle is both a predatory fox and an impoverished farmer, as he sits in "the broken throne of a bankrupt bard." The splendid paradise where the narrator romps is simultaneously a poor, dirty "square of mud and rubbish and bad wood and falling stone, where a bucketful of old and bedraggled hens scratched and laid small eggs." The "pulpit" where Gwilym's inspired sermon is "cried to the heavens" in his deepest voice is a dusty, broken cart in an abandoned barn overrun with mice; but this decrepit building on a mucky hill becomes "a chapel shafted with sunlight," awesome with reverence as the "preacher's" voice becomes "Welsh and singing." The alternate aggrandizement and diminution of the perceptions energize the style as the lyric impulse wars with the satiric impulse in the narrator's voice.

**"Patricia, Edith and Arnold"** • The naïve narrator of the third of the *Portrait of the Artist as a Young Dog* stories, entitled "Patricia, Edith and Arnold," is totally engrossed in his imaginary engine, whose brake is "a hammer in his pocket" and whose fuel is replenished by invisible engineers. As he drives it about the garden, however, he is aware of his maid, Patricia, plotting with the neighbor's servant, Edith, to confront Arnold with the identical letters he wrote to both of them. The girls take the child to the park as it begins to snow; Arnold has been meeting Edith there on Fridays, and Patricia on Wednesdays. As the girls wait for Arnold in the shelter, the boy, disowning them, pretends he is a baker, molding loaves of bread out of snow.

Arnold Matthews, his hands blue with cold, wearing a checked cap but no overcoat, appears and tries to bluff it out. Loudly he says, "Fancy you two knowing each other." The boy rolls a snowman "with a lop-sided dirty head" smoking a pencil, as the situation grows more tense. When Arnold claims that he loves them both, Edith shakes her purse at him, the letters fall out all over the snow, and the snowman collapses. As the boy searches for his pencil, the girls insist that Arnold choose between them. Patricia turns her back, indignantly. Arnold gestures and whispers to Edith behind Patricia's back and then, out loud, chooses Patricia. The boy, bending over his snowman, finds his pencil driven through its head.

Later, during a discussion of lying, the boy tells Patricia that he saw Arnold lying to both of them, and the momentary truce, during which Patricia and Arnold have been walking arm in arm, is over. She smacks and pummels him as he staggers backward and falls. The boy says he has to retrieve the cap that he left near his snowman. He finds Arnold there, rereading the letters that Edith dropped, but does not tell Patricia this. Later, as his frozen hands tingle and his face feels on fire, she comforts him until "the hurting is gone." She acknowledges his pain and her own by saying, "Now we've all had a good cry today." The story achieves its effects through the child's detachment. Totally absorbed in his play, he registers the behavior of the adults, participating in their sorrows without fully comprehending them. In spite of his age-appropriate egocentricity and his critical remarks about her girth (her footprints as large as a horse's), he expresses deep affection for her and such concern as he is capable of, given the puzzling circumstances.

**"The Fight"** • The narrator of "The Fight" is an exuberant adolescent. Although he is fourteen, he deliberately adds a year to his age, lying for the thrill of having to be on guard to avoid detection. The self-conscious teenager is continually inventing scenarios in which he assumes various heroic postures. The story tells of his finding an alter ego, as gifted as he, through whom he can confirm his existence, with whom he can share his anxieties, collaborate imaginatively, and play duets. The opening incident illustrates Dylan's testing himself against the adults about him. He is engaged in a staring contest with a cranky old man who lives beside the schoolyard when a strange boy pushes him down. They fight. Dylan gives Dan a bloody nose and gets a black eye in return. Admiring each other's injuries as evidence of their own manliness, they become fast friends.

Dylan postures, first as a prizefighter, then as a pirate. When a boy ridicules him at school the next day, he has a revenge fantasy of breaking his leg, then of being a famous surgeon who sets it with "a rapid manipulation, the click of a bone," while the grateful mother, on her knees, tearfully thanks him. Assigned a vase to draw in art class, the boys sketch inaccurate versions of naked girls instead. "I drew a wild guess below the waist." This boyish sexual curiosity leads him mentally to undress even Mrs. Bevan, the minister's wife, whom he meets later at supper at Dan's house, but he gets frightened when he gets as far as the petticoats.

Dan shows Dylan the seven historical novels he wrote before he was twelve, plays the piano for him, and lets him make a cat's noise on his violin; Dylan reads Dan his poems out of his exercise book. They share feelings, such as their ambivalences toward their mothers, a love tinged with embarrassment. They decide to edit a paper. Back upstairs, after supper, they imitate the self-important Mr. Bevan and discuss the time Mrs. Bevan tried to fling herself out the window. When she joins them later, they try to induce her to repeat this by pointedly opening the window and inviting her to admire the view. When he has to leave at 9:30, Dan announces that he "must finish a string trio tonight," and Dylan counters that he is "working on a long poem about the princes of Wales." On these bravura promises, the story closes.

**"A Prospect of the Sea"** • Thomas called these luminous remembrances of his youth "portions of a provincial autobiography." The stories he wrote earlier, drafts of which exist in "The Red Notebook," which he kept from December, 1933, to October, 1934, were not published until later. Considered obscure, violent, and surrealistic, the stories are difficult because of the use of narrative devices borrowed from lyric poetry. In "A Prospect of the Sea," for example, the scenery seems to contract and expand. A boy lying in a cornfield on a summer day sees a country girl with berry-stained mouth, scratched legs, and dirty fingernails jump down from a tree, startling the birds. The landscape shrinks, the trees dwindle, the river is compressed into a drop, and the yellow field diminishes into a square "he could cover with his hand." As he masters his fear and sees she is only "a girl in a torn cotton frock" sitting cross-legged on the grass, things assume their proper size. As she makes erotic advances, his terror rises again, and everything becomes magnified. Each leaf becomes as large as a man, every trough in the bark of the tree seems as vast as a channel, every blade of grass looks as high as a house. This apparent contraction and expansion of the external world is dependent upon the protagonist's internal state.

Thomas uses another device commonly employed in lyric poetry, the literalized metaphor. Because a thing seems like another, it is depicted as having been transformed into that other thing. For example, the "sunburned country girl" frightens the lonely boy as if she were a witch; thus, in his eyes, she becomes one. "The stain on her lips was blood, not berries; and her nails were not broken but sharpened sideways, ten black scissorblades ready to snip off his tongue." Finally, not only space and character are subject to transformations but also time. As the narrator fantasizes union with this girl, he attains a mystical vision of history unrolling back to Eden. The story ends as it began; she disappears into the sea. He had imagined, at the beginning, as he dabbled his fingers in the water, that a drowned storybook princess would emerge from the waves. The apparent obscurities are resolved by seeing the plot of this story as simply the daydreams of a lonely boy on a summer's day.

**"The Orchards"** • "The Orchards" is another prose-poem about a man's attempt to record a vision in words. Marlais has a repetitive dream about blazing apple trees guarded by two female figures who change from scarecrows to women. He tries and fails to shape this into a story, and finally sets out on a quest. Striding through eleven valleys, he reaches the scene he has dreamed of, where he reenacts the kissing of the maiden as the orchard catches fire, the fruit falls as cinders, and she and her sister change to scarecrows. These smoldering trees may be related to the sacrificial fires of the Welsh druids on Midsummer Day. The woman figure might be connected with Olwedd, the Welsh Venus, associated with the wild apple. Marlais's adventure, however, is a mental journey undertaken by the creative writer through the landscape of his mind, and the temporal and spatial fluctuations are the projections of that mind, mythicized.

**"The Tree"** • "The Tree" illustrates this same process. A gardener tells a boy the story of Jesus, reading the Bible in his shed by candlelight. While he is mending a rake with wire, he relates the twelve stages of the cross. The boy wants to know the secrets inside the locked tower to which the bearded gardener has the key. On Christmas Eve, the gardener unlocks the room through whose windows the boy can see the Jarvis Hills to the east. The gardener says of this "Christmas present" in a tone which seems prophetic: "It is enough that I have given you the key."

On Christmas morning, an idiot with ragged shoes wanders into the garden, "bearing the torture of the weather with a divine patience." Enduring the rain and the wind, he sits down under the elder tree. The boy, concluding that the gardener had not lied and that the secret of the tower was true, runs to get the wire to reenact the crucifixion. The old man's obsessive religiosity has been transmitted to the boy, who takes it literally: "A tree" has become "The Tree," "a key" has become "The Key," and a passive beggar stumbling from the east has become Christ inviting his martyrdom.

**"The Visitor"** • "The Visitor" is the story of a dying poet, Peter, tended lovingly by Rhiannon, who brings him warm milk, reads to him from William Blake, and at the end pulls the sheet over his face. Death is personified as Callaghan, whose visit he anticipates as his limbs grow numb and his heart slows. Callaghan blows out the candles with his gray mouth, and, lifting Peter in his arms, flies with him to the Jarvis Valley where they watch worms and death-beetles undoing "brightly and minutely" the animal tissues on the shining bones through whose sockets flowers sprout, the blood seeping through the earth to fountain forth in springs of water. "Peter, in his ghost, cried with joy." This is the same assurance found in Thomas's great elegies: Death is but the reentry of the body into the processes of nature. Matter is not extinguished, but transformed into other shapes whose joyous energies flourish forever.

*Ruth Rosenberg*
*With updates by Ann D. Garbett*

## Other major works

PLAY: *Under Milk Wood: A Play for Voices*, pr. 1953 (public reading), pr. 1954 (radio play), pb. 1954, pr. 1956 (staged; musical settings by Daniel Jones).

NOVELS: *The Death of the King's Canary*, 1976 (with John Davenport).

MISCELLANEOUS: *"The Doctor and the Devils," and Other Scripts*, 1966 (two screenplays and one radio play).

NONFICTION: *Letters to Vernon Watkins*, 1957 (Vernon Watkins, editor); *Selected Letters of Dylan Thomas*, 1966 (Constantine FitzGibbon, editor); *Poet in the Making: The Notebooks of Dylan Thomas*, 1968 (Ralph Maud, editor); *Twelve More Letters by Dylan Thomas*, 1969 (FitzGibbon, editor); *The Collected Letters*, 1985 (Paul Ferris, editor).

POETRY: *Eighteen Poems*, 1934; *Twenty-five Poems*, 1936; *The Map of Love*, 1939; *New Poems*, 1943; *Deaths and Entrances*, 1946; *Twenty-six Poems*, 1950; *Collected Poems, 1934-1952*, 1952; *In Country Sleep*, 1952; *The Poems of Dylan Thomas*, 1971 (Daniel Jones, editor).

RADIO PLAYS: *Quite Early One Morning*, 1944; *The Londoner*, 1946; *Return Journey*, 1947; *Quite Early One Morning*, 1954 (twenty-two radio plays).

SCREENPLAYS: *No Room at the Inn*, 1948 (with Ivan Foxwell); *Three Weird Sisters*, 1948 (with Louise Birt and David Evans); *The Doctor and the Devils*, 1953; *The Beach at Falesá*, 1963; *Twenty Years A'Growing*, 1964; *Me and My Bike*, 1965; *Rebecca's Daughters*, 1965.

## Bibliography

Ackerman, John. *Dylan Thomas: His Life and Work*. New York: St. Martin's Press, 1996. Biography describing the life and writings of Thomas.

_____. *Welsh Dylan: Dylan Thomas's Life, Writing, and His Wales*. 2d ed. Bridgend, Wales: Seren, 1998. This biography of Dylan looks at his homeland, Wales, and shows how the area influenced his writings.

Davies, Walford. *Dylan Thomas*. Philadelphia: Open University Press, 1986. Biography and an introduction are followed by several chapters on the poems: poems on poetry, early poetry, comparisons of early and late poems, "Fern Hill," and the last poems. The final chapter attempts to put Thomas's work in context and to draw some conclusions regarding the poet in relationship to society, his style, and the way he uses language. Good notes contain bibliographical references.

_____. *A Reference Companion to Dylan Thomas*. Westport, Conn.: Greenwood Press, 1998. Valuable aid to understanding Thomas's troubled life and enduring body of work. Begins with an insightful biography that provides a useful context for studying his writings. The second section provides a systematic overview of his works, while the third section summarizes the critical and scholarly response to his writings. The volume concludes with a bibliography of the most helpful general studies.

Ferris, Paul. *Dylan Thomas: The Biography*. Washington, D.C.: Counterpoint, 2000. This excellent biography contains material found in American archives and also those of the British Broadcasting Corporation. Ferris interviewed more than two hundred people who either knew Thomas or worked with him. He attempts to separate the facts from the legendary reputation of Thomas. This book elaborates on, and enhances, the "approved" biography by Constantine FitzGibbon (*The Life of Dylan Thomas*, 1965), the personal memoirs by Caitlin Thomas (*Leftover Life to Kill*, 1957), and John Malcolm Brinnin (*Dylan Thomas in America*, 1955).

Hardy, Barbara Nathan. *Dylan Thomas: An Original Language.* Athens: University of Georgia Press, 2000. Hardy looks at Thomas's use of language in his writings, including his use of Welsh-derived terms. Includes bibliography and index.

Jones, R. F. G. *Time Passes: Dylan Thomas's Journey to "Under Milk Wood."* Sydney: Woodworm Press, 1994. Account of the literary development of Thomas, including analysis of *Under Milk Wood.* Includes bibliography and index.

Korg, Jacob. *Dylan Thomas.* Rev. ed. New York: Twayne, 1992. Basic biography of Thomas that covers his life and works. Includes bibliography and index.

Lycett, Andrew. *Dylan Thomas: A New Life.* Woodstock, N.Y.: Overlook Press, 2004. Major new Thomas biography that is well researched and much acclaimed.

May, Charles E., ed. *Masterplots II: Short Story Series, Revised Edition.* 8 vols. Pasadena, Calif.: Salem Press, 2004. Designed for student use, this reference set contains articles providing detailed plot summaries and analyses of five short stories by Thomas: "After the Fair" (vol. 1), "The Enemies" (vol. 2), "The Fight" (vol. 3), "The Peaches" (vol. 6), and "A Story" (vol. 7).

Sinclair, Andrew. *Dylan the Bard: A Life of Dylan Thomas.* New York: Thomas Dunne Books, 2000. Sinclair provides the story of Thomas's life as a poet and writer. Includes bibliography and index.

# James Thurber

**Born:** Columbus, Ohio; December 8, 1894
**Died:** New York, New York; November 2, 1961

**Principal short fiction** • *Is Sex Necessary? Or, Why We Feel the Way We Do*, 1929 (with E. B. White); *The Owl in the Attic, and Other Perplexities*, 1931; *The Seal in the Bedroom, and Other Predicaments*, 1932; *My Life and Hard Times*, 1933; *The Middle-Aged Man on the Flying Trapeze*, 1935; *Let Your Mind Alone!, and Other More or Less Inspirational Pieces*, 1937; *The Last Flower: A Parable in Pictures*, 1939; *Fables for Our Time and Famous Poems Illustrated*, 1940; *My World—And Welcome to It!*, 1942; *The Great Quillow*, 1944; *The Thurber Carnival*, 1945; *The White Deer*, 1945; *The Beast in Me, and Other Animals: A New Collection of Pieces and Drawings About Human Beings and Less Alarming Creatures*, 1948; *The Thirteen Clocks*, 1950; *Thurber Country: A New Collection of Pieces About Males and Females, Mainly of Our Own Species*, 1953; *Further Fables for Our Time*, 1956; *Alarms and Diversions*, 1957; *The Wonderful O*, 1957; *Lanterns and Lances*, 1961; *Credos and Curios*, 1962.

**Other literary forms** • James Thurber's more than twenty published volumes include plays, stories, sketches, essays, verse, fables, fairy tales for adults, reminiscences, biography, drawings, and cartoons.

**Achievements** • James Thurber's writings are widely known and admired in English-speaking countries, and his drawings have a world following. He has been compared with James Joyce in his command of and playfulness with English, and he invites comparison with most of his contemporaries, many of whom he parodies at least once in his works. He greatly admired Henry James, referring to him often in his works and parodying him masterfully several times, for example, in "Something to Say." Although Thurber is best known as a humorist (often with the implication that he need not be taken seriously as an artist), his literary reputation has grown steadily. His short story "The Secret Life of Walter Mitty" became an instant classic after it appeared in 1939 and was subsequently reprinted in *Reader's Digest*. After his death in 1961, several major studies and a volume in the Twentieth Century Views series have appeared, all arguing that Thurber should rank with the best American artists in several fields, including the short story. In 1980, "The Greatest Man in the World" was chosen for dramatization in the American Short Story series of the Public Broadcasting Service. Thurber received numerous awards for his work, including honorary degrees from Kenyon College (1950), Williams College (1957), and Yale University (1953), as well as the Antoinette Perry Award for the revue, *A Thurber Carnival* (1960). His drawings were included in art shows worldwide. He was the first American after Mark Twain to be invited to *Punch*'s Wednesday Luncheon (1958).

**Biography** • On December 8, 1894, James Grover Thurber was born in Columbus, Ohio, where he spent his childhood except for a two-year stay in Washington, D.C. In Columbus, he absorbed the midwestern regional values that remained important to him all of his life: a liberal idealism, a conservative respect for the family, a belief in the agrarian virtues of industry and independence, and a healthy skepticism about the human potential for perfecting anything. He lost his left eye in a childhood accident that eventually led to almost complete blindness forty years later. He attended but did not graduate from Ohio State University, where he met Elliott Nugent, who was crucial in helping and encouraging Thurber to write. Thurber began his writing career as a journalist, earning his living primarily as a reporter in Ohio and France before he joined *The New Yorker* in 1927. There his friendship with E. B. White provided opportunities for him to perfect and publish the stories he had been working on since college. Within five years of beginning at *The New Yorker*, he became one of the best-known humorists in America. He married Althea Adams on May 20, 1922, and they had one daughter before their divorce in 1935. He married Helen Wismer on June 25, 1935. Despite impaired vision that seriously interfered with his work, beginning in the early 1940's, Thurber nevertheless continued writing, though he gave up drawing in 1951. He published more than twenty volumes in his lifetime and left many works uncollected at his death. He died of pneumonia on November 2, 1961, a month after suffering a stroke.

**Analysis** • James Thurber is best known as the author of humorous sketches, stories, and reminiscences dealing with urban bourgeois American life. To discuss Thurber as an artist in the short-story form is difficult, however, because of the variety of things he did that might legitimately be labeled short stories. His essays frequently employ stories and are "fictional" in recognizable ways. His "memoirs" in *My Life and Hard Times* are clearly fictionalized. Many of his first-person autobiographical sketches are known to be "fact" rather than fiction only through careful biographical research. As a result, most of his writings can be treated as short fiction. Thurber seemed to prefer to work on the borderlines between conventional forms.

There is disagreement among critics as to the drift of the attitudes and themes reflected in James Thurber's work. The poles are well represented by Richard C. Tobias on the one hand and the team of Walter Blair and Hamlin Hill on the other. Tobias argues that Thurber comically celebrates the life of the mind: "Thurber's victory is a freedom within law that delights and surprises." Blair and Hill, in *America's Humor* (1978), see Thurber as a sort of black humorist laughing at his own destruction, "a humorist bedeviled by neuroses, cowed before the insignificant things in his world, and indifferent to the cosmic ones. He loses and loses and loses his combats with machines, women, and animals until defeat becomes permanent." Although Tobias sees women as vital forces in Thurber's work, Hill and Blair see Thurber as essentially a misogynist bewailing the end of the ideal of male freedom best portrayed in 1950's Western film and pathetically reflected in the fantasies of Walter Mitty. In fact, it seems that critics' opinions regarding Thurber's attitudes about most subjects vary from one text to the next, but certain themes seem to remain consistent. His weak male characters do hate strong women, but the men are often weak because they accept the world in which their secret fantasies are necessary and, therefore, leave their women no choice but to try to hold things together. When a woman's strength becomes arrogance as in "The Catbird Seat" and "The Unicorn in the Garden," the man often defeats her with the active power of his imagination.

Characterizing Thurber as a Romantic, Robert Morsberger lists some themes he sees pervading Thurber's writing: a perception of the oppression of technocracy and of the arrogance of popular scientism especially in their hostility to imagination; an antirational but not anti-intellectual approach to modern life; a belief in the power of the imagination to preserve human value in the face of contemporary forms of alienation; and a frequent use of fear and fantasy to overcome the dullness of his characters' (and readers') lives.

**"The Secret Life of Walter Mitty"** • "The Secret Life of Walter Mitty" is Thurber's best-known work of short fiction. Its protagonist, the milquetoast Walter Mitty, lives in a reverie consisting of situations in which he is a hero: commander of a navy hydroplane, surgeon, trial witness, bomber pilot, and condemned martyr. The dream is clearly an escape from the external life which humiliatingly interrupts it: his wife's mothering, the arrogant competence of a parking attendant and policeman, the humiliating errands of removing tire chains, buying overshoes, and asking for puppy biscuits. In his dreams, he is Lord Jim, the misunderstood hero, "inscrutable to the last"; in his daily life he is a middle-aged husband enmeshed in a web of the humdrum. Tobias sees Mitty as ultimately triumphant over dreary reality.

Blair and Hill see Mitty as gradually losing grip of the real world and slipping into psychosis. Whether liberated or defeated by his imagination, Mitty is clearly incompetent and needs the mothering his wife gives him. Often described as an immoral and malicious woman, she is actually just the wife he needs and deserves; she seems to exist as a replacement ego to keep him from catching his death of cold as he somnambulates. The story's artfulness is readily apparent in the precise choice and arrangement of details such as sounds, objects, and images that connect fantasy and reality. The technical devices are virtually the same as those used by William Faulkner and Joyce to indicate shifts in levels of awareness in their "free-association internal monologues." Mitty has become a representative figure in modern culture like T. S. Eliot's Prufrock and Faulkner's Quentin Compson, although perhaps more widely known. Although many of Thurber's stories are similar to this one in theme and form, they are astonishingly diverse in subject, situation, and range of technique.

**"The Black Magic of Barney Haller"** • Another large group of Thurber stories might be characterized as fictionalized autobiography. One of the best of these sketches is "The Black Magic of Barney Haller" in *The Middle-Aged Man on the Flying Trapeze*. In this story, "Thurber" exorcises his hired man, a Teuton whom lightning and thunder always follow and who mutters imprecations such as "Bime by I go hunt grotches in de voods," and "We go to the garrick now and become warbs." The narrator becomes convinced that despite his stable and solid appearance, Barney is a necromancer who will transform reality with his incantations. At any moment, Barney will reveal his true devilish form and change "Thurber" into a warb or conjure up a grotch. It does not comfort him to learn the probable prosaic meanings of Haller's spells, even to see the crotches under the heavy peach tree branches. At the end of the story, he feels regret that the only man he knows who could remove the wasps from his garret has departed.

The humor of these incidents is clear, and a humorous meaning emerges from them. The narrator would rather hide in *Swann's Way*, reading of a man who makes himself in his book, but he feels threatened by the external supernatural power of another's language to re-create the world. He first attempts exorcism with Robert Frost, well-known for having successfully disposed of a hired man. He quotes "The Pasture" in an attempt to make the obscure clear, but succeeds only in throwing a fear that mirrors his own into Barney. This gives "Thurber" his clue; in the next attempt he borrows from Lewis Carroll and the American braggart tradition, asserting his own superior power as a magician of words, "Did you happen to know that the mome rath never lived that could outgrabe me?" The man with the superior control of language, the man of superior imagination, really is in control; he *can* become a playing card at will to frighten off black magicians. This story is typical of Thurber in its revelation of the fantastic in the commonplace, its flights of language play, and its concern for the relations among reality, self, imagination, and language. *My Life and Hard Times* is the best-known collection of fictional/autobiographical sketches.

**"The Moth and the Star"** • Also an author of fables, Thurber published two collections of fables. "The Moth and the Star" is a typical and often anthologized example. A moth spends a long life trying to reach a star, defying his disappointed parents' wish that he aspire normally to get himself scorched on a street lamp. Having outlived his family, he gains in old age "a deep and lasting pleasure" from the illusion that he has actually reached the distant star: "Moral: Who flies afar from the sphere of our sorrow is here today and here tomorrow." The moth and the star suggest images in F. Scott Fitzgerald's *The Great Gatsby* (1925), one of Thurber's favorite books, but in partial contrast to that book, this story echoes the import of the great artist of the "Conclusion" of Henry David Thoreau's *Walden* (1854). The aspiring idealist who rejects the suicidal life of material accumulation and devotes himself to some perfect work ultimately conquers time and enriches life whether or not he produces any valuable object. Because the moth, like the artist of Kouroo, succeeds and is happy, this story seems more optimistic than *The Great Gatsby*. Many of the fables are more cynical or more whimsical, but all are rich in meaning and pleasure like "The Moth and the Star."

Critics and scholars have noted ways in which Thurber's career and writings parallel Mark Twain's. For example, both, as they grew older, grew more interested in fables and fairy tales. In the latter, Thurber was perhaps the more successful, publishing four fantasy stories for adults in the last twenty years of his life. Completed while blindness was descending upon him, these stories are characterized by heightened poetic language, highly original variations on the fairy formulae, sparkling humor, and a common theme: in the words of Prince Jorn, hero of *The White Deer*, "Love's miracle enough." Love is the key that frees imagination by giving it strength to do, and strength of imagination makes the wasteland fertile. The fairy tales may be seen as intentional responses to Eliot's vision of the wasteland in his famous poem of 1922, perhaps from a point of view similar to that of Percy Bysshe Shelley's *A Defence of Poetry*

(1840). Although "The Secret Life of Walter Mitty" and *Further Fables for Our Time* may be seen as affirming the view of modern life as a wasteland, the fairy tales suggest that the ash heap of modern culture is escapable. It seems especially significant that the mode of escape is represented in tales of magic in remote settings.

***The White Deer*** • *The White Deer* opens in the third period in King Clode's memory of waiting for the depleted game of his hunting grounds to replenish. The story develops in triads, the central one being the three perilous tasks set for the three sons of King Clode to determine which shall claim the hand of the fair princess who materializes when the king and his sons corner the fleet white deer in the enchanted forest. The sons complete their tasks simultaneously, but, in the meantime, King Clode determines that the nameless Princess is not a disenchanted woman but an enchanted deer. When the returned sons are told of this, Thag and Gallow refuse her. If denied love three times, she would be a deer forever, but Jorn accepts her: "What you have been, you are not, and what you are, you will forever be. I place this trophy in the hands of love. . . . You hold my heart." This acceptance transforms her into a new and lovelier princess, Rosanore of the Northland, and the April fragrance of lilacs fills the air suggesting direct opposition to the opening of Eliot's *The Waste Land:* "April is the cruellest month, breeding/Lilacs out of the dead land." As King Clode later sees the full wisdom and beauty of Rosanore, he repeats, "I blow my horn in waste land." Echoes of Eliot show up repeatedly in the fairy tales, but the greater emphasis falls on the powers of love and imagination, which in this fairy world almost inevitably blossom in beauty and happiness.

The cast of secondary characters and the perilous labors provide opportunities to characterize wittily the world in need of magic. There are an incompetent palace wizard as opposed to the true wizards of the forest, an astronomer-turned-clockmaker who envisions encroaching darkness ("It's darker than you think"), and a royal recorder who descends into mad legalese when the Princess's spell proves to be without precedent. Gallow's labor is especially interesting because he must make his way through a vanity fair bureaucracy in order to conquer a sham dragon, a task that tests his purse and persistence more than his love. This task allows a satire of the commercial values of modern culture. Each of the fairy tales contains similar delights as well as bizarre and beautiful flights of language: the Sphinx asks Jorn, "What is whirly?/ What is curly?/Tell me, what is pearly early?" and in a trice, Jorn replies, "Gigs are whirly,/ Cues are curly/ and the dew is pearly early."

*Terry Heller*

## Other major works
PLAYS: *The Male Animal,* pr., pb. 1940 (with Elliott Nugent); *Many Moons,* pb. 1943; *A Thurber Carnival,* pr. 1960 (revue).

NONFICTION: *The Thurber Album,* 1952; *The Years with Ross,* 1959; *Selected Letters of James Thurber,* 1982; *The Thurber Letters: The Wit, Wisdom, and Surprising Life of James Thurber,* 2003 (Harrison Kinney and Rosemary A. Thurber, editors).

## Bibliography
Grauer, Neil A. *Remember Laughter: A Life of James Thurber.* Lincoln: University of Nebraska Press, 1994. Biography that examines the context of Thurber's work. Provides an interesting discussion of the background to the writing of "The Secret

Life of Walter Mitty" and its reception when first published in *The New Yorker.*

Holmes, Charles S., ed. *Thurber: A Collection of Critical Essays.* Englewood Cliffs, N.J.: Prentice-Hall, 1974. This useful collection includes twenty-five critical and biographical essays, as well as a chronology and a brief annotated bibliography.

Kaufman, Anthony. "'Things Close In': Dissolution and Misanthropy in 'The Secret Life of Walter Mitty.'" *Studies in American Fiction* 22 (Spring, 1994): 93-104. Discusses dissolution and misanthropy in the story; argues that Mitty's withdrawal is symptomatic not of mild-mannered exasperation with a trivial world but of anger; concludes that Mitty is the misanthrope demystified and made middle-class—the suburban man who, unable to imagine or afford the drama of a retreat into the wilderness, retreats inward.

Kenney, Catherine McGehee. *Thurber's Anatomy of Confusion.* Hamden, Conn.: Archon Books, 1984. Survey of Thurber's creative world, including discussions of his most characteristic works. Discusses *Fables for Our Time* and such stories as "The Greatest Man in the World" and "The Secret Life of Walter Mitty." Argues that the latter examines the impotent world of modern urban America, embodying all of the elements of Thurber's fictional world.

Kinney, Harrison. *James Thurber: His Life and Times.* New York: Henry Holt, 1995. Biography that focuses largely on Thurber's relationship to the development of *The New Yorker* magazine. Discusses how Thurber made use of overheard conversation, wordplay, and literary allusions in his stories. Discusses Thurber's obsession with the war between the sexes in his prose and cartoons.

Long, Robert Emmet. *James Thurber.* New York: Continuum, 1988. This biographical and critical study divides Thurber's works into drawings, fiction, autobiography, fables, fairy tales, and occasional pieces, giving each a chapter. Complemented by a bibliography.

Morsberger, Robert E. *James Thurber.* New York: Twayne, 1964. Morsberger sketches Thurber's life and then analyzes his works, looking at his contributions to various art forms and his characteristic themes. Contains a chronology of Thurber's life and a brief annotated bibliography.

Prinsky, Norman. "The Secret Life of Walter Mitty." In *Masterplots II: Short Story Series,* edited by Charles E. May. Rev. ed. Vol. 6. Pasadena, Calif.: Salem Press, 2004. Analysis of "The Secret Life of Walter Mitty" with sections on themes and meaning and style and technique. Also includes a detailed synopsis of the story.

Reisman, Rosemary M. Canfield. "The Catbird Seat." In *Masterplots II: Short Story Series,* edited by Charles E. May. Rev. ed. Vol. 1. Pasadena, Calif.: Salem Press, 2004. Student-friendly analysis of "The Catbird Seat" that covers the story's themes and style and includes a detailed synopsis.

Thurber, James. *My Life and Hard Times.* New York: Harper Perennial, 1999. First published in 1933, this amusing, semifictional collection of autobiographical essays focuses on Thurber's early life and his eccentric relatives. Columnist Russell Baker called it "possibly the shortest and most elegant autobiography ever written."

Tobias, Richard Clark. *The Art of James Thurber.* Athens: Ohio University Press, 1970. Tobias studies Thurber's themes and worldview, with special attention to his methods and techniques in creating humor.

# Leo Tolstoy

**Born:** Yasnaya Polyana, Russia; September 9, 1828
**Died:** Astapovo, Russia; November 20, 1910

**Principal short fiction** • *Sevastopolskiye rasskazy*, 1855-1856 (*Sebastopol*, 1887); *The Kreutzer Sonata, The Devil, and Other Tales*, 1940; *Notes of a Madman, and Other Stories*, 1943; *Tolstoy Tales*, 1947; *Tolstoy's Short Fiction*, 1991; *Divine and Human, and Other Stories*, 2000.

**Other literary forms** • Leo Tolstoy is most famous as the author of two superb novels, *Voyna i mir* (1865-1869; *War and Peace*, 1886) and *Anna Karenina* (1875-1878; English translation, 1886). He wrote one other full-length novel, *Voskreseniye* (1899; *Resurrection*, 1899), and a number of novellas, such as *Destvo* (1852; *Childhood*, 1862), *Otrochestvo* (1854; *Boyhood*, 1886), *Yunost'* (1857; *Youth*, 1886), *Kazaki* (1863; *The Cossacks*, 1872), and *Khadzi-Murat* (1911; *Hadji Murad*, 1911). His fiction tends to overshadow his achievement as a dramatist; his plays include *Vlast tmy* (1887; *The Power of Darkness*, 1888) and *Plody prosveshcheniya* (1889; *The Fruits of Enlightenment*, 1891).

**Achievements** • Leo Tolstoy is one of the undisputed titans of fiction, recognized by friend and foe alike as a great artist and man. He is Homeric in the epic sweep of *War and Peace* and *Anna Karenina*; in his stress on the primacy of human beings' senses and physical acts; in the clarity, freshness, and gusto with which he presents his world; in his celebration of nature's processes, from brute matter to the stars; in his union of an omniscient perspective with a detached vision. Unlike Homer, however, he often shows war as wanton carnage resulting from the vainglory and stupidity of a nation's leaders.

Although most critical evaluations of Tolstoy's writings are highly laudatory, he has been reproached by some interpreters for his disparagement of science, technology, and formal education, his hostility to aesthetics and the life of the mind, and most of all for his insistence, in his later works, on dictating programs of moral and religious belief to his readers. As a writer, his greatest achievement is to convey an insight into the living moment that renders with unequaled verisimilitude the course of human passions and the pattern of ordinary actions, enabling him to present a comprehensive, coherent, and usually convincing sense of life. His influence, while not as pervasive as that of his rival Fyodor Dostoevski, is evident in the works of Maxim Gorky, D. H. Lawrence, Ernest Hemingway, Giuseppe Tomasi di Lampedusa, Ignazio Silone, Isaac Babel, Mikhail Sholokhov, Aleksandr Solzhenitsyn, and Boris Pasternak when he composed his novel, *Doktor Zhivago* (1957; *Doctor Zhivago*, 1958).

**Biography** • Leo Nikolayevich Tolstoy was born on September 9, 1828, to a retired army officer, Count Nikolay Ilyich Tolstoy, and a wealthy princess, Maria Nikolaevna Bolkonskaya, who was descended from Russia's first ruling dynasty. His birthplace was a magnificent estate 130 miles south of Moscow, Yasnaya Polyana (serene meadow). Throughout his life, particularly from the late 1850's, when he settled there, this beautiful manorial land, featuring an avenue of lime trees and several lakes, was a romance he kept reinventing, lodged at the center of his self. He disliked urban civilization and industrialization, instead preferring with increasing fidelity the rural simplicities and patriarchal order that had governed the lives of his ancestors and that gave him commanding knowledge of the ways of the landowners and peasants who dominate his writings.

Tolstoy's mother died when he was two, his father when he was nine. He was lovingly brought up by an aunt, Tatyana, who became the model for Sonya in *War and Peace,* just as his parents sat for the portraits of Nicholas Rostov and Princess Maria in that novel. Aunt Tatyana both built the boy's confidence and indulged all his wishes, inclining him to extremes beginning in childhood. He largely wasted several years at the University of Kazan in drinking, gambling, and wenching, then joined an artillery unit in the Caucasus in 1851. That same year, he began working on his first short novel, *Childhood,* to be followed by *Boyhood* and *Youth.* These works are thinly disguised autobiographical novellas, which unfold a highly complicated moral consciousness.

As a writer, Tolstoy is an inspired solipsist, identifying all other humans in examining his flesh and spirit. His art is essentially confessional, representing the strenuous attempt of a complex and exacting man to reconcile himself with himself. His diary, which he began in 1845, reveals what was to be an inveterate thirst for rational and moral justification of his life. It includes a list of puritanical Rules of Life, which he would update during the tormented periods of guilt that followed his lapses. The biographer Henri Troyat called him "a billy-goat pining for purity." The demands of his senses, mind, and spirit were to contest one another in his character as long as he lived.

Tolstoy served bravely in the Crimean War until 1856, also writing his *Sebastopol* stories as well as a number of other military tales. When he returned to European Russia, he found himself lionized as his country's most promising young author. He passed the years 1856-1861 shuttling between St. Petersburg, Moscow, Yasnaya Polyana, and foreign countries. His two trips abroad disgusted him with what he considered the selfishness and materialism of European bourgeois civilization. In 1859, he founded a school for peasant children at Yasnaya Polyana; in 1862, he launched a pedagogical periodical there; both followed a Rousseauistic model that glorified children's instincts, ignored their discipline, and insisted that intellectuals should learn from the common people, instead of vice versa.

In 1862, the thirty-four-year-old Tolstoy married the eighteen-year-old Sonya Andreyevna Behrs. Family life became his religion, and the union was happy for its first fifteen years, producing thirteen children. He dramatized the stability of marriage and family life in *War and Peace* (written 1863-1869), which his wife was to copy out seven times. Sonya efficiently managed Yasnaya Polyana, often served as Tolstoy's secretary, and nursed him through illnesses. She never recovered from the shock she received, however, a week before their wedding, when he insisted she read every entry of his diary, which recorded not only his moral struggles but also seventeen years of libidinous conduct.

Unhappy times followed the composition of *War and Peace:* the deaths of Aunt Tatyana, a favorite son, and several other relatives; quarrels with Sonya; illness; and depression. *Anna Karenina* (written 1873-1877) is a more somber and moralizing book, with the certainty of death hovering over it, and with sexual passion both given its due and dramatized as destructive to happiness. The male protagonist Levin's search for faith is a pale outline of Tolstoy's own spiritual journey, which next led him to write, between 1879 and 1882, an account of his emotional and ethical pilgrimage entitled *Ispoved* (1884; *A Confession*, 1885).

Shortly after finishing *Anna Karenina*, Tolstoy suffered a shattering midlife crisis that brought him close to suicide. Even though he had much to value—good health, a loving wife, family, fame, wealth, genius—life nevertheless seemed to him a cruel lie, purposeless, fraudulent, empty. For answers, he turned to philosophers, to educated people, and finally to the uneducated but religious peasants whose faith made their lives possible, and he decided to become a religious believer, although rejecting most ecclesiastical dogma.

*A Confession* is the best introduction to the spiritual struggle that Tolstoy was to wage for his remaining thirty years, which he spent in a

Library of Congress

glaringly public retirement. Trying to live up to his principles of purity and simplicity, he stripped his personal demands to the barest necessities, dressed and often worked as a peasant, published doctrines of moral improvement in both tracts and tales, signed over to his wife the right to manage his copyrights as well as his property, and renounced (not always successfully) almost all institutions, his title, concert- and theater-going, meat, alcohol, tobacco, hunting, and even sex. He became the high priest of a cult of Christian anarchy, professing the moral teachings of the Gospel and Sermon on the Mount while rejecting the divinity of Christ and the authority of the Church, which excommunicated him for blasphemy in 1901.

Some typical titles of Tolstoy's didactic last years are *V chom moya vera* (1884; *What I Believe*, 1885), "Gde lyubov', tam i Bog" ("Where Love Is, God Is") and "Mnogo li cheloveku zemli nuzhno?" ("How Much Land Does a Man Need?"). His best-known narrative was the tendentious three-part novel *Resurrection*, which is as long as, but far inferior to, *Anna Karenina*. Its protagonist, Nekhlyudov, experiences remorse after having seduced a peasant woman and expiates his transgression by adopting a moral life. Of greatest interest to literary critics is the book-length essay, *Chto takoye iskusstvo?* (1898; *What Is Art?*, 1898), in which Tolstoy rejects all art based on other than gospel ethics and concludes that only the Old Testament's story of Joseph and primitive popular art will satisfy his standards.

Even in his doctrinaire phase, however, Tolstoy managed to produce great stories and novellas, particularly *The Death of Ivan Ilyich*, "Khozyain i rabotnik" ("Master and Man"), *The Kreutzer Sonata*, and *Hadji Murad*. He also wrote a powerful naturalistic tragedy, *The Power of Darkness*, which featured adultery and infanticide in a somber peasant setting. By contrast, *The Fruits of Enlightenment* is a satiric, farcical comedy revolving around the foibles of the gentry and the land hunger of the peasantry.

Tolstoy's last years were often mired in squabbles with his wife and some of his children, intrigues concerning his legacy, and bitter enmity between Sonya Tolstoy and his chief disciple, Vladimir Chertkov, who became Tolstoy's close confidant. By 1909, the marriage had become extremely stressful, with Countess Tolstoy repeatedly threatening suicide. On November 9, 1910, Leo Tolstoy, driven to distraction, fled his wife and family; on November 13, he was taken ill with what became pneumonia, at the rail junction of nearby Astapovo, and died in the stationmaster's bed there on November 20. His death was mourned as a loss in every Russian family.

**Analysis** • Leo Tolstoy's ego embraces the world, so that he is always at the center of his fictive creation, filling his books with his struggles, personae, problems, questions, and quests for answers, and above all with his notion of life as an ethical search as strenuous as the pursuit of the Holy Grail. He does not try to puzzle or dazzle; his work is not a clever riddle to be solved or a game to be played but a rich realm to be explored. He disdains the kind of exterior purism practiced by Gustave Flaubert and Henry James among others, which concentrates on the inner lives of individuals— although he is superbly skilled at psychological perception. His aim, rather, is to discover, as far as he can, the essential truth of life's meaning, the revelation to be gained at the core of the vast mesh of human relations. What energizes his work is his conviction that this truth is good, and that, once discovered, it will resolve the discords and conflicts that plague humanity.

In Tolstoy's art, the natural, simple, and true is always pitted against the artificial, elaborate, and false, the particular against the general, knowledge gained from observation against assertions of borrowed faiths. His is the gift of direct vision, of fundamental questions and of magical simplicity—perhaps too simple, as a distinguished historian of ideas has indicated. Isaiah Berlin, in a famous essay titled "The Hedgehog and the Fox," sees Tolstoy as torn between his pluralism (the fox, perceiving reality as varied, complex, and multiple) and monism (the hedgehog, reducing life's fullness to one single truth, the infinity of sensory data to the finite limits of a single mind). Tolstoy, Berlin concludes, was a pluralist in his practice but a monist in his theory, who found himself unable to reconcile the foxiness of his multifarious awareness with his hedgehoglike need to discover one all-embracing answer to its myriad problems.

**"The Raid"** • Tolstoy's first stories are set in the Caucasus, where he spent the years 1851 to 1854, with many of the officers and soldiers who he met serving as thinly disguised models. In "Nabeg: Razskaz volontera" ("The Raid: A Volunteer's Story"), he poses several problems: What is the nature of courage? By what tests does one determine bravery or cowardice? What feelings cause a man to kill his fellow? The first-person narrator discusses these questions with a Captain Khlopov (derived from a Captain Khilkovsky in Tolstoy's diary) and illustrates different types of courage among the military characters. Tolstoy deflates warfare, emphasizing ordinary details and casual, matter-of-fact fortitude rather than dashingly proud heroism. His descriptions of nature are simple, concrete, and expert. The story's most powerful scene has a dying young ensign pass from carefree bravado to dignified resignation as he encounters his end.

*Sebastopol* **Sketches** • The element of eyewitness reportage is carried over from the Caucasian tales to the three *Sebastopol* sketches, which are fiction passing as war dispatches. Tolstoy took part in the Crimean War (1854-1856) as a sublieutenant, with Russia fighting a complex series of actions against a multiple enemy composed of not only Turkish but also some British, French, and Sardinian troops. Although aggressively patriotic, he was appalled by the disorganization of his country's military forces, with the average Russian peasant soldier poorly armed, trained, and led, while many company commanders nearly starved their men by pocketing much of the money allocated for their food.

"Sevastopol v dekabre" ("Sebastopol in December") has no characters and no particular topography. The first-person narrator constructs a guidebook homily out of lived experience, familiarly addressing readers, inviting them to listen to his frontline experiences as he wanders from Sebastopol's bay and dockside to a military hospital filled with shrieking, often multilated soldiers. Says the speaker,

> . . . you will see war not as a beautiful, orderly, and gleaming formation, with music and beaten drums, streaming banners and generals on prancing horses, but war in its authentic expression—as blood, suffering and death.

Tolstoy concludes this sketch with a stirring salute to the epic heroism of Sebastopol's residents and Russian defenders. Yet a somber awareness of death's imminence, as the surgeon's sharp knife slices into his patients' flesh, pervades the sketch.

In "Sevastopol v mae" ("Sebastopol in May"), Tolstoy sharply denounces the vainglory of militarism, stressing the futility of the fighting and the madness of celebrating war as a glorious adventure. The passage describing the death by shellfire of an officer is a superb tour de force, with the author using interior monologue to have the lieutenant crowd his many hopes, fears, memories, and fantasies into a few seconds. The speaker comes to consider war as senseless, horrifying, but also—given human nature—almost inevitable. He concludes that the only hero he can find is the truth. This is perhaps the finest of Tolstoy's military tales, anticipating the battle and death scenes of *War and Peace*.

In the third narrative, "Sebastopol in August," Tolstoy uses well-developed characters to unify an episodic plot. He focuses on two brothers whose personalities contrast but who are both killed in action. He also strikes a note of shame and anger at Russia's abandonment of the city and the consequent waste of many thousands of lives. He celebrates, however, the quiet heroism of countless common soldiers who risked and often met death with calm nobility.

**"Two Hussars"** • Before Tolstoy began *War and Peace* in 1863, he wrote a number of long stories or novellas, which he called *povesti*, defined as "A literary narrative of lesser size than a novel." Their compass is usually too small to accommodate the didacticism that his longer works absorb painlessly. One successful story that avoids moralizing is "Dva gusara" ("Two Hussars"). Its first half is devoted to the officer-father, the second to his son. Twenty years apart, they enact the same sequence of card playing, drinking, and philandering, in the same small town, meeting the same people. Their characters, however, differ drastically. The father is gallant, generous, honorable, charming. The son is mean, cold, calculating, cowardly. The father's temperament is natural and open. The son's is contrived and devious, corrupted by decadent society. As always with Tolstoy, he gives his allegiance to the authentic and intuitive, while sardonically scorning the artificial and scheming.

***Family Happiness*** • In *Family Happiness*, Tolstoy treats a problem to which he was to return throughout his career: the place of women, both at home and in society. He had courted a much younger and very pretty girl, Valerya Arseneva, but had become irritated by her fondness for high society and had broken off the relationship. He transforms the experience into a narrative by the young woman, Masha, in the fashion of Charlotte Brontë's novel *Jane Eyre* (1847), which he had read and admired. Now married and a mother, Masha recalls, in the story's first half, her courtship by a man who knew her dead father, considered himself her guardian as she grew up, and was thirty-five to her seventeen when they married. Tolstoy magnificently captures the rapturous chemistry of first love as the girl awakens to womanhood. By the story's second half, however, he undermines her dreams of romantic happiness as she becomes addicted to the whirl of urban high society, driving her husband into rural retreat and seclusion. Toward the end, at home in the country after disillusionments in the city, she and he agree to a different sort of marriage than they envisioned at its start, basing it not on passion but on companionship and parenthood. Tolstoy has here sounded some of his most pervasive notes: Sophistication is evil, simplicity is good; the city is decadent, the country is healthy; and romance is dangerous, often a "charming nonsense," while marriage, though a necessary institution, should never be sentimentalized.

**"Strider"** • The story now called "Kholstomer" ("Strider") was originally translated into English as "Kholstomer: The Story of a Horse," because Tolstoy modeled his equine, first-person narrator on a horse by that name celebrated for his enormous stride and speed. The author humanizes his outcast animal, which is consistently stigmatized as a piebald and a gelding, in a keenly compassionate manner, with Strider's sorrowful life made a parable of protest against unjust punishment of those who are somehow different. "He was old, they were young. He was lean, they were sleek; he was miserable, they were gay; and so he was quite alien to them, an outsider, an utterly different creature whom it was impossible for them to pity." Strider's victimization by greedy, selfish owners enables Tolstoy to lash the evils of private property, using an equine perspective to expose its immorality.

The second phase of Tolstoy's production of short fiction follows his two great novels and the tremendous spiritual crisis chronicled in *A Confession*. It was an extremely profound change for an author. The sublime artist comes to repudiate almost all art; the nobleman now lives like a peasant; the wealthy, titled country gentleman seeks to abandon his property, preaching humility and asceticism; the marvelous novelist and story writer prefers the roles of educational reformer, religious leader, social sage, cultural prophet. Yet Tolstoy's artistic instincts refuse to atrophy, and he manages to create different yet also masterful works, less happy and conventional, uncompromising, sometimes perverse, always powerful, preoccupied with purity, corruption, sin, sex, and death. His late stories express his Rousseauistic hostility to such institutions as the state, which forces citizens to pay taxes and serve in the military; the church, which coerces its communicants by fear and superstition; private property, whereby one person owns another; and modern art, which is elitist. The creative gold nevertheless continues to flow from Tolstoy's pen, despite his moralistic resistance to aesthetics, in such novellas as *The Death of Ivan Ilyich*, *The Kreutzer Sonata*, and the story "Master and Man."

**The Death of Ivan Ilyich** • *The Death of Ivan Ilyich,* perhaps his finest story, was Tolstoy's first published work after his conversion. It is more schematic and deliberate than the earlier tales, more selective and condensed in the choice of descriptive and analytic detail. It is a parable of a life badly lived, with Tolstoy here allying his highest art with an exigent passion for establishing the most profound and encompassing truths.

Ivan Ilyich is a cautious, correct, typical representative of his social class. He has achieved success in his profession of judge, in love, in marriage, in his family, and in his friendships, or so appearances indicate. Yet when he reviews his past, confronted with the inescapability of a cancer-ridden death, he slowly arrives at the realization that he has led a life of selfishness, shallowness, smugness, and hypocrisy. Significantly, his surname, Golovin, is derived from the Russian word for "head." He has excluded any deep feelings, as he has lived according to principles of pleasantness and propriety, conforming to the values of his upper-middle-class social sphere in his striving for status, materialism, bureaucratic impersonality and power, decorous appearance, and pleasure.

In part 1, which begins with the announcement of Ivan Ilyich's death, Tolstoy's tone is caustically satiric. Ivan's wife/widow, Praskovya Fedorovna, defines the nature of his loveless home life, grieving formally for her loss and accepting colleagues' condolences while really concerned with the cost of the grave site and the possibility of increasing her widow's pension. Ivan Ilyich, however, deserves no better. He is shown as a prisoner of his cherished possessions who wanted Praskovya primarily for her property, secondarily for her correct social position and good looks. The density of things dominates Ivan Ilyich's feelings and conduct, pain and pleasure, happiness and misery. His highest moment comes with the furnishing of a new house; and his fall comes from reaching to hang a drape when he is on a ladder. Symbolically, his fall is one from pride and vanity.

The physicians enter to examine Ivan Ilyich's bruised side. They pursue their profession much as he does, from behind well-mannered, ritualistic masks. Ivan Ilyich soon discovers that not only his doctors but also his wife, daughter, colleagues, and friends all refuse him the empathy and compassion that he increasingly needs; they act on the same principle of self-interested pleasure that he has followed. As his physical suffering grows, he experiences the emotional stages that modern psychology accepts as characteristic of responses to lingering terminal illness: denial, loneliness, anger, despondency, and, finally, acceptance. He begins to drop his protective disguises and to realize that his existence has consisted of evasions of self-knowledge, of love, of awareness of the deepest needs of others. His fall into the abyss of death thus brings him to spiritual birth.

At the nadir of Ivan Ilyich's suffering, partial grace comes to him through the care of his servant, Gerasim. He is, like Platon Karataev in *War and Peace*, one of those simple, spontaneous, kindly souls whom Tolstoy venerates. In contrast to the sterile pretensions of Ivan Ilyich's social circle, Gerasim, modest and strong, personifies the Tolstoyan principle of living for others. He is in every sense a "breath of fresh air," showing his master unstinting compassion as he exemplifies the health of youth and naturally loving behavior.

Inspired by Gerasim's devotion, Ivan Ilyich becomes capable of extending compassion to his wife and son. When his condition takes a final, fatal turn, as he feels himself slowly sucked into the bottom of death's sack, he comes to the realization that his life has been trivial, empty, worthless. Two hours before his death, he stops trying to justify it and instead takes pity on his wife, son, and himself. He dies loving rather than hating, forgiving rather than whining, at last surrendering his egoism. Both the story and Ivan Ilyich's life thus end on a note of serenity and joyous illumination. Tolstoy shows that profound consciousness of death can bring one to the communion of true brotherhood. Through his relentless pain, Ivan Ilyich discovers the truth about himself, akin to Prince Andrey in *War and Peace.*

**The Kreutzer Sonata** • *The Kreutzer Sonata,* like *The Death of Ivan Ilyich,* is a condensed masterpiece of harrowing intensity, a poem of the poignant pains of the flesh. Tolstoy presents the nature of marriage more directly and comprehensively than any other writer. In *Family Happiness,* he tries to define its benefits and banes; in *War and Peace,* he celebrates it; in *Anna Karenina,* he upholds yet also questions it; in *The Kreutzer Sonata,* he denounces it vehemently. Though he previously advocated marriage as the morally and socially legitimate release for sexual needs, by the late 1880's, his new views on morality, as well as his own increasingly burdensome marriage, caused him to equate sexuality with hostility and sinfulness and to regard sexual passion as degrading, undermining human beings' spiritual self.

The novella's protagonist, Pozdnyshev, confesses on a train journey that he murdered his wife on suspicion—groundless, as circumstances indicate—of her adultery with an amateur violinist with whom she, a pianist, enjoyed playing duets—such as Ludwig van Beethoven's "Kreutzer Sonata." In the spring of 1888, a performance of this work did take place in Tolstoy's Moscow residence. He proposed to the great realistic painter also present, Ilya Repin, that the artist should paint a canvas, while he would write a story, on the theme of marital jealousy. Although Tolstoy fulfilled the bargain, Repin did not. The tale was submitted to the state censor in 1888; Czar Alexander III, who read a copy, issued an imperial banning order. Sonya Tolstoy thereupon removed some of the story's sexual explicitness, and the czar permitted its publication, in bowdlerized form, in 1891. Not until the 1933 Jubilee Edition of Tolstoy's works was the text issued in its original form. Yet even in its toned-down version, it aroused a storm of controversy among readers.

Pozdnyshev relates his conduct to a lightly sketched narrator. His dramatic monologue is powerful and polemical, although his arguments are often exaggerated and inconsistent. The point of his narrative is that sex is sinful, that those who submit to its drives often become vicious and, in Pozdnyshev's case, murderous. Even in marriage, the protagonist insists, sex is ugly, repulsive, and destructive. Despite the deranged character of Pozdnyshev and the manifest injustice of many of his views, the story is disturbing, forceful, and gripping, as he shows how his sexual lust degraded his character and ruined his marriage. Some critics have interpreted the structure of the tale as equivalent to the sonata form, falling into three movements with a slow introduction and the final chapter as a coda. Tolstoy was himself an accomplished pianist.

In a long, uncompromising afterword to the story, Tolstoy addresses the controversy it caused and clearly links Pozdnyshev's views—but not his pathological personality—to his. He argues that carnal love lowers human beings to animalistic conduct, advocates chastity within as well as outside marriage, denounces society for featuring erotic allure, and dismisses marriage itself as a trap for humanity's finest energies. Men and women should replace conjugal relations "with the pure relations that exist between a brother and a sister." Only thus would they behave as true Christians. Tolstoy thus dismisses sex as relevant—let alone fundamental—to human behavior.

Rather, he regards it as a diabolic temptation sent to divert human beings' purpose from seeking the kingdom of God on earth.

**"Master and Man"** • In his moralistic monograph, *What Is Art?*, Tolstoy asks for writing that is easily understandable, whose subject matter is religious, situations universal, style simple, and technique accessible. None of his successful works embodies these criteria more faithfully than "Master and Man," which is essentially a morality play based on the New Testament. The master is Vasíli Andréevich Brekhunov: selfish, overbearing, coarse, rich, rapacious, the biblical gatherer of wealth who neglects his soul. The servant is Nikíta, a reformed drunkard, who is humane, sensitive, skilled in his work, strong, meek, kindly, rich in spirit though poor in pocket. The contrast between them is stark, with Tolstoy stressing the unambiguous and heavily symbolic nature of the novella: two opposed sorts of men, two opposed sets of moral values, and the conversion of the master to the ethics of his man. The man of flesh and the man of spirit join in the journey of life and the confrontation with death.

Brekhunov, a merchant proud of his ability to drive a hard bargain, sets off with Nikíta on a business trip to make a down payment on a grove. He can consider nothing but his possessions and how to increase them; his relationships to others are governed by materialistic calculations. On their trip, the pair find themselves immersed in a raging snowstorm, which obliterates all landmarks and turns the landscape into a perilous Wood of Error, a moral Wasteland, through which they must make life's passage. Tolstoy masterfully uses the storm for its emblematic qualities. It "buries" the travelers in snowdrifts, is cold like death, turns the substantial into the spectral and vice versa. They lose their way as Brekhunov insists on movements to the left, since men find their reward only on the right hand of God. As Brekhunov urges his horse away from the sled, after having (temporarily) deserted Nikíta, he can only come around in a circle to the same spot, marked by wormwood stalks—wormwood being identified with sin and punishment in Revelation. He is ritualistically confronted with himself in the person of a horse thief, for Brekhunov has been cheating Nikíta of his wages and has stolen a large sum of money from his church to buy the grove.

Nikíta accepts his master's wrong turns without anger or reproof, resigns himself to the snowstorm, and patiently prepares to wait it out when they are forced to settle down for the night in their sled. Around midnight, ill-clad and half-frozen, meekly awaiting likely death before morning, Nikíta asks his master to give the wages owed him to his family and to "Forgive me for Christ's sake!" Finally, moved to pity by Nikíta's words, Brekhunov opens his heavy fur coat and lies down on top of his servant, covering Nikíta with both his coat and body as he sobs.

Just before dawn Brekhunov has a visionary dream, in which "it seemed to him that he was Nikíta and Nikíta was he, and that his life was not in himself but in Nikíta." He wonders why he used to trouble himself so greatly to accumulate money and possessions. At noon the next day, peasants drag both men out of the snow. Brekhunov is frozen to death; Nikíta, though chilled, is alive.

Some critics have faulted the story's ending because Tolstoy has inadequately prepared the reader for Brekhunov's sudden adoption of Christian humility, brotherhood, and self-sacrifice, since he has previously shown not the slightest inclination toward moral regeneration. Be that as it may, most of the tale is enormously impressive in the power of its sensuous description as the snowstorm isolates the couple from ordinary existence, strips them of external comforts, exposes them to the presence of death, forces them to encounter their inmost selves.

Tolstoy's celebration of Brekhunov's redemption through fellowship is his answer to a universe that he has feared all of his life as he confronts the horror of nonexistence conveyed by death. Master and man—or man and man, or man and woman—should cling to each other, love each other, forgive each other. Will such conduct vault their souls into immortality? Tolstoy desperately hopes so.

*Gerhard Brand*

## Other major works

CHILDREN'S LITERATURE: *Azbuka*, 1872; *Novaya azbuka*, 1875 (*Stories for My Children*, 1988); *Russkie knigi dlya chteniya*, 1875; *Classic Tales and Fables for Children*, 2002 (includes selections from *Azbuka* and *Novaya azbuka*).

PLAYS: *Vlast tmy*, pb. 1887 (*The Power of Darkness*, 1888); *Plody prosveshcheniya*, pr. 1889 (*The Fruits of Enlightenment*, 1891); *I svet vo tme svetit*, pb. 1911 (*The Light Shines in Darkness*, 1923); *Zhivoy trup*, pr., pb. 1911 (*The Live Corpse*, 1919); *The Dramatic Works*, pb. 1923.

NOVELS: *Detstvo*, 1852 (*Childhood*, 1862); *Otrochestvo*, 1854 (*Boyhood*, 1886); *Yunost'*, 1857 (*Youth*, 1886); *Semeynoye schast'ye*, 1859 (*Family Happiness*, 1888); *Kazaki*, 1863 (*The Cossacks*, 1872); *Voyna i mir*, 1865-1869 (*War and Peace*, 1886); *Anna Karenina*, 1875-1877 (English translation, 1886); *Smert' Ivana Il'icha*, 1886 (*The Death of Ivan Ilyich*, 1887); *Kreytserova sonata*, 1889 (*The Kreutzer Sonata*, 1890); *Voskreseniye*, 1899 (*Resurrection*, 1899); *Khadzi-Murat*, wr. 1904, pb. 1911 (*Hadji Murad*, 1911).

MISCELLANEOUS: *The Complete Works of Count Tolstoy*, 1904-1905 (24 volumes); *Polnoye sobraniye sochinenii*, 1928-1958 (90 volumes); *Tolstoy Centenary Edition*, 1928-1937 (21 volumes).

NONFICTION: *Ispoved'*, 1884 (*A Confession*, 1885); *V chom moya vera*, 1884 (*What I Believe*, 1885); *O zhizni*, 1888 (*Life*, 1888); *Kritika dogmaticheskogo bogosloviya*, 1891 (*A Critique of Dogmatic Theology*, 1904); *Soedinenie i perevod chetyrekh evangeliy*, 1892-1894 (*The Four Gospels Harmonized and Translated*, 1895-1896); *Tsarstvo Bozhie vnutri vas*, 1893 (*The Kingdom of God Is Within You*, 1894); *Chto takoye iskusstvo?*, 1898 (*What Is Art?*, 1898); *Tak chto zhe nam delat?*, 1902 (*What to Do?*, 1887); *O Shekspire i o drame*, 1906 (*Shakespeare and the Drama*, 1906); *The Diaries of Leo Tolstoy, 1847-1852*, 1917; *The Journal of Leo Tolstoy, 1895-1899*, 1917; *Tolstoi's Love Letters*, 1923; *The Private Diary of Leo Tolstoy, 1853-1857*, 1927; "*What Is Art?*" *and Essays on Art*, 1929; *L. N. Tolstoy o literature: Stati, pisma, dnevniki*, 1955; *Lev Tolstoy ob iskusstve i literature*, 1958; *Last Diaries*, 1960.

## Bibliography

Bayley, John. *Leo Tolstoy*. Plymouth, England: Northcote House, 1997. Criticism and interpretation of Tolstoy's work.

Bloom, Harold, ed. *Leo Tolstoy*. New York: Chelsea House, 1986. Collection of critical essays. The views expressed give a good sampling of the wide range of opinions about Tolstoy prevalent among Western critics. Many of these critics assign a prominent place in literary history to Tolstoy, comparing him to, among others, Homer and Johann Wolfgang von Goethe. Includes bibliography.

Gustafson, Richard F. *Leo Tolstoy, Resident and Stranger: A Study in Fiction and Theology*. Princeton, N.J.: Princeton University Press, 1986. Gustafson seeks to rescue Tolstoy from those who would classify him solely as a realist. By focusing on what he sees as the inherently and uniquely Russian attributes of Tolstoy's writing, Gustafson re-unites the preconversion artist and the postconversion religious thinker and prophet. The study's bibliography is divided between books devoted to Tolstoy and those focusing on Eastern Christian thought.

Jahn, Gary R. *The Death of Ivan Ilich: An Interpretation.* New York: Twayne, 1993. After providing a summary and critique of previous criticism on Tolstoy's most famous story, Jahn examines the context of the story within other works by Tolstoy to ar-gue that the story is an affirmation of life rather than a document of despair.

May, Charles E., ed. *Masterplots II: Short Story Series, Revised Edition.* 8 vols. Pasadena, Calif.: Salem Press, 2004. Designed for student use, this reference set contains articles providing detailed plot summaries and analyses of eight short stories by Tolstoy: "Alyosha the Pot" (vol. 1); "The Death of Ivan Ilyich" (vol. 2); "How Much Land Does a Man Need?" (vol. 4); "Master and Man" (vol. 5); "The Raid: A Volun-teer's Story" (vol. 6); and "The Snow-Storm," "Three Deaths," and "The Three Hermits" (vol. 7).

Orwin, Donna Tussig. *Tolstoy's Art and Thought, 1847-1880.* Princeton, N.J.: Princeton University Press, 1993. Divided into three parts, which coincide with the first three decades of Tolstoy's literary career, Orwin's study attempts to trace the origins and growth of the Russian master's ideas. After focusing on Tolstoy's initial cre-ative vision, Orwin goes on to analyze, in depth, his principal works.

Seifrid, Thomas. "Gazing on Life's Page: Perspectival Vision in Tolstoy." *PMLA* 113 (May, 1998): 436-448. Suggests that the typical visual situation in Tolstoy's fiction is perspectival; argues that Tolstoy's impulse can be linked with the material na-ture of books and that this linkage has implications for Russian culture as well as for the relation between the verbal and the visual in general.

Smoluchowski, Louise. *Lev and Sonya: The Story of the Tolstoy Marriage.* New York: G. P. Putnam's Sons, 1987. With the publication of Sonya Tolstoy's diaries it became ap-parent that in order to understand Tolstoy, it is necessary to understand his mar-riage to the extraordinary Sonya. Smoluchowski does a good job of retelling the story, relying mainly on the words of the principals themselves.

Steiner, George. *Tolstoy or Dostoevsky: An Essay in the Old Criticism.* 2d ed. New Haven, Conn.: Yale University Press, 1996. This welcome reappearance of a classic study of the epic versus the dramatic, first published in 1959, carries only a new preface. In it, however, Steiner makes a compelling case for the reprinting, in the age of deconstructionism, of this wide-ranging study not just of individual texts, but of contrasting worldviews.

Wasiolek, Edward. *Tolstoy's Major Fiction.* Chicago: University of Chicago Press, 1978. Having written a superb study of Fyodor Dostoevski's fiction, Wasiolek has com-posed an equally first-rate critique of Tolstoy's. He concentrates on thorough anal-yses of ten Tolstoyan works, including *Family Happiness, The Death of Ivan Ilyich,* and "Master and Man." His is a close and acute reading, influenced by Russian Formalists and by Roland Barthes. A twenty-page chronicle of Tolstoy's life and work is illuminating.

# William Trevor

**Born:** Mitchelstown, County Cork, Ireland; May 24, 1928

**Principal short fiction** • *The Day We Got Drunk on Cake, and Other Stories*, 1967; *The Ballroom of Romance, and Other Stories*, 1972; *The Last Lunch of the Season*, 1973; *Angels at the Ritz, and Other Stories*, 1975; *Lovers of Their Time, and Other Stories*, 1978; *Beyond the Pale, and Other Stories*, 1981; *The Stories of William Trevor*, 1983; *The News from Ireland, and Other Stories*, 1986; *Family Sins, and Other Stories*, 1990; *Collected Stories*, 1992; *Ireland: Selected Stories*, 1995; *Marrying Damian*, 1995 (limited edition); *Outside Ireland: Selected Stories*, 1995; *After Rain*, 1996; *The Hill Bachelors*, 2000; *A Bit on the Side*, 2004; *Dressmaker's Child*, 2005; *Cheating at Canasta*, 2007.

**Other literary forms** • Though probably best known as a writer of short stories, William Trevor has also written television and radio scripts, plays, and numerous novels. Among his novels, *The Old Boys, Miss Gomez and the Brethren, Elizabeth Alone* (1973), *The Children of Dynmouth* (1976), *Fools of Fortune* (1983), *Felicia's Journey* (1994), and *Death in Summer* (1998) have been particularly praised. He has also written two nonfiction works, *A Writer's Ireland: Landscape in Literature* (1984) and *Excursions in the Real World* (1993). His productivity has continued, unabated, into his seventies. In addition to publishing four new collections of short stories after reaching that age, he has published three more novels: *Death in Summer* (1998), *The Story of Lucy Gault* (2002), and *My House in Umbria* (2003).

**Achievements** • William Trevor is widely regarded as one of the finest storytellers and craftsmen writing in English. In Great Britain, his work has long been widely and favorably reviewed and has frequently been adapted for radio and television broadcast by the British Broadcasting Corporation. In 1964, Trevor's second novel, *The Old Boys*, was awarded the Hawthornden Prize; his fourth collection, *Angels at the Ritz, and Other Stories*, was hailed by writer Graham Greene as "one of the finest collections, if not the best, since James Joyce's *Dubliners.*" In addition, Trevor has won the Royal Society of Literature Award, the Allied Irish Banks' Prize for Literature, and the Whitbread Literary Award; he is also a member of the Irish Academy of Letters. In 1979, "in recognition for his valuable services to literature," Trevor was named an honorary Commander, Order of the British Empire and in the same year received the Irish Community Prize. In 1980 and 1982, he received the Giles Cooper Award for radio plays; in 1983, he received a Jacob Award for a teleplay. He received D.Litt. degrees from the University of Exeter, Trinity College in Dublin, the University of Belfast, and the National University of Ireland in Cork. Trevor received the Sunday Express Book of the Year Award in 1994 for *Felicia's Journey*. In the United States, knowledge of Trevor's work increased markedly when *The Stories of William Trevor*, an omnibus collection, was published in 1983 and received wide and highly enthusiastic reviews.

**Biography** • The son of a bank manager, William Trevor was born William Trevor Cox in Ireland's County Cork. He spent much of his childhood living in small Irish towns and attending a series of boarding and day schools that included St. Columba's in Dublin. After earning a bachelor's degree in history from Dublin's Trinity College, Trevor, a Protestant, began work as a sculptor and schoolmaster, taking his first job as an instructor of history in Armagh, Northern Ireland. In 1952, Trevor married Jane Ryan and moved to England, where he spent the next eight years teaching art at two prestigious public schools—first at Rugby and then at Taunton. Between 1960 and 1965, Trevor worked as a copywriter at an advertising agency in London; he simultaneously began devoting an increasing portion of his free time to the writing of fiction. By the early 1970's, following the appearance of several novels and a steady stream of stories in such publications as *Encounter, The New Yorker,* and *London Magazine,* Trevor's reputation was secure. The father of two sons, Trevor settled in Devon and continued to write full time.

**Analysis** • Like his novels, William Trevor's short stories generally take place in either England or the Republic of Ireland. For the most part, Trevor focuses on middle-class or lower-middle-class figures whose lives have been characterized by loneliness, disappointment, and pain. His stories feature tight organization and lean but detailed prose. Their very "average" characters are made interesting by Trevor's careful attention to the traits and quirks that make them individuals, to the memories and regrets they have of the past. Trevor, often wry and always detached, refuses to sentimentalize any of them; he does not, however, subject them to ridicule. Their struggles reveal the author's deep curiosity about the manifold means by which people foil themselves or, more rarely, manage not to do so. Many of Trevor's characters are trapped in jobs or familial circumstances that are dull or oppressive or both; many retreat frequently to fond memories or romantic fantasies. Trevor rarely mocks the men and women who inhabit his fiction, nor does he treat them as mere ciphers or automatons. In fact, like James Joyce, to whom he is often compared, Trevor assumes a detached authorial stance, but occasionally and subtly he makes it clear that he is highly sympathetic to the plight of underdogs, self-deluders, and the victims of abuse and deceit. Invariably, his principal characters are carefully and completely drawn—and so are the worlds they inhabit. Few contemporary writers of short fiction can render atmosphere and the subtleties of personality as precisely and as tellingly as William Trevor. Few can capture so accurately and wittily the rhythms and nuances of everyday speech. Though its themes can be somber and settings quite bleak, Trevor's brilliantly paced and carefully sculpted fiction consistently moves, amuses, and invigorates.

**"The General's Day"** • One of Trevor's earliest stories, "The General's Day," illustrates with particular clarity the darkest side of his artistic vision. Contained in *The Day We Got Drunk on Cake, and Other Stories,* "The General's Day" centers on a decorated and now-retired military man who, at the age of seventy-eight, has never quite come to grips with his retirement and so spends his days wandering around the local village looking for something to do. On the day of the story, a sunny Saturday in June, General Suffolk greets the day with energy and resolution but ends by simply killing time in the local tea shop, where he musters what is left of his once-celebrated charm and manages to persuade a woman—"a thin, middle-aged person with a face like a faded photograph"—to join him for drinks at the local hotel. There, fueled by gin, General Suffolk flirts so blatantly and clumsily with the woman that she flees, "her face like a beetroot." Fueled by more gin, the lonely man becomes increasingly obnoxious. After suffering a few more rejections and humiliations, he finally stumbles back home, where he is mocked further by his "unreliable servant," Mrs. Hinch, a crude woman who habitually cuts corners and treats herself to secretive swigs of the general's expensive South African sherry. In the story's final scene, General Suffolk, "the hero of Roeux and Monchy-le-Preux," is shown leaning and weeping on his cleaning woman's fat arm as she laughingly helps him back to his cottage. "My God Almighty," General Suffolk, deflated, mutters, "I could live for twenty years."

**"An Evening with John Joe Dempsey"** • Trevor often portrays older men and women who make stoic adjustments to the present while living principally in the past. He also sometimes focuses on children and adolescents who use vividly constructed daydreams as a means of escaping dreary surroundings or obtuse parents who are themselves sunk in the deadness of their cramped and predictable lives. In "An Evening with John Joe Dempsey," from *The Ballroom of Romance, and Other Stories*, Trevor's central figure is a boy of fifteen who lives in a small house in a small Irish town where, daily, he sits in a dull classroom in preparation for a dead-end job at the nearby sawmills. John Joe lives with his widowed mother, a wiry, chronically worried woman, whose principal interest in life is to hover protectively about her only son. John Joe escapes his mother's smothering solicitations by wandering about the town with Quigley, a rather elderly dwarf reputed to be, as one local puts it, "away in the head." Quigley likes to fire John Joe's already active imagination by regaling the boy with detailed descriptions of the sexual vignettes he claims to have witnessed while peeping through area windows. In his own daydreams, John Joe dallies with many of the same sizable matrons whom Quigley likes to portray in compromising positions. One of them, Mrs. Taggart, "the wife of a postman," is a tall, "well-built" woman who in John Joe's fantasies requires repeated rescuing from a locked bathroom in which she stands unblushingly nude. Like many of Trevor's characters, John Joe is thus a convincing mix of the comic and the pathetic. If his incongruous sexual fantasies are humorous, the rest of his life looks decidedly grim. In the story's particularly effective closing scene, Trevor portrays John Joe in his bed, in the dark, thinking again of impossible erotic romps with wholly unobtainable women, feeling

> more alive than ever he was at the Christian Brothers' School . . . or his mother's kitchen, more alive than ever he would be at the sawmills. In his bed he entered a paradise: it was grand being alone.

**"Nice Day at School"** • In "Nice Day at School," from the same collection, Trevor's principal character is a girl of fourteen, Eleanor, who lives on a housing estate with her cranky, chain-smoking mother and her father, a former professional wrestler who now works as a nightclub bouncer and likes to claim that his work has made him the trusted friend of many celebrities, including Rex Harrison, Mia Farrow, Princess Margaret, and Anthony Armstrong-Jones. Though Eleanor is embarrassed by her father's obviously exaggerated accounts of his encounters with the rich and famous, she is much given to vivid imaginings of her own. Bombarded daily by saccharine pop songs and the more blatantly sexual chatter of her friends, Eleanor thinks obsessively of her ideal lover:

> a man whose fingers were long and thin and gentle, who'd hold her hand in the aeroplane. Air France to Biarritz. And afterwards she'd come back to a flat where the curtains were the colour of lavender, the same as the walls, where gas fires glowed and there were rugs on natural-wood floors, and the telephone was pale blue.

Subtly, however, Trevor indicates that Eleanor is not likely to find a lover so wealthy and suave. Like her friends and most girls of the same social class, this daughter of a bloated bouncer and a bored, gin-sipping housewife will instead settle for someone like Denny Price, the young butcher's apprentice with "blubbery" lips, who once moved his rough hand up and down her body "like an animal, a rat gnawing at her, prodding her and poking."

**"Office Romances"** • Trevor often focuses on women who find themselves pursued by or entangled with insensitive or calculating men. In "Office Romances," from *Angels at the Ritz, and Other Stories,* Trevor's central character is Angela Hosford, a typist who works quite anonymously in a large London office appointed with "steel-framed reproductions" and "ersatz leather" sofas and chairs. At the age of twenty-six, Angela is pleasant but plain and myopic: She wears contact lenses that give her eyes a slightly "bulgy look." Her pursuer, Gordon Spelle, is, at thirty-eight, tall and "sleek," but his left eyelid droops a bit, and the eye it covers is badly glazed. While watching old films on television when she was fourteen, Angela developed a crush on the American actor Don Ameche and had imagined "a life with him in a cliff-top home she'd invented, in California." Now, she finds herself drawn to the deliberately "old fashioned" Spelle and at one point imagines herself "stroking his face and comforting him because of his bad eye." One day, after his flatteries succeed in rendering Angela both "generous and euphoric," Spelle manages to lure her into a dark and empty office, where—muttering "I love you," repeatedly—he makes love to her, inelegantly, on the floor. Angela finds this experience "not even momentarily pleasurable, not once," but afterward she basks in the memory of Spelle's heated professions of love. Angela eventually takes a job elsewhere, convinced that Spelle's passion for her "put him under a strain, he being married to a wife who was ill." Like many of Trevor's characters, she understandably decides not to look past her comforting delusions; she refuses to accept the well-known fact that Spelle was "notorious" and "chose girls who were unattractive because he believed such girls, deprived of sex for long periods of time, were an easier bet."

**"Lovers of Their Time"** • The vast gulf that often separates romantic fantasy from unsavory fact is similarly revealed in the title story of *Lovers of Their Time, and Other Stories.* In this piece, set in the 1960's, Trevor's lovers are Norman Britt, a mild-mannered travel agent with "a David Niven moustache," and a young woman, Marie, who tends the counter at Green's the Chemist's. Norman and Marie meet regularly in one of Trevor's favorite fictional locations—a dark pub filled with a wide array of drinkers, talkers, and dreamers.

**"The Drummer Boy"** • In that same place, in "The Drummer Boy," the two listen to Beatles songs and talk of running away with each other to some romantic foreign country—an event they realize is not likely to materialize. Marie is single, but Norman is married to the loud and bawdy Hilda, who spends the better part of her life sipping cheap wine and watching police dramas on the television and who has previously hinted that she is quite content in the odd marital arrangement that Norman loathes. Thus, at Norman's instigation, the two lovers begin to rendezvous more intimately at the nearby hotel, the Great Western Royal. More specifically, they begin to sneak into a large, infrequently used bathroom, "done up in marble," on the hotel's second floor. Here, luxuriating in an enormous tub, they talk hopefully of happier days that, unfortunately, never arrive. Hilda dismisses her husband's request for a divorce by telling him, "You've gone barmy, Norman"; Marie, tired of waiting, weds "a man in a brewery." Thus, as the years pass, Norman is left with a nostalgic longing not only for Marie but also for that brief period in the 1960's when playful risk-taking was much in the air. Often, while riding "the tube" to work, Norman

> would close his eyes and with the greatest pleasure that remained to him he would recall the delicately veined marble and the great brass taps, and the bath that was big enough for two. And now and again he heard what happened to be the sound of distant music, and the voices of the Beatles celebrating a bathroom love, as they had celebrated Eleanor Rigby and other people of that time.

**"Flights of Fancy"** • This allusion to a popular and bittersweet Beatles song is especially appropriate in yet another Trevor story about two thoroughly average and lonely people whose lives have not often been marked by episodes of great passion. In "Flights of Fancy," also from *Lovers of Their Time, and Other Stories*, Trevor's principal character, Sarah Machaen, is yet another Rigby-like character destined, one assumes, to spend the rest of her life uneasily alone. Sarah, a clergyman's daughter, is an executive secretary in a large London firm that manufactures lamps; she visits museums, sings in a Bach choir, and is "a popular choice as a godmother." Well into middle age, Sarah is quite content with the externals of her life and gradually has become "reconciled to the fact that her plainness wasn't going to go away." Sometimes, however, she gets lonely enough to daydream of marriage—perhaps to an elderly widower or a blind man. Ironically, the one person who does express a romantic interest in Sarah is another woman, a young and pretty but unschooled factory worker called Sandra Pond. Sarah is shocked at the very idea of lesbianism, yet she cannot stop her mind from "throwing up flights of fancy" in which she pictures herself sharing her flat with Sandra and introducing her to London's many cultural delights. Though her shyness and acute sense of propriety prompt her to reject Sandra's clumsy but clearly genuine professions of love, Sarah is haunted by the sense that she has perhaps passed up her last chance for passion and romance.

**"Broken Homes"** • "Broken Homes," also from *Lovers of Their Time, and Other Stories*, is one of Trevor's most powerful stories. Its principal character, Mrs. Malby, lives with her two budgerigars in a little flat that is scrupulously neat and prettily painted. Mrs. Malby, a widow, lost both of her sons thirty years earlier during World War II; now, at the age of eighty-seven, she has come to terms with her own impending death and wants nothing more than to spend her remaining days in familiar surroundings, her faculties intact. Unfortunately, Mrs. Malby's flat is destroyed and her serenity threatened by a squad of loud and insensitive teenagers from a nearby comprehensive school—"an ugly sprawl of glass and concrete buildings," Mrs. Malby recalls, full of "children swinging along the pavements, shouting obscenities." As part of a community relations scheme, the teenagers have been equipped with mops and sponges and brushes and sent out into the neighborhood in search of good deeds to perform. Mrs. Malby politely asks these obnoxious adolescents to do nothing more than wash her walls, but they treat her with condescension and contempt, and while she is out, they proceed to make a complete mess of her apartment, splattering its walls and floors with bright yellow paint. The students' "teacher," an obtuse and "untidily dressed" bureaucrat, patronizingly assures Mrs. Malby that the damage is slight.

He reminds her that, in any event, one must make allowances for the children of "broken homes."

Perhaps more than any of his other stories, "Broken Homes" reveals Trevor's sympathy for the plight of the elderly and his acute awareness of the infirmities and insecurities that accompany old age. The story certainly reveals a strong suspicion that, by the mid-1970's, the British welfare state had become both inefficient and rudely intrusive. Indeed, "Broken Homes" is informed by the subtly expressed sense—not uncommon in Trevor's later fiction—that contemporary Great Britain and Ireland have grown increasingly crass and tacky and that the old social fabric is rapidly unraveling.

**"The Paradise Lounge"** • Arguably, "The Paradise Lounge," from *Beyond the Pale, and Other Stories*, is Trevor's most representative story. Set principally in the small bar of Keegan's Railway hotel, in "a hilly provincial town" in the Republic of Ireland, "The Paradise Lounge" shifts its focus between two recognizably Trevoresque figures. One of them, Beatrice, is thirty-two; the other, Miss Doheny, is in her eighties. Beatrice—who wanted to be an actor once—drives often to Keegan's and its adjoining Paradise Lounge to rendezvous with her lover, a middle-aged businessman already married. Miss Doheny, one of the locals, goes regularly to the lounge for a bit of company and several good, stiff drinks. The two have never formally met. Yet Beatrice—observing Miss Doheny from across the room—is convinced that the old woman is an intriguing figure with a fascinating and no doubt satisfyingly romantic past; she does not realize that Miss Doheny is not only lonely but also full of anger and regret. Miss Doheny, in turn, envies Beatrice's freedom—her ability, in a more liberated and enlightened age, to enter into a friendly sexual affair without running the risk of paralyzing guilt and ostracism. She does not realize that the younger woman's affair has grown stale and mechanical and that by her own estimation Beatrice is about to engage in nothing more than a "mess of deception and lies."

*After Rain* • The twelve stories of *After Rain* concern how marriage and family ties constrain, bewilder, confound, or, occasionally, help their characters. For instance, a woman's attempt to invigorate the life of her best friend by encouraging an affair ends the friendship; a young man refuses to visit his parents for his birthday because he is jealous of their deep love for each other; a pregnant young woman is forced to marry a man she hardly knows to save the family reputation; a barren wife spends her days drinking herself insensate while fantasizing about her husband's mistress; a Protestant family shrinks in shame when one son claims that a dead Roman Catholic saint has visited him; a retired couple is helpless and dismayed when an old friend, a hopeless reprobate, courts their daughter. As in Trevor's earlier volumes, the central characters, however muddled in their behavior, usually learn some truth about themselves or recognize a fundamental change in their lives. The tone is taut but not judgmental; the reader is invited to share their emotions rather than laugh at or deplore their plight. The imagery of home, religion, and occupation frequently invests commonplace dramas with broad moral power.

In "The Piano Tuner's Wife," the opening story, a blind piano tuner remarries after his first wife dies. Violet, the second wife, was rejected decades earlier when the piano tuner married her rival, Belle. Now Violet at last succeeds but finds that Belle's memory and style of managing the husband's affairs haunts the marriage at every turn. Violet sets out to efface Belle by contradicting many of the things the first wife told their husband about the countryside and people around them. The piano tuner recognizes her conduct for what it is, self-assertion, and accepts it calmly. In his marriages, as in his work, he seeks harmony. In the title story, "After Rain," Harriet has fled to an Italian resort because of a failed love affair, the same resort that her parents took her to as a child. In the sweltering heat, she feels oppressed by her life. The reader learns of her astonished shock, still disturbing her more than a decade later, at her parents' divorce; she has had previous promising love affairs that all fizzled inexplicably; she cannot be other than distant to her fellow vacationers. To relieve her tedium, she visits a nearby church. There a painting of the Annunciation, vividly colored and showing a rain-swept landscape in the background, lifts her out of her self-absorption. Meanwhile, a hard rain has broken the afternoon heat. Returning to the resort in the refreshing coolness, she suddenly sees her life in a new light, as if she has had an annunciation of her own. She realizes that she has frightened away her lovers by needing too much from love, a reaction to her parents' failed marriage. The annunciation is of her own solitude.

*Brian Murray*
*With updates by Roger Smith, Eugene S. Larson, and the Editors*

**Other major works**

PLAYS: *The Elephant's Foot*, pr. 1965; *The Girl*, pr. 1967 (televised), pr., pb. 1968 (staged); *A Night Mrs. da Tanka*, pr. 1968 (televised), pr., pb. 1972 (staged); *Going Home*, pr. 1970 (radio play), pr., pb. 1972 (staged); *The Old Boys*, pr., pb. 1971; *A Perfect Relationship*, pr. 1973; *Marriages*, pr. 1973; *The Fifty-seventh Saturday*, pr. 1973; *Scenes from an Album*, pr. 1975 (radio play), pr., pb. 1981 (staged).

ANTHOLOGY: *The Oxford Book of Irish Short Stories*, 1989.

NOVELS: *A Standard of Behaviour*, 1958; *The Old Boys*, 1964; *The Boarding-House*, 1965; *The Love Department*, 1966; *Mrs. Eckdorf in O'Neil's Hotel*, 1969; *Miss Gomez and the Brethren*, 1971; *Elizabeth Alone*, 1973; *The Children of Dynmouth*, 1976; *Other People's Worlds*, 1980; *Fools of Fortune*, 1983; *Nights at the Alexandra*, 1987; *The Silence in the Garden*, 1988; *Juliet's Story*, 1991; *Two Lives*, 1991; *Felicia's Journey*, 1994; *Death in Summer*, 1998; *The Story of Lucy Gault*, 2002; *My House in Umbria*, 2003.

NONFICTION: *A Writer's Ireland: Landscape in Literature*, 1984; *Excursions in the Real World*, 1993.

RADIO PLAYS: *Beyond the Pale*, 1980; *Autumn Sunshine*, 1982.

**Bibliography**

Bonaccorso, Richard. "William Trevor's Martyrs for Truth." *Studies in Short Fiction* 34 (Winter, 1997): 113-118. Discusses two types of Trevor characters: those who try to evade the truth and those who gravitate, often in spite of themselves, toward it; argues that the best indicators of the consistency of Trevor's moral vision may be his significant minority, those characters who find themselves pursuing rather than fleeing truth.

Gitzen, Julian. "The Truth-Tellers of William Trevor." *Critique: Studies in Modern Fiction* 21, no. 1 (1979): 59-72. Gitzen claims that most critics of Trevor's work have found it in the comedic tradition, sometimes dark and at other times more compassionate in its humor, but he argues that, if it is comic, it is also melancholic in its journey from "psychological truth" to "metaphysical mystery."

Haughey, Jim. "Joyce and Trevor's Dubliners: The Legacy of Colonialism." *Studies in Short Fiction* 32 (Summer, 1995): 355-365. Compares how James Joyce's "Two Gallants" and Trevor's "Two More Gallants" explore the complexities of Irish identity; argues that Trevor's story provides an updated commentary on the legacy of Ireland's colonial experience. Both stories reveal how Irish men, conditioned by colonization, are partly responsible for their sense of cultural alienation and inferiority.

MacKenna, Dolores. *William Trevor: The Writer and His Work.* Dublin: New Island, 1999. Offers some interesting biographical details; includes a bibliography and an index.

May, Charles E., ed. *Masterplots II: Short Story Series, Revised Edition.* 8 vols. Pasadena, Calif.: Salem Press, 2004. Designed for student use, this reference set contains articles providing detailed plot summaries and analyses of five short stories by Trevor: "Angels at the Ritz," "The Ballroom of Romance," and "Beyond the Pale" (vol. 1); "Death in Jerusalem" (vol. 2); and "Going Home" (vol. 3).

Morrison, Kristin. *William Trevor.* New York: Twayne, 1993. General introduction to Trevor's fiction, focusing on a conceptual "system of correspondences" often manifested in Trevor's work by a rhetorical strategy of "significant simultaneity" and a central metaphor of the Edenic garden. Through close readings of Trevor's major works, including such short stories as "Beyond the Pale" and "The News from Ireland," Morrison examines the overall unity of his fiction.

Paulson, Suzanne Morrow. *William Trevor: A Study of the Short Fiction.* New York: Twayne, 1993. This introduction to Trevor's stories examines four common themes from Freudianism to feminism: psychological shock, failed child/parent relationships, patriarchal repressiveness, and materialism in the modern world. Also contains an interview with Trevor and a number of short reviews of his stories.

Schiff, Stephen. "The Shadows of William Trevor." *The New Yorker* 68, no. 45 (December 28, 1992/January 4, 1993): 158-163. A profile of the writer and his works. Emphasizes Trevor's Irish heritage.

Schirmer, Gregory A. *William Trevor: A Study in His Fiction.* London: Routledge and Kegan Paul, 1990. One of the first full-length studies of Trevor's fictional writings. Schirmer notes the tension in Trevor's works between morality and the elements in contemporary society that make morality almost an impossibility, with lonely alienation the result. He also discusses Trevor as an outsider, both in Ireland and in England. An excellent study. Includes bibliographical references.

# Ivan Turgenev

**Born:** Orel, Russia; November 9, 1818
**Died:** Bougival, France; September 3, 1883

**Principal short fiction** • *Zapiski okhotnika*, 1852 (*Russian Life in the Interior*, 1855; better known as *A Sportsman's Sketches*, 1932); *Povesti i rasskazy*, 1856; *First Love, and Other Stories*, 1989.

**Other literary forms** • In addition to *A Sportsman's Sketches*, Ivan Turgenev published several other short stories and novellas individually. His main contribution, however, was six novels, some of which are among the best written in Russian, especially *Ottsy i deti* (1862; *Fathers and Sons*, 1867). He also wrote poems, poems in prose, and plays, one of which, *Mesyats v derevne* (1855; *A Month in the Country*, 1924), is still staged regularly in Russian theaters.

**Achievements** • Ivan Turgenev's opus is not particularly large, yet with about four dozen stories and novellas and his brief novels, he became one of the best writers not only in Russian but also in world literature. Turgenev was a leading force in the Russian realistic movement of the second half of the nineteenth century. Together with Nikolai Gogol, Fyodor Dostoevski, Leo Tolstoy, and Anton Chekhov, he built the reputation that Russian literature enjoys in the world. Perhaps more than other writers, he was responsible for acquainting foreign readers with Russian literature, and because he spent most of his adult life abroad, he was an esteemed figure in the international literary life.

Turgenev was also instrumental in arousing the sensitivity and consciousness of his compatriots, because he dealt with such burning social issues as the plight of Russian peasantry, in *A Sportsman's Sketches*; the "superfluous man" in Russian society, in "The Diary of a Superfluous Man"; the fixation of Russians with revolution, in *Rudin* (1856; English translation, 1947); the decaying nobility in *Dvoryanskoye gnezdo* (1859; *Liza*, 1869; better known as *A House of Gentlefolk*, 1894); and the age-old conflict between generations, in *Fathers and Sons*.

Turgenev also excelled in his style, especially in the use of the language. Albert Jay Nock called him "incomparably the greatest of artists in fiction," and Virginia Woolf termed his works as being "curiously of our own time, undecayed and complete in themselves." His reputation, despite some fluctuations, endures.

**Biography** • Ivan Sergeyevich Turgenev was born on November 9, 1818, in the central Russian town of Orel, into a small gentry family. His father was a loving, easygoing country squire, while his mother was an overbearing woman of whom Turgenev had many unpleasant memories. He spent his childhood at the family estate, Spasskoe, which he visited every summer even after the family moved to Moscow. He received tutoring at home and later graduated from the University of St. Petersburg in 1837. He continued his studies in Berlin, acquiring a master's degree in philosophy. His stay in Berlin marks the beginning of a lifelong shuffle between his homeland and the European countries, especially France, Germany, England, and Italy. On one visit to

France, he met a French woman, Pauline Viardot, with whom he had a close relationship the rest of his life despite her being married. After serving briefly in the Ministry of Interior, he lived the remainder of his life off his estate income following his parents' death.

Turgenev started to write early, and in 1843, at the age of twenty-five, he published a long narrative poem, *Parasha*, written in imitation of Alexander Pushkin. He soon abandoned poetry for prose, although his reverence for Pushkin and the poetic slant remained constant in his writings. His stories about the dismal life of Russian peasants were much more successful, attracting the attention of readers and critics alike. When the collection of those stories, *A Sportsman's Sketches*, was published in 1852, his reputation as a promising young writer was firmly established. A successful play, *A Month in the Country*, added to his reputation. As his reputation grew, he became friends with many leading writers and critics—Vissarion Belinsky, Nikolai Nekrasov, Tolstoy, Aleksandr Herzen, Dostoevski, and others—but these friendships were often interspersed with heated arguments and enmity. Because of his connections in Europe and a pronounced liberal outlook, he was summoned on several occasions before the investigation committees back in Russia. He was always exonerated, however, and he continued to travel between Russia and Europe.

Turgenev never married, but he had several affairs, while Viardot remained the love of his life, and he was thought to have been the father of a son born to her. The steady stream of successful novels and stories enhanced the esteem in which he was held both at home and abroad. At the same time, he carried on a spirited debate with Russian intellectuals, advocating liberal reforms in Russian society, especially those concerning the plight of peasants, many of whom were still kept as serfs. When they were liberated in 1861, it was believed that not a small merit belonged to Turgenev and his efforts toward their emancipation.

Toward the end of his life, Turgenev kept writing and publishing, though at a slower pace. He also worked on the preparation of his collected works and continued to live in a ménage à trois with Viardot and her husband. During his last visit to Russia in the summer of 1881, he visited Tolstoy at Yasnaya Polyana. His health began to deteriorate in 1882, and, after several months of a serious illness, he died at the Viardots' estate in Bougival, near Paris, on September 3, 1883. As his friend Henry James wrote, "his end was not serene and propitious, but dark and almost violent." Turgenev's body was taken to Russia, where he was buried with great honors in St. Petersburg.

**Analysis** • The reputation of Ivan Turgenev as a short-story writer is based in equal measure on his stories about Russian peasant life and on stories about other segments of society. Although differing greatly in subject matter and emphasis, they nevertheless share the same mastery of storytelling and style and language. Turgenev wrote stories about the peasants early in his career, revealing his familiarity with life in the countryside and his preoccupation with liberal causes. As he grew older and traveled to Europe, his horizons expanded, and he became more interested in topics transcending his provincial outlook. His acquired cosmopolitanism was also reflected in his turning toward personal concerns of love, alienation, and psychological illumination of his characters. The last story that he wrote, "Klara Milich" ("Clara Milich"), takes him to the realm of the fantastic and supernatural, to life after death, and even to the bizarre twists of the human mind.

*A Sportsman's Sketches* • Turgenev's stories about Russian peasants are contained primarily in his collection *A Sportsman's Sketches.* As the title implies (the accurate translation is "notes of a hunter"), the twenty-five tales are more like notes and sketches than full-blown stories with plot and characterization. It is one of the few examples in world literature where the entire collection of separate and independent stories has a thematic unity; another example of this unity is Isaac Babel's *Konormiia* (1926; *Red Cavalry,* 1929). The unifying theme is the hard life of Russian peasants— many generations of whom had lived as serfs for centuries—and the neglect of their well-being on the part of their owners. Despite its innocuous title, chosen to mislead the censors, the collection provoked admiration as well as heated debates. It is credited with speeding up the process of the serfs' emancipation.

The stories are set in the countryside around Turgenev's family estate at the middle of the nineteenth century. They are told by the same narrator, a landowner, in fact the thinly disguised author himself. During his tireless hunting trips, Turgenev met various characters, mostly peasants, many of whom told stories worth listening to. The authentic human quality of the settings and marvelous characterization, rather than the social message, make the stories enduring literature.

The author approaches his characters with an open mind. He observes their demeanor "with curiosity and sympathy" and listens to their concerns and complaints without much comment, with a few questions for his own clarification. He refrains from passing judgment and avoids social criticism or satire. Through such unobtrusiveness, he gains the characters' confidence and allows them to talk freely, making the stories more believable. More important, he does not idealize the peasants; instead, he attempts to penetrate the crust of everyday appearances.

The woman in the story "Ermolai i mel'nichikha" ("Yermolai and the Miller's Wife"), whose freedom had been bought by her husband, talks nonchalantly about her hard lot and the lack of love in her life. Yet beneath her story, the reader senses deep melancholy and hopelessness, reinforced by the author's remark to his hunting companion, "It seems she is ailing," and by the companion's retort, "What else should she be?" The burly, taciturn forest warden in the story "Biriuk" ("The Wolf"), who lives alone, excels in protecting the forest from the poachers, and is feared and hated by the peasants, who are not above stealing wood from the landowner. He cannot be bribed and plays no favorites, finding the only pleasure in doing his job. Yet when he catches a poor peasant trying to fell a tree, he lets him go because it is hunger that drove him to thievery. In one of Turgenev's best stories, "Zhivye Moshchi"

("A Living Relic"), a young woman, dying of a fatal illness, gives the impression of total helplessness, yet she is nourished until her untimely death by her naïve religion and love of life. In all these stories, appearances are deceiving and the observer-narrator is able to get to the core of his characters.

Not all characters have an adversarial relationship with their fate. The two friends in "Khor'i Kalynich" ("Khor and Kalynich") epitomize the two halves of a Russian character. Khor is a practical, down-to-earth man who has found success in life. Kalynich is a sensitive soul living in unison with nature, a dreamer who revels in simple pleasures, without worrying about more complex aspects of life. The doctor in "Uezdnyi lekar" ("The Country Doctor"), called to the sickbed of a young girl, falls in love with her, and his love is returned, but he realizes that he cannot save the young girl. He finds solace in the discovery that the girl has satisfied her own craving for love in the last moments of her life. Thus, the results are not as important as the efforts to avoid or alleviate the blows, no matter how unsuccessful the efforts may be.

Peasants are not the only characters drawing the author's attention. The landowners, who wield the power of life and death over their serfs, also appear in several stories. For the most part, they are depicted with much less sympathy and understanding, despite the author's own social origin. In "Dva pomeshchika" ("Two Landowners"), both characters show negative traits: One, a major-general, is a social clown; the other is an insensitive brute, who thinks that a peasant will always be a peasant and who uses a homespun "philosophy" that "if the father's a thief, the son's a thief too . . . it's blood that counts." The author seems to be saying that, with such a negative attitude, no improvement of the peasants' lot is possible. "Gamlet Shchigrovskogo uezda" ("Hamlet of the Shchigrovsky District") offers an even stronger castigation of the serf-owning class. Here, an intelligent and sensitive landowner fails to find understanding among his peers for his attempts to improve the lot of everybody. In a Dostoevskian fashion, he is forced to act like a buffoon in hopes of gaining attention that way. Turgenev's position here sounds very much like a sharp satire against the existing state of affairs, but, as mentioned, he abstains from open and direct criticism, thus making his points even more effective.

Not all of the stories in *A Sportsman's Sketches* are bleak or hopeless. The two best stories of the collection are also the most positive. In "Bezhin lug" ("Bezhin Meadow"), Turgenev relates his evening encounter with five young boys taking care of the horses in the countryside. Sitting by the fire in the evening, they tell one another fantastic stories, to amuse and even frighten one another. The narrator is impressed by the boys' natural demeanor, straightforwardness, bravery, and, above all, rich imagination of which folktales are spun. The author seems to imply that the future of the country is secure if judged by the young who are to inherit it.

The second story, "Pevtsy" ("The Singers"), is even more uplifting. In another chance encounter, the narrator stumbles across an inn in the barely accessible backwoods. He is treated with a singing competition among the inn patrons unlike any other he had experienced. Turgenev uses the diamond-in-the-rough theme to show where the real talent can be found. As the narrator leaves the inn, he hears the people's voices calling each other from one hill to another—a possible explanation of where the marvelous singers learn how to sing. These stories, along with a few others, strike a balance between the negative and the positive aspects of the life depicted in the book.

Surrounded and suffused by nature, Turgenev reacts to it by stating his position concerning human beings in nature. He expresses his admiration for nature by using strikingly detailed descriptions, emphasizing colors, sounds, and scents. His subtlety of observation is complemented by genuine lyricism and careful use of a melodic, rhythmical language. Despite these ornamental features, however, the reader is tempted to view the author's notion of nature as being rather unfeeling and indifferent toward humankind, in the best tradition of Georg Brandes' theory of *la grande indifférent*. A closer look, however, reveals that nature in Turgenev's works shows the difference in degree, not in kind, and that for him, humankind is a part of nature, not outside it. Only in unison with nature can human beings fulfill their potential, in which case nature is not indifferent but, on the contrary, very helpful, as seen in the example of the singers in the aforementioned story.

Other artistic merits of these stories (which Turgenev was able to maintain throughout his writing career) can be found in his careful and delicate choice of suggestive and descriptive words; in the sketchy but pithy psychological portraiture; in the uncomplicated plot structure, consisting usually of an anecdote or episode; in the natural, calm, matter-of-fact narration; and in the effective imagery that is not strained or artificial. Superior craftsmanship goes hand in hand with the "social message" here, preventing the stories from being dated or used for inartistic purposes.

**"The Diary of a Superfluous Man"** • The second group of Turgenev's tales strikes an altogether different path, although a kinship with his earlier stories can be easily detected. Among many stories outside the cycle of *A Sportsman's Sketches*, eight deserve to be singled out, either for the significance of their contents or for their artistic merit, or both. An early story, "Dnevnik lishnega cheloveka" ("The Diary of a Superfluous Man"), despite its relative immaturity, has a significance that surpasses its artistic quality. It is here that Turgenev coined the phrase "a superfluous man," which would reverberate throughout Russian literature of the nineteenth and twentieth centuries. Even though the superfluous man theme had been used before Turgenev by Pushkin's Eugene Onegin in the novel in verse by the same name and by Mikhail Lermontov's Pechorin in *Geroy nashego vremeni* (1840; *A Hero of Our Times*, 1854), it was Turgenev who made the phrase a literary byword. The story presages Dostoevski's *Zapiski iz podpolya* (1864; *Letters from the Underworld*, 1913; better known as *Notes from the Underground*, 1918).

Turgenev's "superfluous man" is a young scion of erstwhile wealthy landowners, who writes a diary knowing that he will soon die of a disease. To compound his misery, he is rejected in his love for a beautiful neighbor. The excessive introspection of the "hero" and his inability to cope with reality make this story primarily a psychological character study and not a social statement, as some of Turgenev's works of the same kind would become later.

**"Mumu"** • Perhaps the best known of Turgenev's stories, "Mumu" comes the closest in spirit to the collection *A Sportsman's Sketches*. A deaf-mute servant loses the girl he loves when he is forced into marrying another woman. Later, he is ordered to kill his beloved dog because its barking is disturbing his mistress's sleep. Drawing the character of the insensitive mistress after his mother, Turgenev castigates the insensitivity of the entire serf-owning class. The story does not sink into sentimental bathos primarily because of the remarkable characterization of the servant as an ultimate sufferer, underscoring the proverbial capacity for suffering of an entire nation. Moreover, by arousing overwhelming pity for the deaf-mute, Turgenev clearly places the blame for this human and social injustice at the door of the unfeeling gentry.

**"King Lear of the Steppes"** • "Stepnoi Korol' Lir" ("King Lear of the Steppes") is another story that in its countryside setting shows kinship with *A Sportsman's Sketches.* Yet it is entirely different in the subject matter, spirit, and atmosphere. In a takeoff on William Shakespeare's tragedy, the story shows children behaving toward their father in a similar manner. The atmosphere here, however, is typically Russian. Harlov, a descendant of a Russianized Swedish family, suffers the same indignity and ingratitude at the hands of his daughters, and he takes similar revenge upon them, but the tragedy is not relieved or ennobled. Turgenev shows a fine sense for plot, and the dialogues—more excessive than usual for him—are in line with the dramatic nature of its model. Artistically, this story is almost a masterpiece, keeping the reader in suspense until the end.

**"Asya"** • Love is an overriding theme in Turgenev's later stories. "Asya" ("Asya") and "Pervaya lyubov" ("First Love") are the best representatives of Turgenev's love stories. Both are told in the first person, tempting one to attribute to them autobiographical character, which may not be totally unjustified. "Asya" is set in a German town where the narrator (perhaps Turgenev) comes across two compatriots, a brother and a sister.

As the story unfolds, the narrator is increasingly attracted to the woman and develops genuine love feelings, yet he is unable to declare his love openly, vacillating constantly until every chance for consummation is lost. Turgenev was known to have been indecisive in his love affairs, as illustrated by his strange attachment to the Viardot couple. Seen from that angle, the autobiographical element becomes very plausible, but there is more to the story than simply Turgenev's indecisiveness. At this stage of his development, Turgenev had published only one book of short stories and one novel, and he was beset by doubts and indecision, not only in his love relationships but also in his literary aspirations, all too similar to those of the narrator in "Asya." As he himself said,

> There are turning points in life, points when the past dies and something new is born; woe to the man who doesn't know how to sense these turning points and either holds on stubbornly to a dead past or seeks prematurely to summon to life what has not yet fully ripened.

The story reflects the wrenching doubts and soul-searching of the protagonist, which did not enable him to take a resolute stance toward the young woman, who herself was searching for a more assuring love. Thus, the love between Asya and the narrator was doomed to failure almost before it began. The two part, and the only thing left is a bittersweet memory of what might have been.

Perhaps Turgenev was not yet ready to give the story the adequate treatment that it deserves. This is evidenced in the fact that Asya, wistful and charming though she may be, is not developed fully as a character. Turgenev will return soon to a similar theme and develop it to the fullest in his novel *A House of Gentlefolk.* It is also worth mentioning that "Asya" is another example of the theme of the superfluous man, which started with "The Diary of a Superfluous Man."

**"First Love"** • "First Love" is a better love story because both the plot and the characters are more fully developed. It involves a rivalry between a young man and his father, vying for the affection of the same woman, Zinaida. In Turgenev's own admission, the story is autobiographical; as he wrote about it in a letter, "It is the only thing that still gives me pleasure, because it is life itself, it was not made up. . . . 'First Love' is part of my experience." Aside from this candid admission, the story has a wide appeal to all, both young and old; to the young because the first love is always cherished the most (the only true love, according to Turgenev), and to the old because it offers a vicarious pleasure of a last triumph.

It invariably evokes a bittersweet nostalgia in everyone. It also presents a plausible, even if not too common, situation. Turgenev controls with a sure hand the delicate relationships between the three partners in this emotional drama fraught with the awakening of manhood in an adolescent, with the amorous playfulness of a young woman who is both a temptress and a victim, and with the satisfaction of a conquest by a man entering the autumn of his life. Similarly, the author handles tactfully a potentially explosive situation between the loving father and adoring son, producing no rancor in aftermath. The story is a throwback to Romanticism, which had already passed in Russian literature and elsewhere at the time of the story's publication. The story ends in a Turgenev fashion—unhappily for everyone concerned. All these attributes make "First Love" one of the best love stories in world literature.

**"The Song of Triumphant Love"** • Twenty years later, Turgenev would write another love story, "Pesn' torzhestvuiushchei liubvi" ("The Song of Triumphant Love"), which differs from "First Love" in many respects. It again deals with a love relationship in a ménage à trois (it seems that Turgenev was constantly reliving his own predicament with the Viardot couple), but the similarities stop there. The setting is in sixteenth-century Ferrara, and the male players—members of ancient patrician families—are on equal footing, even if one is a husband and the other a suitor. The ending is much more than unhappy: It is downright tragic. What makes this story decisively different from other love stories by Turgenev is the introduction of a supernatural element manifesting itself in the woman's conceiving, not by intercourse, but by the platonic desire and the singing of a song by the unsuccessful suitor.

"The Song of Triumphant Love" marks the transition to a more esoteric subject matter in Turgenev's writing. He had written fantastic stories before ("Prizraki," or "Phantoms"), but in the last decade of his life, he employed the supernatural with increasing frequency. In "Stuk . . . stuk . . . stuk . . ." ("Knock . . . Knock . . . Knock . . ."), he deals with a suicidal urge that borders on the supernatural. In his last story, "Clara Milich," he tells of a man who has fallen in love with a woman after her death. Turgenev believed that there is a thin line dividing the real and the fantastic and that the fantastic stories people tell have happened in real life. As he said, "Wherever you look, there is the drama in life, and there are still writers who complain that all subjects have been exhausted." Had he lived longer, most likely he would have tried to reconcile real life with so-called fantasy and the supernatural.

*Vasa D. Mihailovich*

**Other major works**

PLAYS: *Neostorozhnost,* pb. 1843 (*Carelessness,* 1924); *Bezdenezhe,* pb. 1846, pr. 1852 (*A Poor Gentleman,* 1924); *Kholostyak,* pr. 1849 (*The Bachelor,* 1924); *Nakhlebnik,* wr. 1849, pb. 1857, pr. 1862 (*The Family Charge,* 1924); *Zavtrak u predvoditelya,* pr. 1849, pb. 1856 (*An Amicable Settlement,* 1924); *Mesyats v derevne,* wr. 1850, pb. 1855, pr. 1872 (*A Month in the Country,* 1924); *Razgovor na bolshoy doroge,* pr. 1850, pb. 1851 (*A Conversation on the Highway,* 1924); *Gde tonko, tam i rvyotsya,* wr. 1851, pr. 1912 (*Where It Is*

*Thin, There It Breaks*, 1924); *Provintsialka*, pr. 1851 (*A Provincial Lady*, 1934); *Vecher v Sorrente*, wr. 1852, pr. 1884, pb. 1891 (*An Evening in Sorrento*, 1924); *The Plays of Ivan Turgenev*, pb. 1924; *Three Plays*, pb. 1934.

NOVELS: *Rudin*, 1856 (*Dimitri Roudine*, 1873; better known as *Rudin*, 1947); *Asya*, 1858 (English translation, 1877); *Dvoryanskoye gnezdo*, 1859 (*Liza*, 1869; also as *A Nobleman's Nest*, 1903; better known as *A House of Gentlefolk*, 1894); *Nakanune*, 1860 (*On the Eve*, 1871); *Pervaya lyubov*, 1860 (*First Love*, 1884); *Ottsy i deti*, 1862 (*Fathers and Sons*, 1867); *Dym*, 1867 (*Smoke*, 1868); *Veshniye vody*, 1872 (*Spring Floods*, 1874; better known as *The Torrents of Spring*, 1897); *Nov*, 1877 (*Virgin Soil*, 1877); *The Novels of Ivan Turgenev*, 1894-1899 (15 volumes).

MISCELLANEOUS: *The Works of Iván Turgenieff*, 1903-1904 (6 volumes); *The Essential Turgenev*, 1994.

NONFICTION: "Gamlet i Don Kikhot," 1860 ("Hamlet and Don Quixote," 1930); *Literaturnya i zhiteyskiya vospominaniya*, 1880 (*Literary Reminiscences and Autobiographical Fragments*, 1958); *Letters*, 1983 (David Lowe, editor); *Turgenev's Letters*, 1983 (A. V. Knowles, editor).

POETRY: *Parasha*, 1843; *Senilia*, 1882, 1930 (better known as *Stikhotvoreniya v proze*; *Poems in Prose*, 1883, 1945).

## Bibliography

Allen, Elizabeth Cheresh. *Beyond Realism: Turgenev's Poetics of Secular Salvation*. Stanford, Calif.: Stanford University Press, 1992. Argues that readers should not turn to Turgenev merely for transparent narratives of nineteenth-century Russian life; attempts to expose the unique imaginative vision and literary patterns in Turgenev's work. Discusses Turgenev's development of narrative techniques in *A Sportsman's Sketches*, analyzing several of the major stories, such as "Bezhin Meadow" and "The Singers."

Brodianski, Nina. "Turgenev's Short Stories: A Reevaluation." *Slavonic and East European Review* 32, no. 78 (1953): 70-91. In this brief but thorough and stimulating study, Brodianski examines Turgenev's short stories in general, their themes, structure, and psychological illumination of characters, as well as his philosophy (as much as there is of it) and his literary theories about the short story. Inasmuch as it reevaluates some long-standing opinions about Turgenev, it serves a good purpose.

Brouwer, Sander. *Character in the Short Prose of Ivan Sergeevic Turgenev*. Atlanta: Rodopi, 1996. Excellent look at Turgenev's characters in the short fiction.

Gregg, Richard. "Turgenev and Hawthorne: The Life-Giving Satyr and the Fallen Faun." *Slavic and East European Journal* 41 (Summer, 1997): 258-270. Discusses Nathaniel Hawthorne's influence on Turgenev and comments on the common motif that their "mysterious" stories shared (the uncanny spell, curse, or blight). Claims that Turgenev's explicit admiration for those works of Hawthorne in which that motif is to be found attests a bond of sympathy between the two writers.

Kagan-Kans, Eva. "Fate and Fantasy: A Study of Turgenev's Fantastic Stories." *Slavic Review* 18 (1969): 543-560. Kagan-Kans traces Turgenev's treatment of fantasy and supernatural elements in his stories, as well as the role of fate and dreams. She also examines Turgenev's relationship with other writers, especially the Romanticists, and their influence on him as evidenced in individual stories, especially those dealing with fantasy and the supernatural.

Lowe, David A., ed. *Critical Essays on Ivan Turgenev.* Boston: G. K. Hall, 1989. Collection of essays on Turgenev's literary works. Bibliography and index.

May, Charles E., ed. *Masterplots II: Short Story Series, Revised Edition.* 8 vols. Pasadena, Calif.: Salem Press, 2004. Designed for student use, this reference set contains articles providing detailed plot summaries and analyses of five short stories by Turgenev: "Bezhin Meadow" (vol. 1), "The District Doctor" (vol. 2), "Hamlet of the Shchigrovsky District" (vol. 3), "A Living Relic" (vol. 4), and "Yermolai and the Miller's Wife" (vol. 8).

Seeley, Frank Friedeberg. *Turgenev: A Reading of His Fiction.* New York: Cambridge University Press, 1991. Seeley prefaces his thorough study of Turgenev's fiction with an outline of Turgenev's life and a survey of his poetry and plays. This volume incorporates later findings and challenges some established views, especially the traditional notion of the "simplicity" of Turgenev's works. Seeley stresses the psychological treatment that Turgenev allotted to his characters.

Sheidley, William E. "'Born in Imitation of Someone Else': Reading Turgenev's 'Hamlet of the Shchigrovsky District' as a Version of Hamlet." *Studies in Short Fiction* 27 (Summer, 1990): 391-398. Discusses the character Vasily Vasilyevych as the most emphatic and the most pathetic of the Hamlet types in *A Sportsman's Sketches.* Contends that in a striking flash of metafictional irony, Vasily recognizes himself as the walking embodiment of the Hamlet stereotype. Sheidley points out the different implications of the Hamlet character in Elizabethan tragedy and nineteenth century character sketch.

Woodward, James B. *Turgenev's "Fathers and Sons."* London: Bristol Classical Press, 1996. Part of the Critical Studies in Russian Literature series, this is an excellent study of the novel. Provides bibliographical references and an index.

# Mark Twain

**Born:** Florida, Missouri; November 30, 1835
**Died:** Redding, Connecticut; April 21, 1910

**Principal short fiction** • *The Celebrated Jumping Frog of Calaveras County, and Other Sketches*, 1867; *Mark Twain's (Burlesque) Autobiography and First Romance*, 1871; *Mark Twain's Sketches: New and Old*, 1875; *Punch, Brothers, Punch! and Other Sketches*, 1878; *The Stolen White Elephant, and Other Stories*, 1882; *Merry Tales*, 1892; *The £1,000,000 Bank-Note, and Other New Stories*, 1893; *The Man That Corrupted Hadleyburg, and Other Stories and Essays*, 1900; *King Leopold's Soliloquy: A Defense of His Congo Rule*, 1905; *The $30,000 Bequest, and Other Stories*, 1906; *The Curious Republic of Gondour, and Other Whimsical Sketches*, 1919; *The Complete Short Stories of Mark Twain*, 1957 (Charles Neider, editor); *Letters from the Earth*, 1962; *Selected Shorter Writings of Mark Twain*, 1962; *Mark Twain's Satires and Burlesques*, 1967 (Franklin R. Rogers, editor); *Mark Twains's Which Was the Dream? and Other Symbolic Writings of the Later Years*, 1967 (John S. Tuckey, editor); *Mark Twain's Hannibal, Huck and Tom*, 1969 (Walter Blair, editor); *Mark Twain's Fables of Man*, 1972 (Tuckey, editor); *Life as I Find It*, 1977 (Neider, editor); *Early Tales and Sketches*, 1979-1981 (2 volumes; Edgar Marquess Branch and Robert H. Hirst, editors); *A Murder, a Mystery, and a Marriage*, 2001 (Roy Blount, Jr., editor).

**Other literary forms** • As a professional writer who felt the need for a large income, Mark Twain published more than thirty books and left many uncollected pieces and manuscripts. He tried every genre, including drama, and even wrote some poetry that is seldom read. His royalties came mostly from subscription books sold door to door, especially five travel volumes. For more than forty years, he occasionally sold material, usually humorous sketches, to magazines and newspapers. He also composed novels, philosophical dialogues, moral fables, and maxims, as well as essays on a range of subjects which were weighted more toward the social and cultural than the belletristic but which were nevertheless often controversial.

**Achievements** • Certainly one of the most beloved and most frequently quoted American writers, Mark Twain earned that honor by creating an original and nearly inimitable style that is thoroughly American. Although he tried nearly every genre from historical fiction to poetry to quasi-scientific fantasy, his novels about boyhood on the Mississippi, *The Adventures of Tom Sawyer* and *Adventures of Huckleberry Finn*, are the works that permanently wove his celebrity status into the fabric of American culture. During his own lifetime, he received numerous honors including honorary degrees from Yale University and the University of Missouri. His proudest moment, however, was in 1907, when Oxford University awarded him an honorary LL.D. He was so proud of his scarlet doctor's gown that he wore it to his daughter's wedding.

**Biography** • Born Samuel Langhorne Clemens in Missouri in 1835, Mark Twain adopted his famous pen name twenty-seven years later, while working as a reporter in western Nevada. Throughout the rest of his life, he signed his pen name to virtually all his writings but never hid the fact that his real name was Clemens.

After his education was cut short by the death of a stern father who had more ambition than success, at the age of eleven Mark Twain was apprenticed to a newspaper office, which, except for the money earned from four years of piloting on the Mississippi, supplied most of his income until 1868. Then, he quickly won eminence as a lecturer and author before his marriage to wealthy Olivia Langdon in 1870 led to a memorably comfortable and active family life which included three daughters. Although always looking to his writing for income, he increasingly devoted energy to business affairs and investments until his publishing house declared bankruptcy in 1894. After his world lecture tour of 1895-1896, he became one of the most admired figures of his time and continued to earn honors until his death in 1910.

**Analysis** • Many readers find Mark Twain most successful in briefer works, including his narratives, because they were not padded to fit some extraneous standard of length. His best stories are narrated by first-person speakers who are seemingly artless, often so convincingly that critics cannot agree concerning the extent to which their ingenuousness is the result of Twain's self-conscious craft. Although deeply divided himself, Twain seldom created introspectively complex characters or narrators who are unreliable in the Conradian manner. Rather, just as Twain alternated between polarities of attitude, his characters tend to embody some extreme unitary state either of villainy or (especially with young women) of unshakable virtue. Therefore, they too seldom interact effectively. Except when adapting a plot taken from oral tradition, Twain does better with patently artificial situations, which his genius for suggesting authentic speech makes plausible enough. In spite of their faults, Twain's stories captivate the reader with their irresistible humor, their unique style, and their spirited characters who transfigure the humdrum with striking perceptions.

**"The Celebrated Jumping Frog of Calaveras County"** • "The Celebrated Jumping Frog of Calaveras County" is generally regarded as Twain's most distinctive story, although some readers may prefer Jim Baker's bluejay yarn, which turns subtly on the psyche of its narrator, or Jim Blaine's digressions from his grandfather's old ram, which reach a more physical comedy while evolving into an absurdly tall tale. In "The Celebrated Jumping Frog of Calaveras County," Jim Smiley's eagerness to bet on anything in the mining camp may strain belief, but it is relatively plausible that another gambler could weigh down Smiley's frog, Daniel Webster, with quailshot and thus win forty dollars with an untrained frog. Most attempts to find profundity in this folk anecdote involve the few enveloping sentences attributed to an outsider, who may represent the literate easterner being gulled by Simon Wheeler's seeming inability to stick to his point. The skill of the story can be more conclusively identified, from the deft humanizing of animals to the rising power and aptness of the imagery. Especially adroit is the deadpan manner of Wheeler, who never betrays whether he himself appreciates the humor and the symmetry of his meanderings. Twain's use of the oral style is nowhere better represented than in "The Celebrated Jumping Frog of Calaveras County," which exemplifies the principles of the author's essay "How to Tell a Story."

**"A True Story"** • In 1874, Twain assured the sober *Atlantic Monthly* that his short story "A True Story" was not humorous, although in fact it has his characteristic sparkle and hearty tone. Having been encouraged by the contemporary appeal for local color, Twain quickly developed a narrator with a heavy dialect and a favorite folk-saying that allows a now-grown son to recognize his mother after a separation of thirteen years. While she, in turn, finds scars confirming their relationship on his wrist and head, this conventional plot gains resonance from Rachel's report of how her husband and seven children had once been separated at a slave auction in Richmond. Contemporaries praised "A True Story" for its naturalness, testimony that Twain was creating more lifelike blacks than any other author by allowing them greater dignity, and Rachel is quick to insist that slave families cared for one another just as deeply as any white families. Her stirringly recounted memories challenged the legend of the Old South even before that legend reached its widest vogue, and her spirit matched her "mighty" body so graphically that "A True Story" must get credit for

Library of Congress

much more craftsmanship than is admitted by its subtitle, "Repeated Word for Word as I Heard It."

**"The Facts Concerning the Recent Carnival of Crime in Connecticut"** • In "The Facts Concerning the Recent Carnival of Crime in Connecticut," in which Twain again uses first-person narration with a flawless touch for emphasizing the right word or syllable, the main character closely resembles the author in age, experience, habits, and tastes. Of more significance is the fact that the story projects Twain's lifelong struggles with, and even against, his conscience. Here the conscience admits to being the "most pitiless enemy" of its host, whom it is supposed to "improve" but only tyrannizes with gusto while refusing to praise the host for anything. It makes the blunder, however, of materializing as a two-foot dwarf covered with "fuzzy greenish mold" who torments the narrator with intimate knowledge of and contemptuous judgments on his behavior. When beloved Aunty Mary arrives to scold him once more for his addiction to tobacco, his conscience grows so torpid that he can gleefully seize and destroy it beyond any chance of rebirth. Through vivid yet realistic detail, "The Facts Concerning the Recent Carnival of Crime in Connecticut" dramatizes common musings about shame and guilt along with the yearnings some persons feel for release from them. If it maintains too comic a tone to preach nihilism or amorality, it leaves readers inclined to view conscience less as a divine agent than as part of psychic dynamics.

**"The £1,000,000 Bank-Note"** • The shopworn texture of "The £1,000,000 Bank-Note" reveals Twain's genius for using the vernacular at a low ebb. Narrated by the protagonist, this improbable tale is set in motion by two brothers who disagree over what would happen if some penniless individual were lent a one-million-pound bill (then the equivalent of five million U.S. dollars) for thirty days. To solve their argument, they engage in an experiment with a Yankee, Henry Adams, a stockbroker's clerk stranded in London. Coincidence thickens when, having managed by the tenth day of the experiment to get invited to dinner by an American minister, Adams unknowingly meets the stepdaughter of one of the brothers and woos and wins her that very night. Having just as nimbly gained a celebrity that makes every merchant eager to extend unlimited credit, he endorses a sale of Nevada stocks that enables him to show his future father-in-law that he has banked a million pounds of his own. The overall effect is cheerfully melodramatic and appeals to fantasies about windfalls of money; the reader can share Adams's pleasure in the surprise and awe he arouses by pulling his banknote out of a tattered pocket. It can be argued that the story indicts a society in which the mere show of wealth can so quickly raise one's standing, but Twain probably meant Adams to deserve respect for his enterprise and shrewdness when his chance came.

**"The Man That Corrupted Hadleyburg"** • "The Man That Corrupted Hadleyburg" is one of the most penetrating of Twain's stories. It achieves unusual depth of character and, perhaps by giving up the first-person narrator, a firm objectivity that lets theme develop through dialogue and incident. It proceeds with such flair that only a third or fourth reading uncovers thin links in a supposedly inescapable chain of events planned for revenge by an outsider who had been insulted in Hadleyburg, a town smugly proud of its reputation for honesty.

Stealthily he leaves a sack of counterfeit gold coins which are to be handed over to the fictitious resident who once gave a needy stranger twenty dollars and can prove it by recalling his words at the time. Next, the avenger sends nineteen leading citizens a letter which tells each of them how to claim the gold, supposedly amounting to forty thousand dollars. During an uproarious town meeting studded with vignettes of local characters, both starchy and plebeian, eighteen identical claims are read aloud; the nineteenth, however, from elderly Edward Richards, is suppressed by the chairman, who overestimates how Richards once saved him from the community's unjust anger. Rewarded by the stranger and made a hero, Richards is actually tormented to death, both by pangs of conscience and by fear of exposure. Hadleyburg, however, has learned a lesson in humility and moral realism and shortens its motto from the Lord's Prayer to run: "Lead Us into Temptation."

"The Man That Corrupted Hadleyburg" exhibits Twain's narrative and stylistic strengths and also dramatizes several of his persistent themes, such as skepticism about orthodox religion, ambivalence toward the conscience but contempt for rationalizing away deserved guilt, and attraction to mechanistic ideas. The story raises profound questions which can never be settled. The most useful criticism asks whether the story's determinism is kept consistent and uppermost—or, more specifically, whether the reform of Hadleyburg can follow within the patterns already laid out. The ethical values behind the story's action and ironical tone imply that people can in fact choose to behave more admirably.

In printing the story, *Harper's Monthly* may well have seen a Christian meliorism, a lesson against self-righteous piety that abandons true charity. The revised motto may warn that the young, instead of being sheltered, should be educated to cope with fallible human nature. More broadly, the story seems to show that the conscience can be trained into a constructive force by honestly confronting the drives for pleasure and self-approval that sway everyone.

Many of these same themes reappear in quasi-supernatural sketches such as "Extract from Captain Stormfield's Visit to Heaven." Twain never tired of toying with biblical characters, particularly Adam and Eve, or with parodies of Sunday-school lessons. He likewise parodied most other genres, even those which he himself used seriously. In his most serious moods he preached openly against cruelty to animals in "A Dog's Tale" and "A Horse's Tale," supported social or political causes, and always came back to moral choices, as in "Was It Heaven or Hell?" or "The $30,000 Bequest." Notably weak in self-criticism, he had a tireless imagination capable of daringly unusual perspectives, a supreme gift of humor darkened by brooding over the enigmas of life, and an ethical habit of thought that expressed itself most tellingly through character and narrative.

*Louis J. Budd*
*With updates by Leslie A. Pearl and the Editors*

## Other major works

NOVELS: *The Gilded Age*, 1873 (with Charles Dudley Warner); *The Adventures of Tom Sawyer*, 1876; *The Prince and the Pauper*, 1881; *Adventures of Huckleberry Finn*, 1884; *A Connecticut Yankee in King Arthur's Court*, 1889; *The American Claimant*, 1892; *The Tragedy of Pudd'nhead Wilson*, 1894; *Tom Sawyer Abroad*, 1894; *Personal Recollections of Joan of Arc*, 1896; *Tom Sawyer, Detective*, 1896; *A Double-Barrelled Detective Story*, 1902; *Extracts from Adam's Diary*, 1904; *A Horse's Tale*, 1906; *Eve's Diary, Translated from the Original Ms*, 1906; *Extract from Captain Stormfield's Visit to Heaven*, 1909; *The Mysterious Stranger*, 1916 (revised as *The Chronicle of Young Satan*, 1969, by Albert Bigelow Paine and Frederick A. Duneka); *Report from Paradise*, 1952 (Dixon Wecter, editor); *Simon Wheeler, Detective*, 1963; *Mark Twain's Mysterious Stranger Manuscripts*, 1969 (William M. Gibson, editor).

PLAYS: *Colonel Sellers*, pr., pb. 1874 (adaptation of his novel *The Gilded Age*); *Ah Sin*, pr. 1877 (with Bret Harte); *Is He Dead?: A Comedy in Three Acts*, pb. 2003 (Shelley Fisher Fishkin, editor).

NONFICTION: *The Innocents Abroad*, 1869; *Roughing It*, 1872; *A Tramp Abroad*, 1880; *Life on the Mississippi*, 1883; *Following the Equator*, 1897 (also known as *More Tramp Abroad*); *How to Tell a Story, and Other Essays*, 1897; *My Début as a Literary Person*, 1903; *What Is Man?*, 1906; *Christian Science*, 1907; *Is Shakespeare Dead?*, 1909; *Mark Twain's Speeches*, 1910 (Albert Bigelow Paine, editor); *Europe and Elsewhere*, 1923 (Paine, editor); *Mark Twain's Autobiography*, 1924 (2 volumes; Paine, editor); *Mark Twain's Notebook*, 1935 (Paine, editor); *Letters from the Sandwich Islands, Written for the Sacramento Union*, 1937 (G. Ezra Dane, editor); *Mark Twain in Eruption*, 1940 (Bernard DeVoto, editor); *Mark Twain's Travels with Mr. Brown*, 1940 (Franklin Walker and G. Ezra Dane, editors); *Mark Twain to Mrs. Fairbanks*, 1949 (Dixon Wecter, editor); *The Love Letters of Mark Twain*, 1949 (Wecter, editor); *Mark Twain of the Enterprise: Newspaper Articles and Other Documents, 1862-1864*, 1957 (Henry Nash Smith and Frederick Anderson, editors); *Traveling with the Innocents Abroad: Mark Twain's Original Reports from Europe and the Holy Land*, 1958 (Daniel Morley McKeithan, editor; letters); *Mark Twain-Howells Letters: The Correspondence of Samuel L. Clemens and William D. Howells, 1872-1910*, 1960 (Henry Nash Smith and William M. Gibson, editors); *The Autobiography of Mark Twain*, 1961 (Charles Neider, editor); *Mark Twain's Letters to His Publishers, 1867-1894*, 1967 (Hamlin Hill, editor); *Clemens of the Call: Mark Twain in San Francisco*, 1969 (Edgar M. Branch, editor); *Mark Twain's Correspondence with Henry Huttleston Rogers,*

*1893-1909,* 1969 (Lewis Leary, editor); *A Pen Warmed-Up in Hell: Mark Twain in Protest,* 1972; *Mark Twain's Notebooks and Journals,* 1975-1979 (3 volumes); *Mark Twain Speaking,* 1976 (Paul Fatout, editor); *Mark Twain Speaks for Himself,* 1978 (Fatout, editor); *Mark Twain's Letters,* 1988-2002 (6 volumes; Edgar Marquess Branch, et al., editors); *Mark Twain's Own Autobiography: The Chapters from the "North American Review,"* 1990 (Michael J. Kiskis, editor); *Mark Twain's Aquarium: The Samuel Clemens Angelfish Correspondence, 1905-1910,* 1991 (John Cooley, editor); *Mark Twain: The Complete Interviews,* 2006.

MISCELLANEOUS: *The Writings of Mark Twain,* 1922-1925 (37 volumes); *The Portable Mark Twain,* 1946 (Bernard De Voto, editor); *Collected Tales, Sketches, Speeches, and Essays, 1853-1891,* 1992 (Louis J. Budd, editor); *Collected Tales, Sketches, Speeches, and Essays, 1891-1910,* 1992 (Budd, editor).

## Bibliography

Briden, Earl F. "Twainian Pedagogy and the No-Account Lessons of 'Hadleyburg.'" *Studies in Short Fiction* 28 (Spring, 1991): 125-234. Argues that within the context of Twain's skepticism about man's capacity for moral education, "The Man That Corrupted Hadleyburg" is not a story about a town's redemptive lessons of sin but rather an exposé about humanity's inability to learn morality from either theory or practice, abstract principle or moral pedagogy.

Camfield, Gregg. *The Oxford Companion to Mark Twain.* New York: Oxford University Press, 2003. Collection of original essays, including several by other scholars, on diverse aspects of Twain's life and writing, with encyclopedia reference features.

Emerson, Everett. *Mark Twain: A Literary Life.* Philadelphia: University of Pennsylvania Press, 2000. Complete revision of Emerson's *The Authentic Mark Twain* (1984), this masterful study traces the development of Twain's writing against the events in his life and provides illuminating discussions of many individual works.

LeMaster, J. R., and James D. Wilson, eds. *The Mark Twain Encyclopedia.* New York: Garland, 1993. Comprehensive reference work broadly similar in organization to Rasmussen's *Mark Twain A to Z,* differing in devoting most of its space to literary analysis. Very useful for studying aspects of Twain's writing.

Leonard, James S., ed. *Making Mark Twain Work in the Classroom.* Durham, N.C.: Duke University Press, 1999. Collection of essays by leading Twain scholars designed for students and teachers. Special attention is given to *A Connecticut Yankee in King Arthur's Court, Joan of Arc, Innocents Abroad,* and *Adventures of Huckleberry Finn.*

May, Charles E., ed. *Masterplots II: Short Story Series, Revised Edition.* 8 vols. Pasadena, Calif.: Salem Press, 2004. Designed for student use, this reference set contains articles providing detailed plot summaries and analyses of six short stories by Twain: "The Celebrated Jumping Frog of Calaveras County" (vol. 1), "The Chronicle of Young Satan" (vol. 2), "Jim Baker's Bluejay Yarn" (vol. 4), "The Man That Corrupted Hadleyburg" and "The £1,000,000 Bank-Note" (vol. 5), and "A True Story: Repeated Word for Word as I Heard It" (vol. 7).

Messent, Peter B. *The Short Works of Mark Twain: A Critical Study.* Philadelphia: University of Pennsylvania Press, 2001. Detailed exploration of Twain's shorter works that takes the innovative approach of examining how Twain planned the individual collections in which they were first published in book form.

Rasmussen, R. Kent. *Bloom's How to Write About Mark Twain.* New York: Chelsea House, 2008. Practical guide to writing student essays on Mark Twain, with several hundred general and specific suggestions on ten major works, including the jumping frog story, "The Man That Corrupted Hadleburg," and "The War Prayer." Includes a general introduction to writing on Mark Twain. Each chapter has a lengthy bibliography.

————————. *Critical Companion to Mark Twain: A Literary Reference to His Life and Work*. 2 vols. New York: Facts On File, 2007. Greatly expanded revision of *Mark Twain A to Z* (1995), which has been hailed as the most impressive reference tool on Mark Twain available. Virtually every character, theme, place, and biographical fact can be researched in these compendious volumes. Contains the most complete chronology ever compiled. Among the new features in this edition are lengthy analytical essays on individual works, a glossary of unusual words used by Twain, and a greatly expanded and annotated bibliography.

Sloane, David E. E. *Student Companion to Mark Twain*. New York: Greenwood Press, 2001. Essays on aspects of Twain's life, with special chapters on individual books.

Wilson, James D. *A Reader's Guide to the Short Stories of Mark Twain*. Boston: G. K. Hall, 1987. Detailed summaries and analyses of sixty-five stories, including several stories that appear within Twain's travel books. Perhaps the best single-volume work on Mark Twain's short fiction.

Wonham, Henry B. *Mark Twain and the Art of the Tall Tale*. New York: Oxford University Press, 1993. Discusses how Twain used the tall-tale conventions of interpretive play, dramatic encounters, and the folk community. Focuses on the relationship between storyteller and audience in Twain's canon.

# Anne Tyler

**Born:** Minneapolis, Minnesota; October 25, 1941

**Principal short fiction** • "The Common Courtesies," 1968; "Who Would Want a Little Boy?," 1968; "With All Flags Flying," 1971; "The Bride in the Boatyard," 1972; "Spending," 1973; "The Base-Metal Egg," 1973; "Half-Truths and Semi-Miracles," 1974; "A Knack for Languages," 1975; "Some Sign That I Ever Made You Happy," 1975; "The Geologist's Maid," 1975; "Your Place Is Empty," 1976; "Average Waves in Unprotected Waters," 1977; "Foot-Footing On," 1977; "Holding Things Together," 1977; "Uncle Ahmad," 1977; "Under the Bosom Tree," 1977; "Linguistics," 1978; "Laps," 1981; "The Country Cook," 1982; "Teenage Wasteland," 1983; "Rerun," 1988; "A Woman Like a Fieldstone House," 1989; "People Who Don't Know the Answers," 1991.

**Other literary forms** • Anne Tyler published the first novel of seventeen novels, *If Morning Ever Comes*, in 1964. Later titles include *Searching for Caleb* (1976), *Earthly Possessions* (1977), *Morgan's Passing* (1980), *Dinner at the Homesick Restaurant* (1982), *The Accidental Tourist* (1985), *Breathing Lessons* (1988), *Saint Maybe* (1991), *Ladder of Years* (1995), *A Patchwork Planet* (1998), *Back When We Were Grownups* (2001), *The Amateur Marriage* (2004), and *Digging to America* (2006). Tyler has also published many nonfiction articles and essays about writing and writers. Hundreds of her book reviews have appeared in national periodicals. She has also written a children's book, *Tumble Tower* (1993), which was illustrated by her daughter Mitra Modarressi.

**Achievements** • At Duke University, Anne Tyler won the Anne Flexner Award for creative writing. In 1966, she won the *Mademoiselle* magazine award for showing promise as a writer. In 1969 and 1972, she won O. Henry Awards for the short stories "Common Courtesies" and "With All Flags Flying." In 1977, she received a citation from the American Academy of Arts and Letters for her novel *Earthly Possessions*. In 1980, *Morgan's Passing* won her the Janet Heidinger Kafka Prize. In 1982, Tyler was nominated for the Pulitzer Prize for her novel *Dinner at the Homesick Restaurant*, which won a PEN/Faulkner Award for fiction. In 1985, she won the National Book Critics Circle Award for *The Accidental Tourist*, and in 1988, the film version won four Academy Award nominations. That same year Tyler was a National Book Award finalist for *Breathing Lessons*, the novel for which she won the Pulitzer Prize for Literature in 1989. *Breathing Lessons*, *Saint Maybe*, and *Ladder of Years* were Book-of-the-Month Club selections.

Tyler's novel *The Accidental Tourist* was adapted for the screen in 1988, as was her 1970 novel *A Slipping-Down Life* in 1999. *Earthly Possessions*, *Saint Maybe*, and *Breathing Lessons* were all adapted to television dramas.

**Biography** • When Anne Tyler was seven, her parents moved to Celo, a Quaker commune in North Carolina, to raise their family in a quiet, isolated environment. Anne and her two brothers were schooled at home. Tyler became an avid reader, and her favorite book was *The Little House* (1942) by Virginia Lee Burton. Unable to support the family adequately at Celo, Tyler's parents moved to Raleigh in 1952, where her father worked as a research chemist, and her mother became a social worker. The Tylers were activists in the Civil Rights movement, opposed the death penalty, and, as Quaker pacifists, opposed U.S. involvement in war. With this background, it is surprising that Tyler's writing reveals no political or social ideology, other than her portrayal of the family as a basic unit in society.

Tyler attended high school in Raleigh, where Mrs. Peacock, her English teacher, taught literature with a dramatic flair and inspired Anne's desire to become a writer. At the age of sixteen, she entered Duke University on scholarship, majoring in Russian studies and literature, and graduated Phi Beta Kappa in 1961. At Duke, Professors Reynolds Price and William Blackburn recognized her talent. Eudora Welty's conversational dialogue, southern settings, and gentle satire also influenced Tyler.

Tyler attended Columbia University but did not finish her master's degree. While working in the library at Duke University, she met Taghi Modarressi, an Iranian medical student, and married him in 1963. After he completed his residency in child psychiatry at McGill University in Canada, the couple moved to Baltimore, Maryland, where they established a permanent home and produced two daughters, Tezh and Mitra. After Taghi Modarressi died there of lymphoma in April, 1997, Tyler continued to reside in, and set her fiction in, Baltimore.

As a full-time wife and mother, Tyler wrote and published many short stories and book reviews. Always time-oriented and well organized, she wrote when the children were napping or at school. She has said that her early novels are flawed because normal family distractions interfered with her concentration while she was writing them. In 1970, her novels began to attract readers and critics, and by 1980, her reputation as a mature writer was secure.

Tyler maintains disciplined work methods. She begins writing after breakfast and continues for seven hours daily until late afternoon. She keeps a file of ideas, interesting people, and newspaper articles. Then she plans a story, using charts, pictures, and doodles. She imagines life inside her characters' skins, until they come alive for her. Tyler writes early drafts in longhand because the flow of her pen stimulates creativity; then she writes final drafts on a word processor. When she finishes a project, she rests and enjoys gardening and her family. Her two greatest fears are blindness and arthritis, diseases affecting the senses of sight and touch. As Tyler's skill and success as a novelist has grown, her prolific production of short stories and articles has declined.

**Analysis** • Classified by critics as a southern writer, Anne Tyler focuses on modern families and their unique relationships. Her underlying theme is that time inexorably changes the direction of people's lives. The past determines the present and the present determines the future. Her stories show that life moves in generational cycles and that conflicts almost inevitably arise as time passes and settings change. Within families, the perspective of love evolves, children grow up and leave home, and death and grief sever connections. When a character's freedom is restricted by too many demands on energy or resources, the individual must make choices, adapt to changing circumstances, and endure insecurity and hardship before reaching a temporary equilibrium. Tyler says that life is a "web, crisscrossed by strings of love and need and worry." Her humanistic worldview focuses on individuals, isolated and unable to communicate complex emotions such as love, grief, despair, or guilt. Missed connections, language, social class, age, religious beliefs, ethnicity, and other barriers prevent communication.

Tyler is always aware of the writer/reader connection. What draws a reader are "concrete details, carefully layered to create complexity and depth, like real life." Characters must be individuals with unique qualities, and their dialogue must flow like conversation. Tyler often uses multiple points of view as a third-person observer. She says she is able to assume a convincing masculine persona in her narrative because most human experience has no particular gender. She makes effective use of flashbacks, in which a character's memory travels to the past and links it to the present and future.

**"Your Place Is Empty"** • The idea for this story occurred when Tyler accompanied her husband, Taghi Modarressi, to Iran to meet his large family. Before the journey, Tyler, like the character Elizabeth, taught herself Persian and spoke it well enough to communicate on a surface level, but she soon discovered that mere words could not express complex emotions or overcome her feelings of being an outsider in a foreign culture.

The situation is reversed in "Your Place Is Empty." Mrs. Ardavi arrives in the United States for a six-month visit with her son Hassan, his American wife Elizabeth, and their small daughter. Hassan has lived in the United States for twelve years and is a successful doctor. Upon arrival at the airport, his mother does not recognize him. She reminds him that his place at home is still empty and urges him to return to Iran. Hassan has not forgotten his heritage, but he has changed, an underlying theme of the story.

Another theme shows how conflicts arise when people from different cultures cannot adapt. At first Elizabeth tries to make Mrs. Ardavi welcome, but soon language and culture become barriers to communication. As Mrs. Ardavi attempts to express her personality and infuse her son's home with Iranian customs, Elizabeth feels resentful and isolated, as if her freedom within her own home is restricted. Food preparation symbolizes their conflict. Elizabeth serves bacon, a taboo food for Mrs. Ardavi, who clutters Elizabeth's kitchen with spices and herbs, pots and pans, as she prepares Hassan's favorite lamb stew. She thinks that Elizabeth's meals are inadequate and that she is a negligent mother. Like an unsuccessful arbiter, Hassan stands between his mother and Elizabeth.

Tyler uses a narrative point of view that shifts between Mrs. Ardavi and Elizabeth. Insight into both women's personalities evokes reader sympathy, especially for Mrs. Ardavi. In flashbacks, she recalls her traditional Muslim girlhood; an arranged marriage to a man she never loved; his prolonged illness and death; grief over her oldest son's unhappy marriage and his untimely death; problems with the spoiled and pregnant wife of her youngest son; and the small comfort of "knowing her place" within the family circle of thirteen sisters who gossip and drink tea each afternoon. Elizabeth expresses resentment at her mother-in-law's interference with icy silence, zealous housecleaning, and private complaints to Hassan. Realizing that the situation has reached an impasse, Hassan suggests that for the duration of her visit, Mrs. Ardavi move to a nearby apartment, away from the intimacy of his family. Unable to find "her place" in her son's American home, Mrs. Ardavi returns to Iran.

**"Average Waves in Unprotected Waters"** • This story shows how the passage of time causes physical and emotional changes for Bet, a single mother, and Arnold, her mentally disabled son. Avery Blevins, Bet's "grim and cranky" husband, deserts her after a doctor diagnoses their baby as mentally disabled, the result of a fateful genetic error. Without family (her parents are dead), Bet supports herself and her child at a low-paying job. Arnold's increasingly wild tantrums force her to place him in a state hospital. Bet's landlady and longtime baby-sitter is a kindly woman, who has grown too old to control Arnold's aggressive behavior. His lack of response to her tears and special gift of cookies when he leaves indicates his infantile emotional level. On the train he enjoys watching the conductor scold a black woman for trying to ride without a ticket and cheers loudly as if they are actors in a television comedy. Arnold ignores the hospital setting and the nurse until his mother leaves. Then, like a small child, he screams loudly enough for Bet to hear him in the driveway as she climbs into a taxi. The train is late; so Bet dries her tears and watches strangers draping bunting on a speaker's stand in preparation for a ceremony dedicat-

© Diana Walker

ing the antiquated depot's restoration. She observes their actions while she waits for the train to take her life in a new direction.

Tyler describes how the passage of time erodes concrete objects and compares it to changing human relationships. The shabby boardinghouse has peeling layers of wallpaper, symbolic of passing time and the people who once lived there. Bet is worn down physically and emotionally by Arnold's hyperactive behavior, his short attention span, and his loud, incoherent speech. Marble steps at the mental hospital are worn down by the feet of care-givers and patients who have climbed them. The hospital dormitory is stripped of color and warmth. Only a small, crooked clown picture indicates that children might live there. The nurse disengages emotionally when Bet tries to tell her about Arnold's unique qualities. The train conductor, taxi driver, and station attendant are coldly impersonal, showing lack of empathy for Bet and Arnold. In the past, they have witnessed many arrivals and departures like Bet's and no longer respond to them.

The title "Average Waves in Unprotected Waters" indicates how the main characters, Bet and Arnold, adapt to "waves" in their lives. Bet faces disappointments and griefs, just as she once allowed "ordinary" breakers in the ocean to slam against her body, "as if staunchness were a virtue." The waves are not life-threatening; they are unhappy experiences to which she and Arnold must adapt in environments of "unprotected waters." Bet must endure life without family, goals, or resources, and Arnold must endure life in an impersonal mental hospital without his mother's love and protection.

**"Teenage Wasteland"** • Originally published in *Seventeen* magazine, this story shows how lack of communication between a troubled adolescent and his parents results in tragedy. Tyler's title, "Teenage Wasteland," comes from a popular song by the musical group the Who. Contributing factors to fifteen-year-old Donnie's "wasted" life include Daisy and Matt's inept parenting skills, a tutor's destructive influence, and Donnie's changing needs as an adolescent. Poor grades, petty thefts, smoking and drinking, and truancy are symptoms of Donnie's low self-esteem.

Tyler tells the story from a third-person point of view, limited to Daisy, a mother who agonizes over her guilt and inadequacies as a parent. Significantly, Matt, the father, does not get directly involved in guiding or disciplining his son. Neither parent is able to talk to Donnie about his personal problems. They focus on academic performance. At first, the parents make strict rules, and Daisy helps Donnie complete his assignments. However, her best efforts result in minimal improvement and cause major emotional storms.

Humiliated and unable to cope, Daisy takes Donnie to see Cal, a young counselor and tutor whose office is in his house, where other students lounge around, playing basketball and listening to rock music by the Who. Cal "marches to a different drummer" and encourages Donnie and other adolescents under his tutelage to rebel from "controlling" adults, like parents and school authorities. Accepting responsibility for one's actions, setting goals, and studying are not part of Cal's agenda. Donnie gradually withdraws from his family in favor of "hanging out" at Cal's with teenagers like himself.

Donnie is expelled from the private school he attends after authorities find beer and cigarettes in his locker, and his academic performance drops even lower. Instead of going home, he runs to Cal's. Donnie claims it was a "frame up," and Cal excuses the boy by saying that the school violated his civil rights. Angry and frustrated, Daisy takes Donnie home and enrolls him in public school, where he finishes the semester. Miserable and friendless, Donnie runs away, his youth wasted, and Daisy wonders what went wrong.

**"People Who Don't Know the Answers"** • This story, published in *The New Yorker*, is a revised chapter from Tyler's novel *Saint Maybe*. Doug Bedloe, a recently retired schoolteacher, realizes that nobody has the final answers to life's mysteries. The passage of time changes everything. To fill the void in his life, he tries several boring and unproductive hobbies. Then he becomes interested in some foreign students who live across the street. Like actors in a comedy, they enjoy a casual lifestyle and are fascinated by American gadgets, music, language, and clothing, far different from the "real" life and family responsibilities they have known in distant lands.

Doug compares their experimental lifestyle to his own static existence. Seen through the foreigners' window screen, his house reminds him of a framed needlepoint picture, something "cozy, old-fashioned, stitched in place forever." Yet Doug's family has changed. His wife Bee has become disabled with arthritis. Death has taken their oldest son Danny, whose children now live with them. Beastie, Doug's old dog and companion, is buried under the azalea. Adult siblings, Ian and Claudia, have gradually assumed family authority. Doug feels physically fit, but his life has no anchor. His past is gone, and he must somehow endure the present.

Ian invites his family to a picnic sponsored by the Church of the Second Chance, viewed by some as a cult, or "alternative religion." Brother Emmett and church members have helped Ian endure his overwhelming sense of guilt over Danny's accidental death and support his role as surrogate father to Danny's children. Doug acknowledges that sharing one's joys and sorrows would benefit him, but Bee remains cynical. Doug's past and the present reality make him feel split, like the foreigners' old car, parked half inside their garage with the faulty automatic door bisecting it.

*Martha E. Rhynes*
*With updates by the Editors*

**Other major works**

CHILDREN'S LITERATURE: *Tumble Tower,* 1993 (illustrations by Mitra Modarressi).
NOVELS: *If Morning Ever Comes,* 1964; *The Tin Can Tree,* 1965; *A Slipping-Down Life,* 1970; *The Clock Winder,* 1972; *Celestial Navigation,* 1974; *Searching for Caleb,* 1976; *Earthly Possessions,* 1977; *Morgan's Passing,* 1980; *Dinner at the Homesick Restaurant,* 1982; *The Accidental Tourist,* 1985; *Breathing Lessons,* 1988; *Saint Maybe,* 1991; *Ladder of Years,* 1995; *A Patchwork Planet,* 1998; *Back When We Were Grownups,* 2001; *The Amateur Marriage,* 2004; *Digging to America,* 2006.

**Bibliography**

Bail, Paul. *Anne Tyler: A Critical Companion.* Westport, Conn.: Greenwood Press, 1998. Part of a series of reference books about popular contemporary writers, this book contains a biography, literary influences on Anne Tyler, and individual chapters that discuss twelve of Tyler's novels. General analysis includes how her novels fit into southern regional literature, women's literature, and popular culture, as well as critiques from feminist and multicultural points of view. Bail also discusses plot, characters, themes, literary devices, historical settings, and narrative points of view as they apply to individual novels. The book concludes with an extensive bibliography.

Croft, Robert W. *Anne Tyler: A Bio-Bibliography.* Westport, Conn.: Greenwood Press, 1995. Part of a series focusing on American authors, this book is divided into two parts: a biography which includes four chapters, each followed by endnotes. It concludes with an extensive bibliography, divided into primary and secondary sources, with a list of Anne Tyler's papers at Duke University. "A Setting Apart" concerns her childhood in a commune, teen years in Raleigh, college at Duke, and early writing. "The Only Way Out" refers to her feelings of isolation during her early marriage and motherhood and how writing her first novels and short stories kept her in touch with the real world. "Rich with Possibilities" refers to her life in Baltimore, the setting of most of her stories, her book reviews, and discussion of her middle-period novels. "A Border Crossing" deals with Tyler's fame and recurring themes in her novels.

Harper, Natalie. "Teenage Wasteland." In *Masterplots II: Short Story Series,* edited by Charles E. May. Rev. ed. Vol. 7. Pasadena, Calif.: Salem Press, 2004. Analysis of "Teenage Wasteland" with sections on themes and meaning and style and technique. Also includes a detailed synopsis of the story.

Robertson, Mary F. "Anne Tyler: Medusa Points and Contact Points." In *Contemporary American Women Writers: Narrative Strategies,* edited by Catherine Rainwater and William J. Scheick. Lexington: University Press of Kentucky, 1985. Discussion of the narrative form of Tyler's novels, focusing on her disruption of the conventional expectations of family novels.

Salwak, Dale, ed. *Anne Tyler as Novelist.* Iowa City: University of Iowa Press, 1994. Collection of essays addressing Tyler's development, attainments, and literary reputation.

Stephens, C. Ralph, ed. *The Fiction of Anne Tyler.* Jackson: University Press of Mississippi, 1990. Collection of essays selected from papers given in 1989 at the Anne Tyler Symposium in Baltimore and representing a range of interests and approaches.

Thorndike, Jonathan L. "The Artificial Family." In *Masterplots II: Short Story Series,* edited by Charles E. May. Rev. ed. Vol. 1. Pasadena, Calif.: Salem Press, 2004. Student-friendly analysis of "The Artificial Family" that covers the story's themes and style and includes a detailed synopsis.

Tyler, Anne. "Still Just Writing." In *The Writer on Her Work: Contemporary Women Writers Reflect on Their Art and Situation.* Edited by Janet Sternberg. New York: W. W. Norton, 1980. Tyler's personal essay explains how she keeps her life balanced. Writing fiction draws her into an imaginary world, but being a wife and mother keeps her anchored to the *real* world of home and family. Writing novels takes much time and concentration, so she has gradually given up writing short stories. Revised chapters from some of her novels appear in periodicals as short stories. She has reduced the number of book reviews she writes because she fears her lack of enthusiasm will not give books and authors a fair analysis.

Voelker, Joseph C. *Art and the Accidental in Anne Tyler.* Columbia: University of Missouri Press, 1989. The first book-length study of Anne Tyler's fiction, this volume focuses on the development of Tyler's aesthetics and her treatment of character, particularly her view of selfhood as mystery and of experience as accidental.

# John Updike

**Born:** Shillington, Pennsylvania; March 18, 1932

**Principal short fiction** • *The Same Door*, 1959; *Pigeon Feathers, and Other Stories*, 1962; *Olinger Stories: A Selection*, 1964; *The Music School*, 1966; *Museums and Women, and Other Stories*, 1972; *Problems, and Other Stories*, 1979; *Three Illuminations in the Life of an American Author*, 1979; *Too Far to Go: The Maples Stories*, 1979; *The Chaste Planet*, 1980; *Bech Is Back*, 1982; *The Beloved*, 1982; *Trust Me*, 1987; *Brother Grasshopper*, 1990 (limited edition); *The Afterlife, and Other Stories*, 1994; *Licks of Love: Short Stories and a Sequel, "Rabbit Remembered,"* 2000; *The Complete Henry Bech: Twenty Stories*, 2001; *The Early Stories, 1953-1975*, 2003.

**Other literary forms** • A prolific and versatile writer, John Updike is an accomplished novelist, best known for his "Rabbit" tetralogy, but he is also the author of *The Centaur* (1963), which fuses myth and realism in middle-class America; *Couples* (1968), which examines the social and sexual mores of a modern American town; *The Coup* (1978), in which the narrator is writing, in memoirs, the history of an imaginary African nation; and *Roger's Version* (1986) and *S* (1988), which are creative reworkings of the situation of Nathaniel Hawthorne's *The Scarlet Letter* (1850). His later novels include *Brazil* (1994), *Toward the End of Time* (1997), *Bech at Bay: A Quasi-Novel* (1998), *Gertrude and Claudius* (2000), *Seek My Face* (2002), *Villages* (2004), and *Terrorist* (2006).

Updike has also published many books of verse, including *Americana, and Other Poems* (2001); a play (*Buchanan Dying*, 1974), and scores of reviews and critical essays on literature, music, and painting. His nonfiction books include *Golf Dreams: Writings on Golf* (1996), *More Matter: Essays and Criticism* (1999), and *Still Looking: Essays on American Art* (2005).

**Achievements** • *The Centaur* won for John Updike the National Book Award in 1964. He was elected to the National Institute of Arts and Letters, the youngest man to receive the honor at that time. "The Bulgarian Poetess" won an O. Henry Award in 1966.

*Rabbit Is Rich* (1981) won an American Book Award and a Pulitzer Prize, while *Hugging the Shore: Essays and Criticism* (1983), a nine-hundred-page volume, won the National Book Critics Circle Award. In 1991, *Rabbit at Rest* won a Pulitzer Prize, and in 1995, it received the Howells Medal. In 1996, Updike's *In the Beauty of the Lilies* (1996) won the Ambassador Book Award, and the next year Updike received the Campion Award. In 1998, he earned the Harvard Arts First Medal and the National Book Medal for Distinguished Contribution to American Letters.

**Biography** • John Updike was born in 1932, the only child of Wesley Updike, a cable splicer who lost his job in the Depression and had to support his family on a meager teacher's salary ($1,740 per year), and Linda Grace Updike, an aspiring writer. The family moved to Plowville from Shillington, Pennsylvania, in 1945 to live on the farm of Updike's maternal grandparents. Updike recalls that a gift subscription at that time to *The New Yorker*, a Christmas present from an aunt, was a significant factor in his decision to become an artist. In high school, he drew for the school paper, wrote articles and poems, and demonstrated sufficient academic gifts to be awarded a full scholarship to Harvard University, which he entered in 1950.

At college, Updike majored in English, became editor of the prestigious Harvard *Lampoon*, and graduated with honors in 1954. That year, *The New Yorker* accepted a poem and a story, an event that Updike remembered as "the ecstatic breakthrough of my literary life." After graduation, Updike and his wife of one year, Mary Pennington, a fine arts major from Radcliffe, spent 1955 in Oxford, where Updike held a Knox Fellowship. When E. B. White offered him a job as a staff writer with *The New Yorker*, Updike accepted and spent the next two years contributing brief, witty pieces to the "Talk of the Town" section at the front of the magazine. During this time, he worked on the manuscript of a six-hundred-page book, which he decided not to publish because it had "too many of the traits of a first novel." When his second child was born, he believed that he needed a different setting in which to live and work (the literary world in New York seemed "unnutritious and interfering") and moved to Ipswich, Massachusetts, where he found "the space" to write "the Pennsylvania thing," which became the novel *The Poorhouse Fair* (1959), and his first collection of short stories, *The Same Door*.

Choosing to work in a rented office in downtown Ipswich, Updike began an extremely active literary career that would continue for several decades. The first book in the Rabbit series, *Rabbit, Run*, was published in 1960, the same year in which the last of Updike's four children was born. *Rabbit, Run* caught the attention of the reading public with its combination of sexual candor and social insight, but *The Centaur* was Updike's first real success with serious critics, winning the National Book Award in 1964. That same year, Updike was elected a member of the National Institute of Arts and Letters. During 1964 and 1965, Updike traveled in Eastern Europe, the source for his first story about Henry Bech ("The Bulgarian Poetess"), who became a kind of slightly displaced version of himself in the guise of a Jewish writer from New York. Further travels to Africa led to other Bech stories as well as *The Coup*, but Updike generally remained in Ipswich, involved in local affairs, writing constantly, and using the beach to find the sun, which was the only cure at that time for a serious case of psoriasis. The second Rabbit book, *Rabbit Redux*, was published in 1971, and short-story collections appeared regularly. During the late 1960's, Updike sold the screen rights to his novel *Couples* for a half-million dollars (the film was not produced).

After fifteen years, Updike and his wife ended their marriage, and in 1974 he moved to Boston, returning to the North Shore area in 1976, the year before he married Martha Bernhard. In 1977, Updike published his fifth volume of verse, *Tossing and Turning*, from a major press, and in 1979, two collections of short stories that he had written during the emotional turmoil of the last years of his marriage and its conclusion were issued as *Problems, and Other Stories* and *Too Far to Go*. The latter volume included all the stories about a couple named Maples whose lives were a literary transmutation of aspects of Updike's first marriage. Updike continued his energetic and inventive career through the 1980's, writing two novels imaginatively derived from Hawthorne's *The Scarlet Letter*, possibly completing the Rabbit series with *Rabbit at Rest* (1990) and collecting another nine hundred pages of essays in *Odd Jobs* (1991). In 1991, *Rabbit at Rest* won a Pulitzer Prize, and Updike continued to garner awards throughout the 1990's. He is known as one of the United States' leading writers.

**Analysis** • From the beginning of his career as a writer, John Updike demonstrated his strengths as a brilliant stylist and a master of mood and tone whose linguistic facility has sometimes overshadowed the dimensions of his vision of existence in the twentieth century. His treatment of some of the central themes of modern times—sexual and social politics, the nature of intimate relationships, the collapse of traditional values, the uncertainty of the human condition as the twentieth century drew to a close—is as revealing and compelling as that of any of his contemporaries. Although he is regarded mainly as a novelist, the short story may well be his true métier, and his ability to use its compressed structure to generate intensity and to offer succinct insight has made his work a measure of success for writers of short fiction, an evolving example of the possibilities of innovation and invention in a traditional narrative form.

© Davis Freeman

*The Same Door* **and** *Pigeon Feathers, and Other Stories* • Always eloquent about his aspirations and intentions—as he is about almost everything he observes—John Updike remarked to Charles Thomas Samuels in an interview in 1968 that some of the themes of his work are "domestic fierceness within the middle class, sex and death as riddles for the thinking animal, social existence as sacrifice, unexpected pleasures and rewards, corruption as a kind of evolution," and that his work is "meditation, not pontification." In his short fiction, his meditations have followed an arc of human development from the exuberance of youth to the unsettling revelations of maturity and on toward the uncertainties of old age, a "curve of sad time" (as he ruefully described the years from 1971 to 1978, when his first marriage failed), which contains the range of experience of an extremely incisive, very well-educated, and stylistically brilliant man who has been able to reach beyond the limits of his own interesting life to capture the ethos of an era.

Updike's artistic inclinations were nurtured by his sensitive, supportive parents, who recognized his gifts and his needs, while the struggles of his neighbors in rural Pennsylvania during the Depression left him with a strong sense of the value of community and the basis for communal cohesion in a reliable, loving family. At Harvard, his intellectual capabilities were celebrated and encouraged, and in his first job with *The New Yorker,* his ability to earn a living through his writing endowed his entire existence with an exhilaration that demanded expression in a kind of linguistic rapture. The 1950's marked the steepest incline in time's curve, and his first two collections, *The Same Door* and *Pigeon Feathers, and Other Stories,* while primarily covering his youth and adolescence in the town of Shillington (which he calls Olinger), are written from the perspective of the young man who overcame the limitations of an economically strained and culturally depleted milieu to marry happily, begin a family, and capitalize on his talents in the profession that he adored. There is no false sentimentality about Olinger or the narrowness of some its citizens. Updike always saw right through the fakery of the chamber of commerce manipulators who disguised their bigotry and anti-intellectualism with pitches to patriotism, but the young men in these stories often seem destined to overcome whatever obstacles they face to move toward the promise of some artistic or social reward.

In "Flight," a high school senior is forced to relinquish his interest in a classmate because of his mother's pressures and his social status, but the loss is balanced by his initial venture into individual freedom. "The Alligators" depicts a moment of embarrassed misperception, but in the context of the other stories, it is only a temporary setback, an example of awkwardness that might, upon reflection, contribute to the cultivation of a subtler sensibility. "The Happiest I've Been" epitomizes the author's attitude at a pivotal point in his life, poised between the familiar if mundane streets of his childhood and the infinite expanse of a world beyond, enjoying the lingering nostalgia he feels for home ground, which he can carry in memory as he moves on to a wider sphere of experience. These themes are rendered with a particular power in the often-anthologized "A&P" and in "Wife-Wooing," both from *Pigeon Feathers, and Other Stories*.

**"A&P"** • As in many of his most effective stories, in "A&P" Updike found a voice of singular appropriateness for his narrative consciousness—a boy of nineteen from a working-class background who is working as a checkout clerk at the local A&P grocery store. The store stands for the assembly-line numbness that is a part of the lockstep life that seems to be the likely destiny of all the young men in the town, and it serves as a means of supply for a nearby resort area. When three young women pass the boy's register, he is enchanted by "the queen," a girl who appears "more than pretty," and when she is ordered to dress properly by the store manager on her next visit ("Girls, this isn't the beach"), Sammy feels compelled to deliver a declaration of passionate defense of their innocence. Frustrated by the incipient stodginess and puritanical repression of the entire town and moved by his heart-driven need to make some kind of chivalrous gesture, he finds that his only recourse is to mumble "I quit" as the girls leave the store.

Lengel, the aptly named manager-curmudgeon, speaking for unreasoning minor authority, uses several power trips to maintain his petty tyranny, but Sammy refuses to back down, even when Lengel presents the ultimate guilt ploy, "You don't want to do this to your Mom and Dad." This is an appeal to conformist quiescence, and Sammy, like most of Updike's protagonists, is susceptible to the possibility of hurting or disgracing his family in a small, gossip-ridden community. When Lengel warns him, "You'll feel this for the rest of your life," Sammy recognizes the validity of his threat but realizes that, if he backs down now, he will always back down in similar situations. Frightened and uncertain, he finds the resolve to maintain his integrity by carrying through his gesture of defiance. He knows that he will have to accept the consequences of his actions, but this is the true source of his real strength. Acknowledging that now "he felt how hard the world was going to be to me hereafter," his acceptance of the struggle is at the root of his ability to face challenges in the future. As if to ratify his decision, Lengel is described in the last paragraph reduced to Sammy's slot, "checking the sheep through," his visage "dark gray and his back stiff." If the reward for selling out is a life like Lengel's, then even an act that no one but its agent appreciates (the girls never notice their champion) is better than the defeat of submerging the self in the despair of denial.

**"Wife-Wooing"** • "Wife-Wooing" is the real reward for acting according to principle. If the A&P is the symbol of enclosure and the girl a figure for the wonder of the cosmos beyond, then marriage to a woman who incarnates the spirit of wonder contains the possibilities for paradise. The mood of ecstasy is established immediately by the narrator's declaration of devotion, "OH MY LOVE. Yes. Here we sit, on warm broad floor-boards, before a fire. . . ." He is a man whose marriage, in its initial stages, is informed by what seems like an exponential progression of promise. Thus, although he has "won" his mate, he is impelled to continue to woo her as a testament to his continuing condition of bliss, of his exultation in the sensuality of the body's familiar but still mysterious terrain—its "absolute geography." The evocative description of the couple together—framed in images of light and warmth—is sufficient to convey the delight they share, but what makes the story noteworthy is Updike's employment and investigation of the erotics of language as a register of feeling. The mood of arousal becomes a kind of celebration of the words that describe it, so that it is the "irrefutably magical life language leads with itself" that becomes the substance of erotic interest.

Updike, typically, recalls James Joyce, using Blazes Boylan's word "smackwarm" from "the legendary, imperfectly explored grottoes of *Ulysses*" to let loose a chain of linguistic associations beginning with a consideration of the root etymology of "woman"—the "wide w, the receptive o. Womb." Located in a characteristically masculine perspective (almost inevitable considering Updike's background and the historical context), the narrator envisions himself as a warrior/hunter in prehistoric times, and in a brilliantly imaginative, affectionate parody of Anglo-Saxon alliterative verse, Updike continues to express the husband's exultation through the kind of linguistic overdrive that makes his mastery of styles the focus of admiration (and envy) of many of his peers. Beneath the wordplay and the almost self-congratulatory cleverness, however, there is still another level of intent. Once the element of erotic power in language itself has been introduced, Updike is free to employ that language in an investigation of sensuality that strains at the bounds of what was acceptable in 1960. His purpose is to examine a marriage at the potentially dangerous seven-year point, to recall the sexual history of the couple, and to show how the lessons of mutual experience have enabled them to deepen their erotic understanding as the marriage progressed.

Continuing to use language to chart the erogenous regions of the mind and body, Updike arranges a series of puns ("Oh cunning trick") so that the dual fascination of love—for wife, words—is expressed in intertwined images of passion. The story concludes with the husband leaving for work in the cold stone of a city of "heartless things," then returning to the eternal mystery of woman/wooing, where, as Robert Creeley's poem "The Wife" expresses it, he knows "two women/ and the one/ is tangible substance,/ flesh and bone," while "the other in my mind/ occurs."

*The Henry Bech stories* • Updike's energetic involvement with the dimensions of life—the domestic and the artistic—crested on a curve of satisfaction for him as the 1950's drew to a close. The chaotic explosion of countercultural diversity that took place in the 1960's fractured the comforting coordinates of a world with which Updike had grown very familiar, and he began to find himself in an adversary position both toward the confines of bourgeois social values and toward the sprawling uncertainty of a country in entropic transition. As a means of confronting this situation at a remove that would permit some aesthetic distance from his displeasure, Updike created Henry Bech, an urban, blocked Jewish writer seemingly the polar opposite of the now urbane Updike but actually only a slight transmutation of his own sensibility. Bech is much more successful in managing the perils of the age than Harry Angstrom, who represents Updike's peevish squareness in *Rabbit Redux*, and the "interview" "Bech Meets Me" (November, 1971) is a jovial display of Updike's witty assessment of his problems and goals.

The individual Bech stories, beginning with "The Bulgarian Poetess" (from *The Music School*), which covers Updike's experiences on a trip to Eastern Europe sponsored by the State Department, generally work as separate entities, but they are linked sufficiently that there is a clear progression in *Bech: A Book*, while *Bech Is Back* is closer to a novel than a collection of short fiction and *Bech at Bay* is classified as long fiction. Through the personae of Henry Bech and Rabbit Angstrom, among others, Updike maintained a distinct distance from the political and incipient personal turmoil that he was experiencing.

**The Music School** • In *The Music School*, the stories include fond recollections of a positive, recent past, as in "The Christian Roommates" (which "preserved" aspects of his Harvard experience), or tentative excursions into the malaise of the times, as in the fascinating dissection of psychoanalytic methods offered by "My Lover Has Dirty Fingernails" and in the unusual venture into the possibilities of renewal in a natural setting of "The Hermit." In this story, the prickly, idiosyncratic spirit of the New England individualist and environmentalist Henry David Thoreau is expressed as an urge to escape from the social realities of *success*—an essentially forlorn quest for a larger sense of life than "they" will permit and an attempt to explore the possibility of a mystical essence beyond the attainment of intellectual power.

**Museums and Women, and Other Stories** • Although Updike spoke admiringly of the "splendid leafiness" of Pennsylvania and could evoke the mood of Scotland's highland moors (as in "Macbech") with typical facility, his central subject has always been the nature of relationships. In *Museums and Women, and Other Stories*, he returned to the consequences of marked changes in the social climate and his personal life that could not be avoided by fictional explorations of subsidiary concerns. The story "When Everyone Was Pregnant" is a paean to an old order passing into history, a celebration of years of relative pleasure and satisfaction that he calls "the Fifties" but which actually encompass the first half of the century. "*My* Fifties," he labels them, positioning himself at the center of a benign cosmos, where tests were passed ("Entered them poor and left them comfortable. Entered them chaste and left them a father") and life was relatively uncomplicated. The paragraphs of the story are like a shorthand list of bounty ("Jobs, houses, spouses of our own"), and the entire era is cast in an aura of innocence, a prelude to a sudden shock of consciousness that utterly changed everything. The factors that caused the shift are never identified, leaving the narrator bewildered ("Now: our babies drive cars, push pot, shave, menstruate, riot for peace, eat macrobiotic"), but the alteration in perception is palpable and its ramifications ("Sarah looks away" after fifteen shared years) unavoidable.

The last section of *Museums and Women, and Other Stories* contains five stories under the subhead "The Maples." Updike eventually published seventeen stories about Richard and Joan Maple, a family with four children that might be said to approximate Updike's first marriage, in *Too Far to Go*, and the narrative thread that becomes apparent in the full collection is the transition from optimism and contentment to uncertainty and fracture. A story that registers the process of psychological displacement particularly well is the last one in *Museums and Women, and Other Stories*, "Sublimating," in which the Maples have decided to give up sex, which they have mistakenly identified as the "only sore point" in their marriage. Since nearly all that Updike has written on the subject indicates that sex is at the heart of everything that matters in a relationship, the decision—as Updike assumed would be obvious to everyone but the parties involved—was a false solution that could only aggravate the problem. What becomes apparent as the story progresses is that everything in the relationship has become a pretext for disguising true feeling, but the desperation of the participants makes their methods of camouflage sympathetic and understandable.

Unable to accept that change in both parties has permanently altered their position, Richard and Joan repeat strategies that have previously revitalized their marriage, but nothing can be successful, since the actors no longer fit their roles. The procedures of the past cannot be recapitulated, and their efforts produce a series of empty rituals that leave the Maples exhausted and angry. Using external remedies for internal maladies (the purchase of an old farmhouse, impulsive acquisition of trivia), bantering about each other's lovers to reignite passion, turning their children into would-be allies, exchanging barbed, bitchy, and self-regarding comments, the Maples are more baffled than destructive, but both of them are aware that they will eventually have to confront the fact that they have no solution. Sublimation is ultimately suppression of truth, and Richard Maple's description of the people in a pornographic film house on Forty-second Street in Manhattan as perpetual spectators, who watch unseeing while meaningless acts of obscenity occur in the distance, stands as an emblem of stasis and nullity, a corollary to the paralysis that engulfs the couple. Joan Maple's final comment on their current state, a pathetic observation about the "cleansing" aspects of their nonsensual behavior, brings the story to a conclusion that is warped with tension, a situation that Richard Maple's comment, "we may be on to something," does nothing to relieve.

**Problems, and Other Stories** • Updike's next collection, *Problems, and Other Stories*, contains a prefatory note that begins, "Seven years since my last short story collection? There must have been problems." The central problem has been the end of Updike's first marriage and the removal of the core of certainty that the domestic structure of his family provided. The unraveling of the threads that were woven through a lifetime of intelligent analysis and instinctual response called everything into question and opened a void that had been lurking near the surface of Updike's work. Updike was far too perceptive ever to assume that a stable family was possible for everyone or that it would provide answers for everything. From the start of the Rabbit tetralogy, the strains inherent in an ongoing marital arrangement were examined closely, but the dissolution of his own primary household drew several specific responses that expanded the range and depth of his short fiction. First, the sad facts of the separation and divorce were handled in the last Maple stories.

"Separating" recounts the parents' attempts to explain the situation to their children. It is written in bursts of lacerating dialogue, a conversation wrought in pain and doubt that concludes with a child posing the tormenting, unanswerable query "*Why?*" to Richard Maple. "Here Come the Maples" presents the ceremony of the divorce as a reverse marriage, complete with programmed statements forcing the couple to agree by saying "I do." The jaunty tone of the proceedings does not totally mask the looming cloud of uncertainty that covers the future. Then, the artist turned toward his work for sustenance. In "From the Journal of a Leper," Updike projects his psychic condition into the life of a potter who is afflicted with a serious skin disease akin to his own. The fear of leprosy stands for all of his doubts before an unknown universe no longer relatively benign; his work provides some compensation but is intricately connected to his psychological stability; a woman with whom he is developing a relationship improves and complicates the situation. The story is open-ended, but in a forecast of the direction Updike has begun to chart for his protagonists, the artist recognizes the necessity of standing alone, dependent ultimately on his own strength. The final words may be more of a self-directed exhortation than a summary of actuality, but they represent a discernible goal: "I am free, as other men. I am whole."

**"Transaction"** • The difficulties of freedom and the elusiveness of wholeness are explored in "Transaction," one of Updike's most powerful stories. In *The Paris Review* interview with Charles Thomas Samuels, Updike said:

> About sex in general, by all means let's have it in fiction, as detailed as needs be, but real, real in its social and psychological connections. Let's take coitus out of the closet and off the altar and put it on the continuum of human behavior.

The transaction of the title involves a man in his middle years, married but alone in a city labeled "N—," in December at a conference, who somewhat impulsively picks up a prostitute and takes her to his hotel room. What exactly he is seeking is not entirely clear, because the cold, mechanical city and the "raffish army of females" occupying the streets are as much threat as promise and his temporary liberty to act as he chooses is undercut by his feelings of isolation and loneliness. Regarding his actions as a version of an exploratory adventure in which he is curious about how he will react and tempted not only by lust but also by the desire to test his virility and validity in establishing a human connection with the girl, he is moving into unknown country, where his usual persuasive strategies have no relevance. The "odorless metal" of the room mocks his efforts to re-create the warmth of a home in an anonymous city, and the false bravado of other men around him reminds him of the insecurity that lies beneath the bluster. Even what he calls the "paid moral agent" of his imagination—that is, his mostly vestigial conscience—is summoned briefly only as a source of comforting certainty in the uncharted, shifting landscape he has entered.

The man's initial investment in the room and in purchasing some aspect of the girl's time does not permit him to exercise any influence on their transaction, a reminder that his generally successful life (marriage, money, status) counts for less than he had thought. The language of commerce that he has mastered does not contain a vocabulary for expressing his current feelings. Ruled by old habits, the preliminary stages of the transaction are a capsule courtship, but he finds that his solicitations are subject to scorn or rebuke. The girl wavers in his imagination between alluring innocence and forbidding authority, an amalgam of a dream lover who accepts him and an indifferent critic who reinforces the mechanical motif by calling his genitals "them" and prepares for their assignation "with the deliberateness of an insult or the routine of marriage." Although Updike uses his extensive abilities of description to render the physical attributes of the girl in vivid detail, she does not seem sexually attractive—an implicit comment on the failure of erotic potential when it is restricted to the external surface, as well as a subtle dig at the magazine *Oui* (a *Playboy* clone), where the story originally appeared. Without the spontaneity of mutual discovery, the transaction becomes clinical and antierotic, an unnatural or perverse use of human capability.

The man is aware of the inadequacy of his supplications. He has been using the strategies of commerce—a mix of supposedly ingratiating self-pity and cold calculation—and when these fail he tries false compliance, then bogus amiability. In desperation, because of a severe reduction in sexual potence, he begins to "make love" to her, and in a shift in tone that Updike handles with characteristic smoothness, the writing becomes lyrical as the man becomes fully involved, and the woman finally responds freely and openly. Old habits intrude, however, and the man's heightened virility causes a reversion to his familiar self. He stops producing pleasure and seeks it again as his due. His excitement has been transformed from authentic passion to calculation, the transaction back on its original terms. Both parties to the agreement have reached a level of satisfaction (he is a successful sexual athlete, and she has met the terms of the contract), and, when she offers to alter the original bargain in a mixture of self-interest and genuine generosity, he is unable to make a further break away from a lifetime of monetary measure. He contents himself with small gestures of quasi gallantry that carry things back toward the original situation of customer and salesperson. Thus, the true cost of real freedom is gradually becoming apparent. He feels an urge to go beyond the transactional to the honestly emotional, but he is hindered by fear, and his instincts are frozen. The residue of the encounter is a dreadful shrinking of his sense of the universe. "She had made sex finite," he thinks, but in actuality, it is only his cramped view of his own possibilities that he sees.

**"Trust Me"** • "Transaction" marks the beginning of a phase of maturity in Updike's work in which recollection of an earlier time of certitude, confidence, and optimism is still possible, but in which a search for new modes of meaning is gradually taking precedence. "Deaths of Distant Friends," from *Trust Me*, which appeared in an anthology of *Best American Short Stories*, is a finely wrought philosophical meditation— exactly the sort of story cautious anthologists often include, a minor-key minirequiem for a grand past with only a twist of rue at the conclusion to relieve the sentimental mood. "The Egg Race," from *Problems, and Other Stories*, is somewhat more severe in its recollection of the past. Here, the origins of the problems of the present are traced with some tolerance of human need back to the narrator's father.

The title story, "Trust Me," is closer to the mood of middle-life angst that informs many of the stories. Again, the narrator reconsiders the past in an effort to determine the cause of the emptiness of the present, but in his attempts to explain the failure of faith in his life, he reveals (to himself) that his parents did not trust each other, that his first wife did not trust the modern world, that his child did not trust him, that with his girlfriend he does not trust himself, and that with a psychotropic agent, he does not (or cannot) trust his senses so he ultimately cannot trust his perceptions. Logically, then, he cannot know, with surety, anything at all. His predicament is a part of a larger vision of loss that directs many stories in the volume, as Updike's characters attempt to cope with a deterioration of faith that revives some of the earlier questions of a religious nature that formed an important dimension of Updike's writing in books such as *The Poorhouse Fair* (1959) or *A Month of Sundays* (1975). The situation has changed somewhat, though, since the more traditional religious foundations that Updike seemed to trust earlier have become less specifically sound, even if the theological questions they posed still are important. The newfound or sensed freedom that is glimpsed carries a terrifying burden of singularity.

**"Slippage"** • "Slippage" conveys this feeling through its metaphors of structural fragility. A "not quite slight earthquake" awakens a man who is "nauseated without knowing why." His wife, a much younger woman, is hidden under the covers, "like something dead on the road," an image of nullity. Blessed or cursed with a memory that "extended so much further back in time than hers," he feels she is preparing them prematurely for senility. At the age of sixty, he sees his life as a series of not-quite-achieved plateaus. His work as a scholar was adequate but not all that it might have been, and his "late-capitalist liberal humanism" now seems passé. Even his delight in the sensual has been shaken, "though only thrice wed." Updike depicts him in his confusion as "a flake of consciousness lost within time's black shale" and extends the metaphor of infirmity to a loose molar and a feeling that his children are "a tiny, hard, slightly shrivelled core of disappointment." In the story's denouement, the man meets a woman at a party; she excites him, but it turns out that she is "quite mad," an ultimate betrayal of his instincts. At the close, he lies in bed again, anticipating another earth tremor and feeling its unsettling touch in his imagination.

**"The City"** • The aura of discouragement that "Slippage" projects is balanced by another of Updike's most forceful stories, "The City" (also from *Trust Me*). Recalling both "Transaction" with its portrayal of a business traveler alone in an urban wasteland and several later stories in which illness or disease disarms a man, "The City" places Carson—a "victim of middle-aged restlessness—the children grown, the long descent begun"—in a hospital, where he must face a battery of tests to determine the cause of a vague stomach pain. Confronted by doctors, nurses, orderlies, other patients, and fellow sufferers, none of whom he knows, Carson is alone and helpless in an alien environment. The hospital works as a fitting figure for the absurdity and complexity of the postmodern world. The health professionals seem like another species, and Carson's physical pain is a symbol of his spiritual discomfort as he proceeds with the useless repetition of his life's requirements. From the nadir of a debilitating operation, Carson begins to overcome the indignity and unreality of his plight. He becomes fascinated with people who are unknown to him, like a beautiful black nurse whose unfathomable beauty expands the boundaries of his realm. He calls upon his lifelong training as a stoic WASP and determines not to make a fuss about his difficulties. He finds his "curiosity about the city revived" and develops a camaraderie with other patients, a community of the wounded. His removal from the flow of business life—he is a computer parts salesman fluent in techno-babble—helps him regain an ironic perspective that enables him to regard his estranged daughter's ignorance of his crisis as "considerate and loving" because it contributes to the "essential solitude" he now enjoys.

In a poetic excursion into Carson's mind, Updike illustrates the tremendous satisfaction available to a person with an artistic imagination capable of finding meaning in any pattern of life's variety. Carson makes the necessary leap of faith required to "take again into himself the miracle of the world" and seizes his destiny from a mechanized, indifferent cosmos. In a reversal of the curve of decline that was the trajectory of Updike's thought from the problems of the early 1970's through the 1980's, Carson is depicted at the end of "The City" as a version of existential man who can, even amid doubt and uncertainty, find a way to be "free" and "whole"—at least as much as the postmodern world permits.

*The Afterlife, and Other Stories* • The central character in many of the stories collected in *The Afterlife, and Other Stories* has a superficial autobiographical relationship to Updike, including having moved from the city to the country as a child and having desired to return to the city. In the award-winning "A Sandstone Farmhouse," Joey Robinson visits his mother's farmhouse and watches her die as the farmhouse deteriorates. After she dies, he discovers that the farmhouse was his true home: "He had always wanted to be where the action was, and what action there was, it turned out, had been back there." "The Other Side of the Street" involves a protagonist, Rentschler, returning to his childhood home and seeing it from a house across the street, where he goes to have some papers notarized. He discovers that one of his childhood friends still lives next door to the notary's house. As he leaves, he sees what used to be his house "lit up as if to welcome a visitor, a visitor, it seemed clear to him, long expected and much beloved." He thus experiences a kind of homecoming. The final story in the collection, "Grandparenting," is another tale in the Maple saga. Divorced and married to others, both Richard and Joan (now Vanderhaven) Maple are present when their daughter Judith has her first baby. In spite of the divorce, the Maples still continue as a family.

Central to *The Afterlife, and Other Stories* is the family as seen from the perspective of an aging male. Story after story deals with people aging and dying. One, "The Man Who Became a Soprano," treats a group who get together to play recorders. As members of the group begin to form liaisons that end in divorce, and some move away, the group itself agrees to play a concert for an elderly audience at the Congregational church. The concert is a success, but it signals the end of the recorder group.

"The Afterlife," the first story in the collection, focuses on Carter Billings. His and his wife Joan's best friends, the Egglestons, move to England. During the first night of a visit there, Carter awakens and, wandering through the hall, tumbles down the stairs. "Then something—some*one*, he felt—hit him a solid blow in the exact center of his chest," and he finds himself standing on a landing on the stairway. The next morning he decides that he actually bumped into the knob of a newel post. Nonetheless, after the experience his life seems charged with new feeling. It is as though he has had some kind of taste of the afterlife so that he is now "beyond" all earthly matters.

*Leon Lewis*
*With updates by Richard Tuerk and the Editors*

## Other major works

PLAYS: *Three Texts from Early Ipswich: A Pageant*, pb. 1968; *Buchanan Dying*, pb. 1974, pr. 1976.

ANTHOLOGY: *The Best American Short Stories of the Century*, 2000.

NOVELS: *The Poorhouse Fair*, 1959; *Rabbit, Run*, 1960; *The Centaur*, 1963; *Of the Farm*, 1965; *Couples*, 1968; *Bech: A Book*, 1970; *Rabbit Redux*, 1971; *A Month of Sundays*, 1975; *Marry Me: A Romance*, 1976; *The Coup*, 1978; *Rabbit Is Rich*, 1981; *The Witches of Eastwick*, 1984; *Roger's Version*, 1986; *S.*, 1988; *Rabbit at Rest*, 1990; *Memories of the Ford*

*Administration*, 1992; *Brazil*, 1994; *In the Beauty of the Lilies*, 1996; *Toward the End of Time*, 1997; *Bech at Bay: A Quasi-Novel*, 1998; *Gertrude and Claudius*, 2000; *Seek My Face*, 2002; *Villages*, 2004; *Terrorist*, 2006.

NONFICTION: *Assorted Prose*, 1965; *Picked-Up Pieces*, 1975; *Hugging the Shore: Essays and Criticism*, 1983; *Just Looking: Essays on Art*, 1989; *Self-Consciousness: Memoirs*, 1989; *Odd Jobs: Essays and Criticism*, 1991; *Golf Dreams: Writings on Golf*, 1996; *More Matter: Essays and Criticism*, 1999; *Still Looking: Essays on American Art*, 2005.

POETRY: *The Carpentered Hen, and Other Tame Creatures*, 1958; *Telephone Poles, and Other Poems*, 1963; *Dog's Death*, 1965; *Verse*, 1965; *Bath After Sailing*, 1968; *The Angels*, 1968; *Midpoint, and Other Poems*, 1969; *Seventy Poems*, 1972; *Six Poems*, 1973; *Cunts (Upon Receiving the Swingers Life Club Membership Solicitation)*, 1974; *Query*, 1974; *Tossing and Turning*, 1977; *Sixteen Sonnets*, 1979; *Five Poems*, 1980; *Jester's Dozen*, 1984; *Facing Nature*, 1985; *Mites, and Other Poems in Miniature*, 1990; *A Helpful Alphabet of Friendly Objects*, 1995; *Americana, and Other Poems*, 2001.

## Bibliography

Donahue, Peter. "Pouring Drinks and Getting Drunk: The Social and Personal Implications of Drinking in John Updike's 'Too Far to Go.'" *Studies in Short Fiction* 33 (Summer, 1996): 361-367. Argues that drinking, in the stories, moves from a conventional social pastime to an extension of the couple's private discord, significantly changing how they view and interact with each other; their drinking habits expose the degree to which alcohol use is connected to the specific gender roles and family dynamics of the middle-class suburban world the Maples occupy.

Luscher, Robert M. *John Updike: A Study of the Short Fiction*. New York: Twayne, 1993. Introduction to Updike's short fiction, dealing with his lyrical technique, his experimentation with narrative structure, his use of the short-story cycle convention, and the relationship between his short fiction and his novels. Includes Updike's comments on his short fiction and previously published critical essays representing a variety of critical approaches.

Macnaughton, William R., ed. *Critical Essays on John Updike*. Boston: G. K. Hall, 1982. Comprehensive, eclectic collection, including essays by writers such as Alfred Kazin, Anthony Burgess, and Joyce Carol Oates, who provide reviews, and various Updike experts who have written original essays. Contains a survey of bibliographies and an assessment of criticism and scholarship.

May, Charles E., ed. *Masterplots II: Short Story Series, Revised Edition*. 8 vols. Pasadena, Calif.: Salem Press, 2004. Designed for student use, this reference set contains articles providing detailed plot summaries and analyses of nine short stories by Updike: "A&P" and "Ace in the Hole" (vol. 1), "The Gun Shop" (vol. 3), "Leaves" and "Lifeguard" (vol. 4), "Pigeon Feathers" and "A Sandstone Farmhouse" (vol. 6), "Tomorrow and Tomorrow and So Forth" (vol. 7), and "Walter Briggs" (vol. 8).

Miller, D. Quentin. *John Updike and the Cold War: Drawing the Iron Curtain*. Columbia: University of Missouri Press, 2001. Studies the influence of Cold War society and politics in forming Updike's worldview.

Newman, Judie. *John Updike*. New York: St. Martin's Press, 1988. Part of the Modern Novelists series, Newman covers the long fiction with facility and insight and offers a solid foundation for understanding Updike's primary concerns throughout his writing. Contains a good, comprehensive introduction and a judicious bibliography.

Pinsker, Sanford. "The Art of Fiction: A Conversation with John Updike." *The Sewanee Review* 104 (Summer, 1996): 423-433. Updike discusses the visual artists who have inspired him, how his academic experiences helped to shape his writing, and how he regards criticism of his work.

Pritchard, William H. *Updike: America's Man of Letters.* South Royalton, Vt.: Steerforth Press, 2000. Biography of the novelist, whom Pritchard sees as the heir to such American storytellers as William Dean Howells and Henry James, alone in a sea of metafiction.

Rogers, Michael. "The Gospel of the Book: *LJ* Talks to John Updike." *Library Journal* 124, no. 3 (February 15, 1999): 114-116. Updike expounds on books, contemporary writers, and the state of publishing at the end of the twentieth century.

Schiff, James A. *John Updike Revisited.* New York: Twayne, 1998. General introduction surveying all of Updike's work but focusing on his fiction in the late 1990's. The chapter on the short story is relatively brief, with short analyses of such stories as "A&P" and "Separating."

Tallent, Elizabeth. *Married Men and Magic Tricks: John Updike's Erotic Heroes.* Berkeley, Calif.: Creative Arts, 1982. Offers, in Judie Newman's words, "a ground-breaking exploration of the erotic dimensions of selected works." A long-needed analysis that includes a feminist perspective missing from much previous Updike criticism.

# Helena María Viramontes

**Born:** East Los Angeles, California; February 26, 1954

**Principal short fiction** • *The Moths, and Other Stories*, 1985; "Miss Clairol," 1987; "Tears on My Pillow," 1992; "The Jumping Bean," 1993.

**Other literary forms** • Helena María Viramontes is the author of two novels: *Under the Feet of Jesus* (1995), which she dedicated to the memory of civil rights activist César Chávez, and *Their Dogs Came with Them* (2000). With María Herrera-Sobek, she edited two anthologies, *Chicana Creativity and Criticism: Creative Frontiers in American Literature* and *Chicana (W)rites: On Word and Film* (1995).

**Achievements** • Helena María Viramontes won a National Endowment for the Arts grant in 1989 and received the John Dos Passos Prize for Literature for 1995.

**Biography** • Helena María Viramontes was born on February 26, 1954, in East Los Angeles, California, a city that has served as the setting for most of her short fiction. One of nine children in the family, she learned the value of work from an early age. Her father was a construction worker, her mother a homemaker. The Viramontes household was often filled with friends and relatives who had crossed the Mexican border looking for work. In her fiction Viramontes draws on the memories of the stories she heard from these immigrants. As a student at Immaculate Heart College, where she was one of only five Chicanas in her class, Viramontes worked twenty hours a week while carrying a full load of classes. She received a bachelor's degree in 1975 with a major in English literature. In 1977 her short story "Requiem for the Poor" won first prize for fiction in a contest sponsored by *Statement Magazine* of California State University, Los Angeles. In 1978 "The Broken Web" was the first-place winner, and in 1979 "Birthday" won first prize in the Chicano Literary Contest at the University of California at Irvine. "The Broken Web" and "Birthday" appear in her collection of short stories *The Moths, and Other Stories*. She received a master of fine arts degree in the creative writing program of the University of California at Irvine. She became an assistant professor of English at Cornell University in Ithaca, New York. She has served as editor of the cultural magazine *Chismearte* and coordinator of the Los Angeles Latino Writers Association.

**Analysis** • In her short stories Helena María Viramontes provides a vision of Hispanic women in American society, presenting female characters whose lives are limited by the patriarchy of Hispanic society and the imposition of religious values. She provides a humanistic and caring approach to the poor and downtrodden women who inhabit the working-class world of her fiction. She deals with the issues of abortion, aging, death, immigration, divorce, and separation. The stories in *The Moths, and Other Stories* are arranged in the order of the stages in a woman's life, beginning with the story of a young girl in "The Moths" moving on to stories of women in the later stage of life. Near the end of the collection, "Snapshots" is the story of a divorced woman who feels that she has wasted her life in the mundane and demanding trivia of housework. "Neighbors" depicts an elderly woman, isolated and living in fear of the young men in the neighborhood.

**"The Moths"** • "The Moths" is the story of a young Chicana girl who finds a safe refuge in caring for her aging grandmother, her abuelita. Constantly in trouble at home, fighting with her sisters, and receiving whippings, the rebellious fourteen-year-old girl finds a purpose for her life as she works with her grandmother to plant flowers and grow them in coffee cans. Viramontes describes in detail how the two women nurture the plants as they form a world of their own, away from the dominating force of the girl's father.

The story contains elements of the Magical Realism that characterizes much contemporary Third World American literature. When her more feminine sisters call her "Bull Hands" because her hands are too large and clumsy for the fine work of embroidery or crocheting, the girl feels her hands begin to grow. As her grandmother soothes the hands in a balm of dried moth wings and Vicks, the girl feels her hands shrink back to normal size. Another example of Magical Realism occurs at the end of the story, when the image of the moths is realized as they fly out of the dead grandmother's mouth.

The women exist in a world of wild lilies, jasmine, heliotrope, and cilantro, working with mayonnaise jars and coffee cans. The vines of chayotes wind around the pillars of the grandmother's house, climbing to the roof and creating the illusion that the house is "cradled" in vines, safe and protected. In her own home the girl's Apá, her father, forces her to go to church by banging on the table, threatening to beat her, and lashing out at her mother, her Amá. In one brief scene Viramontes is able to portray the brutal hold the father has on the family. In contrast to this household, the grandmother's house, devoid of a masculine presence, is a place of peace and growth. When the grandmother dies, the girl finds her, and she bathes her grandmother's body in a ceremony. As she performs this ritual, the girl sees the old scars on the woman's back, evidence that she, too, had suffered beatings.

**"Snapshots"** • As the story opens, Olga Ruiz, a woman whose husband has left her, reflects on her life and admits that it was the "small things in life" that made her happy: "ironing straight arrow creases" on her husband's work shirts and cashing in coupons. Now that she has reached middle age, she realizes that she has wasted her life in the pursuit of housework with nothing to show for all her efforts. Now that she is alone, a hopeless lethargy has set in, and she seems unable to cope with her new circumstances. Marge, her daughter, tries to get her involved with projects, pleading "Please. Mother. Knit. Do something."

As she pores over the snapshots in family albums, Olga sees that she has been "longing for a past that never actually existed." The title of the story refers to more than the actual snapshots. Olga sees snapshots as ghosts and feels "haunted by the frozen moments." She remembers her grandmother's fear that snapshots would steal a person's soul, and she recounts how her grandfather tried to take a family picture with his new camera; not knowing how to operate it, he took the film out and expected it to develop in the sunlight. As the story ends, Olga, fearing that her grandmother was right, decides that if she finds a picture of her grandmother, she will destroy it.

Viramontes paints a portrait of a woman who has devoted her life to being a good wife and mother, cooking, cleaning, taking care of others, and then in her middle years has been abandoned. Her husband has remarried, and her son-in-law is tired of her calls to her daughter, Marge. At one point he takes the phone away from Marge and says, "Mrs. Ruiz, why don't you leave us alone." A few minutes later, Dave, her former husband calls and asks her to "leave the kids alone." After a lifetime of hard work, Olga has been left alone, feeling that her life was worthless.

**"Neighbors"** • "Neighbors," the last story in the collection, tells the story of Aura Rodriguez, an isolated seventy-three-year-old woman who lives in fear of the young men in her neighborhood, who have vowed to get even with her for calling the police on them. Realizing that she must take care of herself, she gets a gun and sits in a chair facing the door, ready to protect herself. This story opens with a description of a neighborhood that has "slowly metamorphosed into a graveyard." Aura believes in living within her own space and expects her neighbors to do the same.

In the words of Fierro, Aura's old neighbor, Viramontes repeats the metaphor of the graveyard that she used at the beginning of the story. Fierro remembers the quiet hills and old homes that existed before the government destroyed the houses and covered the land with "endless freeway" that "paved over his sacred ruins, his secrets, his graves . . . his memories." The story is filled with realistic details such as the description of Aura's "Ben Gay scented house slipper."

**"The Cariboo Café"** • Conflict in Central America is the focus of "The Cariboo Café," in which a woman from El Salvador has suffered the loss of her child at the hands of government officials. Interwoven with the story of her grief is the story of the cook, who suffers from loneliness after losing his wife and son, and the terrified illegal immigrants who fear capture by the police. The woman from El Salvador, who has been mourning the loss of her small son for several years, mistakenly believes that one of the immigrants in the café is her son.

In the first segment of this three-part story, Sonya and her brother Macky, children of illegal immigrants, are frightened when they see a police officer seizing a man on the street. Trained to fear the police, the children run to the café for protection. In the second part, the narrator is the cook, who has shown immigration agents where the immigrants are hiding even though they have been regular customers. The narrator of the third part is the Salvadoran woman whose young son was taken by army officials. After numerous attempts to find her son, the woman moved across the Mexican border to the United States. In the final, violent confrontation when the police enter the café, the woman fights them, identifying them with the army officials who took her son. Viramontes tells this complex story through shifting points of view to reveal different perspectives as she shows the power of oppressive governments.

*Judith Barton Williamson*

## Other major works

ANTHOLOGIES: *Chicana Creativity and Criticism: Charting New Frontiers in American Literature*, 1987, revised 1996 (with María Herrera-Sobek); *Chicana (W)rites: On Word and Film*, 1995 (with Herrera-Sobek).

NOVELS: *Under the Feet of Jesus*, 1995; *Their Dogs Came with Them*, 2000.

NONFICTION: "Nopalitos: The Making of Fiction," 1989; "Why I Write," 1995.

## Bibliography

Bair, Barbara J. "The Cariboo Café." In *Masterplots II: Short Story Series*, edited by Charles E. May. Rev. ed. Vol. 1. Pasadena, Calif.: Salem Press, 2004. Analysis of "The Cariboo Café" with sections on themes and meaning and style and technique. Also includes a detailed synopsis of the story.

_____. "The Moths." In *Masterplots II: Short Story Series*, edited by Charles E. May. Rev. ed. Vol. 5. Pasadena, Calif.: Salem Press, 2004. Student-friendly analysis of "The Moths" that covers the story's themes and style and includes a detailed synopsis.

Carbonell, Ana Maria. "From Llarona to Gritona: Coatlicue in Feminist Tales by Viramontes and Cisneros." *MELUS* 24 (Summer, 1999): 53-74. Analyzes the representations of the Mexican goddess Coatlicue and the folkloric figure of the wailing ghost La Llarona in the works of Mexican American women writers Viramontes and Sandra Cisneros.

Green, Carol Hurd, and Mary Grimley Mason. *American Women Writers*. New York: Continuum, 1994. The editors provide a brief biographical sketch as well as an analysis of the short stories in *The Moths*. They emphasize the portrayal of Chicana women with their strengths and weaknesses as they struggle with the restrictions placed on them because they are women. They note that many of the characters pay a price for rebelling against traditional values.

Moore, Deborah Owen. "La Llorona Dines at the Cariboo Cafe: Structure and Legend in the Works of Helena María Viramontes." *Studies in Short Fiction* 35 (Summer, 1998): 277-286. Contrasts the distant and close-up narrative perspectives in Viramontes's work.

Richards, Judith. "Chicano Creativity and Criticism: New Frontiers in American Literature." *College Literature* 25 (Spring, 1998): 182. In this review of the anthology edited by Viramontes and María Herrera-Sobek, Richards argues that the book provides a good starting place for those who want to evaluate the Chicana literary movement. Points to the emergence of urban working-class women as protagonists, the frequent use of child and adolescent narrators, and autobiographical formats that focus on unresolved issues as characteristics of Chicana literature.

Saldívar-Hull, Sonia. "Helena María Viramontes." *Dictionary of Literary Biography*. Chicano Writers series. Detroit: Gale Research, 1992. Summarizes and analyzes several stories from *The Moths*, stressing the cultural and religious traditions that restrict women's lives. Discusses the patriarchal privileges that the father assumes in the story when he shouts at his daughter "'Tu eres mujer'" (you are a woman) in order to control her. Calls "Snapshots" a "scathing critique of the politics of housework" and refers to the divorced Olga as "an alienated laborer whose value has decreased."

Swyt, Wendy. "Hungry Women: Borderlands Mythos in Two Stories by Helena María Viramontes." *MELUS* 23 (Summer, 1998): 189-201. Discusses the short stories "The Broken Web" and "Cariboo Café."

Yarbo-Bejarano, Yvonne. *Introduction to "The Moths, and Other Stories."* Houston, Tex.: Arte Público Press, 1995. Discusses Viramontes's portrayal of women characters who struggle against the restrictions placed on them by the Chicano culture, the church, and the men in these women's lives. Provides a brief analysis of each story in the collection, showing that the stories deal with problems Chicana women face at various stages of their lives. Notes that, although Viramontes addresses the problems of racial prejudice and economic struggles, the emphasis is on the cultural and social values that shape these women and suggests that most of the stories involve the conflict between the female character and the man who represents an oppressive authority figure.

# Kurt Vonnegut

**Born:** Indianapolis, Indiana; November 11, 1922
**Died:** New York, New York; April 11, 2007

**Principal short fiction** • *Canary in a Cat House*, 1961; *Welcome to the Monkey House*, 1968; *Bagombo Snuff Box: Uncollected Short Fiction*, 1999.

**Other literary forms** • Kurt Vonnegut published numerous volumes, including essays, short stories, the plays *Happy Birthday, Wanda June* and *Between Time and Timbuktu: Or, Prometheus-5, a Space Fantasy* (1972), and the novels on which his reputation is principally based. His best-known novels include *The Sirens of Titan* (1959), *Cat's Cradle* (1963), *Slaughterhouse-Five: Or, The Children's Crusade, a Duty-Dance with Death* (1969), and *Breakfast of Champions* (1973), and he published *Timequake* in 1997. His last long fictional work, *God Bless You, Dr. Kevorkian* (1999) is a novella. The last book he published during his lifetime, *A Man Without a Country* (2005), is a small collection of essays he published over the previous five years. Many of these contain autobiographical reflections and express his views on contemporary politics.

**Achievements** • For many years, the popular success of the writing of Kurt Vonnegut exceeded critical recognition of his work. With his earlier work labeled as science fiction and published in paperback editions and popular magazines such as *Ladies' Home Journal* and *The Saturday Evening Post*, critical attention was delayed. In 1986, he received the Bronze Medallion from Guild Hall. He later was given lecturer and honorary professorial positions at distinguished universities. More important, his insightful and sympathetic treatment of the psychologically and morally disabled victims of the modern world earned him a reputation as one of the great humanist writers of his time.

**Biography** • Although not specifically an autobiographical writer, Kurt Vonnegut drew frequently on facts and incidents from his own life in his writing. The youngest in a family of three children, Kurt Vonnegut was born and reared in Indianapolis, Indiana. While serving in the army as an infantry scout during World War II, he was taken prisoner by the Germans and interned at Dresden, Germany, at the time of the 1945 Allied firebombing of the city that cost 135,000 lives. He survived only through the ironic circumstance of being quartered in an underground meat locker. This episode contributed much toward his authorial distance: After returning to that meat locker forty-three years later in 1998, Vonnegut commented that he was one of the few who could recall the destruction of an Atlantis.

Although the destruction of Dresden became a recurring motif in Vonnegut's work, not until twenty-three years later could he bring himself to write the novel of his war experiences, *Slaughterhouse-Five*. Almost three decades later, he revisited that subject in *Timequake*. After World War II, Vonnegut worked in public relations for General Electric in Schenectady, New York (called "Ilium" in his fiction), before leaving in 1950 to devote himself full-time to his writing. In 1945, he married Jane Marie Cox, settling in Cape Cod, where they reared their own three children and the three children of

Vonnegut's deceased sister, Alice. In 1972, he moved to New York City and was divorced from Cox early in 1974. He married the photographer Jill Krementz in November, 1979, and they adopted a daughter, Lily. They were divorced in 1991.

When Vonnegut published *Timequake* in 1997, he declared that it would be his last book. Two years later, however, he published a volume of previously uncollected stories, *Bagombo Snuff Box*; a volume on his ideas about writing, *Like Shaking Hands with God*; and the novella *God Bless You, Dr. Kevorkian*. *A Man Without a Country* was his final book during his lifetime. He died on April 11, 2007, shortly after sustaining a head injury during a fall in his New York City home.

**Analysis** • After the publication of his masterpiece, *Slaughterhouse-Five*, however, the work of Kurt Vonnegut received increasingly serious critical commentary. He emerged as a consistent commentator on American culture through the second half of the twentieth century. His short stories range from satiric visions of grotesque future societies, which are extensions of modern societies, and portrayals of ordinary people, which reassert the stability of middle-class values. In his novels, the social satire predominates, and Vonnegut blends whimsical humor and something approaching despair as he exposes the foibles of American culture and a world verging on destruction through human thoughtlessness. As in the short stories, however, attention to an unheroic protagonist doing his or her best and to the value of "common human decency" persists.

Best known for his novels, Vonnegut acknowledged the ancillary interest of short stories for him. In the preface to his collection of short stories *Welcome to the Monkey House*, he describes the stories as "work I sold in order to finance the writing of the novels. Here one finds the fruits of Free Enterprise." Vonnegut's blunt comment, however, does not imply that the stories can be dismissed out of hand. The themes of the stories are the themes and concerns of all his work. Again, in the preface to *Welcome to the Monkey House*, Vonnegut describes those concerns in a characteristically tough style. He recalls a letter his brother sent him shortly after bringing his firstborn home from the hospital: "Here I am," that letter began, "cleaning the s— off of practically everything." Of his sister, Vonnegut tells us that she died of cancer: "her dying words were 'No pain.' Those are good dying words. . . . I realize now that the two main themes of my novels were stated by my siblings: 'Here I am cleaning the s— off of practically everything' and 'No pain.'" These terms apply equally well to the themes of Vonnegut's short stories. His muckraking is frequently social satire; his concern is with the alleviation of human suffering.

© Jill Krementz

Vonnegut's short stories generally fall into two broad categories: those that are science fiction, and those that are not. The science fiction characteristically pictures a future society controlled by government and technology, whose norms have made human life grotesque. The protagonist is often an outlaw who has found such norms or conventions intolerable.

In contrast, Vonnegut's stories that are not science fiction regularly affirm social norms. Ordinary life in these stories is simply not threatened by large-scale social evil. Some of these stories indeed depict the victims of society—refugees, displaced persons, juvenile delinquents—but primarily they show such people's efforts to recover or establish conventional lives. It is within the context of conventional life that Vonnegut's protagonists can achieve those qualities which in his view give a person stability and a sense of worth. These are the qualities of modesty, considerateness (which he often calls common human decency), humor, order, and pride in one's work. They are values interfered with, in the science-fiction stories, by governmental and technological controls.

Vonnegut resented any dismissal of his work merely because it is science fiction, a kind of writing he described as incorporating "technology in the human equation." In the novel, *God Bless You, Mr. Rosewater* (1965), Eliot Rosewater speaks for Vonnegut when he delivers an impassioned, drunken, and impromptu defense of the genre before a convention of science-fiction writers:

I love you sons of bitches. . . . You're all I read any more. . . . You're the only ones with guts enough to *really* care about the future, who *really* notice what machines do to us, what wars do to us, what cities do to us, what big, simple ideas do to us, what tremendous misunderstandings, mistakes, accidents and catastrophes do to us.

In Eliot Rosewater's opinion, society's "greatest prophet" is an obscure writer of science fiction named Kilgore Trout, a recurring character in Vonnegut's fiction. His masterpiece, the work for which he will be revered in the far future, is a book entitled *2BR02B*, a rephrasing of Hamlet's famous question.

**"Welcome to the Monkey House"** • The story of *2BR02B*, in Vonnegut's précis, corresponds closely to his own short story, "Welcome to the Monkey House." Vonnegut writes of his fictional character, "Trout's favorite formula was to describe a perfectly hideous society, not unlike his own, and then, toward the end, to suggest ways in which it could be improved." The approach describes Vonnegut's writing as well. *2BR02B* predicates an America crippled by automation and overpopulation. Machines have taken over most jobs, leaving people idle and feeling "silly and pointless." The government's solution has been to encourage patriotic suicide. Ethical Suicide Parlors have been widely established, each identifiable by its purple roof and each located next to a Howard Johnson's restaurant (with its orange roof), where the prospective client is entitled to a free last meal.

This is also the world of "Welcome to the Monkey House." The story takes place in Cape Cod in an unspecified future time. Fourteen Kennedys, by now, have served as presidents of the United States or of the world. There is a world government; in fact, in this world, Vonnegut writes, "practically everything was the Government." Most people look twenty-two years old, thanks to the development of antiaging shots. The population of the world numbers seventeen billion people. For Vonnegut, the world's dilemma is the result of advanced technology combined with backward human attitudes. Suicide is voluntary, but everyone, under law, must use "ethical" birth control pills that, in fact, control not birth but sexuality. Their effect is to make people numb below the waist, depriving them not of the ability to reproduce, "which would have been unnatural and immoral," but rather of all pleasure in sex. "Thus did science and morals go hand in hand," Vonnegut ironically concludes.

The kind of morality that could produce these pills is exemplified in J. Edgar Nation, their inventor. Walking through the Grand Rapids Zoo with his eleven children one Easter, he had been so offended by the behavior of the animals that he promptly developed a pill "that would make monkeys in the springtime fit things for a Christian family to see." In the opinion of Billy the Poet, a renegade in this society, throughout history those people most eager "to tell everybody exactly how God Almighty wants things here on Earth" have been unaccountably terrified of human sexuality.

Billy the Poet's special campaign is to deflower hostesses in Ethical Suicide Parlors, who are all, as part of their qualifications for the job, "plump and rosy" virgins at least six feet tall. Their uniform is a purple body stocking "with nothing underneath" and black leather boots. In this world, only death is permitted to be seductive. Billy's modus operandi is to single out a hostess and send her some bawdy doggerel, calculated to offend (and to excite) narrow sensibilities. Nancy McLuhan, his present target, is more intrigued than she will admit to herself. Billy kidnaps her and takes her to his current hideout, the old Kennedy compound at Hyannis Port, now "a museum of how life had been lived in more expansive times. The museum was closed." The original lawn is now green cement; the harbor is blue cement. The whole of the compound is covered by an enormous plastic geodesic dome through which light can filter. The only "light" in which an earlier graciousness can now be seen is colored by the world's pervasive vulgarity. The current world president, named "Ma" Kennedy but not the "real thing," keeps a sign reading "Thimk!" on the wall of her office in the Taj Mahal.

Nancy's encounter with Billy is not the licentious orgy she expects but an approximation of an old-fashioned wedding night. Billy explains to her that most people only gradually develop a full appreciation of their sexuality. Embarrassed and confused, she tries conscientiously to resist her comprehension of his motives. As he leaves, Billy offers Nancy another poem, this time the famous sonnet by Elizabeth Barrett Browning that begins "How do I love thee? Let me count the ways." The implication is that sexuality is one dimension of human love sorely lacking in their world. Far from being obscene, that love pursues a larger "ideal Grace," in the words of the poem, wholly unavailable either to the vulgarity of "Ma" Kennedy or to the narrow-minded purity of J. Edgar Nation. Billy also leaves with Nancy a bottle of birth-control pills that will not hamper sexual enjoyment. On the label are printed the words "WELCOME TO THE MONKEY HOUSE." If Browning's poem risks sentimentality, the story ends in a comic readjustment of the reader's sense of proportion. Sex need not be humorless; the reader need not view himself and the human condition with the chilling seriousness and inflated self-importance of J. Edgar Nation. The reader is left with the impression that Nancy McLuhan has begun her conversion. There is a measure of hope in this world where, as Billy assures her, the "movement is growing by leaps and bounds."

**"Harrison Bergeron"** • Governmental domination of private life is nearly total, however, in the world of "Harrison Bergeron," whose inhabitants are tortured and shackled as a matter of course, all in the name of equality. In the United States of 2081, equality of all persons has been mandated by the 211th, 212th, and 213th

Amendments to the Constitution. People are not merely equal under the law, but "equal every which way." Those people of "abnormal" capacities must wear equalizing disabilities at all times. Hazel Bergeron is a person of average intelligence, which means that "she couldn't think about anything except in short bursts." Her husband, George, however, as a man of superior intelligence, has to wear a "mental handicap radio" in his ear which broadcasts at twenty-second intervals strident noises designed to break his concentration: burglar alarms, sirens, an automobile collision, or a twenty-gun salute. A strong man as well, George wears "forty-seven pounds of bird shot in a canvas bag" padlocked around his neck.

Neither George nor his wife is able to recall that their fourteen-year-old son, Harrison, has just been arrested. They are watching on television a performance by ballerinas also weighted down with bird shot and masked to disguise their beauty. As a law-abiding couple, George and Hazel have only fleeting suspicions that the system is a bad one. If not for such handicaps, George says, "pretty soon we'd be right back to the dark ages again, with everybody competing against everybody else." When the television announcer cannot deliver a news bulletin because he—"like all announcers"—has a serious speech impediment, Hazel's response is a well-meaning platitude, "He tried. That's the big thing." A ballerina, disguising her "unfair" voice, reads the announcement for him: Harrison Bergeron, "a genius and an athlete," has escaped from jail.

Suddenly Harrison bursts into the television studio. A "walking junkyard," he wears tremendous earphones, thick glasses, three hundred pounds of scrap metal, a rubber ball on his nose, and black caps on his teeth. In this reductio ad absurdum of the ideal of equality, the technology is pointedly silly. "I am the Emperor!" Harrison cries, and tears off his handicaps, revealing a man who "would have awed Thor, the god of thunder." Harrison is rival to the gods. A ballerina joins him as his empress. Freed of her restraints, she is "blindingly beautiful." Whatever the reader may perceive as ultimate human beauty, Harrison and the ballerina are that. Together the two of them dance in "an explosion of joy and grace" equally as fantastic as the shackles they have thrown off. They leap thirty feet to kiss the ceiling and hover midair to embrace each other, "neutralizing gravity with love and pure will." They have defied the laws of the land, the law of gravity, the laws of motion. They dance out the soaring aspiration of the human spirit, for a moment made triumphantly manifest.

The United States Handicapper General, ironically named Diana Moon Glampers, then breaks into the television studio and shoots them both. Her ruthless efficiency is in marked contrast to the bumbling capabilities of everyone else. The reader is suddenly aware that the idea of equality has been made an instrument of social control. Clearly some are allowed to be more equal than others. In their home, Harrison's parents are incapable of either grief or joy. They resume their passive, acquiescent lives, having forgotten the entire scene almost as soon as they witnessed it.

If the conventional life depicted in Vonnegut's work other than his science fiction has not been made this grotesque by technology and government, it is, nevertheless, also humdrum and uninspiring. These limitations, however, are more than compensated for by the fact that ordinary people feel useful, not superfluous, and they are capable of sustaining love. This dynamic is especially true of "Poor Little Rich Town," first published in *Collier's* and reprinted in *Bagombo Snuff Box*. In this story an entire village rejects the wisdom of an efficiency expert, Newell Cady. The bonds of community love win over logic, because the townspeople do not want the postmistress to lose her job.

**"Go Back to Your Precious Wife and Son"** • In "Go Back to Your Precious Wife and Son" the narrator's occupation is selling and installing "aluminum combination storm windows and screens" and occasionally a bathtub enclosure. He marks as "the zenith of [his] career" an order for a glass door for a film star's bathtub specially fixed with a life-sized picture of the film star's face on it. He is comically intent on installing the enclosure and on doing the job well, even as the star's household disintegrates around him. Yet if it is funny, the narrator's pride in his mundane work is also the basis of stability in his life, a stability visibly lacking in the apparently glamorous life of Gloria Hilton, the film star. Also installing two windows for her, he says about them,

> The Fleetwood Trip-L-Trak is our first-line window, so there isn't anything quick or dirty about the way we put them up. . . . You can actually fill up a room equipped with Fleetwoods with water, fill it clear up to the ceiling, and it won't leak—not through the windows, anyway.

While the narrator is at work in the bathroom, Gloria Hilton is engaged in dismissing her fifth husband. She speaks to him, as she always speaks, in a series of fatuous clichés. She tells him, "You don't know the meaning of love," after earlier seducing him away from his family with the words, "Dare to be happy, my poor darling! Oh, darling, we were *made* for each other!" She had then promptly announced to the press that the two of them were moving to New Hampshire "to find ourselves." In the narrator's (and the reader's) only glimpse of Gloria Hilton, she is without makeup ("she hadn't even bothered to draw on eyebrows") and dressed in a bathrobe. He decides, "that woman wasn't any prettier than a used studio couch." Her actual commonplaceness and utter self-absorption are patent.

Gloria's hapless fifth husband is a writer, George Murra, of whom she had expected no less than "the most beautiful scenario anybody in the history of literature has ever written for me." In the constant publicity and tempestuousness of their lives together, however, he has been unable to work at all. He had been lured by a hollow glamour, she by the possibility of greater self-glorification. The superficiality of their marriage is revealed in his references to her as "Miss Hilton," and her contemptuous parting words: "Go on back to your precious wife and your precious son."

In a long drinking session together after Gloria leaves, Murra explains to the narrator his earlier dreams of breaking free from the petty marital squabbles, the financial worries, the drab responsibility and sameness of conventional life. The narrator momentarily and drunkenly succumbs to the appeal of the glamorous life; when he staggers home he immediately offends his wife. Murra is now repentant and nearly desperate for the forgiveness of his son, living at a nearby preparatory school. When the boy arrives to visit his father, it is apparent that the hurt and bitterness of his father's desertion have made him rigid with intolerant rectitude. The situation looks hopeless until the narrator (back to finish his job) suggests to Murra that he topple the boy from his pedestal with a kick in the pants. The gambit works, the family is reconciled, and the narrator returns home, having agreed to exchange bathtub doors with Murra. He finds his own wife gone and his own son stuffily self-righteous; but his wife returns, her equanimity restored. The new bathtub enclosure with Gloria's face on it amuses his wife. She is exactly Gloria's height; when she showers, the film star's face on the door forms a "mask" for her. Gloria's glamour is all mask and pose; but his wife's good humor is genuine. The ordinary lives of the narrator and his wife have provided them with exactly what Gloria lacks and what Murra and his son need to recover: the saving grace of humor, tolerance, and a sense of proportion.

***Bagombo Snuff Box*** • The 1999 publication of *Bagombo Snuff Box* presented again several of the previous stories, plus others that achieved magazine exposure in the 1950's and 1960's but had since been forgotten. In the introduction to this volume, Vonnegut explains that his stories are "a bunch of Buddhist catnaps" designed to slow the pulse and breathing and allow one's troubles to fade away. He also provides his eight rules for writing stories in this introduction. Only three of the twenty-three stories here could be construed as futuristic. The title story focuses on a braggart who attempts to win favor with a former wife by false exaggeration of the exotic snuffbox, which her son quickly identifies as a common item. As in his previous work, the high and mighty are deflated and the average person is ennobled. George M. Helmholtz, a band director, is the qualified hero of three of these stories. An authorial "coda" at the end of the volume argues for the importance of the "Middle West" of Ohio and Indiana.

Despite the fact that most of Vonnegut's short stories are not science fiction and similarly applaud conventional life, the happy triumph of kindness and work seems contrary to the thrust of his novels. What he values remains the same, but the prospect of realizing those values becomes more desperate as the vision of normalcy recedes. The crises of the planet are too extreme and the capabilities of technology too great for Vonnegut to imagine a benign society in the future which could foster those values.

Vonnegut's novels are often described as "black humor," wholly unlike the generous good humor of "Go Back to Your Precious Wife and Son." This is another label that annoys the author ("just a convenient tag for reviewers"), but his description of black humor recalls his own lonely rebels whose cause is seriously overmatched by the monolithic enemy: "Black humorists' holy wanderers find nothing but junk and lies and idiocy wherever they go." Vonnegut said that the writer functions like the canaries coal miners took with them into the mines "to detect gas before men got sick." He must serve society as an early-warning system so that one can work to improve the human condition while one still may.

*Martha Meek*
*With updates by Peter J. Reed, Scott D. Vander Ploeg, and the Editors*

**Other major works**

CHILDREN'S LITERATURE: *Sun Moon Star*, 1980 (with Ivan Chermayeff).

PLAY: *Penelope*, pr. 1960, revised pr., pb. 1970 (as *Happy Birthday, Wanda June*).

NOVELS: *Player Piano*, 1952; *The Sirens of Titan*, 1959; *Mother Night*, 1961; *Cat's Cradle*, 1963; *God Bless You, Mr. Rosewater: Or, Pearls Before Swine*, 1965; *Slaughterhouse-Five: Or, The Children's Crusade, a Duty-Dance with Death*, 1969; *Breakfast of Champions: Or, Goodbye Blue Monday*, 1973; *Slapstick: Or, Lonesome No More!*, 1976; *Jailbird*, 1979; *Deadeye Dick*, 1982; *Galápagos*, 1985; *Bluebeard*, 1987; *Hocus Pocus*, 1990; *Timequake*, 1997; *God Bless You, Dr. Kevorkian*, 1999 (novella).

NONFICTION: *Wampeters, Foma, and Granfalloons (Opinions)*, 1974; *Palm Sunday: An Autobiographical Collage*, 1981; *Conversations with Kurt Vonnegut*, 1988; *Fates Worse than Death: An Autobiographical Collage of the 1980's*, 1991; *Like Shaking Hands with God: A Conversation About Writing*, 1999 (with Lee Stringer); *A Man Without a Country*, 2005.

TELEPLAY: *Between Time and Timbuktu: Or, Prometheus-5, a Space Fantasy*, 1972.

## Bibliography

Allen, William Rodney. *Understanding Kurt Vonnegut.* Columbia: University of South Carolina Press, 1991. Allen's study, part of the Understanding Contemporary American Literature series, places Vonnegut, and especially *Slaughterhouse-Five*, in the literary canon. Contains an annotated bibliography and an index.

Boon, Kevin A., ed. *At Millennium's End: New Essays on the Work of Kurt Vonnegut.* Albany: State University of New York Press, 2001. Collection of eleven essays examining the novelist's moral vision.

Goldstein, Marc. "EPICAC." In *Masterplots II: Short Story Series*, edited by Charles E. May. Rev. ed. Vol. 2. Pasadena, Calif.: Salem Press, 2004. Analysis of "EPICAC" with sections on themes and meaning and style and technique. Also includes a detailed synopsis of the story.

Klinkowitz, Jerome, Julie Huffman-Klinkowitz, and Asa B. Pieratt, Jr. *Kurt Vonnegut, Jr.: A Comprehensive Bibliography.* Hamden, Conn.: Archon Books, 1987. Authoritative bibliography of works by and about Vonnegut. Lists Vonnegut's works in all their editions, including the short stories in their original places of publication, dramatic and cinematic adaptations, interviews, reviews, secondary sources, and dissertations.

_____. *Vonnegut in Fact: The Public Spokesmanship of Personal Fiction.* Columbia: University of South Carolina Press, 1998. Klinkowitz makes a case for Vonnegut as a sort of redeemer of the novelistic form, after writers such as Philip Roth declared it dead. He traces Vonnegut's successful integration of autobiography and fiction in his body of work. Provides an extensive bibliography and an index.

Klinkowitz, Jerome, Julie Huffman-Klinkowitz, Asa B. Pieratt, Jr., and John Somer, eds. *The Vonnegut Statement.* New York: Delacorte Press, 1973. Collection of essays by various authors, which establishes the nature and sources of Vonnegut's reputation at this important juncture. Analyzes his career from his college writing to the short fiction, and through the novels to *Slaughterhouse-Five*. Includes an interview and a bibliography. The most important accounting of his career through its first two decades.

Labin, Linda L. "Harrison Bergeron." In *Masterplots II: Short Story Series*, edited by Charles E. May. Rev. ed. Vol. 3. Pasadena, Calif.: Salem Press, 2004. Student-friendly analysis of "Harrison Bergeron" that covers the story's themes and style and includes a detailed synopsis.

Leeds, Marc. *The Vonnegut Encyclopedia: An Authorized Compendium.* Westport, Conn.: Greenwood Press, 1995. Concordance and encyclopedia identifying Vonnegut's most frequently recurring images and all his characters; indispensable for serious students of Vonnegut.

Merrill, Robert, ed. *Critical Essays on Kurt Vonnegut.* Boston: G. K. Hall, 1990. Comprehensive collection of essays on Vonnegut's works and career, which includes reviews, previously published essays, and articles commissioned for this work. The extensive introduction traces in detail Vonnegut's career and critical reception from the beginnings to 1990.

Mustazza, Leonard, ed. *The Critical Response to Kurt Vonnegut.* Westport, Conn.: Greenwood Press, 1994. Presents a brief history of the critical response to Vonnegut, and critical reviews.

Reed, Peter J. *The Short Fiction of Kurt Vonnegut.* Westport, Conn.: Greenwood Press, 1997. Critical study of the author's short fiction. Includes a bibliography and an index.

Reed, Peter J. and Marc Leeds, eds. *The Vonnegut Chronicles: Interviews and Essays.* Westport, Conn.: Greenwood Press, 1996. Vonnegut discusses, among other topics, postmodernism and experimental fiction. Includes a bibliography and an index.

# Alice Walker

**Born:** Eatonton, Georgia; February 9, 1944

**Principal short fiction** • *In Love and Trouble: Stories of Black Women*, 1973; *You Can't Keep a Good Woman Down*, 1981; *The Complete Stories*, 1994; *Alice Walker Banned*, 1996 (stories and commentary).

**Other literary forms** • Alice Walker is known for her achievements in both prose and poetry; in addition to several short-story collections, she has published several novels, volumes of poetry, collections of essays, and children's books. Her novels *The Third Life of Grange Copeland* (1970), *Meridian* (1976), *The Color Purple* (1982), *The Temple of My Familiar* (1989), *Possessing the Secret of Joy* (1992), *By the Light of My Father's Smile* (1998), *Now Is the Time to Open Your Heart* (2004), examine the struggles of African Americans—especially women—against destruction by a racist society.

Walker's poetry is collected in *Once: Poems* (1968), *Five Poems* (1972), *Revolutionary Petunias, and Other Poems* (1973), *Goodnight, Willie Lee, I'll See You in the Morning: Poems* (1979), *Horses Make a Landscape Look More Beautiful* (1984), *Her Blue Body Everything We Know: Earthling Poems, 1965-1990* (1991), *A Poem Traveled Down My Arm* (2003), and *Absolute Trust in the Goodness of the Earth: New Poems* (2003). *In Search of Our Mothers' Gardens: Womanist Prose* (1983) is a collection of essays important to an understanding of Walker's purposes and methods as well as the writers influential on her fiction. A later collection of nonfiction prose is *Living by the Word: Selected Writings, 1973-1987* (1988). Walker also wrote *Langston Hughes: American Poet* (1974), *To Hell with Dying* (1988), *Finding the Green Stone* (1991), and *There Is a Flower at the Tip of My Nose Smelling Me* (2006) for children. Walker also edited an anthology titled *I Love Myself When I Am Laughing . . . and Then Again When I Am Looking Mean and Impressive: A Zora Neale Hurston Reader* (1979) that did much to revive interest in the fiction of Zora Neale Hurston, the writer whom she considers one of the major influences on her fiction.

**Achievements** • From the beginning of her career, Alice Walker has been an award-winning writer. Her first published essay, "The Civil Rights Movement: What Good Was It?" won first prize in *The American Scholar*'s annual essay contest in 1967. That same year she won a Merrill writing fellowship. Her first novel was written on a fellowship at the MacDowell Colony in New Hampshire. In 1972, she received a doctoral degree from Russell Sage College. *Revolutionary Petunias, and Other Poems* was nominated for a National Book Award and won the Lillian Smith Award of the Southern Regional Council in 1973. *In Love and Trouble* won the Richard and Hinda Rosenthal Award from the American Institute of Arts and Letters in 1974. *The Color Purple*, which remained on *The New York Times* list of best-sellers for more than twenty-five weeks, was nominated for the National Book Critics Circle Award and won both an American Book Award and the Pulitzer Prize for Fiction. Walker's many honors include a National Endowment for the Arts grant in 1969 and 1977, a Radcliffe Institute Fellowship in 1971-1973, and a John Simon Guggenheim Memorial Foundation Fellowship in 1977-1978. In 1984, she received a Best Books for Young Adults citation from the American Library Association for *In Search of Our Mothers' Gardens*. She has also won the O. Henry Award (1986), the Langston Hughes Award (1989), the Nora Astorga Leadership Award (1989), the Fred Cody Award for lifetime achievement (1990), the Freedom to Write Award (1990), the California Governor's Arts Award (1994), and the Literary Ambassador Award (1998).

**Biography** • Alice Malsenior Walker was born in Eatonton, Georgia, to sharecropper parents on February 9, 1944. She attended Spelman College in Atlanta on scholarship, transferring to Sarah Lawrence College in New York, from which she graduated in 1965. While working in the Civil Rights movement in Mississippi in the summer of 1966, she met Melvyn Rosenman Levanthal, an attorney, whom she married in 1967. After residing for seven years in Jackson, Mississippi, the couple returned to the East in 1974, where Walker served as a contributing editor to *Ms.* magazine. The two were divorced in 1976, sharing joint custody of a daughter, Rebecca. Walker cofounded a publishing house in Navarro, California, Wild Trees Press. She has been a writer-in-residence and a teacher of black studies at Jackson State College (1968-1969), a lecturer in literature at Wellesley College and the University of Massachusetts at Boston (1972-1973), a distinguished writer in the African American studies department at the University of California at Berkeley (1982), and a Fannie Hurst Professor of Literature at Brandeis University (1982). She coproduced a 1992 film documentary, *Warrior Marks*, directed by Pratibha Parmar, a film she narrated and for which she wrote the script. Walker settled in Mendocino, California, where she continued to write and remained politically active.

**Analysis** • The heroism of black women in the face of turmoil of all kinds rings from both volumes of Alice Walker's short stories like the refrain of a protest song. *In Love and Trouble* reveals the extremes of cruelty and violence to which poor black women are often subjected in their personal relationships, while the struggles in *You Can't Keep a Good Woman Down* reflect the social upheavals of the 1970's.

*In Love and Trouble* • Such subjects and themes lend themselves to a kind of narrative that is filled with tension. The words "love" and "trouble," for example, in the title of the first collection, identify a connection that is both unexpected and almost inevitable. Each of the thirteen stories in this collection is a vivid confirmation that every kind of love known to woman brings its own kind of suffering. Walker is adept at pairing such elements so as to create pronounced and revealing contrasts or intense conflicts. One such pair that appears in many of these short stories is a stylistic one and easy to see: the poetry and prose that alternate on the page. Another unusual combination at work throughout the short fiction may be called the lyrical and the sociological. Like the protest song, Walker's stories make a plea for justice made more memorable by its poetic form. She breathes rhythmic, eloquent language into the most brutish and banal abuses.

These two elements—similarity of subject matter and the balance of highly charged contraries—produce a certain unity within each volume. Yet beyond this common ground, the stories have been arranged so as to convey a progression of interconnected pieces whose circumstances and themes repeat, alternate, and overlap rather like a musical composition. The first three stories of *In Love and Trouble*, for example, are all about married love; the next two are about love between parent and child; then come three stories in which black-white conflict is central; the fourth group concerns religious expression; and the last three stories focus on initiation. Other themes emerge and run through this five-set sequence, linking individual motifs and strengthening the whole. Jealousy is one of those motifs, as is the drive for self-respect, black folkways, and flowers, in particular the rose and the black-eyed Susan.

Four stories suggest the breadth of Walker's imagination and narrative skills. "Roselily" strikes an anticipatory note of foreboding. "The Child Who Favored Daughter" is an equally representative selection, this time of the horrific destruction of the black woman. "The Revenge of Hannah Kemhuff" is as cool and clear as "The Child Who Favored Daughter" is dark and fevered. The narrator recounts a tale of Voodoo justice, specifically crediting Zora Neale Hurston, author of *Mules and Men* (1935). The final story in this collection, "To Hell with Dying," is an affirmative treatment of many themes Walker has developed elsewhere more darkly.

**"Roselily"** • "Roselily" takes place on a front porch surrounded by a crowd of black folk, in sight of Highway 61 in Mississippi during the time it takes to perform a wedding ceremony. As the preacher intones the formal words, the bride's mind wanders among the people closest to her there—the bridegroom, the preacher, her parents, sisters, and children. The groom's religion is not the same as hers, and she knows that he disapproves of this gathering. She speculates uneasily about their future life together in Chicago, where she will wear a veil, sit on the women's side of his church, and have more babies. She is the mother of four children already but has never been

Courtesy, *The Eatonton Messenger*

married. He is giving her security, but he intends, she realizes, to remake her into the image he wants. Even the love he gives her causes her great sadness, as it makes her aware of how unloved she was before. At last, the ceremony over, they stand in the yard, greeting well-wishers, he completely alien, she overcome with anxiety. She squeezes his hand for reassurance but receives no answering signal from him.

Poetic and fairy tale elements intensify the ambivalence felt by the bride in this magnetic mood piece. First, there are the ceremonial resonances of the words between the paragraphs of narrative, stately and solemn like a slow drumbeat. As these phrases alternate with Roselily's thoughts, a tension develops. At the words *"Dearly Beloved,"* a daydream of images begins to flow, herself a small girl in her mother's fancy dress, struggling through "a bowl of quicksand soup"; the words *"we are gathered here"* suggest to her the image of cotton, waiting to be weighed, a Mississippi ruralness she knows the bridegroom finds repugnant; *"in the sight of God"* creates in her mind the image of God as a little black boy tugging at the preacher's coattail. Gradually, a sense of foreboding builds. At the words *"to join this man and this woman"* she imagines "ropes, chains, handcuffs, his religion." The bridegroom is her rescuer, like Prince Charming, and is ready to become her Pygmalion. Like Sleeping Beauty, Roselily is only dimly aware of exchanging one form of confinement, of enchantment, for another. At the end of the ceremony, she awakes to his passionate kiss and a terrible sense of being wrong.

**"The Child Who Favored Daughter"** • Although "Roselily" is a subtle story of a quiet inner life, "The Child Who Favored Daughter" records the circumstances of a shocking assault. It begins, also, on a front porch. A father waits with a shotgun on a hot afternoon for his daughter to walk from the school bus through the front yard. He is holding in his hand a letter she had written to her white lover. Realizing what her father knows, the girl comes slowly down the dusty lane, pausing to study the black-eyed Susans. As his daughter approaches, the father is reminded of his sister, "Daughter," who also had a white lover. His intense love for his sister had turned to bitterness when she gave herself to a man by whom he felt enslaved; his bitterness poisoned all of his relationships with women thereafter. He confronts the girl on the porch with the words "White man's slut!" then beats her with a stable harness and leaves her in the shed behind the house. The next morning, failing to make her deny the letter and struggling to suppress his "unnameable desire," he slashes off her breasts. As the story ends, he sits in a stupor on the front porch.

This story of perverted parental love and warring passions explores the destructive power of jealousy and denial. Its evil spell emanates from the father's unrepented and unacknowledged desire to possess his sister. He is haunted by her when he looks at his own daughter. Once again, a strongly lyrical style heightens the dominant tone, in this case, horror. Short lines of verse, like snatches of song interspersed with the narrative, contrast sharply in their suggestion of pure feeling with the tightly restrained prose. The daughter's motif associates her with the attraction of natural beauty: *"Fire of earth/ Lure of flower smells/ The sun."* The father's theme sounds his particular resignation and doom: *"Memories of years/ Unknowable women—/ sisters/ spouses/ illusions of soul."* The resulting trancelike confrontation seems almost inevitable, the two moving through a pattern they do not control, do not understand.

**"The Revenge of Hannah Kemhuff"** • In "The Revenge of Hannah Kemhuff," a woman who has lost husband, children, and self-respect, all because a charity worker denied her food stamps, comes to the seer Tante Rosie for peace of mind. Tante Rosie assures the troubled woman that the combined powers of the Man-God and the Great Mother of Us All will destroy her enemy. Tante Rosie's apprentice, who narrates the story, teaches Mrs. Kemhuff the curse-prayer printed in Zora Neale Hurston's *Mules and Men*. Then she sets about to collect the necessary ingredients for the conjure: Sarah Sadler Holley's feces, water, nail parings. Her task seems to become almost impossible when her mentor tells her that these items must be gained directly from the victim herself. Nevertheless, with a plan in mind, the young woman approaches Mrs. Holley, tells her that she is learning the profession from Tante Rosie, and then asks her to prove that she, as she claims, does not believe in "rootworking." It is only a short while until Mrs. Kemhuff dies, followed a few months later by Mrs. Holley, who had, after the visit of the apprentice, taken to her bedroom, eating her nails, saving her fallen hair, and collecting her excrement in plastic bags and barrels.

This is the first story in the collection in which the black community comes into conflict with the white. It is a conflict of religious traditions and a strong statement in recognition of something profound in African folkways. Mrs. Holley failed Mrs. Kemhuff years before in the greatest of Christian virtues, that of charity. Mrs. Kemhuff, though now reconciled to her church, cannot find peace and seeks the even greater power of ancient conjure to restore her pride. Like other African American writers who have handled this subject, Walker first acknowledges that Voodoo is widely discounted as sheer superstition, but then her story argues away all rational objections. Mrs. Holley does not die as the result of hocus-pocus but because of her own radical belief, a belief in spite of herself. There is something else about this story that is different from those at the beginning of the collection. Instead of a dreamy or hypnotic action, alert characters speak and think purposefully, clearly, one strand of many evolving patterns that emerge as the stories are read in sequence.

**"To Hell with Dying"** • "To Hell with Dying" is the last story in the collection and a strong one. A more mellow love-and-trouble story than most preceding it, it features a male character who is not the villain of the piece. Mr. Sweet Little is a melancholy man whom the narrator has loved from childhood, when her father would bring the children to Mr. Sweet's bedside to rouse him from his depression with a shout: "To hell with dying! These children want Mr. Sweet!" Because the children were so successful in "reviving" Mr. Sweet with their kisses and tickling and cajoling ways, they were not to learn for some time what death really meant. Years pass. Summoned from her doctoral studies in Massachusetts, the twenty-four-year-old narrator rushes to Mr. Sweet's bedside, where she cannot quite believe that she will not succeed. She does induce him to open his eyes, smile, and trace her hairline with his finger as he once did. Still, however, he dies. His legacy to her is the steel guitar on which he played away his blues all those years, that and her realization that he was her first love.

It is useful to recognize this story as an initiation story, like the two that precede it, "The Flowers" and "We Drink the Wine in France." Initiation stories usually involve, among other things, an unpleasant brush with reality, a new reality. A child, adolescent, or young adult faces an unfamiliar challenge and, if successful, emerges at a new level of maturity or increased status. Always, however, something is lost, something must be given up. As a very small girl, the narrator remembers, she did not understand quite what was going on during their visits to the neighbor's shack. When she was somewhat older, she felt the weight of responsibility for the dying man's survival. At last, after she has lost her old friend, she is happy, realizing how important they were to each other. She has successfully negotiated her initiation into the mysteries of love and death, as, in truth, she had already done to the best of her ability at those earlier stages. This often-reprinted story is a culmination of the struggle between Death and Love for the lives of the girls and women, really for all the blacks of *In Love and Trouble,* one which well represents Walker's talent and demonstrates her vision of blacks supporting and affirming one another in community.

***You Can't Keep a Good Woman Down*** • *You Can't Keep a Good Woman Down* is her salute to black women who are pushing ahead, those who have crossed some barriers and are in some sense champions. There are black women who are songwriters, artists, writers, students in exclusive Eastern schools; they are having abortions, teaching their men the meaning of pornography, coming to terms with the death of a father, on one hand, or with the meaning of black men raping white women, on the other. Always, they are caught up short by the notions of whites. In other words, all the political, sexual, racial, countercultural issues of the 1970's are in these stories, developed from what Walker calls the "womanist" point of view.

This set of stories, then, is somewhat more explicitly sociological than the first and somewhat less lyrical, and it is also more apparently autobiographical, but in a special sense. Walker herself is a champion, so her life is a natural, even an inescapable, source of material. Walker-the-artist plays with Walker-the-college-student and Walker-the-idealistic-teacher, as well as with some of the other roles she sees herself as having occupied during that decade of social upheaval. Once a writer's experience has become transformed within a fictive world, it becomes next to impossible to think of the story's events as either simply autobiography or simply invention. The distinction has been deliberately blurred. It is because Walker wants to unite her public and private worlds, her politics and her art, life as lived and life as imagined, that, instead of poetry, these stories are interspersed with autobiographical parallels, journal entries, letters, and other expressions of her personality. There are three stories that deserve special attention, "Nineteen Fifty-Five," "Fame," and "Source." To begin with, they serve as checkpoints for the collection's development, from the essentially simple and familiar to the increasingly complex and strange, from 1955 to 1980. Furthermore, these stories are independently memorable.

**"Nineteen Fifty-Five"** • The opening story, "Nineteen Fifty-Five," is presented from the perspective of a middle-aged blues singer, Gracie Mae Still, whose signature song, recorded by a young white man named Traynor, brings him fame and fortune. Gracie Mae records her impressions of Traynor in a journal, beginning with their first meeting in 1955 and continuing until his death in 1977. Over the years, the rock-and-roll star (obviously meant to suggest Elvis Presley) stays in touch with the matronly musician, buying her lavish gifts—a white Cadillac, a mink coat, a house—and quizzing her on the real meaning of her song. From the army, he writes to tell her that her song is very much in demand, and that everyone asks him what he thinks it means, really. As time goes by and his life disappoints him, he turns to the song, as if it were a touchstone that could give his life meaning. He even arranges an appearance for himself and Gracie Mae on the variety show hosted by Johnny Carson, with some half-developed notion of showing his fans what the real thing is and how he aspires to it. If he is searching for a shared experience of something true and moving with his audience, however, he is to be disappointed again. His fans applaud only briefly, out of politeness, for the originator of the song, the one who really gives it life, then squeal wildly for his imitation, without any recognition of what he wanted them to understand. That is the last time the two musicians see each other.

In part, this story is about the contribution that black music made to the spirit of the times and how strangely whites transformed it. The white rock-and-roll singer, who seems as much in a daze as some of the women of *In Love and Trouble*, senses something superior in the original blues version, but he misplaces its value, looking for some meaning to life that can be rolled up in the nutshell of a lyric. In contrast to the bemused Traynor, Gracie Mae is a down-to-earth champion, and her dialect looks forward to Walker's masterful handling of dialect in *The Color Purple*. She repeatedly gives Traynor simple and sensible advice when he turns to her for help, and she has her own answer to the mystery of his emptiness: "Really, I think, some peoples advance *so* slowly."

**"Fame"** • The champion of "Fame" is Andrea Clement White, and the events take place on one day, when she is being honored, when she is being confronted by her own fame. She is speaking to a television interviewer as the story begins. The old woman tells the young interviewer that in order to look at the world freshly and creatively, an artist simply cannot be famous. When reminded by the young woman that she herself is famous, Andrea Clement White is somewhat at a loss. As the interview continues its predictable way, the novelist explaining once again that she writes about people, not their color, she uneasily asks herself why she does not "*feel* famous," why she feels as though she has not accomplished what she set out to do.

The highlight of the day is to be a luncheon in her honor, at which her former colleagues, the president, and specially invited dignitaries, as well as the generally detested former dean, will all applaud her life accomplishments (while raising money). All the while, the lady of the hour keeps a bitingly humorous commentary running in her mind. Her former students in attendance are "numbskulls," the professors, "mediocre." Out loud, she comments that the president is a bore. No matter how outrageous her behavior, she is forgiven because of her stature; when she eats her Rock Cornish hen with her hands, the entire assembly of five hundred follows suit. At last, however, the spleen and anxious bravado give way to something out of reach of the taint of fame: a child singing an anonymous slave song. Recalled to her dignity, the honored guest is able to face her moment in the limelight stoically.

In this comic story of the aggravations and annoyances that beset the publicly recognized artist, Walker imagines herself as an aging novelist who does not suffer fools gladly. She puts the artist's inner world on paper so that something of her gift for storytelling and her habits of mind become visible. The stress of the occasion and being brought into forced contact with her former president and dean trigger her aggressive imagination, and her innate narrative gift takes over. She visualizes using her heavy award as a weapon against the repulsive, kissing dean, hearing him squeal, and briefly feels gleeful. The story, however, is something more than simply a comic portrait of the artist's foibles. When Andrea Clement White questions herself about her own sense of fame, admits her own doubts, she is searching for something certain, as Traynor is searching in "Nineteen Fifty-five," though not so blindly. Like him, she is called out of the mundane by a meaningful song.

**"Source"** • The last story of *You Can't Keep a Good Woman Down* is "Source," which connects the social conscience of an antipoverty worker in Mississippi with the expanding consciousness of the alternative lifestyle as practiced on the West Coast. Two friends, Irene and Anastasia had attended college together in New York. When funding for Irene's adult-education project was cut, she traveled to San Francisco for a change of scene, to be met by Anastasia, living on welfare with some friends named Calm, Peace, and their baby, Bliss, all under the guidance of a swami named Source. The two young women had been unable to find any common ground, Irene believing in collective action and Anastasia believing that people choose to suffer and that nothing can be changed. After walking out on a meeting with Source, Irene was asked to leave. Years later, the two meet again in Alaska, where Irene is lecturing to educators. Anastasia is now living with an Indian and "passing" for white. This time, the two women talk more directly, of color, of Anastasia's panic when she is alone, of her never being accepted as a black because of her pale skin. Irene is brought to face her own part in this intolerance and to confess that her reliance on government funding was every bit as insecure as had been Anastasia's reliance on Source. Their friendship restored and deepened, the two women embrace.

The title of this story suggests a theme that runs throughout the entire collection, the search for a center, a source of strength, meaning, or truth. This source is very important to the pioneer, but it can be a false lure. When Irene recognizes that she and Anastasia were both reaching out for something on which to depend, she states what might be taken as the guiding principle for the champion: "*any* direction that is away from ourselves is the wrong direction." This final portrait of a good woman who cannot be kept down is a distinctively personal one. Women who are not distracted by external influences and who are true to themselves and able to open themselves to one another will triumph.

Walker's short fiction adds a new image to the pantheon of American folk heroes: the twentieth century black woman, in whatever walk of life, however crushed or blocked, still persevering. Even those who seem the most unaware, the most poorly equipped for the struggle, are persevering, because, in their integrity, they cannot do otherwise. The better equipped know themselves to be advocates. They shoulder their dedication seriously and cheerfully. They are the fortunate ones; they understand that what they do has meaning.

**"Everyday Use"** • One of the more widely anthologized of Walker's stories, "Everyday Use" addresses the issues of identity and true cultural awareness and attacks the "hyper-Africanism" much in vogue during the 1960's and 1970's as false and shallow. The occasion of the story is Dee's brief trip back to her home, ostensibly to visit with her mother and her sister, Maggie, who was left seriously scarred in the fire of suspicious origin that destroyed their home years earlier. Dee's real purpose, however, is to acquire some homemade quilts and other artifacts of her culture so that she can display them in her home as tokens of her "authenticity," her roots in the soil of rural Georgia. She wears a spectacular dashiki and wishes to be called by an "African" name; she is accompanied by a man who likewise affects "African" dress, hairstyle, naming tradition, and handshaking routines. Walker's tongue is firmly in her cheek as she portrays these two characters in vivid contrast with Mama and Maggie, whose lives are simple, close to the earth, and genuine. Despite (or perhaps because of) Mama's sacrifices and hard work to send Dee off to acquire an education in the outside world, Dee reveals a fundamental selfishness and lack of understanding of her culture and family and, her purposes thwarted, leaves without the quilts in a cloud of dust and disdain. Mama and Maggie sit in their neat yard, its dirt surface carefully raked, enjoying the shade and their snuff together "until it was time to go in the house and go to bed."

Walker's control of style and tone is nowhere more certain than in this powerful and economical story. Here she shows that family, tradition, and strength are to be found in the items of everyday use that have survived the fires of prejudice, from whatever source, and illuminate the true meaning of family and love and forgiveness. Despite the truth of Dee's parting statement that "it really is a new day for us," Walker leaves no doubt that the promise of that new day will be dimmed if traditions are exploited rather than understood and cherished. Maggie, after all, learned how to quilt from her grandmother and her great aunt and thus has a much surer sense of her own identity than her sister.

*Rebecca R. Butler*
*With updates by D. Dean Shackelford and Theodore C. Humphrey*

**Other major works**

CHILDREN'S LITERATURE: *Langston Hughes: American Poet*, 1974; *To Hell with Dying*, 1988; *Finding the Green Stone*, 1991; *There Is a Flower at the Tip of My Nose Smelling Me*, 2006.

EDITED TEXT: *I Love Myself When I Am Laughing . . . and Then Again When I Am Looking Mean and Impressive: A Zora Neale Hurston Reader*, 1979.

NOVELS: *The Third Life of Grange Copeland*, 1970; *Meridian*, 1976; *The Color Purple*, 1982; *The Temple of My Familiar*, 1989; *Possessing the Secret of Joy*, 1992; *By the Light of My Father's Smile*, 1998; *Now Is the Time to Open Your Heart*, 2004.

NONFICTION: *In Search of Our Mothers' Gardens: Womanist Prose*, 1983; *Living by the Word: Selected Writings, 1973-1987*, 1988; *Warrior Marks: Female Genital Mutilation and the Sexual Blinding of Women*, 1993 (with Pratibha Parmar); *The Same River Twice: Honoring the Difficult*, 1996; *Anything We Love Can Be Saved: A Writer's Activism*, 1997; *The Way Forward Is with a Broken Heart*, 2000; *Sent by Earth: A Message from the Grandmother Spirit After the Attacks on the World Trade Center and Pentagon*, 2001.

POETRY: *Once: Poems*, 1968; *Five Poems*, 1972; *Revolutionary Petunias, and Other Poems*, 1973; *Goodnight, Willie Lee, I'll See You in the Morning: Poems*, 1979; *Horses Make a Landscape Look More Beautiful*, 1984; *Her Blue Body Everything We Know: Earthling Poems, 1965-1990 Complete*, 1991; *A Poem Traveled Down My Arm*, 2003; *Absolute Trust in the Goodness of the Earth: New Poems*, 2003.

MISCELLANEOUS: *We Are the Ones We Have Been Waiting For: Inner Light in a Time of Darkness—Meditations*, 2006.

**Bibliography**

Bates, Gerri. *Alice Walker: A Critical Companion*. Westport, Conn.: Greenwood Press, 2005. Well-crafted biography that discusses Walker's major works, tracing the themes of her novels to her life.

Bauer, Margaret D. "Alice Walker: Another Southern Writer Criticizing Codes Not Put to 'Everyday Use.'" *Studies in Short Fiction* 29 (Spring, 1992): 143-151. Discusses parallels between Walker's *In Love and Trouble* and stories by William Faulkner, Katherine Anne Porter, Eudora Welty, and Flannery O'Connor. Argues that Walker, like these other southern writers, examines the tendency to support social and religious codes at the expense of individual fulfillment.

Bloxham, Laura J. "Alice [Malsenior] Walker." In *Contemporary Fiction Writers of the South*, edited by Joseph M. Flora and Robert Bain. Westport, Conn.: Greenwood Press, 1993. General introduction to Walker's "womanist" themes of oppression of black women and change through affirmation of self. Provides a brief summary and critique of previous criticism of Walker's work.

Borgmeier, Raimund. "Alice Walker: 'Everyday Use.'" In *The African-American Short Story: 1970 to 1990*, edited by Wolfgang Karrer and Barbara Puschmann-Nalenz. Trier, Germany: Wissenschaftlicher Verlag Trier, 1993. Detailed discussion of the generic characteristics of one of Walker's best-known stories. Analyzes the tension between the typical unheard-of occurrence and everyday reality as well as the story's use of a central structural symbol.

Dieke, Ikenna, ed. *Critical Essays on Alice Walker.* New York: Greenwood Press, 1999. Especially well suited for use in college literature classrooms, this collection gives particular attention to Walker's poetry and her developing ecofeminism.

Gates, Henry Louis, Jr., and K. A. Appiah, eds. *Alice Walker: Critical Perspectives Past and Present*. New York: Amistad, 1993. Contains reviews of Walker's first five novels and critical analyses of several of her works of short and long fiction. Also includes two interviews with Walker, a chronology of her works, and an extensive bibliography of essays and texts.

Lauret, Maria. *Alice Walker.* New York: St. Martin's Press, 2000. Provocative discussions of Walker's ideas on politics, race, feminism, and literary theory. Of special interest is the exploration of Walker's literary debt to Zora Neale Hurston, Virginia Woolf, and even Bessie Smith.

McKay, Nellie. "Alice Walker's 'Advancing Luna—and Ida B. Wells': A Struggle Toward Sisterhood." In *Rape and Representation*, edited by Lynn A. Higgins and Brenda R. Silver. New York: Columbia University Press, 1991. Shows how the story allows readers to see how women's cross-racial relationships are controlled by systems of white male power. The story helps its audience understand why black women fail to provide group support for feminists of the antirape movement in spite of their own historical oppression by rape.

May, Charles E., ed. *Masterplots II: Short Story Series, Revised Edition.* 8 vols. Pasadena, Calif.: Salem Press, 2004. Designed for student use, this reference set contains articles providing detailed plot summaries and analyses of six short stories by Walker: "Everyday Use" and "Her Sweet Jerome" (vol. 3); "Kindred Spirits" (vol. 4); and "Strong Horse Tea," "A Sudden Trip Home in the Spring," and "To Hell with Dying" (vol. 7).

Petry, Alice Hall. "Walker: The Achievement of the Short Fiction." In *Alice Walker: Critical Perspectives Past and Present*, edited by Henry Louis Gates, Jr., and K. A. Appiah. New York: Amistad, 1993. Skeptical analysis of Walker's short fiction that contrasts the successful and focused achievement of *In Love and Trouble* (1973) with the less satisfying *You Can't Keep a Good Woman Down* (1981). Petry argues that the latter collection suffers in many places from unfortunate unintentional humor, trite and clichéd writing, and reductionism, and a confusion of genres that perhaps owes much to her being a "cross-generic writer."

White, Evelyn C. *Alice Walker: A Life.* New York: W. W. Norton, 2004. The life and accomplishments of Walker are chronicled in this biography through interviews with Walker, her family, and friends.

Winchell, Donna Haisty. *Alice Walker.* New York: Twayne, 1992. Provides a comprehensive analysis of Walker's short and long fiction. A brief biography and chronology precede the main text of the book. Each chapter refers to specific ideas and themes within Walker's works and focuses on how Walker's own experiences define her characters and themes. Following the narrative is a useful annotated bibliography.

# Robert Penn Warren

**Born:** Guthrie, Kentucky; April 24, 1905
**Died:** West Wardsboro, near Stratton, Vermont; September 15, 1989

**Principal short fiction** • *Blackberry Winter*, 1946; *The Circus in the Attic, and Other Stories*, 1947.

**Other literary forms** • In addition to his short fiction, Robert Penn Warren published ten novels, several volumes of poetry, a play, a biography, two collections of critical essays, three historical essays, three influential textbooks, several children's books, two studies of race relations in America, one memoir, and several book-length treatises on literature.

**Achievements** • Honored as a major American poet and novelist, Robert Penn Warren displayed uncommon versatility in significant contributions to almost every literary genre. His work has been translated worldwide, and his short stories are widely anthologized. Although he is best known for his novel *All the King's Men* (1946), which won the Pulitzer Prize, he was most prolific as a poet whose awards included two Pulitzer Prizes and an appointment as America's first poet laureate. Three of his novels have been filmed, and one of them, *All the King's Men*, has been presented in operatic form.

The subject of Warren's fiction, and much of his poetry, is southern rural life in the late nineteenth and early twentieth centuries. He reveals a rootedness in his subject and its values, a concern for moral issues, and a gift for dialogue and environmental detail that lends distinctiveness to his work. His short stories, for example, are set down in rich, vigorous style, and they delineate the flow of time, the influence of past on present, and the painful necessity of self-knowledge.

**Biography** • Robert Penn Warren was educated at Guthrie High School. In 1925, he graduated from Vanderbilt University in Nashville, Tennessee, where he was associated with the Fugitive Group of poets. He did graduate work at the University of California (M.A., 1927), Yale University, and Oxford, and as a Rhodes scholar (D.Litt., 1930). In 1930, he contributed an essay, *I'll Take My Stand*, to the Agrarian symposium. Between 1935 and 1942, he was an editor of the *Southern Review* and was influential in the articulation and practice of the New Criticism. After an active career as a professor of English at a number of American colleges and universities, he retired from Yale in 1973. His first marriage to Emma Brescia in 1930 ended in divorce in 1950. He and his second wife, the writer Eleanor Clark, herself a National Book Award winner, had one son and one daughter.

Warren won the Pulitzer Prize for Fiction in 1947, the Pulitzer Prize for Poetry in 1958 and 1979, and the National Book Award in 1958. From 1944 to 1945, he held the Chair of Poetry at the Library of Congress. In 1952 he was elected to the American Philosophical Society; in 1959 to the American Academy of Arts and Letters; and in 1972 to the American Academy of Arts and Sciences. In 1967, he received the Bollingen Prize in Poetry, and in 1970 the National Medal for Literature and the Van

Wyck Brooks Award. In 1974, he was chosen to deliver the third Annual Jefferson Lecture in the Humanities. In 1975 he received the Emerson-Thoreau Award of the American Academy of Arts and Sciences; the next year the Copernicus Award from the Academy of American Poets; and in 1977 the Harriet Monroe Prize for Poetry. Other awards included the Shelley Memorial Prize and the Presidential Medal of Freedom. In 1986, Warren achieved the unique distinction of becoming the first official "poet laureate" (by act of Congress) of the United States. Warren's life spanned almost the whole twentieth century. After producing a rich final harvest of work from the mid-1970's to the mid-1980's, he died in 1989 at the age of eighty-four at his summer residence in Vermont. He left to posterity a canon of outstanding creative effort.

**Analysis** • Many of Robert Penn Warren's stories feature an adult protagonist's introspective, guilty recollections of imperishable childhood events, of things done or left undone or simply witnessed with childish innocence.

**"Blackberry Winter"** • "Blackberry Winter" (the literal reference is to an unseasonable, late spring cold snap) opens with a nine-year-old boy's unbroken, secure world, a small community permeated with the presence and warmth of protective loved ones. A vaguely sinister city-clothed stranger happens by and is given a job burying drowned chicks and poults by the boy's mother. Later the boy watches with his father and neighboring farmers as a dead cow, the yoke still around her neck, bobs down a flooding creek past fields of ruined tobacco plants. Then the boy finds a somehow shocking heap of litter washed out from under the house of his father's black help. Dellie, who lives there, is sick in bed with "woman-mizry," and after calling him to her side, gives her son little Jebb a sudden, "awful" slap. Big Jebb predicts that the cold snap will go on and that everything and everyone will die, because the Lord is tired of sinful people.

Later on, when the boy's father explains that he cannot afford to hire any help now but offers the stranger fifty cents for a half day's work, the stranger curses the farm and leaves, followed by the curious boy, whom he also curses. "You don't stop following me and I cut yore throat, you little son-of-a-bitch." "But I did follow him," the narrator tells us, "all the years." At the end of the story all the sureties of the boy's world have been threatened, and in the epilogue we learn that the farm was soon lost, his parents died, and little Jebb has gone to prison. The narrator has learned that the essence of time is the passing away of things and people; he has been exposed to natural and moral evil.

**"When the Light Gets Green"** • "When the Light Gets Green" (the reference is to a peculiar, ominous shade of greenish light just before a storm) recalls "Blackberry Winter" in its setting, characterization, and theme, as well as in its retrospective point of view. The story's first two sentences display the technique: "My grandfather had a long white beard and sat under the cedar tree. The beard, as a matter of fact, was not very long and not very white, only gray, but when I was a child. . . ." Grandfather Barden had served as a Confederate cavalry captain in the Civil War (1861-1865); he had been a hero, but now he is old and thin and his blue jeans hang off his shrunken hips and backside. During a bad hailstorm in the summer of 1914 which threatens his son-in-law's tobacco crop, the old man has a stroke and collapses, and later upstairs in his room waits to die—unloved, as he believes. His is the necessarily uncomprehending and hopeless fight that love and pride put up against time and change. His grandson, who visits him but cannot speak, suffers the guilt of having tried and failed both to feel and to communicate the impossible love the old man needed.

Mr. Barden, as we learn in the epilogue, lived until 1918, by which time other catastrophes had intervened—the farm sold, his son-in-law fighting in France, where he would soon be killed, his daughter working in a store. "I got the letter about my grandfather, who died of the flu," the story concludes, "but I thought about four years back, and it didn't matter much." The now adult narrator is puzzled and shamed by his failure and betrayal of his grandfather. In the dual perspective of the story Warren infuses a self-condemnatory ambivalence toward the old man which gives to the narrative the quality of expiation.

**"Prime Leaf"** • "Prime Leaf," Warren's first published story, derives from the Kentucky tobacco wars of the first decade of the twentieth century, in which tobacco farmers organized in an attempt to secure higher prices from the tobacco buyers. The focus of the story is upon contention within the Hardin family, most directly between Old Man Hardin and Big Thomas, his son, but also involving Thomas's wife and young son. Old Man Hardin leaves the farmers' association rather than support the use of force against those members who object to the association's price fixing. Big Thomas, whom he had originally persuaded to join the association, refuses to resign immediately. Their reconciliation occurs only after Big Thomas wounds one of a party of barn-burning night riders raiding the Hardins' property. Big Thomas decides that he will wait at home for the sheriff, but his father urges him to ride into town to justice, and on the way Big Thomas is ambushed and killed. The opposition of father and son is a contest between idea and fact, between idealism and pragmatism. Old Man Hardin is a kind and morally upright man but is also notably detached, remote, and unyielding. To his idealism is opposed his son's stubborn practicality, born of hard experience.

In delineating the conflict of the two men, with its tragic and ironic outcome, Warren did not espouse the beliefs of either, but focused on the incompleteness of each. Old Man Hardin, embodying the rocklike integrity of the gentleman-farmer tradition, places an unwise reliance on what he still—despite much evidence to the contrary—takes to be the due processes of law. He cannot save his son and is in a way responsible for his death. Big Thomas, firing at the night riders until his rifle jams, before yielding to his father, does not resolve in acceptable fashion the problem of ends and means.

**"The Circus in the Attic"** • "The Circus in the Attic" is a long and crowded tale about the meaning—or apparent meaninglessness—of history. It features, appropriately enough, a would-be local historian, Bolton Lovehart, a frail, frustrated man of aristocratic antecedents, whose deepest desire is simply to be free and himself. The only child of a weak father and an almost cannibalistically possessive mother, Bolton as a boy makes several doomed gestures of resistance. To his mother's subsequent horror, he participates in a riverbank baptismal ceremony; later he runs off with a carnival but is immediately retrieved. During his first year at college his now widowed mother has a heart attack; such at least is her story, although she will not allow a specialist to examine her and treats her son's suggestion as treason. In any event, Bolton does not return to college and life closes in on him. He begins to see a young woman, but, realizing that Bolton's mother has the stronger hold, she deliberately seduces and then abandons him.

Establishing the context of local history back to the first white settlers, Warren provides a series of vivid and ironic vignettes, one of which distinguishes between the official, heroic, United Daughters of the Confederacy version of the Civil War battle of Bardsville and the half-comic, half-sordid truth of the unremarkable little affair. One of the heroes, Cash Perkins, full of liquor, climbed on the wrong horse, a particularly mean one, and was carried, helpless and roaring, directly into Yankee rifle range. The truth of the other memorialized hero, Seth Sykes, was somewhat more involved. He cared nothing for Secession, said so publicly, and lost a stomp-and-gouge fight over it. Then he said he hoped the Yankees would come, which they soon did, to take his corn, for which they offered him a note. He would have none of it; he had offered them meat but not his corn. He resisted and was killed. Of the official versions of these two

Robert A. Ballard, Jr.

deaths, Warren wrote, "People always believe what truth they have to believe to go on being the way they are."

Bolton Lovehart's major resource and consolation is the painstaking creation of a tiny circus—complete with animals and clowns and trapeze artists and a lion tamer—which he carves in the attic office where he is supposedly composing his study of local history. Upon his mother's death (finally, she does have a heart attack), it appears that he may at last enter into a life of his own. Shortly before World War II, Bolton marries, finds a hero in his braggart stepson, a posthumous Medal of Honor winner, and becomes for a time in his reflected energy and glory a current affairs expert and historian of sorts. His wife, however, who has been unfaithful to him, is killed in an automobile crash, his stepson is taken from him, and at last he returns to the creation of those small, inanimate, innocent, wooden objects whose world alone he cherishes, controls, and understands. Bolton Lovehart's is less a fully human life than a kind of pathetic facsimile. His study of Bardsville's past—and by extension, humans' study of history—seems to assert that historical causation and "truth" are unknowable, that all humans are equally unimportant, and that all people are trapped in their own dark compulsions.

Warren is commonly identified as a southern writer and associated with such other premier representatives of that area as William Faulkner and Eudora Welty. So long as "southern" is not equated with "regionalist" in the limiting sense of that term, the description is accurate if not very illuminating. In another sense, however, as is apparent in his short fiction, Warren was a provincial, at least insofar as he retained an attachment to and an awareness of generally humanistic values—moral, social, and theological—often regarded as a vital part of the region's heritage. Thus the frequently noticeable tension between stylistic understatement (apparent in passages quoted earlier) and thematic intensity characteristic of the stories seems a reflection of a pull between the old humanistic conception of human wholeness and a naturalistic belief in the fragmented and unintegrated nature of human experience.

Warren published his last short story, "The Circus in the Attic," in 1947; thereafter he published as stories fourteen prepublication excerpts from his novels. Although in his nearly twenty years as a short-story writer Warren produced some fine work, both the author and a good many of his readers have found his achievement in short fiction less satisfying than that in other genres, notably poetry and the novel.

Explanations for his limited success in and his dissatisfaction with short fiction might start with the fact that when he wrote many of the stories collected in *The Circus in the Attic, and Other Stories*, he was a beginner, at least in fiction. It is also the case, as Warren conceded, that he wrote for the quick buck, which did not come. Most of the stories did not represent major efforts; as Arthur Miller has said of his own short stories, they were what came easier. Finally, and most importantly, the form itself seems to have inhibited Warren's natural talents and inclinations.

In writing stories in the 1930's and 1940's, Warren appears to have backed into what was for him an unhappy compromise; stories were neither long enough nor short enough, offered neither the satisfying extensive scope of the novel nor the demanding intensive concision of the poem. Short stories might occasionally serve as sketches for novels ("Prime Leaf," discussed earlier, is the prototype of Warren's first published novel, *Night Rider*, 1939), but Warren found that the overlap between the short story and the poem was bad for him, that stories consumed material that would otherwise have become poems. Thus he said, "Short stories are out for me."

Despite such demurs, however, Warren's achievement in the short story is that of a major talent. Warren's ear never failed him; the voices from the past and of the present always ring true. No one writing in his day had a better ear—one could almost say recollection, if one did not know Warren's age—for the voices of late nineteenth and early twentieth century America. His eyes were open to both the panorama and to the smallest evocative detail: from the trapper looking across the mountains to the West to the cracked and broken shoe of a tramp. He was intensely alive to the natural world. This is not to say simply that the natural backgrounds of the stories are vividly realized and accurately observed, although Warren was here the equal of Ernest Hemingway or Faulkner, but that such observation and realization provide the bases for those effects characteristic of his stories, for the evocation of atmosphere, for tonal modulation, and for symbolic representation.

*Allen Shepherd*
*With updates by Christian H. Moe*

## Other major works

PLAYS: *Proud Flesh*, pr. 1947; *All the King's Men*, pr. 1958 (adaptation of his novel).

ANTHOLOGIES: *An Approach to Literature*, 1936 (with Cleanth Brooks and John Thibault Purser); *Understanding Poetry: An Anthology for College Students*, 1938 (with Brooks); *Understanding Fiction*, 1943 (with Brooks); *Faulkner: A Collection of Critical Essays*, 1966; *Randall Jarrell, 1914-1965*, 1967 (with Robert Lowell and Peter Taylor); *American Literature: The Makers and the Making*, 1973 (with R. W. B. Lewis).

NOVELS: *Night Rider,* 1939; *At Heaven's Gate,* 1943; *All the King's Men,* 1946; *World Enough and Time: A Romantic Novel,* 1950; *Band of Angels,* 1955; *The Cave,* 1959; *Wilderness: A Tale of the Civil War,* 1961; *Flood: A Romance of Our Time,* 1964; *Meet Me in the Green Glen,* 1971; *A Place to Come To,* 1977.

NONFICTION: *John Brown: The Making of a Martyr,* 1929; *Modern Rhetoric,* 1949 (with Cleanth Brooks); *Segregation: The Inner Conflict in the South,* 1956; *Selected Essays,* 1958; *The Legacy of the Civil War: Meditations on the Centennial,* 1961; *Who Speaks for the Negro?,* 1965; *Democracy and Poetry,* 1975; *Portrait of a Father,* 1988; *New and Selected Essays,* 1989; *Cleanth Brooks and Robert Penn Warren: A Literary Correspondence,* 1998 (James A. Grimshaw, Jr., editor); *Selected Letters of Robert Penn Warren,* 2000-2001 (2 volumes; William Bedford Clark, editor).

POETRY: *Thirty-six Poems,* 1935; *Eleven Poems on the Same Theme,* 1942; *Selected Poems, 1923-1943,* 1944; *Brother to Dragons: A Tale in Verse and Voices,* 1953; *Promises: Poems, 1954-1956,* 1957; *You, Emperors, and Others: Poems, 1957-1960,* 1960; *Selected Poems: New and Old, 1923-1966,* 1966; *Incarnations: Poems, 1966-1968,* 1968; *Audubon: A Vision,* 1969; *Or Else: Poem/Poems, 1968-1974,* 1974; *Selected Poems 1923-1975,* 1976; *Now and Then: Poems, 1976-1978,* 1978; *Brother to Dragons: A New Version,* 1979; *Ballad of a Sweet Dream of Peace,* 1980 (with Bill Komodore); *Being Here: Poetry 1977-1980,* 1980; *Rumor Verified: Poems, 1979-1980,* 1981; *Chief Joseph of the Nez Percé,* 1983; *New and Selected Poems, 1923-1985,* 1985; *The Collected Poems of Robert Penn Warren,* 1998 (John Burt, editor).

## Bibliography

Bloom, Harold, ed. *Robert Penn Warren.* New York: Chelsea House, 1986. This collection of essays on Warren's work considers both the poetry and the fiction.

Blotner, Joseph. *Robert Penn Warren: A Biography.* New York: Random House, 1997. Blotner's is the first of what will almost certainly be many biographies following Warren's death in 1989. Blotner began his work while Warren was still alive and had the good fortune to have the cooperation not only of his subject but also of the larger Warren family. Blotner's book is straightforward and chronological; it makes a good beginning.

Clark, William Bedford, ed. *Critical Essays on Robert Penn Warren.* Boston: G. K. Hall, 1981. Comprehensive collection of criticism by leading literary scholars of Warren's major work as novelist, poet, biographer, and essayist. Among the contributors are Harold Bloom, Malcolm Cowley, Carlos Baker, John Crowe Ransom, and Randall Jarrell. The collection includes a valuable 1969 interview with Warren by Richard Sale.

Dietrich, Bryan. "Christ or Antichrist: Understanding Eight Words in 'Blackberry Winter.'" *Studies in Short Fiction* 29 (Spring, 1992): 215-220. Discusses the final line of the story, "But I did follow him, all the years," by analyzing and critiquing previous critical interpretations of the line and by providing a religious reading of the tramp as Antichrist; suggests that the young protagonist of the story follows in the footsteps of disillusionment.

Ferriss, Lucy. "Sleeping with the Boss: Female Subjectivity in Robert Penn Warren's Fiction." *The Mississippi Quarterly* 48 (Winter, 1994/1995): 147-167. Part of a special issue on Warren; suggests a feminist reading of Warren's fiction, discussing significant women characters who have sexual liaisons with men of power and wealth; argues that Warren's ability to risk the profound disruption of masculine authority either by admitting female "selves" or by exposing the self-other dialectic as unreliable demonstrates his faith in the continuing resilience of interpretation.

Glenn, Jonathan A. "When the Light Gets Green." In *Masterplots II: Short Story Series*, edited by Charles E. May. Rev. ed. Vol. 8. Pasadena, Calif.: Salem Press, 2004. Analysis of "When the Light Gets Green" with sections on themes and meaning and style and technique. Also includes a detailed synopsis of the story.

Madden, David, ed. *The Legacy of Robert Penn Warren*. Baton Rouge: Louisiana State University Press, 2000. Collection of critical and biographical essays on Warren's life and work. Includes bibliographical references and an index.

May, Charles E. "Blackberry Winter." In *Masterplots II: Short Story Series*, edited by Charles E. May. Rev. ed. Vol. 1. Pasadena, Calif.: Salem Press, 2004. Student-friendly analysis of "Blackberry Winter" that covers the story's themes and style and includes a detailed synopsis.

Millichap, Joseph R. *Robert Penn Warren: A Study of the Short Fiction*. New York: Twayne, 1992. Millichap examines fourteen stories and two essays by Warren and maintains that the short works provide a window into Warren's longer and better-known writings.

Ruppersburg, Hugh. *Robert Penn Warren and the American Imagination*. Athens: University of Georgia Press, 1990. Ruppersburg considers the Warren opus an attempt to define a national identity. He focuses, in particular, on *Brother to Dragons*, *Audubon: A Vision*, and *Chief Joseph of the Nez Percé*. Subscribing to Warren's notion that he was not a historical writer, Ruppersburg also attempts to place Warren in a contemporary context, emphasizing such modern American concerns as civil rights and nuclear warfare.

Watkins, Floyd C., John T. Hiers, and Mary Louise Weaks, eds. *Talking with Robert Penn Warren*. Athens: University of Georgia Press, 1990. Collection of twenty-four interviews, extending from 1953 to 1985, in which Warren talks about his work with characteristic honesty, openness, folksiness, and wit from the joint perspective of writer, interpreter, and critic. The group of interviewers includes Ralph Ellison, Marshall Walker, Bill Moyers, Edwin Harold Newman, Floyd C. Watkins, and Eleanor Clark.

# Eudora Welty

**Born:** Jackson, Mississippi; April 13, 1909
**Died:** Jackson, Mississippi; July 23, 2001

**Principal short fiction** • *A Curtain of Green, and Other Stories*, 1941; *The Wide Net, and Other Stories*, 1943; *The Golden Apples*, 1949; *Short Stories*, 1950; *Selected Stories of Eudora Welty*, 1954; *The Bride of the Innisfallen, and Other Stories*, 1955; *Moon Lake, and Other Stories*, 1980; *The Collected Stories of Eudora Welty*, 1980; *Retreat*, 1981.

**Other literary forms** • In addition to her many short stories, Eudora Welty published novels, essays, reviews, an autobiography, a fantasy story for children, and a volume of photographs of Mississippi during the Depression, *One Time, One Place: Mississippi in the Depression, A Snapshot Album* (1971), taken during her stint as photographer and writer for the Works Progress Administration. Several posthumous volumes of her work have also been published, including *On Writing* (2002), a collection of her essays about literature, and a memoir, *Some Notes on River Country* (2003).

**Achievements** • Eudora Welty possessed a distinctive voice in southern, and indeed in American, fiction. Her vibrant, compelling evocation of the Mississippi landscape, which was her most common setting, led to comparisons between her work and that of other eminent southern writers such as William Faulkner, Carson McCullers, and Flannery O'Connor. Welty's graceful, lyrical fiction, however, lacks the pessimism that characterizes much of established southern writing, and though her settings are distinctly southern, her themes are universal and do not focus on uniquely southern issues.

The honors and awards that Welty amassed throughout her long career are so many as to defy complete listing in a short space. Among her major achievements are four O. Henry Awards for her short stories (first prizes in 1942, 1943, and 1968, and a second prize in 1941), two Guggenheim Fellowships (1942, 1949), honorary lectureships at Smith College (1952) and the University of Cambridge (1955), election to the National Institute of Arts and Letters (1952) and to the American Academy of Arts and Letters (1971), honorary LL.D. degrees from the University of Wisconsin (1954) and Smith College (1956), a term as honorary consultant to the Library of Congress (1958-1961), the William Dean Howells Medal of the American Academy of Arts and Letters for *The Ponder Heart* (1954), the Gold Medal for Fiction of the National Institute of Arts and Letters (1972), the Pulitzer Prize in fiction (awarded in 1973 for her 1972 novel *The Optimist's Daughter*), the National Medal of Literature and Medal of Freedom (1981), the National Medal of Arts (1986), the naming of the Jackson Public Library in her honor (1986), and a Rea Award (1992).

**Biography** • Eudora Welty was born on April 13, 1909, in Jackson, Mississippi. In the Welty household, reading was a favorite pastime, and Welty recalls in her autobiography, *One Writer's Beginnings* (1984), both being read to often as a young child and becoming a voracious reader herself. Her recollections of her early life are of a loving and protective family and of a close, gossip-prone community in which she developed

Frank Hains/Courtesy, Mississippi Department of Archives and History

her lifelong habit of watching, listening to, and observing closely everything around her. Her progressive and understanding parents encouraged her in her education, and in 1925, she enrolled at the Mississippi State College for Women. After two years there, she transferred to the University of Wisconsin and graduated with a bachelor's degree in English in 1929.

Welty subsequently studied advertising at the Columbia University Business School; her father had recommended to her that if she planned to be a writer, she would be well advised to have another skill to which she could turn in case of need. During the Depression, however, she had little success finding employment in the field of advertising. She returned to Mississippi and spent the next several years working variously as a writer for radio and as a society editor. In 1933, she began working for the Works Progress Administration, traveling throughout Mississippi, taking photographs, interviewing people, and writing newspaper articles. She later credited this experience with providing her with much material for her short stories as well as sharpening her habit of observation. During these working years, she wrote short stories and occasionally traveled to New York in an effort to interest publishers in her work, with little success. Her first short story, "Death of a Traveling Salesman," was published in 1936 by a "little" magazine called *Manuscript.* Her ability as a writer soon attracted the attention of Robert Penn Warren and Cleanth Brooks, editors of *The Southern Review,* and over the next years her writing appeared in that magazine as well as in *The New Yorker, The Atlantic Monthly,* and *The Sewanee Review.*

Welty's first collection of short stories, *A Curtain of Green, and Other Stories,* appeared in 1941, with a preface by Katherine Anne Porter. Welty's reputation as an important southern writer was established with this first volume, and, at the urging of her editor and friend John Woodburn, who encouraged her to write a longer work of fiction, she followed it with her fabular novel *The Robber Bridegroom* in 1942. Thenceforth, she continued with a fairly steady output of fiction, and with each successive publication, her stature as a major American writer grew. Although fiction was her primary field, she wrote many essays and critical reviews and dabbled in the theater. In addition to stage adaptations of *The Robber Bridegroom* and *The Ponder Heart,* she collaborated on a musical (never produced) entitled *What Year Is This?* and wrote several short theatrical sketches. In 1984, her autobiography, *One Writer's Beginnings,* appeared and quickly became a best-seller.

Welty spent most of her life living in, observing, and writing about Jackson and the

Mississippi Delta country. Her frequent visits to New York, and her travels in France, Italy, Ireland, and England (where she participated in a conference on American studies at the University of Cambridge in 1955) provided her with material for those few stories that are set outside her native Mississippi. From time to time, she lectured or taught but in general preferred the quiet and privacy of her lifelong home of Jackson. Welty died of pneumonia in the place of her birth, Jackson, Mississippi, on July 23, 2001, at the age of ninety-two.

**Analysis** • Although some dominant themes and characteristics appear regularly in Eudora Welty's fiction, her work resists categorization. The majority of her stories are set in her beloved Mississippi Delta country, of which she paints a vivid and detailed picture, but she is equally comfortable evoking such diverse scenes as a northern city or a transatlantic ocean liner. Thematically, she concerns herself both with the importance of family and community relations and, paradoxically, with the strange solitariness of human experience. Elements of myth and symbol often appear in her work, but she uses them in shadowy, inexplicit ways. Perhaps the only constant in Welty's fiction is her unerring keenness of observation, both of physical landscape and in characterization, and her ability to create convincing psychological portraits of an immensely varied cast of characters.

**"Death of a Traveling Salesman"** • One of her earliest stories, "Death of a Traveling Salesman," tells of a commercial traveler who loses his way in the hill country of Mississippi and accidentally drives his car into a ravine. At the nearest farm dwelling, the salesman finds a simple, taciturn couple who assist him with his car and give him a meal and a place to stay for the night. The unspoken warmth in the relationship of the couple is contrasted with the salesman's loneliness, and he repeatedly worries that they can hear the loud pounding of his heart, physically weakened from a recent illness and metaphorically empty of love. When he leaves their house in the morning, his heart pounds loudest of all as he carries his bags to his car; frantically he tries to stifle the sound and dies, his heart unheard by anyone but himself.

**"A Worn Path"** • Another relatively early story, "A Worn Path," recounts an ancient black woman's long and perilous journey on foot from her remote rural home to the nearest town. The frail old woman, called Phoenix, travels slowly and painfully through a sometimes hostile landscape, described in rich and abundant detail. She overcomes numerous obstacles with determination and good humor. Into the vivid, realistic description of the landscape and journey, Welty interweaves characteristically lyrical passages describing Phoenix's fatigue-induced hallucinations and confused imaginings. When Phoenix reaches the town, she goes to the doctor's office, and it is revealed that the purpose of her journey is to obtain medicine for her chronically ill grandson. A poignant scene at the story's close confirms the reader's suspicion of Phoenix's extreme poverty and suggests the likelihood that her beloved grandson will not live long; old Phoenix's dignity and courage in the face of such hardship, however, raise the story from pathos to a tribute to her resilience and strength of will. Like her mythical namesake, Phoenix triumphs over the forces that seek to destroy her.

**"Why I Live at the P.O."** • "Why I Live at the P.O." is a richly comic tale of family discord and personal alienation, told in the first person in idiomatic, naturalistic language that captures the sounds and patterns of a distinctive southern speech. It is one of the earliest examples of Welty's often-used narrative technique, what she calls the "monologue that takes possession of the speaker." The story recounts how Sister, the intelligent and ironic narrator, comes to fall out with her family over incidents arising from her younger sister Stella-Rondo's sudden reappearance in their small southern town, minus her husband and with a two-year-old "adopted" child in tow.

Welty's flair for comedy of situation is revealed as a series of bizarrely farcical episodes unfolds. Through the irritable Stella-Rondo's manipulative misrepresentations of fact and Sister's own indifference to causing offense, Sister earns the ire of her opinionated and influential grandfather Papa-Daddy, her gullible, partisan mother, and her short-tempered Uncle Rondo. Sister responds by removing all of her possessions from communal use in the home and taking up residence in the local post office, where she is postmistress. Inability to communicate is a recurrent theme in Welty's short fiction; in this case, it is treated with a controlled hilarity that is chiefly comic but that nevertheless reveals the pain of a family's disunity. This story is one of the best examples of Welty's gift for comic characterization, her gentle mockery of human foibles, and her ear for southern idiom and expression.

**"Keela, the Outcast Indian Maiden"** • Although Welty disliked having the term "gothic" applied to her fiction, "Keela, the Outcast Indian Maiden" has a grotesque quality that characterizes much of southern gothic writing. Steve, a former circus sideshow barker, has enlisted the help of Max in finding a small, clubfooted black man who used to be exhibited in the sideshow as "Keela, the Outcast Indian Maiden." As a sideshow freak, he was forced to behave savagely and eat live chickens. Max has brought Steve to the home of Little Lee Roy, who is indeed the man Steve seeks.

As Little Lee Roy looks on, Steve tells Max the disgusting details of the sideshow act and explains how Little Lee Roy was ill-treated by the circus until a kind spectator rescued the victim from his degrading existence. Although he persistently refers to Little Lee Roy as "it" and, unlike Max, refuses to address Little Lee Roy directly, Steve expresses guilt and regret over his role in Little Lee Roy's exploitation. There are subtle resonances of the South's troubled legacy in the way the obviously culpable Steve tries to diminish his role in this ugly episode of oppression by pleading ignorance. He claims that he never knew that the sideshow freak was a normal man and not the savage beast that he was displayed as being in the circus.

The simpleminded Little Lee Roy, however, reacts to these reminders of his bizarre past with uncomprehending glee; he seems to have forgotten the pain and unpleasantness of his life with the circus and remembers it only as a colorful adventure. Steve cannot expiate his guilt; he has nothing to offer Little Lee Roy to compensate him for his brutal treatment. He says awkwardly to Max, "Well, I was goin' to give him some money or somethin', I guess, if I ever found him, only now I ain't got any." After the white men's departure, Little Lee Roy's children return, but they hush him when he tries to tell them about the visitors who came to talk to him about "de old times when I use to be wid de circus." The ugly incidents have left no scar on their simple victim; rather, it is the victimizer who suffers an inescapable burden of guilt and shame.

**"The Wide Net"** • "The Wide Net" is a fabular tale of the mysteries of human relationships and the potency of the natural world. Young William Wallace returns home from a night on the town to find a note from his pregnant wife saying that she has gone to drown herself in the river. William Wallace assembles a motley collection of men and boys to help him drag the river. The river's power as a symbol is apparent in the meaning that it holds for the many characters: To youngsters Grady and Brucie it is the grave of their drowned father; to the rough, carefree Malones, it is a fertile source of life, teeming with catfish to eat, eels to "rassle," and alligators to hunt; to the philosophical and somewhat bombastic Doc, it signifies that "the outside world is full of endurance." It is also, the river-draggers discover, the home of the primeval "king of the snakes."

Throughout the story, Welty deliberately obscures the nature of William Wallace's relationship with his wife, the history behind her threat, and even whether William Wallace truly believes his wife has jumped in the river. Characteristically, Welty relies on subtle hints and expert manipulation of tone rather than on open exposition to suggest to her readers the underpinnings of the events that she describes. This deliberate vagueness surrounding the facts of the young couple's quarrel lends the story the quality of a fable or folktale. The young lover must undergo the test of dragging the great river, confronting the king of snakes, and experiencing a kind of baptism, both in the river and in the cleansing thunderstorm that drenches the searchers, before he is worthy of regaining his wife's love.

Like a fable, the story has an almost impossibly simple and happy ending. William Wallace returns from the river to find his welcoming wife waiting calmly at home. They have a brief, affectionate mock quarrel that does not specifically address the incident at all, and they retire hand in hand, leaving the reader to ponder the mystery of their bond.

**"Livvie"** • "Livvie" has a lyrical, fabular quality similar to that of "The Wide Net." Livvie is a young black woman who lives with her elderly husband, Solomon, on a remote farm far up the old Natchez Trace. The strict old husband is fiercely protective of his young bride and does not allow her to venture from the yard or to talk with—or even see—other people. The inexperienced Livvie, however, is content in Solomon's comfortable house, and she takes loving care of him when his great age finally renders him bedridden. One day, a white woman comes to her door, selling cosmetics. Livvie is enchanted with the colors and scents of the cosmetics but is firm in her insistence that she has no money to buy them. When the saleswoman leaves, Livvie goes into the bedroom to gaze on her ancient, sleeping husband. Desire for wider experience and a more fulfilling life has been awakened in her, and as her husband sleeps, she disobeys his strictest command and wanders off down the Natchez Trace.

There, she comes upon a handsome, opulently dressed young man named Cash, whom she leads back to Solomon's house. When Solomon awakes and sees them, he is reproachful but resigned to her need for a younger man, asking God to forgive him for taking such a young girl away from other young people. Cash steals from the room, and as Livvie gazes on the frail, wasted body of Solomon, he dies. In a trancelike shock, Livvie drops Solomon's sterile, ticking watch; after momentary hesitation, she goes outside to join Cash in the bright light of springtime.

"Livvie" is almost like a fairy tale in its use of simple, universal devices. The beautiful young bride, the miserly old man who imprisons her, the strange caller who brings temptation, and the handsome youth who rescues the heroine are all familiar, timeless characters. Welty broadens the references of her story to include elements of myth and religion. Young Cash, emerging from the deep forest dressed in a bright green coat and green-plumed hat, could be the Green Man of folklore, a symbol of springtime regeneration and fertility. In contrasting youth with age and old with new, Welty subtly employs biblical references. Old Solomon thinks rather than feels but falls short of his Old Testament namesake in wisdom. Youthful Cash, redolent of spring, tells Livvie that he is "ready for Easter," the reference ostensibly being to his new finery but suggesting new life rising to vanquish death. The vague, dreamy impressionism of "Livvie," which relies on image and action rather than dialogue to tell the story (except in the scenes featuring the saleswoman), adds to this folktale-like quality.

**"A Still Moment"** • In "A Still Moment," Welty uses historical characters to tell a mystically imaginative tale. Lorenzo Dow, the New England preacher, James Murrell, the outlaw, and John James Audubon, the naturalist and painter, were real people whom Welty places in a fictional situation. Dow rides with an inspired determination to his evening's destination, a camp meeting where he looks forward to a wholesale saving of souls. With single-minded passion, he visualizes souls and demons crowding before him in the dusky landscape. Dow's spiritual intensity is both compared and contrasted to the outlook of the outlaw Murrell, who shadows Dow along the Natchez Trace. Murrell considers his outlawry in a profoundly philosophical light, seeing each murder as a kind of ceremonial drawing out and solving of the unique "mystery" of each victim's being. Audubon, like Dow and Murrell, has a strange and driving intensity that sets him apart from other men. His passion is the natural world; by meticulously observing and recording it, he believes that he can move from his knowledge to an understanding of all things, including his own being.

The three men are brought together by chance in a clearing, each unaware of the others' identities. As they pause, a solitary white heron alights near them in the marsh. As the three men stare in wonder at the snowy creature, Welty identifies for the reader the strange similarity of these outwardly diverse men: "What each of them had wanted was simply *all*. To save all souls, to destroy all men, to see and record all life that filled this world." The simple and beautiful sight of the heron, however, causes these desires to ebb in each of them; they are transfixed and cleansed of desire. Welty uses the heron as a symbol of the purity and beauty of the natural world, which acts as a catalyst for her characters' self-discovery. Oddly, it is Audubon, the lover of nature, who breaks the spell. He reaches for his gun and shoots the bird, to add to his scientific collection. The magic of the moment is gone, and the lifeless body of the bird becomes a mere sum of its parts, a dull, insensate mass of feathers and flesh.

Audubon, his prize collected, continues on his way, and the horrified Dow hurries away toward his camp meeting, comforted by the vivid memory of the bird's strange beauty. The dangerous Murrell experiences an epiphanic moment of self-realization; the incident has reminded him poignantly of all men's separateness and innocence, a thought that reconfirms in him his desire to waylay and destroy. It is only through a brief but intense moment of shared feeling and experience that the men can recognize their essential loneliness. As in "The Wide Net" and "Livvie," the most important communication must be done without words.

**"Moon Lake"** • "Moon Lake" is from the collection *The Golden Apples*, the stories of which are nearly all set in or around the mythical community of Morgana, Mississippi, and feature a single, though extensive, cast of characters. Thematically, it shares with "A Still Moment" the sense of the paradoxical oneness and interconnectedness of the human condition. The story describes a sequence of events at a camp for girls at the lake of the story's title. The characteristically lushly detailed landscape is both beautiful and dangerous, a place where poisonous snakes may lurk in the blackberry brambles and where the lake is a site for adventure but also a brown-watered, bug-infested morass with thick mud and cypress roots that grasp at one's feet.

The story highlights the simultaneous attraction and repulsion of human connection. Antipathies abound among the group assembled at the lake: The lake's Boy Scout lifeguard, Loch, feels contempt for the crowd of young girls; the Morgana girls look down on the orphan girls as ragged thieves; rivalry and distrust crops up among individual girls. The sensitive Nina yearns for connection and freedom from connection at the same time; she envies the lonely independence of the orphans and wishes to be able to change from one persona to another at will, but at the same time she is drawn to Easter, the "leader" of the orphans, for her very qualities of separateness and disdain for friendship.

Nina and her friend Jinny Love follow Easter to a remote part of the lake in an unsuccessful attempt to cultivate her friendship, and when they return to where the others are swimming, Easter falls from the diving platform and nearly drowns. The near-drowning becomes a physical acting out of the story's theme, the fascinating and inescapable but frightening necessity of human connection. Without another's help, Easter would have died alone under the murky water, but Loch's lengthy efforts to resuscitate the apparently lifeless form of Easter disgust the other girls. The quasi-sexual rhythm of the resuscitation is made even more disturbing to the girls by its violence: Loch pummels Easter with his fists, and blood streams from her mud-smeared mouth as he flails away astride her. The distressing physical contact contrasts with the lack of any emotional connection during this scene. One orphan, a companion of Easter, speculates that if Easter dies she gets her winter coat, and gradually the other girls grow bored of the spectacle and resent the interruption of their afternoon swim. Jinny Love's mother, appearing unexpectedly at the camp, is more concerned with the lewdness that she imputes to Loch's rhythmic motions than with Easter's condition and she barks at him, "Loch Morrison, get off that table and shame on you." Nina is the most keenly aware of the symbolic significance of the incident and of the peril of connection; she reflects that "Easter had come among them and had held herself untouchable and intact. For one little touch could smirch her, make her fall so far, so deep."

### "The Whole World Knows"

"The Whole World Knows" • Another story from *The Golden Apples* is "The Whole World Knows," which features the adult Jinny Love Stark, whom readers have met as a child in "Moon Lake," and Ran McLain, who appears briefly in "Moon Lake" and other stories in this collection. The story addresses the inescapable net of personal and community relations and the potentially stifling and limiting nature of small-town life. Welty uses a monologue form similar to the one in "Why I Live at the P.O.," but in this story, told by Ran, the tone is lamenting and confessional rather than comically outraged.

Ran and Jinny are married but have separated, ostensibly over Jinny's infidelity. They both remain in the claustrophobically small town of Morgana, living in the same street and meeting occasionally in the town's bank, where Ran works alongside Jinny's lover, Woody Spights. On the surface, the story centers on Ran's developing relationship with a Maideen Sumrall, a foolish, chattering young country girl with whom he has taken up as a way of revenging himself on his wayward wife. The true focus, however, is on the causes of the deterioration of Ran's marriage to the lively, enthusiastic Jinny, revealed obliquely through other events in the story. The reasons for Jinny's initial infidelity are only hinted at; her irrepressibly joyous and wondering outlook is contrasted with Ran's heavy and brooding nature, indicating a fundamental incompatibility. Ran's careless and selfish use of Maideen, to whom he is attracted because she seems a young and "uncontaminated" version of Jinny, suggests a dark side to his nature that may be at the root of their estrangement. There is a vague suggestion, never clearly stated, that Ran may have been unfaithful to Jinny first. The merry, carefree Jinny baffles and infuriates Ran, and he fantasizes about violently murdering both Jinny and her lover, Woody. His true victim, however, is Maideen, the vulnerable opposite of the unflappable, independent Jinny. After Ran roughly consummates his shabby affair with the semi-willing Maideen, he wakes to find her sobbing like a child beside him. Readers learn in another story that Maideen eventually commits suicide. The story ends inconclusively, with neither Ran nor Jinny able or even entirely willing to escape from their shared past, the constricted community of Morgana being their all-knowing "whole world" of the story's title. As in "Moon Lake," true connection is a paradox, at once impossible, inescapable, desirable, and destructive.

**"Where Is the Voice Coming From?"** • "Where Is the Voice Coming From?" was originally published in *The New Yorker,* and it remained uncollected until the appearance of the complete *The Collected Stories of Eudora Welty* in 1980. In it, Welty uses a fictional voice to express her views on the civil rights struggle in the South. The story, written in 1963 in response to the murder of Medgar Evers in Welty's hometown of Jackson, is told as a monologue by a southern white man whose ignorance and hate for African Americans is depicted as chillingly mundane. He tells how, enraged by black activism in the South, he determines to shoot a local civil rights leader. He drives to the man's home late on an unbearably hot summer night, waits calmly in hiding until the man appears, and then shoots him in cold blood. The callous self-righteousness of the killer and his unreasoning hate are frighteningly depicted when he mocks the body of his victim, saying "Roland? There was only one way left for me to be ahead of you and stay ahead of you, by Dad, and I just taken it. . . . We ain't never now, never going to be equals and you know why? One of us is dead. What about that, Roland?" His justification for the murder is simple: "I done what I done for my own pure-D satisfaction." His only regret is that he cannot claim the credit for the killing.

Welty scatters subtle symbols throughout the story. The extremely hot weather, which torments the killer, reflects the social climate as the civil rights conflict reaches a kind of boiling point. To the killer, the street feels as hot under his feet as the barrel of his gun. Light and dark contrast in more than just the black and white skins of the characters: The stealthy killer arrives in a darkness that will cloak his crime and he finds light shining forth from the home of his prey, whose mission is to enlighten. When the killer shoots his victim, he sees that "something darker than him, like the wings of a bird, spread on his back and pulled him down."

Unlike most of Welty's fiction, "Where Is the Voice Coming From?" clearly espouses a particular viewpoint, and the reader is left with no doubt about the writer's intention in telling the story. The story, however, embodies the qualities that typify Welty's fiction: the focus on the interconnections of human society; the full, sharp characterization achieved in a minimum of space; the detailed description of the physical landscape that powerfully evokes a sense of place; the ear for speech and idiom; and the subtle, floating symbolism that insinuates rather than announces its meaning.

*Catherine Swanson*
*With updates by the Editors*

## Other major works

CHILDREN'S LITERATURE: *The Shoe Bird*, 1964.

NOVELS: *The Robber Bridegroom*, 1942; *Delta Wedding*, 1946; *The Ponder Heart*, 1954; *Losing Battles*, 1970; *The Optimist's Daughter*, 1972.

MISCELLANEOUS: *Stories, Essays, and Memoir*, 1998; *Early Escapades*, 2005 (Patti Carr Black, editor).

NONFICTION: *Music from Spain*, 1948; *The Reading and Writing of Short Stories*, 1949; *Place in Fiction*, 1957; *Three Papers on Fiction*, 1962; *One Time, One Place: Mississippi in the Depression, a Snapshot Album*, 1971; *A Pageant of Birds*, 1974; *The Eye of the Story: Selected Essays and Reviews*, 1978; *Ida M'Toy*, 1979; *Miracles of Perception: The Art of Willa Cather*, 1980 (with Alfred Knopf and Yehudi Menuhin); *Conversations with Eudora Welty*, 1984 (Peggy Whitman Prenshaw, editor); *One Writer's Beginnings*, 1984; *Eudora Welty: Photographs*, 1989; *A Writer's Eye: Collected Book Reviews*, 1994 (Pearl Amelia McHaney, editor); *More Conversations with Eudora Welty*, 1996 (Prenshaw, editor); *Country Churchyards*, 2000; *On William Hollingsworth, Jr.*, 2002; *On Writing*, 2002 (includes essays originally published in *The Eye of the Story*); *Some Notes on River Country*, 2003; *On William Faulkner*, 2003.

## Bibliography

Devlin, Albert J. *Eudora Welty's Chronicle: A Story of Mississippi Life*. Jackson: University Press of Mississippi, 1983. Devlin analyzes certain works, such as *Delta Wedding*, in great detail. He offers insightful criticism and suggests that Welty's writing contains a historical structure, spanning from the territorial era to modern times.

*Georgia Review* 53 (Spring, 1999). A special issue on Welty celebrating her ninetieth birthday, with articles by a number of writers, including Doris Betts, as well as a number of critics and admirers of Welty.

Kaplansky, Leslie A. "Cinematic Rhythms in the Short Fiction of Eudora Welty." *Studies in Short Fiction* 33 (Fall, 1996): 579-589. Discusses the influence of film technique on Welty's short fiction; argues that in taking advantage of cinematic rhythm in her stories, Welty developed her mastery of technique and style.

Marrs, Suzanne. *Eudora Welty: A Biography*. Orlando, Fla.: Harcourt, 2005. Literary biography provides insight into Welty's life and writing and serves to refute some popular conceptions of the writer.

_____. *One Writer's Imagination: The Fiction of Eudora Welty*. Baton Rouge: Louisiana State University Press, 2002. Combination of critical analysis and memoir, written by a long-time friend of Welty who is also a scholar and the archivist of Welty's papers. Discusses the effects of both close personal relationships and social and political events on Welty's imagination and writing.

May, Charles E., ed. *Masterplots II: Short Story Series, Revised Edition*. 8 vols. Pasadena, Calif.: Salem Press, 2004. Designed for student use, this reference set contains articles providing detailed plot summaries and analyses of thirteen short stories by Welty: "Death of a Traveling Salesman" (vol. 2); "Keela, the Outcast Indian

Maiden" (vol. 4); "A Memory" and "No Place for You, My Love" (vol. 5); "Petrified Man," "A Piece of News," and "Powerhouse" (vol. 6); "Shower of Gold" (vol. 7); and "A Visit of Charity," "The Wide Net," "Where Is the Voice Coming From?," "Why I Live at the P.O.," and "A Worn Path" (vol. 8).

*Mississippi Quarterly* 50 (Fall, 1997). A special issue on Welty, with essays comparing Welty to William Faulkner, Edgar Allan Poe, and Nathaniel Hawthorne, and discussions of the women in Welty's stories, her political thought, her treatment of race and history.

Prenshaw, Peggy Whitman, ed. *Conversations with Eudora Welty.* Jackson: University Press of Mississippi, 1984. Collection of interviews with Welty spanning the years 1942-1982. Welty talks frankly and revealingly with interviewers such as William F. Buckley, Jr., and Alice Walker about her fiction and her life, addressing such topics as her methods of writing, her southern background, her love of reading, and her admiration for the works of writers such as William Faulkner, Elizabeth Bowen, and Katherine Anne Porter.

Waldron, Ann. *Eudora Welty: A Writer's Life.* New York: Doubleday, 1998. The first full-length biography of Welty, but one that was done without her authorization or permission; provides a great deal of detail about Welty's life and literary career but derives commentary about Welty's work from reviews and other previous criticism.

Weston, Ruth D. *Gothic Traditions and Narrative Techniques in the Fiction of Eudora Welty.* Baton Rouge: Louisiana State University Press, 1994. Discusses Welty's use of the gothic tradition in her fiction; provides original readings of a number of Welty's short stories.

# Edith Wharton

**Born:** New York, New York; January 24, 1862
**Died:** St.-Brice-sous-Forêt, France; August 11, 1937

**Principal short fiction** • *The Greater Inclination*, 1899; *Crucial Instances*, 1901; *The Descent of Man*, 1904; *The Hermit and the Wild Woman*, 1908; *Tales of Men and Ghosts*, 1910; *Xingu, and Other Stories*, 1916; *Here and Beyond*, 1926; *Certain People*, 1930; *Human Nature*, 1933; *The World Over*, 1936; *Ghosts*, 1937; *The Collected Short Stories of Edith Wharton*, 1968; *Collected Stories, 1891-1910*, 2001 (Maureen Howard, editor); *Collected Stories, 1911-1937*, 2001 (Howard, editor).

**Other literary forms** • Edith Wharton's prolific career includes the publication of novels, novellas, short stories, poetry, travel books, criticism, works on landscaping and interior decoration, a translation, an autobiography, and wartime pamphlets and journalism. Her novel *The Age of Innocence* (1920) was awarded the Pulitzer Prize in 1921. Several of her works have been adapted for the stage, including *The Age of Innocence* and the novels *Ethan Frome* (1911), *The House of Mirth* (1905), and *The Old Maid* (1924). The dramatization of *The Old Maid* was awarded the Pulitzer Prize for drama in 1935. Films based on Edith Wharton's works include *The House of Mirth, The Glimpses of the Moon* (1922), and *The Old Maid*.

**Achievements** • Edith Wharton's talent in affording her reader an elegant, well-constructed glance at upper-class New York and European society won for her high esteem from the earliest years of her career. The novel *The House of Mirth* was her first best-seller and, along with *Ethan Frome* and *The Age of Innocence*, is considered to be one of her finest works. During World War I, Wharton served the Allied cause in Europe by organizing relief efforts and caring for Belgian orphans, work for which she was inducted into the French Legion of Honor in 1916 and the Order of Leopold (Belgium) in 1919. In the United States, the 1920's would see Wharton's literary career flower. In 1921, she became the first woman to receive the Pulitzer Prize, awarded to her for *The Age of Innocence*; in 1923, she also became the first female recipient of an honorary degree of doctor of letters from Yale University; in 1927, she was nominated for the Nobel Prize in Literature; in 1928, her novel *The Children* was the Book-of-the-Month Club selection for September. By 1930, Wharton was one of the most highly regarded American authors of the time and was elected to the American Academy of Arts and Letters. After Wharton's death in 1937, her fiction was not as widely read by the general public as it was during her lifetime. Feminist literary scholars, however, have reexamined Wharton's works for their unmistakable portrayal of women's lives in the early twentieth century.

**Biography** • Edith Wharton was born Edith Newbold Jones, a member of a family occupying the highest level of society. Like most girls of her generation and social class, she was educated at home. At the age of twenty-three she married a wealthy young man, Edward Wharton; they had no children. Wharton divided her time between writing and her duties as a society hostess. Her husband, emotionally unstable, suffered several nervous breakdowns, and in 1913, they were divorced. Wharton spent a great deal of time in Europe; after 1912 she returned to America only once, to accept the honorary degree of doctor of letters from Yale University in 1923. During World War I, Wharton was very active in war work in France, for which she was made a Chevalier of the Legion of Honor in 1916. Realizing that after her death her friends would suppress much of her real personality in their accounts of her life, and wanting the truth to be told, Wharton willed her private papers to Yale University, with instructions that they were not to be published until 1968. These papers revealed a totally unexpected side of Wharton's character: passionate, impulsive, and vulnerable. This new view of the author has had a marked effect on subsequent interpretations of her work.

**Analysis** • Because many of Edith Wharton's characters and themes resemble those of Henry James, her work has sometimes been regarded as derivative of his. Each of these authors wrote a number of stories regarding such themes as the fate of the individual who challenges the standards of society, the effect of commercial success on an artist, the impact of European civilization on an American mentality, and the confrontation of a public personality with his own private self. Further, both James and Wharton used ghost stories to present, in allegorical terms, internal experiences which would be difficult to dramatize in a purely realistic way. Wharton knew James and admired him as a friend and as a writer, and some of her early short stories—those in *The Greater Inclination* and *Crucial Instances*, for example—do resemble James's work. As she matured, however, Wharton developed an artistic viewpoint and a style which were distinctly her own. Her approach to the themes which she shared with James was much more direct than his: She took a more sweeping view of the action of a story and omitted the myriad details, qualifications, and explanations which characterize James's work.

It is not surprising that Wharton and James developed a number of parallel interests. Both writers moved in the same rather limited social circle and were exposed to the same values and to the same types of people. Not all their perceptions, however, were identical since Wharton's viewpoint was influenced by the limitations she experienced as a woman. She was therefore especially sensitive to such subtle forms of victimization as the narrowness of a woman's horizons in her society, which not only denied women the opportunity to develop their full potential but also burdened men with disproportionate responsibilities. This theme, which underlies some of her best novels—*The House of Mirth* is a good example—also appears in a number of her short stories, such as "The Rembrandt."

**"The Rembrandt"** • The narrator of "The Rembrandt" is a museum curator whose cousin, Eleanor Copt, frequently undertakes acts of charity toward the unfortunate. These acts of charity, however, often take the form of persuading someone else to bear the brunt of the inconvenience and expense. As "The Rembrandt" opens, Eleanor persuades her cousin to accompany her to a rented room occupied by an elderly lady, the once-wealthy Mrs. Fontage. This widowed lady, who has suffered a number of financial misfortunes, has been reduced from living in palatial homes to now living in a dingy room. Even this small room soon will be too expensive for her unless she can sell the one art treasure she still possesses: an unsigned Rembrandt. The supposed Rembrandt, purchased under highly romantic circumstances during the Fontages' honeymoon in Europe, turns out to be valueless. The curator, however, is moved by the dignity and grace with which Mrs. Fontage faces her situation, and he cannot bring himself to tell her that the painting is worthless. He values it at a thousand dollars, reasoning that he himself cannot be expected to raise that much money. When he realizes that his cousin and Mrs. Fontage expect him to purchase the painting on behalf of the museum, he temporizes.

Meanwhile, Eleanor interests an admirer of hers, Mr. Jefferson Rose, in the painting. Although he cannot really spare the money, Rose decides to buy the painting as an act of charity and as an investment. Even after the curator confesses his lie to Rose, the young man is determined to relieve Mrs. Fontage's misery. The curator, reasoning that it is better to defraud an institution than an

Library of Congress

individual, purchases the painting for the museum. The only museum official who might question his decision is abroad, and the curator stores the painting in the museum cellar and forgets it. When the official, Crozier, returns, he asks the curator whether he really considers the painting valuable. The curator confesses what he has done and offers to buy the painting from the museum. Crozier then informs the curator that the members of the museum committee have already purchased the painting privately, and beg leave to present it to the curator in recognition of his kindness to Mrs. Fontage.

Despite its flaws in structure and its somewhat romantic view of the business world, "The Rembrandt" shows Wharton's concern with the relationship between helpless individuals and the society which produced them. Her portrait of Mrs. Fontage is especially revealing—she is a woman of dignity and breeding, whose pride and training sustain her in very difficult circumstances. That very breeding, however, cripples Mrs. Fontage because of the narrowness which accompanies it. She is entirely ignorant of the practical side of life, and, in the absence of a husband or some other head of the family, she is seriously handicapped in dealing with business matters. Furthermore, although she is intelligent and in good health, she is absolutely incapable of contributing to her own support. In this very early story, Wharton applauds the gentlemen who live up to the responsibility of caring for such women. Later, Wharton will censure the men and the women whose unthinking conformity to social stereotypes has deprived women like Mrs. Fontage of the ability to care for themselves and has placed a double burden on the men.

**"The Eyes"** • As Wharton matured, her interest in victimization moved from the external world of society to the internal world of the individual mind. She recognized the fact that adjustment to life sometimes entails a compromise with one's private self which constitutes a betrayal. One of her most striking portrayals of that theme is in "The Eyes." This tale employs the framework of a ghost story to dramatize an internal experience. The story's aging protagonist, Andrew Culwin, has never become part of life, or allowed an involvement with another human being to threaten his absolute egotism. One evening, as his friends amuse themselves by telling tales of psychic events they have witnessed, Culwin offers to tell a story of his own. He explains that as a young man he once flirted with his naïve young cousin Alice, who responded with a seriousness which alarmed him. He immediately announced a trip to Europe; but, moved by the grace with which she accepted her disappointment, Culwin proposed to her and was accepted. He went to bed that evening feeling his self-centered bachelorhood giving way to a sense of righteousness and peace. Culwin awakened in the middle of the night, however, and saw in front of him a hideous pair of eyes. The eyes, which were sunken and old, had pouches of shriveled flesh beneath them and red-lined lids above them, and one of the lids drooped more than the other. These eyes remained in the room all night, and in the morning Culwin fled, without explanation, to a friend's house. There he slept undisturbed and made plans to return to Alice a few days later. Thereupon the eyes returned, and Culwin fled to Europe. He realized that he did not really want to marry Alice, and he devoted himself to a self-centered enjoyment of Europe.

After two years, a handsome young man arrived in Rome with a letter of introduction to Culwin from Alice. This young man, Gilbert Noyes, had been sent abroad by his family to test himself as a writer. Culwin knew that Noyes's writing was worthless, but he temporized in order to keep the handsome youth with him. He also pitied Noyes because of the dull clerk's job which waited for him at home. Finally, Culwin told Noyes that his work had merit, intending to support the young man himself if necessary. That night, the eyes reappeared; and Culwin felt, along with his revulsion, a disquieting sense of identity with the eyes, as if he would some day come to understand all about them. After a month, Culwin cruelly dismissed Noyes, who went home to his clerkship; Culwin took to drink and turned up years later in Hong Kong, fat and unshaven. The eyes then disappeared and never returned.

Culwin's listeners perceive what the reader perceives: The eyes that mock Culwin's rare attempts to transform his self-centered existence into a life of involvement with someone else are in fact his own eyes, looking at him from the future and mocking him with what he would become. The eyes also represent Culwin's lesser self, which would in time take over his entire personality. Even in his youth, this lesser self overshadows Culwin's more humane impulses with second thoughts of the effect these impulses are likely to have on his comfort and security. The story ends as Culwin, surprised by his friends' reaction to his story, catches sight of himself in a mirror, and realizes the truth.

**"After Holbein"** • Wharton's twin themes of social and self-victimization are joined most effectively in a later story which many readers consider her best: "After Holbein." The title refers to a series of woodcuts by Hans Holbein the Younger, entitled "The Dance of Death." They show the figure of death, represented by a skeleton, insinuating himself into the lives of various unsuspecting people. One of these engravings, entitled "Noblewoman," features a richly dressed man and woman following the figure of death.

The story begins with a description of an elderly gentleman, Anson Warley, who has been one of the most popular members of New York society for more than thirty years. In the first three pages of the story, the reader learns that Warley fought, long ago, a battle between his public image and his private self; and the private self lost. Warley gradually stopped staying at home to read or meditate and found less and less time to talk quietly with intellectual friends or scholars. He became a purely public figure, a frequenter of hot, noisy, crowded rooms. His intellect gave itself entirely to the production of drawing-room witticisms, many of them barbed with sarcasm. On the evening that the story takes place, Warley finds himself reminded of one of these sallies of his. Some years earlier, Warley, who had been dodging the persistent invitations of a pompous and rather boring society hostess, finally told his circle of friends that the next time he received a card saying "Mrs. Jasper requests the pleasure," he would reply, "Mr. Warley declines the boredom." The remark was appreciated at the time by the friends who heard it; but in his old age Warley finds himself hoping that Mrs. Jasper never suffered the pain of hearing about it.

At this point in the story, Wharton shifts the scene to a mansion on Fifth Avenue, where a senile old woman prepares herself for an imaginary dinner party. She wears a grotesque purple wig, and broad-toed orthopedic shoes under an ancient purple gown. She also insists on wearing her diamonds to what she believes will be another triumph of her skill as a hostess. This woman is the same Mrs. Jasper whom Warley has been avoiding for years. She is now in the care of an unsympathetic young nurse and three elderly servants. Periodically, the four employees go through the charade of preparing the house and Mrs. Jasper for the dinner parties which she imagines still take place there.

While Mrs. Jasper is being dressed for her illusory dinner party, Anson Warley is preparing to attend a real one. Despite his valet's protests concerning his health, Warley not only refuses to stay at home but also insists on walking up Fifth Avenue in the freezing winter night. Gradually he becomes confused and forgets his destination. Then he sees before him Mrs. Jasper's mansion, lighted for a dinner party, and in his confusion, he imagines he is to dine there. He arrives just as Mrs. Jasper's footman is reading aloud the list of guests whom Mrs. Jasper thinks she has invited.

When dinner is announced, Warley and Mrs. Jasper walk arm in arm, at a stately processional gait, to the table. The footman has set the table with heavy blue and white servants' dishes, and he has stuffed newspapers instead of orchids into the priceless Rose Dubarry porcelain dishes. He serves a plain meal and inexpensive wine in the empty dining room. Lost in the illusion, however, Warley and Mrs. Jasper imagine that they are consuming a gourmet meal at a luxuriously appointed table in the presence of a crowd of glittering guests. They go through a ritual of gestures and conversation which does indeed resemble the *danse macabre* for which the story is named. Finally, Mrs. Jasper leaves the table exhausted and makes her way upstairs to her uncomprehending and chuckling nurse. Warley, equally exhausted and equally convinced that he has attended a brilliant dinner party, steps out into the night and drops dead.

"After Holbein" is a powerful story primarily because of the contrasts it establishes. In the foreground are the wasted lives of Warley and Mrs. Jasper, each of whom has long given up all hope of originality or self-realization for the sake of being part of a nameless, gilded mass. The unsympathetic nurse, who teases Mrs. Jasper into tears, acts not from cruelty but from her inability to comprehend, in her own hopeful youth, the tragedy of Mrs. Jasper's situation. This nurse is contrasted with Mrs. Jasper's elderly maid, Lavinia, who conceals her own failing health out of loyalty to her mistress, and who is moved to tears by Mrs. Jasper's plight. Even the essential horror of the story is intensified by the contrasting formality and restraint of its language and by the tight structuring which gives the plot the same momentum of inevitability as the movements of a formal dance.

Warley and Mrs. Jasper have been betrayed from within and from without. They have traded their private selves for public masks, and have spent their lives among others who have made the same bargain. Lavinia's recollections suggest to the reader that Mrs. Jasper subordinated her role as mother to her role as hostess; and her children, reared in that same world, have left her to the care of servants. Her friends are dead or bedridden, or they have forgotten her. She exists now, in a sense, as she has always existed: as a grotesque figure in a world of illusion.

Warley, too, has come to think of himself only in terms of his social reputation—he will not accept the reality of his age and infirmity. Thus, as he drags one leg during his icy walk along Fifth Avenue, he pictures a club smoking room in which one of his acquaintances will say, "Warley? Why, I saw him sprinting up Fifth Avenue the other night like a two-year-old; that night it was four or five below." Warley has convinced himself that whatever is said in club smoking rooms by men in good society is real. None of the acquaintances, however, to whom he has given his life is with him when he takes that final step; and it would not have mattered if anyone had been there. Warley is almost inevitably and irrevocably alone at last.

Wharton's eleven volumes of short stories, spanning thirty-nine years, record her growth in thought and in style. They offer the entertainment of seeing inside an exclusive social circle which was in many respects unique and which no longer exists as Wharton knew it. Some of Wharton's stories are trivial and some are repetitive; but her best stories depict, in the inhabitants of that exclusive social world, experiences and sensations which are universal.

*Joan DelFattore*
*With updates by Mary F. Yudin*

### Other major works

NOVELS: *The Touchstone*, 1900; *The Valley of Decision*, 1902; *Sanctuary*, 1903; *The House of Mirth*, 1905; *Madame de Treymes*, 1907; *The Fruit of the Tree*, 1907; *Ethan Frome*, 1911; *The Reef*, 1912; *The Custom of the Country*, 1913; *Summer*, 1917; *The Marne*, 1918; *The Age of Innocence*, 1920; *The Glimpses of the Moon*, 1922; *A Son at the Front*, 1923; *Old New York*, 1924 (4 volumes; includes *False Dawn*, *The Old Maid*, *The Spark*, and *New Year's Day*); *The Mother's Recompense*, 1925; *Twilight Sleep*, 1927; *The Children*, 1928; *Hudson River Bracketed*, 1929; *The Gods Arrive*, 1932; *The Buccaneers*, 1938.

NONFICTION: *The Decoration of Houses*, 1897 (with Ogden Codman, Jr.); *Italian Villas and Their Gardens*, 1904; *Italian Backgrounds*, 1905; *A Motor-Flight Through France*, 1908; *Fighting France from Dunkerque to Belfort*, 1915; *French Ways and Their Meaning*, 1919; *In Morocco*, 1920; *The Writing of Fiction*, 1925; *A Backward Glance*, 1934; *The Letters of Edith Wharton*, 1988; *The Uncollected Critical Writings*, 1997 (Frederick Wegener, editor); *Yrs. Ever Affly: The Correspondence of Edith Wharton and Louis Bromfield*, 2000 (Daniel Bratton, editor).

POETRY: *Verses*, 1878; *Artemis to Actæon*, 1909; *Twelve Poems*, 1926.

## Bibliography

Ammons, Elizabeth. *Edith Wharton's Argument with America.* Athens: University of Georgia Press, 1980. Ammons proposes that Wharton's "argument with America" concerns the freedom of women, an argument in which she had a key role during three decades of significant upheaval and change. This engaging book examines the evolution of Wharton's point of view in her novels and discusses the effect of World War I on Wharton. Contains a notes section.

Banta, Martha. "The Ghostly Gothic of Wharton's Everyday World." *American Literary Realism: 1870-1910* 27 (Fall, 1994): 1-10. An analysis of Wharton's ghost story "Afterward" and her novella *Ethan Frome* as illustrative of the nineteenth century craving for a circumscribed experience of the bizarre.

Beer, Janet. *Kate Chopin, Edith Wharton, and Charlotte Perkins Gilman: Studies in Short Fiction.* London: Macmillan, 1997. Beer devotes two chapters to Wharton's short fiction, focusing primarily on the novellas in one chapter and the regional stories about New England in the other.

Benstock, Shari. *No Gifts from Chance: A Biography of Edith Wharton.* New York: Charles Scribner's Sons, 1994. As the first substantial biography of Wharton to appear in nearly two decades, Benstock's study is informed by her investigation of a variety of primary sources that have become available in recent years.

Fracasso, Evelyn E. *Edith Wharton's Prisoner of Consciousness: A Study of Theme and Technique in the Tales.* Westport, Conn.: Greenwood Press, 1994. Analyzes stories from three periods of Wharton's career. Focuses on her technique in treating the theme of imprisonment. Deals with people trapped by love and marriage, imprisoned by the dictates of society, victimized by the demands of art and morality, and paralyzed by fear of the supernatural.

Gawthrop, Betty G. "Roman Fever." In *Masterplots II: Short Story Series,* edited by Charles E. May. Rev. ed. Vol. 6. Pasadena, Calif.: Salem Press, 2004. Analysis of "Roman Fever" with sections on themes and meaning and style and technique. Also includes a detailed synopsis of the story.

Lane, James B. "The Other Two." In *Masterplots II: Short Story Series,* edited by Charles E. May. Rev. ed. Vol. 6. Pasadena, Calif.: Salem Press, 2004. Student-friendly analysis of "The Other Two" that covers the story's themes and style and includes a detailed synopsis.

Lewis, R. W. B. *Edith Wharton: A Biography.* 2 vols. New York: Harper and Row, 1975. Extensive study on Wharton, whom Lewis calls "the most renowned writer of fiction in America." Notes that Wharton thoughtfully left extensive records, made available through the Beinecke Library at Yale, on which this biography is based. Essential reading for serious scholars of Wharton or for those interested in her life and how it shaped her writing.

Nettels, Elsa. *Language and Gender in American Fiction: Howells, James, Wharton, and Cather.* Charlottesville: University Press of Virginia, 1997. Nettels examines American writers struggling with the problems of patriarchy.

Young, Judy Hale. "The Repudiation of Sisterhood in Edith Wharton's 'Pomegranate Seed.'" *Studies in Short Fiction* 33 (Winter, 1996): 1-11. Argues that the story is an indictment of the woman writer who perpetuates the state of noncommunication among women; claims the story is Wharton's anti-manifesto of female writing. In it, she presents her notion of just what the woman who writes must not do.

# Joy Williams

**Born:** Chelmsford, Massachusetts; February 11, 1944

**Principal short fiction** • *Taking Care: Short Stories,* 1982; *Escapes: Stories,* 1990; "Craving," 1991; "The Route," 1992; "Marabou," 1993; *Honored Guest: Stories,* 2004.

**Other literary forms** • Although Joy Williams is known mainly for her short fiction, she is also the author of the novels *State of Grace* (1973), *The Changeling* (1978), *Breaking and Entering* (1988), and *The Quick and the Dead* (2000) and two volumes of nonfiction: *Florida Keys: A History and Guide* (1986) and *Ill Nature: Rants and Reflections on Humanity and Other Animals* (2001). She has also written travel articles for *Esquire* magazine, including "How to Do and Undo Key West" (February, 1996), "Nantucket Now" (September, 1996), "Desert Flower" (January, 1997), and "No Place Like Home" (March, 1997).

**Achievements** • Joy Williams has established herself as one of the preeminent practitioners of the short-story form in the United States. Along with Raymond Carver, Richard Ford, and a handful of other writers, she has perfected a style and content which accurately render life in late twentieth century America. It is not a pretty picture she paints: In Williams's stories, characters cannot communicate, couples cannot connect, and children are being abandoned or reared by others.

Williams has been the recipient of numerous awards in her career, including a John Simon Guggenheim Memorial Foundation Fellowship in 1974. Her stories regularly appear in the leading U.S. literary journals—*Esquire, The New Yorker, Grand Street*—and many have been collected in the annual *The Best American Short Stories* or *Prize Stories: The O. Henry Awards* collections and in other prime anthologies of contemporary American fiction.

**Biography** • Born in 1944, Joy Williams grew up in the small Maine town of Cape Elizabeth, where both her father and her grandfather were Congregational ministers. She holds degrees from Marietta College, in Ohio, and from the University of Iowa. Married to Rust Hills, the writer and fiction editor at *Esquire,* she has one daughter, Caitlin. She has taught in the writing programs at several leading U.S. universities (including the University of California at Irvine and the University of Arizona) and has settled into homes in Arizona and Florida.

**Analysis** • Joy Williams is a short-story writer with a dark vision encased in a clean prose style. Although a few of her stories have an experimental, almost surrealistic form, and often a wry, ironic tone, the bulk fall into what can be called the realist mode, minimalist division: Williams deals with American family life in the last third of the twentieth century, focusing on troubles, handicaps, and incompletions. She interests readers in these subjects without divulging all the information that they might ordinarily want or need about the characters and their situations. What further distinguishes her stories is a prose style that is clean but highly metaphorical, for the images and motifs of the stories often carry the meaning more deeply than the action or exposition.

Hers is not a reassuring portrait of contemporary American life. The families are often dysfunctional, physically as well as psychologically: parents abandon children, by leaving or by dying, and children wander in life without guidance. Alcohol is a cause of the unhappiness as well as its hoped-for cure. In nearly all her stories, love is being sought but is rarely found and nearly as rarely expressed. Characters seem unable to ask the questions that might free them from their unhappiness; the best they can hope for is an escape to some other state, physical or emotional. Disabilities, addictions, dead animals, arguments in restaurants, and car accidents abound in Williams's stories.

Williams's first collection *Taking Care* contains stories published in the 1970's and early 1980's in *The New Yorker, Partisan Review, The Paris Review, Esquire, Ms.*, and other leading vehicles of contemporary American fiction. These stories show a firmness and subtlety that have marked Williams's style over her entire career (although there was probably more range here than in her second collection). The themes that would mark that career are clearly established in this first collection. Although many of the stories are riveting in their subject matter, they leave readers with a sense of hollowness and futility. There are few resolutions in Williams, even early in her career, but there are the tensions, violence, and disconnections that mark most of her stories.

**"Taking Care"** • In the title story, Jones, a preacher, is "taking care" of two generations: a wife dying of leukemia and a six-month-old baby girl whom his daughter has left him to care for before fleeing to Mexico. Jones baptizes his granddaughter and then brings his wife back from the hospital; in the last line of the story, "Together they enter the shining rooms"—rooms made "shining" by Jones's love and care. This epiphanic ending, however, cannot erase all the abandonment and death. Jones is surely "taking care" of more than his required load in this life, and there is a heaviness, a spiritual sadness, that is expressed appropriately in Williams's flat, terse prose style.

Other stories in *Taking Care* have similar themes and forms. In "Traveling to Pridesup," three sisters in their eighties and nineties, "in a big house in the middle of Florida," find a baby abandoned in a feed bag on their mailbox. In the journey in their old Mercedes to find someone to help, Lavinia gets them lost, drives hundreds of miles in circles, and finally crashes. In a tragicomic mix reminiscent of Flannery O'Connor, the story ends with a painful revelation, "the recognition that her life and her long, angry journey through it, had been wasteful and deceptive and unnecessary."

"Winter Chemistry," features two students who spy on their teacher every night and inadvertently kill him when they are caught. "Shepherd" concerns a young woman who cannot get over the death of her German shepherd and who will probably lose her boyfriend because of it. ("'We are all asleep and dreaming, you know,'" he tells her in a speech that might apply to characters in other stories in *Taking Care*. "'If we could ever actually comprehend our true position, we would not be able to bear it, we would have to find a way out.'") In "The Farm," alcohol, infidelities, and the accidental killing of a hitchhiker will destroy the central couple. "Breakfast," too, has many of the stock Williams ingredients: parents who abandon their children, a half-blind dog, and characters who are both alcoholic and lacking direction.

Possibly the only difference in *Taking Care* from Williams's later fiction is that there appears to be more humor in these early stories, and more effort by Williams to perfect a wry, ironic style. ("The Yard Boy," for example, is a surreal caricature of a kind of New Age spiritual character.) Yet the other landmarks are there as well: The style is often flat and cryptic, events and incidents seem to have more a symbolic than a representational quality, and people pass by one another without touching or talking. There is little love in these stories (even in those that are supposedly love stories), but often a violence beneath the surface that is constantly threatening to bubble up and destroy the characters or kill their animals (as in "Preparation for a Collie" or "Woods"). People rarely have names; rather, they are "the woman," "her lover," "the child." Williams writes easily about children, but hers are children who are wandering in an adult world without supervision or love (as in "Train" or "The Excursion.") Williams works here in the great American tradition of Sherwood Anderson's *Winesburg, Ohio* (1919), in which characters become what Anderson called "grotesques." Williams writes of grotesques as well, of bizarre characters who are lost or losing or obsessive, and whom nothing, apparently, will save.

*Escapes* • These elements can be found throughout the title story of Williams's second collection, *Escapes*. The narrator, a young girl, describes the time when her alcoholic mother (abandoned by the father) took her to see a magician. The mother, drunk, wanders onto the stage and has to be removed. Layers of escape, both literal and metaphorical, characterize this story: the father's abandonment of his dysfunctional family; the magician's illusions ("Houdini was more than a magician, he was an escape artist"); the mother's addiction to alcohol; and the daughter's dreams of escaping her lot: "I got out of this situation," Lizzie writes in the last line of the story, "but it took me years."

Williams's later short fiction is unique not only for this bleak view of human nature, in which people are shown trapped and searching for some inexpressible transcendence, but also for a prose style that is both less and more than it appears: less because, like other minimalists whom Williams resembles (such as Raymond Carver and Ann Beattie), she draws only the outlines of the action and leaves the characters' backgrounds to the reader's imagination and more because Williams manipulates metaphors and motifs in such a way that they carry a heavy weight of meaning in her stories. In "Escapes," for example, the old magician's illusion of sawing a woman in half becomes the vehicle for the story's theme: The alcoholic mother tells her daughter that she witnessed that trick performed by Houdini when she was a child. She wanted to be that lady, "sawed in half, and then made whole again!" Her subsequent intrusion into the show by walking onstage is her attempt to escape by realizing that dream, "to go and come back," but the dream is impossible to realize and therefore self-destructive. The usher escorts mother and daughter out of the theater, assuring the drunken woman that she can "pull [herself] through." She will not, however, succeed in reconstructing herself and her life, and in the end, the reader suspects, the daughter will escape only by abandoning the mother.

The stories in *Escapes* thus seem to work at cross-purposes: Although the prose style is clean and uncluttered, the motifs and metaphors lead readers to meanings beneath the surface, to a depth that is full of horror and despair. In the second story, "Rot" (first reprinted in the O. Henry Prize collection of 1988), these concerns and formal characteristics continue. Dwight persuades his wife, who is twenty-five years younger than he is, to allow him to park the vintage Thunderbird he has just bought in their living room. The car is full of rot and rust—a symbol, readers may suspect, of the couple's marriage. The reader learns little about these characters, what they do or where they are headed; instead, symbolism replaces information: The rusting car was found in a parking lot with its owner dead inside it; now Dwight sits in the car in the living room and looks dead.

The other stories in *Escapes* take a similar approach: "The Skater," which was chosen to appear in the 1985 collection *Best American Short Stories*, presents a family, parents and a daughter, on a tour of East Coast prep schools. It slowly becomes apparent that the sickness at the heart of this family is the memory of the daughter—like the skater of the title who glides in and out of the story at several points—who died the previous year; the parents simply want Molly to be away from the sadness of their home.

The young woman in "Lulu" puts an old couple to bed after all three have gotten drunk one morning; she then attempts to drive off with their boa constrictor, apparently searching for love (she wonders, "Why has love eluded me"). In "Health," a twelve-year-old girl is undergoing ultraviolet treatments to help her recover from tuberculosis but is surprised by a man who walks in during one of her tanning sessions, as she lies naked on the couch. The grandmother of "The Blue Men" tries, in part through use of alcohol, to assuage her grief over her dead son, who was executed for murdering a police officer. "The Last Generation," the collection's closing story, depicts a father, numbing his pain over his wife's death through drink and work and neglecting his own children.

Williams's bleak vision is mitigated only by the sureness of her prose and the symbolic poetry of her language. "Bromeliads," in which a young mother abandons her new baby to her parents, becomes the central metaphor of the story's meaning. As the young woman explains, bromeliads are "thick glossy plants with extraordinary flowers. . . . They live on nothing. Just the air and the wind"—a perfect description of the mother herself.

In "White," a couple has moved from Florida to Connecticut to escape the memory of their two babies, who have died. They cannot, however, escape their grief, even in alcohol and evasion. At a party they throw for a departing Episcopal priest, the husband describes a letter that the couple has recently received from the woman's father; after the greeting, the letter contains nothing, "just a page, blank as the day is long." The letter becomes a symbol for the missed communication, the things that are not said and that may in fact be inexpressible, abandonment and death among them.

In the end, readers are left with the bleakness of Williams's stories—despite a minimalist style and a use of metaphor that almost negates that vision. Only "Honored Guest" differs in that it implies affirmation of life through a character's likening those alive to honored guests. Nevertheless, Williams remains one of the more highly regarded short-fiction writers in modern-day America, often anthologized and the recipient of numerous awards. Along with Raymond Carver, Ann Beattie, Richard Ford, and a handful of other contemporaries, she continues to produce works that are read by university students and the general public alike, and younger writers emulate her polished style.

*David Peck*
*With updates by Mary H. Bruce and the Editors*

**Other major works**

NOVELS: *State of Grace*, 1973; *The Changeling*, 1978; *Breaking and Entering*, 1988; *The Quick and the Dead*, 2000.

NONFICTION: *Florida Keys: A History and Guide*, 1986; *Ill Nature: Rants and Reflections on Humanity and Other Animals*, 2001.

**Bibliography**

Cooper, Rand Richards. "The Dark at the End of the Tunnel." *The New York Times*, January 21, 1990. In this detailed review of *Escapes*, Cooper focuses on the quirky, ominous world they create; discusses several stories, arguing that "The Blue Men" and the title story are the strongest.

Heller, Zoe. "Amazing Moments from the Production Line." *The Independent*, July 21, 1990, p. 28. In this review of *Escapes*, Heller complains that Williams's style has become a mannerism, but singles out "In the Route" as a story that is more interesting than the other formulaic pieces in the collection.

Hills, Rust. Review of *State of Grace. Esquire* 80 (July, 1973): 26, 28. Hills recognizes that Williams has a problem with structure but praises her language: "open the novel to virtually any page and you'll instantly see it—a kind of strange phosphorescent style describing disquieting, dark and funny goings-on. Sentences are brilliant, gorgeous, surprising."

*Kirkus Reviews.* Review of *Escapes.* 57 (November 15, 1989): 1633. This anonymous reviewer recognizes that "Williams' weird, seemingly anesthetized, protagonists are usually in flight: from inexorable fate, from the oppressive past, from reality itself."

Kornblatt, Joyce. "Madness, Murder, and the Surrender of Hope." Review of *Taking Care. The Washington Post Book World*, March 21, 1982, 4. Noting her similarity to Flannery O'Connor and Joyce Carol Oates, the reviewer here sees the redemptive qualities of Williams's work, for in the "fragile gestures" of these stories, "we glimpse, merely glimpse, an order of being that eschews randomness, that ascribes value, that insists on love in the face of destructiveness."

Malinowski, Sharon. "Joy Williams." In *Contemporary Authors*, edited by Deborah A. Straub. Vol. 22. Detroit: Gale Research, 1988. Good summary of Williams's career, including long passages from reviews of her novels and her short-story collections through 1982. "In Williams's fiction, the ordinary events of daily life are susceptible to bizarre turns of horror and individuals are lost in their private selves, unable to comprehend the forces which shape their lives. Although Williams occasionally alleviates her bleak vision with humor, a sense of hopelessness and despair remains central to her work."

May, Charles E., ed. *Masterplots II: Short Story Series, Revised Edition.* 8 vols. Pasadena, Calif.: Salem Press, 2004. Designed for student use, this reference set contains articles providing detailed plot summaries and analyses of four short stories by Williams: "The Farm" and "Health" (vol. 3), and "Taking Care" and "Train" (vol. 7).

Williams, Joy. "Joy Williams." Interview by Molly McQuade. *Publishers Weekly* 237 (January 26, 1990): 400-401. This brief but wide-ranging interview allows Williams to talk about her career and her sense of her own writing; words, for example, are intended "to affect the reader in unexpected, mysterious, subterranean ways. The literal surface has to be *very* literal—smooth and exact—yet what makes it strange is what's teeming underneath. Stories should be something other than they appear to be. . . . They should make you uncomfortable."

# Tennessee Williams

**Born:** Columbus, Mississippi; March 26, 1911
**Died:** New York, New York; February 25, 1983

**Principal short fiction** • *One Arm, and Other Stories*, 1948; *Hard Candy: A Book of Stories*, 1954; *The Knightly Quest: A Novella and Four Short Stories*, 1967; *Eight Mortal Ladies Possessed: A Book of Stories*, 1974; *Collected Stories*, 1985.

**Other literary forms** • In addition to his three dozen collected and uncollected stories, Tennessee Williams wrote two novels, a book of memoirs, a collection of essays, two volumes of poetry, numerous short plays, a screenplay, and more than twenty full-length dramas. Among the most important of his plays are *The Glass Menagerie* (1944), *A Streetcar Named Desire* (1947), *Cat on a Hot Tin Roof* (1955), and *The Night of the Iguana* (1961).

**Achievements** • Tennessee Williams's most obvious achievements in literature lie in the field of drama, where he is considered by many to be America's greatest playwright, a standing supported by two Pulitzer Prizes, a Commonwealth Award, a Medal of Freedom (presented by President Jimmy Carter), and an election in 1952 to a lifetime membership in the National Institute of Arts and Letters. Williams himself, however, believed that his short fiction contained some of his best writing. Indeed, besides stories appearing in his own collections, Williams published stories in many of America's most prestigious magazines, including *The New Yorker* and *Esquire*, and many have been selected for various anthologies, including three in Martha Foley's *Best American Short Stories* annual anthologies. Williams's short stories and plays alike dramatize the plight of the "fugitive," the sensitive soul punished by a harsh, uncaring world; in the stories, however, readers find specific and frequent voice given to a theme and subject only hinted at in Williams's drama, at least until his later, less memorable, plays: the plight of the homosexual in a bigoted society.

**Biography** • Descended on his mother's side from a southern minister and on his father's from Tennessee politicians, Thomas Lanier (Tennessee) Williams moved with his family from Mississippi to St. Louis shortly after World War I. He attended the University of Missouri and Washington University, finally graduating from the University of Iowa. After odd jobs in the warehouse of a shoe factory, ushering at a movie house, and even a stint screenwriting in Hollywood, he turned full-time writer in the early 1940's, encouraged by grants from the Group Theatre and Rockefeller Foundation. Despite purchasing a home in Key West, Florida, in 1950, Williams spent most of the remainder of his life living for short periods in a variety of locales in Europe, the United States, and Mexico. His two Pulitzer Prizes early in his career, plus four Drama Critics Circle Awards, solidified Williams's reputation as a playwright; the quality of his writing declined, however, after the early 1960's, in great part as a result of drug dependency. He died, alone, in a New York City hotel room in 1983.

**Analysis** • Although during his lifetime Tennessee Williams was commonly held to be without peer among America's—many would say the world's—playwrights, he began his career writing short fiction, with a story entitled "The Vengeance of Nitocris" in *Weird Tales* in 1928. As late as 1944, when his first theatrical success was in rehearsal, George Jean Nathan reportedly observed that Williams "didn't know how to write drama, that he was really just a short-story writer who didn't understand the theatre." In proportion to the worldwide audience familiar with Williams's dramas, only a handful know more than a story or two, usually from among the ones later transformed into stage plays. Seven of Williams's full-length dramas, in fact, had their genesis in the fiction: *The Glass Menagerie* in "Portrait of a Girl in Glass"; *Summer and Smoke* (1947) in "The Yellow Bird"; *Cat on a Hot Tin Roof* in "Three Players of a Summer Game"; *The Night of the Iguana* and *Kingdom of Earth* (1968) in stories of the same names; *The Milk Train Doesn't Stop Here Anymore* (1963) in "Man Bring This Up Road"; and *Vieux Carré* (1977) in "The Angel in the Alcove" and "Grand."

**"The Night of the Iguana"** • The play *The Night of the Iguana* is sufficiently different from its progenitor to indicate how Williams rethought his material in adapting it to another medium. Both works portray a spinsterish artist, Miss Jelkes; but while Hannah in the play has fought for and achieved inner peace, Edith's harsher name in the story belies her edginess, neurosis, and lack of "interior poise." Having channeled her own "morbid energy" into painting, she discerns in the contrasting "splash of scarlet on snow . . . a flag of her own unsettled components" warring within her. When a servant at the Costa Verde hotel tethers an iguana to the veranda, Edith recoils hysterically from such brutality against "one of God's creatures," taking its suffering as proof of a grotesque "universe . . . designed by the Marquis de Sade."

This picture of cosmic indifference, even malevolence, occurs in a handful of Williams's stories, most notably in "The Malediction," in which the lonely Lucio exists in a meaningless universe verging on the absurd, ruled by a God "Who felt that something was wrong but could not correct it, a man Who sensed the blundering sleepwalk of time and hostilities of chance" and "had been driven to drink." Edith finds God personified in a violent storm "like a giant bird lunging up and down on its terrestrial quarry, a bird with immense white wings and beak of godlike fury."

Edith's fellow guests at the hotel are two homosexual writers. Squeamish and yet attracted by the forbidden nature of their relationship, Edith insinuates herself into their company only to become the object of a desperate attack on her "demon of virginity" by the older of the two. Although she has earlier hinted that she always answers, with understanding, cries for help from a fellow sufferer, she ferociously fends off his pathetic advances, metaphorically associated with the predatory "bird of blind white fury." Afterward, however, once the younger man has mercifully cut loose the iguana, Edith feels her own "rope of loneliness had also been severed," and—instead of drawing back in "revulsion" from "the spot of dampness" left on her belly by the older writer's semen—exclaims "Ah, life," evidently having reached through this epiphanic moment a new acceptance and integration of her sexuality. Yet, unlike Hannah, whose compassionate response to Shannon in the play is for him a saving grace and who can affirm, along with Williams, that "Nothing human disgusts me unless it's unkind, violent," Edith's inability to answer unselfishly the older man's need—the cardinal sin in Williams—may have permanently maimed him by destroying his self-respect.

Williams does not always capitalize fully on his gift for writing dialogue in his stories. For all its interest in light of the later play, the pace of "The Night of the Iguana" is curiously desultory and enervated, which might not have been true if the story had been written from Edith's point of view. Williams does indeed prove adept at handling first-person narration in several autobiographical tales, whose content seems hardly distinguishable at times from the sections of the *Memoirs* (1975).

**"The Resemblance Between a Violin Case and a Coffin"** • Williams can become annoyingly self-conscious when, in authorial intrusions analogous to the nonrepresentational techniques that deliberately destroy the illusion of reality in his dramas, he breaks the narrative line in a dozen or so stories to interject comments about himself as writer manipulating his materials, sometimes apologizing for his awkwardness in handling the short-story form, or for play-

Sam Shaw/Courtesy, New Directions Publishing

ing too freely with chronology or radically shifting tone. At times these stories provide some notion of Williams's aesthetic theories and practice, as when, in "Three Players of a Summer Game," for example, he discusses the method by which the artist orders experience by a process that distorts and "yet . . . may be closer than a literal history could be to the hidden truth of it." These "metafictional" asides might indicate his conception of character portrayal. On that point—while without qualms at employing clinical details when necessary—Williams insists, in "Hard Candy," on the need for "indirection" and restraint rather than "a head-on violence that would disgust and destroy" if he is to remain nonjudgmental and respect the "mystery" at the heart of character.

An almost identical comment occurs in "The Resemblance Between a Violin Case and a Coffin," part of a small group of *rites de passage* stories in the Williams canon. The story centers on a love triangle of sorts as the young narrator faces the destruction of the "magical intimacy" with his pianist sister as she enters adolescence—that "dangerous passage" between the "wild country of childhood" and the "uniform world of adults"—and turns her attentions toward a fellow musician, Richard Miles. It is as if she has deserted the narrator and "carried a lamp into another room [he] could not enter." He resents the "radiant" Richard, but also feels a frightening prepubescent physical attraction for the older boy. Like many of Williams's adult neurotics whose libidinous desires rebel against their Puritan repressions, the narrator longs to touch Richard's skin, yet recoils in shame and guilt from the boy's offer of his hand as if it were somehow "impure." Seeing Richard play the violin, however, provides an epiphany as the narrator "learns the will of life to transcend the single body" and perceives the connection between Eros and Thanatos. For the narrator equates the act of playing the phallic violin with "making love," and the violin case to "a little black coffin made for a child or doll." He mourns the loss of youth and innocence and the birth of the knowledge of sin and death.

Tom, the authorial voice in *The Glass Menagerie*, confesses to "a poet's weakness for symbols," and one of Williams's own hallmarks has always been an extensive use of visual stage symbolism—"the natural speech of drama." As he remarks in one of his essays, it can "say a thing more directly and simply and beautifully than it could be said in words"; he employs symbols extensively, however, in only a handful of stories, although he does rely heavily on figurative language. In the earlier stories the imagery is ordinarily controlled and striking, as, for example, in this line (reminiscent of Karl Shapiro's "cancer, simple as a flower, blooms") describing the doctor's tumor from "Three Players of a Summer Game": "An awful flower grew in his brain like a fierce geranium that shattered its pot." In the more recent tales, however, Williams's diction frequently becomes overwrought and demonstrates some lack of control, falling into what he criticizes elsewhere in the same essay as "a parade of images for the sake of images."

If the mood of "The Resemblance Between a Violin Case and a Coffin" is tender and elegiac, the tone of a much later *rite de passage* story, "Completed," is chilling, but no less haunting and memorable. Miss Rosemary McCord, a student at Mary, Help a Christian School, is a withdrawn debutante subjected by her unsympathetic mother to a pathetic and bizarre coming-out dance. The onset of menstruation has been late in coming for Rosemary, and when it finally does arrive, she is pitifully unprepared for it. Ironically, the fullness of physical development in Rosemary coincides with a death wish; her only "purpose in life is to complete it quick." Her one understanding relative, the reclusive Aunt Ella, deliberately retreats from the external world through morphine; the drug brings her comforting apparitions of the Virgin Mary and tears of peace. Rosemary goes to live with her, aware that she has been taken captive and yet willingly submissive, ready to be calmed through drugs and her own reassuring visions of the Virgin. Her life—apparently the latest of several variations on that of Williams's own sister—is over before it began. Perhaps it is, however, only in such a sheltered, illusory life that this fragile, sensitive girl can exist.

**"Sabbatha and Solitude"** • The other "passage" that threads through Williams's stories is that from life to death, obsessed as he is with what he terms "a truly awful sense of impermanence," with the debilitating effects of time on both physical beauty and one's creative powers, and the sheer tenacity necessary if one is to endure at least spiritually undefeated. In "Sabbatha and Solitude," the aging poetess (undoubtedly semi-autobiographical) finds that the process of composition is a trial not unlike the Crucifixion that results only in "a bunch of old repeats," while in the picaresque "Two on a Party," the blond and balding queen and hack screenwriter exist at the mercy of that "worst of all enemies . . . the fork-tailed, cloven-hoofed, pitchfork-bearing devil of Time."

**"Completed"** • "Completed" is one of Williams's few later stories—"Happy August the Tenth" is another—that can stand alongside some of his earliest as a fully successful work. Just as there was a noticeable diminution in the power of his later dramas compared with the ones from *The Glass Menagerie* through *The Night of the Iguana*, so, too, each successive volume of short fiction was less impressive than its predecessor. As Williams's vision of the universe darkened and became more private, the once elegiac tone acquired a certain stridency and sharp edge; and as Williams developed a tough, self-protective shell of laughter as a defense against his detractors, some of the dark humor—what he once called the "jokes of the condemned"—became directed toward the pathetic grotesques who increasingly peopled his works, whereas once there was only compassion.

**"Desire and the Black Masseur"** • Thus, two of the most representative stories, "One Arm" and "Desire and the Black Masseur," neither of which, significantly, has ever been dramatized, appeared in his first collection. Unquestionably the most macabre of all his tales is "Desire and the Black Masseur," which details the fantastic, almost surreal sadomasochistic relationship between the insecure, sexually repressed Anthony Burns and an unnamed black masseur at a men's bath. Burns, whose name blends that of a Christian saint with the suggestion of consummation by fire—here metaphoric—suffers from an overly acute awareness of his own insignificance, as well as of his separateness and lack of completeness as a human being. Williams views the latter as an inescapable fact of the human condition and proposes three means available to compensate for it: art, violent action, or surrendering oneself to brutal treatment at the hands of others. Burns chooses the third path, submitting himself as if in a dream, finding at the punishing hands of the masseur first pain, then orgasmic pleasure, and ultimately death. Although the masseur thus secures a release from his pent-up hatred of his white oppressors, this tale should not be construed as a social comment reflecting Williams's attitude toward black/white relations, hardly even peripherally a concern in his work, despite his being a southern writer.

Blacks figure importantly in only two other stories. In the ribald "Miss Coynte of Greene," the title character's long-frustrated female eroticism erupts into nymphomania, her pleasure intensified by the dark skin of her sexual partners. In "Mama's Old Stucco House," Williams's gentlest foray into the black/white terrain, the failed artist Jimmy Krenning is cared for physically and emotionally after his own mother's death by the black girl Brinda and her Mama, the latter having always functioned as his surrogate mother.

That "Desire and the Black Masseur" is to be read on levels other than the literal appears clear when Williams places its climax at the end of the Lenten Season. The death and devouring of Burns becomes a ritual of expiation, a kind of black mass and perversion of the sacrifice on Calvary, even accomplished in biblical phraseology. Indeed, counterpointed with it is a church service during which a self-proclaimed Fundamentalist preacher exhorts his congregation to a frenzy of repentance. What Williams has written, then, is not only a psychological study of man's subconscious desires and an allegory of the division between innocence and evil within all men but also a parable exposing how excessive emphasis on guilt and the need for punishment at the hands of a vengeful God have destroyed the essential New Testament message of love and forgiveness. So Burns's strange rite of atonement stands as a forceful indictment of a Puritanism that creates a dark god of hate as a reflection of one's own obsession with evil, which is one of the recurrent emphases in almost all of Williams's important dramas, especially *Suddenly Last Summer* (1958) and *The Night of the Iguana*.

**"One Arm"** • Something of the obverse, the possibility for transcending one's knowledge of evil and isolation, occurs in "One Arm," the quintessential—and perhaps the finest—Williams story, in which can be discerned nearly all the central motifs that adumbrate not only his fiction but also his plays. Oliver Winemiller, a former light heavyweight champion who in an accident two years earlier lost an arm, is one of Williams's "fugitive kind," a lonely misfit, cool, impassive, now tasting, like Brick in *Cat on a Hot Tin Roof*, "the charm of the defeated." Since all he possessed was his "Apollo-like beauty," after his physical mutilation he undergoes a psychological and emotional change; feeling that he has lost "the center of his being," he is filled with self-loathing and disgust. He enters on a series of self-destructive sexual encounters, finally committing a murder for which he is sentenced to die.

While in confinement awaiting execution, he receives letters from all over the country from his male lovers, confessing that he had aroused deep feelings in them, that he had effected a "communion" with them that would have been, if he had only recognized it, a means of "personal integration" and "salvation." If it was not until very late in his dramas that Williams openly treated homosexuality with sympathy, in his stories his unapologetic and compassionate attitude existed from the very first. Oliver's epiphany, that he had been loved, liberates him from his self-imposed insularity; ironically, however, this rebirth makes his approaching death harder to accept. On the eve of his execution, he recognizes that the Lutheran minister who visits him has used religion as an escape from facing his own sexuality, and he desperately hopes that by forcing the minister to come to terms with himself and his "feelings" he can thereby somehow repay his debt to all those who had earlier responded to him with kindness. The minister, however, recognizing a forbidden side of himself and still suffering guilt over his adolescent sexual awakening during a dream of a golden panther, which Oliver reminds him of, refuses to give Oliver a massage and rushes from his cell. Oliver goes to his execution with dignity, gripping the love letters tightly between his things as a protection from aloneness.

The doctors performing the autopsy see in Oliver's body the "nobility" and purity of an "antique sculpture." Yet Williams reminds his readers in the closing line that "death has never been much in the way of completion." Although the work of art is immutable, it is not alive as only the emotionally responsive person can be, for the true artist in Williams is the person who goes out unselfishly to answer the cry for help of others, and the real work of art is the bond of communion that is formed by that response. Thus "One Arm" incorporates virtually all of Williams's major attitudes, including his somewhat sentimental valuation of the lost and lonely; his romantic glorification of physical beauty and worship of sexuality as a means of transcending aloneness; his castigation of Puritan repression and guilt that render one selfish and judgmental; and his Hawthornian abhorrence of the underdeveloped heart that prevents one from breaking out of the shell of the ego to respond with infinite compassion to all God's misbegotten creatures.

Although Williams's stories, with their frequent rhetorical excesses, their sometimes awkward narrative strategies, and their abrupt shifts in tone, technically do not often approach the purity of form of Oliver's statue, they do, nevertheless—as all good fiction must—surprise the reader with their revelations of the human heart and demand that the reader abandon a simplistic perspective and see the varieties of human experience. What in the hands of other writers might seem a too specialized vision, frequently becomes in Williams's work affectingly human and humane.

*Thomas P. Adler*
*With updates by Dennis Vannatta*

## Other major works

PLAYS: *Fugitive Kind*, pr. 1937, pb. 2001; *Spring Storm*, wr. 1937, pr., pb. 1999; *Not About Nightingales*, wr. 1939, pr., pb. 1998; *Battle of Angels*, pr. 1940, pb. 1945; *I Rise in Flame, Cried the Phoenix*, wr. 1941, pb. 1951, pr. 1959 (one act); *This Property Is Condemned*, pb. 1941, pr. 1946 (one act); *The Lady of Larkspur Lotion*, pb. 1942 (one act); *The Glass Menagerie*, pr. 1944, pb. 1945; *Twenty-seven Wagons Full of Cotton*, pb. 1945, pr. 1955 (one act); *You Touched Me*, pr. 1945, pb. 1947 (with Donald Windham); *A Streetcar Named Desire*, pr., pb. 1947; *Summer and Smoke*, pr. 1947, pb. 1948; *American Blues*, pb. 1948 (collection); *Five Short Plays*, pb. 1948; *The Long Stay Cut Short: Or, The Unsatisfactory Supper*, pb. 1948 (one act); *The Rose Tattoo*, pr. 1950, pb. 1951; *Camino Real*, pr., pb. 1953; *Cat on a Hot Tin Roof*, pr., pb. 1955; *Sweet Bird of Youth*, pr. 1956, pb. 1959 (based on *The Enemy: Time*); *Orpheus Descending*, pr. 1957, pb. 1958 (revision of *Battle of Angels*); *Suddenly Last Summer*, pr., pb. 1958; *Period of Adjustment*, pr. 1959, pb. 1960; *The Enemy: Time*, pb. 1959; *The Night of the Iguana*, pr., pb. 1961; *The Milk Train Doesn't Stop Here Anymore*, pr. 1963, revised pb. 1976; *The Eccentricities of a Nightingale*, pr., pb. 1964 (revised of *Summer and Smoke*); *Slapstick Tragedy: "The Mutilated" and "The Gnädiges Fräulein,"* pr. 1966, pb. 1970 (one acts); *The Two-Character Play*, pr. 1967, pb. 1969; *The Seven Descents of Myrtle*, pr., pb. 1968 (as *Kingdom of Earth*); *In the Bar of a Tokyo Hotel*, pr. 1969, pb. 1970; *Confessional*, pb. 1970; *Dragon Country*, pb. 1970 (collection); *Out Cry*, pr. 1971, pb. 1973 (revised of *The Two-Character Play*); *The Theatre of Tennessee Williams*, pb. 1971-1981 (7 volumes); *Small Craft Warnings*, pr., pb. 1972 (revised of *Confessional*); *Vieux Carré*, pr. 1977, pb. 1979; *A Lovely Sunday for Creve Coeur*, pr. 1979, pb. 1980; *Clothes for a Summer Hotel*, pr. 1980; *A House Not Meant to Stand*, pr. 1981; *Something Cloudy, Something Clear*, pr. 1981, pb. 1995.

NOVELS: *The Roman Spring of Mrs. Stone*, 1950; *Moise and the World of Reason*, 1975.

NONFICTION: *Memoirs*, 1975; *Where I Live: Selected Essays*, 1978; *Five O'Clock Angel: Letters of Tennessee Williams to Maria St. Just, 1948-1982*, 1990; *The Selected Letters of Tennessee Williams*, 2000-2004 (2 volumes; Albert J. Devlin and Nancy M. Tischler, editors); *Notebooks*, 2006 (Margaret Bradham Thornton, editor).

POETRY: *In the Winter of Cities*, 1956; *Androgyne, Mon Amour*, 1977; *The Collected Poems of Tennessee Williams*, 2002.

SCREENPLAYS: *The Glass Menagerie*, 1950 (with Peter Berneis); *A Streetcar Named Desire*, 1951 (with Oscar Saul); *The Rose Tattoo*, 1955 (with Hal Kanter); *Baby Doll*, 1956; *Suddenly Last Summer*, 1960 (with Gore Vidal); *The Fugitive Kind*, 1960 (with Meade Roberts; based on *Orpheus Descending*); *Stopped Rocking, and Other Screenplays*, 1984.

## Bibliography

Bloom, Harold, ed. *Tennessee Williams*. New York: Chelsea House, 1987. This collection of critical essays carries an introduction by Bloom that places Williams in the dramatic canon of American drama and within the psychological company of Hart Crane and Arthur Rimbaud. Authors in this collection take traditional thematic and historical approaches, noting Williams's "grotesques," his morality, his irony, his work in the "middle years," and the mythical qualities in his situations and characters.

Kolin, Philip C. *The Tennesse Williams Encyclopedia*. Westport, Conn.: Greenwood Press, 2004. Useful guide to Williams and his work. In 160 informative entries, Williams scholars offer the reader a wealth of information.

Leverich, Lyle. *Tom: The Unknown Tennessee Williams*. New York: Crown Publishers, 1995. This first volume of a two-volume biography traces Williams's life for the first thirty-three years. Draws on previously unpublished letters, journals, and note-books. Discusses Williams's focus on how society has a destructive influence on sensitive people and his efforts to change drama into an unrealistic form.

Martin, Robert A., ed. *Critical Essays on Tennessee Williams.* New York: G. K. Hall, 1997. Excellent, accessible collection of criticism of Williams's works.

May, Charles E., ed. *Masterplots II: Short Story Series, Revised Edition.* 8 vols. Pasadena, Calif.: Salem Press, 2004. Designed for student use, this reference set contains articles providing detailed plot summaries and analyses of four short stories by Williams: "Happy August the Tenth" and "The Field of Blue Children" (vol. 3), "The Resemblance Between a Violin Case and a Coffin" (vol. 6), and "Three Players of a Summer Game" (vol. 7).

Pagan, Nicholas. *Rethinking Literary Biography: A Postmodern Approach to Tennessee Williams.* Madison, N.J.: Fairleigh Dickinson University Press, 1993. Discusses the symbolism of Williams's characters in relation to his life.

Spoto, Donald. *The Kindness of Strangers: The Life of Tennessee Williams.* Reprint. New York: Da Capo Press, 1998. Spoto's lively chronicle details Williams's encounters with such diverse influences as the Group Theatre, Frieda and D. H. Lawrence, Senator Joseph R. McCarthy, Fidel Castro, Hollywood stars, and the homosexual and drug subcultures of Key West. Forty-two pages of notes, bibliography, and index make this study a valuable resource for further scholarship.

Tischler, Nancy Marie Patterson. *Student Companion to Tennessee Williams.* Westport, Conn.: Greenwood Press, 2000. A well-known Williams scholar brings together the playwright's biography and critical assessments of his works to provide students with a thorough introduction and appreciation of Williams's achievements.

Vannatta, Dennis. *Tennessee Williams: A Study of the Short Fiction.* Boston: Twayne, 1988. The only book-length study of Williams's short fiction. Contains a selection of essays concerning Williams's short fiction by various scholars and a selection of Williams's own letters, essays, and reviews.

Williams, Dakin, and Shepherd Mead. *Tennessee Williams: An Intimate Biography.* New York: Arbor House, 1983. One of the more bizarre duos in biographical writing, Williams (Tennessee's brother) and Mead (Tennessee's childhood friend) produce a credible biography in a highly readable, well-indexed work. Their account of the playwright also helps to capture his almost schizophrenic nature. A solid index and extensive research assist the serious scholar and general reader.

# William Carlos Williams

**Born:** Rutherford, New Jersey; September 17, 1883
**Died:** Rutherford, New Jersey; March 4, 1963

**Principal short fiction** • *The Knife of the Times, and Other Stories*, 1932; *Life Along the Passaic River*, 1938; *Make Light of It: Collected Stories*, 1950; *The Farmers' Daughters: The Collected Stories of William Carlos Williams*, 1961; *The Doctor Stories*, 1984; *The Collected Stories of William Carlos Williams*, 1996.

**Other literary forms** • Best known as a poet, William Carlos Williams nevertheless wrote in a variety of literary forms (some of them defying categorization) including poetry, novels, short stories, prose poetry, essays, autobiography, and plays. *Paterson*, his extended poem published in four separate volumes (1946-1951), with a fifth volume serving as a commentary (1958), is his most famous and enduring work.

**Achievements** • William Carlos Williams received numerous awards, including the Dial Award in 1926, the National Book Award in 1950, the Bollingen Award in 1953, and, posthumously, the Pulitzer Prize in poetry in 1963.

**Biography** • After attending public schools in New Jersey, spending time in Europe, and then finishing high school in New York, William Carlos Williams enrolled in the University of Pennsylvania's Medical School in 1902. While completing his medical degree there, he met Ezra Pound, Hilda Doolittle, and the painter Charles Demuth. In 1910, he began work as a general practitioner in Rutherford, New Jersey; in addition to this practice, from 1925 on he became a pediatrician at Passaic General Hospital. Williams held these positions until several strokes forced him to retire in 1951. His medical and literary careers always coexisted. In 1909, he had his first volume, *Poems*, privately published. As his reputation grew, he traveled to Europe several times and encountered such writers as James Joyce, Gertrude Stein, and Ford Madox Ford. He married Florence Herman in 1912, and they had two sons. Williams died on March 4, 1963, in his beloved Rutherford.

**Analysis** • William Carlos Williams is one of the major figures of literary modernism whose peers included Ezra Pound and Wallace Stevens. Highly influenced by the visual arts and the imagist movement, Williams's work was marked by a rejection of metaphysics, characterized by his famous dictum: "No ideas/ But in things." Williams's objective approach to literature is reflected in the coarse realism of his short stories. His prose shares the basic principles of his poetic theory: use of an American idiom, adherence to a locale, communication through specifics, and belief in organic form. The pastiche effects of Williams's poetry and prose had a profound influence on the next generation of American literary modernists, particularly the so-called Objectivist School, which included Louis Zukofsky, George Oppen, Carl Rakosi, and Charles Reznikoff.

M. L. Rosenthal claims that William Carlos Williams's short stories "are often vital evocations of ordinary American reality—its toughness, squalor, pathos, intensities."

As such, this short fiction tends to exhibit distinctive characteristics. First, its style is the American idiom, with heavy reliance on dialogue and speech rhythm. Second, Williams almost inevitably writes of his own locale and stresses the Depression's dramatic effect on ordinary working people. Third, as he shows in his poem "A Sort of a Song," there should be "No ideas/ But in things"; in other words, details should suggest underlying ideas, not vice versa. Fourth, Williams himself is often present, but as a doctor, never as a poet; thus biography and autobiography constitute important plot elements. Last, the author allows plot to develop organically, which affects length (the tales range from one to thirty pages) and structure (the stories may appear diffuse or highly compressed).

Williams published two main short-story anthologies: *The Knife of the Times, and Other Stories* and *Life Along the Passaic River.* In 1950, he collected these and other stories into a single volume called *Make Light of It*; then, in 1961, this was superseded by his complete collected stories entitled *The Farmers' Daughters.* Although these stories may indicate progressive technical sophistication or experimentation, they all treat "the plight of the poor" (as Williams says on several occasions) or the physician's frequently ambiguous role of healing the sick within an infected society.

**"Old Doc Rivers"** • On the choice of title for his first short-story anthology, Williams observes, "The times—that was the knife that was killing them" (the poor). A typical story is "Old Doc Rivers," which provides a full background on one rural general practitioner. It also contains a strong autobiographical element because the narrator is a younger doctor (apparently Williams). An enormously complex picture emerges of Doc Rivers: efficient, conscientious, humane, yet simultaneously crude, cruel, and addicted to drugs and alcohol. The story builds this portrait by piling up specifics about the physician's personal and professional lives and interweaving case studies among the young doctor-narrator's comments. The narrator is astonished by Rivers's psychological sharpness, intuition for the correct diagnosis, and ability to inspire blind faith in his patients. As with many Williams tales, the reader's moral response is ambiguous, for when sober, Rivers is not a good doctor, yet when drunk or doped, he is at least as good as anyone else. The plot follows a roughly chronological structure which charts Rivers's gradual mental and physical decline. This story's particular strengths are its narrator voice, concrete details, re-creation of dialogue, and exploration of the doctor-patient relationship.

**"Jean Beicke"** • Williams further considers the physician-patient relationship in "Jean Beicke" and "A Face of Stone," representative of his second short-fiction collection. Told by a pediatrician-narrator (but this time an established, not a beginning, doctor), "Jean Beicke" is set in a children's ward during the Depression and recounts the story of a "scrawny, misshapen, worthless piece of humanity." Although Jean is desperately ill, she wins the hearts of the physicians and nurses by her sheer resilience: "As sick as she was," the narrator marvels, "she took her grub right on time every three hours, a big eight ounce bottle of milk and digested it perfectly." Yet little Jean's symptoms puzzle the medics, and despite initial improvement, she finally dies. Up to this point, doctors and readers alike have been ignorant of her previous history, but when her mother and aunt visit the dying infant, it is learned that she is the third child of a woman whose husband deserted her. As her aunt says, "It's better off dead—never was any good anyway." After the autopsy, the doctors discover they have completely misdiagnosed Jean. The storyteller ends the tale like this:

> I called the ear man and he came down at once. A clear miss, he said. I think if we'd gone in there earlier, we'd have saved her.
> For what? said I. Vote the straight Communist ticket. Would it make us any dumber? said the ear man.

Williams thought "Jean Beicke" was "the best short story I ever wrote." One reason is its involved narrator, whose sophisticated social conscience (why cure these Depression babies only to return them to a sick society?) contrasts with the nurses' instinctive (but perhaps naïve) humanitarianism. The story's careful structure takes us from external details—Jean's misshapen body, tiny face, and pale blue eyes—to internal ones—in the postmortem—and so suggests that beneath society's superficial ills lie fundamental, perhaps incurable, troubles. Once again, Williams shows his skill for catching the speech patterns of ordinary Americans, especially in the monologue of Jean's aunt. Finally, the author's main achievement is to individualize yet not sentimentalize Jean and to dramatize her life-and-death struggle so that it matters to him—and to the reader.

**"A Face of Stone"** • In "A Face of Stone," the doctor-narrator becomes the main character. A harried family doctor, he finds himself at the end of a busy morning confronted by a young Jewish couple. The husband, one of "the presuming poor," insists that he examine their baby, while the wife maintains an expressionless, stony face. As the doctor approaches the baby boy, his mother clutches him closer and is extremely reluctant to relinquish him. Frustrated and tired, the doctor is brusque and patronizing. When he eventually looks at the child, he discovers that it is quite healthy. During the winter, the people request a house call, but he refuses to go; then, in the spring, they return and still protest that the child is unwell. Conquering his annoyance at their persistence, the family doctor checks the boy and says that he simply needs to be fed regularly and weaned.

Now the physician expects the consultation to finish, but the young Jew asks him to examine his wife. The doctor is by this time exhausted and furious; however, he starts to check this passive, poverty-stricken, physically unattractive woman. Then, almost accidentally, he discovers she is a Polish Jew who has lost her whole family. Immediately, he forgets her ugliness, grasps her intense anxiety for her baby, and realizes the strong bond between wife and husband: "Suddenly I understood his half shameful love for the woman and at the same time the extent of her reliance on him. I was touched." The woman smiles for the first time when the doctor prescribes pain-killers for her varicose veins and she senses that she can trust him.

This story effectively dramatizes the shifting reactions among patients and doctors as they try to establish a successful relationship. Often, a physician may exploit his position of power (as this one does at the beginning) and forget that his clients are human. If he does, he turns into Doc Rivers at his worst. The best relationship occurs when both parties move beyond stereotypes to view each other as individuals. Because the doctor narrates the tale, the reader follows his process of discovery, so when he stops stereotyping the couple, the reader does too. Williams once again successfully uses dialogue to convey character interaction. Also, as in "Jean Beicke," he reveals people through detail (such as the woman's ripped dress, bowlegs, and high-heeled, worn-out shoes).

**"The Farmers' Daughters"** • Williams composed few notable short stories after *Life Along the Passaic River,* mainly because he diverted his energies into longer projects (novels, plays, and *Paterson*). From the early 1940's to the mid-1950's, however, he worked on a long short story which he eventually called "The Farmers' Daughters" (and whose title he used for his collected short fiction). The title characters are Helen and Margaret, two southern women who have been (and continue to be) betrayed by their men. Their similar background and experience form the basis of an enduring, unshakable friendship that terminates only with Margaret's death. Technically, this is one of Williams's best stories: It unfolds quickly in a "paragraph technique" as the narrator—once more a doctor—re-creates the women's conversations and letters, then links them chronologically with his own comments. The teller refers to himself in the third person, so that most of the time the story progresses through dialogue. This extract, in which Margaret and the doctor chat, illustrates the strength of using direct, idiomatic speech:

> What's your favorite flower, Margaret?
> Why?
> I just want to know.
> What's yours?
> No. Come on—don't be so quick on the trigger so early in the evening. I think I can guess. Petunias! (emphasizing the second syllable.) God knows I've seen enough of them. No. Red roses. Those are really what I love.

Unlike Williams's previous stories, "The Farmers' Daughters" relies on complex character depiction and development rather than on plot or theme.

Most short-story writers merely write, but Williams left behind theoretical as well as practical evidence of his interest in the genre. *A Beginning on the Short Story (Notes)* (1950) outlines his basic tenets: truthfulness, unsentimentality, and simplicity. "The finest short stories," he states, "are those that raise . . . one particular man or woman, from that Gehenna, the newspapers, where at last all men are equal, to the distinction of being an individual." From the herd of humanity, Williams succeeds in individualizing Doc Rivers, little Jean Beicke, the Jewish couple, Margaret, Helen, and all his various doctor-narrators.

*Kathryn Zabelle Derounian*
*With updates by William E. Grim*

## Other major works

PLAYS: *A Dream of Love*, pb. 1948; *Many Loves, and Other Plays*, pb. 1961.

NOVELS: *The Great American Novel*, 1923; *A Voyage to Pagany*, 1928; *White Mule*, 1937; *In the Money*, 1940; *The Build-up*, 1952.

MISCELLANEOUS: *The Descent of Winter*, 1928 (includes poetry, prose, and anecdotes); *Imaginations*, 1970 (includes poetry, fiction, and nonfiction).

NONFICTION: *In the American Grain*, 1925; *A Novelette, and Other Prose*, 1932; *The Autobiography of William Carlos Williams*, 1951; *Selected Essays of William Carlos Williams*, 1954; *The Selected Letters of William Carlos Williams*, 1957; *I Wanted to Write a Poem: The Autobiography of the Works of a Poet*, 1958; *The Embodiment of Knowledge*, 1974; *A Recognizable Image*, 1978; *William Carlos Williams, John Sanford: A Correspondence*, 1984; *William Carlos Williams and James Laughlin: Selected Letters*, 1989; *Pound/Williams: Selected Letters of Ezra Pound and William Carlos Williams*, 1996 (Hugh Witemeyer, editor); *The Correspondence of William Carlos Williams and Louis Zukofsky*, 2003 (Barry Ahearn, editor); *The Humane Particulars: The Collected Letters of William Carlos Williams and Kenneth Burke*, 2003 (James H. East, editor).

POETRY: *Poems*, 1909; *The Tempers*, 1913; *Al Que Quiere!*, 1917; *Kora in Hell: Improvisations*, 1920; *Sour Grapes*, 1921; *Spring and All*, 1923; *Collected Poems, 1921-1931*, 1934; *An Early Martyr, and Other Poems*, 1935; *Adam & Eve & The City*, 1936; *The Complete Collected Poems of William Carlos Williams, 1906-1938*, 1938; *The Broken Span*, 1941; *The Wedge*, 1944; *Paterson*, 1946-1958; *The Clouds*, 1948; *Selected Poems*, 1949; *Collected Later Poems*, 1950, 1963; *Collected Earlier Poems*, 1951; *The Desert Music, and Other Poems*, 1954; *Journey to Love*, 1955; *Pictures from Brueghel*, 1962; *Selected Poems*, 1985; *The Collected Poems of William Carlos Williams: Volume I, 1909-1939*, 1986; *The Collected Poems of William Carlos Williams: Volume II, 1939-1962*, 1988.

TRANSLATIONS: *Last Nights of Paris*, 1929 (of Philippe Soupault; with Raquel Hélène Williams); *A Dog and the Fever*, 1954 (of Francisco de Quevedo; with Raquel Hélène Williams).

## Bibliography

Axelrod, Steven Gould, and Helen Deese, eds. *Critical Essays on William Carlos Williams.* New York: G. K. Hall, 1995. Solid collection of essays.

Beck, John. *Writing the Radical Center: William Carlos Williams, John Dewey, and American Cultural Politics.* Albany: State University of New York Press, 2001. Analyzes Williams's political convictions as reflected in his writings, and compares them with those of philosopher John Dewey.

Bremen, Brian A. *William Carlos Williams and the Diagnostics of Culture.* New York: Oxford University Press, 1993. Examination of the development of Williams's poetry, focused on his fascination with the effects of poetry and prose, and his friendship with Kenneth Burke. Using Burke's and Williams's writings and correspondence, and the works of contemporary critics, Bremen looks at how the methodological empiricism in Williams's poetic strategy is tied to his medical practice.

Gish, Robert. *William Carlos Williams: A Study of the Short Fiction.* Boston: Twayne, 1989. Very fine single-volume study of Williams's substantial contributions to the short story and the essay.

Haisty, Donna B. "The Use of Force." In *Masterplots II: Short Story Series*, edited by Charles E. May. Rev. ed. vol. 8. Pasadena, Calif.: Salem Press, 2004. Analysis of "The Use of Force" with sections on themes and meaning and style and technique. Also includes a detailed synopsis of the story.

Lenhart, Gary, ed. *The Teachers and Writers Guide to William Carlos Williams.* New York: Teachers & Writers Collaborative, 1998. Offers more than a dozen practical and innovative essays on using Williams's work to inspire writing by students and adults, including the use of both his classics and his neglected later poems.

Sayre, Henry M. *The Visual Text of William Carlos Williams.* Urbana: University of Illinois Press, 1983. Sayre ably demonstrates the influence that modernist painters and photographers had on Williams's poetry and prose, and he examines the visual effects of the graphic presentation of Williams's poetry on the printed page.

Wagner, Linda W. "Williams' 'The Use of Force': An Expansion." *Studies in Short Fiction* 4 (Summer, 1967): 351-353. Disagrees with the rape interpretation of the story, arguing that nothing could be further from the Doctor's intention and that his use of force can be attributed to other reasons.

Whitaker, Thomas R. *William Carlos Williams.* Rev. ed. Boston: Twayne, 1989. Whitaker's discussion of the short stories in chapter 6 of this general introduction to Williams's life and art focuses primarily on the stories in *The Knife of the Times*; includes a brief discussion of the oral style of the stories and the transformation of their anecdotal core.

Williams, William Carlos. *Interviews with William Carlos Williams.* Edited by Linda Wagner-Martin. New York: New Directions, 1976. Contains an introduction by Linda Wagner-Martin. Williams speaks candidly about himself and his work. Includes bibliographical references and an index.

# Tobias Wolff

**Born:** Birmingham, Alabama; June 19, 1945

**Principal short fiction** • *In the Garden of the North American Martyrs*, 1981; *Back in the World*, 1985; *The Stories of Tobias Wolff*, 1988; *The Night in Question*, 1996.

**Other literary forms** • In addition to his short stories, Tobias Wolff has also published several works of long fiction: *Ugly Rumours* (1975), *The Barracks Thief* (1984), and *Old School* (2003). One of his best-known works is his memoir, *This Boy's Life* (1989). He has also edited six volumes of short-story anthologies, ranging from *Matters of Life and Death: New American Stories* in 1983 to *Writers Harvest 3* in 2000.

**Achievements** • The quality of his work has earned for Wolff much critical respect and numerous literary prizes. He received a Wallace Stegner Fellowship in 1975-1976 to study creative writing at Stanford University, and even before he published his first book, he won creative writing grants from the National Endowment for the Arts (1978, 1985), a Mary Roberts Rinehart grant (1979), and an Arizona Council on the Arts and Humanities fellowship in creative writing (1980). He has also won several O. Henry Awards (1980, 1981, and 1985) and a John Simon Guggenheim Memorial Foundation Fellowship (1982). Wolff's *In the Garden of the North American Martyrs* received the St. Lawrence Award for Fiction (1982), his *The Barracks Thief* (1984) took the PEN/Faulkner Award for Fiction (1985), and he won the Rea Award for short stories (1989).

Wolff's *This Boy's Life: A Memoir* (1989) won *The Los Angeles Times* book prize for biography and the Ambassador Book Award of the English-Speaking Union and was a finalist for the National Book Critics Circle Award. It was also brought to the screen in 1993 in a film that starred Leonardo DiCaprio as Wolff himself. Wolff's *In Pharaoh's Army: Memories of the Lost War* (1994) won *Esquire*-Volvo-Waterstone's Prize for Nonfiction and was a finalist for both the National Book Award (1994) and *The Los Angeles Times* Book Award for biography (1995). He has also received a Whiting Foundation Award (1990), a Lila Wallace-*Reader's Digest* Award (1994), and a Lyndhurst Foundation Award (1994).

**Biography** • Readers are lucky to have two prime sources dealing with Tobias Jonathan Ansell Wolff's parents and Wolff's early life: Wolff's own memoir and a recollection of his father entitled *The Duke of Deception: Memories of My Father* (1979), written by Wolff's older brother, the novelist Geoffrey Wolff. Together, these works portray a remarkable family, though Rosemary Loftus Wolff, Wolff's mother, wryly observed that if she had known so much was going to be told, she might have watched herself more closely.

The one who bore watching, however, was Wolff's inventive father, a genial Gatsby-like figure who, in pursuit of the good life, forged checks, credentials, and his own identity. He began as Arthur Samuels Wolff, a Jewish doctor's son and boarding-school expellee, but later emerged as Arthur Saunders Wolff, an Episcopalian and Yale University graduate. A still later reincarnation was as Saunders Ansell-Wolff III.

On the basis of forged credentials, he became an aeronautical engineer and rose to occupy an executive suite. During his time, however, he also occupied a number of jail cells. Still, he showed remarkable creativity in his fabrications, so perhaps it is not surprising that both his sons became writers of fiction. Family life with him was something of a roller coaster, exciting but with many ups and downs. Eventually, this instability led to the family's breakup in 1951: Twelve-year-old Geoffrey remained with the father, while the mother took five-year-old Tobias, who had been born June 19, 1945, in Birmingham, Alabama, one of several locations where the family had chased the American Dream. Henceforth reared separately, sometimes a country apart, the two boys were not reunited until Geoffrey's final year at Princeton University.

Meanwhile, Tobias and his mother lived first in Florida, then in Utah, and finally in the Pacific Northwest, where his mother remarried. The stays in Utah and the Pacific Northwest are recounted in *This Boy's Life*, which covers Wolff's life from the age of ten until he left for Hill School in Pottstown, Pennsylvania, where he faked his references in order to be accepted. He attended Hill School for a time but did not graduate and instead ended up joining the military. From 1964 to 1968, Wolff served in the U.S. Army Special Forces and toured Vietnam as an adviser to a South Vietnamese unit, experiences he recounted in his second volume of memoirs, *In Pharaoh's Army*. After this service, deterred by the antiwar movement in the United States, he traveled to England, where he enrolled at Oxford University. He received a bachelor's degree with first class honors from Oxford University in 1972.

Returning to the United States, he worked first as a reporter for *The Washington Post*, then at various restaurant jobs in California, and finally entered the Stanford University creative writing program. He received a master's degree from Stanford in 1978. While at Stanford, he met and became friends with other writers, including Raymond Carver, and taught for a period of time. While pursuing his own writing, Wolff has taught creative writing at Goddard College, Arizona State University, and Syracuse University. In 1975, he married Catherine Dolores Spohn, a teacher and social worker; they had two sons, Michael and Patrick.

**Analysis** • Tobias Wolff is an outstanding contemporary craftsman of the American short story. Working slowly, sometimes taking months and countless drafts, he polishes each story into an entertaining, gemlike work that reads with deceptive ease. He has said, in interviews, that he needs time to get to know his characters but that the finished story no longer holds any surprises for him. For the reader, the result is full of surprises, insights, humor, and other line-by-line rewards, particularly in character portrayal and style. The influences on his work—his friend Raymond Carver and earlier masters such as Guy de Maupassant, Anton Chekhov, Sherwood Anderson, Ernest Hemingway, and Flannery O'Connor—indicate the company Wolff intends to keep.

No overriding theme, message, or agenda seems to unite Wolff's work—only his interest in people, their quirks, their unpredictability, their strivings and failings, and their predicaments as human beings. Despite their dishonesty and drug use, most of his characters fall within the range of a very shaky middle-class respectability or what passes for it in contemporary America. Although most of them do not hope for much, many still have troubles separating their fantasies from reality. Despite their dried-up souls, vague remnants of Judeo-Christian morality still rattle around inside their rib cages, haunting them with the specter of moral choice (Wolff himself is a Roman Catholic). It is perhaps emblematic that a considerable amount of action in his stories occurs inside automobiles hurtling across the landscape (except when they break down or fly off the road).

Wolff himself has called his stories autobiographical (just as his memoirs are somewhat fictionalized), but this seems true only in a broad sense. Wolff goes on to say that many of his characters reflect aspects of himself and that he sometimes makes use of actual events. According to Wolff, "The Liar" mirrors himself as a child: The story is about a boy who reacts to his father's death by becoming a pathological liar. A story that appears to make use of an actual event is "The Missing Person," about a priest who, to impress his drinking buddy, fabricates a story about killing a man with his bare hands. Before he knows it, the buddy has spread the news to the nuns. Wolff related a similar story about himself in an *Esquire* magazine article ("Raymond Carver Had His Cake and Ate It Too," September, 1989), recalling his friend Carver after Carver's death from cancer. In a tale-swapping competition with Carver, known for his bouts with alcohol, Wolff bested his friend by fabricating a story about being addicted to heroin; aghast, Carver repeated the story, and people began regarding Wolff with pity and sorrow.

**"Our Story Begins"** • A truly autobiographical story titled "Our Story Begins" (a double or triple entendre) probably gives a more typical view of Wolff's sources of inspiration: uncanny powers of observation and a good ear. In this story, Charlie, an aspiring writer, who barely supports himself by working as a busboy in a San Francisco restaurant, is discouraged and about ready to quit. On his way home through one of those notorious San Francisco fogs, however, he stops at a coffeehouse. There he overhears a conversation between a woman, her husband, and another man. The man tells a story about a Filipino taxi driver's fantastic love obsession with a local woman, and the trio are identified as a love triangle themselves. Charlie soaks it all in with his cappuccino, then, newly inspired by these riches, heads home through the fog. Wolff brings these stories to a close with a patented ending: A Chinese woman carrying a live lobster rushes past, and a foghorn in the bay is likewise an omen that "at any moment anything might be revealed."

*In the Garden of the North American Martyrs* • Wolff's patented ending is an updated open version of O. Henry's surprise ending, which wrapped things up with a plot twist. Wolff's endings are usually accomplished with a modulation of style, a sudden opening out into revelation, humor, irony, symbolism, or lyricism. Such an ending is illustrated by "Next Door," the first story of *In the Garden of the North American Martyrs*. A quiet couple are scandalized by the goings-on next door, where everybody screams and fights and the husband and wife make love standing up against the refrigerator. To drown out these raucous neighbors, the couple turns up their television volume, goes to bed, and watches the film *El Dorado*. Lying next to his wife, the husband becomes sexually aroused, but she is unresponsive. The seemingly uneventful story ends when the husband suddenly imagines how he would rewrite the movie—an ambiguous ending that suggests both his desire for some of the lusty, disorderly life next door (and in the movie) and the quiet, passionless fate that he is probably doomed to endure.

The next story, "Hunters in the Snow," perhaps Wolff's best, is much more eventful and has an unforgettable ending. The story is set in the wintry fields of the Northwest, where three deer hunters, supposedly old buddies, rib and carp and play practical jokes on one another. The ringleader, Kenny, who is driving his old truck, is unmerciful to Frank and especially to Tub. Tub, however, wreaks a terrible revenge when one of Kenny's practical jokes backfires and, through a misunderstanding, Tub shoots him, inflicting a gruesome gut wound. Frank and Tub throw Kenny into the back of the pickup truck and head off over unfamiliar country roads for the hospital fifty miles away. After a while, Frank and Tub become cold from the snow blowing through a hole in the windshield and stop at a tavern for a beer, where they strike up a sympathetic conversation with each other. Leaving the directions to the hospital on the table, they hit the road again. A little farther on, Frank and Tub have to stop at the next tavern for another beer and, this time, a warm meal. Self-absorbed, they continue their discoveries that they have much in common and become real pals. Meanwhile, Kenny is cooling in the back of the truck, and the story ends when they get under way again:

> As the truck twisted through the gentle hills the star went back and forth between Kenny's boots, staying always in his sight. "I'm going to the hospital," Kenny said. But he was wrong. They had taken a different turn a long way back.

The title story, "In the Garden of the North American Martyrs," shows that academics can be just as cruel as hunters (or, in this case, the Iroquois Indians). The story's protagonist is Mary, a mousy historian who has a terrible teaching job at a college in the rainy Northwest. She is invited by her friend Louise—who is a member of the history faculty of a posh college in upstate New York, Iroquois country—to interview for a job opening there. When Mary arrives on campus, she finds that she has been cruelly exploited: The interview was only a setup to fulfill a college requirement that a woman be interviewed for every job opening. As the story ends, Mary changes the topic of her demonstration lecture and—before horrified faculty and students assembled in the college's modernized version of the long house—delivers a grisly account of how the Iroquois "took scalps and practiced cannibalism and slavery" and "tortured their captives."

Two other memorable stories in Wolff's first collection explore the bittersweet possibilities of relationships that never come to fruition. In "Passenger," the strictly behaved protagonist, Glen, is conned into giving a ride to the aging flower child Bonnie and her dog Sunshine. They become a working unit in the car, like an informal but close-knit family, and the reader sees that they are good for each other but realizes that the relationship probably would not last much longer than the day's journey; the probability is symbolized by a hair-raising incident along the way, when the dog leaps on the driver, Glen, causing the car to go spinning down the wet highway out of control. In "Poaching," a real family gets together again, briefly: A divorced woman visits her former husband and their small son. It is clear that husband and wife should reunite for their own good and the good of the child, but neither will make the first move—even though they sleep together in the same bed. The state of their relationship is symbolized by an old beaver who tries to build his lodge in a pond on the property and is quickly shot.

***Back in the World*** • The stories in *Back in the World*, Wolff's second collection, are not quite as finished as the ones in his first but include several worth noting. The title is a phrase used by American soldiers in Vietnam to refer to home. Ironically, from Wolff's stories it appears that "back in the world" is also a crazy battle zone. Besides "The Missing Person" and "Our Story Begins," other stories that stand out are "Coming Attractions," "Desert Breakdown, 1968," and "The Rich Brother."

"Coming Attractions," the collection's first story, showcases a precocious teenage girl who is every parent's nightmare. She shoplifts and makes random anonymous phone calls late at night: For example, she calls and wakes an unfortunately named Mr. Love, sixty-one years old, and gets him excited about winning a big contest. First, however, he has to answer the question: "Here's the question, Mr. Love. I lie and steal and sleep around. What do you think about that?" Still, she reveals another side of herself at the end, when she dives to the bottom of an ice-cold swimming pool in the middle of the night and fishes out an abandoned bike for her little brother.

The two other stories feature cars. In "Desert Breakdown, 1968," the car of a young family fresh back from Germany—a former American soldier, his pregnant German wife, and their first child—breaks down at an isolated service station in the Mojave desert. The locals do not lift a hand to help, except for a woman who runs the station, and the husband is tempted to abandon his young family there. The story demonstrates that men cannot be depended on, but women are quite capable of taking care of themselves: The German wife beats up one of the local cowboys, and the station operator goes out and shoots rabbits for dinner. In "The Rich Brother," the collection's last story, the lifestyles of two brothers clash. The rich brother drives to a distant religious commune to rescue his young brother, but on the way home, they quarrel, and the rich brother abandons the young one along the roadside. As the story ends, however, the rich brother is having second thoughts, afraid to get home and face the questions of his wife: "Where is he? Where is your brother?"

***The Night in Question*** • The fifteen stories in *The Night in Question* again display Wolff's command of dialogue, expressive detail, and meticulous plotting. The plots frequently turn on situational irony, and the endings show the principal characters suffering unexpectedly because of their behavior. That behavior devolves from self-delusion. The disparity between characters' intentions and the consequences of their actions creates conflict that at times skirts the bizarre but is moving and provocative in the end.

The "Other Miller" illustrates Wolff's use of a surprise ending to reveal the source of self-delusion. Miller, a young soldier, is told that his mother has died. He is delighted because he believes that the authorities have mistaken him for another Miller in his battalion. He plays along in order to get emergency leave and amuses himself with the sympathy of other soldiers. He never believes his mother has died because she is young and, more important, he is obsessed with punishing her for remarrying after his father's death. His enlistment, in fact, had been meant to punish her. Not until he opens the door to his home does the truth force its way through his childish spite. The only mistake, all along, has been his; his mother now dead, he has only punished himself with his bitter love.

In some stories the ending is foreshadowed, gradually intensifying for the reader the emotional state of the protagonists. "The Life of the Body" concerns an aging preparatory school English teacher. A romantic, he loves the classics and is liberal in applying their themes to modern social problems. The story opens in a bar. He is drunk, makes a pass at a pretty young veterinarian, and is beaten up by her boyfriend. The next day, heroically bruised, he does not correct the rumors among his students that he has been mugged by a gang. He tells the truth to a friend and admits his foolishness but continues to pursue the veterinarian despite her hostility and dangerous boyfriend. As the story ends, she relents slightly, just enough to give him hope for more adventure and romance. However irrational his actions, he deeply craves direct experience. The title story, "The Night in Question," similarly heightens suspense in order to depict a complex emotional state with devastating power. Frank and Frances grew up under a violently abusive father. As adults, they seem familiar literary types: Frank has been the wild youth who now has gotten religion; Frances is the long-suffering, practical big sister. In the story, Frank repeats to Frances a sermon he has heard about a man who must choose between saving his beloved son and a passenger train. Frances will have none of the story's pat message about choice and trust in the heavenly Father. It becomes ever clearer as she listens that she is spiritually alive only when she is protecting her brother. In fact, as their names suggest—Frank (Francis) and Frances—their earthly father's violence has welded them into a single spiritual being. The story makes the psychological concept of codependency potently eerie.

Like Wolff's earlier collections, *The Night in Question* portrays the predicaments of human intercourse vividly and conveys their psychological or philosophical consequence by suggestion. Wolff rarely sermonizes. If he comments at all, he usually comments indirectly, through symbolism or his patented ending. Above all, Wolff is a lover of good stories and is content to tell them and let them stand on their own.

*Harold Branam*

**Other major works**

ANTHOLOGIES: *Matters of Life and Death: New American Stories*, 1983; *The Picador Book of Contemporary American Stories*, 1993; *The Best American Short Stories, 1994*, 1994; *The Vintage Book of Contemporary American Short Stories*, 1994; *Best New American Voices*, 2000; *Writers Harvest 3*, 2000.

NOVELS: *Ugly Rumours*, 1975; *The Barracks Thief*, 1984; *Old School*, 2003.

NONFICTION: *This Boy's Life*, 1989; *In Pharaoh's Army: Memories of the Lost War*, 1994.

**Bibliography**

Challener, Daniel D. *Stories of Resilience in Childhood: The Narratives of Maya Angelou, Maxine Hong Kingston, Richard Rodrigues, John Edgar Wideman, and Tobias Wolff*. New York: Garland, 1997. Compares the poverty-stricken childhoods of several notable writers, analyzing what led them to overcome early hardship and go on to literary greatness. Includes a bibliography and index.

Desmond, John F. "Catholicism in Contemporary American Fiction." *America* 170, no. 17 (1994): 7-11. Notes Wolff's Christian ethos and comments on his use of liars and lying as means of exploring the manipulation of reality in his fiction.

Hannah, James. *Tobias Wolff: A Study of the Short Fiction*. Twayne's Studies in Short Fiction 64. New York: Twayne, 1996. Good critical study of the short fiction of Tobias Wolff.

Kelly, Colm L. "Affirming the Indeterminable: Deconstruction, Sociology, and Tobias Wolff's 'Say Yes.'" *Mosaic* 32 (March, 1999): 149-166. In response to sociological approaches to literature, argues that stories like Wolff's are polysemous and therefore not reducible to any single interpretation; provides a deconstructive reading of the story, setting it off against three possible readings derived from current sociological theory, in order to show how the story deconstructs the theories that attempt to explain it.

May, Charles E., ed. *Masterplots II: Short Story Series, Revised Edition*. 8 vols. Pasadena, Calif.: Salem Press, 2004. Designed for student use, this reference set contains articles providing detailed plot summaries and analyses of five short stories by Wolff: "Hunters in the Snow," "In the Garden of the North American Martyrs," and "The Liar" (vol. 4); and "The Rich Brother" and "Say Yes" (vol. 6).

Peters, Joanne M., and Jean W. Ross. "Tobias Wolff (Jonathan Ansell)." In *Contemporary Authors*, edited by Hal May. Vol. 117. Detroit: Gale Research, 1986. Peters gives a brief overview of Wolff's work, but more important is the interview by Ross. In the interview, Wolff talks about his reasons for writing short stories, the writers who have influenced him, his working methods and sources of inspiration, his own reading, and his teaching of creative writing.

Prose, Francine. "The Brothers Wolff." *The New York Times Magazine*, February 5, 1989, 22. Prose's fine article, which is also collected in *The New York Times Biographical Service* (February, 1989), introduces the writing of the Wolff brothers, Geoffrey and Tobias. Traces how they grew up apart but became inseparable, even bearing striking resemblances to each other. The article also provides background on their parents, particularly their father.

Wolff, Tobias. "A Forgotten Master: Rescuing the Works of Paul Bowles." *Esquire* 103 (May, 1986): 221-223. Wolff's article not only helps rescue a forgotten master but also provides an index of what Wolff values in writing. He praises Bowles for the mythic quality of his stories, the clarity of his language, his ability to shift moods at will, and his ability to depict a wide range of international characters. He feels that Bowles's pessimism might have contributed to his lack of popularity.

_____. Interview by Nicholas A. Basbanes. *Publishers Weekly* 241 (October 24, 1994): 45-46. A brief biographical sketch and survey of Wolff's career; Wolff discusses his writing habits and his works.

_____. "An Interview with Tobias Wolff." *Contemporary Literature* 31 (Spring, 1990): 1-16. Wolff discusses lying in his story "The Liar" and the nature of "winging it" in his story "In the Garden of the North American Martyrs." Wolff also talks about the fable aspect of his story "The Rich Brother," as well as his fiction about the Vietnam War.

# Virginia Woolf

**Born:** London, England; January 25, 1882
**Died:** The River Ouse, near Rodmell, Sussex, England; March 28, 1941

**Principal short fiction** • *Two Stories*, 1917 (one by Leonard Woolf); *Kew Gardens*, 1919; *The Mark on the Wall*, 1919; *Monday or Tuesday*, 1921; *A Haunted House, and Other Short Stories*, 1943; *Mrs. Dalloway's Party*, 1973 (Stella McNichol, editor); *The Complete Shorter Fiction of Virginia Woolf*, 1985.

**Other literary forms** • Besides authoring short stories, Virginia Woolf was an acute and detailed diarist (her diary entries occupy five volumes in the authoritative collected edition); a prolific letter writer (six volumes in the authoritative collected edition); a biographer; a perceptive, original, and argumentative essayist and reviewer (her collected essays fill six volumes in the authoritative edition); and a pioneer of the modern novel in her ten works of long prose fiction, which include the acknowledged classics *Mrs. Dalloway* (1925), *To the Lighthouse* (1927), and *The Waves* (1931).

**Achievements** • A distinguished and distinctive prose stylist, Virginia Woolf excelled in fiction, nonfiction, and her own unique hybrid of these genres in her two whimsical books *Orlando: A Biography* (1928) and *Flush: A Biography* (1933), which are variously categorized as fiction, nonfiction, or "other" by critics of her work. In nonfiction, essays such as "The Death of the Moth," "How Should One Read a Book?" and "Shakespeare's Sister" have been widely anthologized, and in their vividness, imagery, and keen analysis of daily life, literature, society, and women's concerns assure Woolf a place in the history of the essay.

In fiction, Woolf's classic novels, sharing much in style and theme with the nonfiction, have overshadowed the short stories. Reacting against the realistic and naturalistic fiction of her time, Woolf often emphasized lyricism, stream of consciousness, and the irresolute slice of life in both her novels and her stories, though she wrote more conventional fiction as well. Whether the conventional "well-made" or the experimental stream-of-consciousness variety, many of her approximately fifty short stories are accomplished works of art. Because of their precise and musical prose style, irony, ingenious spiral form (with narrative refrains), reversal or revelatory structure, and exploration of human nature and social life, they deserve to be better known and to be studied for themselves and not just for what they may reveal about the novels.

**Biography** • Virginia Woolf was born as Adeline Virginia Stephen and grew up in the household of her father, Leslie Stephen, a Victorian and Edwardian literary lion who was visited by many prominent writers of the time. The importance of books in her life is reflected in many of the short stories, such as "Memoirs of a Novelist," "The Evening Party," and "A Haunted House"; her father's extensive personal library provided much of her education, along with some private tutoring (especially in Greek). Despite Katherine Stephen, niece of Leslie Stephen, being the principal of Newnham College at the University of Cambridge (reflected in the story "A

Woman's College from Outside"), Virginia was denied a formal college education because of persistent ill health (emotional and physical), as well as her father's male bias in this matter, all of which is echoed with mild irony in "Phyllis and Rosamond" (about two sisters who resemble Virginia and Vanessa Stephen, lacking a college education) and "A Society" (in which the character Poll, lacking a college education, receives her father's inheritance on condition that she read all the books in the London Library).

The early death of Woolf's mother, Julia, in 1895, the repeated sexual molestation by her half brother George Duckworth, her father's transformation of Virginia's sisters Stella and Vanessa into surrogate mothers after Julia's death, and her own attachments to women such as Violet Dickinson and, later, Vita Sackville-West culminated in Virginia's cool and ambivalent sexuality, reflected by the general absence of sexual passion in many of the short stories as well as by what Woolf herself described as the "Sapphism" of "Moments of Being: 'Slater's Pins Have No Points.'" The more regular element of her adolescence and generally happy life with Leonard Woolf, whom she married in 1912, was the social round of upper-middle-class life, including horticultural outings in London (reflected in "Kew Gardens"), parties, private concerts, and theater-going (as in "The Evening Party," "The String Quartet," the Mrs. Dalloway party cycle of stories, "Uncle Vanya," and "The Searchlight"), and excursions to the country (as in "In the Orchard"), seashore (as in "Solid Objects" and "The Watering Place"), or foreign resorts (as in "A Dialogue upon Mount Pentelicus" and "The Symbol").

Clustering around Virginia and her sister Vanessa, when they moved to a house in the Bloomsbury district after Leslie Stephen's death in 1904, was a group of talented writers, artists, and intellectuals who came to be known as the Bloomsbury Group and were generally among the avant-garde in arts and letters. (This period is portrayed in "Phyllis and Rosamond.") Many intellectuals from the group continued to associate with Virginia and Leonard Woolf after their marriage, and some, such as T. S. Eliot, had books published by the Hogarth Press, which was set up by the Woolfs in 1917. Indeed, all Virginia Woolf's short stories in book form have been published in England by this press.

In 1919, the Woolfs, for weekend and recreational use, took a country cottage called Monks House, whose reputation for being haunted evoked "A Haunted House" and whose vicinity, Rodmell (as well as Leonard Woolf, by name), is jocularly referred to in "The Window and the Parrot: A True Story." Because of numerous family deaths as well as, later, the strain and letdown of completing her novels and the anxiety from World Wars I and II (referred to in many of the stories, and responsible in 1940 for the destruction of the Woolfs' London house), Woolf had been and continued to be subject to mental breakdowns. The motifs of liquid's destructiveness and death by drowning in several of the stories ("Solid Objects," "A Woman's College from Outside," "The Widow and the Parrot," "The New Dress," "The Introduction," "A Simple Melody," "The Fascination of the Pool") were actualized when, in early 1941, Woolf, at the onset of another breakdown, drowned herself in the Ouse River, near Rodmell and Monks House.

**Analysis** • Perhaps related to her mental condition is Virginia Woolf's interest in perception and perspective, as well as their relationship to imagination, in many stories. In two short avant-garde pieces—"Monday or Tuesday" (six paragraphs) and "Blue and Green" (two paragraphs, one for each color)—Woolf attempts to convey

Courtesy, D.C. Public Library

the reality of the urban and natural worlds through discrete, apparently disconnected associative impressions.

**"Monday or Tuesday" and "Blue and Green"** • In "Monday or Tuesday," a series of contrasts between up and down, spatially free timelessness (a lazily flying heron) and restrictive timeliness (a clock striking), day and night, inside and outside, present experience and later recollection of it conveys the ordinary cycle of life suggested by the title and helps capture its experiential reality, the concern expressed by the refrain question that closes the second, fourth, and fifth paragraphs: "and truth?"

Similar contrasts inform the two paragraphs describing the blue and green aspects of reality and the feelings associated with them in "Blue and Green." These two colors are dominant and symbolic throughout Woolf's short stories. Differing perspectives, which are almost cinematic or painterly, also structure "In the Orchard," as each of the story's three sections, dealing with a woman named Miranda sleeping in an orchard, focuses on, in order, the sleeping Miranda in relation to her physical surroundings, the effect of the physical surroundings on Miranda's dreaming (and thus the interconnection between imagination and external world), and finally a return to the physical environment, with a shift in focus to the orchard's apple trees and birds. The simultaneity and differing angle of the three perspectives are suggested by the narrative refrain that closes each section, a sentence referring to Miranda jumping upright and exclaiming that she will be late for tea.

The ability of the imagination, a key repeated word in Woolf's short stories, to perceive accurately the surrounding world is an issue in many of the stories. In "The Mark on the Wall," a narrator is led into associative musings from speculating about the mark, only to discover, with deflating irony, that the source of the imaginative ramblings is in reality a lowly snail (with the further concluding ironic reversal being an unexpected reference to World War I, whose seriousness undercuts the narrator's previous whimsical free associations). Even more difficult is the imagination's perception of people (who and what individuals really are) in the surrounding world. This is the chief problem of the biographer, a task at which Woolf herself was successful, though not the self-centered and somewhat dishonest novelist's biographer who narrates "Memoirs of a Novelist." In the four stories "An Unwritten Novel," "Moments of Being: 'Slater's Pins Have No Points,'" "The Lady in the Looking Glass: A Reflection," and "The Shooting Party," a major character or the narrator is led through small details into imaginative flights about the life and personality of an individual—only, in the story's concluding reversal, to be proved incorrect or be left very doubtful about the picture or account created. Likewise showing a connection between the literary artist's problem of depicting the truth and the imagination's problem in probing reality is the story "The Three Pictures," in which the first picture, of a sailor's homecoming to a welcoming wife, leads the narrator to imagine further happy events, undercut by the second and third pictures revealing the sailor's death from a fever contracted overseas and the despair of his wife.

The problem of "and truth?" (as phrased in "Monday or Tuesday") can be comically superficial, as in the narrator's wasted sympathetic imaginings in "Sympathy" in response to a newspaper account of Humphrey Hammond's death, only to discover in the story's conclusion that the article referred to the elderly father rather than the son (with ironic undercutting of the genuineness of the narrator's sympathy because of her chagrin about the "deception" and "waste"). In contrast, in "The Fascination of the Pool," the deeply evocative imagery and symbolism of never-ending layers of stories absorbed by a pool over time, and always going inexhaustibly deeper, have a meditative and melancholic solemnity.

**"Kew Gardens"** • Related to imagination and art (which may or may not bridge the gap between human beings), as well as to social criticism and feminist issues (whether roles and identities unite or divide, fulfill or thwart people), is the motif of isolation and alienation in many of the stories. In "Kew Gardens," the first paragraph's twice-repeated detail of the heart-and-tongue shape of the colorful plants symbolizes the potential of love and communication to effect communion, while the colors projected by the flowers from sunlight on various things (mentioned in the first and last paragraphs) symbolize the various couples' imaginations projected on the environs. In the social context of the park, however, the four sets of strollers are isolated from one another, as is the other major "character" described, the snail; each is solipsistically involved in its own affairs. Only in the fourth set, a romantic young couple, do love and communication seem to promise, though not guarantee, the hope of communion.

**"Solid Objects"** • In "Solid Objects," the first paragraph's emphasis on a changing perspective (a black dot on the horizon becomes four-legged and then two men) symbolizes how the protagonist's, John's, perspective changes from imaginative engagements with people, politics, and ideas, to engagements with small things or concrete objects, beginning with his discovery at the beach of a smooth, irregular fragment of glass. While Charles, John's friend, at the beach casts flat slate stones into the water, aware of objects only as a means of allowing physical action and release, John becomes attached to them with the child's and artist's fascination, which lures him away from the practical and pragmatic adult world of action and politics, in which he had a bright future. John thus becomes alienated from all those around him, including Charles. Symbolically during their last encounter, both end up conversing at cross purposes, neither person understanding the other.

**"A Haunted House" and "Lappin and Lapinova"** • "A Haunted House" and "Lappin and Lapinova" show, respectively, success and failure in human communion. The former story uses the convention of the ghost story and gothic fiction, almost satirically or ironically, to suggest the broader theme of the mystery of the human heart. Implicitly two kinds of mystery are contrasted: the mystery of ghosts, haunted houses, secret treasures, and so on, and the real, important mystery of what is most worthwhile in the universe—the ghostly couple's lesson at the story's close that the house's hidden treasure is love, "the light in the heart." The implicitly living couple presumably have love, paralleling the ghostly couple's bond. The cyclical repetitions in the story help convey, stylistically, the pulsation or beating of the human heart, the seat of this love. In contrast, the married couple in "Lappin and Lapinova" become alienated because the husband cannot genuinely share in the wife's imaginative fantasy of the two of them as rabbit and hare, reverting to his pragmatic and stolid family heritage and an arrogant masculine impatience.

**Mrs. Dalloway Party Cycle** • Most of the nine stories constituting the Mrs. Dalloway party cycle ("Mrs. Dalloway in Bond Street," "The New Dress," "Happiness," "Ancestors," "The Introduction," "Together and Apart," "The Man Who Loved His Kind," "A Simple Melody," "A Summing Up") naturally deal, by their focus on a social occasion, with communion or alienation, as suggested by the title "Together and Apart." In "Mrs. Dalloway in Bond Street," the title character remains isolated or insulated from the surrounding world, symbolized by the gloves that she is going to buy (perhaps for the party), by her general disregard of traffic and other phenomena while she muses about the death of a recent acquaintance, and by her disregard of a literal explosion that ends the story (though paradoxically she communes with an acquaintance by remembering and uttering the name while ignoring the explosion). At the party itself, Mabel Waring, the protagonist of "The New Dress," is alienated because her new dress, owing to her limited means, seems a failure and source of embarrassment; Stuart Elton, protagonist of "Happiness," remains withdrawn in himself to preserve an egocentric equilibrium that is his happiness; Mrs. Vallance, protagonist of "Ancestors," is alienated by the superficial and undignified talk and values of the young around her, in contrast to her past. Woolf's feminist concerns about the unjust subordination and oppression of women (prominent in "Phyllis and Rosamond," "The Mysterious Case of Miss V.," "The Journal of Mistress Joan Martyn," "A Society," "A Woman's College from Outside," and "The Legacy") are suggested by the isolation and alienation of Lily Everit, who feels inadequate when introduced to Bob Brinsley, symbol of thoughtless male power and conceit. Despite Everit's esteemed essay writing (paralleling Woolf's), Brinsley negligently assumes that she must, as a woman, write poetry, as his initial question shows. Everit feels crushed, stifled, and silenced by the weight of masculine accomplishment in the arts and sciences.

Two impromptu pairings in the Dalloway party cycle—Roderick Serle and Ruth Anning of "Together and Apart," and Prickett Ellis and Miss O'Keefe of "The Man Who Loved His Kind"—achieve temporary communion: Serle and Anning when they imaginatively attune to each other, sharing profound emotions about experiences in Canterbury; Ellis and O'Keefe when the latter concurs with the former's concern about the poor excluded from affairs such as Mrs. Dalloway's party. These couples, however, driven apart at story's end by the evening's experience—Serle and Anning when the former is mockingly accosted by a female acquaintance, and Ellis and O'Keefe when the former fails, with some self-centered posturing, to appreciate the latter's understanding of the need for beauty and imagination in the life lived at all social levels. Only the protagonists of the last two stories of the cycle, George Carslake in "A Simple Melody" and Sasha Latham in "A Summing Up," achieve a transcendence over isolation and alienation. Carslake melds all the partygoers and himself through a blend of imagination, art, and nature by meditating on a beautiful painting of a heath in the Dalloways' house and imagining the various partygoers on a walk there that reduces them all to fundamentally decent human beings coalesced in a common enterprise. Like Carslake, Latham achieves wisdom by fixing on inanimate objects, the Dalloways' beautiful Queen Anne house (art) and a tree in the garden (nature), and meditating on them; like Carslake, Latham sees people admirably united in motion—in her reverie, adventures and survivors sailing on the sea.

*Norman Prinsky*

**Other major works**

NOVELS: *Melymbrosia*, wr. 1912, pb. 1982, revised pb. 2002 (early version of *The Voyage Out*; Louise DeSalvo, editor); *The Voyage Out*, 1915; *Night and Day*, 1919; *Jacob's Room*, 1922; *Mrs. Dalloway*, 1925; *To the Lighthouse*, 1927; *Orlando: A Biography*, 1928; *The Waves*, 1931; *Flush: A Biography*, 1933; *The Years*, 1937; *Between the Acts*, 1941.

NONFICTION: *The Common Reader: First Series*, 1925; *A Room of One's Own*, 1929; *The Common Reader: Second Series*, 1932; *Three Guineas*, 1938; *Roger Fry: A Biography*, 1940; *The Death of the Moth, and Other Essays*, 1942; *The Moment, and Other Essays*, 1947; *The Captain's Death Bed, and Other Essays*, 1950; *A Writer's Diary*, 1953; *Letters: Virginia Woolf and Lytton Strachey*, 1956; *Granite and Rainbow*, 1958; *Contemporary Writers*, 1965; *Collected Essays, Volumes 1-2*, 1966; *Collected Essays, Volumes 3-4*, 1967; *The Flight of the Mind: The Letters of Virginia Woolf, Vol. I, 1888-1912*, 1975 (pb. in U.S. as *The Letters of Virginia Woolf, Vol. I: 1888-1912*, 1975; Nigel Nicolson, editor); *The London Scene: Five Essays*, 1975; *Moments of Being*, 1976 (Jeanne Schulkind, editor); *The Question of Things Happening: The Letters of Virginia Woolf, Vol. II, 1912-1922*, 1976 (pb. in U.S. as *The Letters of Virginia Woolf, Vol. II: 1912-1922*, 1976; Nicolson, editor); *A Change of Perspective: The Letters of Virginia Woolf, Vol. III, 1923-1928*, 1977 (pb. in U.S. as *The Letters of Virginia Woolf, Vol. III: 1923-1928*, 1978; Nicolson, editor); *Books and Portraits*, 1977; *The Diary of Virginia Woolf*, 1977-1984 (5 volumes; Anne Olivier Bell, editor); *A Reflection of the Other Person: The Letters of Virginia Woolf, Vol. IV, 1929-1931*, 1978 (pb. in U.S. as *The Letters of Virginia Woolf, Vol. IV: 1929-1931*, 1979; Nicolson, editor); *The Sickle Side of the Moon: The Letters of Virginia Woolf, Vol. V, 1932-1935*, 1979 (pb. in U.S. as *The Letters of Virginia Woolf, Vol. V: 1932-1935*, 1979; Nicolson, editor); *Leave the Letters Til We're Dead: The Letters of Virginia Woolf, Vol. VI, 1936-1941*, 1980 (Nicolson, editor); *The Essays of Virginia Woolf*, 1987-1994 (4 volumes); *Carlyle's House and Other Sketches*, 2003 (David Bradshaw, editor).

**Bibliography**

Baldwin, Dean R. *Virginia Woolf: A Study of the Short Fiction*. Boston: Twayne, 1989. Baldwin's lucid parallels between Woolf's life experiences and her innovative short-story techniques contribute significantly to an understanding of both the author and her creative process. The book also presents the opportunity for a comparative critical study by furnishing a collection of additional points of view in the final section. A chronology, a bibliography, and an index supplement the work.

Barrett, Eileen, and Patricia Cramer, eds. *Virginia Woolf: Lesbian Readings*. New York: New York University Press, 1997. This collection of conference papers features two essays on Woolf's stories: one on Katherine Mansfield's presence in Woolf's story "Moments of Being," and one that compares lesbian modernism in the stories of Woolf with lesbian modernism in the stories of Gertrude Stein.

Bleishman, Avrom. "Forms of the Woolfian Short Story." In *Virginia Woolf: Revaluation and Continuity*, edited by Ralph Freedman. Berkeley: University of California Press, 1980. In twenty-six pages, abstract theoretical issues concerning genre are discussed; then several stories are divided into the two categories of linear (for example, "The New Dress" and "Kew Gardens") and circular (for example, "The Duchess" and "Lappin and Lapinova") in form.

Briggs, Julia. *Virginia Woolf: An Inner Life*. Orlando, Fla.: Harcourt, 2005. Thorough biography of Woolf, shedding light on her creative process as well as her own perceptions of her work.

Dalsimer, Katherine. *Virginia Woolf: Becoming a Writer*. New Haven, Conn.: Yale University Press, 2002. Woolf has long been associated with psychoanalysis as the first English-language publisher of Sigmund Freud. Dalsimer, a psychoanalyst herself, analyzes Woolf's writings in all genres to uncover the psychology that underlies her literary persona.

Dick, Susan, ed. Introduction to *The Complete Shorter Fiction of Virginia Woolf*. 2d ed. San Diego: Harcourt Brace Jovanovich, 1989. Along with classification of stories into traditional ones and fictional reveries, with affinities in works of nineteenth century writers such as Thomas De Quincey and Anton Chekhov, invaluable notes are given on historical, literary, and cultural allusions, as well as textual problems, for every story.

Head, Dominic. "Experiments in Genre." In *The Modernist Short Story: A Study in Theory and Practice*. Cambridge, England: Cambridge University Press, 1992. Head discusses Woolf's search for a narrative texture that would adequately portray her notion of life as amorphous.

Heilbrun, Carolyn G. *Women's Lives: The View from the Threshold*. Toronto: University of Toronto Press, 1999. This volume discusses George Eliot, Woolf, Willa Cather, and Harriet Beecher Stowe. Focuses on the female view and feminism in literature.

King, James. *Virginia Woolf*. New York: W. W. Norton, 1995. Literary biography that relates Woolf's life to her work. Shows how the chief sources of her writing were her life, her family, and her friends.

Lee, Hermione. *Virginia Woolf*. New York: Alfred A. Knopf, 1997. Detailed biography of Woolf, her complex family relationships, her lifelong battle with mental illness, and her relationship to the Bloomsbury group.

May, Charles E., ed. *Masterplots II: Short Story Series, Revised Edition*. 8 vols. Pasadena, Calif.: Salem Press, 2004. Designed for student use, this reference set contains articles providing detailed plot summaries and analyses of four short stories by Woolf: "A Haunted House" (vol. 3), "The Mark on the Wall" (vol. 5), and "The Symbol" and "Together and Apart" (vol. 7).

Roe, Sue, and Susan Sellers, eds. *The Cambridge Companion to Virginia Woolf*. New York: Cambridge University Press, 2000. Landmark collection of essays by leading scholars that addresses the full range of Woolf's intellectual perspectives—literary, artistic, philosophical, and political.

# Richard Wright

**Born:** Roxie, Mississippi; September 4, 1908
**Died:** Paris, France; November 28, 1960

**Principal short fiction** • *Uncle Tom's Children: Four Novellas*, 1938 (expanded as *Uncle Tom's Children: Five Long Stories*, 1938); *Eight Men*, 1961.

**Other literary forms** • Although Richard Wright is best known for his novel *Native Son* (1940), his nonfiction works, such as the two volumes of his autobiography *Black Boy: A Record of Childhood and Youth* (1945) and *American Hunger* (1977) along with books such as *Twelve Million Black Voices* (1941) and *White Man, Listen!* (1957), have proven to be of lasting interest. He developed a Marxist ideology while writing for the Communist *Daily Worker*, which was very influential on his early fiction, notably *Native Son* and *Uncle Tom's Children*, but which culminated in an article, "I Tried to Be a Communist," first published by the *Atlantic Monthly* in 1944. Although he abandoned Marxist ideology, he never abandoned the idea that protest is and should be at the heart of great literature.

**Achievements** • Richard Wright is often cited as being the founder of the post-World War II African American novel. The works of James Baldwin and Ralph Ellison owe a direct debt to the work of Wright, and his role in inspiring the Black Arts movement of the 1960's is incalculable. Further, he was one of the first African American novelists of the first half of the twentieth century to capture a truly international audience. Among his many honors were a Guggenheim Fellowship in 1939 and the Spingarn Award from the National Association for the Advancement of Colored People (NAACP) in 1941 for his novel, *Native Son*. This novel, which James Baldwin said was "unquestionably" the "most powerful and celebrated statement we have had yet of what it means to be a Negro in America," along with the first volume of his autobiography and the stories in *Uncle Tom's Children*, constitute Wright's most important lasting contributions to literature. His plots usually deal with how the harrowing experience of racial inequality transforms a person into a rebel—usually violent, and usually randomly so. The more subtle achievement of his fiction, however, is the psychological insight it provides into the experience of oppression and rebellion.

**Biography** • The poverty, racial hatred, and violence that Richard Nathaniel Wright dramatizes in fiction come directly from his own experience as the child of an illiterate Mississippi sharecropper. Richard was six years old when his father was driven off the land and the family moved to a two-room slum tenement in Memphis, Tennessee. The father deserted the family there. Richard's mother, Ella Wright, got a job as a cook, leaving Richard and his younger brother Alan alone in the apartment. When his mother became ill, the brothers were put in an orphanage. An invitation for Ella and the boys to stay with a more prosperous relative in Arkansas ended in panic and flight when white men shot Uncle Hoskins, who had offered the Wrights a home. The family lived for some time with Richard's grandparents, stern Seventh-day Adventists. In this grim, repressive atmosphere, Richard became increasingly violent and rebellious.

Although he completed his formal education in the ninth grade, the young Richard read widely, especially Stephen Crane, Fyodor Dostoevski, Marcel Proust, T. S. Eliot, and Gertrude Stein. The family eventually migrated to Chicago. Wright joined the Communist Party in 1933, and, in 1937 in New York City, became editor of the *Daily Worker.* The publication of *Uncle Tom's Children, Native Son,* and *Black Boy* brought Wright fame both in the United States and in Europe. In 1945, at the invitation of the French government, Wright went to France and became friends with Jean-Paul Sartre, Simone de Beauvoir, and other existentialists. His next novel, *The Outsider* (1953), has been called the first existential novel by an American writer. Wright traveled widely, lectured in several countries, and wrote journalistic accounts of his experiences in Africa and Spain. He died unexpectedly in Paris of amoebic dysentery, probably contracted in Africa or Indonesia under conditions his friend and biographer Margaret Walker, in *Richard Wright: Daemonic Genius* (1988), believes indicate at least medically questionable decisions, or, possibly, homicide.

**Analysis** • "Fire and Cloud" in *Uncle Tom's Children* is perhaps the best representative of Richard Wright's early short fiction. It won first prize in the 1938 *Story* magazine contest which had more than four hundred entries, marking Wright's first triumph with American publishers. Charles K. O'Neill made a radio adaptation of the story after it appeared in *American Scenes.*

**"Fire and Cloud"** • Unlike the later works concerning black ghetto experience, "Fire and Cloud" has a pastoral quality, recognizing the strong bond of the southern black to the soil and the support he has drawn from religion. Wright reproduces faithfully the southern black dialect in both conversation and internal meditations. This use of dialect emphasizes the relative lack of sophistication of rural blacks. His protagonist, Reverend Taylor, is representative of the "old Negro," who has withstood centuries of oppression, sustained by hard work on the land and humble faith in a merciful God.

Wright's attitude toward religion, however, is ambivalent. Although he recognizes it as contributing to the quiet nobility of the hero, it also prevents Taylor from taking effective social action when his people are literally starving. The final triumph of Reverend Taylor is that he puts aside the conciliatory attitude which was part of his religious training and becomes a social activist. Instead of turning the other cheek after being humiliated and beaten by white men, he embraces the methods of his Marxist supporters, meeting oppression with mass demonstration. Strength of numbers proves more effective and appropriate for getting relief from the bigoted white establishment than all his piety and loving kindness. Early in the story Taylor exclaims "The good Lawds gonna clean up this ol worl some day! Hes gonna make a new Heaven n a new Earth!" His last words, however, are "Freedom belongs t the strong!"

The situation of the story no doubt reflects Wright's early experience when his sharecropper father was driven off the plantation. Taylor's people are starving because the white people, who own all the land, have prohibited the blacks from raising food on it. No matter how Taylor pleads for relief, the local white officials tell him to wait and see if federal aid may be forthcoming. When two communist agitators begin pushing Taylor to lead a mass demonstration against the local government, white officials have Taylor kidnapped and beaten, along with several deacons of his church. Instead of intimidating them, this suffering converts them to open confrontation. As the communists promised, the poor whites join the blacks in the march, which

forces the white authorities to release food to those facing starvation.

The story's strength lies in revealing through three dialogues
the psychological dilemma of the
protagonist as opposing groups
demand his support. He resists
the communists initially because
their methods employ threat of
open war on the whites—"N tha
ain Gawds way!" The agitators say
he will be responsible if their
demonstration fails through lack
of numbers and participants are
slaughtered. On the other hand,
the mayor and chief of police
threaten Taylor that they will hold
him personally responsible if any
of his church members join the
march. After a humiliating and futile exchange with these men, Taylor faces his own church deacons,
who are themselves divided and
look to him for leadership. He
knows that one of their number,
who is just waiting for a chance to
oust him from his church, will run

Library of Congress

to the mayor and police with any evidence of Taylor's insubordination. In a pathetic
attempt to shift the burden of responsibility that threatens to destroy him no matter
what he does, he reiterates the stubborn stand he has maintained with all three
groups: He will not order the demonstration, but he will march with his people if
they choose to demonstrate. The brutal horse-whipping that Taylor endures as a result of this moderate stand convinces him of the futility of trying to placate everybody. The Uncle Tom becomes a rebel.

Critics sometimes deplore the episodes of raw brutality described in graphic detail in Wright's fiction, but violence is the clue here to his message. Behind the white
man's paternalistic talk is the persuasion of whip and gun. Only superior force can
cope with such an antagonist.

**"The Man Who Lived Underground"** • Wright's best piece of short fiction is "The
Man Who Lived Underground." Although undoubtedly influenced by Dostoevski's
underground man and by Franz Kafka's "K," the situation was based on a prisoner's
story from *True Detective* magazine. The first version appeared in 1942 in *Accent* magazine under the subtitle "Two Excerpts from a Novel." This version began with a description of the life of a black servant, but Wright later discarded this opening in favor of the dramatic scene in which an unnamed fugitive hides from the police by
descending into a sewer. This approach allowed the story to assume a more universal,
symbolic quality. Although racist issues are still significant, the protagonist repre-

sents that larger class of all those alienated from their society. Eventually the fugitive's name is revealed as Fred Daniels, but so completely is he absorbed into his Everyman role that he cannot remember his name when he returns to the upper world. His progress through sewers and basements becomes a quest for the meaning of life, parodying classic descents into the underworld and ironically reversing Plato's allegory of the cave.

Although Plato's philosopher attains wisdom by climbing out of the cave where men respond to shadows on the cave wall, Wright's protagonist gains enlightenment because of his underground perspective. What he sees there speaks not to his rational understanding, however, but to his emotions. He moves among symbolic visions which arouse terror and pity—a dead baby floating on the slimy water whose "mouth gaped black in a soundless cry." In a black church service spied on through a crevice in the wall, the devout are singing "Jesus, take me to your home above." He is overwhelmed by a sense of guilt and intuits that there is something obscene about their "singing with the air of the sewer blowing in on them." In a meat locker with carcasses hanging from the ceiling, a butcher is hacking off a piece of meat with a bloody cleaver. When the store proprietor goes home, Fred emerges from the locker and gorges on fresh fruit, but he takes back with him into the sewer the bloody cleaver—why he does not know.

When Fred breaks through a wall into the basement of a movie house, the analogy to Plato's myth of the cave becomes explicit. He comes up a back stair and sees jerking shadows of a silver screen. The Platonic urge to enlighten the people in the theater, who are bound to a shadow world, merges with messianic images. In a dream he walks on water and saves a baby held up by a drowning woman, but the dream ends in terror and doubt as he loses the baby and his ability to emulate Christ. All is lost and he himself begins to drown.

Terror and pity are not the only emotions that enlarge his sensibilities in this underground odyssey. As he learns the peculiar advantages of his invisibility, he realizes that he can help himself to all kinds of gadgets valued by that shadow world above ground. He collects them like toys or symbols of an absurd world. He acquires a radio, a light bulb with an extension cord, a typewriter, a gun, and finally, through a chance observation of a safe being opened by combination, rolls of hundred dollar bills, containers of diamonds, watches, and rings. His motivation for stealing these articles is not greed but sheer hilarious fun at acquiring objects so long denied to persons of his class.

In one of the most striking, surrealist scenes in modern literature, Fred delightedly decorates his cave walls and floor with these tokens of a society which has rejected him. "They were the serious toys of the men who lived in the dead world of sunshine and rain he had left, the world that had condemned him, branded him guilty." He glues hundred dollar bills on his walls. He winds up all the watches but disdains to set them (for he is beyond time, freed from its tyranny). The watches hang on nails along with the diamond rings. He hangs up the bloody cleaver, too, and the gun. The loose diamonds he dumps in a glittering pile on the muddy floor. Then as he gaily tramps around, he accidentally/on purpose, stomps on the pile, scattering the pretty baubles over the floor. Here, indeed, is society's cave of shadows, and only he realizes how absurd it all is.

When the euphoria of these games begins to pall, Fred becomes more philosophical, perceiving the nihilistic implications of his experience. "Maybe *any*thing's right, he mumbled. Yes, if the world as men had made it was right, then anything else was right, any act a man took to satisfy himself, murder, theft, torture." In his unlettered, blundering way, he is groping toward Ivan Karamazov's dark meditation: "If there is no God, then all things are permissible." Fred becomes convinced of the reality of human guilt, however, when he witnesses the suicide of the jewelry store's night watchman, who has been blamed for the theft he himself committed. At first, the scene in which police torture the bewildered man to force a confession strikes Fred as hilariously funny, duplicating his own experience. When the wretched man shoots himself before Fred can offer him a means of escape, however, Fred is shocked into a realization of his own guilt.

The protagonist ultimately transcends his nihilism, and like Platonic realism's philosopher who returns to the cave out of compassion for those trapped there, Fred returns to the "dead world of sunshine and rain" to bear witness to the Truth. Like the philosopher who is blinded coming out of the light into cave darkness, Fred seems confused and stupid in the social world above ground. When he is thrown out of the black church, he tries inarticulately to explain his revelation at the police station where he had been tortured and condemned. The police think he is crazy, but because they now know they accused him unjustly, they find his return embarrassing. Fred euphorically insists that they accompany him into the sewer so that they, too, can experience the visions that enlightened him. When he shows them his entrance to the world underground, one of the policemen calmly shoots him and the murky waters of the sewer sweep him away.

This ironic story of symbolic death and resurrection is unparalleled in its unique treatment of existential themes. Guilt and alienation lead paradoxically to a tragic sense of human brotherhood, which seems unintelligible to "normal" people. The man who kills Fred Daniels is perhaps the only person who perceives even dimly what Daniels wants to do. "You've got to shoot this kind," he says. "They'd wreck things."

*Katherine Snipes*
*With updates by Thomas Cassidy*

**Other major works**

PLAY: *Native Son: The Biography of a Young American*, pr. 1941 (with Paul Green).

NOVELS: *Native Son*, 1940; *The Outsider*, 1953; *Savage Holiday*, 1954; *The Long Dream*, 1958; *Lawd Today*, 1963.

MISCELLANEOUS: *Works*, 1991 (2 volumes).

NONFICTION: *Twelve Million Black Voices: A Folk History of the Negro in the United States*, 1941 (photographs by Edwin Rosskam); *Black Boy: A Record of Childhood and Youth*, 1945; *Black Power: A Record of Reactions in a Land of Pathos*, 1954; *The Color Curtain*, 1956; *Pagan Spain*, 1957; *White Man, Listen!*, 1957; *American Hunger*, 1977; *Richard Wright Reader*, 1978 (Ellen Wright and Michel Fabre, editors); *Conversations with Richard Wright*, 1993 (Keneth Kinnamon and Michel Fabre, editors).

POETRY: *Haiku: This Other World*, 1998 (Yoshinobu Hakutani and Robert L. Tener, editors).

**Bibliography**

Butler, Robert. *"Native Son": The Emergence of a New Black Hero*. Boston: Twayne, 1991. Critical but accessible look at the seminal novel. Includes bibliographical references and index.

_____. *The World of Richard Wright.* Jackson: University Press of Mississippi, 1985. Collection of Michel Fabre's essays on Wright. A valuable resource, though not a sustained, full-length study. It contains two chapters on individual short stories by Wright, including the short story "Superstition." Supplemented by an appendix.

Felgar, Robert. *Richard Wright.* Boston: Twayne, 1980. General biographical and critical source, this work devotes two chapters to the short fiction of Wright.

Hakutani, Yoshinobu. *Richard Wright and Racial Discourse.* Columbia: University of Missouri Press, 1996. This study of Wright's fiction as racial discourse and the product of diverse cultures devotes one chapter to Wright's *Uncle Tom's Children*, focusing primarily on racial and cultural contexts of "Big Boy Leaves Home."

Kinnamon, Kenneth. *The Emergence of Richard Wright.* Urbana: University of Illinois Press, 1972. Study of Wright's background and development as a writer, up until the publication of *Native Son*.

_____. *A Richard Wright Bibliography: Fifty Years of Criticism and Commentary: 1933-1982.* Westport, Conn.: Greenwood Press, 1988. Mammoth annotated bibliography (one of the largest annotated bibliographies ever assembled on an American writer), which traces the history of Wright criticism. This bibliography is invaluable as a research tool.

_____, ed. *Critical Essays on Richard Wright's "Native Son."* New York: Twayne, 1997. Divided into sections of reviews, reprinted essays, and new essays. Includes discussions of Wright's handling of race, voice, tone, novelistic structure, the city, and literary influences. Index but no bibliography.

May, Charles E., ed. *Masterplots II: Short Story Series, Revised Edition.* 8 vols. Pasadena, Calif.: Salem Press, 2004. Designed for student use, this reference set contains articles providing detailed plot summaries and analyses of four short stories by Wright: "Big Boy Leaves Home" and "Bright and Morning Star" (vol. 1), and "The Man Who Lived Underground" and "The Man Who Was Almost a Man" (vol. 5).

Rand, William E. "The Structure of the Outsider in the Short Fiction of Richard Wright and F. Scott Fitzgerald." *CLA Journal* 40 (December, 1996): 230-245. Compares theme, imagery, and form of Fitzgerald's "The Diamond as Big as the Ritz" with Wright's "The Man Who Lived Underground" in terms of the treatment of the outsider. Argues that both Fitzgerald and Wright saw themselves as outsiders—Wright because of race and Fitzgerald because of economic class.

Walker, Margaret. *Richard Wright: Daemonic Genius.* New York: Warner, 1988. Critically acclaimed study of Wright's life and work written by a friend and fellow novelist. Not a replacement for Michel Fabre's biography but written with the benefit of several more years of scholarship on issues that include the medical controversy over Wright's death. Walker is especially insightful on Wright's early life, and her comments on Wright's short fiction are short but pithy. Includes a useful bibliographical essay at the end.

# Terms and Techniques

*Aestheticism:* European literary movement, with its roots in France, that was predominant in the 1890's. It denied that art needed to have any utilitarian purpose and focused on the slogan "art for art's sake." The doctrines of aestheticism were introduced to England by Walter Pater and can be found in the plays of Oscar Wilde and the short stories of Arthur Symons. In American literature, the ideas underlying the aesthetic movement can be found in the short fiction of Edgar Allan Poe.

*Allegory:* Literary mode in which characters in a narrative personify abstract ideas or qualities and so give a second level of meaning to the work, in addition to the surface narrative. Two famous examples of allegory are Edmund Spenser's *The Faerie Queene* (1590, 1596) and John Bunyan's *The Pilgrim's Progress from This World to That Which Is to Come,* Part I (1678). Modern examples may be found in Nathaniel Hawthorne's story "The Artist of the Beautiful" and the stories and novels of Franz Kafka.

*Allusion:* Reference to a person or event, either historical or from a literary work, which gives another literary work a wider frame of reference and adds depth to its meaning. For example, Sylvia Townsend Warner's story "Winter in the Air" gains greater suggestiveness from the frequent allusions to William Shakespeare's play *The Winter's Tale* (c. 1610-1611), and her story "Swans on an Autumn River" is enriched by a number of allusions to the poetry of William Butler Yeats.

*Ambiguity:* Capacity of language to suggest two or more levels of meaning within a single expression, thus conveying a rich, concentrated effect. Ambiguity has been defined by William Empson in *Seven Types of Ambiguity* (1930) as "any verbal nuance, however, slight, which gives room for alternative reactions to the same piece of language." It has been suggested that because of the short story's highly compressed form, ambiguity may play a more important role in the form than it does in the novel.

*Anachronism:* Event, person, or thing placed outside—usually earlier than—its proper historical era. Shakespeare uses anachronism in *King John* (c. 1596-1597), *Antony and Cleopatra* (c. 1606-1607), and *Julius Caesar* (c. 1599-1600). Mark Twain employed anachronism to comic effect in *A Connecticut Yankee in King Arthur's Court* (1889).

*Anecdote:* Short narration of a single interesting incident or event. An anecdote differs from a short story in that it does not have a plot, relates a single episode, and does not range over different times and places.

*Antagonist:* Character in fiction who stands in opposition, or rivalry, to the protagonist. In Shakespeare's *Hamlet, Prince of Denmark* (c. 1600-1601), for example, King Claudius is the antagonist of Hamlet.

*Anthology:* Collection of prose or poetry, usually by various writers. Often serves to introduce the work of little-known authors to a wider audience.

*Aphorism:* Short, concise statement that states an opinion, precept, or general truth, such as Alexander Pope's "Hope springs eternal in the human breast."

*Apostrophe:* Direct address to a person (usually absent), inanimate entity, or abstract quality. Examples are the first line of William Wordsworth's sonnet "London,

1802," "Milton! Thou should'st be living at this hour," and King Lear's speech in Shakespeare's *King Lear* (c. 1605-1606), "Blow, winds, and crack your cheeks! rage! blow!"

*Archetypal theme:* Recurring thematic patterns in literature. Common archetypal themes include death and rebirth (Samuel Taylor Coleridge's *The Rime of the Ancient Mariner,* 1798), paradise-Hades (Coleridge's "Kubla Khan"), the fatal woman (Guy de Maupassant's "Doubtful Happiness"), the earth goddess ("Yanda" by Isaac Bashevis Singer), the scapegoat (D. H. Lawrence's "The Woman Who Rode Away"), and the return to the womb (Flannery O'Connor's "The River").

*Archetype:* Term used by psychologist Carl Jung to describe what he called "primordial images," which exist in the "collective unconscious" of humankind and are manifested in myths, religion, literature, and dreams. Now used broadly in literary criticism to refer to character types, motifs, images, symbols, and plot patterns recurring in many different literary forms and works. The embodiment of archetypes in a work of literature can make a powerful impression on the reader.

*Atmosphere:* Mood or tone of a work; it is often associated with setting but can also be established by action or dialogue. The opening paragraphs of Poe's "The Fall of the House of Usher" and James Joyce's "Araby" provide good examples of atmosphere created early in the works and pervading the remainder of the story.

*Black humor:* General term of modern origin that refers to a form of "sick humor" that is intended to produce laughter out of the morbid and the taboo. Examples are the works of Joseph Heller, Thomas Pynchon, Günter Grass, and Kurt Vonnegut.

*Burlesque:* Work that, by imitating attitudes, styles, institutions, and people, aims to amuse. Burlesque differs from satire in that it aims to ridicule simply for the sake of amusement rather than for political or social change.

*Caricature:* Form of writing that focuses on unique qualities of a person and then exaggerates and distorts those qualities in order to ridicule the person and what he or she represents. Contemporary writers, such as Flannery O'Connor, have used caricature for serious and satiric purposes in such stories as "Good Country People" and "A Good Man Is Hard to Find."

*Character type:* Term can refer to the convention of using stock characters, such as the *miles gloriosus* (braggart soldier) of Renaissance and Roman comedy, the figure of vice in medieval morality plays, or the clever servant in Elizabethan comedy. It can also describe "flat" characters (the term was coined by E. M. Forster) in fiction who do not grow or change during the course of the narrative and who can be easily classified.

*Climax:* Similar to crisis, the moment in a work of fiction at which the action reaches a turning point and the plot begins to be resolved. Unlike crisis, the term is also used to refer to the moment in which the reader's emotional involvement with the work reaches its point of highest intensity.

*Comic story:* Form encompassing a wide variety of modes and inflections, such as parody, burlesque, satire, irony, and humor. Frequently, the defining quality of comic characters is that they lack self-awareness; the reader tends not to identify with them but perceives them from a detached point of view, more as objects than persons.

*Conflict:* Struggle that develops as a result of the opposition between the protagonist and another person, the natural world, society, or some force within the self. In short fiction, the conflict is most often between the protagonist and some strong force either within the protagonist or within the given state of the human condition.

*Conte:* French for tale, a conte was originally a short adventure tale. In the nineteenth century, the term was used to describe a tightly constructed short story. In England, the term is used to describe a work longer than a short story and shorter than a novel.

*Crisis:* Turning point in the plot, at which the opposing forces reach the point that a resolution must take place.

*Criticism:* Study and evaluation of works of literature. Theoretical criticism, as for example in Aristotle's *De poetica,* c. 334-323 B.C.E. (*Poetics,* 1705), sets out general principles for interpretation. Practical criticism (Coleridge's lectures on Shakespeare, for example) offers interpretations of particular works or authors.

*Deconstruction:* Literary theory, primarily attributed to French critic Jacques Derrida, which has spawned a wide variety of practical applications, the most prominent being the critical tactic of laying bare a text's self-reflexivity, that is, showing how it continually refers to and subverts its own way of meaning.

*Defamiliarization:* Term coined by the Russian Formalists to indicate a process by which the writer makes the reader perceive the concrete uniqueness of an object, event, or idea that has been generalized by routine and habit.

*Denouement:* Literally, "unknotting"; the conclusion of a drama or fiction, when the plot is unraveled and the mystery solved.

*Detective story:* A "classic" detective story (or "mystery") is a highly formalized and logically structured mode of fiction in which the focus is on a crime solved by a detective through interpretation of evidence and clever reasoning. Many modern practitioners of the genre, however, such as Raymond Chandler, Patricia Highsmith, and Ross Macdonald, have placed less emphasis on the puzzle-like qualities of the detective story and have focused instead on characterization, theme, and other elements of mainstream fiction. The form was first developed in short fiction by Edgar Allan Poe; Jorge Luis Borges has also used the convention in short stories.

*Deus ex machina:* Latin, meaning "god out of the machine." In the Greek theater, it referred to the use of a god lowered out of a mechanism onto the stage to untangle the plot or save the hero. It has come to signify any artificial device for the easy resolution of dramatic difficulties.

*Device:* Any technique used in literature in order to gain a specific effect. Poets use the device of figurative language, for example, while novelists may use foreshadowing, flashback, and so on, in order to create desired effects.

*Dialogics:* Theory that fiction is a dialogic genre in which many different voices are held in suspension without becoming merged into a single authoritative voice. Developed by Russian critic Mikhail Bakhtin.

*Didactic literature:* Literature that seeks to instruct, give guidance, or teach a lesson. Didactic literature normally has a moral, religious, or philosophical purpose, or it will expound a branch of knowledge (as in Vergil's *Georgics,* c. 37-29 B.C.E.; English translation, 1589). It is distinguished from imaginative works, in which the aesthetic product takes precedence over any moral intent.

*Diegesis:* Hypothetical world of a story, as if it actually existed in real space and time. It is the illusory universe of the story created by its linguistic structure.

*Doppelgänger:* Double or counterpart of a person, sometimes endowed with ghostly qualities. A fictional doppelgänger often reflects a suppressed side of his or her personality, as in Fyodor Dostoevski's novella *Dvoynik* (1846; *The Double*, 1917) and the short stories of E. T. A. Hoffmann. Isaac Bashevis Singer and Jorge Luis Borges, among other modern writers, have also employed the doppelgänger with striking effect.

*Dream vision:* Allegorical form common in the Middle Ages, in which the narrator or a character falls asleep and dreams a dream that becomes the actual framed story. Subtle variations of the form have been used by Hawthorne in "Young Goodman Brown" and by Poe in "The Pit and the Pendulum."

*Dualism:* Theory that the universe is explicable in terms of two basic, conflicting entities, such as good and evil, mind and matter, or the physical and the spiritual.

*Effect:* Total, unified impression, or impact, made upon the reader by a literary work. Every aspect of the work—plot, characterization, style, and so on—is seen to directly contribute to this overall impression.

*Epiphany:* A literary application of this religious term was popularized by James Joyce in his book *Stephen Hero* (1944): "By an epiphany he meant a sudden spiritual manifestation, whether in the vulgarity of speech or of gesture or in a memorable phase of the mind itself." Many short stories since Joyce's collection *Dubliners* (1914) have been analyzed as epiphanic stories in which a character or the reader experiences a sudden revelation of meaning.

*Essay:* Brief prose work, usually on a single topic, that expresses the personal point of view of the author. The essay is usually addressed to a general audience and attempts to persuade the reader to accept the author's ideas.

*Essay-sketch tradition:* The earliest sketches can be traced to the Greek philosopher Theophrastus in 300 B.C.E., whose character sketches influenced seventeenth and eighteenth century writers in England, who developed the form into something close to the idea of character in fiction. The essay has an equally venerable history, and, like the sketch, had an impact on the development of the modern short story.

*Exemplum:* Brief anecdote or tale introduced to illustrate a moral point in medieval sermons. By the fourteenth century these exempla had expanded into exemplary narratives. Geoffrey Chaucer's "The Nun's Priest's Tale" and "The Pardoner's Tale" are exempla.

*Existentialism:* Philosophy and attitude of mind that gained wide currency in religious and artistic thought after the end of World War II. Typical concerns of existential writers are human beings' estrangement from society, their awareness that the world is meaningless, and their recognition that one must turn from external props to the self. The writings of Albert Camus and Franz Kafka provide examples of existentialist beliefs.

*Exposition:* Part or parts of a work of fiction that provide necessary background information. Exposition not only provides the time and place of the action but also introduces readers to the fictive world of the story, acquainting them with the ground rules of the work. In the short story, exposition is usually elliptical.

*Fable:* One of the oldest narrative forms. Usually takes the form of an analogy in which animals or inanimate objects speak to illustrate a moral lesson. The most famous examples are the fables of Aesop, a Greek who used the form orally around 600 B.C.E.

*Fabulation:* Term coined by Robert Scholes and used in contemporary literary criticism to describe novels radically experimental in subject matter, style, and form. Like the Magical Realists, fabulators mix realism with fantasy. The works of Thomas Pynchon, John Barth, Donald Barthelme, and William Gass provide examples.

*Fairy tale:* Form of folktale in which supernatural events or characters are prominent. Fairy tales usually depict realms of reality beyond those of the natural world and in which the laws of the natural world are suspended. Among the most famous creators of fairy tales are Germany's Brothers Grimm.

*Fantastic:* The Bulgarian Critic Tzvetan Todorov defines the fantastic as a genre that lies between the uncanny and the marvelous. Whereas the marvelous presents an event that cannot be explained by the laws of the natural world and the uncanny presents an event that is the result of hallucination or illusion, the fantastic exists as long as the reader cannot decide which of these two applies. Henry James's *The Turn of the Screw* (1898) is an example of the fantastic.

*Figurative language:* Any use of language that departs from the usual or ordinary meaning to gain a poetic or otherwise special effect. Figurative language embodies various figures of speech, such as irony, metaphor, simile, and many others.

*Flashback:* Scene that depicts an earlier event; it can be presented as a reminiscence by a character in a story, or it can simply be inserted into the narrative.

*Folktale:* Short prose narrative, usually handed down orally, found in all cultures of the world. The term is often used interchangeably with myth, fable, and fairy tale.

*Form:* Organizing principle in a work of literature, the manner in which its elements are put together in relation to its total effect. The term is sometimes used interchangeably with structure and is often contrasted with content: If form is the building, content is what is in the building and what the building is specifically designed to express.

*Frame story:* Story that provides a framework for another story (or stories) told within it. The form is ancient and is used by Geoffrey Chaucer in *The Canterbury Tales* (1387-1400). In modern literature, the technique has been used by Henry James in *The Turn of the Screw* (1898), Joseph Conrad in *Heart of Darkness* (1902), and John Barth in *Lost in the Funhouse* (1968).

*Framework:* When used in connection with a frame story, the framework is the narrative setting, within which other stories are told. The framework may also have a plot of its own. More generally, the framework is similar to structure, referring to the general outline of a work.

*Gendered:* When a work is approached as thematically or stylistically specific to male or female characteristics or concerns, it is said to be "gendered."

*Genre study:* Concept of studying literature by classification and definition of types or kinds, such as tragedy, comedy, epic, lyrical, and pastoral. First introduced by Aristotle in *Poetics*, the genre principle has been an essential concomitant to the basic proposition that literature can be studied scientifically.

*Gothic genre:* Form of fiction developed in the late eighteenth century which focuses on horror and the supernatural. Examples include the short fiction of Edgar Allan Poe. In modern literature, the gothic genre can be found in the fiction of Truman Capote.

*Grotesque:* Characterized by a breakup of the everyday world by mysterious forces, the form differs from fantasy in that the reader is not sure whether to react with humor or horror. Examples include the stories of E. T. A. Hoffmann and Franz Kafka.

*Hyperbole:* Greek term for "overshooting" that refers to the use of gross exaggeration for rhetorical effect, based on the assumption that the reader will not be persuaded of the literal truth of the overstatement. Can be used for serious or comic effect.

*Imagery:* Often defined as the verbal stimulation of sensory perception. Although the word betrays a visual bias, imagery, in fact, calls on all five senses. In its simplest form, imagery re-creates a physical sensation in a clear, literal manner; it becomes more complex when a writer employs metaphor and other figures of speech to re-create experience.

*In medias res:* Latin phrase used by Horace, meaning literally "into the midst of things" that refers to a literary technique of beginning the narrative when the action has already begun. The term is used particularly in connection with the epic, which traditionally begins *in medias res.*

*Initiation story:* Story in which protagonists, usually children or young persons, go through an experience, sometimes painful or disconcerting, that carries them from innocence to some new form of knowledge and maturity. William Faulkner's "The Bear," Nathaniel Hawthorne's "Young Goodman Brown," Alice Walker's "To Hell with Dying," and Robert Penn Warren's "Blackberry Winter" are examples of the form.

*Interior monologue:* Defined as the speech of a character designed to introduce the reader directly to the character's internal life, the form differs from other monologues in that it attempts to reproduce thought before any logical organization is imposed upon it. An example is Molly Bloom's long interior monologue at the conclusion of James Joyce's *Ulysses.*

*Irrealism:* Term often used to refer to modern or postmodern fiction that is presented self-consciously as a fiction or fabulation rather than a mimesis of external reality. The best-known practitioners of irrealism are John Barth, Robert Coover, and Donald Barthelme.

*Leitmotif:* From the German, meaning "leading motif." Any repetition—of a word, phrase, situation, or idea—that occurs within a single work or group of related works.

*Literary short story:* Term that was current in American criticism in the 1940's to distinguish the short fiction of Ernest Hemingway, Eudora Welty, Sherwood Anderson, and others from the popular pulp and slick fiction of the day.

*Local color:* Term that usually refers to a movement in literature, especially in the United States, in the latter part of the nineteenth century. The focus was on the environment, atmosphere, and milieu of a particular region. For example, Mark Twain wrote about the Mississippi region; Sarah Orne Jewett wrote about New England. The term can also be used to refer to any work that represents the characteristics of a particular region.

*Lyric short story:* Form in which the emphasis is on internal changes, moods, and feelings. The lyric story is usually open-ended and depends on the figurative language generally associated with poetry. Examples of lyric stories are the works of Ivan Turgenev, Anton Chekhov, Katherine Mansfield, Sherwood Anderson, Conrad Aiken, and John Updike.

*Malaprop/Malapropism:* Malapropism occurs when one word is confused with another because of a similarity in sound between them. The term is derived from the character Mistress Malaprop in Richard Brinsley Sheridan's *The Rivals* (1775), who, for example, uses the word "illiterate" when she really means "obliterate" and mistakes "progeny" for "prodigy."

*Märchen:* German fairy tales, as collected in the works of Wilhelm and Jacob Grimm or in the works of nineteenth century writers such as Novalis and E. T. A. Hoffmann.

*Metafiction:* Refers to fiction that manifests a reflexive tendency, such as Vladimir Nabokov's *Pale Fire* (1962), and John Fowles's *The French Lieutenant's Woman* (1969). The emphasis is on the loosening of the work's illusion of reality to expose the reality of its illusion. Such terms as "irrealism," "postmodernist fiction," and "antifiction" are also used to refer to this type of fiction.

*Metaphor:* Figure of speech in which two dissimilar objects are imaginatively identified (rather than merely compared) on the assumption that they share one or more qualities: "She is the rose, the glory of the day" (Edmund Spenser). The term is often used in modern criticism in a wider sense to identify analogies of all kinds in literature, painting, and film.

*Metonymy:* Figure of speech in which an object that is closely related to a word comes to stand for the word itself, such as when one says "the White House" when meaning the "president."

*Minimalist movement:* School of fiction writing that developed in the late 1970's and early 1980's and that John Barth has characterized as the "less is more school." Minimalism attempts to convey much by saying little, to render contemporary reality in precise, pared-down prose that suggests more than it directly states. Leading minimalist writers are Raymond Carver and Ann Beattie. A character in Beattie's short story "Snow" (in *Where You'll Find Me*, 1986) seems to sum up minimalism: "Any life will seem dramatic if you omit mention of most of it."

*Mise en abême:* Small story inside a larger narrative that echoes or mirrors the larger narrative, thus containing the larger within the smaller.

*Modern short story:* Literary form that dates from the nineteenth century and is associated with Edgar Allan Poe (who is often credited with inventing the form) and Nathaniel Hawthorne in the United States, Honoré de Balzac in France, and E. T. A. Hoffmann in Germany. In his influential critical writings, Poe defined the short story as being limited to "a certain unique or single effect," to which every detail in the story should contribute.

*Monologue:* Any speech or narrative presented by one person. It can sometimes be used to refer to any lengthy speech, in which one person monopolizes the conversation.

*Motif:* Incident or situation in a story that serves as the basis of its structure, creating by repetition and variation a patterned recurrence and consequently a general theme. Russian Formalist critics distinguish between bound motifs, which cannot be omitted without disturbing the thematic structure of the story, and unbound motifs, which serve merely to create the illusion of external reality. In this sense, motif is the same as leitmotif.

*Myth:* Anonymous traditional story, often involving supernatural beings or the interaction between gods and human beings and dealing with the basic questions of how the world and human society came to be as they are. Myth is an important term in contemporary literary criticism. Northrop Frye, for example, has said that "the typical forms of myth become the conventions and genres of literature." By this, he means that the genres of comedy, romance, tragedy, and irony (satire) correspond to seasonal myths of spring, summer, autumn, and winter.

*Narrative:* Account in prose or verse of an event or series of events, whether real or imagined.

*Narrative persona:* "Persona" means literally "mask": It is the self created by the author and through whom the narrative is told. The persona is not to be identified with the author, even when the two may seem to resemble each other. The narrative persona in George Gordon, Lord Byron's *Don Juan* (1819-1824), for example, may express many sentiments of which Byron would have approved, but he is nevertheless a fictional creation who is distinct from the author.

*Narratology:* Theoretical study of narrative structures and ways of meaning. Most all major literary theories have a branch of study known as narratology.

*Narrator:* Character who recounts the narrative. There are many different types of narrators: The first-person narrator is a character in the story and can be recognized by his or her use of "I"; third-person narrators may be limited or omniscient. In the former, the narrator is confined to knowledge of the minds and emotions of one or, at most, a few characters. In the latter, the narrator knows everything, seeing into the minds of all the characters. Rarely, second-person narration may be used. (An example can be found in Edna O'Brien's *A Pagan Place*, 1973.)

*Novel:* Fictional prose form, longer than a short story or novelette. The term embraces a wide range of types, but the novel usually includes a more complicated plot and a wider cast of characters than the short story. The focus is often on the development of individual characterization and the presentation of a social world and a detailed environment.

*Novella, Novelette, Novelle, Nouvelle:* These terms all refer to the form of fiction that is longer than a short story and shorter than a novel. *Novella*, the Italian term, is the term usually used to refer to English-language works in this genre, such as Joseph Conrad's *Heart of Darkness* (1902) and Henry James's *The Turn of the Screw* (1898). *Novelle* is the German term; *nouvelle* the French; "novelette" the British. The term "novel" derives from these terms.

*Oral tale:* Wide-ranging term that can include everything from gossip to myths, legends, folktales, and jokes. Among the terms used by Stith Thompson to classify oral tales (*The Folktale*, 1951) are *Märchen*, fairy tale, household tale, *conte populaire*, novella, hero tale, local tradition, migratory legend, explanatory tale, humorous anecdote, and merry tale.

*Oral tradition:* Material that is transmitted by word of mouth, often through chants or songs, from generation to generation. Homer's epics, for example, were originally passed down orally and employ formulas to make memorization easier. Often, ballads, folklore, and proverbs are also passed down in this way.

*Parable:* Short, simple, and usually allegorical story that teaches a moral lesson. In the West, the most famous parables are those told in the Gospels by Jesus Christ.

*Paradox:* Statement that initially seems to be illogical or self-contradictory yet eventually proves to embody a complex truth. In New Criticism, the term is used to embrace any complexity of language that sustains multiple meanings and deviates from the norms of ordinary language usage.

*Parody:* Literary work that imitates or burlesques another work or author for the purpose of ridicule. Twentieth century parodists include E. B. White and James Thurber.

*Periodical essay/sketch:* Informal in tone and style and applied to a wide range of topics, the periodical essay originated in the early eighteenth century. It is associated in particular with Joseph Addison and Richard Steele and their informal periodical, *The Spectator.*

*Personification:* Figure of speech which ascribes human qualities to abstractions or inanimate objects, as in these lines by W. H. Auden: "There's Wrath who has learnt every trick of guerrilla warfare,/ The shamming dead, the night-raid, the feinted retreat." Richard Crashaw's "Hope, thou bold taster of delight" is another example.

*Plot:* Way in which authors arrange their material not only to create the sequence of events in a play or story but also to suggest how those events are connected in a cause-and-effect relationship. There is a great variety of plot patterns, each of which is designed to create a particular effect.

*Point of view:* Perspective from which a story is presented to the reader. In simplest terms, it refers to whether narration is first person (directly addressed to the reader as if told by one involved in the narrative) or third person (usually a more objective, distanced perspective).

*Postcolonial:* Literary approach that focuses on English-language texts from countries and cultures formerly colonized or dominated by the United States or the British Empire, and other European countries. Postcolonialists focus on the literature of such regions as Australia, New Zealand, Africa, or South America, and such cultural groups as African Americans and Native Americans.

*Postmodern:* Although this term is so broad it is interpreted differently by many different critics, it basically refers to a trend by which the literary work calls attention to itself as an artifice rather than a mirror held up to external reality.

*Protagonist:* Originally, in the Greek drama, the "first actor," who played the leading role. The term has come to signify the most important character in a drama or story. It is not unusual for a work to contain more than one protagonist.

*Pun:* Puns occur when words that have similar pronunciations have entirely different meanings. The results may be surprise recognition of unusual or striking connections, or, more often, humorously accidental connections.

*Realism:* Literary technique in which the primary convention is to render an illusion of fidelity to external reality. Realism is often identified as the primary method of the novel form; the realist movement in the late nineteenth century coincided with the full development of the novel form.

*Rhetorical device:* Rhetoric is the art of using words clearly and effectively, in speech or writing, in order to influence or persuade. A rhetorical device is a figure of speech, or way of using language, employed to this end. It can include such elements as choice of words, rhythms, repetition, apostrophe, invocation, chiasmus, zeugma, antithesis, and the rhetorical question (a question to which no answer is expected).

*Rogue literature:* From Odysseus to Shakespeare's Autolocus to Huckleberry Finn, the rogue is a common literary type. He is usually a robust and energetic comic or satirical figure whose roguery can be seen as a necessary undermining of the rigid complacency of conventional society. The picaresque novel (*pícaro* is Spanish for "rogue"), in which the picaro lives by his wits, is perhaps the most common form of rogue literature.

*Romance:* Originally, any work written in Old French. In the Middle Ages, romances were about knights and their adventures. In modern times, the term has also been used to describe a type of prose fiction in which, unlike the novel, realism plays little part. Prose romances often give expression to the quest for transcendent truths. Examples of the form include Nathaniel Hawthorne's *The Scarlet Letter* (1850) and Herman Melville's *Moby Dick* (1851).

*Romanticism:* Movement of the late eighteenth and nineteenth centuries which exalted individualism over collectivism, revolution over conservatism, innovation over tradition, imagination over reason, and spontaneity over restraint. Romanticism regarded art as self-expression; it strove to heal the cleavage between object and subject and expressed a longing for the infinite in all things. It stressed the innate goodness of human beings and the evils of the institutions that would stultify human creativity.

*Satire:* Form of literature that employs the comedic devices of wit, irony, and exaggeration to expose, ridicule, and condemn human folly, vice, and stupidity. Justifying satire, Alexander Pope wrote that "nothing moves strongly but satire, and those who are ashamed of nothing else are so of being ridiculous."

*Setting:* Circumstances and environment, both temporal and spatial, of a narrative. Setting is an important element in the creation of atmosphere.

*Short story:* Concise work of fiction, shorter than a novella, that is usually more concerned with mood, effect, or a single event than with plot or extensive characterization.

*Simile:* Type of metaphor in which two things are compared. It can usually be recognized by the use of the words "like," "as," "appears," or "seems": "Float like a butterfly, sting like a bee" (Muhammad Ali); "The holy time is quiet as a nun" (William Wordsworth).

*Sketch:* Brief narrative form originating in the eighteenth century, derived from the artist's sketch. The focus of a sketch is on a single person, place, or incident; it lacks a developed plot, theme, or characterization.

*Story line:* Differing from plot, a story line is merely the events that happen; plot is how those events are arranged by the author to suggest a cause-and-effect relationship.

*Stream of consciousness:* Narrative technique used in modern fiction by which an author tries to embody the total range of consciousness of a character, without any authorial comment or explanation. Sensations, thoughts, memories, and associations pour out in an uninterrupted, prerational, and prelogical flow. Examples are James Joyce's *Ulysses* (1922), Virginia Woolf's *To the Lighthouse* (1927), and William Faulkner's *The Sound and the Fury* (1929).

*Structuralism:* Structuralism is based on the idea of intrinsic, self-sufficient structures that do not require reference to external elements. A structure is a system of transformations that involves the interplay of laws inherent in the system itself. The structuralist literary critic attempts, by using models derived from modern linguistic theory, to define the structural principles that operate intertextually throughout the whole of literature as well as principles that operate in genres and in individual works.

*Style:* Style is the manner of expression, or how the writer tells the story. The most appropriate style is that which is perfectly suited to conveying whatever idea, emotion, or other effect that the author wishes to convey. Elements of style include diction, sentence structure, imagery, rhythm, and coherence.

*Tale:* General term for a simple prose or verse narrative. In the context of the short story, a tale is a story in which the emphasis is on the course of the action rather than on the minds of the characters.

*Tall tale:* Humorous tale popular in the American West; the story usually makes use of realistic detail and common speech, while telling a tale of impossible events that most often focus on a single legendary, superhuman figure, such as Paul Bunyan or Davy Crockett.

*Theme:* Loosely defined as what a literary work means, theme is the underlying idea, the abstract concept, that the author is trying to convey: "the search for love," "the growth of wisdom," or some such formulation. The theme of William Butler Yeats's poem "Sailing to Byzantium," for example, might be interpreted as the failure of the attempt to isolate oneself within the world of art.

*Tone:* Strictly defined, tone is the authors' attitudes toward their subjects, their personas, themselves, their audiences, or their societies. The tone of a work may be serious, playful, formal, informal, morose, loving, ironic, and so on; it can be thought of as the dominant mood of a work, and it plays a large part in the total effect.

*Trope:* Literally "turn" or "conversion"; a figure of speech in which a word or phrase is used in a way that deviates from the normal or literal sense.

*Verisimilitude:* When used in literary criticism, verisimilitude refers to the degree to which a literary work gives the appearance of being true or real, even though the events depicted may in fact be far removed from the actual.

*Vignette:* Sketch, essay, or brief narrative characterized by precision, economy, and grace. The term can also be applied to brief short stories, less than five hundred words long.

*Yarn:* Oral tale or a written transcription of what purports to be an oral tale. The yarn is usually a broadly comic tale, the classic example of which is Mark Twain's bluejay yarn. The yarn achieves its comic effect by juxtaposing realistic detail and incredible events; tellers of the tale protest that they are telling the truth; listeners know differently.

*Bryan Aubrey*
*Updated by Charles E. May*

# Time Line

| Date and place of birth | Name |
|---|---|
| June or July, 1313; Florence or Certaldo (now in Italy) | Giovanni Boccaccio |
| c. 1343; London(?), England | Geoffrey Chaucer |
| | |
| April 3, 1783; New York, New York | Washington Irving |
| January 4, 1785; Hanau, Hesse-Kassel (now in Germany) | Jacob Grimm |
| February 24, 1786; Hanau, Hesse-Kassel (now in Germany) | Wilhelm Grimm |
| | |
| September 27, 1803; Paris, France | Prosper Mérimée |
| July 4, 1804; Salem, Massachusetts | Nathaniel Hawthorne |
| April 2, 1805; Odense, Denmark | Hans Christian Andersen |
| | |
| January 19, 1809; Boston, Massachusetts | Edgar Allan Poe |
| March 31, 1809; Sorochintsy, Ukraine, Russian Empire (now in Ukraine) | Nikolai Gogol |
| | |
| November 9, 1818; Orel, Russia | Ivan Turgenev |
| August 1, 1819; New York, New York | Herman Melville |
| | |
| November 11, 1821; Moscow, Russia | Fyodor Dostoevski |
| December 12, 1821; Rouen, France | Gustave Flaubert |
| September 9, 1828; Yasnaya Polyana, Russia | Leo Tolstoy |
| | |
| November 30, 1835; Florida, Missouri | Mark Twain |
| August 25, 1836; Albany, New York | Bret Harte |
| | |
| June 24, 1842; Horse Cave Creek, Ohio | Ambrose Bierce |
| April 15, 1843; New York, New York | Henry James |
| September 3, 1849; South Berwick, Maine | Sarah Orne Jewett |
| August 5, 1850; Château de Miromesnil, France | Guy de Maupassant |
| November 13, 1850; Edinburgh, Scotland | Robert Louis Stevenson |
| | |
| February 8, 1851; St. Louis, Missouri | Kate Chopin |
| December 3, 1857; Near Berdyczów, Podolia, Poland | Joseph Conrad |
| June 20, 1858; Cleveland, Ohio | Charles Waddell Chesnutt |
| | |
| May 22, 1859; Edinburgh, Scotland | Arthur Conan Doyle |
| January 29, 1860; Taganrog, Russia | Anton Chekhov |
| September 14, 1860; West Salem, Wisconsin | Hamlin Garland |

| Date and place of birth | Name |
|---|---|
| January 24, 1862; New York, New York | Edith Wharton |
| September 11, 1862; Greensboro, North Carolina | O. Henry |
| December 30, 1865; Bombay, India | Rudyard Kipling |
| June 28, 1867; Girgenti (now Agrigento), Sicily, Italy | Luigi Pirandello |
| December 18, 1870; Akyab, Myanmar (formerly Burma) | Saki |
| | |
| November 1, 1871; Newark, New Jersey | Stephen Crane |
| April 25, 1873; Charlton, Kent, England | Walter de la Mare |
| December 7, 1873; Back Creek Valley, Virginia | Willa Cather |
| January 25, 1874; Paris, France | W. Somerset Maugham |
| May 29, 1874; London, England | G. K. Chesterton |
| June 6, 1875; Lübeck, Germany | Thomas Mann |
| January 12, 1876; San Francisco, California | Jack London |
| September 13, 1876; Camden, Ohio | Sherwood Anderson |
| January 4, 1878; Folkestone, Kent, England | A. E. Coppard |
| January 1, 1879; London, England | E. M. Forster |
| | |
| January 25, 1882; London, England | Virginia Woolf |
| February 2, 1882; Dublin, Ireland | James Joyce |
| July 3, 1883; Prague, Bohemia (now in Czech Republic) | Franz Kafka |
| September 17, 1883; Rutherford, New Jersey | William Carlos Williams |
| March 6, 1885; Niles, Michigan | Ring Lardner |
| April 17, 1885; Rungsted, Denmark | Isak Dinesen |
| September 11, 1885; Eastwood, Nottinghamshire, England | D. H. Lawrence |
| October 14, 1888; Wellington, New Zealand | Katherine Mansfield |
| August 5, 1889; Savannah, Georgia | Conrad Aiken |
| May 15, 1890; Indian Creek, Texas | Katherine Anne Porter |
| | |
| January 7, 1891; Eatonville, Florida | Zora Neale Hurston |
| August 22, 1893; West End, New Jersey | Dorothy Parker |
| July 13, 1894; Odessa, Ukraine, Russian Empire (now in Ukraine) | Isaac Babel |
| December 8, 1894; Columbus, Ohio | James Thurber |
| August 28, 1896; Gort na gCapell, Aran Islands, Ireland | Liam O'Flaherty |
| September 24, 1896; St. Paul, Minnesota | F. Scott Fitzgerald |
| September 25, 1897; New Albany, Mississippi | William Faulkner |
| April 23, 1899; St. Petersburg, Russia | Vladimir Nabokov |
| June 7, 1899; Dublin, Ireland | Elizabeth Bowen |
| July 21, 1899; Oak Park, Illinois | Ernest Hemingway |
| August 24, 1899; Buenos Aires, Argentina | Jorge Luis Borges |
| February 22, 1900; Cork, Ireland | Seán O'Faoláin |
| December 16, 1900; Ipswich, England | V. S. Pritchett |
| | |
| February 1, 1902; Joplin, Missouri | Langston Hughes |
| February 19, 1902; St. Paul, Minnesota | Kay Boyle |
| February 27, 1902; Salinas, California | John Steinbeck |

| Date and place of birth | Name |
|---|---|
| 1903; Cork City, Ireland | Frank O'Connor |
| February 22, 1903; Toronto, Ontario, Canada | Morley Callaghan |
| February 1, 1904; Brooklyn, New York | S. J. Perelman |
| July 14 or November 21, 1904; Leoncin, Poland | Isaac Bashevis Singer |
| October 2, 1904; Berkhamsted, Hertfordshire, England | Graham Greene |
| April 24, 1905; Guthrie, Kentucky | Robert Penn Warren |
| October 10, 1906; Madras, India | R. K. Narayan |
| August 31, 1908; Fresno, California | William Saroyan |
| September 4, 1908 ; Born: Roxie, Mississippi | Richard Wright |
| October 12, 1908; Old Saybrook, Connecticut | Ann Petry |
| April 13, 1909; Jackson, Mississippi | Eudora Welty |
| August 3, 1909; East Orland, Maine | Walter Van Tilburg Clark |
|  |  |
| March 26, 1911; Columbus, Mississippi | Tennessee Williams |
| May 27, 1912; Quincy, Massachusetts | John Cheever |
| June 11, 1912; East Walpole, Massachusetts | Mary Lavin |
| January 14, 1913; Omaha, Nebraska | Tillie Olsen |
| March 1, 1914; Oklahoma City, Oklahoma | Ralph Ellison |
| April 26, 1914; Brooklyn, New York | Bernard Malamud |
| August 26, 1914; Brussels, Belgium | Julio Cortázar |
| October 27, 1914; Swansea, Wales | Dylan Thomas |
| June 10, 1915; Lachine, Quebec, Canada | Saul Bellow |
| January 8, 1917; Trenton, Tennessee | Peter Taylor |
| February 19, 1917; Columbus, Georgia | Carson McCullers |
| July 8, 1917; Jacksonville, Illinois | J. F. Powers |
| December 16, 1917; Minehead, Somerset, England | Arthur C. Clarke |
| February 1, 1918; Edinburgh, Scotland | Muriel Spark |
| January 1, 1919; New York, New York | J. D. Salinger |
| October 22, 1919; Kermānshāh, Persia (now Bākhtarān, Iran) | Doris Lessing |
| December 14, 1919; San Francisco, California | Shirley Jackson |
| August 22, 1920; Waukegan, Illinois | Ray Bradbury |
|  |  |
| August 11, 1922; Montreal, Quebec, Canada | Mavis Gallant |
| November 11, 1922; Indianapolis, Indiana | Kurt Vonnegut |
| December 11, 1922; New York, New York | Grace Paley |
| July 14, 1923; Near Fremont, Ohio | James Purdy |
| November 20, 1923; Springs, Transvaal, South Africa | Nadine Gordimer |
| August 2, 1924; New York, New York | James Baldwin |
| September 30, 1924; New Orleans, Louisiana | Truman Capote |
| January 14, 1925; Tokyo, Japan | Yukio Mishima |
| March 25, 1925; Savannah, Georgia | Flannery O'Connor |
| August 14, 1926; Fredericksburg, Virginia | Alice Adams |
| May 7, 1927; Cologne, Germany | Ruth Prawer Jhabvala |
| March 4, 1928; Nottingham, England | Alan Sillitoe |
| March 6, 1928; Aracataca, Colombia | Gabriel García Márquez |
| April 4, 1928; St. Louis, Missouri | Maya Angelou |

**Date and place of birth**

| | |
|---|---|
| **Name** | |

April 17, 1928; New York, New York — Cynthia Ozick
May 24, 1928; Mitchelstown, County Cork, Ireland — William Trevor
October 21, 1929; Berkeley, California — Ursula K. Le Guin
November 16, 1930; Ogidi, Nigeria — Chinua Achebe
December 15, 1930; Tuamgraney, County Clare, Ireland — Edna O'Brien

April 7, 1931; Philadelphia, Pennsylvania — Donald Barthelme
July 10, 1931; Wingham, Ontario, Canada — Alice Munro
February 4, 1932; Charles City, Iowa — Robert Coover
March 18, 1932; Shillington, Pennsylvania — John Updike
August 22, 1935; Norwich, Connecticut — E. Annie Proulx
August 11, 1936; Lake Charles, Louisiana — Andre Dubus
May 25, 1938; Clatskanie, Oregon — Raymond Carver
June 16, 1938; Lockport, New York; — Joyce Carol Oates
March 25, 1939; New York, New York — Toni Cade Bambara
November 18, 1939; Ottawa, Ontario, Canada — Margaret Atwood
March 28, 1940; Newton, Massachusetts — Russell Banks
May 1, 1940; Mayfield, Kentucky — Bobbie Ann Mason
July 27, 1940; Calcutta, West Bengal, India — Bharati Mukherjee

October 25, 1941; Minneapolis, Minnesota — Anne Tyler
April 10, 1942; Chicago, Illinois — Stuart Dybek
August 2, 1942; Lima, Peru — Isabel Allende
February 9, 1944; Eatonton, Georgia — Alice Walker
February 11, 1944; Chelmsford, Massachusetts — Joy Williams
June 19, 1945; Birmingham, Alabama — Tobias Wolff
September 8, 1947; Washington, D.C. — Ann Beattie
December 2, 1948; Peekskill, New York — T. Coraghessan Boyle
May 25, 1949; Saint Johns, Antigua — Jamaica Kincaid

December 14, 1951; Chicago, Illinois — Amy Hempel
February 19, 1952; Oakland, California — Amy Tan
February 26, 1954; East Los Angeles, California — Helena María Viramontes
June 7, 1954; Little Falls, Minnesota — Louise Erdrich
December 20, 1954; Chicago, Illinois — Sandra Cisneros
April 8, 1955; Annapolis, Maryland — Barbara Kingsolver

October 7, 1966; Spokane Indian Reservation, Wellpinit, Washington — Sherman Alexie

# INDEX

# Index